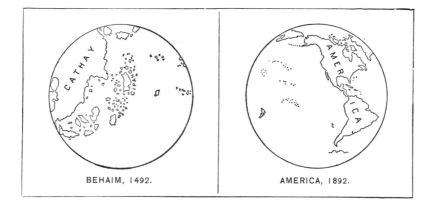

BEHAIM, 1492.      AMERICA, 1892.

# CHRISTOPHER COLUMBUS

## AND HOW HE RECEIVED AND IMPARTED THE SPIRIT OF DISCOVERY

BY

## JUSTIN WINSOR

They that go down to the sea in ships,
that do business in great waters, these
see the works of the Lord and his wonders in the deep. — *Psalms*, cvii. 23, 24

LONGMEADOW
P R E S S

1992

This special reprint edition
in honor of the
500th Anniversary of
Christopher Columbus'
discovery of America
is published
by

Longmeadow Press
201 High Ridge Road
Stamford, CT  06904

in association with

Platinum Press Inc.
311 Crossways Park Drive
Woodbury, NY  11797

ISBN  0-681-41381-6

098765432

Printed in USA


Library of Congress Cataloging-in-Publication Data

Winsor, Justin, 1831-1897.
    Christopher Columbus and how he received and imparted the
spirit of discovery / by Justin Winsor. -- 2nd ed.
    p.  cm.
    Originally published: Boston: Houghton Mifflin, 1892.
    "A Platinum Press book."
    Includes index.
    ISBN  0-681-41381-6
    1. Columbus, Christopher  2. America -- Discovery, and
exploration-Spanish. 3. Explorers -- America -- Biography.
4. Explorers -- Spain -- Biography. I. Title.
E111.W79  1992
970.01'5'092 — dc20
    [B]                                              92-13732
                                                        CIP

## To FRANCIS PARKMAN, LL. D.,

### THE HISTORIAN OF NEW FRANCE.

———

DEAR PARKMAN : —

You and I have not followed the maritime peoples of western Europe in planting and defending their flags on the American shores without observing the strange fortunes of the Italians, in that they have provided pioneers for those Atlantic nations without having once secured in the New World a foothold for themselves.

When Venice gave her Cabot to England and Florence bestowed Verrazano upon France, these explorers established the territorial claims of their respective and foster motherlands, leading to those contrasts and conflicts which it has been your fortune to illustrate as no one else has.

When Genoa gave Columbus to Spain and Florence accredited her Vespucius to Portugal, these adjacent powers, whom the Bull of Demarcation would have kept asunder in the new hemisphere, established their rival races in middle and southern America, neighboring as in the Old World ; but their contrasts and conflicts have never had so worthy a historian as you have been for those of the north.

The beginnings of their commingled history I have tried to relate in the present work, and I turn naturally to associate in it the name of the brilliant historian of FRANCE AND ENGLAND IN NORTH AMERICA with that of your obliged friend,

*Justin Winsor*

CAMBRIDGE, *June, 1890.*

# CONTENTS AND ILLUSTRATIONS.

# CHRISTOPHER COLUMBUS.

## CHAPTER I.

### SOURCES, AND THE GATHERERS OF THEM.

In considering the sources of information, which are original, as distinct from those which are derivative, we must place first in importance the writings of Columbus himself. We may place next the documentary proofs belonging to private and public archives.

Harrisse points out that Columbus, in his time, acquired such a popular reputation for prolixity that a court fool of Charles the Fifth linked the discoverer of the Indies with <sub>His</sub> Ptolemy as twins in the art of blotting. He wrote <sub>prolixity.</sub> as easily as people of rapid impulses usually do, when they are not restrained by habits of orderly deliberation. He has left us a mass of jumbled thoughts and experiences, which, unfortunately, often perplex the historian, while they of necessity aid him.

Ninety-seven distinct pieces of writing by the hand of Columbus either exist or are known to have existed. Of <sub>His</sub> such, whether memoirs, relations, or letters, sixty- <sub>writings.</sub> four are preserved in their entirety. These include twenty-four which are wholly or in part in his own hand. All of them have been printed entire, except one which is in the Biblioteca Colombina, in Seville, the *Libro de las Proficias*, written apparently between 1501 and 1504, of which only part is in Columbus's own hand. A second document, a memoir addressed to Ferdinand and Isabella, before June, 1497, is now in the collection of the Marquis of San Roman at Madrid, and was printed for the first time by Harrisse in his *Christophe Colomb*. A third and fourth are in the public archives in Madrid, being letters addressed to the Spanish monarchs: one without date in 1496 or 1497, or perhaps earlier, in 1493, and the

other February 6, 1502; and both have been printed and given
in facsimile in the *Cartas de Indias*, a collection published by

MANUSCRIPT OF COLUMBUS.

[From a MS. in the Biblioteca Colombina, given in Harrisse's *Notes on Columbus*.]

the Spanish government in 1877.   The majority of the existing
private papers of Columbus are preserved in Spain, in the
hands of the present representative of Columbus, the Duke of
Veragua, and these have all been printed in the great collection of Navarrete.   They consist, as enumerated by Harrisse in
his *Columbus and the Bank of Saint George*, of the following
pieces: a single letter addressed about the year 1500 to Ferdinand and Isabella; four letters addressed to Father Gaspar
Gorricio, — one from San Lucar, April 4, 1502; a second from
the Grand Canaria, May, 1502; a third from Jamaica, July 7,
1503; and the last from Seville, January 4, 1505; — a memorial addressed to his son, Diego, written either in December,
1504, or in January, 1505; and eleven letters addressed also to
Diego, all from Seville, late in 1504 or early in 1505.

Without exception, the letters of Columbus of which we have
knowledge were written in Spanish.   Harrisse has
conjectured that his stay in Spain made him a better
master of that language than the poor advantages of his early
life had made him of his mother tongue.

All in
Spanish.

Columbus was more careful of the documentary proofs of his titles and privileges, granted in consequence of his <sub>His privileges.</sub> discoveries, than of his own writings. He had more solicitude to protect, by such records, the pecuniary and titular rights of his descendants than to preserve those personal papers which, in the eyes of the historian, are far more valuable. These attested evidences of his rights were for a while inclosed in an iron chest, kept at his tomb in the monastery of Las Cuevas, near Seville, and they remained down to 1609 in the custody of the Carthusian friars of that convent. At this date, Nuño de Portugallo having been declared the heir to the estate and titles of Columbus, the papers were transferred to his keeping; and in the end, by legal decision, they passed to that Duke of Veragua who was the grandfather of the present duke, who in due time inherited these public memorials, and now preserves them in Madrid.

In 1502 there were copies made in book form, known as the *Codex Diplomaticus*, of these and other pertinent documents, raising the number from thirty-six to forty-four. These copies were attested at Seville, by order of the Admiral, who then aimed to place them so that the record of his deeds and rights should not be lost. Two copies seem to have been sent by him through different channels to Nicoló Oderigo, the Genoese ambassador in Madrid; and in 1670 both of these copies came from a descendant of that ambassador as a gift to the Republic of Genoa. Both of these later disappeared from its archives. A third copy was sent to Alonso Sanchez de Carvajal, the factor of Columbus in Española, and this copy is not now known. A fourth copy was deposited in the monastery of Las Cuevas, near Seville, to be later sent to Father Gorricio. It is very likely this last copy which is mentioned by Edward Everett in a note to his oration at Plymouth (Boston, 1825, p. 64), where, referring to the two copies sent to Oderigo as the only ones made by the order of Columbus, as then understood, he adds: " Whether the two manuscripts thus mentioned be the only ones in existence may admit of doubt. When I was in Florence, in 1818, a small folio manuscript was brought to me, written on parchment, apparently two or three centuries old, in binding once very rich, but now worn, containing a series of documents in Latin and Spanish, with the following title on the first blank page : ' Treslado de las Bullas del Papa Alexandro VI., de la concession de las Indias y los titulos, privilegios y cedulas reales, que se dieron a Christoval Colon.' I was led by this title to purchase the book." After referring to the *Codice*, then just published, he adds : " I was surprised to find my manuscript, as far as it goes, nearly identical in its contents with that of Genoa, supposed to be one of the only two in existence. My manuscript consists of almost eighty closely written folio pages, which coincide precisely with the text of the first thirty-seven documents, contained in two hundred and forty pages of the Genoese volume."

Caleb Cushing says of the Everett manuscript, which he had examined before he wrote of it in the *North American Review*, October, 1825, that, " so far as it goes, it is a much more perfect one than the Oderigo manuscript, as several passages which Spotorno was unable to decipher in the latter are very plain and legible in the former, which indeed is in most complete preservation." I am sorry to learn from Dr. William Everett that this manuscript is not at present easily accessible.

Of the two copies named above as having disappeared from the archives of Genoa, Harrisse at a late day found one in the archives of the Ministry of Foreign Affairs in Paris. It had been taken to Paris in 1811, when Napoleon I. caused the archives of Genoa to be sent to that city, and it was not returned when the chief part of the documents was recovered by Genoa in 1815. The other copy was in 1816 among the papers of Count Cambiaso, and was bought by the Sardinian government, and given to the city of Genoa, where it is now deposited in a marble *custodia*, which, surmounted by a bust of Columbus, stands at present in the main hall of the palace of the municipality. This " custodia " is a pillar, in which a door of gilded bronze closes the receptacle that contains the relics, which are themselves inclosed in a bag of Spanish leather, richly embossed. A copy of this last document was made and placed in the archives at Turin.

These papers, as selected by Columbus for preservation, were

Their publication by Spotorno.

edited by Father Spotorno at Genoa, in 1823, in a volume called *Codice diplomatico Colombo-Americano*, and published by authority of the state. There was an English edition at London, in 1823; and a Spanish at Havana, in 1867. Spotorno was re-printed, with additional matter, at Genoa, in 1857, as *La Tavola di Bronzo, il pallio di seta, ed il Codice Colomboamericano, nuovamente illustrati per cura di Giuseppe Banchero.*

This Spotorno volume included two additional letters of Columbus, not yet mentioned, and addressed, March 21, 1502, and December 27, 1504, to Oderigo. They were found pasted in the duplicate copy of the papers given to Genoa, and are now preserved in a glass case, in the same custodia. A third letter, April 2, 1502, addressed to the governors of the bank of St. George, was omitted by Spotorno; but it is given by Harrisse in his *Columbus and the Bank of Saint George* Letters to the Bank of St. George. (New York, 1888). This last was one of two letters, which Columbus sent, as he says, to the bank, but the other has not been found. The history of the one preserved is traced by Harrisse in the work last mentioned, and there are

THE GENOA CUSTODIA.

# CHRISTOPHER COLUMBUS.

COLUMBUS'S LETTER, APRIL 2, 1502, ADDRESSED TO THE BANK OF ST. GEORGE IN GENOA.

[Reduced in size by photographic process.]

lithographic and photographic reproductions of it. Harrisse's work just referred to was undertaken to prove the forgery of a manuscript which has within a few years been offered for sale, either as a duplicate of the one at Genoa, or as the original. When represented as the original, the one at Genoa is pronounced a facsimile of it. Harrisse seems to have proved the forgery of the one which is seeking a purchaser.

Some manuscript marginalia found in three different books, used by Columbus and preserved in the Biblioteca Colombina at Seville, are also remnants of the auto-graphs of Columbus. These marginal notes are in copies of Æneas Sylvius's *Historia Rerum ubique gestarum* (Venice, 1477) of a Latin version of Marco Polo (Antwerp, 1485 ?), and of Pierre d'Ailly's *De Imagine Mundi* (perhaps 1490), though there is some suspicion that these last-mentioned notes may be those of Bartholomew, and not of Christopher, Columbus. These books have been particularly described in José Silverio Jorrin's *Varios Autografos ineditos de Cristóbal Colon*, published at Havana in 1888. In May, 1860, José Maria Fernandez y Velasco, the librarian of the Biblioteca Colombina, discovered a Latin text of the letter of Toscanelli, written by Columbus in this same copy of Æneas Sylvius. He believed it a Latin version of a letter originally written in Italian; but it was left for Harrisse to discover that the Latin was the original draft. A facsimile of this script is in Harrisse's *Fernando Colon* (Seville, 1871), and specimens of the marginalia were first given by Harrisse in his *Notes on Columbus*, whence they are reproduced in part in the *Narrative and Critical History of America* (vol. ii.).

*Marginalia.*

*Toscanelli's letter.*

It is understood that, under the auspices of the Italian government, Harrisse is now engaged in collating the texts and preparing a national memorial issue of the writings of Columbus, somewhat in accordance with a proposition which he made to the Minister of Public Instruction at Rome in his *Le Quatrième Centenaire de la Découverte du Nouveau Monde* (Genoa, 1887).

*Harrisse's memorial of Columbus.*

There are references to printed works of Columbus which I have not seen, as a *Declaracion de Tabla Navigatoria*, annexed to a treatise, *Del Uso de la Carta de Navegar*, by Dr. Grajales ; a *Tratado de las Cinco Zonas Habitables*, which Humboldt found it very difficult to find.

*Columbus's printed works.*

Of the manuscripts of Columbus which are lost, there are

His lost writings.

traces still to be discovered. One letter, which he dated off the Canaries, February 15, 1493, and which

ANNOTATIONS BY COLUMBUS ON THE *IMAGO MUNDI.*
[From Harrisse's *Notes on Columbus.*]

must have contained some account of his first voyage, is only known to us from an intimation of Marino Sanuto that it was included in the *Chronica Delphinea.* It is probably from an imperfect copy of this last in the library at Brescia, that the letter in question was given in the book's third part (A. D. 1457–1500), which is now missing. We know also, from a letter still preserved (December 27, 1504), that there must be a letter somewhere, if not destroyed, sent by him respecting his fourth voyage, to Messer Gian Luigi Fieschi, as is supposed, the same who led the famous conspiracy against the house of Doria. Other letters, Columbus tells us, were sent at times to the Signora Madonna Catalina, who was in some way related to Fieschi.

In 1780, Francesco Pesaro, examining the papers of the Council of Ten, at Venice, read there a memoir of Columbus, setting forth his maritime project; or at least Pesaro was so understood by Marin, who gives the story at a later day in the seventh volume of his history of Venetian commerce. As Harrisse remarks, this paper, if it could be discovered, would prove the most interesting of all Columbian documents, since it would probably be found to fall within a period, from 1473 to 1487, when we have little or nothing authentic respecting Columbus's life. Indeed, it might happily elucidate a stage in the development of the Admiral's cosmographical views of which we know nothing.

We have the letter which Columbus addressed to Alexander VI., in February, 1502, as preserved in a copy made by his son Ferdinand; but no historical student has ever seen the Commentary, which he is said to have written after the manner of Cæsar, recounting the haps and mishaps of the first voyage, and which he is thought to have sent to the ruling Pontiff. This act of duty, if done after his return from his last voyage, must have been made to Julius the Second, not to Alexander.

Irving and others seem to have considered that this Cæsarian performance was in fact, the well-known journal of the first voyage; but there is a good deal of difficulty in identifying that which we only know in an abridged form, as made by Las Casas, with the narrative sent or intended to be sent to the Pope.

Journal of his first voyage.

Ferdinand, or the writer of the *Historie*, later to be mentioned, it seems clear, had Columbus's journal before him, though he excuses himself from quoting much from it, in order to avoid wearying the reader.

The original " journal " seems to have been in 1554 still in the possession of Luis Colon. It had not, accordingly, at that date been put among the treasures of the Biblioteca Colombina. Thus it may have fallen, with Luis's other papers, to his nephew and heir, Diego Colon y Pravia, who in 1578 entrusted them to Luis de Cardona. Here we lose sight of them.

Las Casas's abridgment in his own handwriting, however, has come down to us, and some entries in it would seem to indicate that Las Casas abridged a copy, and not the original. It was, up to 1886, in the library of the Duke of Orsuna, in Madrid, and was at that date bought by the Spanish government. While it was in the possession of Orsuna, it was printed by Varnhagen, in his *Verdadera Guanahani* (1864). It was clearly used by Las Casas in his own *Historia*, and was also in the hands of Ferdinand, when he wrote, or outlined, perhaps, what now passes for the life of his father, and Ferdinand's statements can sometimes correct or qualify the text in Las Casas. There is some reason to suppose that Herrera may have used the original. Las Casas tells us that in some parts, and particularly in describing the landfall and the events immediately succeeding, he did not vary the words of the original. This Las Casas abridgment was in the archives of the Duke del Infantado, when Navarrete discovered its importance, and edited it as early as 1791, though it was not given to the public till Navarrete published his *Coleccion* in 1825. When this journal is read, even as we have it, it is hard to imagine that Columbus could have intended so disjointed a performance to be an imitation of the method of Cæsar's *Commentaries*.

The American public was early given an opportunity to judge of this, and of its importance. It was by the instigation of George Ticknor that Samuel Kettell made a translation of the text as given by Navarrete, and published it in Boston in 1827, as a *Personal Narrative of the first Voyage of Columbus to America, from a Manuscript recently discovered in Spain.*

We also know that Columbus wrote other concise accounts of his discovery. On his return voyage, during a gale, on Feb-

*Abridged by Las Casas.*

ruary 14, 1493, fearing his ship would founder, he prepared a statement on parchment, which was incased in wax, put in a barrel, and thrown overboard, to take the chance of washing ashore. A similar account, protected in like manner, he placed on his vessel's poop, to be washed off in case of disaster. Neither of these came, as far as is known, to the notice of anybody. They very likely simply duplicated the letters which he wrote on the voyage, intended to be dispatched to their destination on reaching port. The dates and places of these letters are not reconcilable with his journal. He was apparently approaching the Azores, when, on February 15, he dated a letter "off the Canaries," directed to Luis de Santangel. So false a record as "the Canaries" has never been satisfactorily explained. It may be imagined, perhaps, that the letter had been written when Columbus supposed he would make those islands instead of the Azores, and that the place of writing was not changed. It is quite enough, however, to rest satisfied with the fact that Columbus was always careless, and easily erred in such things, as Navarrete has shown. The postscript which is added is dated March 14, which seems hardly probable, or even possible, so that March 4 has been suggested. He professes to write it on the day of his entering the Tagus, and this was March 4. It is possible that he altered the date when he reached Palos, as is Major's opinion. Columbus calls this a second letter. Perhaps a former letter was the one which, as already stated, we have lost in the missing part of the *Chronica Delphinea.*

**Descriptions of his first voyage.**

The original of this letter to Santangel, the treasurer of Aragon, and intended for the eyes of Ferdinand and Isabella, was in Spanish, and is known in what is thought to be a contemporary copy, found by Navarrete at Simancas; and it is printed by him in his *Coleccion*, and is given by Kettell in English, to make no other mention of places where it is accessible. Harrisse denies that this Simancas manuscript represents the original, as Navarrete had contended. A letter dated off the island of Santa Maria, the southernmost of the Azores, three days after the letter to Santangel, February 18, essentially the same, and addressed to Gabriel Sanchez, was found in what seemed to be an early copy, among the papers of the Colegio Mayor de Cuenca. This text was

**Letter to Santangel.**

**Letter to Sanchez.**

printed by Varnhagen at Valencia, in 1858, as *Primera Epistola del Almirante Don Cristóbal Colon*, and it is claimed by him that it probably much more nearly represents the original of Columbus's own drafting.

Printed editions. There was placed in 1852 in the Biblioteca Ambrosiana at Milan, from the library of Baron Pietro Custodi, a printed edition of this Spanish letter, issued in 1493, perhaps somewhere in Spain or Portugal, for Barcelona and Lisbon have been named. Harrisse conjectures that Sanchez gave his copy to some printer in Barcelona. Others have contended that it was not printed in Spain at all. No other copy of this edition has ever been discovered. It was edited by Cesare Correnti at Milan in 1863, in a volume called *Lettere autografe di Cristoforo Colombo, nuovamente stampate*, and was again issued in facsimile in 1866 at Milan, under the care of Girolamo d'Adda, as *Lettera in lingua Spagnuola diretta da Cristoforo Colombo a Luis de Sant-Angel*. Major and Becher, among others, have given versions of it to the English reader, and Harrisse gives it side by side with a French version in his *Christophe Colomb* (i. 420), and with an English one in his *Notes on Columbus*.

This text in Spanish print had been thought the only avenue of approach to the actual manuscript draft of Columbus, till very recently two other editions, slightly varying, are said to have been discovered, one or both of which are held by some, but on no satisfactory showing, to have preceded in issue, probably by a short interval, the Ambrosian copy.

One of these newly alleged editions is on four leaves in quarto, and represents the letter as dated on February 15 and March 14, and its cut of type has been held to be evidence of having been printed at Burgos, or possibly at Salamanca. That this and the Ambrosian letter were printed one from the other, or independently from some unknown anterior edition, has been held to be clear from the fact that they correspond throughout in the division of lines and pages. It is not easily determined which was the earlier of the two, since there are errors in each corrected in the other. This unique four-leaf quarto was a few months since offered for sale in London, by Ellis and Elvey, who have published (1889) an English translation of it, with annotations by Julia E. S. Rae. It is now understood to be in the possession of a New York collector. It is but fair to say that suspicions of its genuineness have been entertained; indeed, there can be scarce a doubt that it is a modern fabrication.

The other of these newly discovered editions is in folio of two leaves, and was the last discovered, and was very recently held by Maisonneuve of Paris at 65,000 francs, and has since been offered by Quaritch in London for £1,600. It is said to have been discovered in Spain, and to have been printed at Barcelona; and this last fact is thought to be apparent from the Catalan form of some of the Spanish, which has disappeared in the Ambrosian text. It also gives the dates February 15 and March 14. A facsimile edition has been issued under the title *La Lettre de Christophe Colomb, annonçant la Découverte du Nouveau Monde*.

Caleb Cushing, in the *North American Review* in October, 1825, refers to newspaper stories then current of a recent sale of a copy of the Spanish text in London, for £33 12s. to the Duke of Buckingham. It cannot now be traced.

Harrisse finds in Ferdinand's catalogue of the Biblioteca Colombina what was probably a Catalan text of this Spanish letter; but it has disappeared from the collection. Catalan text.

Bergenroth found at Simancas, some years ago, the text of another letter by Columbus, with the identical dates already given, and addressed to a friend; but it conveyed nothing not known in the printed Spanish texts. Letter found by Bergenroth. He, however, gave a full abstract of it in the *Calendar of State Papers relating to England and Spain*.

Columbus is known, after his return from the second voyage, to have been the guest of Andrès Bernaldez, the Cura de los Palacios, and he is also known to have placed papers in this friend's hands; and so it has been held Columbus gives papers to Bernaldez. probable by Muñoz that another Spanish text of Columbus's first account is embodied in Bernaldez's *Historia de los Reyes Católicos*. The manuscript of this work, which gives thirteen chapters to Columbus, long remained unprinted in the royal library at Madrid, and Irving, Prescott, and Humboldt all used it in that form. It was finally printed at Granada in 1856, as edited by Miguel Lafuente y Alcántara, and was reprinted at Seville in 1870. Harrisse, in his *Notes on Columbus*, gives an English version of this section on the Columbus voyage.

These, then, are all the varieties of the Spanish text of Columbus's first announcement of his discovery which
Varieties of the Spanish text. are at present known. When the Ambrosian text
was thought to be the only printed form of it, Varn-
hagen, in his *Carta de Cristóbal Colon enviada de Lisboa á
Barcelona en Marzo de 1493* (Vienna, 1869; and Paris, 1870),
collated the different texts to try to reconstruct a possible
original text, as Columbus wrote it. In the opinion of Major
no one of these texts can be considered an accurate transcript
of the original.

There is a difference of opinion among these critics as to the
Origin of the Latin text. origin of the Latin text which scholars generally cite
as this first letter of Columbus. Major thinks this
Latin text was not taken from the Spanish, though similar to it;
while Varnhagen thinks that the particular Spanish text found
in the Colegio Mayor de Cuenca was the original of the Latin
version.

There is nothing more striking in the history of the years
immediately following the discovery of America than
Transient fame of the discovery. the transient character of the fame which Columbus
acquired by it. It was another and later generation
that fixed his name in the world's regard.

Harrisse points out how some of the standard chroniclers of
the world's history, like Ferrebouc, Regnault, Galliot du Pré,
and Fabian, failed during the early half of the sixteenth century to make any note of the acts of Columbus; and he could
find no earlier mention among the German chroniclers than that
of Heinrich Steinhowel, some time after 1531. There was even
great reticence among the chroniclers of the Low Countries; and
in England we need to look into the dispatches sent thence by
the Spanish ambassadors to find the merest mention
English mentions of it. of Columbus so early as 1498. Perhaps the reference to him made eleven years later (1509), in an
English version of Brandt's *Shyppe of Fools*, and another
still ten years later in a little native comedy called *The New
Interlude*, may have been not wholly unintelligible. It was not
till about 1550 that, so far as England is concerned, Columbus
really became a historical character, in Edward Hall's *Chronicle*.

Speaking of the fewness of the autographs of Columbus

which are preserved, Harrisse adds: "The fact is that Columbus was very far from being in his lifetime the important personage he now is ; and his writings, which then commanded neither respect nor attention, were probably thrown into the waste-basket as soon as received."

Nevertheless, substantial proof seems to exist in the several editions of the Latin version of this first letter, which were issued in the months immediately following the return of Columbus from his first voyage, as well as in the popular versification of its text by Dati in two editions, both in October, 1493, besides another at Florence in 1495, to show that for a brief interval, at least, the news was more or less engrossing to the public mind in certain confined areas of Europe. Before the discovery of the printed editions of the Spanish text, there existed an impression that either the interest in Spain was less than in Italy, or some effort was made by the Spanish government to prevent a wide dissemination of the details of the news.

Editions of the Latin text.

The two Genoese ambassadors who left Barcelona some time after the return of Columbus, perhaps in August, 1493, may possibly have taken to Italy with them some Spanish edition of the letter. The news, however, had in some form reached Rome in season to be the subject of a papal bull on May 3d. We know that Aliander or Leander de Cosco, who made the Latin version, very likely from the Sanchez copy, finished it probably at Barcelona, on the 29th of April, not on the 25th as is sometimes said. Cosco sent it at once to Rome to be printed, and his manuscript possibly conveyed the first tidings, to Italy, — such is Harrisse's theory, — where it reached first the hands of the Bishop of Monte Peloso, who added to it a Latin epigram. It was he who is supposed to have committed it to the printer in Rome, and in that city, during the rest of 1493, four editions at least of Cosco's Latin appeared. Two of these editions are supposed to be printed by Plannck, a famous Roman printer ; one is known to have come from the press of Franck Silber. All but one were little quartos, of the familiar old style, of three or four black-letter leaves ; while the exception was a small octavo with woodcuts. It is Harrisse's opinion that this pictorial edition was really printed at Basle. In Paris, during the same time or shortly after, there were three editions of a similar appearance, all from one press. The latest of all, brought to light but recently, seems to have been printed by a distinguished

¶ Epiſtola Chriſtofori Colom : cui etas noſtra multũ debet: de Inſulis Indie ſupra Gangem nuper inuentis·Ad quas perquirendas octauo antea menſe auſpicijs τ ere inuictiſſimi Fernandi Hiſpaniarum Regis miſſus fuerat:ad Magnificum dñm Raphaelem Sanxis:eiuſdem ſereniſſimi Regis Teſaurariũ miſſa: quam nobilis ac litteratus vir Aliander de Coſco ab Hiſpano ideomate in latinum conuertit : tertio kals Maij·M·cccc·xciij· Pontificatus Alexandri Sexti Anno primo·

Quoniam ſuſcepte prouintie rem perfectam me cõſecutum fuiſſe gratum tibi fore ſcio: has conſtitui exarare: que te vniuſcuiuſ cõ rei in hoc noſtro itinere geſte inuentecõ ad/ moneant: Tricefimotertio die poſt cõ Gadibus diſceſſi in mare Indicũ perueni:vbi plurimas inſulas innumeris habitatas hol minibus repperi:quarum omnium pro foeliciſſmo Rege noſtro preconio celebrato τ vexillis extenſis contradicente nemine poſ/ ſeſſionem accepi:prime cõ earum diui Saluatoris nomen impo/ ſui:euius fretus auxilio tam ad hanc: cõ ad ceteras alias peruel nimus·Eam ꝟo Indi Guanabanin vocant·Aliarum etiã vnam quan cõ nouo nomine nuncupaui·Quippe aliã inſulam Sancte Marie Conceptionis·aliam Fernandinam · aliam Hyſabellam· aliam Iohanam·τ ſic de reliquis appellari iuſſi·Quamprimum in eam inſulam quã dudum Iohanã vocari dixi appulimus:iu xta eius littus occidentem verſus aliquantulum proceſſi:tam cõ eam magnã nullo reperto fine inueni:vt non inſulam: ſed conti nentem: Chatai prouinciam eſſe crediderim:nulla tñ videns op/ pida municipiaue in maritimis ſita confinib? preter aliquos vi/ cos τ predia ruſtica:cum quoꝝ incolis loqui nequibam·quare fi mul ac nos videbant ſurripiebant fugam· Progrediebar vltra: exiſtimans aliquã me vrbem villaſue inuenturum·Deni cõ vides cõ longe admodum progreſſis nibil noui emergebat:τ bmõi via nos ad Septentrionem deferebat: cõ ipſe fugere exoptabã:terris etenim regnabat bruma: ad Auſtrũm cõ erat in voto cõtendere:

FIRST PAGE, COLUMBUS'S FIRST LETTER, LATIN EDITION, 1493.
[From the Barlow copy, now in the Boston Public Library.]

Flemish printer, Thierry Martens, probably at Antwerp. It

is not improbable that other editions printed in all these or other cities may yet be found. It is noteworthy that nothing was issued in Germany, as far as we know, before a German version of the letter appeared at Strassburg in 1497.

The text in all these Latin editions is intended to be the same. But a very few copies of any edition, and only a single copy of two or three of them, are known. The Lenox, the Carter-Brown, and the Ives libraries in this country are the chief ones possessing any of them, and the collections of the late Henry C. Murphy and Samuel L. M. Barlow also possessed a copy or two, the edition owned by Barlow passing in February, 1890, to the Boston Public Library. This scarcity and the rivalry of collectors would probably, in case any one of them should be brought upon the market, raise the price to fifteen hundred dollars or more. The student is not so restricted as this might imply, for in several cases there have been modern facsimiles and reprints, and there is an early reprint by Veradus, annexed to his poem (1494) on the capture of Granada. The text usually quoted by the older writers, however, is that embodied in the *Bellum Christianorum Principum* of Robertus Monarchus (Basle, 1533).

In these original small quartos and octavos, there is just enough uncertainty and obscurity as to dates and printers, to lure bibliographers and critics of typography into research and controversy; and hardly any two of them agree in assigning the same order of publication to these several issues. Order of The present writer has in the second volume of the publication. *Narrative and Critical History of America* grouped the varied views, so far as they had in 1885 been made known. The bibliography to which Harrisse refers as being at the end of his work on Columbus was crowded out of its place and has not appeared; but he enters into a long examination of the question of priority in the second chapter of his last volume. The earliest English translation of this Latin text appeared in the *Edinburgh Review* in 1816, and other issues have been variously made since that date.

We get some details of this first voyage in Oviedo, which we do not find in the journal, and Vicente Yañez Pinzon and Hernan Perez Matheos, who were companions of Columbus, are said to be the source of this additional matter.    The testimony

Additional
sources re-
specting the
first voyage. in the lawsuit of 1515, particularly that of Garcia Hernandez, who was in the " Pinta," and of a sailor named Francisco Garcia Vallejo, adds other details.

There is no existing account by Columbus himself of his ex-

Second voy-
age. periences during his second voyage, and of that cruise along the Cuban coast in which he supposed himself to have come in sight of the Golden Chersonesus.    The *Historie* tells us that during this cruise he kept a journal, *Libro del Segundo Viage*, till he was prostrated by sickness, and this itinerary is cited both in the *Historie* and by Las Casas.    We also get at second-hand from Columbus, what was derived from him in conversation after his return to Spain, in the account of these explorations which Bernaldez has embodied in his *Reyes Católicos*.    Irving says that he found these descriptions of Bernaldez by far the most useful of the sources for this period, as giving him the details for a picturesque narrative.    On disembarking at Cadiz in June, 1495, Columbus sent to his sovereigns two dispatches, neither of which is now known.

It was in the collection of the Duke of Veragua that Navar-

Columbus's
letters. rete discovered fifteen autograph letters of Columbus, four of them addressed to his friend, the Father Gaspar Gorricio, and the rest to his son Diego.    Navarrete speaks of them when found as in a very deplorable and in parts almost unreadable condition, and severely taxing, for deciphering them, the practiced skill of Tomas Gonzalez, which had been acquired in the care which he had bestowed on the archives of Simancas.    It is known that two letters addressed to Gorricio in 1498, and four in 1501, beside a single letter addressed in the last year to Diego Colon, which were in the iron chest at Las Cuevas, are not now in the archives of the Duke of Veragua ; and it is further known that during the great lawsuit of Columbus's heirs, Cristoval de Cardona tampered with that chest, and was brought to account for the act in 1580.    Whatever he removed may possibly some day be found, as Harrisse thinks, among the notarial records of Valencia.

Two letters of Columbus respecting his third voyage are only

Third voy-
age. known in early copies ; one in Las Casas's hand belonged to the Duke of Orsuna, and the other addressed to the nurse of Prince Juan is in the Custodia collection at Genoa.    Both are printed by Navarrete.

Columbus, in a letter dated December 27, 1504, mentions a relation of his fourth voyage with a supplement, which he Fourth voyage. had sent from Seville to Oderigo ; but it is not known.
We are without trace also of other letters, which he wrote at Dominica and at other points during this voyage. We do know, however, a letter addressed by Columbus to Ferdinand and Isabella, giving some account of his voyage to July 7, 1503. The lost Spanish original is represented in an early copy, which is printed by Navarrete. Though no contemporary Spanish edition is known, an Italian version was issued at Venice in 1505, as *Copia de la Lettera per Colombo mandata.* This was reprinted with comments by Morelli, at Bassano, in 1810, and the title which this librarian gave it of *Lettera Rarissima* has clung to it, in most of the citations which refer to it.

Peter Martyr, writing in January, 1494, mentions just having received a letter from Columbus, but it is not known to exist.

Las Casas is said to have once possessed a treatise by Columbus on the information obtained from Portuguese Las Casas uses Columbus's papers. and Spanish pilots, concerning western lands ; and he also refers to *Libros de Memorias del Almirante.* He is also known by his own statements to have had numerous autograph letters of Columbus. What has become of them is not known. If they were left in the monastery of San Gregorio at Valladolid, where Las Casas used them, they have disappeared with papers of the convent, since they were not among the archives of the suppressed convents, as Harrisse tells us, which were entrusted in 1850 to the Academy of History at Madrid.

In his letter to Doña Juana, Columbus says that he has deposited a work in the Convent de la Mejorada, in Work on the Arctic pole. which he has predicted the discovery of the Arctic pole. It has not been found.

Harrisse also tells us of the unsuccessful search which he has made for an alleged letter of Columbus, said in Gun- Missing letters. ther and Schultz's handbook of autographs (Leipzig, 1856) to have been bought in England by the Duke of Buckingham ; and it was learned from Tross, the Paris bookseller, that about 1850 some autograph letters of Columbus, seen by him, were sent to England for sale.

After his return from his first voyage, Columbus prepared a
Columbus's map and an accompanying table of longitudes and lati-
maps.        tudes for the new discoveries. They are known to
have been the subject of correspondence between him and the
queen.

There are various other references to maps which Columbus
had constructed, to embody his views or show his discoveries.
Not one, certainly to be attributed to him, is known, though
Ojeda, Niño, and others are recorded as having used, in their
explorations, maps made by Columbus. Peter Martyr's language does not indicate that Columbus ever completed any
chart, though he had, with the help of his brother Bartholomew,
begun one. The map in the Ptolemy of 1513 is said by Santarem to have been drawn by Columbus, or to have been based
on his memoranda, but the explanation on the map seems rather
to imply that information derived from an admiral in the service of Portugal was used in correcting it, and since Harrisse
has brought to light what is usually called the Cantino map,
there is strong ground for supposing that the two had one prototype.

Let us pass from records by Columbus to those about him.
We owe to an ancient custom of Italy that so much
Italian no-
tarial rec- has been preserved, to throw in the aggregate no small
ords.      amount of light on the domestic life of the family in
which Columbus was the oldest born. During the fourteen
years in which his father lived at Savona, every little business
act and legal transaction was attested before notaries, whose
records have been preserved filed in *filzas* in the archives of
the town.

These *filzas* were simply a file of documents tied together by
a string passed through each, and a *filza* generally embraced a
year's accumulation. The photographic facsimile which Harrisse gives in his *Columbus and the Bank of Saint George*, of
the letter of Columbus preserved by the bank, shows how the
sheet was folded once lengthwise, and then the hole was made
midway in each fold.

We learn in this way that, as early as 1470 and later, Columbus stood security for his father. We find him in 1472 the
witness of another's will. As under the Justinian procedure

the notary's declaration sufficed, such documents in Italy are not rendered additionally interesting by the autograph of the witness, as they would be in England. This notarial resource is no new discovery. As early as 1602, thirteen documents drawn from similar depositaries were printed at Genoa, in some annotations by Giulio Salinerio upon Cornelius Tacitus. Other similar papers were discovered by the archivists of Savona, Gian Tommaso and Giambattista Belloro, in 1810 (reprinted, 1821) and 1839 respectively, and proving the general correctness of the earlier accounts of Columbus's younger days given in Gallo, Senarega, and Giustiniani. It is to be regretted that the original entries of some of these notarial acts are not now to be found, but patient search may yet discover them, and even do something more to elucidate the life of the Columbus family in Savona.

There has been brought into prominence and published lately a memoir of the illustrious natives of Savona, written by a lawyer, Giovanni Vincenzo Verzellino, Savona. who died in that town in 1638. This document was printed at Savona in 1885, under the editorial care of Andrea Astengo; but Harrisse has given greater currency to its elucidations for our purpose in his *Christophe Colomb et Savone* (Genoa, 1877).

Harrisse is not unwisely confident that the nineteen documents — if no more have been added — throwing light Genoa notarial records. on minor points of the obscure parts of the life of Columbus and his kindred, which during recent years have been discovered in the notarial files of Genoa by the Marquis Marcello Staglieno, may be only the precursors of others yet to be unearthed, and that the pages of the *Giornale Ligustico* may continue to record such discoveries as it has in the past.

The records of the Bank of Saint George in Genoa have yielded something, but not much. In the state archives of Genoa, preserved since 1817 in the Palazzetto, we Records of the Bank of St. George. might hope to find some report of the great discovery, of which the Genoese ambassadors, Francesco Marchesio and Gian Antonio Grimaldi, were informed, just as they were taking leave of Ferdinand and Isabella for returning to Italy; but nothing of that kind has yet been brought to light there ; nor was it ever there, unless the account which Senarega gives in the narrative printed in Muratori was borrowed thence. We may hope, but probably in vain, to have these public archives determine if Columbus really offered to serve his native country in a voyage of discovery. The inquirer is more fortunate if he explores what there is left of the archives of the old abbey of St. Stephen, which, since the suppression of the convents in 1797, have been a part of the public papers, for he can find in them some help in solving some pertinent questions.

Harrisse tells us in 1887 that he had been waiting two years Vatican ar- for permission to search the archives of the Vatican. chives. What may yet be revealed in that repository, the world waits anxiously to learn. It may be that some one shall yet discover there the communication in which Ferdinand and Isabella announced to the Pope the consummation of the hopes of Columbus. It may be that the diplomatic correspondence covering the claims of Spain by virtue of the discovery of Columbus, and leading to the bull of demarcation of May, 1493, may yet be found, accompanied by maps, of the highest interest in interpreting the relations of the new geography. There is no assurance that the end of manuscript disclosures has yet come. Hidden Some new bit of documentary proof has been found manu- at times in places quite unexpected. The number of scripts. Italian observers in those days of maritime excitement living in the seaports and trading places of Spain and Portugal, kept their home friends alert in expectation by reason of such Letters appetizing news. Such are the letters sent to Italy about Co- by Hanibal Januarius, and by Luca, the Florentine lumbus. engineer, concerning the first voyage. There are similar transient summaries of the second voyage. Some have been found in the papers of Macchiavelli, and others had been arranged by Zorzi for a new edition of his documentary collection. These have all been recovered of recent years, and Harrisse himself, Gargiolli, Guerrini, and others, have been instrumental in their publication.

It was thirty-seven years after the death of Columbus before, Spanish under an order of Charles the Fifth, February 19, archives. 1543, the archives of Spain were placed in some sort of order and security at Simancas. The great masses of papers filed by the crown secretaries and the Councils of the

Indies and of Seville, were gradually gathered there, but not until many had been lost. Others apparently disappeared at a later day, for we are now aware that many to which Herrera refers cannot be found. New efforts to secure the preservation and systematize the accumulation of manuscripts were made by order of Philip the Second in 1567, but it would seem without all the success that might have been desired. Towards the end of the last century, it was the wish of Charles the Third that all the public papers relating to the New World <sub>Simancas</sub> should be selected from Simancas and all other places <sub>and Seville.</sub> of deposit and carried to Seville. The act was accomplished in 1788, when they were placed in a new building which had been provided for them. Thus it is that to-day the student of Columbus must rather search Seville than Simancas for new documents, though a few papers of some interest in connection with the contests of his heirs with the crown of Castile may still exist at Simancas. Thirty years ago, if not now, as Bergenroth tells us, there was little comfort for the student of history in working at Simancas. The papers are preserved <sub>Simancas.</sub> in an old castle, formerly belonging to the admirals of Castile, which had been confiscated and devoted to the uses of such a repository. The one large room which was assigned for the accommodation of readers had a northern aspect, and .as no fires were allowed, the note-taker found not infrequently in winter the ink partially congealed in his pen. There was no imaginable warmth even in the landscape as seen from the windows, since, amid a treeless waste, the whistle of cold blasts in winter and a blinding African heat in summer characterize the climate of this part of Old Castile.

Of the early career of Columbus, it is very certain that something may be gained at Simancas, for when Bergenroth, sent by the English government, made search there to illustrate the relations of Spain with England, and published his results, with the assistance of Gayangos, in 1862–1879, as a *Calendar of Letters, Despatches, and State Papers relating to Negotiations between England and Spain,* one of the earliest entries of his first printed volume, under 1485, was a complaint of Ferdinand and Isabella against a Columbus — some have supposed it our Christopher — for his participancy in the piratical service of the French.

ARCHIVO DE SIMANCAS.
[From Parcerisa and Quadrado's *España.*]

Harrisse complains that we have as yet but scant knowledge of what the archives of the Indies at Seville may con- Seville. tain, but they probably throw light rather upon the successors of Columbus than upon the career of the Admiral himself.

The notarial archives of Seville are of recent construction, the gathering of scattered material having been first Seville ordered so late as 1869. The partial examination notarial records. which has since been made of them has revealed some slight evidences of the life of some of Columbus's kindred, and it is quite possible some future inquirer will be rewarded for his diligent search among them.

It is also not unlikely that something of interest may be brought to light respecting the descendants of Columbus who have lived in Seville, like the Counts of Gelves ; but little can be expected regarding the life of the Admiral himself.

The personal fame of Columbus is much more intimately con- nected with the monastery of Santa Maria de las Cue- Santa Maria vas. Here his remains were transported in 1509 ; and de las Cue- vas. at a later time, his brother and son, each Diego by name, were laid beside him, as was his grandson Luis. Here in an iron chest the family muniments and jewels were kept, as has been said. It is affirmed that all the documents which might have grown out of these transactions of duty and precau- tion, and which might incidentally have yielded some biograph- ical information, are nowhere to be found in the records of the monastery. A century ago or so, when Muñoz was working in these records, there seems to have been enough to repay his exertions, as we know by his citations made between 1781 and 1792.

The national archives of the Torre do Tombo, at Lisbon, begun so far back as 1390, are well known to have Portuguese been explored by Santarem, then their keeper, pri- archives. Torre do marily for traces of the career of Vespucius ; but so Tombo. intelligent an antiquary could not have forgotten, as a second- ary aim, the acts of Columbus. The search yielded him, how- ever, nothing in this last direction ; nor was Varnhagen more fortunate. Harrisse had hopes to discover there the corre- spondence of Columbus with John the Second, in 1488 ; but the

search was futile in this respect, though it yielded not a little
respecting the Perestrello family, out of which Columbus took
his wife, the mother of the heir of his titles.  There is even
hope that the notarial acts of Lisbon might serve a similar purpose to those which have been so fruitful in Genoa and Savona.
There are documents of great interest which may be yet obscurely hidden away, somewhere in Portugal, like the letter
from the mouth of the Tagus, which Columbus on his return in
March, 1493, addressed to the Portuguese king, and the diplomatic correspondence of John the Second and Ferdinand of
Aragon, which the project of a second voyage occasioned, as
well as the preliminaries of the treaty of Tordesillas.

There may be yet some hope from the archives of Santo
Domingo itself, and from those of its Cathedral, to
Santo Do-
mingo      trace in some of their lines the descendants of the
archives.
Admiral through his son Diego.  The mishaps of nature and war have, however, much impaired the records.  Of
Columbus himself there is scarce a chance to learn anything
Lawsuit      here.  The papers of the famous lawsuit of Diego
papers.     Colon with the crown seem to have escaped the attention of all the historians before the time of Muñoz and
Navarrete.  The direct line of male descendants of the Admiral ended in 1578, when his great-grandson, Diego Colon
y Pravia, died on the 27th January, a childless man.  Then
began another contest for the heritage and titles, and it lasted
for thirty years, till in 1608 the Council of the Indies judged
the rights to descend by a turn back to Diego's aunt Isabel,
and thence to her grandson, Nuño de Portugallo, Count of
Gelves.  The excluded heirs, represented by the children of a
sister of Diego, Francisca, who had married Diego Ortegon,
were naturally not content ; and out of the contest which followed we get a large mass of printed statements and counter
statements, which used with caution, offer a study perhaps of
some of the transmitted traits of Columbus.  Harrisse names
and describes nineteen of these documentary memorials, the
last of which bears date in 1792.  The most important of them
all, however, is one printed at Madrid in 1606, known as *Memorial del Pleyto*, in which we find the descent of the true and
spurious lines, and learn something too much of the scandalous
life of Luis, the grandson of the Admiral, to say nothing of the

illegitimate taints of various other branches. Harrisse finds assistance in working out some of the lines of the Admiral's descendants, in Antonio Caetano de Sousa's *Historia Genealogica da Casa Real Portugueza* (Lisbon, 1735–49, in 14 vols.).

The most important collection of documents gathered by individual efforts in Spain, to illustrate the early his- The Muñoz tory of the New World, was that made by Juan Bau- collection. tista Muñoz, in pursuance of royal orders issued to him in 1781 and 1788, to examine all Spanish archives, for the purpose of collecting material for a comprehensive History of the Indies. Muñoz has given in the introduction of his history a clear statement of the condition of the different depositories of archives in Spain, as he found them towards the end of the last century, when a royal order opened them all to his search. A first volume of Muñoz's elaborate and judicious work was issued in 1793, and Muñoz died in 1799, without venturing on a second volume to carry the story beyond 1500, where he had left it. He was attacked for his views, and there was more or less of a pamphlet war over the book before death took him from the strife ; but he left a fragment of the second volume in manuscript, and of this there is a copy in the Lenox Library in New York. Another copy was sold in the Brinley sale. The Muñoz collection of copies came in part, at least, at some time after the collector's death into the hands of Antonio de Uguina, who placed them at the disposal of Irving ; and Ternaux seems also to have used them. They were finally deposited by the Spanish government in the Academy of History at Madrid. Here Alfred Demersey saw them in 1862–63, and described them in the *Bulletin* of the French Geographical Society in June, 1864, and it is on this description as well as on one in Fuster's *Biblioteca Valenciana*, that Harrisse depends, not having himself examined the documents.

Martin Fernandez de Navarrete was guided in his career as a collector of documents, when Charles the Fourth
made an order, October 15, 1789. that there should be The Navar-rete collec-tion. such a work begun to constitute the nucleus of a library and museum. The troublous times which succeeded interrupted the work, and it was not till 1825 that Navarrete brought out the first volume of his *Coleccion de los Viages y Descubrimientos que hicieron por Mar los Españoles desde*

*Fines del Siglo XV.*, a publication which a fifth volume completed in 1837, when he was over seventy years of age.

Any life of Columbus written from documentary sources must reflect much light from this collection of Navarrete, of which the first two volumes are entirely given to the career of the Admiral, and indeed bear the distinctive title of *Relaciones, Cartas y otros Documentos*, relating to him.

Navarrete was engaged thirty years on his work in the archives of Spain, and was aided part of the time by

The researches of Navarrete. Muñoz the historian, and by Gonzales the keeper of the archives at Simancas. His researches extended to all the public repositories, and to such private ones as could be thought to illustrate the period of discovery. Navarrete has told the story of his searches in the various archives of Spain, in the introduction to his *Coleccion*, and how it was while searching for the evidences of the alleged voyage of Maldonado on the Pacific coast of North America, in 1588, that he stumbled upon Las Casas's copies of the relations of Columbus, for his first and third voyages, then hid away in the archives of the Duc del Infantado ; and he was happy to have first brought them to the attention of Muñoz.

There are some advantages for the student in the use of the French edition of Navarrete's *Relations des Quatre Voyages entrepris par Colomb*, since the version was revised by Navarrete himself, and it is elucidated, not so much as one would wish, with notes by Rémusat, Balbi, Cuvier, Jomard, Letronne, St. Martin, Walckenaer, and others. It was published at Paris in three volumes in 1828. The work contains Navarrete's accounts of Spanish pre-Columbian voyages, of the later literature on Columbus, and of the voyages of discovery made by other efforts of the Spaniards, beside the documentary material respecting Columbus and his voyages, the result of his continued labors. Caleb Cushing, in his *Reminiscences of Spain* in 1833, while commending the general purposes of Navarrete, complains of his attempts to divert the indignation of posterity from the selfish conduct of Ferdinand, and to vindicate him from the charge of injustice towards Columbus. This plea does not find to-day the same sympathy in students that it did sixty years ago.

Father Antonio de Aspa of the monastery of the Mejorada,

formed a collection of documents relating to the discovery of the New World, and it was in this collection, now preserved in the Academy of History at Madrid, that Navarrete discovered that curious narration of the second voyage of Columbus by Dr. Chanca, which had been sent to the chapter of the Cathedral, and which Navarrete included in his collection. It is thought that Bernaldez had used this Chanca narrative in his *Reyes Católicos*.

Madrid Academy of History.

Navarrete's name is also connected, as one of its editors, with the extensive *Coleccion de Documentos Ineditos para la Historia de España*, the publication of which was begun in Madrid in 1847, two years before Navarrete's death. This collection yields something in elucidation of the story to be here told; but not much, except that in it, at a late day, the *Historia* of Las Casas was first printed.

Coleccion de Documentos Ineditos.

In 1864, there was still another series begun at Madrid, *Coleccion de Documentos Ineditos relativos al Descubrimiento, Conquista y Colonizacion de las Posesiones Españolas en América y Oceania*, under the editing of Joaquin Pacheco and Francisco de Cárdenas, who have not always satisfied students by the way in which they have done their work. Beyond the papers which Navarrete had earlier given, and which are here reprinted, there is not much in this collection to repay the student of Columbus, except some long accounts of the Repartimiento in Española.

The latest documentary contribution is the large folio, with an appendix of facsimile writings of Columbus, Vespucius, and others, published at Madrid in 1877, by the government, and called *Cartas de Indias*, in which it has been hinted some use has been made of the matter accumulated by Navarrete for additional volumes of his *Coleccion*.

Cartas de Indias.

Dies diei apponit, & manifeftat verbum & nox nocti diminuit & nunciat fcientiam.

Nõ eft verbú lamentationis, & nõ funt fermones tumultus & non audiuntur voces eorum. In omnem terram extenfi funt effectus eorum, & in fines orbis omnia verba eorum, foli pofuit tabernaculum.

Illumiatione aũti illos. Et ipfe i mane tanq fponfus procedes de thalamo fuo pulcherrime, & dum diuiditur dies letatur vt gigas, & obferuat ad currendam in fortitudine viam occafus: vefptini. Ab extremitatibus

D. Et in fines mundi uerba eorum, Saltem téporibus noftris qbs mirabili aufu Chriftophori columbi genuenfis, alter pene orbis repertus eft chriftianorumq3 cetui aggregatus. At uetoquoniam Columbus frequéter pdicabat fe a Deo electum ut periptum adimpleretur hec prophetia. non alienu exiftimaui uitam ipfius hoc loco incerte. Igitur Chriftophorus cognomento columbus patria genuenfis, uilibus ortus parentibus, noftra etate fuit qui fua induftria, plus retrarum & peflagi exploauerit paues mé fibus, quam penereñ oui omñes mortales umuerfis retro actis

PART OF A PAGE IN THE GIUSTINIANI PSALTER, SHOWING THE BEGINNING OF THE EARLIEST PRINTED LIFE OF COLUMBUS.

# CHAPTER II.

WE may most readily divide by the nationalities of the writers our enumeration of those who have used the material which has been considered in the previous chapter. We begin, naturally, with the Italians, the countrymen of Columbus. We may look first to three Genoese, and it has been shown that while they used documents apparently now lost, they took nothing from them which we cannot get from other sources ; and they all borrowed from common originals, or from each other. Two of these writers are Antonio Gallo, the official chronicler of the Genoese Republic, on the first and second voyages of Columbus, and so presumably writing before the third was made, and Bartholomew Senarega on the affairs of Genoa, both of which recitals were published by Muratori, in his great Italian collection. The third is Giustiniani, the Bishop of Ncbbio, who, publishing in 1516, at Genoa, a polyglot Psalter, added, as one of his elucidations of the nineteenth psalm, on the plea that Columbus had often boasted he was chosen to fulfill its prophecy, a brief life of Columbus, in which the story of the humble origin of the navigator has in the past been supposed to have first been told. The other accounts, it now appears, had given that condition an equal prominence. Giustiniani was but a child when Columbus left Genoa, and could not have known him ; and taking, very likely, much from hearsay, he might have made some errors, which were repeated or only partly corrected in his Annals of Genoa, published in 1537, the year following his own death. It is not found, however, that the sketch is in any essential particular far from correct, and it has been confirmed by recent investigations. The English of it is given in Harrisse's *Notes on Columbus* (pp. 74–79). The statements of the Psalter respecting Columbus were reckoned with other things so false that the Senate of

<small>Contempo-rary notices.</small>

<small>Giustiniani.</small>

Genoa prohibited its perusal and allowed no one to possess it,
— at least so it is claimed in the *Historie* of 1571; but no one
has ever found such a decree, nor is it mentioned by any who
would have been likely to revert to it, had it ever existed.

The account in the *Collectanea* of Battista Fulgoso (sometimes written Fregoso), printed at Milan in 1509, is of scarcely
any original value, though of interest as the work of another
Genoese. Allegetto degli Allegetti, whose *Ephemerides* is also
published in Muratori, deserves scarcely more credit, though he
seems to have got his information from the letters of Italian
merchants living in Spain, who communicated current news to
their home correspondents. Bergomas, who had pub-
Bergomas. lished a chronicle as early as 1483, made additions to
his work from time to time, and in an edition printed at Venice,
in 1503, he paraphrased Columbus's own account of his first
voyage, which was reprinted in the subsequent edition of 1506.
In this latter year Maffei de Volterra published a commentary
at Rome, of much the same importance. Such was the filtering
process by which Italy, through her own writers, acquired contemporary knowledge of her adventurous son.

The method was scarcely improved in the condensation of
Jovius (1551), or in the traveler's tales of Benzoni (1565).

Harrisse affirms that it is not till we come down to the
Casoni, Annals of Genoa, published by Filippo Casoni, in
1708. 1708, that we get any new material in an Italian
writer, and on a few points this last writer has adduced documentary evidence, not earlier made known. It is only when we
pass into the present century that we find any of the countrymen of Columbus undertaking in a sustained way to tell the
whole story of Columbus's life. Léon had noted that at some
time in Spain, without giving place and date, Columbus had
printed a little tract, *Declaracion de Tabla Navigatoria;* but
no one before Luigi Bossi had undertaken to investigate the
writings of Columbus. He is precursor of all the
Bossi. modern biographers of Columbus, and his book was
published at Milan, in 1818. He claimed in his appendix to
have added rare and unpublished documents, but Harrisse
points out how they had all been printed earlier.

Bossi expresses opinions respecting the Spanish nation that
are by no means acceptable to that people, and Navarrete not

infrequently takes the Italian writer to task for this as for his many errors of statement, and for the confidence which he places even in the pictorial designs of De Bry as historical records.

There is nothing more striking in the history of American discovery than the fact that the Italian people furnished to Spain Columbus, to England Cabot, and to France Verrazano; and that the three leading powers of Europe, following as maritime explorers in the lead of Portugal, who could not dispense with Vespucius, another Italian, pushed their rights through men whom they had borrowed from the central region of the Mediterranean, while Italy in its own name never possessed a rood of American soil. The adopted country of each of these Italians gave more or less of its own impress to its foster child. No one of these men was so impressible as Columbus, and no country so much as Spain was likely at this time to exercise an influence on the character of an alien. Humboldt has remarked that Columbus got his theological fervor in Andalusia and Granada, and we can scarcely imagine Columbus in the garb of a Franciscan walking the streets of free and commercial Genoa as he did those of Seville, when he returned from his second voyage.

The latest of the considerable popular Italian lives of Columbus is G. B. Lemoyne's *Colombo e la Scoperta dell' America,* issued at Turin, in 1873.

We may pass now to the historians of that country to which Columbus betook himself on leaving Italy; but about all to be found at first hand is in the chronicle of João II. of Portugal, as prepared by Ruy de Pina, the archivist of the Torre do Tombo. At the time of the voyage of Columbus Ruy was over fifty, while Garcia de Resende was a young man then living at the Portuguese court, who in his *Choronica,* published in 1596, did little more than borrow from his elder, Ruy; and Resende in turn furnished to João de Barros the staple of the latter's narrative in his *Decada da Asia,* printed at Lisbon, in 1752.

We find more of value when we summon the Spanish writers. Although Peter Martyr d'Anghiera was an Italian, Muñoz reckons him a Spaniard, since he was naturalized in Spain.

Spanish writers. He was a man of thirty years, when, coming from Rome, he settled in Spain, a few years before Columbus attracted much notice. Martyr had been borne thither Peter Martyr. on a reputation of his own, which had commended his busy young nature to the attention of the Spanish court. He took orders and entered upon a prosperous career, proceeding by steps, which successively made him the chaplain of Queen Isabella, a prior of the Cathedral of Granada, and ultimately the official chronicler of the Indies. Very soon after his arrival in Spain, he had disclosed a quick eye for the changeful life about him, and he began in 1488 the writing of those letters which, to the number of over eight hundred, exist to attest his active interest in the events of his day. These events he continued to observe till 1525. We have no more vivid source of the contemporary history, particularly as it concerned the maritime enterprise of the peninsular peoples. He wrote fluently, and, as he tells us, sometimes while waiting for dinner, and necessarily with haste. He jotted down first and unconfirmed reports, and let them stand. He got news by hearsay, and confounded events. He had candor and sincerity enough, however, not to prize his own works above their true value. He knew Columbus, and, his letters readily reflect what interest there was in the exploits of Columbus, immediately on his return from his first voyage ; but the earlier preparations of the navigator for that voyage, with the problematical characteristics of the undertaking, do not seem to have made any impression upon Peter Martyr, and it is not till May of 1493, when the discovery had been made, and later in September, that he chronicles the divulged existence of the newly discovered islands. The three letters in which this wonderful intelligence was first communicated are printed by Harrisse in English, in his *Notes on Columbus*. Las Casas tells us how Peter Martyr got his accounts of the first discoveries directly from the lips of Columbus himself and from those who accompanied him ; but he does not fail to tell us also of the dangers of too implicitly trusting to all that Peter says. From May 14, 1493, to June 5, 1497, in twelve separate letters, we read what this observer has to say of the great navigator who had suddenly and temporarily stepped into the glare of notice. These and other letters of

Peter Martyr have not escaped some serious criticism. There are contradictions and anachronisms in them that have forcibly helped Ranke, Hallam, Gerigk, and others to count the text which we have as more or less changed from what must have been the text, if honestly written by Martyr. They have imagined that some editor, willful or careless, has thrown this luckless accompaniment upon them. The letters, however, claimed the confidence of Prescott, and have, as regards the parts touching the new discoveries, seldom failed to impress with their importance those who have used them. It is the opinion of the last examiner of them, J. H. Mariéjol, in his *Peter Martyr d'Anghera* (Paris, 1887), that to read them attentively is the best refutation of the skeptics. Martyr ceased to refer to the affairs of the New World after 1499, and those of his earlier letters which illustrate the early voyage have appeared in a French version, made by Gaffarel and Louvot (Paris, 1885).

The representations of Columbus easily convinced Martyr that there opened a subject worthy of his pen, and he set about composing a special treatise on the discoveries in the New World, and, under the title of *De Orbe Novo*, it occupied his attention from October, 1494, to the day of his death. For the earlier years he had, if we may believe him, not a little help from Columbus himself; and it would seem from his one hundred and thirty-five epistles that he was not altogether prepared to go with Columbus, in accounting the new islands as lying off the coast of Asia. He is particularly valuable to us in treating of Columbus's conflicts with the natives of Española, and Las Casas found him as helpful as we do.

These *Decades*, as the treatise is usually called, formed enlarged bulletins, which, in several copies, were transmitted by him to some of his noble friends in Italy, to keep them conversant with the passing events.

A certain Angelo Trivigiano, into whose hands a copy of some of the early sections fell, translated them into easy, Trivigiano. not to say vulgar, Italian, and sent them to Venice, in four different copies, a few months after they were written; and in this way the first seven books of the first decade fell into the hands of a Venetian printer, who, in April, 1504, brought out a little book of sixteen leaves in the dialect of that region, known in bibliography as the *Libretto de Tutta la Navigation de Re de Spagna de le Isole et Terreni novamente trovati.* This publication is known to us in a single copy lacking a title, in the Biblioteca Marciana.   Here we have the first account of the new discoveries, written upon report, and supplementing the narrative of Columbus himself.   We also find in this little narrative some personal details about Columbus, not contained in the same portions when embodied in the larger *De Orbe Novo* of Martyr, and it may be a question if somebody who acted as editor to the Venetian version may not have added them to the translation.   The story of the new discoveries attracted enough notice to make Zorzi or Montalboddo — if one or the other were its editor — include this Venetian version of Martyr bodily in the collection of voyages which, as *Paesi novamente retrovati*, was published at Vicentia somewhere about November, 1507.   It is, perhaps, a measure of the interest felt in the undertakings of Columbus, not easily understood at this day, that it took fourteen years for a scant recital of such events to work themselves into the context of so composite a record of discovery as the *Paesi* proved to be ; and still more remarkable it may be accounted that the story could be told with but few actual references to the hero of the transactions, "Columbus, the Genoese."   It is not only the compiler who is so reticent, but it is the author whence he borrowed what he had to say, Martyr himself, the observer and acquaintance of Columbus, who buries the discoverer under the event.   With such an augury, it is not so strange that at about the same time in the little town of St. Dié, in the Vosges, a sequestered teacher could suggest a name derived from that of a follower of Columbus, Americus Vespucius, for that part of the new lands then brought into prominence.   If the documentary proofs of Columbus's priority had given to the Admiral's name the same prominence which the event received, the result might not, in the end, have been so discouraging to justice.

Martyr, unfortunately, with all his advantages, and with his access to the archives of the Indies, did not burden his recital with documents.   He was even less observant of the lighter traits that interest those eager for news than might have been expected, for the busy chaplain was a gossip by nature : he liked to retail hearsays and rumors ; he enlivened his letters with personal characteristics; but in speaking of Columbus he is singularly reticent upon all that might picture the man to us as he lived.

When, in 1534, these portions of Martyr's *Decades* were combined with a summary of Oviedo, in a fresh publica- Oviedo. tion, there were some curious personal details added to Ramusio. Martyr's narrative; but as Ramusio is supposed to have edited the compilation, these particulars are usually accredited to that author. It is not known whence this Italian compiler could have got them, and there is no confirmation of them elsewhere to be found. If these additions, as is supposed, were a foreign graft upon Martyr's recitals, the staple of his narrative still remains not altogether free from some suspicions that, as a writer himself, he was not wholly frank and trustworthy. At least a certain confusion in his method leads some of the critics to discover something like imposture in what they charge as a habit of antedating a letter so as to appear prophetic; while his defenders find in these same evidences of incongruity a sign of spontaneity that argues freshness and sincerity.

The confidence which we may readily place in what is said of Columbus in the chronicle of Ferdinand and Isa- Bernaldez. bella, written by Andrès Bernaldez, is prompted by his acquaintance with Columbus, and by his being the recipient of some of the navigator's own writings from his own hands. He is also known to have had access to what Chanca and other companions of Columbus had written. This country curate, who lived in the neighborhood of Seville, was also the chaplain of the Archbishop of Seville, a personal friend of the Admiral, and from him Bernaldez received some help. He does not add much, however, to what is given us by Peter Martyr, though in respect to the second voyage and to a few personal details Bernaldez is of some confirmatory value. The manuscript of his narrative remained unprinted in the royal library at Madrid till about thirty-five years ago; but nearly all the leading writers have made use of it in copies which have been furnished.

In coming to Oviedo, we encounter a chronicler who, as a writer, possesses an art far from skillful. Muñoz laments that

his learning was not equal to his diligence. He finds him of
Oviedo. little service for the times of Columbus, and largely
because he was neglectful of documents and pursued
uncritical combinations of tales and truths. With all his vagaries he is a helpful guide. "It is not," says Harrisse, "that
Oviedo shows so much critical sagacity, as it is that he col-
lates all the sources available to him, and gives the reader the
clues to a final judgment." He is generally deemed honest,
though Las Casas thought him otherwise. The author of the
*Historie* looks upon him as an enemy of Columbus, and would
make it appear that he listened to the tales of the Pinzons,
who were enemies of the Admiral. His administrative services
in the Indies show that he could be faithful to a trust, even at
the risk of popularity. This gives a presumption in favor of
his historic fairness. He was intelligent if not learned, and
a power of happy judgments served him in good stead, even
with a somewhat loose method of taking things as he heard
them. He further inspires us with a certain amount of confidence, because he is not always a hero-worshiper, and he does
not hesitate to tell a story, which seems to have been in circulation, to the effect that Columbus got his geographical ideas
from an old pilot. Oviedo, however, refrains from setting the
tale down as a fact, as some of the later writers, using little of
Oviedo's caution, and borrowing from him, did. His opportunities of knowing the truth were certainly exceptional, though it
does not appear that he ever had direct communication with the
Admiral himself. He was but a lad of fifteen when we find
him jotting down notes of what he saw and heard, as a page in
attendance upon Don Juan, the son of the Spanish sovereigns,
when, at Barcelona, he saw them receive Columbus after his
first voyage. During five years, between 1497 and 1502, he was
in Italy. With that exception he was living within the Spanish court up to 1514, when he was sent to the New World, and
passed there the greater part of his remaining life. While he
had been at court in his earlier years, the sons of Columbus,
Diego and Ferdinand, were his companions in the pages' ante-
room, and he could hardly have failed to profit by their acquaintance. We know that from the younger son he did
derive not a little information. When he went to America,
some of Columbus's companions and followers were still living,

— Pinzon, Ponce de Leon, and Diego Velasquez, — and all these could hardly have failed to help him in his note-taking. He also tells us that he sought some of the Italian compatriots of the Admiral, though Harrisse judges that what he got from them was not altogether trustworthy. Oviedo rose naturally in due time into the position of chronicler of the Indies, and tried his skill at first in a descriptive account of the New World. A command of Charles the Fifth, with all the facilities which such an order implied, though doubtless in some degree embarrassed by many of the documentary proofs being preserved rather in Spain than in the Indies, finally set him to work on a *Historia General de las Indias,* the opening portions of which, and those covering the career of Columbus, were printed at Seville in 1535. It is the work of a consistent though not blinded admirer of the Discoverer, and while we might wish he had helped us to more of the proofs of his narrative, his recital is, on the whole, one to be signally grateful for.

Gomara, in the early part of his history, mixed up what he took from Oviedo with what else came in his way, with an avidity that rejected little.

But it is to a biography of Columbus, written by his youngest son, Ferdinand, as was universally believed up to 1871, that all the historians of the Admiral have been mainly indebted for the personal details and other circumstances which lend vividness to his story. As the book has to-day a good many able defenders, notwithstanding the discredit which Harrisse has sought to place upon it, it is worth while to trace the devious paths of its transmission, and to measure the burden of confidence placed upon it from the days of Ferdinand to our own.

*Historie* ascribed to Ferdinand Columbus.

The rumor goes that some of the statements in the Psalter note of 1516, particularly one respecting the low origin of the Admiral, disturbed the pride of Ferdinand to such a degree that this son of Columbus undertook to leave behind him a detailed account of his father's career, such as the Admiral, though urged to do it, had never found time to write. Ferdinand was his youngest son, and was born only three or four years before his father left Palos. There are two dates given for his birth, each apparently on good authority, but these are a year apart.

The language of Columbus's will, as well as the explicit statements of Oviedo and Las Casas, leaves no reasonable ground for doubting his illegitimacy. Bastardy was no bar to heirship in Spain, if a testator chose to make a natural son his heir, as Columbus did, in giving Ferdinand the right to his titles after the failure of heirs to Diego, his legitimate son. Columbus's influence early found him a place as a page at court, and during the Admiral's fourth voyage, in 1502–1504, the boy accompanied his father, and once or twice at a later day he again visited the Indies. When Columbus died, this son inherited many of his papers; but if his own avowal be believed, he had neglected occasions in his father's lifetime to question the Admiral respecting his early life, not having, as he says, at that time learned to have interest in such matters. His subsequent education at court, however, implanted in his mind a good deal of the scholar's taste, and as a courtier in attendance upon Charles the Fifth he had seasons of travel, visiting pretty much every part of Western Europe, during which he had opportunities to pick up in many places a large collection of books. He often noted in them the place and date of purchase, so that it is not difficult to learn in this way something of his wanderings.

*Career of Ferdinand Columbus.*

The income of Ferdinand was large, or the equivalent of what Harrisse calls to-day 180,000 francs, which was derived from territorial rights in San Domingo, coming to him from the Admiral, increased by slave labor in the mines, assigned to him by King Ferdinand, which at one time included the service of four hundred Indians, and enlarged by pensions bestowed by Charles the Fifth.

It has been said sometimes that he was in orders; but Harrisse, his chief biographer, could find no proof of it. Oviedo describes him in 1535 as a person of "much nobility of character, of an affable turn and of a sweet conversation."

When he died at Seville, July 12, 1539, he had amassed a collection of books, variously estimated in contemporary accounts at from twelve to twenty thousand volumes. Harrisse, in his *Grandeur et Décadence de la Colombine* (2d ed., Paris, 1885), represents Ferdinand as having searched from 1510 to 1537 all the principal book marts of Europe. He left these books by will to his minor nephew, Luis

*Biblioteca Colombina.*

Colon, son of Diego, but there was a considerable delay before Luis renounced the legacy, with the conditions attached. Legal proceedings, which accompanied the transactions of its executors, so delayed the consummation of the alternative injunction of the will that the chapter of the Cathedral of Seville, which was to receive the library in case Don Luis declined it, did not get possession of it till 1552.

The care of it which ensued seems to have been of a varied nature. Forty years later a scholar bitterly complains that it was inaccessible. It is known that by royal command certain books and papers were given up to enrich the national archives, which, however, no longer contain them. When, in 1684, the monks awoke to a sense of their responsibility and had a new inventory of the books made, it was found that the collection had been reduced to four or five thousand volumes. After the librarian who then had charge of it died in 1709, the collection again fell into neglect. There are sad stories of roistering children let loose in its halls to make havoc of its treasures. There was no responsible care again taken of it till a new librarian was chosen, in 1832, who discovered what any one might have learned before, that the money which Ferdinand left for the care and increase of the library had never been applied to it, and that the principal, even, had disappeared. Other means of increasing it were availed of, and the loss of the original inestimable bibliographical treasures was forgotten in the crowd of modern books which were placed upon its shelves. Amid all this new growth, it does not appear just how many of the books which descended from Ferdinand still remain in it. Something of the old carelessness — to give it no worse name — has despoiled it, even as late as 1884 and 1885, when large numbers of the priceless treasures still remaining found a way to the Quay Voltaire and other marts for old books in Paris, while others were disposed of in London, Amsterdam, and even in Spain. This outrage was promptly exposed by Harrisse in the *Revue Critique*, and in two monographs, *Grandeur et Décadence*, etc., already named, and in his *Colombine et Clément Marot* (Paris, 1886); and the story has been further recapitulated in the accounts of Ferdinand and his library, which Harrisse has also given in his *Excerpta Colombiana: Bibliographie de Quatre Cents Pièces Gothiques*

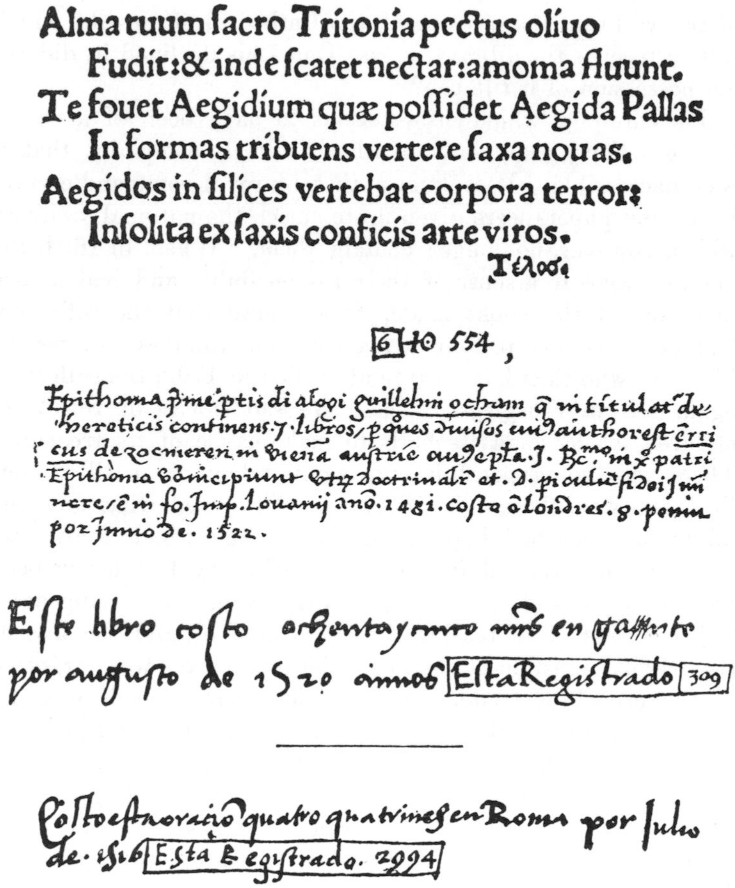

Alma tuum facro Tritonia pectus oliuo
  Fudit:& inde fcatet nectar:amoma fluunt.
Te fouet Aegidium quæ poffidet Aegida Pallas
  In formas tribuens vertere faxa nouas.
Aegidos in filices vertebat corpora terror:
  Infolita ex faxis conficis arte viros.
                     Τέλος

6 ꝉ 554 ,

Epithoma  p̃me p̃tis di alogi guillelmi ocham q̃ intitulat de
hereticis continens.7 libros/ pq̃ues duifos eñ authorest erri
cus derocmeren in viena auftrie aufepta.J. Bc̃. mxpatri
Epithoma cõincipiunt ct17 dottrinale et. d. picoliefidoiJm
nere e ñ in fo. Jm̃p. Louanij añd. 1481. cofta ãlondres. g pẽniñ
por Jmnio de. 1522.

Efte libro cofto orgentaymuro miñs en gaffuito
por auguſto de 1520 ãnnob EftaRegiftrado 309

---

Cofto eftnoracio qnatro qnatvinefen Roma por Julio
de. 1516 Efta Egiftrado. 2994

SPECIMENS OF THE NOTES OF FERDINAND COLUMBUS ON HIS BOOKS.
[From Harrisse's *Grandeur et Décadence de la Colombine* (Paris, 1885).]

*Francaises, Italiennes et Latines du Commencement du XVI Siecle* (Paris, 1887), an account of book rarities found in that library.

We are fortunate, nevertheless, in having a manuscript catalogue of it in Ferdinand's own hand, though not a complete one, for he died while he was making it. This library, as well as what we know of his writings and of the reputation which he bore among his contemporaries, many of whom speak of him and of his library with approbation, shows us that a habit, careless of inquiry in his boyhood, gave place in his riper years to study and respect for learning. He is said by the inscription on his tomb to have composed an extensive work on the New World and his father's finding of it, but it has disappeared. Neither in his library nor in his catalogue do we find any trace of the life of his father which he is credited with having prepared. None of his friends, some of them writers on the New World, make any mention of such a book. There is in the catalogue a note, however, of a life of Columbus written about 1525, of which the manuscript is credited to Ferdi- Perez de nand Perez de Oliva, a man of some repute, who died Oliva. in 1530. Whether this writing bore any significant relation to the life which is associated with the owner of the library is apparently beyond discovery. It can scarcely be supposed that it could have been written other than with Ferdinand's cognizance. That there was an account of the Admiral's career, quoted in Las Casas and attributed to Ferdinand Columbus, and that it existed before 1559, seems to be nearly certain. A manuscript of the end of the sixteenth century, by Gonzalo Argote de Molina, mentions a report that Ferdinand had written a life of his father. Harrisse tells us that he has seen a printed book catalogue, apparently of the time of Muñoz or Navarette, in which a Spanish life of Columbus by Ferdinand Columbus is entered; but the fact stands without any explanation or verification. Spotorno, in 1823, in an introduction to his collection of documents about Columbus, says that the manuscript of what has passed for Ferdinand's memoir of his father was taken from Spain to Genoa by Luis Colon, the Duke of Veragua, son of Diego and grandson of Christopher Columbus. It is not known that Luis ever had any personal relations with Ferdinand, who died while Luis was still in Santo Domingo.

It is said that it was in 1568 that Luis took the manuscript to Genoa, but in that year he is known to have been living elsewhere. He had been arrested in Spain in 1558 for having three wives, when he was exiled to Oran, in Africa, for ten years, and he died in 1572. Spotorno adds that the manuscript afterwards fell into the hands of a patrician, Marini, from whom Alfonzo de Ullua received it, and translated it into Italian. It is shown, however, that Marini was not living at this time. The original Spanish, if that was the tongue of the manuscript, then disappeared, and the world has only known it in this Italian *Historie*, published in 1571. Whether the copy brought to Italy had been in any way changed from its original condition, or whether the version then made public fairly represented it, there does not seem any way of determining to the satisfaction of everybody. At all events, the world thought it had got something of value and of authority, and in sundry editions and retranslations, with more or less editing and augmentation, it has passed down to our time — the last edition appearing in 1867 — unquestioned for its service to the biographers of Columbus. Muñoz hardly knew what to make of some of "its unaccountable errors," and conjectured that the Italian version had been made from "a corrupt and false copy;" and coupling with it the "miserable" Spanish rendering in Barcia's *Historiadores*, Muñoz adds that "a number of falsities and absurdities is discernible in both." Humboldt had indeed expressed wonder at the ignorance of the book in nautical matters, considering the reputation which Ferdinand held in such affairs. It began the Admiral's story in detail when he was said to be fifty-six years of age. It has never been clear to all minds that Ferdinand's asseveration of a youthful want of curiosity respecting the Admiral's early life was sufficient to account for so much reticence respecting that formative period. It has been, accordingly, sometimes suspected that a desire to ignore the family's early insignificance rather than ignorance had most to do with this absence of information. This seems to be Irving's inference from the facts.

In 1871, Henry Harrisse, who in 1866 had written of the book, "It is generally accepted with some latitude," made the first assault on its integrity, in his *Fer-*

*Character of the Historie.*

*Attacked by Harrisse.*

*nando Colon*, published in Seville, in Spanish, which was followed the next year by his *Fernand Colomb*, in the original
French text as it had been written, and published at Paris.
Harrisse's view was reënforced in the *Additions* to his *Bibliotheca Americana Vetustissima*, and he again reverted to the
subject in the first volume of his *Christophe Colomb*, in 1884.
In the interim the entire text of Las Casas's *Historia* had been
published for the first time, rendering a comparison of the two
books more easy. Harrisse availed himself of this facility of
examination, and made no abatement of his confident disbe-
lief. That Las Casas borrowed from the *Historie*, or rather that
the two books had a common source, Harrisse thinks satisfactorily shown. He further throws out the hint that this source,
or prototype, may have been one of the lost essays of Ferdinand, in which he had followed the career of his father; or indeed, in some way, the account written by Oliva may have
formed the basis of the book. He further implies that, in the
transformation to the Italian edition of 1571, there were engrafted upon the narrative many contradictions and anachronisms, which seriously impair its value. Hence, as he contends,
it is a shame to impose its authorship in that foreign shape
upon Ferdinand. He also denies in the main the story of its
transmission as told by Spotorno.

So much of this book as is authentic, and may be found to be
corroborated by other evidence, may very likely be due to the
manuscript of Oliva, transported to Italy, and used as the
work of Ferdinand Columbus, to give it larger interest than
the name of Oliva would carry; while, to gratify prejudices and
increase its attractions, the various interpolations were made,
which Harrisse thinks — and with much reason — could not
have proceeded from one so near to Columbus, so well informed,
and so kindly in disposition as we know his son Ferdinand
to have been.

So iconoclastic an outburst was sure to elicit vindicators of
the world's faith as it had long been held. In counter publications, Harrisse and D'Avezac, the latter an eminent French authority on questions of this period, fought out their battle, not
without some sharpness. Henry Stevens, an old antagonist of Harrisse, assailed the new views with his Defended by
Stevens and
accustomed confidence and rasping assertion. Oscar others.

Peschel, the German historian, and Count Circourt, the French student, gave their opposing opinions; and the issue has been joined by others, particularly within a few years by Prospero Peragallo, the pastor of an Italian church in Lisbon, who has pressed defensive views with some force in his *L'Auten- ticità delle Historie di Fernando Colombo* (1884), and later in his *Cristoforo Colombo et sua Famiglia* (1888). It is held by some of these later advocates of the book that parts of the original Spanish text can be identified in Las Casas. The controversy has thus had two stages. The first was marked by the strenuousness of D'Avezac fifteen years ago. The second sprang from the renewed propositions of Harrisse in his *Christophe Colomb*, ten years later. Sundry critics have summed up the opposing arguments with more or less tendency to oppose the iconoclast, and chief among them are two German scholars: Professor Max Büdinger, in his *Acten zur Columbus' Geschichte* (Wien, 1886), and his *Zur Columbus Literatur* (Wien, 1889); and Professor Eugen Gelcich, in the *Zeitschrift der Gesellschaft für Erdkunde zu Berlin* (1887).

Harrisse's views cannot be said to have conquered a position; but his own scrutiny and that which he has engendered in others have done good work in keeping the *Historie* constantly subject to critical caution. Dr. Shea still says of it: "It is based on the same documents of Christopher Columbus which Las Casas used. It is a work of authority."

Reference has already been made to the tardy publication of the narrative of Las Casas. Columbus had been dead

Las Casas.

something over twenty years, when this good man set about the task of describing in this work what he had seen and heard respecting the New World, — or at least this is the generally accredited interval, making him begin the work in 1527; and yet it is best to remember that Helps could not find any positive evidence of his being at work on the manuscript before 1552. Las Casas did not live to finish the task, though he labored upon it down to 1561, when he was eighty-seven years old. He died five years later. Irving, who made great use of Las Casas, professed to consult him with that caution which he deemed necessary in respect to a writer given to prejudice and overheated zeal. For the period of Columbus's public life

(1492–1506), no other one of his contemporaries gives us so much of documentary proof. Of the thirty-one papers, falling within this interval, which he transcribed into his pages nearly in their entirety, — throwing out some preserved in the archives of the Duke of Veragua, and others found at Simancas or Seville, — there remain seventeen, that would be lost to us but for this faithful chronicler. How did he command this rich resource? As a native of Seville, Las Casas had come there to be consecrated as bishop in 1544, and again in 1547, after he had quitted the New World forever. At this time the family papers of Columbus, then held for Luis Colon, a minor, were locked up in a strong box in the custody of the monks of the neighboring monastery of Las Cuevas. There is no evidence, however, that the chest was opened for the inspection of the chronicler. He also professes to use original letters sent by Columbus to Ferdinand and Isabella, which he must have found in the archives at Valladolid before 1545, or at Simancas after that date. Again he speaks of citing as in his own collection attested copies of some of Columbus's letters.

In 1550, and during his later years, Las Casas lived in the monastery of San Gregorio, at Valladolid, leaving it only for visits to Toledo or Madrid, unless it was for briefer visits to Simancas, not far off. Some of the documents, which he might have found in that repository, are not at present in those archives. It was there that he might have found numerous letters which he cites, but which are not otherwise known. From the use Las Casas makes of them, it would seem that they were of more importance in showing the discontent and querulousness of Columbus than as adding to details of his career. Again it appears clear that Las Casas got documents in some way from the royal archives. We know the journal of Columbus on his first voyage only from the abridgment which Las Casas made of it, and much the same is true of the record of his third voyage.

In some portion, at least, of his citations from the letters of Columbus, there may be reason to think that Las Casas took them at second hand, and Harrisse, with his belief in the derivative character of the *Historie* of Ferdinand Columbus, very easily conjectures that this primal source may have been the manuscript upon which the compiler of the *Historie* was equally dependent. One kind of reasoning which Harrisse uses is this: If Las Casas had used the original Latin of the correspondence with Toscanelli, instead of the text of this supposed Spanish

LAS CASAS.

prototype, it would not appear in so bad a state as it does in Las Casas's book.

If this missing prototype of the *Historie* was among Ferdinand's books in his library, which had been removed from his house in 1544 to the convent of San Pablo in Seville, and was not removed to the cathedral till 1552, it may also have happened that along with it he used there the *De Imagine Mundi* of Pierre d'Ailly, Columbus's own copy of which was, and still is, preserved in the Biblioteca Colombina, and shows the Admiral's own manuscript annotations.

It was in the chapel of San Pablo that Las Casas had been consecrated as bishop in 1544, and his associations with the monks could have given easy access to what they held in custody, — too easy, perhaps, if Harrisse's supposition is correct, that they let him take away the map which Toscanelli sent to Columbus, and which would account for its not being in the library now.

We know, also, that Las Casas had use of the famous letter respecting his third voyage, which the Admiral ad- His opportunities. dressed to the nurse of the Infant Don Juan, and which was first laid before modern students when Spotorno printed it, in 1823. We further understand that the account of the fourth voyage, which students now call, in its Italian form, the *Lettera Rarissima*, was also at his disposal, as were many letters of Bartholomew, the brother of Columbus, though they apparently only elucidate the African voyage of Diaz.

In addition to these manuscript sources, Las Casas shows that, as a student, he was familiar with and appreciated the decades of Peter Martyr, and had read the accounts of Columbus in Garcia de Resende, Barros, and Castañeda, — to say nothing of what he may have derived from the supposable prototype of the *Historie*. It is certain that his personal acquaintance brought him into relations with the Admiral himself, — for he accompanied him on his fourth voyage, — with the Admiral's brother, son, and son's wife; and moreover his own father and uncle had sailed with Columbus. There were, among his other acquaintances, the Archbishop of Seville, Pinzon, and other of the contemporary navigators. It has been claimed by some, not accurately, we suspect, that Las Casas had also accompanied Columbus on his third voyage. Notwithstanding all these opportunities of acquiring a thorough intimacy with the story of Columbus, it is contended by Harrisse that the aid afforded by Las Casas disappoints one; and that all essential data with which his narrative is supplied can be found else-

where, nearer the primal source.   This condition arises, as he
Character of  thinks, from the fact that the one engrossing purpose
his writings.  of Las Casas — his aim to emancipate the Indians from
a cruel domination — constantly stood in the way of a critical
consideration of the other aspects of the early Spanish contact
with the New World.   It was while at the University of Salamanca that the father of Las Casas gave the son an Indian
slave, one of those whom Columbus had sent home; and it was
taken from the young student when Isabella decreed the undo-
ing of Columbus's kidnapping exploits.   It was this event
which set Las Casas to thinking on the miseries of the poor
natives, which Columbus had planned, and which enables us to
discover, in the example of Las Casas, that the customs of the
time are not altogether an unanswerable defense of the time's
inhumanity and greed.

As is well known, all but the most recent writers on Spanish-
American history have been forced to use this work of Las
Casas in manuscript copies, as a license to print such an  exposure of Spanish cruelty could not be obtained till 1875, when
the *Historia* was first printed at Madrid.

Herrera, so far as his record concerns Columbus, simply gives
us what he takes from Las Casas.   He was born about
Herrera.  the time that the older writer was probably making
his investigations.   Herrera did not publish his results, which
are slavishly chronological in their method, till half a century
later (1601-15).   Though then the official historiographer of the
Indies, with all the chances for close investigation which that
situation afforded him, Herrera failed in all ways to make the
record of his *Historia* that comprehensive and genuine source
of the story of Columbus which the reader might naturally look
for.   The continued obscuration of Las Casas by reason of the
long delay in printing his manuscript served to give Herrera,
through many generations, a prominence as an authoritative
source which he could not otherwise have had.   Irving, when
he worked at the subject, soon discovered that Las Casas stood
behind the story as Herrera told it, and accordingly the American writer resorted by preference to such a copy of the manuscript of Las Casas as he could get.   There is a manifest
tendency in Herrera to turn Las Casas's qualified statements
into absolute ones.

The personal contributions of the later writers, Muñoz and Navarrete, have been already considered, in speaking Later Spanish writers. of the diversified mass of documentary proofs which accompany or gave rise to their narratives.

The *Colon en España* of Tomas Rodriguez Pinilla (Madrid, 1884) is in effect a life of the Admiral; but it ignores much of the recent critical and controversial literature, and deals mainly with the old established outline of events.

Among the Germans there was nothing published of any importance till the critical studies of Forster, Peschel, German writers. and Ruge, in recent days. De Bry had, indeed, by his translations of Benzoni (1594) and Herrera (1623), familiarized the Germans with the main facts of the career of Columbus. During the present century, Humboldt, in his *Examen Critique de l'Histoire et de la Geographie du* Humboldt. *Nouveau Continent,* has borrowed the language of France to show the scope of his critical and learned inquiries into the early history of the Spanish contact in America, and has left it to another hand to give a German rendering to his labors. With this work by Humboldt, brought out in its completer shape in 1836–39, and using most happily all that had been done by Muñoz and Navarrete to make clear both the acts and environments of the Admiral, the intelligence of our own time may indeed be said to have first clearly apprehended, under the light of a critical spirit, in which Irving was deficient, the true significance of the great deeds that gave America to Europe. Humboldt has strikingly grouped the lives of Toscanelli and Las Casas, from the birth of the Florentine physician in 1397 to the death of the Apostle to the Indians in 1566, as covering the beginning and end of the great discoveries of the fifteenth and sixteenth centuries.

It is also to be remarked that this service of broadly, and at the same time critically, surveying the field was the work of a German writing in French; while it is to an American citizen writing in French that we owe, in more recent years, such a minute collation and examination of every original source of information as set the labors of Henry Harrisse, for Henry Harrisse. thoroughness and discrimination, in advance of any critical labor that has ever before been given to the career and character of Christopher Columbus. Without the aid of his researches, as embodied in his *Christophe Colomb* (Paris, 1884), it would have been quite impossible for the present writer to have reached conclusions on a good many mooted points in the history of the Admiral and of his reputation. Of almost equal usefulness have been the various subsidiary books and tracts which Harrisse has devoted to similar fields.

Harrisse's books constitute a good example of the constant change of opinion and revision of the relations of facts which are going on incessantly in the mind of a vigilant student in recondite fields of research. The progress of the correction of error respecting Columbus is illustrated continually in his series of books on the great navigator, beginning with the *Notes on Columbus* (N. Y., 1866), which have been intermittently published by him during the last twenty-five years.

Harrisse himself is a good deal addicted to hypotheses; but they fare hard at his hands if advanced by others.

The only other significant essays which have been made in French have been a series of biographies of Columbus, emphasizing his missionary spirit, which have been aimed to prepare the way for the canonization of the great navigator, in recognition of his instrumentality in carrying the cross to the New World. That, in the spirit which characterized the age of discovery, the voyage of Columbus was, at least in profession, held to be one conducted primarily for that end does not, certainly, admit of dispute. Columbus himself, in his letter to Sanchez, speaks of the rejoicing of Christ at seeing the future redemption of souls. He made a first offering of the foreign gold by converting a mass of it into a cup to hold the sacred host, and he spent a wordy enthusiasm in promises of a new crusade to wrest the Holy Sepulchre from the Moslems. Ferdinand and Isabella dwelt upon the propagandist spirit of the enterprise they had sanctioned, in their appeals to the Pontiff to confirm their worldly gain in its results. Ferdinand, the son of the Admiral, referring to the family name of Colombo, speaks of his father as like Noah's dove, carrying the olive branch and oil of baptism over the ocean. Professions, however, were easy; faith is always exuberant under success, and the world, and even the Catholic world, learned, as the ages went on, to look upon the

*French writers.*

*Attempted canonization of Columbus.*

spirit that put the poor heathen beyond the pale of humanity as not particularly sanctifying a pioneer of devastation. It is the world's misfortune when a great opportunity loses any of its dignity; and it is no great satisfaction to look upon a person of Columbus's environments and find him but a creature of questionable grace. So his canonization has not, with all the endeavors which have been made, been brought about. The most conspicuous of the advocates of it, with a crowd of imitators about him, has been Antoine François Félix Valalette, Comte Roselly de Lorgues, who began in 1844

Roselly de Lorgues.

ROSELLY DE LORGUES.

to devote his energies to this end. He has published several books on Columbus, part of them biographical, and all of them, including his *Christoph Colomb* of 1864, mere disguised supplications to the Pope to order a deserved sanctification. As contributions to the historical study of the life of Columbus, they are of no importance whatever. Every act and saying of the Admiral capable of subserving the purpose in view are simply made the salient points of a career assumed to be holy. Columbus was in fact of a piece, in this respect, with the age in which he lived. The official and officious religious profession of the time belonged to a period which invented the Inquisition and extirpated a race in order to send them to heaven. None knew this better than those, like Las Casas, who mated their faith with charity of act. Columbus and Las Casas had little in common.

The *Histoire Posthume de Colomb*, which Roselly de Lorgues finally published in 1885, is recognized even by Catholic writers as a work of great violence and indiscretion, in its denunciations of all who fail to see the saintly character of Columbus. Its inordinate intemperance gave a great advantage to Cesario Fernandez Duro in his examination of De Lorgues's position, made in his *Colon y la Historia Postuma*.

Columbus was certainly a mundane verity. De Lorgues tells us that if we cannot believe in the supernatural we cannot understand this worldly man. The writers who have followed him, like Charles Buet in his *Christophe Colomb* (Paris, 1886), have taken this position. The Catholic body has so far summoned enough advocates of historic truth to prevent the result which these enthusiasts have kept in view, notwithstanding the seeming acquiescence of Pius IX. The most popular of the idealizing lives of Columbus is probably that by Auguste, Marquis de Belloy, which is tricked out with a display of engravings as idealized as the text, and has been reproduced in English at Philadelphia (1878, 1889). It is simply an ordinary rendering of the common and conventional stories of the last four centuries. The most eminent Catholic historical student of the United States, Dr. John Gilmary Shea, in a paper on this century's estimates of Columbus, in the *American Catholic Quarterly Review* (1887), while referring to the "imposing array of members of the hierarchy" who have urged the beatification of Columbus, added, "But calm official scrutiny of the question was required before permission could be given to introduce the cause;" and this permission has not yet been given, and the evidence in its favor has not yet been officially produced.

France has taken the lead in these movements for canonization, ostensibly for the reason that she needed to make some reparation for snatching the honor of naming the New World from Columbus, through the printing-presses of Saint Dié and Strassburg. A sketch of the literature which has followed this movement is given in Baron van Brocken's *Des Vicissitudes Posthumes de Christophe Colomb, et de sa Beatification Possible* (Leipzig et Paris, 1865).

Of the writers in English, the labors of Hakluyt and Purchas only incidentally touched the career of Colum- English bus; and it was not till Stevens issued his garbled writers. version of Herrera in 1725, that the English public got the record of the Spanish historian, garnished with something that did not represent the original. This book of Stevens is responsible for not a little in English opinion respecting the Spanish age of discovery, which needs in these later days to be qualified. Some of the early collections of voyages, like those of Churchill, Pinkerton, and Kerr, included the story of the *Historie* of 1571. It was not till Robertson, in 1777, published Robertson. the beginning of a contemplated *History of America* that the English reader had for the first time a scholarly and justified narrative, which indeed for a long time remained the ordinary source of the English view of Columbus. It was, however, but an outline sketch, not a sixth or seventh part in extent of what Irving, when he was considering the subject, thought necessary for a reasonable presentation of the subject. Robertson's footnotes show that his main dependence for the story of Columbus was upon the pages of the *Historie* of 1571, Peter Martyr, Oviedo, and Herrera. He was debarred the help to be derived from what we now use, as conveying Columbus's own record of his story. Lord Grantham, then the British ambassador at Madrid, did all the service he could, and his secretary of legation worked asssiduously in complying with the wishes which Robertson preferred; but no solicitation could at that day render easily accessible the archives at Simancas. Still, Robertson got from one source or another more than it was pleasant to the Spanish authorities to see in print, and they later contrived to prevent a publication of his work in Spanish.

The earliest considerable recounting of the story of Columbus in America was by Dr. Jeremy Belknap, who, Jeremy having delivered a commemorative discourse in Bos- Belknap.

ton in 1792, before the Massachusetts Historical Society, afterward augmented his text when it became a part of his well-
known *American Biography*, a work of respectable standing
for the time, but little remembered to-day.

It was in 1827 that Washington Irving published his *Life*
Washington    *of Columbus*, and he produced a book that has long
Irving.    remained for the English reader a standard biography.
Irving's canons of historical criticism were not, however, such
as the fearless and discriminating student to-day would ap-
prove.    He commended Herrera for " the amiable and pardonable error of softening excesses," as if a historian sat in a con-
fessional to deal out exculpations.    The learning which probes
long established pretenses and grateful deceits was not acceptable to Irving.    " There is a certain meddlesome spirit," he
says, " which, in the garb of learned research, goes prying about
the traces of history, casting down its monuments, and marring
and mutilating its fairest trophies.    Care should be taken to
vindicate great names from such pernicious erudition."

Under such conditions as Irving summoned, there was little
chance that a world's exemplar would be pushed from his ped-
estal, no matter what the evidence.    The *vera pro gratis* in
personal characterization must not assail the traditional hero.
And such was Irving's notion of the upright intelligence of a
historian.

Mr. Alexander H. Everett, who was then the minister of the
United States at Madrid, saw a chance of making a readable
book out of the journal of Columbus as preserved by Las Casas,
and recommended the task of translating it to Irving, then in
Europe.    This proposition carried the willing writer to Madrid,
where he found comfortable quarters, with quick sympathy of
intercourse, under the roof of a Boston scholar then living
there, Obadiah Rich.    The first two volumes of the documentary work of Navarrete coming out opportunely, Irving was not
long in determining that, with its wealth of material, there was
a better opportunity for a newly studied life of Columbus than
for the proposed task.    So Irving settled down in Madrid to
the larger endeavor, and soon found that he could have other
assistance and encouragement from Navarrete himself, from the
Duke of Veragua, and from the then possessor of the papers
of Muñoz.    The subject grew under his hands.    " I had no

idea," he says, " of what a complete labyrinth I had entangled myself in." He regretted that the third volume of Navarrete's book was not far enough advanced to be serviceable; but he worked as best he could, and found many more facilities than Robertson's helper had discovered. He went to the Biblioteca Colombina, and he even brought the annotations of Columbus in the copy of Pierre d'Ailly, there preserved, to the attention of its custodians for the first time; almost feeling himself the discoverer of the book, though it was known to him that Las Casas, at least, had had the advantage of using these minutes of Columbus. Irving knew that his pains were not unavailing, at any rate, for the English reader. " I have woven into my book," he says, " many curious particulars not hitherto known concerning Columbus; and I think I have thrown light upon some points of his character which have not been brought out by his former biographers." One of the things that pleased the new biographer most was his discovery, as he felt, in the account by Bernaldez, that Columbus was born ten years earlier than had been usually reckoned; and he supposed that this increase of the age of the discoverer at the time of his voyage added much greater force to the characteristics of his career. Irving's book readily made a mark. Jeffrey thought that its fame would be enduring, and at a time when no one looked for new light from Italy, he considered that Irving had done best in working, almost exclusively, the Spanish field, where alone " it was obvious " material could be found.

When Alexander H. Everett, pardonably, as a godfather to the work, undertook in January, 1829, to say in the *North American Review* that Irving's book was a delight of readers, he anticipated the judgment of posterity; but when he added that it was, by its perfection, the despair of critics, he was forgetful of a method of critical research that is not prone to be dazed by the prestige of demigods.

In the interval between the first and second editions of the book, Irving paid a visit to Palos and the convent of La Rabida, and he got elsewhere some new light in the papers of the lawsuit of Columbus's heirs. The new edition which soon followed profited by all these circumstances.

Irving's occupation of the field rendered it both easy and gracious for Prescott, when, ten years later (1837), he published

his *Ferdinand and Isabella*, to say that his predecessor had
stripped the story of Columbus of the charm of novelty ; but he was not quite sure, however, in the privacy
of his correspondence, that Irving, by attempting to continue the
course of Columbus's life in detail after the striking crisis of the
discovery, had made so imposing a drama as he would have
done by condensing the story of his later years.   In this Prescott shared something of the spirit of Irving, in composing history to be read as a pastime, rather than as a study of completed truth.   Prescott's own treatment of the subject is scant,
as he confined his detailed record to the actions incident to the
inception and perfection of the enterprise of the Admiral, to
the doings in Spain or at court.   He was, at the same time,
far more independent than Irving had been, in his views of the
individual character round which so much revolves, and the
reader is not wholly blinded to the unwholesome deceit and
overweening selfishness of Columbus.

Prescott.

Within twenty years Arthur Helps approached the subject
from the point of view of one who was determined, as
he thought no one of the writers on the subject of the
Spanish Conquest had been, to trace the origin of, and responsibility for, the devastating methods of Spanish colonial government; " not conquest only, but the result of conquest, the
mode of colonial government which ultimately prevailed, the ex-
tirpation of native races, the introduction of other races, the
growth of slavery, and the settlement of the *encomiendas*, on
which all Indian society depended."   It is not to Helps, therefore, that we are to look for any extended biography of Columbus; and when he finds him in chains, sent back to Spain, he
says of the prisoner, " He did not know how many wretched
beings would have to traverse those seas, in bonds much worse
than his ; nor did he foresee, I trust, that some of his doings
would further all this coming misery."   It does not appear from
his footnotes that Helps depended upon other than the obvious
authorities, though he says that he examined the Muñoz collection, then as now in the Royal Academy of History at Madrid.

Arthur
Helps.

The last scholarly summary of Columbus's career previous to
the views incident to the criticism of Harrisse on the
*Historie* of 1571 was that which was given by R. H.

R. H. Major.

Major, in the second edition of his *Select Letters of Columbus* (London, 1870).

There have been two treatments of the subject by Americans within the last twenty years, which are characteristic. The *Life and Achievements of the So-called Christopher Colum-bus* (New York, 1874), by Aaron Goodrich, mixes Aaron Good-that unreasoning trust and querulous conceit which is rich. so often thrown into the scale when the merits of the discover-ers of the alleged Vinland are contrasted with those of the imagined Indies. With a craze of petulancy, he is not able to see anything that cannot be twisted into defamation, and his book is as absurdly constant in derogation as the hallucinations of De Lorgues are in the other direction.

When Hubert Howe Bancroft opened the story of his Pacific States in his *History of Central America* (San Fran- H. H. Ban-cisco, 1882), he rehearsed the story of Columbus, but croft. did not attempt to follow it critically except as he tracked the Admiral along the coasts of Honduras, Nicaragua, and Costa Rica. This writer's estimate of the character of Columbus con-veys a representation of what the Admiral really was, juster than national pride, religious sympathy, or kindly adulation has usually permitted. It is unfortunately, not altogether chaste in its literary presentation. His characterization of Irving and Prescott in their endeavors to draw the character of Columbus has more merit in its insight than skill in its drafting.

The brief sketch of the career of Columbus, and the exami-nation of the events that culminated in his maritime risks and developments, as it was included in the *Narrative and Critical History of America* (vol. ii., Boston, 1885), gave Winsor. the present writer an opportunity to study the sources and trace the bibliographical threads that run through an ex-tended and diversified literature, in a way, it may be, not earlier presented to the English reader. If any one desires to compass all the elucidations and guides which a Bibliog-thorough student of the career and fame of Columbus raphy of Co-would wish to consider, the apparatus thus referred to, lumbus. and the footnotes in Harrisse's *Christophe Colomb* and in his other germane publications, would probably most essentially shorten his labors. Harrisse, who has prepared, but not yet published, lists of the books devoted to Columbus *exclusively*, says that they number about six hundred titles. The literature which treats of him incidentally is of a vast extent.

In concluding this summary of the commentaries upon the life of Columbus, the thought comes back that his career has been singularly subject to the gauging of opinionated chroniclers. The figure of the man, as he lives to-day in the mind of the general reader, in whatever country, comports in the main with the characterizations of Irving, De Lorgues, or Goodrich. These last two have entered upon their works with a determined purpose, the Frenchman of making a saint, and the American a scamp, of the great discoverer of America. They each, in their twists, pervert and emphasize every trait and every incident to favor their views. Their narratives are each without any background of that mixture of incongruity, inconsistency, and fatality from which no human being is wholly free. Their books are absolutely worthless as historical records. That of Goodrich has probably done little to make proselytes. That of De Lorgues has infected a large body of tributary devotees of the Catholic Church.

*Varied estimates of Columbus.*

The work of Irving is much above any such level ; but it has done more harm because its charms are insidious. He recognized at least that human life is composite ; but he had as much of a predetermination as they, and his purpose was to create a hero. He glorified what was heroic, palliated what was unheroic, and minimized the doubtful aspects of Columbus's character. His book is, therefore, dangerously seductive to the popular sense. The genuine Columbus evaporates under the warmth of the writer's genius, and we have nothing left but a refinement of his clay. The *Life of Columbus* was a sudden product of success, and it has kept its hold on the public very constantly ; but it has lost ground in these later years among scholarly inquirers. They have, by their collation of its narrative with the original sources, discovered its flaccid character. They have outgrown the witcheries of its graceful style. They have learned to put at their value the repetitionary changes of stock sentiment, which swell the body of the text, sometimes, provokingly.

Out of the variety of testimony respecting the person of the adult Columbus, it is not easy to draw a picture that his contemporaries would surely recognize. Likeness we have none that can be proved beyond a question the result of any sitting, or even of any acquaintance. If we were called upon to picture him as he stood on San Salvador, we might figure a man of impressive stature with lofty, not to say austere, bearing, his face longer by something more than its breadth, his cheek bones high, his nose aquiline, his eyes a light gray, his complexion fair with freckles spotting a ruddy glow, his hair once light, but then turned to gray. His favorite garb seems to have been the frock of a Franciscan monk. Such a figure would not conflict with the descriptions which those who knew him, and those who had questioned his associates, have transmitted to us, as we read them in the pages ascribed to Ferdinand, his son; in those of the Spanish historian, Oviedo; of the priest Las Casas; and in the later recitals of Gomara and Benzoni, and of the official chronicler of the Spanish Indies, Antonio Herrera. The oldest description of all is one made in 1501, in the unauthorized version of the first decade of Peter Martyr, emanating, very likely, from the translator Trivigiano, who had then recently come in contact with Columbus.

Turning from these descriptions to the pictures that have been put forth as likenesses, we find not a little difficulty in reconciling the two. There is nothing that unmistakably goes back to the lifetime of Columbus except the figure of St. Christopher, which makes a vignette in colors on the mappemonde, which was drawn in 1500, by one of Columbus's pilots, Juan de la Cosa, and is now preserved in Madrid. It has been fondly claimed that Cosa transferred the features of his master to the lineaments of the saint; but the assertion is wholly without proof.

Paolo Giovio, or, as better known in the Latin form, Paulus Jovius, was old enough in 1492 to have, in later life, remembered the thrill of expectation which ran for the moment through parts of Europe, when the letter of Columbus describing his voyage was published in Italy, where Jovius was then a schoolboy. He was but an infant, or perhaps not born when Columbus left Italy. So the interest of

*Portraits of Columbus.*

*Columbus's person.*

*La Cosa's St. Christopher.*

*Jovius's gallery.*

ST. CHRISTOPHER.
[The vignette of La Cosa's map.]

Jovius in the Discoverer could hardly have arisen from any other associations than those easily suggestive to one who, like Jovius, was a student of his own times. Columbus had been dead ten years when Jovius, as a historian, attracted the notice of Pope Leo X., and entered upon such a career of prosperity

JOVIUS'S COLUMBUS, THE EARLIEST ENGRAVED LIKENESS.

that he could build a villa on Lake Como, and adorn it with a gallery of portraits of those who had made his age famous. That he included a likeness of Columbus among his heroes there seems to be no doubt. Whether the likeness was painted from life, and by whom, or modeled after an ideal, more or less accordant with the reports of those who may have known the Genoese, is entirely beyond our knowledge. As a historian

Jovius professed the right to distort the truth for any purpose that suited him, and his conceptions of the truth of portraiture may quite as well have been equally loose. Just a year before his own death, Jovius gave a sketch of Columbus's career in his *Elogia Virorum Illustrium*, published at Florence in 1551 ; but it was not till twenty-four years later, in 1575, that a new edition of the book gave wood-cuts of the portraits in the gallery of the Como villa, to illustrate the sketches, and that of Columbus appeared among them. This engraving, then, is the oldest likeness of Columbus presenting any claims to consideration. It found place also, within a year or two, in what purported to be a collection of portraits from the Jovian gallery ; and the engraver of them was Tobias Stimmer, a Swiss designer, who stands in the biographical dictionaries of artists as born in 1534, and of course could not have assisted his skill by any knowledge of Columbus, ·on his own part. This picture, to which a large part of the very various likenesses called those of Columbus can be traced, is done in the bold, easy handling common in the wood-cuts of that day, and with a precision of skill that might well make one believe that it preserves a dashing verisimilitude to the original picture. It represents a full-face, shaven, curly-haired man, with a thoughtful and somewhat sad countenance, his hands gathering about the waist a priest's robe, of which the hood has fallen about his neck. If there is any picture to be judged authentic, this is best entitled to that estimation.

Connection with the Como gallery is held to be so significant of the authenticity of any portrait of Columbus that it is claimed for two other pictures, which are near enough alike to have followed the same prototype, and which are not, except in garb, very unlike the Jovian wood-cut. As copies of the Como original in features, they may easily have varied in apparel. One of these is a picture preserved in the gallery at Florence, — a well-moulded, intellectual head, full-faced, above a closely buttoned tunic, or frock, seen within drapery that falls off the shoulders. It is not claimed to be the Como portrait, but it may have been painted from it, perhaps by Christofano dell' Altissimo, some time before 1568. A copy of it was made for Thomas Jefferson, which, having hung for a while at Monticello, came at last to Boston, and passed into the gallery of the Massachusetts Historical Society.

The Florence picture.

The picture resembling this, and which may have had equal claims of association with the Jovian gallery, is one now pre-

THE FLORENCE COLUMBUS.

served in Madrid, and the oldest canvas representing Columbus that is known in Spain. It takes the name of the Yanez por-

trait from that of the owner of it, from whom it was bought in
The Yanez picture. Granada, in 1763. Representing, when brought to notice, a garment trimmed with fur, there has been disclosed upon it, and underlying this later paint, an original,

THE YANEZ COLUMBUS.

close-fitting tunic, much like the Florence picture; while a further removal of the superposed pigment has revealed an inscription, supposed to authenticate it as Columbus, the discoverer of the New World. It is said that the Duke of Veragua holds it to be the most authentic likeness of his ancestor.

Another conspicuous portrait is that given by De Bry in the
De Bry's picture. larger series of his Collection of Early Voyages. De Bry claims that it was painted by order of King Ferdinand, and that it was purloined from the offices of the Council of the Indies in Spain, and brought to the Netherlands, and in this way fell into the hands of that engraver and editor. It bears little resemblance to the pictures already mentioned; nor does it appear to conform to the descriptions of Columbus's

person. It has a more rugged and shorter face, with a profusion of closely waved hair falling beneath an ugly, angular cap. De Bry engraved it, or rather published it, in 1595, twenty

**COLUMBUS.**

[A reproduction of the so-called Capriolo cut given in Giuseppe Banchero's *La Tavola di Bronzo*, (Genoa, 1857), and based on the Jovian type.]

years after the Jovian wood-cut appeared, and we know of no engraving intervening. No one of the generation that was old enough to have known the navigator could then have survived, and the picture has no other voucher than the professions of the engraver of it.

These are but a few of the many pictures that have been
Other portraits.
made to pass, first and last, for Columbus, and the only ones meriting serious study for their claims. The American public was long taught to regard the effigy of Columbus as that of a bedizened courtier, because Prescott se-

DE BRY'S COLUMBUS.

lected for an engraving to adorn his *Ferdinand and Isabella* a picture of such a person, which is ascribed to Parmigiano, and is preserved in the Museo Borbonico, at Naples. Its claims long ago ceased to be considered. The traveler in Cuba sees
Havana monument.
in the Cathedral at Havana a monumental effigy, of which there is no evidence of authenticity worthy of consideration. The traveler in Italy can see in Genoa, placed on the cabinet which was made to hold the manuscript titles

of Columbus, a bust by Peschiera.  It has the negative merit of having no relation to any of the alleged portraits; but represents the sculptor's conception of the man, Peschiera's bust.

THE BUST OF COLUMBUS ON THE TOMB AT HAVANA.

guided by the scant descriptions of him given to us by his contemporaries.

If the reader desires to see how extensive the field of research is, for one who can spend the time in tracing all the clues connected with all the representations which pass for Columbus, he can make a beginning, at least, under the guidance of the essay on the portraits which the present writer contributed to the *Narrative and Critical History of America*, vol. ii.

When Columbus, in 1502, ordered a tenth of his income to be paid annually to the Bank of St. George, in Genoa, for the purpose of reducing the tax upon corn, wine, and other provisions, the generous act, if it had been carried out, would have entitled him to such a recognition as a public benefactor as the bank was accustomed to bestow. The main hall of the palace of this institution commemorates such patriotic efforts by showing a sitting statue for the largest benefactors; a standing figure for lesser gifts, while still lower gradations of charitable help are indicated in busts, or in mere inscriptions on a mural tablet. It has been thought that posterity, curious to see the great Admiral as his contemporaries saw him, suffers with the state of Genoa, in not having such an effigy, by the neglect or inattention which followed upon the announced purpose of Columbus. We certainly find there to-day no such visible proof of his munificence or aspect. Harrisse, while referring to this deprivation, takes occasion, in his *Bank of St. George* (p. 108), to say that he does not " believe that the portrait of Columbus was ever drawn, carved, or painted from the life." He contends that portrait-painting was not common in Spain, in Columbus's day, and that we have no trace of the painters, whose work constitutes the beginning of the art, in any record, or authentic effigy, to show that the person of the Admiral was ever made the subject of the art. The same writer indicates that the interval during which Columbus was popular enough to be painted extended over only six weeks in April and May, 1493. He finds that much greater heroes, as the world then determined, like Boabdil and Cordova, were not thus honored, and holds that the portraits of Ferdinand and Isabella, which editions of Prescott have made familiar, are really fancy pictures of the close of the sixteenth century.

# CHAPTER III.

## THE ANCESTRY AND HOME OF COLUMBUS.

No one has mastered so thoroughly as Harrisse the intricacies of the Columbus genealogy. A pride in the name of Colombo has been shared by all who have borne it or have had relationship with it, and there has been a not un-worthy competition among many branches of the common stock to establish the evidences of their descent in connection, more or less intimate, with the greatest name that has signalized the family history.

The name Colombo.

This reduplication of families, as well as the constant recurrence of the same fore-names, particularly common in Italian families, has rendered it difficult to construct the genealogical tree of the Admiral, and has given ground for drafts of his pedigree, acceptable to some, and disputed by other claimants of kinship.

There was a Gascon-French subject of Louis XI., Guillaume de Casanove, sometimes called Coulomp, Coullon, Co-lon, in the Italian accounts Colombo, and Latinized as Columbus, who is said to have commanded a fleet of seven sail, which, in October, 1474, captured two galleys belonging to Ferdinand, king of Sicily. When Leibnitz published, for the first time, some of the diplomatic correspondence which ensued, he interjected the fore-name Christophorus in the references to the Columbus of this narrative. This was in his *Codex Juris Gentium Diplomaticus*, published at Hannover in 1693. Leibnitz was soon undeceived by Nicolas Thoynard, who explained that the corsair in question was Guillaume de Casanove, vice-admiral of France, and Leibnitz disavowed the imputation upon the Genoese navigator in a subsequent volume. Though there is some difference of opinion respecting the identity of Casanove and the capturer of the galleys, there can no longer be any doubt, in the light of pertinent investigations, that the French

The French Colombos.

Colombos were of no immediate kin to the family of Genoa and Savona, as is abundantly set forth by Harrisse in his *Les Colombo de France et d'Italie* (Paris, 1874). Since the French Coullon, or Coulomp, was sometimes in the waters neighboring to Genoa, it is not unlikely that some confusion may arise in separating the Italian from the French Colombos; and it has been pointed out that a certain entry of wreckage in the registry of Genoa, which Spotorno associates with Christopher Columbus, may more probably be connected with this Gascon navigator.

Bossi, the earliest biographer in recent times, considers that a Colombo named in a letter to the Duke of Milan as being in a naval fight off Cyprus, between Genoese and Venetian vessels, in 1476, was the discoverer of the New World. Harrisse, in his *Les Colombo*, has printed this letter, and from it it does not appear that the commander of the Genoese fleet is known by name, and that the only mention of a Colombo is that a fleet commanded by one of that name was somewhere encountered. There is no indication, however, that this commander was Christopher Columbus. The presumption is that he was the roving Casanove.

Leibnitz was doubtless misled by the assertion of the *Historie* of 1571, which allows that Christopher Columbus had sailed under the orders of an admiral of his name and family, and, particularly, was in that naval combat off Lisbon, when, his vessel getting on fire, he swam with the aid of an oar to the Portuguese shore. The doubtful character of this episode will be considered later; but it is more to the purpose here that this same book, in citing a letter, of which we are supposed to have the complete text as preserved by Columbus himself, makes Columbus say that he was not the only admiral which his family had produced. This is a clear reference, it is supposed, to this vice-admiral of France. It is enough to say that the genuine text of this letter to the nurse of Don Juan does not contain this controverted passage, and the defenders of the truth of the *Historie*, like D'Avezac, are forced to imagine there must have been another letter, not now known.

Beside the elder admiral of France, the name of Colombo Junior belonged to another of these French sea-rovers in the fifteenth century, who has been held to be a nephew, or at least a relative, of the elder. He has also sometimes been confounded with the Genoese Columbus.

The younger French admiral.

To determine the exact relationship between the various French and Italian Colombos and Coulons of the fif- teenth century would be hazardous. It is enough to <sup>Genealogy.</sup> say that no evidence that stands a critical test remains to con- nect these famous mariners with the line of Christopher Co- lumbus. The genealogical tables which Spotorno presents, upon which Caleb Cushing enlightened American readers at the time in the *North American Review*, and in which the French family is made to issue from an alleged great-grand- father of Christopher Columbus, are affirmed by Har- <sup>Pretenders.</sup> risse, with much reason, to have been made up not far from 1583, to support the claims of Bernardo and Baldassare (Bal- thazar) Colombo, as pretenders to the rights and titles of the discoverer of the New World.

Ferdinand is made in his own name to say of his father, " I think it better that all the honor be derived to us from his per- son than to go about to inquire whether his father was a mer- chant or a man of quality, that kept his hawks and hounds." Other biographers, however, have pursued the inquiry dili- gently.

In one of the sections of his book on *Christopher Columbus and the Bank of Saint George*, Harrisse has shown <sup>Columbus's</sup> how the notarial records of Savona and Genoa have <sup>family line.</sup> been worked, to develop the early history of the Admiral's family from documentary proofs. These evidences are distinct from the narratives of those who had known him, or who at a later day had told his story, as Gallo, the writer of the *His- torie*, and Oviedo did. Reference has already been made to the prevalence of Colombo as a patronymic in Genoa and the neighboring country at that time. Harrisse in his *Christophe Colomb* has enumerated two hundred of this name in Liguria alone, in those days, who seem to have had no kinship to the family of the Admiral. There appear to have been in Genoa, moreover, four Colombos, and in Liguria, outside of Genoa, six others who bore the name of Christopher's father, Domenico ; but the searchers have not yet found a single other Christoforo. These facts show the discrimination which those who of late years have been investigating the history of the Admiral's fam- ily have been obliged to exercise. There are sixty notarial acts

of one kind and another, out of which these investigators have
constructed a pedigree, which must stand till present knowledge
is increased or overthrown.

What we know in the main is this : Giovanni Colombo, the
grandfather of the Admiral, lived probably in Quinto
al Mare, and was of a stock that seemingly had been
earlier settled in the valley of Fontanabuona, a region east of
Genoa. This is a parentage of the father of Columbus quite
different from that shown in the genealogical chart made by
Napione in 1805 and later; and Harrisse tells us that the notarial acts which were given then as the authority for such other
line of descent cannot now be found, and that there are grave
doubts of their authenticity.

His grand-
father.

It was this Giovanni's son, Domenico, who came from Quinto
(where he left a brother, Antonio) at least as early
as 1439, and perhaps earlier, and settled himself in
the wool-weaver's quarter, so called, in Genoa, where in due
time he owned a house. Thence he seems to have removed to
Savona, where various notarial acts recognize him at a later
period as a Genoese, resident in Savona.

His father.

The essential thing remaining to be proved is that the Domenico Colombo of these notarial acts was the Domenico who
was the father of Christopher Columbus. For this purpose we
must take the testimony of those who knew the genuine Colombos, as Oviedo and Gallo did ; and from their statements
we learn that the father of Christopher was a weaver named
Domenico, who lived in Genoa, and had sons, Christoforo, Bartolomeo, and Giacomo. These, then, are the test conditions,
and finding them every one answered in the Savona-Genoa
family, the proof seems incontestable, even to the further fact
that at the end of the fifteenth century all three brothers had
for some years lived under the Spanish crown.

It is too much to say that this concatenation of identities
may not possibly be overturned, perhaps by discrediting the
documents, not indeed untried already by Peragallo and others,
but it is safe to accept it under present conditions of knowledge ; though we have to trust on some points to the statements of those who have seen what no longer can be found.
Domenico Colombo, who had removed to Savona in 1470, did
not, apparently, prosper there. He and his son Christopher

pursued their trade as weavers, as the notarial records show. Lamartine, in his *Life of Columbus*, speaking of the wool-carding of the time, calls it " a business now low, but then respectable and almost noble," — an idealization quite of a kind with the spirit that pervades Lamartine's book, and a spirit in which it has been a fashion to write of Columbus and other heroes. The calling was doubtless, then as now, simply respectable. The father added some experience, it would seem, in keeping a house of entertainment. The joint profit, however, of these two occupations did not suffice to keep him free from debt, out of which his son Christopher is known to have helped him in some measure. Domenico sold and bought small landed properties, but did not pay for one of them at least. There were fifteen years of this precarious life passed in Savona, during which he lost his wife, when, putting his youngest son to an apprenticeship, he returned in 1484, or perhaps a little earlier, to Genoa, to try other chances. His fortune here was no better. Insolvency still followed him. When we lose sight of him, in 1494, the old man may, it is hoped, have heard rumors of the transient prosperity of his son, and perhaps have read in the fresh little quartos of Plaanck the marvelous tale of the great discovery. He lived we know not how much longer, but probably died before the winter of 1499–1500, when the heirs of Corrado de Cuneo, who had never received due payment for an estate which Domenico had bought in Savona, got judgment against Christopher and his brother Diego, the sons of Domenico, then of course beyond reach in foreign lands.

Within a few years the Marquis Marcello Staglieno, a learned antiquary in Genoa, who has succeeded in throwing much new light on the early life of Columbus from the notarial records of that city, has identified a house in the Vico Dritto Ponticello, No. 37, as the one in which Domenico Colombo lived during the younger years of Christopher's life. The municipality bought this estate in June, 1887, and placed over its door an inscription recording the associations of the spot. Harrisse thinks it not unlikely that the great navigator was even born here. The discovery of his father's ownership of the house seems to have been made by carefully tracing back the title of the land to the time when Domenico owned it. This was rendered surer by tracing the titles of the adjoining estates back to the time of Nicolas Paravania and Antonio Bondi, who, according to the notarial act of 1477, recording Domenico's wife's assent to the sale of the property, lived as Domenico's next neighbors.

If Christopher Columbus was born in this house, that event Columbus took place, as notarial records, brought to bear by the born. Marquis Staglieno, make evident, between October 29, 1446, and October 29, 1451 ; and if some degree of inference be allowed, Harrisse thinks he can narrow the range to the twelve months between March 15, 1446, and March 20, 1447. This is the period within which, by deduction from other statements, some of the modern authorities, like Muñoz, Bossi, and Spotorno, among the Italians, D'Avezac among the French, and Major in England, have placed the event of Columbus's birth without the aid of attested documents. This conclusion has been reached by taking an avowal of Columbus that he had led twenty-three years a sailor's life at the time of his first voyage, and was fourteen years old when he began a seaman's career. The question which complicates the decision is : When did Columbus consider his sailor's life to have ended? If in 1492, as Peschel contends, it would carry his birth back no farther than 1455–56, according as fractions are managed ; and Peschel accepts this date, because he believes the unconfirmed statement of Columbus in a letter of July 7, 1503, that he was twenty-eight when he entered the service of Spain in 1484.

But if 1484 is accepted as the termination of that twenty-three years of sea life, as Muñoz and the others already mentioned say, then we get the result which most nearly accords 1445-1447. with the notarial records, and we can place the birth of Columbus somewhere in the years 1445–47, according as the fractions are considered. This again is confirmed by another of the varied statements of Columbus, that in 1501 it was forty years since, at fourteen, he first took to the sea.

There has been one other deduction used, through which Navarrete, Humboldt, Irving, Roselly de Lorgues, Napi-1435-1437. one, and others, who copy them, determine that his birth must have taken place, by a similar fractional allowance of margin, in 1435–37. This is based upon the explicit statement of Andrès Bernaldez, in his book on the Catholic monarchs of Spain, that Columbus at his death was about seventy years old.

So there is a twenty years' range for those who may be influenced by one line of argument or another in determining the date of the Admiral's birth. Many writers have discussed the arguments; but the weight of authority seems, on the whole, to rest upon the records which are used by Harrisse.

The mother of Columbus was Susanna, a daughter of Giacomo de Fontanarossa, and Domenico married her in the Bisagno country, a region lying east of Genoa. *His mother, brothers, and sister.* She was certainly dead in 1489, and had, perhaps, died as early as 1482, in Savona. Beside Christoforo, this alliance with Domenico Colombo produced four other children, who were probably born in one and the same house. They were Giovanni-Pellegrino, who, in 1501, had been dead ten years, and was unmarried; Bartolomeo, who was never married, and who will be encountered later as Bartholomew; and Giacomo, who when he went to Spain became known as Diego Colon, but who is called Jacobus in all Latin narratives. There was also a daughter, Bianchinetta, who married a cheesemonger named Bavarello, and had one child.

Antonio, the brother of Domenico, seems to have had three sons, Giovanni, Matteo, and Amighetto. They were *His uncle and cousins.* thus cousins of the Admiral, and they were so far cognizant of his fame in 1496 as to combine in a declaration before a notary that they united in sending one of their number, Giovanni, on a voyage to Spain to visit their famous kinsman, the Admiral of the Indies; their object being, most probably, to profit, if they could, by basking in his favor.

If the evidences thus set forth of his family history be accepted, there is no question that Columbus, as he *Born in Genoa.* himself always said, and finally in his will declared, and as Ferdinand knew, although it is not affirmed in the *Historie*, was born in Genoa. Among the early writers, if we except Galindez de Carvajal, who claimed him for Savona, there seems to have been little or no doubt that he was born in Genoa. Peter Martyr and Las Casas affirm it. Bernaldez believed it. Giustiniani asserts it. But when Oviedo, not many years after Columbus's death, wrote, it was become so doubtful where Columbus was born that he mentions five or six towns which claimed the honor of being his birthplace. The claim *Claim for Savona,* for Savona has always remained, after Genoa, that which has received the best recognition. The grounds of such

a belief, however, have been pretty well disproved in Harrisse's *Christophe Colomb et Savone* (Genoa, 1887), and it has been shown, as it would seem conclusively, that, prior to Domenico Colombo's settling in Savona in 1470–71, he had lived in Genoa, where his children, taking into account their known or computed ages, must have been born.   It seems useless to re-
and other places. hearse the arguments which strenuous advocates have, at one time or another, offered in support of the pre-tensions of many other Italian towns and villages to have fur-nished the great discoverer to the world, — Plaisance, Cuccaro, Cogoleto, Pradello, Nervi, Albissola, Bogliasco, Cosseria, Finale, Oneglia, Quinto, Novare, Chiavari, Milan, Modena.   The pre-tensions of some of them were so urgent that in 1812 the Acad-emy of History at Genoa thought it worth while to present the proofs as respects their city in a formal way.   The claims of Cuccaro were used in support of a suit by Balthazar Colombo, to obtain possession of the Admiral's legal rights.   The claim of Cogoleto seems to have been mixed up with the supposed birth of the corsairs, Colombos, in that town, who for a long while were confounded with the Admiral.   There is left in favor of any of them, after their claims are critically examined, nothing but local pride and enthusiasm.

   The latest claimant for the honor is the town of Calvi, in Cor-sica, and this cause has been particularly embraced by the French.   So late as 1882, President Grévy, of the French Re-public, undertook to give a national sanction to these claims by approving the erection there of a statue of Columbus.   The assumption is based upon a tradition that the great discoverer was a native of that place.   The principal elucidator of that claim, the Abbé Martin Casanova de Pioggiola, seems to have a comfortable notion that tradition is the strongest kind of his-torical proof, though it is not certain that he would think so with respect to the twenty and more other places on the Italian coast where similar traditions exist or are said to be current. Harrisse seems to have thought the claim worth refuting in his *Christophe Colomb et La Corse* (Paris, 1888), to say nothing of other examinations of the subject in the *Revue de Paris* and the *Revue Critique*, and of two very recent refutations, one by the Abbé Casabianca in his *Le Berceau de Christophe Colomb et la Corse* (Paris, 1889), and the last word of Harrisse in the *Revue Historique* (1890, p. 182).

# CHAPTER IV.

THE condition of knowledge respecting Columbus's early life was such, when Prescott wrote, that few would dispute his conclusion that it is hopeless to unravel the entanglement of events, associated with the opening of his career. The critical discernment of Harrisse and other recent investigators has since then done something to make the confusion even more apparent by unsettling convictions too hastily assumed. A bunch of bewildering statements, in despite of all that present scholarship can do, is left to such experts as may be possessed in the future of more determinate knowledge. It may well be doubted if absolute clarification of the record is ever to be possible.

The student naturally inquires of the contemporaries of Columbus as to the quality and extent of his early edu- His education, and he derives most from Las Casas and the tion. *Historie* of 1571. It has of late been ascertained that the woolcombers of Genoa established local schools for the education of their children, and the young Christopher may have had his share of their instruction, in addition to whatever he picked up at his trade, which continued, as long as he remained in Italy, that of his father. We know from the manuscripts which have come down to us that Columbus acquired the manual dexterity of a good penman; and if some existing drawings are not apocryphal, he had a deft hand, too, in making a spirited sketch with a few strokes. His drawing of maps, which we are also told about, implies that he had fulfilled Ptolemy's definition of that art of the cosmographer which could represent the cartographic outlines of countries with supposable correctness. He could do it with such skill that he practiced it at one time, as is said, for the gaining of a livelihood. We know, trusting the *Historie*, that he was for a brief period at the University of Pavia,

perhaps not far from 1460, where he sought to understand the
mysteries of cosmography, astrology, and geometry.
Bossi has enumerated the professors in these depart-

At Pavia.

DRAWING ASCRIBED TO COLUMBUS.

ments at that time, from whose teaching Columbus may possibly have profited.   Harrisse with his accustomed distrust,

throws great doubt on the whole narrative of his university experiences, and thinks Pavia at this time offered no peculiar advantages for an aspiring seaman, to be compared with the practical instruction which Genoa in its commercial eminence could at the same time have offered to any sea-smitten boy. It was at Genoa at this very time (1461), that Benincasa was producing his famous sea-charts.

ANDREAS BENINCASA, 1476.
[From St. Martin's *Atlas*.]

After his possible, if not probable, sojourn at Pavia, made transient, it has been suggested but not proved, by the failing fortunes of his father, Christopher returned to Genoa, and then after an uncertain interval entered on his seafaring career. If what passes for his own statement be taken he was at this turn of his life not more than fourteen years old. The attractions of the sea at that period of the <sub>Goes to sea.</sub> fifteenth century were great for adventurous youths. There was a spice of piracy in even the soberest ventures of commerce. The ships of one Christian state preyed on another. Private ventures were buccaneerish, and the hand of the Catalonian and of the Moslem were turned against all. The news which sped from one end of the Mediterranean to the other was of fight and plunder, here and everywhere. Occasionally it was mixed with rumors of the voyages beyond the Straits of Hercules, which told of the Portuguese and their hazards on the African coast towards the equator. Not far from the time when our vigorous young Genoese wool-comber may be supposed to have

embarked on some of these venturesome exploits of the great
inland sea, there might have come jumping from port to port,
westerly along the Mediterranean shores, the story of
Prince Henry, the Navigator. the death of that great maritime spirit of Portugal,
Prince Henry, the Navigator, and of the latest feats
of his captains in the great ocean of the west.

SHIP, FIFTEENTH CENTURY.
[From the *Isolario*, 1547.]

It has been usual to associate the earliest maritime career of
Anjou's expedition. our dashing Genoese with an expedition fitted out in
Genoa by John of Anjou, Duke of Calabria, to re-
cover possession of the kingdom of Naples for his father, Duke
René, Count of Provence. This is known to have been undertaken in 1459–61. The pride of Genoa encouraged the service
of the attacking fleet, and many a citizen cast in his lot with

that naval armament, and embarked with his own subsidiary command. There is mention of a certain doughty captain, Colombo by name, as leading one part of this expeditionary force. He was very likely one of those French corsairs of that name, already mentioned, and likely to have been a man of importance in the Franco-Genoese train. He has, indeed, been sometimes made a kinsman of the wool-comber's son. There is little likelihood of his having been our Christopher himself, then, as we may easily picture him, a red-haired youth, or in life's early prime, with a ruddy complexion, — a type of the Italian which one to-day is not without the chance of encountering in the north of Italy, preserving, it may be, some of that northern blood which had produced the Vikings.

The *Historie* of 1571 gives what purports to be a letter of Columbus describing some of the events of this campaign. It was addressed to the Spanish monarchs in 1495. If Anjou was connected with any service in which Columbus took part, it is easy to make it manifest that it could not have happened later than 1461, because the reverses of that year drove the unfortunate René into permanent retirement. The rebuttal of this testimony depends largely upon the date of Columbus's birth ; and if that is placed in 1446, as seems well established, Columbus, the Genoese mariner, could hardly have commanded a galley in it at fourteen ; and it is still more improbable if, as D'Avezac says, Columbus was in the expedition when it set out in 1459, since the boy Christopher was then but twelve. As Harrisse puts it, the letter of Columbus quoted in the *Historie* is apocryphal, or the correct date of Columbus's birth is not 1446.

It is, however, not to be forgotten that Columbus himself testifies to the tender age at which he began his sea-service, when, in 1501, he recalled some of his early experiences ; but, unfortunately, Columbus was chronically given to looseness of statement, and the testimony of his contemporaries is often the better authority. In 1501, his mind, moreover, was verging on irresponsibility. He had a talent for deceit, and sometimes boasted of it, or at least counted it a merit.

Much investigation has wonderfully confirmed the accuracy of that earliest sketch of his career contained in the Giustiniani Psalter in 1516 ; and it is learned from that narrative that Columbus had attained an adult age when he first went to sea, — and this was one of the statements which the *Historie* of 1571 sought to discredit. If the notarial records of Savona are correct in calling Columbus a wool-comber in 1472, and he was of the Savona family, and born in 1446, he was then twenty-six years old, and of the adult age that is claimed by the Psalter and by other early writers, who either knew or mentioned him, when he began his seafaring life. In that case he could have had no part in the Anjou-René expedition, whose whole story, even with the expositions of Harrisse and Max Büdinger, is shrouded in uncertainties of time and place. That after 1473 he disappears from every notarial record that can be found in Genoa shows, in Harrisse's opinion, that it was not till then that he took to the sea as a profession.

We cannot say that the information which we have of this early seafaring life of Columbus, whenever beginning, is deserving of much credit, and it is difficult to place whatever it includes in chronological order.

We may infer from one of his statements that he had, at some time, been at Scio observing the making of mastic. Certain reports which most likely concern his namesakes, the French corsairs, are sometimes associated with him as leading an attack on Spanish galleys somewhere in the service of Louis XI., or as cruising near Cyprus.

So everything is misty about these early days; but the imagination of some of his biographers gives us abundant precision for the daily life of the school-boy, apprentice, cabin boy, mariner, and corsair, even to the receiving of a wound which we know troubled him in his later years. Such a story of details is the filling up of a scant outline with the colors of an unfaithful limner.

# CHAPTER V.

## THE ALLUREMENTS OF PORTUGAL.

COLUMBUS, disappearing from Italy in 1473, is next found in Portugal, and it is a natural inquiry why an active, adventurous spirit, having tested the exhilaration of 1473. the sea, should have made his way to that outpost of maritime ambition, bordering on the great waters, that had for many ages attracted and puzzled the discoverer and cosmographer. It is hardly to be doubted that the fame of the Portuguese voyaging out upon the vasty deep, or following the western coast of Africa, had for some time been a not unusual topic of talk among the seamen of the Mediterranean. It may be only less probable that an intercourse of seafaring Mediterranean people with the Arabs of the Levant had brought rumors of voyages in the ocean that washed the eastern shores of Africa. Maritime enterprise in Portugal. These stories from the Orient might well have induced some to speculate that such voyages were but the complements of those of the Portuguese in their efforts to solve the problem of the circumnavigation of the great African continent. It is not, then, surprising that a doughty mariner like Columbus, in life's prime, should have desired to be in the thick of such discussions, and to no other European region could he have turned as a wanderer with the same satisfaction as to Portugal.

Let us see how the great maritime questions stood in Portugal in 1473, and from what antecedents they had arisen.

The Portuguese, at this time, had the reputation of being the most expert seamen in Europe, or at least they divided Portuguese it with the Catalans and Majorcans. Their fame seamanship. lasted, and at a later day was repeated by Acosta. These hardy mariners had pushed boldly out, as early as we have any records, into the enticing and yet forbidding Sea of Darkness, Explora- not often perhaps willingly out of sight of land ; but tions on the Sea of storms not infrequently gave them the experience of Darkness.

sea and sky, and nothing else.   The great ocean was an untried
waste for cartography.   A few straggling beliefs in islands
lying westward had come down from the ancients, and the fan-
Marino Sa-   tastic notions of floating islands and steady lands,
nuto, 1306.   upon which the imagination of the Middle Ages
thrived, were still rife, when we find in the map of Marino
Sanuto, in 1306, what may well be considered the beginning of
Atlantic cartography.

There is no occasion to make it evident that the Islands of
The Cana-   the West found by the Phœnicians, the Fortunate
ries.   Islands of Sertorius, and the Hesperides of Pliny were
the Canaries of later times, brought to light after thirteen centuries of oblivion ; but these islands stand in the planisphere of
Sanuto at the beginning of the fourteenth century, to be casually visited by the Spaniards and others for a hundred years
and more before the Norman, Jean de Béthencourt, in the
beginning of the fifteenth century (1402), settled himself on one
of them.   Here his kinspeople ruled, till finally the rival claims
of sovereignty by Spain and Portugal ended in the rights of
Spain being established, with compensating exclusive rights to
Portugal on the African coast.

But it was by Genoese in the service of Portugal, the fame
The Genoese   of whose exploits may not have been unknown to Co-
in Portugal.   lumbus, that the most important discoveries of ocean
islands had been made.

It was in the early part of the fourteenth century that the
Madeira group had been discovered.   In the Lauren-
Madeira.   tian portolano of 1351, preserved at Florence, it is
unmistakably laid down and properly named, and that atlas
has been considered, for several reasons, the work of Genoese,
and as probably recording the voyage by the Genoese Pezagno
for the Portuguese king, — at least Major holds that to be demonstrable.   The real right of the Portuguese to these islands
rests, however, on their rediscovery by Prince Henry's captains
at a still later period, in 1418–20, when Madeira, seen as a
cloud in the horizon from Porto Santo, was approached in a
boat from the smaller island.

It is also from the Laurentian portolano of 1351 that we
know how, at some anterior time, the greater group
Azores.   of the Azores had been found by Portuguese vessels

under Genoese commanders.　We find these islands also in the Catalan map of 1373, and in that of Pizigani of the same period (1367, 1373). Maps.

It was in the reign of Edward III. of England that one Rob-

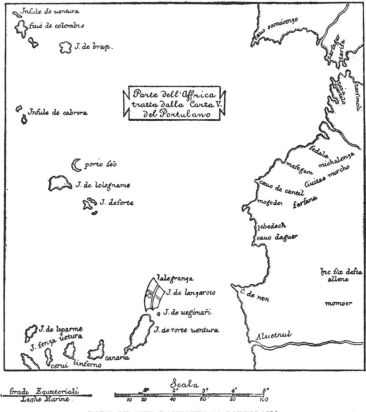

PART OF THE LAURENTIAN PORTOLANO.
[From Major's *Prince Henry.*]

ert Machin, flying from England to avoid pursuit for stealing a wife, accidentally reached the island of Madeira. Robert Here disaster overtook Machin's company, but some Machin. of his crew reached Africa in a boat and were made captives by the Moors.　In 1416, the Spaniards sent an expedition to redeem Christian captives held by these same Moors, and, while bringing them away, the Spanish ship was overcome by a Portuguese navigator, Zarco, and among his prisoners was one

Morales, who had heard, as was reported, of the experiences of Machin. Zarco, a little later, being sent by Prince Henry of
Porto Santo and Madeira rediscovered.
Portugal to the coast of Guinea, was driven out to sea, and discovered the island of Porto Santo; and subsequently, under the prompting of Morales, he rediscovered Madeira, then uninhabited. This was in 1418 or 1419, and though there are some divergences in the different forms of the story, and though romance and anachronism somewhat obscure its truth, the main circumstances are fairly discernible.

This discovery was the beginning of the revelations which the navigators of Prince Henry were to make. A few years later (1425) he dispatched colonists to occupy the two islands, and among them was a gentleman of the household, Bar-
The Perestrello family.
tolomeo Perestrello, whose name, in a descendant, we shall again encounter when, near the close of the century, we follow Columbus himself to this same island of Porto Santo.

It is conjectured that the position of the Azores was laid down on a map which, brought to Portugal from Venice in
Maps.
1428, instigated Prince Henry to order his seamen to rediscover those islands. That they are laid down on Valsequa's Catalan map of 1439 is held to indicate the accomplishment of the prince's purpose, probably in 1432, though it took twenty years to bring the entire group within the knowledge of the Portuguese.

The well-known map of Andrea Bianco in 1436, preserved
Bianco's map, 1436.
in the Biblioteca Marciana at Venice, records also the extent of supposition at that date respecting the island-studded waste of the Atlantic. Between this date and the period of the arrival of Columbus in Portugal, the best known names of the map makers of the Atlantic are those of
Other maps.
Valsequa (1439), Leardo (1448, 1452, 1458), Pareto (1455), and Fra Mauro (1459). This last there will be occasion to mention later.

In 1452, Pedro de Valasco, in sailing about Fayal westerly,
Flores.
seeing and following a flight of birds, had discovered the island of Flores. From what Columbus says in the journal of his first voyage, forty years later, this tracking of the flight of birds was not an unusual way, in these early exploring days, of finding new islands.

Thus it was that down to a period a very little later than the middle of the fifteenth century the Portuguese had been ac-

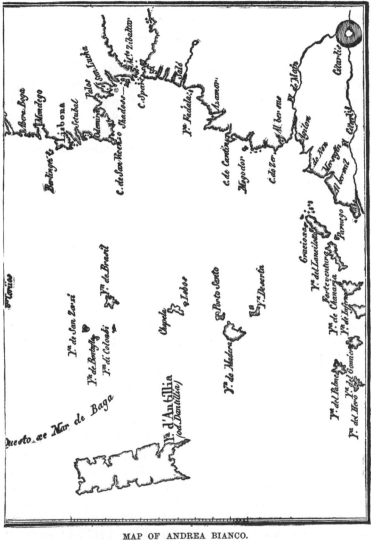

MAP OF ANDREA BIANCO.
[From *Allgem. Geog. Ephemeriden*, Weimar, 1807.]

customing themselves to these hazards of the open ocean. Without knowing it they had, in the discovery of Flores, actually reached the farthest land westerly, which could in the better knowledge of later years be looked upon as the remotest out-post of the Old World.

There was, as they thought, a much larger cosmographical
The African problem lying to the south, — a route to India by a
route to
India. supposable African cape.

For centuries the Orient had been the dream of the philoso-pher and the goal of the merchant. Everything in the East was thought to be on a larger scale than in Europe, — metals were more abundant, pearls were rarer, spices were richer, plants were nobler, animals were statelier. Everything but man was more lordly. He had been fed there so luxuriously that he was believed to have dwindled in character. Europe was the world of active intelligence, the inheritor of Greek and Roman power, and its typical man belonged naturally with the grander ex-ternals of the East. There was a fitness in bringing the better man and the better nature into such relations that the one should sustain and enjoy the other.

The earliest historical record of the peoples of Western Asia
China. with China goes back, according to Yule, to the sec-ond century before Christ. Three hundred years later we find the first trace of Roman intercourse (A. D. 166). With India China had some trade by sea as early as the fourth cen-tury, and with Babylonia possibly in the fifth century. There were Christian Nestorian missionaries there as early as the eighth century, and some of their teachings had been found there by Western travelers in the thirteenth and fourteenth cen-turies. The communication of Ceylon with China was revived in the thirteenth century.

It was in the twelfth century, under the Mongol dynasty, that
Cathay. China became first generally known in Europe, under the name of Cathay, and then for the first time the Western nations received travelers' stories of the kingdom of the great Khan. Two Franciscans, one an Italian, Plano Car-pini, the other a Fleming, Rubruquis, sent on missions for the Church, returned to Europe respectively in 1247 and 1255. It was not, however, till Marco Polo returned from his visit to
Marco Polo. Kublai Khan, in the latter part of the thirteenth cen-tury, that a new enlargement of the ideas of Europe respecting the far Orient took place. The influence of his mar-

velous tales continued down to the days of Columbus, and when the great discoverer came on the scene it was to find the public mind occupied with the hopes of reaching these Eastern realms by way of the south. The experimental and accidental voyagings of the Portuguese on the Atlantic were held to be but preliminary to a steadier progression down the coast of Africa.

Whether the ancients had succeeded in circumnavigating Africa is a question never likely to be definitely settled, and opposing views, as weighed by Bunbury in his *History of Ancient Geography*, are too evenly balanced to allow either side readily to make conquest of judicial minds. It is certain that Hipparchus had denied the possibility of it, and had supposed the Indian Ocean a land-bound sea, Africa extending at the south so as to connect with a southern prolongation of eastern Asia. This view had been adopted by Ptolemy, whose opinions were dominating at this time the Western mind. Nevertheless, that Africa ended in a southern cape seems to have been conceived of by those who doubted the authority of Ptolemy early enough for Sanuto, in 1306, to portray such a cape in his planisphere. If Sanuto really knew of its existence the source of his knowledge is a subject for curious speculation. Not unlikely an African cape may have been surmised by the Venetian sailors, who, frequenting the Mediterranean coasts of Asia Minor, came in contact with the Arabs. These last may have cherished the traditions of maritime explorers on the east coast of Africa, who may have already discovered the great southern cape, perhaps without passing it.

The guiding spirit in this new habit of exploration was that scion of the royal family of Portugal who became famous even-

*(marginal notes)* The African route and the ancients.

The African cape.

Navarrete records that as early as 1393 a company had been formed in Andalusia and Biscay for promoting discoveries down the coast of Africa. It was an effort to secure in the end such a route to Asia as might enable the people of the Iberian peninsula to share with those of the Italian the trade with the East, which the latter had long conducted wholly or in part overland from the Levant. The port of Barcelona had indeed a share in this opulent commerce ; but its product for Spain was insignificant in comparison with that for Italy.

*(marginal note)* African coast discovery, 1393.

The guiding spirit in this new habit of exploration was that scion of the royal family of Portugal who became famous even-

tually as Prince Henry the Navigator, and whose biography
has been laid before the English reader within twenty
years, abundantly elucidated by the careful hand of
Richard H. Major. The Prince had assisted King
João in the attack on the Moors at Ceuta, in 1415, and this
success had opened to the Prince the prospect of possessing the
Guinea coast, and of ultimately finding and passing the anticipated cape at the southern end of Africa.

*Prince Henry, the Navigator.*

This was the mission to which the Prince early in the fifteenth century gave himself. His ships began to crawl down
the western Barbary coast, and each season added to the extent of their explorations, but Cape Bojador for a
while blocked their way, just as it had stayed other
hardy adventurers even before the birth of Henry. "We may
wonder," says Helps, "that he never took personal command
of any of his expeditions, but he may have thought that he
served the cause better by remaining at home, and forming a
centre whence the electric energy of enterprise was communicated to many discoverers and then again collected from them."

*Cape Boja-dor.*

Meanwhile, Prince Henry had received from his father the
government of Algaroe, and he selected the secluded promontory of Sagres, jutting into the sea at the southwestern extremity of Portugal, as his home, going here in
1418, or possibly somewhat later. Whether he so organized his
efforts as to establish here a school of navigation is in dispute,
but it is probably merely a question of what constitutes a
school. There seems no doubt that he built an observatory
and drew about him skillful men in the nautical arts, including
a somewhat famous Majorcan, Jayme. He and his staff of
workers took seamanship as they found it, with its cylindrical
charts, and so developed it that it became in the hands of the
Portuguese the evidence of the highest skill then attainable.

*Sagres.*

Seamanship as then practiced has become an interesting study.
Under the guidance of Humboldt, in his remarkable
work, the *Examen Critique*, in which he couples a
consideration of the nautical astronomy with the needs of this
age of discovery, we find an easy path among the intricacies of
the art. These complications have, in special aspects, been
further elucidated by Navarrete, Margry, and a recent German
writer, Professor Ernst Mayer.

*Art of sea-manship.*

It was just at the end of the thirteenth century (1295) that the *Arte de Navegar* of Raymond Lully, or Lullius, Lully's *Arte* gave mariners a handbook, which, so far as is made *de Navegar.* apparent, was not superseded by a better even in the time of Columbus.

Another nautical text-book at this time was a treatise by John Holywood, a Yorkshire man, who needs to be a little dressed up when we think of him as the Latin- Sacrobosco. ized Sacrobosco. His *Sphera Mundi* was not put into type till

PRINCE HENRY THE NAVIGATOR.
[From a Chronicle in the National Library at Paris.]

1472, just before Columbus's arrival in Portugal, — a work which is mainly paraphrased from Ptolemy's *Almagest.* It was one of the books which, by law, the royal cosmographer of Spain, at a later day, was directed to expound in his courses of instruction.

The loadstone was known in western and northern Europe as early as the eleventh century, and for two or three The load- centuries there are found in books occasional refer- stone. ences to the magnet. We are in much doubt, however, as to the prevalence of its use in navigation.  If we are to believe some writers on the subject, it was known to the Norsemen as early as the seventh century.  Its use in the Levant, derived, doubtless, from the peoples navigating the Indian Ocean, goes back to an antiquity not easily to be limited.

By the year 1200, a knowledge of the magnetic needle, coming

Magnetic needle.

from China through the Arabs, had become common enough in Europe to be mentioned in literature, and in another century its use did not escape record by the chroniclers of maritime progress.  In the fourteenth century, the adventurous spirit of the Catalans and the Normans stretched the scope of their observations from the Hebrides on the north to the west coast of tropical Africa on the south, and to the westward, two fifths across the Atlantic to the neighborhood of the Azores, — voyages made safely under the direction of the magnet.

There was not much difficulty in computing latitude either by

Observations for latitude.

the altitude of the polar star or by using tables of the sun's declination, which the astronomers of the time were equal to calculating.  The astrolabe used for gauging the altitude was a simple instrument, which had been long in use among the Mediterranean seamen, and had been described by Raymond Lullius in the latter part of the thirteenth century.  Before Columbus's time it had been somewhat im-

The astrolabe.

proved by Johannes Müller of Königsberg, who became better known from the Latin form of his native town as Regiomontanus,  He had, perhaps, the best reputation in his day as a nautical astronomer, and Humboldt has explained the importance of his labors in the help which he afforded in an age of discovery.

It is quite certain that the navigators of Prince Henry, and

Dead reckoning.

even Columbus, practiced no artificial method for ascertaining the speed of their ships.  With vessels of the model of those days, no great rapidity was possible, and the utmost a ship could do under favorable circumstances was not usually beyond four miles an hour.  The hourglass gave them the time, and afforded the multiple according as the eye adjusted the apparent number of miles which the ship was making hour by hour.  This was the method by which Columbus, in 1492, calculated the distances, which he recorded day by day in

his journal. Of course the practiced seaman made allowances
for drift in the ocean currents, and met with more or less intelligence the various deterrent elements in beating to windward.

Humboldt, with his keen insight into all such problems concerning their relations to oceanic discoveries, tells us The sea-
in his *Cosmos* how he has made the history of the log man's log.
a subject of special investigation in the sixth volume of his

THE ASTROLABE OF REGIOMONTANUS.

*Examen Critique de l'Histoire de la Géographie*, which, unfortunately, the world has never seen; but he gives, apparently, the
results in his later *Cosmos*.

It is perhaps surprising that the Mediterranean peoples had
not perceived a method, somewhat clumsy as it was, which had
been in use by the Romans in the time of the republic. Though
the habit of throwing the log is still, in our day, kept up on
ocean steamers, I find that experienced commanders quite as
willingly depend on the report of their engineers as to the
number of revolutions which the wheel or screw has made in
the twenty-four hours. In this they were anticipated by these

republicans of Rome who attached wheels of four feet diameter to the sides of their ships and let the passage of the water turn them. Their revolutions were then recorded by a device which threw a pebble into a tally-pot for each revolution.

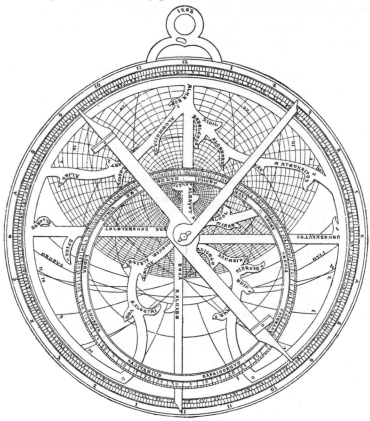

REGIOMONTANUS'S ASTROLABE, 1468.

[After an original in the museum at Nuremberg, shown in E. Mayer's *Die Hilfsmittel der Schiffahrtskunde.*]

From that time, so far as Humboldt could ascertain, down to a period later than Columbus, and certainly after the revival of long ocean voyages by the Catalans, Portuguese, and Normans, there seems to have been no skill beyond that of the eyes in measuring the speed of vessels. After the days of Columbus, it is only when we come to the voyages of Magellan that we find any mention of such a device as a log, which consisted, as his chronicler explains, of some arrangements of cog-wheels and chains carried on the poop.

Such were in brief the elements of seamanship in which Prince Henry the Navigator caused his sailors to be instructed, and which more or less governed the in- Prince Henry's character. strumentalities employed in his career of discovery. He was a man who, as his motto tells us, wished, and was able, to do well. He was shadowed with few infirmities of spirit. He joined with the pluck of his half-English blood — for he was the grandson of John of Gaunt — a training for endurance derived in his country's prolonged contests with the Moor. He was the staple and lofty exemplar of this great age of discovery. He was more so than Columbus, and rendered the adventitious career of the Genoese possible. He knew how to manage men, and stuck devotedly to his work. He respected his helpers too much to drug them with deceit, and there is a straightforward honesty of purpose in his endeavors. He was a trainer of men, and they grew courageous under his instruction. To sail into the supposed burning zone beyond Cape Bojador, and to face the destruction of life which was believed to be inevitable, required a courage quite as conspicuous as to cleave the floating verdure of the Sargasso Sea, on a western passage. It must be confessed that he shared with Columbus those proclivities which in the instigators of African slavery so easily slipped into cruelty. They each believed there was a merit, if a heathen's soul be at stake, in not letting commiseration get the better of piety.

It was not till 1434 that Prince Henry's captains finally passed Cape Bojador. It was a strenuous and daring effort in the face of conceded danger, and under the impulse Cape Bojador passed, 1434. of the Prince's earnest urging. Gil Eannes returned from this accomplished act a hero in the eyes of his master. Had it ever been passed before? Not apparently in any way to affect the importance of this Portuguese enterprise. We can go back indeed, to the expedition of Hanno the Carthaginian, and in the commentaries of Carl Müller and Vivien de St. Martin track that navigator outside the Pillars of Hercules, and follow him southerly possibly to Cape Verde or its vicinity; and this, if Major's arguments are to be accepted, is the only antecedent venture beyond Cape Bojador, though there have been claims set up for the Genoese, the Catalans, and the Dieppese. That the map of Marino Sanuto in 1306, and the so-called Laurentian portolano of 1351, both of which establish a vague southerly limit to Africa, rather give expression to a theory than chronicle the experience of navigators is the opinion of Major. It is of course possible that some indefinite knowledge of oriental tracking of the eastern coast of Africa, and developing its terminal shape southerly, may have passed, as already intimated, with other nautical knowledge, by the Red Sea to the Mediterranean peoples. To attempt to settle the question of any circumnavigation of Africa before the days of Diaz and Da Gama, by the evidence of earlier maps, makes us confront very closely geographical theories on the one hand, and on the other a possible actual knowledge filtered through the Arabs. All this renders it imprudent to assume any tone of certainty in the matter.

SKETCH MAP OF AFRICAN DISCOVERY.

The captains of Prince Henry now began, season by season, to make a steady advance. The Pope had granted to the Portuguese monarchy the exclusive right to discovered lands on this unexplored route to India, and had enjoined all others not to interfere.

In 1441 the Prince's ships passed beyond Cape Blanco, and

Cape Blanco passed, 1441. in succeeding years they still pushed on little by little, bringing home in 1442 some negroes for slaves, the first which were seen in Europe, as Helps supposes, though this is a matter of some doubt.

Cape Verde had been reached by Diniz Dyàz (Fernandez)

Cape Verde reached, 1445. in 1445, and the discovery that the coast beyond had a general easterly trend did much to encourage the Portuguese, with the illusory hope that the way to India was at last opened. They had by this time passed beyond the countries of the Moors, and were coasting along a country inhabited by negroes.

In 1455, the Venetian Cadamosto, a man who proved that he

could write intelligently of what he saw, was induced by Prince Henry to conduct a new expedition, which was led to Cadamosto, the Gambia; so that Europeans saw for the first time 1445. the constellation of the Southern Cross. In the following year, still patronized by Prince Henry, who fitted out one of his vessels, Cadamosto discovered the Cape Verde Islands, or at least his narrative would indicate that he did. By Cape Verde comparison of documents, however, Major has made it Islands. pretty clear that Cadamosto arrogated to himself a glory which belonged to another, and that the true discoverer of the Cape Verde Islands was Diogo Gomez, in 1460. It was on this second voyage that Cadamosto passed Cape Roxo, and reached the Rio Grande.

FRA MAURO'S WORLD, 1439.

In 1457, Prince Henry sent, by order of his nephew and sovereign, Alfonso V., the maps of his captains to Fra Mauro's Venice, to have them combined in a large mappe- maps, 1457.

monde; and Fra Mauro was entrusted with the making of it, in which he was assisted by Andrea Bianco, a famous cartog-

TOMB OF PRINCE HENRY AT BATALHA.
[From Major's *Prince Henry.*]

rapher of the time. This great map came to Portugal the year before the Prince died, and it stands as his final rec- ord, left behind him at his death, November 13, 1460, Prince Henry dies, to attest his constancy and leadership. The pecuni- 1460.

ary sacrifices which he had so greatly incurred in his enterprises had fatally embarrassed his estate. His death was not

as Columbus's was, an obscuration that no one noted; his life was prolonged in the school of seamanship which he had created.

The Prince's enthusiasm in his belief that there was a great southern point of Africa had been imparted to all his followers. Fra Mauro gave it credence in his map by an indication that an Indian junk from the East had rounded the cape with the sun in 1420. In this Mauro map the easterly trend of the coast beyond Cape Verde is adequately shown, but it is m a d e only as the northern shore of a deep gulf indenting the continent. The more southern parts are simply forced into a shape to suit and fill out the circular dimensions of the map.

Within a few years after Henry's death — though some place it earlier — the explorations had been pushed to Sierra Leone and be- Sierra Leone, yond Cape Mezu- Gold Coast. rada. When the revenues of the Gold Coast were farmed out in 1469, it was agreed that dis- covery should be pushed a hun-

STATUE OF PRINCE HENRY AT BELEM.
[From Major's *Prince Henry.*]

dred leagues farther south annually; and by 1474, when the contract expired, Fernam Gomez, who had taken it, La Mina. had already found the gold dust region of La Mina, which Columbus, in 1492, was counseled by Spain to avoid while searching for his western lands.

This, then, was the condition of Portuguese seamanship and of its exploits when Columbus, some time, probably, in 1473, reached Portugal. He found that country so content with the rich product of the Guinea coast that it was some years later before the Portuguese began to push still farther to the south. The desire to extend the Christian faith to heathen, often on the lips of the discoverers of the fifteenth century, was never so powerful but that gold and pearls made them forget it.

# CHAPTER VI.

## COLUMBUS IN PORTUGAL.

It has been held by Navarrete, Irving, and other writers of the older school that Columbus first arrived in Portugal in 1470; and his coming has commonly been connected with a naval battle near Lisbon, in which he escaped from a burning ship by swimming to land with the aid of an oar. It is easily proved, however, that notarial entries in Italy show him to have been in that country on August 7, 1473. We may, indeed, by some stretch of inference, allow the old date to be sustained, by supposing that he really was domiciled in Lisbon as early as 1470, but made occasional visits to his motherland for the next three or four years. *Date of his arrival.* *1470.*

The naval battle, in its details, is borrowed by the *Historie* of 1571 from the *Rerum Venitiarum ab Urbe Condita* of Sabellicus. This author makes Christopher Columbus a son of the younger corsair Colombo, who commanded in the fight, which could not have happened either in 1470, the year usually given, or in 1473–74, the time better determined for Columbus's arrival in Portugal, since this particular action is known to have taken place on August 22, 1485. Those who defend the *Historie*, like D'Avezac, claim that its account simply confounds the battle of 1485 with an earlier one, and that the story of the oar must be accepted as an incident of this supposable anterior fight. The action in 1485 took place when the French corsair, Casaneuve or Colombo, intercepted some richly laden Venetian galleys between Lisbon and Cape St. Vincent. History makes no mention of any earlier action of similar import which could have been the occasion of the escape by swimming; and to sustain the *Historie* by supposing such is a simple, perhaps allowable, hypothesis. *Supposed naval battle.*

Rawdon Brown, in the introduction to his volumes of the *Calendar of State Papers in the Archives of Venice*, has connected Columbus with this naval combat, but, as he later acknowledged to Harrisse, solely on the authority of the *Historie.* Irving has rejected the story. There seems no occasion to doubt its inconsistencies and anachronisms, and, once discarded, we are thrown back upon the notarial evidence in Italy, by which we may venture to accept the date of 1473– 74 as that of the entrance of Columbus into Portugal. Irving, though he discards the associated incidents, accepts the earlier date. Nevertheless, the date of 1473–74 is not taken without some hazard. As it has been of late ascertained that when Columbus left Portugal it was not for good, as was supposed, so it may yet be discovered that it was from some earlier adventure that the buoyancy of an oar took him to the land.

*Probable arrival in 1473-1474.*

This coming of an Italian to Portugal to throw in his lot with a foreign people leads the considerate observer to reflect on the strange vicissitudes which caused Italy to furnish to the western nations so many conspicuous leaders in the great explorations of the fifteenth and sixteenth centuries, without profiting in the slightest degree through territorial return. Cadamosto and Cabot, the Venetians, Columbus, the Genoese, Vespucius and Verrazano, the Florentines, are, on the whole, the most important of the great captains of discovery in this virgin age of maritime exploration through the dark waters of the Atlantic; and yet Spain and Portugal, France and England, were those who profited by their genius and labors.

*Italians as maritime discoverers.*

It is a singular fact that, during the years which Columbus spent in Portugal, there is not a single act of his life that can be credited with an exact date, and few can be placed beyond cavil by undisputed documentary evidence.

It is the usual story, given by his earliest Italian biographers, Gallo and his copiers, that Columbus had found his brother Bartholomew already domiciled in Portugal, and earning a living by making charts and selling books, and that Christopher naturally fell, for a while, into similar occupations. He was not, we are also told, unmindful of his father's distresses in Italy, when he disposed of his small earnings. We likewise know the names of a few of his fellow Genoese settled in Lisbon in traffic, because he speaks of their kindnesses to him, and the help which they had given him (1482) in what would appear to have been commercial ventures.

*Occupation in Portugal.*

It seems not unlikely that he had not been long in the country when the incident occurred at Lisbon which led to his marriage, which is thus recorded in the *Historie.*

During his customary attendance upon divine worship in the Convent of All Saints, his devotion was observed by <sup>His marriage.</sup> one of the pensioners of the monastery, who sought him with such expressions of affection that he easily yielded to her charms. This woman, Felipa Moñiz by name, is said to have been a daughter, by his wife Caterina Visconti, of Bartolomeo Perestrello, a gentleman of Italian origin, who is associated with the colonization of Madeira and Porto Santo. From anything which Columbus himself says and is preserved to us, we know nothing more than that he desired in his will that masses should be said for the repose of her soul; for she was then long dead, and, as Diego tells us, was buried in Lisbon. We learn her name for the first time from Diego's will, in 1509, and this is absolutely all the documentary evidence which we have concerning her. Oviedo and the writers who wrote before the publication of the *Historie* had only said that Columbus had married in Portugal, without further particulars.

But the *Historie*, with Las Casas following it, does not wholly satisfy our curiosity, neither does Oviedo, later, nor <sup>The Perestrellos.</sup> Gomara and Benzoni, who copy from Oviedo. There arises a question of the identity of this Bartolomeo Perestrello, among three of the name of three succeeding generations. Somewhere about 1420, or later, the eldest of this line was made the first governor of Porto Santo, after the island had been discovered by one of the expeditions which had been down the African coast. It is of him the story goes that, taking some rabbits thither, their progeny so quickly possessed the island that its settlers deserted it! Such genealogical information as can be acquired of this earliest Perestrello is against the supposition of his being the father of Felipa Moñiz, but rather indicates that by a second wife, Isabel Moñiz by name, he had the second Bartolomeo, who in turn became the father of our Felipa Moñiz. The testimony of Las Casas seems to favor this view. If this is the Bartolomeo who, having attained his majority, was assigned to the captaincy of Porto Santo in 1473, it could hardly be that a daughter would have been old enough to marry in 1474–75.

The first Bartolomeo, if he was the father-in-law of Columbus, seems to have died in 1457, and was succeeded in 1458, in
command of the island of Porto Santo, by another son-in-law,
Pedro Correa da Cunha, who married a daughter of his first
marriage, — or at least that is one version of this genealogical
complication, — and who was later succeeded in 1473 by the
second Bartolomeo.

The Count Bernardo Pallastrelli, a modern member of the
family, has of late years, in his *Il Suocero e la Moglie di Cristoforo Colombo* (2d ed., Piacenza, 1876), attempted to identify
the kindred of the wife of Columbus. He has examined the
views of Harrisse, who is on the whole inclined to believe that
the wife of Columbus was a daughter of one Vasco Gill Moñiz,
whose sister had married the Perestrello of the *Historie* story.
The successive wills of Diego Columbus, it may be observed,
call her in one (1509) Philippa Moñiz, and in the other (1523)
Philippa Muñiz, without the addition of Perestrello. The genealogical table of the count's monograph, on the other hand,
makes Felipa to be the child of Isabella Moñiz, who was the
second wife of Bartolomeo Pallastrelli, the son of Felipo, who
came to Portugal some time after 1371, from Plaisance, in Italy.
Bartolomeo had been one of the household of Prince Henry,
and had been charged by him with founding a colony at Porto
Santo, in 1425, over which island he was long afterward (1446)
made governor. We must leave it as a question involved in
much doubt.

The issue of this marriage was one son, Diego, but there is
no distinct evidence as to the date of his birth. Sundry incidents go to show that it was somewhere between 1475 and 1479. Columbus's marriage to Doña
Felipa had probably taken place at Lisbon, and not before
1474 at the earliest, a date not difficult to reconcile with the
year (1473–74) now held to be that of his arrival in Portugal. It is supposed that it was while Columbus was living at
Porto Santo, where his wife had some property, that Diego was
born, though Harrisse doubts if any evidence can be adduced
to support such a statement beyond a sort of conjecture on Las
Casas's part, derived from something he thought he remembered Diego to have told him.

The story of Columbus's marriage, as given in the *Historie* and followed by Oviedo, couples with it the belief that it was among the papers of his dead father-in-law, Perestrel- <sub>Perestrello's</sub> lo, that Columbus found documents and maps which <sub>MSS.</sub> prompted him to the conception of a western passage to Asia. In that case, this may perhaps have been the motive which induced him to draw from Paolo Toscanelli that famous letter, which is usually held to have had an important influence on the mind of Columbus.

The fact of such relationship of Columbus with Perestrello is called in question, and so is another incident often <sub>Story of a</sub> related by the biographers of Columbus. This is that <sub>sailor dying in Colum-</sub> an old seaman who had returned from an adventur- <sub>bus's house.</sub> ous voyage westward had found shelter in the house of Columbus, and had died there, but not before he had disclosed to him a discovery he had made of land to the west. This story is not told in any writer that is now known before Gomara (1552), and we are warned by Benzoni that in Gomara's hands this pilot story was simply an invention " to diminish the immortal fame of Christopher Columbus, as there were many who could not endure that a foreigner and Italian should have acquired so much honor and so much glory, not only for the Spanish kingdom, but also for the other nations of the world."'

It is certain, however, that under the impulse of the young art of printing men's minds had at this time become more alive than they had been for centuries to the search for cosmographical views. The old geographers, just at this time, were one by one finding their way into print, mainly in Italy, while the intercourse of that country with Portugal was quickened by the attractions of the Portuguese discoveries. While Columbus was still in Italy, the great popularity of Pomponius Mela began with the first edition in Latin, which was printed at <sub>Pomponius</sub> Milan in 1471, followed soon by other editions in <sub>Mela,</sub> Venice. The *De Situ Orbis* of Strabo had already <sub>Strabo, etc.</sub> been given to the world in Latin as early as 1469, and during the next few years this text was several times reprinted at Rome and Venice. The teaching of the sphericity of the earth in the astronomical poem of Manilius, long a favorite with <sub>Manilius,</sub> the monks of the Middle Ages, who repeated it in <sub>Solinus,</sub> their labored script, appeared in type at Nuremberg at <sub>Ptolemy.</sub> the same time. The *Polyhistor* of Solinus did not long delay to follow.  A Latin version of Ptolemy had existed since 1409, but it was later than the rest in appearing in print, and bears the date of 1475.  These were the newer issues of the Italian and German presses, which were attracting the notice of the learned in this country of the new activities when Columbus came among them, and they were having their palpable effect.

Just when we know not, but some time earlier than this, Al-
Toscanelli's  fonso V. of Portugal had sought, through the medium
theory.      of the monk Fernando Martinez (Fernam Martins), to know precisely what was meant by the bruit of Toscanelli's theory of a westward way to India.  To an inquiry thus vouched Toscanelli had replied to Fernando Martinez (June 25, 1474), some days before a similar inquiry addressed to Toscanelli reached Florence, from Columbus himself, and through the agency of an aged Florentine merchant settled in Lisbon.  It seems probable that no knowledge of Martinez's correspondence with Toscanelli had come to the notice of Columbus ; and that the message which the Genoese sent to the Florentine was due simply to the same current rumors of Toscanelli's views which had attracted the attention of the king.  So in replying
His letter to  to Columbus Toscanelli simply shortened his task by
Columbus.    inclosing, with a brief introduction, a copy of the letter, which he says he had sent " some days before " to Martinez.  This letter outlined a plan of western discovery ; but it is difficult to establish beyond doubt the exact position which the letter of Toscanelli should hold in the growth of Columbus's views.  If Columbus reached Portugal as late as 1473–74, as seems likely, it is rendered less certain that Columbus had grasped his idea anterior to the spread of Toscanelli's theory. In any event, the letter of the Florentine physician would strengthen the growing notions of the Genoese.

As Toscanelli was at this time a man of seventy-seven, and as a belief in the sphericity of the earth was then not unprevalent, and as the theory of a westward way to the East was a necessary concomitant of such views in the minds of thinking men, it can hardly be denied that the latent faith in a westward passage only needed a vigilant mind to develop the theory, and an adventurous spirit to prove its correctness.  The development had been found in Toscanelli and the proof was waiting for Columbus, — both Italians ; but Humboldt points out how the Florentine very likely thought he was communicating with a Portuguese, when he wrote to Columbus.

This letter has been known since 1571 in the Italian text as given in the *Historie*, which, as it turns out, was inexact and overladen with additions. At least such is the inference when we compare this Italian text with a Latin text, supposed to be the original tongue of the letter, which has been discovered of late years in the handwriting of Columbus himself, on the fly-leaf of an Æneas Sylvius (1477), once belonging to Columbus, and still preserved in the Biblioteca Colombina at Seville. The letter which is given in the *Historie* is accompanied by an antescript, which says that the copy had been sent to Columbus at his request, and that it had been originally addressed to Martinez, some time " before the wars of Castile." How much later than the date June 25, 1474, this copy was sent to Columbus, and when it was received by him, there is no sure means of determining, and it may yet be in itself one of the factors for limiting the range of months during which Columbus must have arrived in Portugal.

The extravagances of the letter of Toscanelli, in his opulent descriptions of a marvelous Asiatic region, were safely made in that age without incurring the charge of credulity. Travelers could tell tales then that were as secure from detection as the revealed arcana of the Zuñi have been in our own days. Two hundred towns, whose marble bridges spanned a single river, and whose commerce could incite the cupidity of the world, was a tale easily to stir numerous circles of listeners in the maritime towns of the Mediterranean, wherever wandering mongers of marvels came and went. There were such travelers whose recitals Toscanelli had read, and others whose tales he had heard from their own lips, and these last were pretty sure to augment the wonders of the elder talebearers.

Columbus had felt this influence with the rest, and the tales lost nothing of their vividness in coming to him freshened, as it were, by the curious mind of the Florentine physician. The map which accompanied Toscanelli's letter, and which depicted his notions of the Asiatic coast lying over against that of Spain, is lost to us, but various attempts have been made to restore it, as is done in the sketch annexed. It will be a precious

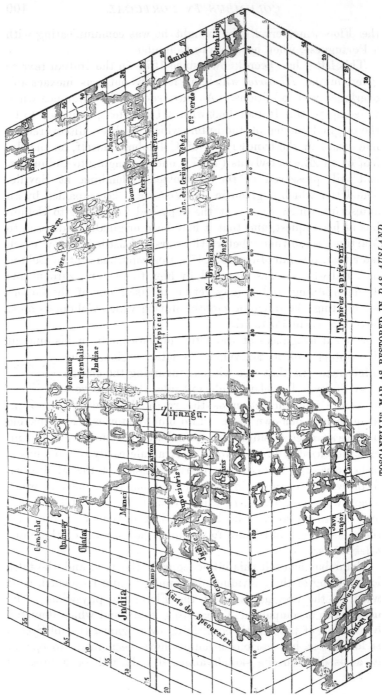

TOSCANELLI'S MAP AS RESTORED IN *DAS AUSLAND*.

memorial, if ever recovered, worthy of study as a reflex, in more concise representation than is found in the text of the letter, of the ideas which one of the most learned cosmographers of his day had imbibed from mingled demonstrations of science and imagination.

It is said that in our own day, in the first stages of a belief in the practicability of an Atlantic telegraphic cable, *The passage* it was seriously claimed that the vast stretch of its ex- *westward.* tension could be broken by a halfway station on Jacquet Island, one of those relics of the Middle Ages, which has disappeared from our ocean charts only in recent years.

Just in the same way all the beliefs which men had had in the island of Antillia, and in the existence of many another visionary bit of land, came to the assistance of *Antillia.* these theoretical discoverers in planning the chances of a desperate voyage far out into a sea of gorgons and chimeras dire. Toscanelli's map sought to direct the course of any one who dared to make the passage, in a way that, in case of disaster to his ships, a secure harbor could be found in Antillia, and in such other havens as no lack of islands would supply.

Ferdinand claimed to have found in his father's papers some statements which he had drawn from Aristotle of Carthaginian voyages to Antillia, on the strength of which the Portuguese had laid that island down in their charts in the latitude of Lisbon, as one occupied by their people in 714, when Spain was conquered by the Moors. Even so recently as the time of Prince Henry it had been visited by Portuguese ships, if records were to be believed. It also stands in the Bianco map of 1436.

There are few more curious investigations than those which concern these fantastic and fabulous islands of the Sea of Darkness. They are connected with views which *Fabulous islands of* were an inheritance in part from the classic times, with *the Atlantic.* involved notions of the abodes of the blessed and of demoniacal spirits. In part they were the aërial creation of popular mythologies, going back to a remoteness of which it is impossible to trace the beginning, and which got a variable color from the popular fancies of succeeding generations. The whole subject is curiously without the field of geography, though entering into all surveys of mediæval knowledge of the earth, and depending very largely for its elucidation on the maps of the fourteenth and fifteenth centuries, whose mythical traces are not beyond recognition in some of the best maps which have instructed a generation still living.

To place the island of the Irish St. Brandan — whose coming there with his monks is spoken of as taking place in the sixth century — in the catalogue of insular entities is to place geography in such a marvelous guise as would have satisfied the monk Philoponus and the rest of the credulous fictionmongers who hang about the skirts of the historic field. But the belief in it long prevailed, and the apparition sometimes came to sailors' eyes as late as the last century.

St. Brandan.

The great island of Antillia, or the Seven Cities, already referred to, was recognized, so far as we know, for the first time in the Weimar map of 1424, and is known in legends as the resort of some Spanish bishops, flying from the victorious Moors, in the eighth century. It never quite died out from the recognition of curious minds, and was even thought to have been seen by the Portuguese, not far from the time when Columbus was born. Peter Martyr also, after Columbus had returned from his first voyage, had a fancy that what the Admiral had discovered was really the great island of Antillia, and its attendant groups of smaller isles, and the fancy was perpetuated when Wytfliet and Ortelius popularized the name of Antilles for the West Indian Archipelago.

Antillia, or the Seven Cities.

Another fleeting insular vision of this pseudo-geographical realm was a smaller body of floating land, very inconstant in position, which is always given some form of the name that, in later times, got a constant shape in the word Brazil. We can trace it back into the portolanos of the middle of the fourteenth century; and it had not disappeared as a survival twenty or thirty years ago in the admiralty charts of Great Britain. The English were sending out expeditions from Bristol in search of it even while Columbus was seeking countenance for his western schemes; and Cabot, at a little later day, was instrumental in other searches.

Brazil Island.

Foremost among the travelers who had excited the interest of Toscanelli, and whose names he possibly brought for the first time to the attention of Columbus, were Marco Polo, Sir John Mandeville, and Nicolas de Conti.

Travelers in the Orient.

It is a question to be resolved only by critical study as to

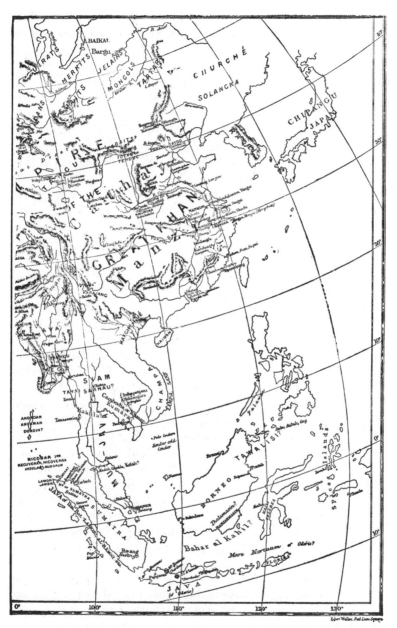

**MODERN EASTERN ASIA, WITH THE OLD AND NEW NAMES.**
[From Yule's *Cathay.*]

what was the language in which Marco Polo first dictated, in
a Genoese prison in 1298, the original narrative of
his experiences in Cathay.    The inquiry has engaged

Marco Polo,

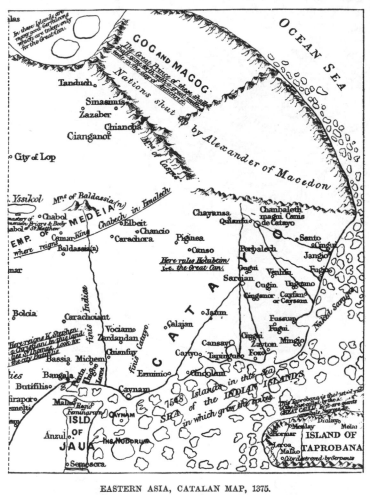

EASTERN ASIA, CATALAN MAP, 1375.

[From Yule's *Cathay*, vol. i.]

the attention of all his editors, and has invited the critical sagacity of D'Avezac.    There seems little doubt that it was written down in French.

There are no references by Columbus himself to the Asiatic travels of Marco Polo, but his acquaintance with the marvelous book of the Venetian observer may safely be assumed. The multiplication of texts of the *Milione* following upon his first dictation, and upon the subsequent revision in 1307, may not, indeed, have caused it to be widely known in various manu-

MARCO POLO.
[From an original at Rome.]

script forms, be it in Latin or Italian. Nor is it likely that Columbus could have read the earliest edition which was put in type, for it was in German in 1477; but there is the interesting possibility that this work of the Nuremberg press may have been known to Martin Behaim, a Nuremberger then in Lisbon, and likely enough to have been a familiar of Columbus. The fact that there is in the Biblioteca Colombina at Seville a copy of the first Latin printed edition (1485) with notes, which seem to be in Columbus's handwriting, may be taken as evidence, that at least in the later years of his study the inspiration which Marco Polo could well have been to him was not wanting; and the story may even be true as told in Navarrete, that Columbus had a copy of this famous book at his side during his first voyage, in 1492.

At the time when Humboldt doubted the knowledge of Columbus in respect to Marco Polo, this treasure of the Colombina was not known, and these later developments have shown how such a question was not to be settled as Humboldt supposed, by the fact that Columbus quoted Æneas Sylvius upon Cipango, and did not quote Marco Polo.

Neither does Columbus refer to the journey and strange stories of Sir John Mandeville, whose recitals came to a generation which was beginning to forget the stories of Marco Polo, and which, by fostering a passion for the marvelous, had readily become open to the English knight's bewildering fancies. The same negation of evidence, however, that satisfied Humboldt as respects Marco Polo will hardly suffice to establish Columbus's ignorance of the marvels which did more, perhaps, than the narratives of any other traveler to awaken Europe to the wonders of the Orient. Bernaldez, in fact, tells us that Columbus was a reader of Mandeville, whose recital was first printed in French at Lyons in 1480, within a few years after Columbus's arrival in Portugal.

It was to Florence, in Toscanelli's time, not far from 1420, that Nicolo di Conti, a Venetian, came, after his long sojourn of a quarter of a century in the far East. In Conti's new marvels, the Florentine scholar saw a rejuvenation of the wonders of Marco Polo. It was from Conti, doubtless, that Toscanelli got some of that confidence in a western voyage which, in his epistle to Columbus, he speaks of as derived from a returned traveler.

Pope Eugene IV., not far from the time of the birth of Columbus, compelled Conti to relate his experiences to Poggio Bracciolini. This scribe made what he could out of the monstrous tales, and translated the stories into Latin. In this condition Columbus may have known the narrative at a later day. The information which Conti gave was eagerly availed of by the cosmographers of the time, and Colonel Yule, the modern English writer on ancient Cathay, thinks that Fra Mauro got for his map more from Conti than that traveler ventured to disclose to Poggio.

Toscanelli, at the time of writing this letter to Columbus, had long enjoyed a reputation as a student of terrestrial and celestial phenomena. He had received, in 1463, the dedica-  Toscanelli's death, 1482. tion by Regiomontanus of his treatise on the quadrature of the circle. He was, as has been said, an old man of seventy-seven when Columbus opened his correspondence with him. It was not his fate to live long enough to see his physical views substantiated by Diaz and Columbus, for he died in 1482.

In two of the contemporary writers, Bartholomew Columbus is credited with having incited his brother Christopher  Columbus confers with others. to the views which he developed regarding a western passage, and these two were Antonio Gallo and Giustiniani, the commentator of the Psalms. It has been of late contended by H. Grothe, in his *Leonardo da Vinci* (Berlin, 1874), that it was at this time, too, when that eminent artist conducted a correspondence with Columbus about a western way to Asia. But there is little need of particularizing other advocates of a belief which had within the range of credible history never ceased to have exponents. The conception was in no respect the merit of Columbus, except as he grasped a tradition, which others did not, and it is strange, that Navarrete in quoting the testimony of Ferdinand and Isabella, of August 8, 1497, to the credit of the discovery of Columbus, as his own proper work, does not see that it was the venturesome, and as was then thought foolhardy, deed to prove the conception which those monarchs commended, and not the conception itself.

We learn from the *Historie* that its writer had found among the papers of Columbus the evidence of the grounds  Columbus writes out reasons for his belief. of his belief in the western passage, as under varying impressions it had been formulated in his mind. These reasons divide easily into three groups: First, those based on deductions drawn from scientific research, and as expressed in the beliefs of Ptolemy, Marinus, Strabo, and Pliny; second, views which the authority of eminent writers had rendered weightier, quoting as such the works of Aristotle, Seneca, Strabo, Pliny, Solinus, Marco Polo, Mandeville, Pierre d'Ailly, and Toscanelli; and third, the stories of sailors as to lands and indications of lands westerly.

From these views, instigated or confirmed by such opinions, Columbus gradually arranged his opinions, in not one of which did he prove to be right, except as regards the sphericity of the earth; and the last was a belief which had been the common property of learned men, and at intervals occupying even the popular mind, from a very early date.

The conception among the Greeks of a plane earth, which
Sphericity was taught in the Homeric and Hesiodic poems, be-
of the earth. gan to give place to a crude notion of a spherical form
at a period that no one can definitely determine, though we find it taught by the Pythagoreans in Italy in the sixth century before Christ. The spherical view and its demonstration passed down through long generations of Greeks, under the sanction of Plato and their other highest thinkers. In the fourth century before Christ, Aristotle and others, by watching the moon's shadow in an eclipse, and by observing the rising and setting of the heavenly bodies in different latitudes, had proved the roundness of the earth to their satisfaction; Eratosthenes first measured a degree of latitude in the third century; Hipparchus, in the second century, was the earliest to establish geographical positions; and in the second century of the Christian era
Transmis- Ptolemy had formulated for succeeding times the gen-
sion of the eral scope of the transmitted belief. During all these
belief in it. centuries it was perhaps rather a possession of the
learned. We infer from Aristotle that the view was a novelty in his time; but in the third century before Christ it began to engage popular attention in the poem of Aratus, and at about 200 B. C. Crates is said to have given palpable manifestation of the theory in a globe, ten feet in diameter, which he constructed.

The belief passed to Italy and the Latins, and was sung by Hyginus and Manilius in the time of Augustus. We find it also in the minds of Pliny, Cicero, Virgil, and Ovid. So the belief became the heirloom of the learned throughout the classic times, and it was directly coupled in the minds of Aristotle, Eratosthenes, Strabo, Seneca, and others with a conviction, more or less pronounced, of an easy western voyage from Spain to India.

No one of the ancient expressions of this belief seems to have
Seneca's clung more in the memory of Columbus than that in
Medea. the *Medea* of Seneca; and it is an interesting confirmation that in a copy of the book which belonged to his son

Ferdinand, and which is now preserved in Seville, the passage is scored by the son's hand, while in a marginal note he has attested the fact that its prophecy of a western passage had been made good by his father in 1492. Though the opinion was opposed by St. Chrysostom in the fourth century, it was taught by St. Augustine and Isidore in the fifth. Cosmas in the sixth century was unable to understand how, if the earth was a sphere, those at the antipodes could see Christ at his coming. That settled the question in his mind. The Venerable Bede, however, in the eighth century, was not constrained by any such arguments, and taught the spherical theory. Jourdain, a modern French authority, has found distinct evidence that all through the Middle Ages the belief in the western way was kept alive by the study of Aristotle; and we know how the Arabs perpetuated the teachings of that philosopher, which in turn were percolated through the Levant to Mediterranean peoples. It is a striking fact that at a time when Spain was bending all her energies to drive the Moor from the Iberian peninsula, that country was also engaged in pursuing those discoveries along the western way to India which were almost a direct result of the Arab preservation of the cosmographical learning of Aristotle and Ptolemy. A belief in an earth-ball had the testimony of Dante in the twelfth century, and it was the well-known faith of Albertus Magnus, Roger Bacon, and the schoolmen, in the thirteenth. It continued to be held by the philosophers, who kept alive these more recent names, and came to Columbus because of the use of Bacon which Pierre d'Ailly had made.

*Cosmas.*

*Bacon, Albertus Magnus, Pierre d'Ailly.*

The belief in the sphericity of the earth carried with it of necessity another, — that the east was to be found in the west. Superstition, ignorance, and fear might magnify the obstacles to a passage through that drear Sea of Darkness, but in Columbus's time, in some learned minds at least, there was no distrust as to the accomplishment of such a voyage beyond the chance of obstacles in the way.

It is true that in this interval of very many centuries there had been lapses into unbelief. There were long periods, indeed, when no one dared to teach the doctrine. Whenever and wherever the Epicureans supplanted the Pythagoreans, the belief fell with the disciples of Pythagoras. There had been, dur-

ing the days of St. Chrysostom and other of the fathers, a decision of the Church against it.   There were doubtless,
as Humboldt says, conservers, during all this time, of
the traditions of antiquity, since the monasteries and

The belief
opposed by
the Church.

ALBERTVS MAGNVS EPI
ſcopus Ratiſponenſis.

*Magnus eram Sophiæ doctor, Præfulgᵹ ſacrorum:*
*Abdita naturæ vis mihi nota liquet.*

M. CCCXXCII.

ALBERTUS MAGNUS.
[From Reusner's *Icones.*]

colleges — even in an age when to be unlearned was more pardonable than to be pagan — were of themselves quite a world
apart from the dullness of the masses of the people.   A hundred

years before Columbus, the inheritor of much of this conservation was the Bishop of Cambray, that Pierre d'Ailly whose *Imago Mundi* (1410) was so often on the lips of Columbus, and out of which it is more than likely that Columbus drank of the knowledge of Aristotle, Strabo, Pierre D'Ailly's *Imago Mundi.* and Seneca, and to a degree greater perhaps than he was aware of he took thence the wisdom of Roger Bacon. It was through the *Opus Majus* (1267) of this English philosopher that western Europe found accessible the stories of the Roger Bacon's *Opus Majus.* "silver walls and golden towers" of Quinsay as described by Rubruquis, the wandering missionary, who in the thirteenth century excited the cupidity of the Mediterranean merchants by his accounts of the inexhaustible treasures of eastern Asia, and which the reader of to-day may find in the collections of Samuel Purchas.

Pierre d'Ailly's position in regard to cosmographical knowledge was hardly a dominant one. He seems to know nothing of Marco Polo, Bacon's contemporary, and he never speaks of Cathay, even when he urges the views which he has borrowed from Roger Bacon, of the extension of Asia towards Western Europe.

Any acquaintance with the *Imago Mundi* during these days of Columbus in Portugal came probably through report, though possibly he may have met with manuscripts of the work; for it was not till after he had gone to Spain that D'Ailly could have been read in any printed edition, the first being issued in 1490.

The theory of the rotundity of the earth carried with it one objection, which in the time of Columbus was sure sooner or later to be seized upon. If, going west, the Rotundity and gravitation. ship sank with the declivity of the earth's contour, how was she going to mount such an elevation on her return voyage? — a doubt not so unreasonable in an age which had hardly more than the vaguest notion of the laws of gravitation, though some, like Vespucius, were not without a certain prescience of the fact.

By the middle of the third century before Christ, Eratosthenes, accepting sphericity, had by astronomical methods studied the extent of the earth's circumference, and, ac- Size of the earth. cording to the interpretation of his results by modern scholars, he came surprisingly near to the actual size, when he exceeded the truth by perhaps a twelfth part. The calculations of Eratosthenes commended themselves to Hipparchus, Strabo, and Pliny. A century later than Eratosthenes, a new calculation, made by Posidonius of Rhodes, reduced the magnitude to a globe of about four fifths its proper size. It was palpably certain to the observant philosophers, from the beginning of their observations on the size of the earth, that the portion known to commerce and curiosity was but a small part of what might yet be known. The unknown, however, is always a terror. Going north from temperate Europe increased the cold, going south augmented the heat; and it was no bold thought for the naturalist to conclude that a north existed in which the cold was unbearable, and a south in which the heat was too great for life. Views like these stayed the impulse for exploration even down to the century of Columbus, and magnified the horrors which so long balked the exploration of the Portuguese on the African coast. There had been intervals, however, when men in the Indian Ocean had dared to pass the equator.

Therefore it was before the age of Columbus that, east and west along the temperate belt, men's minds groped to find new conditions beyond the range of known habitable regions. Strabo, in the first century before Christ, made this habitable zone stretch over 120 degrees, or a third of the circumference of the earth. The corresponding extension of Marinus of Tyre in the second century after Christ stretched over 225 degrees. This geographer did not define the land's border on the ocean at the east, but it was not unusual with the cosmographers who followed him to carry the farthest limits of Asia to what is actually the meridian of the Sandwich Islands. On the west Marinus pushed the Fortunate Islands (Canaries) two degrees and a half beyond Cape Finisterre, failing to comprehend their real position, which for the westernmost, Ferro, is something like nine degrees beyond the farther limits of the main land.

*Unknown regions.*

*Strabo and Marinus on the size of the earth.*

The belt of the known world running in the direction of the equator was, in the conception of Ptolemy, the contemporary of Marinus, about seventy-nine degrees wide, sixteen of these being south of the equatorial line. This was a contraction from the previous estimate of Marinus, who had made it over eighty-seven degrees.

*Ptolemy's view.*

Toscanelli reduced the globe to a circumference of about 18,000 miles, losing about 6,000 miles; and the un- <small>Toscanelli's</small> tracked ocean, lying west of Lisbon, was about one <small>view.</small> third of this distance. In other words, the known world occupied about 240 of the 360 degrees constituting the equatorial length. Few of the various computations of this time gave such scant dimensions to the unknown proportion of the line. The Laon globe, which was made ten or twelve years later than Toscanelli's time, was equally scant. Behaim, who figured out

LAON GLOBE.
[After D'Avezac.]

the relations of the known to the unknown circuit, during the summer before Columbus sailed on his first voyage, reduced what was known to not much more than a third of the whole. It was the fashion, too, with an easy reliance on their genuineness, to refer to the visions of Esdras in support of a belief in the small part — a sixth — of the surface of the globe covered by the ocean.

The problem lay in Columbus's mind thus: he accepted the theory of the division of the circumference of the <small>Views of</small> earth into twenty-four hours, as it had come down <small>Columbus.</small> from Marinus of Tyre, when this ancient astronomer supposed that from the eastern verge of Asia to the western extremity of Europe there was a space of fifteen hours. The discovery of the Azores had pushed the known limit a single hour farther towards the setting sun, making sixteen hours, or two thirds of the circumference of 360 degrees. There were left eight hours, or one hundred and twenty degrees, to represent the space between the Azores and Asia. This calculation in reality brought the Asiatic coast forward to the meridian of California, obliterating the width of the Pacific at that latitude, and reducing by so much the size of the globe as Columbus measured it, on the assumption that Marinus was correct. This, however, he denied. If the *Historie* reports Columbus exactly, he contended that the testimony of Marco Polo and Mandeville carried the verge of Asia so far east that the land distance was more than fifteen hours across; and by as much as this increased the distance, by so much more was the Asiatic shore pushed nearer the coasts of Europe. " We can thus determine," he says, " that India is even neighboring to Spain and Africa."

The calculation of course depended on what was the length
Length of a of a degree, and on this point there was some differ-
degree. ence of opinion. Toscanelli had so reduced a degree's length that China was brought forward on his planisphere till its coast line cut the meridian of the present Newfoundland.

We can well imagine how this undue contraction of the size of the globe, as the belief lay in the mind of Columbus, and as he expressed it later (July 7, 1503), did much to push him forward, and was a helpful illusion in inducing others to venture upon the voyage with him. The courage required to sail out of some Iberian port due west a hundred and twenty de-
Quinsay. grees in order to strike the regions about the great
Chinese city of Quinsay, or Kanfu, Hangtscheufu, and Kingszu, as it has been later called, was more easily summoned than if the actual distance of two hundred and thirty-one degrees had been recognized, or even the two hundred and four degrees necessary in reality to reach Cipango, or Japan. The views of Toscanelli, as we have seen, reduced the duration of risk westward to so small a figure as fifty-two degrees. So it had not been an unusual belief, more or less prominent for many generations, that with a fair wind it required no great run westward to reach Cathay, if one dared to undertake it. If there were no insurmountable obstacles in the Sea of Darkness, it would not be difficult to reach earlier that multitude of

islands which was supposed to fringe the coast of China. It was a common belief, moreover, that somewhere in this void lay the great island of Cipango, — the goal of Columbus's voyage. Sometimes nearer and sometimes farther it lay from the Asiatic coast. Pinzon saw in Rome in 1491 a map which carried it well away from that coast; and if one could find somewhere in the English archives the sea-chart with which Bartholomew Columbus enforced the views of his brother, to gain the support of the English king, it is supposed that it would reveal a somewhat similar location of the coveted island. Here, then, was a space, larger or smaller, as men differently believed, interjacent along this known zone between the ascertained extreme east in Asia and the accepted most distant west at Cape St. Vincent in Spain, as was thought in Strabo's time, or at the Canaries, as was comprehended in the days of Ptolemy. What there was in this unknown space between Spain and Cathay was the problem which balked the philosophers quite as much as that other uncertainty, which concerned what might possibly be found in the southern hemisphere, could one dare to enter the torrid heats of the supposed equatorial ocean, or in the northern wastes, could one venture to sail beyond the Arctic Circle. These curious quests of the inquisitive and learned minds of the early centuries of the Christian era were the prototypes of the actual explorations which it was given in the fifteenth century to the Spaniards and Portuguese respectively to undertake. The commercial rivalry which had in the past kept Genoa and Venice watchful of each other's advantage had by their maritime ventures in the Atlantic passed to these two peninsular nations, and England was not long behind them in starting in her race for maritime supremacy.

It was in human nature that these unknown regions should become those either of enchantment or dismay, according to personal proclivities. It is not necessary to seek far for any reason for this. An unknown stretch of waters was just the place for the resorts of the Gorgons and to find the Islands of the Blest, and to nurture other creations of the literary and spiritual instincts, seeking to give a habitation to fancies. It is equally in human nature that what the intellect

*[marginal notes: Asiatic islands. Cipango. Spanish and Portuguese explorations. Sea of Darkness.]*

has habilitated in this way the fears, desires, and superstitions of men in due time turn to their own use. It was easy, under the stress of all this complexity of belief and anticipation, for this supposable interjacent oceanic void to teem in men's imaginations with regions of almost every imaginable character; and when, in the days of the Roman republic, the Canaries were reached, there was no doubt but the ancient Islands of the Blest had been found, only in turn to pass out of cognizance, and once more to fall into the abyss of the Unknown.

There are, however, three legends which have come down to us from the classic times, which the discovery of America revived with new interest in the speculative excursions of the curiously learned, and it is one of the proofs of the narrow range of Columbus's acquaintance with original classic writers that these legends were not pressed by him in support of his views. The most persistent of these in presenting a question for the physical geographer is the story of Atlantis, traced to a tale told by Plato of a tradition of an island in the Atlantic which eight thousand years ago had existed in the west, opposite the Pillars of Hercules; and which, in a great inundation, had sunken beneath the sea, leaving in mid ocean large mud shoals to impede navigation and add to the terrors of a vast unknown deep. There have been those since the time of Gomara who have believed that the land which Columbus found dry and inhabited was a resurrected Atlantis, and geographers even of the seventeenth century have mapped out its provinces within the usual outline of the American continents. Others have held, and some still hold, that the Atlantic islands are but peaks of this submerged continent. There is no evidence to show that these fancies of the philosopher ever disturbed even the most erratic moments of Columbus, nor could he have pored over the printed Latin of Plato, if it came in his way, till its first edition appeared in 1483, during his stay in Portugal. Neither do we find that he makes any references to that other creation, the land of the Meropes, as figured in the passages cited by Ælian some seven hundred years after Theopompus had conjured up the vision in the fourth century before Christ. Equally ignorant was Columbus, it would appear, of the great Saturnian continent, lying five days west from Britain, which makes a story in Plutarch's *Morals.*

Story of Atlantis.

Land of the Meropes.

Saturnian continent.

We deal with a different problem when we pass from these theories and imaginings of western lands to such records as exist of what seem like attempts in the earliest days to attain by actual exploration the secret of this interjacent void. The Phœnicians had passed the Straits of Gibraltar and found Gades (Cadiz), and very likely attempted to course the Atlantic, about 1100 years before the birth of Christ. Perhaps they went to Cornwall for tin. It may have been by no means impossible for them to have passed among the Azores and even to have reached the American islands and main, as a statement in Diodorus Siculus has been interpreted to signify. Then five hundred years later or more we observe the Carthaginians pursuing their adventurous way outside the Pillars of Hercules, going down the African coast under Hanno to try the equatorial horrors, or running westerly under Hamilko to wonder at the Sargasso sea. Later, the Phœnicians seem to have made some lodgment in the islands off the coasts of northwestern Africa. The Romans in the fourth century before Christ pushed their way out into the Atlantic under Pytheas and Euthymenes, the one daring to go as far as Thule — whatever that was — in the north, and the other to Senegal in the south. It was in the same century that Rome had the strange sight of some unknown barbarians, of a race not recognizable, who were taken upon the shores of the German Ocean, where they had been cast away. Later writers have imagined — for no stronger word can be used — that these weird beings were North American Indians, or rather more probably Eskimos. About the same time, Sertorius, a Roman commander in Spain, learned, as already mentioned, of some salubrious islands lying westward from Africa, and gave Horace an opportunity, in the evil days of the civil war, to picture them as a refuge.

When the Romans ruled the world, commerce lost much of the hazard and enterprise which had earlier instigated international rivalry. The interest in the western ocean subsided into merely speculative concern; and wild fancy was brought into play in depicting its horrors, its demons and shoals, with the intermingling of sky and water.

It is by no means certain that Columbus knew anything of this ancient lore of the early Mediterranean people. There is

*[marginal notes: Earlier voyages on the Atlantic. Phœnicians. Carthaginians. Romans.]*

little or nothing in the early maps of the fifteenth century to
indicate that such knowledge was current among those
who made or contributed to the making of such of
these maps as have come down to us.   The work of
some of the more famous chart makers Columbus could hardly
have failed to see, or heard discussed in the maritime circles of
Portugal; and indeed it was to his own countrymen,
Marino Sanuto, Pizignani, Bianco, and Fra Mauro,
that Portuguese navigators were most indebted for the broad
cartographical treatment of their own discoveries.   At the same
time there was no dearth of legends of the venturesome Genoese,
with fortunes not always reassuring.   There was a story, for
instance, of some of these latter people, who in 1291
had sailed west from the Pillars of Hercules and had
never returned.   Such was a legend that might not have
escaped Columbus's attention even in his own country, associating with it the names of the luckless Tedisio Doria and Ugolino
Vivaldi in their efforts to find a western way to India.   Harrisse, however, who has gone over all the evidence of such a
purpose, fails to be satisfied.

These stories of ocean hazards hung naturally about the seaports of Portugal.

Galvano tells us of such a tale concerning a Portuguese ship,
driven west, in 1447, to an island with seven cities,
where its sailors found the people speaking Portuguese,
who said they had deserted their country on the death of King
Roderigo.   This is the legend of Antillia, already referred to.

Columbus recalled, when afterwards at the Canaries on his
first voyage, how it was during his sojourn in Portugal
that some one from Madeira presented to the Portuguese king a petition for a vessel to go in quest of land, occasionally seen to the westward from that island.   Similar stories
were not unknown to him of like apparitions being familiar in
the Azores.   A story which he had also heard of one Antonio
Leme having seen three islands one hundred leagues west of the
Azores had been set down to a credulous eye, which had been
deceived by floating fields of vegetation.

There was no obstacle in the passing of similar reports around
the Bay of Biscay from the coasts of the Basques, and the story
might be heard of Jean de Echaide, who had found stores of

*Marginal notes:*
Knowledge of such early attempts.
Maps XVth cent.
Genoese voyages, 1291.
Antillia.
Islands seen.

stockfish off a land far oceanward, — an exploit supposed to be commemorated in the island of Stokafixia, which stands far away to the westward in the Bianco map of 1436. All these tales of the early visits of the Basques to what imaginative minds have supposed parts of the American coasts derive much of their perennial charm from associations with a remarkable people. There is indeed nothing improbable in a hardy daring which could have borne the Basques to the Newfoundland shores at almost any date earlier than the time of Columbus.

The Basques.

Fructuoso, writing as late as 1590, claimed that a Portuguese navigator, João Vaz Cortereal, had sailed to the codfish coast of Newfoundland as early as 1464, but Barrow seems to be the only writer of recent times who has believed the tale, and Biddle and Harrisse find no evidence to sustain it.

Newfoundland banks possibly visited.

There is a statement recorded by Columbus, if we may trust the account of the *Historie*, that a sailor at Santa Maria had told him how, being driven westerly in a voyage to Ireland, he had seen land, which he then thought to be Tartary. Some similar experiences were also told to Columbus by Pieter de Velasco, of Galicia; and this land, according to the account, would seem to have been the same sought at a later day by the Cortereals (1500).

Tartary supposed to be seen.

It is not easy to deal historically with long-held traditions. The furbishers of transmitted lore easily make it reflect what they bring to it. To find illustrations in any inquiry is not so difficult if you select what you wish, and discard all else, and the result of this discriminating accretion often looks very plausible. Historical truth is reached by balancing everything, and not by assimilating that which easily suits. Almost all these discussions of pre-Columbian voyagings to America afford illustrations of this perverted method. Events in which there is no inherent untruth are not left with the natural defense of probability, but are proved by deductions and inferences which could just as well be applied to prove many things else, and are indeed applied in a new way by every new upstart in such inquiries. The story of each discoverer before Columbus has been upheld by the stock intimation of white-bearded men, whose advent is somehow mysteri-

Dubious pre-Columbian voyages.

ously discovered to have left traces among the aborigines of every section of the coast.

There was another class of evidence which, as the *Historie* informs us, served some purpose in bringing conviction to the mind of Columbus. Such were the phenomenal washing ashore on European coasts of unknown pines and other trees, sculptured logs, huge bamboos, whose joints could be made into vessels to hold nine bottles of wine, and dead

*Traces of a western land in drift.*

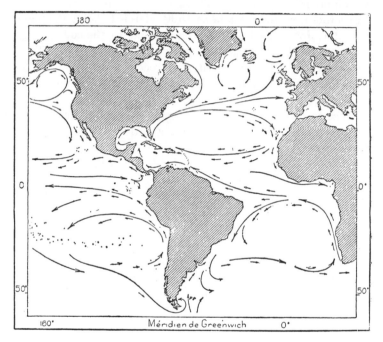

OCEANIC CURRENTS.
[From Reclus's *Amérique Boréale.*]

bodies with strange, broad faces. Even canoes, with living men in them of wonderful aspects, had at times been reported as thrown upon the Atlantic islands. Such events had not been unnoticed ever since the Canaries and the Azores had been inhabited by a continental race, and conjectures had been rife long before the time of Columbus that westerly winds had brought these estrays from a distant land, — a belief more comprehensible at that time than any dependence upon the unsuspected fact that it was the oceanic currents, rather, which impelled these migratory objects. It required the experiences of later Spanish navigators along the Bahama Channel, and those of the French and English farther north upon the Banks of New- Gulf foundland, before it became clear that the currents Stream. of the Atlantic, grazing the Cape of Good Hope and whirling in the Gulf of Mexico, sprayed in a curling fringe in the North Atlantic. This in a measure became patent to Sir Humphrey Gilbert sixty or seventy years after the death of Columbus.

If science had then been equal to the microscopic tasks which at this day it imposes on itself, the question of western lands might have been studied with an interest beyond what attached to the trunks of trees, carved timbers, edible nuts, and seeds of alien plants, which the Gulf Stream is still bringing to the shores of Europe. It might have found in the dust settling upon the throngs of men in the Old World, the shells of animalcules, differing from those known to the observing eye in Europe, which, indeed, had been carried in the upper currents of air from the banks of the Orinoco.

Once in Portugal, Columbus was brought in close contact with that eager spirit of exploration which had sur- Influence of vived the example of Prince Henry and his naviga- Portuguese discoveries tors. If Las Casas was well informed, these Portu- upon Columguese discoveries were not without great influence upon bus. the Genoese's receptive mind. He was now where he could hear the fresh stories of their extending acquaintance with the African coast. His wife's sister, by the accepted accounts, had married Pedro Correa, a navigator not without fame in those days, and a companion in maritime inquiry upon whom Columbus could naturally depend, — unless, as Harrisse decides, he was no navigator at all. Columbus was also at hand to observe the growing skill in the arts of navigation which gave the Portuguese their preëminence. He had not been long in Lisbon when Regiomontanus gave a new power in astro- *Ephemeri-* nomical calculations of positions at sea by publishing *des* of Regiomonhis *Ephemerides*, for the interval from 1475 to 1506, *tanus.* upon which Columbus was yet to depend in his eventful voyage.

The most famous of the pupils of this German mathematician was himself in Lisbon during the years of Columbus's sojourn.

Martin Behaim.

We have no distinct evidence that Martin Behaim, a Nuremberger, passed any courtesies with the Genoese adventurer, but it is not improbable that he did. His

SAMPLES OF THE TABLES OF REGIOMONTANUS, 1474–1506.

position was one that would attract Columbus, who might never have been sought by Behaim. The Nuremberger's standing was, indeed, such as to gain the attention of the Court, and he was thought not unworthy to be joined with the two royal physicians, Roderigo and Josef, on a commission to improve the astrolabe. Their perfected results mark an epoch in the art of seamanship in that age.

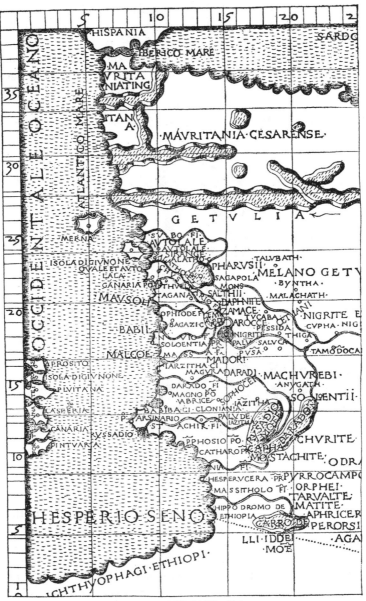

THE AFRICAN COAST, 1478.

[From Nordenskiöld's *Facsimile Atlas*.]

It was a new sensation when news came that at last the Por-
Guinea       tuguese had crossed the equator, in pushing along the
coast, 1482.  African coast.   In January, 1482, they had said their
first mass on the Guinea coast, and the castle of San Jorge da
             Mina was soon built under the new impulse to enter-
The Congo
reached,     prise which came with the accession of João II.   In
1484.        1484 they reached the Congo, under the guidance of
Diogo Cam, and Martin Behaim was of his company.

MARTIN BEHAIM.

These voyages were not without strong allurements to the
Genoese sailor.   He is thought to have been a participant in
some of the later cruises.   The *Historie* claims that he began
to reason, from his new experiences, that if land could be discovered to the south there was much the same chance of like
discoveries in the west.   But there were experiences of other
kinds which, in the interim, if we believe the story, he underwent in the north.

# CHAPTER VII.

## WAS COLUMBUS IN THE NORTH?

THERE is, in the minds of some inquirers into the early discovery of America, no more pivotal incident attaching to the career of Columbus than an alleged voyage made to the vicinity of what is supposed to have been Iceland, in the assigned year of 1477. The incident is surrounded with the confusion that belongs to everything dependent on Columbus's own statements, or on what is put forth as such.

Columbus supposed to have sailed beyond Iceland, 1477.

Our chief knowledge of his voyage is in the doubtful Italian rendering of the *Historie* of 1571, where, citing a memoir by Columbus himself on the five habitable zones, the translator or adapter of that book makes the Admiral say that "in February, 1477, he sailed a hundred leagues beyond the island Tile, which lies under the seventy-third parallel, and not under the sixty-third, as some say." The only evidence that he saw Tile, in sailing beyond it, is in what he further says, that he was able to ascertain that the tide rose and fell twenty-six fathoms, which observation necessitates the seeing of some land, whether Tile or not.

There is no land at all in the northern Atlantic under 73°. Iceland stretches from 64° to 67°; Jan Mayen is too small for Columbus's further description of the island, and is at 71°, and Spitzbergen is at 76°. What Columbus says of the English of Bristol trading at this island points to Iceland; and it is easy, if one will, to imagine a misprint of the figures, an error of calculation, a carelessness of statement, or even the disappearance, through some cataclysm, of the island, as has been suggested.

Inconsistencies in the statement.

Humboldt in his *Cosmos* quotes Columbus as saying of this voyage near Thule that "the sea was not at that time covered with ice," and he credits that statement to the same *Tratado*

MAP OF OLAUS MAGNUS, 1539.
[From Dr. Brenner's Essay.]

*de las Cinco Zonas Habitables* of Columbus, and urges in proof that Finn Magnusen had found in ancient historical sources that in February, 1477, ice had not set in on the southern coast of that island.

Speaking of "Tile," the same narrative adds that "it is west of the western verge of Ptolemy [that is, Ptolemy's world map], and larger than England." This Thyle. expression of its size could point only to Iceland, of all islands in the northern seas.

There are elements in the story, however, not easily reconcilable with what might be expected of an experienced mariner; and if the story is true in its main purpose, there is little more in the details than the careless inexactness, which characterizes a good many of the well-authenticated asseverations of Columbus.

Again the narrative says, "It is true that Ptolemy's Thule is where that geographer placed it, but that it is now called Frislande." Does this mean that the Zeni story had been a matter of common talk forty years after the voyage to their Frisland had been made, and eighty-four years before a later scion of the family published the remarkable narrative in Venice, in 1558? It is possible that the maker of the *Historie* of 1571, in the way in which it was given to the The Zeni's<br>Frisland. world, had interpolated this reference to the Frisland of the Zeni to help sustain the credit of his own or the other book.

A voyage undertaken by Columbus to such high latitudes is rendered in all respects doubtful, to say the least, from the fact that in 1492 Columbus detailed for the eyes of his sovereigns the unusual advantages of the harbors of the new islands which he had discovered, and added that he was entitled to express such an opinion, because his exploration had extended from Guinea on the south to England on the north. It was an occasion when he desired to make his acquaintance seem as wide as the facts would warrant, and yet he does not profess to have been farther north than England. A hundred leagues, moreover, beyond Iceland might well have carried him to the upper Greenland coast, but he makes no mention of other land being seen in those high latitudes.

Thyle and Iceland are made different islands in the Ptolemy

of 1486, which, if it does not prove that Iceland was not then
the same as Thyle in the mind of geographers, shows
that geographical confusion still prevailed at the north.

Thyle and Iceland.

It may be further remarked that Muñoz and others have found no time in Columbus's career to which this voyage to the north could so easily pertain as to a period anterior to his going to Portugal, and consequently some years before the 1477 of the *Historie*.

A voyage to Iceland was certainly no new thing. The English traded there, and a large commerce was maintained with it by Bristol, and had been for many years. A story grew up at a later day, and found expression in Gomara and Wytfliet, that in 1476, the year before this alleged voyage of Columbus, a Danish expedition, under the command of the Pole Kolno, or Skolno, had found in these northern regions an entrance to the straits of Anian, which figure so constantly in later maps, and which opened a passage to the Indies ; but there seems to be no reason to believe that it had any definite foundation, and it could hardly have been known to Columbus. It is also easy to conjecture that Columbus had been impelled to join some English trading vessel from Bristol, through mere nautical curiosity, and even been urged by reports which may have reached him of the northern explorations of the Zeni, long before the accounts were printed. But if he knew anything, he either treasured it up as a proof of his theories, not yet to be divulged, — why is not clear, — or, what is vastly more probable, it never occurred to him to associate any of these dim regions with the coasts of Marco Polo's Cathay.

The English in Iceland.

Kolno.

The Zeni.

There was no lack of stories, even at this time, of venturesome voyages west along the latitude of England and to the northwest, and of these tales Columbus may possibly have heard. Such was the story which had been obscurely recorded, that Madoc, a Welsh chieftain, in the later years of the twelfth century had carried a colony westerly. Nor can it be positively asserted that the Estotiland and Drogeo of the Zeni narrative, then lying in the cabinet of an Italian family unknown, had ever come to his knowledge.

Madoc.

There are stories in the *Historie* of reports which had reached him, that mariners sailing for Ireland had been driven west, and had sighted land which had been supposed to be Tartary, which at a later day was thought to be the Baccalaos of the Cortereals.

The island of Bresil had been floating about the Atlantic, usually in the latitude of Ireland, since the days when the maker of the Catalan planisphere, in 1375, placed it in that sea, and current stories of its existence resulted, at a later day (1480), in the sending from Bristol of an expedition of search, as has already been said.

> Bresil, or Brazil, Island.

Finn Magnusen among the Scandinavian writers, and De Costa and others among Americans, have thought it probable that Columbus landed at Hualfiord, in Iceland. Columbus, however, does not give sufficient ground for any such inference. He says he went beyond Thule, not to it, whatever Thule was, and we only know by his observations on the tides, that he approached dry land.

> Did Columbus land on Thule?

Laing, in his introduction to the *Heimskringla*, says confidently that Columbus " came to Iceland from Bristol, in 1477, on purpose to gain nautical information," — an inference merely, — " and must have heard of the written accounts of the Norse discoveries recorded in " the *Codex Flatoyensis*. Laing says again that as Bishop Magnus is known to have been in Iceland in the spring of 1477, " it is presumed Columbus must have met and conversed with him " !

> Bishop Magnus in Iceland.

A great deal turns on this purely imaginary conversation, and the possibilities of its scope.

The listening Columbus might, indeed, have heard of Irish monks and their followers, who had been found in Iceland by the first Norse visitors, six hundred years before, if perchance the traditions of them had been preserved, and these may even have included the somewhat vague stories of visits to a country somewhere, which they called Ireland the Great. Possibly, too, there were stories told at the firesides of the adventures of a sea-rover, Gunnbiorn by name, who had been driven westerly from Iceland and had seen a strange land, which after some years was visited by Eric the Red ; and there might have been wondrous stories told of this same land, which Eric had called Greenland, in order to lure settlers, where there is some reason to believe yet earlier wanderers had found a home. There might

> The Norse in Iceland.

> Eric the Red.

> Greenland.

possibly have been shown to Columbus an old manuscript chronicle of the kings of Norway, which they called the *Heims-*

*Heims-*     *kringla,* and which had been written by Snorre Stur-
*kringla.*    lason in the thirteenth century; and if he had turned
the leaves with any curiosity, he could have read, or have had
translated for him, accounts of the Norse colonization of Greenland in the ninth century. Where, then, was this Greenland?
Could it possibly have had any connection with that Cathay of
Marco Polo, so real in the vision of Columbus, and which was
supposed to lie above India in the higher latitudes? As a student of contemporary cartography, Columbus would have an-

*Position of*    swered such a question readily, had it been suggested;
*Greenland.*    for he would have known that Greenland had been
represented in all the maps, since it was first recognized at all,
as merely an extended peninsula of Scandinavia, made by a
southward twist to enfold a northern sea, in which Iceland lay.
One certainly cannot venture to say how far Columbus may
have had an acquaintance with the cartographical repertories,
more or less well stocked, as they doubtless were, in the great
commercial centres of maritime Europe, but the knowledge
which we to-day have in detail could hardly have been otherwise than a common possession among students of geography

*Thought to*    then. We comprehend now how, as far back as 1427,
*be a part of*   a map of Claudius Clavus showed Greenland as this
*Europe.*     peninsular adjunct to the northwest of Europe, — a
view enforced also in a map of 1447, in the Pitti palace, and
in one which Nordenskiöld recently found in a Codex of Ptolemy at Warsaw, dated in 1467. A few years later, and certainly before Columbus could have gone on this voyage, we find
a map which it is more probable he could have known, and that
is the engraved one of Nicholas Donis, drawn presumably in
1471, and later included in the edition of Ptolemy published
at Ulm in 1482. The same European connection is here maintained. Again it is represented in the map of Henricus Martellus (1489–90), in a way that produced a succession of
maps, which till long after the death of Columbus continued to
make this Norse colony a territorial appendage of Scandinavian
Europe, betraying not the slightest symptom of a belief that
Eric the Red had strayed beyond the circle of European connections. It is only when we get down to the later years of Co-

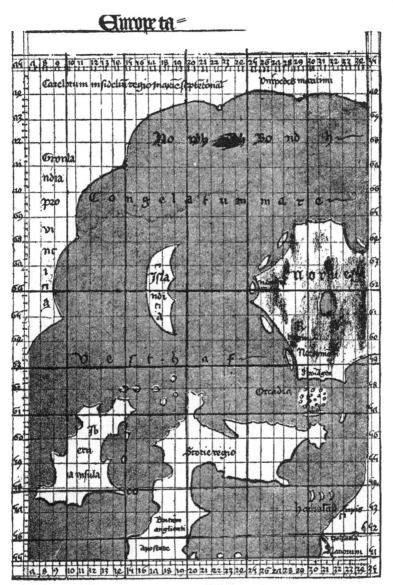

CLAUDIUS CLAVUS, 1427.

[From Nordenskiöld's *Studien.*]

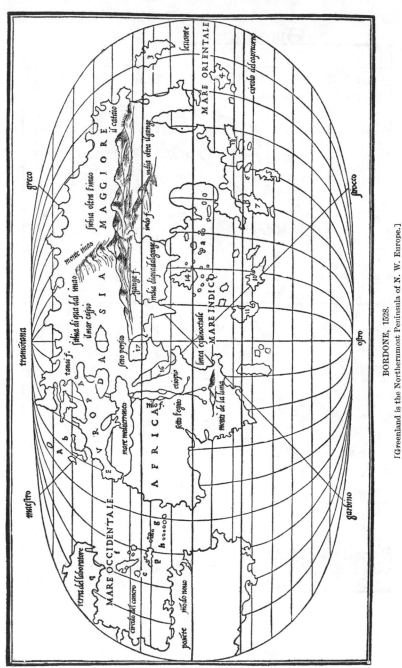

BORDONE, 1528.

[Greenland is the Northernmost Peninsula of N. W. Europe.]

lumbus's life that we find, on a Portuguese chart of 1503, a glimmer of the truth, and this only transiently, though the conception of the mariners, upon which this map was based, probably associated Greenland with the Asiatic main, as Made a part Ruysch certainly did, by a bold effort to reconcile the of Asia. Norse traditions with the new views of his time, when he produced the first engraved map of the discoveries of Columbus and Cabot in the Roman Ptolemy of 1508.

It is thus beyond dispute that if Columbus entertained any views as to the geographical relations of Greenland, which had been practically lost to Europe since communication with it ceased, earlier in the fifteenth century, they were simply those of a peninsula of northern Europe, which could have no connection with any country lying beyond the Atlantic ; for it was not till after his death that any general conception of it associated with the Asiatic main arose. It is quite certain, however, that as the conception began to prevail, after the discovery of the South Sea by Balboa, in 1513, that an interjacent new world had really been found, there was a tendency, as Again made a part of shown in the map of Thorne (1527), representing cur- Europe. rent views in Spain, and in those of Finæus (1531), Ziegler (1532), Mercator (1538), and Bordone (1528–1547), to relegate the position of Greenland to a peninsular connection with Europe.

There is a curious instance of the evolution of the correct idea in the Ptolemy of 1525, and repeated in the same plate as used in the editions of 1535 and 1545. The map was originally engraved to show " Gronlandia " as a European peninsula, but apparently, at a later stage, the word Gronlandia was cut in the corner beside the sketch of an elephant, and farther west, as if to indicate its transoceanic and Asiatic situation, though there was no attempt to draw in a coast line.

Later in the century there was a strife of opinion between the geographers of the north, as represented in the Olaus Later diMagnus map of 1567, who disconnected the country verse views. from Europe, and those of the south, who still united Greenland with Scandinavia, as was done in the Zeno map of 1558. By this time, however, the southern geographers had begun to doubt, and after 1540 we find Labrador and Greenland put in close proximity in many of their maps ; and in this the editors of the Ptolemy of 1561 agreed, when they altered their reëngraved map — as the plate shows — in a way to disconnect Greenland from Scandinavia.

It is not necessary to trace the cartographical history of Greenland to a later day. It is manifest that it was long after Columbus's death when the question was raised of its having any other connection than with Europe, and Columbus could have learned in Iceland nothing to suggest to him that the land of Eric the Red had any connection with the western shores of Asia, of which he was dreaming.

If any of the learned men in Iceland had referred Columbus Discovery of once more to the *Heimskringla*, it would have been to Vinland. the brief entry which it shows in the records as the leading Norse historian made it, of the story of the discovery of Vinland. There he would have read, " Leif also found Vinland the Good," and he could have read nothing more. There was nothing in this to excite the most vivid imagination as to place or direction.

It was not till a time long after the period of Columbus that, so far as we know, any cartographical records of the Scandina- vian views discoveries associated with the Vinland voyages were of Vinland. made in the north; and not till the discoveries of Columbus and his successors were a common inheritance in Europe did some of the northern geographers, in 1570, undertake to reconcile the tales of the sagas with the new beliefs. The testimony of these later maps is presumably the transmitted view then held in the north from the interpretation of the Norse sagas in the light of later knowledge. This testimony is that the " America " of the Spaniards, including Terra Florida and the " Albania " of the English, was a territory south of the Stephanius's Norse region and beyond a separating water, very map, 1570. likely that of Davis' Straits. The map of Sigurd Stephanius of this date (1570) puts Vinland north of the Straits of Belle Isle, and makes it end at the south in a " wild sea," which separates it [B of map] from " America." Torfæus quotes Torlacius as saying that this map of Stephanius's was drawn from ancient Icelandic records. If this cartographical record has its apparent value, it is not likely that Columbus could have seen in it anything more than a manifestation of that vague boreal region which was far remote from the thoughts which possessed him, in seeking a way to India over against Spain.

Beside the scant historic record respecting Vinland which has been cited from the *Heimskringla*, it is further <sub>Dubious</sub> possible that Columbus may have seen that series of <sub>sagas.</sub> sagas which had come down in oral shape to the twelfth century. At this period put into writing, two hundred years after

SIGURD STEPHANIUS, 1570.

the events of the Vinland voyages, there are none of the manuscript copies of these sagas now existing which go back of the fourteenth century. This rendering of the old sagas into script came at a time when, in addition to the inevitable transformations of long oral tradition, there was superadded the romancing spirit then rife in the north, and which had come to them from the south of Europe. The result of this blending of confused tradition with the romancing of the period of the written

preservation has thrown, even among the Scandinavians themselves, a shade of doubt, more or less intense at times, which
envelops the saga record with much that is indistinguishable
from myth, leaving little but the general drift of the story to be
held of the nature of a historic record. The Icelandic editor
of Egel's saga, published at Reikjavik in 1856, acknowledges
this unavoidable reflex of the times when the sagas were reduced to writing, and the most experienced of the recent writers
on Greenland, Henrik Rink, has allowed the untrustworthiness
of the sagas except for their general scope.

Less than a hundred years before the alleged visit of Colum-
Codex bus to Thule, there had been a compilation of some of
Flatoyensis. the early sagas, and this *Codex Flatoyensis* is the
only authority which we have for any details of the Vinland
voyages. It is possible that the manuscript now known is but
one copy of several or many which may have been made at an
early period, not preceding, however, the twelfth century, when
writing was introduced. This particular manuscript was discovered in an Icelandic monastery in the seventeenth century, and
there is no evidence of its being known before. Of course it is
possible that copies may have been in the hands of learned Ice-
landers at the time of Columbus's supposed voyage to the north,
and he may have heard of it, or have had parts of it read to
him. The collection is recognized by Scandinavian writers as
being the most confused and incongruous of similar records;
and it is out of such romancing, traditionary, and conflicting recitals that the story of the Norse voyages to Vinland is made,
Leif if it is made at all. The sagas say that it was six-
Erikson. teen winters after the settlement of Greenland that
Leif went to Norway, and in the next year he sailed to Vinland.
These are the data from which the year A. D. 1000 has been deduced as that of the beginning of the Vinland voyages. The
principal events are to be traced in the saga of Eric the Red,
which, in the judgment of Rask, a leading Norse authority, is
"somewhat fabulous, written long after the event, and taken
from tradition."

Such, then, was the record which, if it ever came to the notice of Columbus, was little suited to make upon him any
impression to be associated in his mind with the Asia of his
dreams. Humboldt, discussing the chances of Columbus's gain-

ing any knowledge of the story, thinks that when the Spanish Crown was contesting with the heirs of the Admiral his rights of discovery, the citing of these northern experiences of Columbus would have been in the Crown's favor, if there had been any conception at that time that the Norse discoveries, even if known to general Europe, had any relation to the geographical problems then under discussion. Similar views have been expressed by Wheaton and Prescott, and there is no evidence that up to the time of Columbus an acquaintance with the Vinland story had ever entered into the body of historical knowledge possessed by Europeans in general. The scant references in the manuscripts of Adam of Bremen (A. D. 1073), of Ordericus Vitalis (A. D. 1140), and of Saxo Grammaticus (A. D. 1200), were not likely to be widely comprehended, even if they were at all known, and a close scrutiny of the literature of Peringskiöld's edition of the subject does not seem to indicate that there was any considerable means of propagating a knowledge of the sagas. the sagas before Peringskiöld printed them in 1697, two hundred years after the time of Columbus. This editor inserted them in an edition of the *Heimskringla* and concealed the patchwork. This deception caused it afterwards to be supposed that the accounts in the *Heimskringla* had been interpolated by some later reviser of the chronicle ; but the truth regarding Peringskiöld's action was ultimately known.

Basing, then, their investigation on a narrative confessedly confused and unauthentic, modern writers have sought to determine with precision the fact of Norse visits to British America, and to identify the localities. The fact that every investigator finds geographical correspondences where he likes, and quite independently of all others, is testimony of itself to the confused condition of the story. The soil of the United States and Nova Scotia contiguous to the Atlantic may now safely be said to have been examined by competent critics sufficiently to affirm that no archæological trace of the presence of the Norse here is discernible. As to such a forbidding coast as that of Labrador, there has been as yet no such familiarity with it by trained archæologists as to render it reasonably certain that some trace may not be found there, and on this account George Bancroft allows the possibility that the Norse may Probabilities. have reached that coast. There remains, then, no evidence beyond a strong probability that the Norse from Greenland crossed Davis' Straits and followed south the American coast. That indisputable archæological proofs may yet be found to establish the fact of their southern course and sojourn is certainly possible. Meanwhile we must be content that there is no testimony satisfactory to a careful historical student, that this course and such sojourn ever took place. A belief in it must rest on the probabilities of the case.

Many writers upon the Norseman discovery would do well to remember the advice of Ampère to present as doubtful what is true, sooner than to give as true what is doubtful.

" Ignorance," says Muñoz, in speaking of the treacherous grounds of unsupported narrative, " is generally accompanied by vanity and temerity."

It is an obvious and alluring supposition that this story should have been presented to Columbus, whatever the effect may have been on his mind. Lowell in a poem pardonably pictures him as saying : —

Did Columbus hear of the saga stories ?

> " I brooded on the wise Athenian's tale
> Of happy Atlantis ; and heard Björne's keel
> Crunch the gray pebbles of the Vinland shore,
> For I believed the poets."

But the belief is only a proposition. Rafn and other extreme advocates of the Norse discovery have made as much as they could of the supposition of Columbus's cognizance of the Norse voyages. Laing seems confident that this contact must have happened. The question, however, must remain unsettled ; and whether Columbus landed in Iceland or not, and whether the bruit of the Norse expeditions struck his ears elsewhere or not, the fact of his never mentioning them, when he summoned every supposable evidence to induce acceptance of his views, seems to be enough to show at least that to a mind possessed as his was of the scheme of finding India by the west the stories of such northern wandering offered no suggestion applicable to his purpose. It is, moreover, inconceivable that Columbus should have taken a course southwest from the Canaries, if he had been prompted in any way by tidings of land in the northwest.

# CHAPTER VIII.

## COLUMBUS LEAVES PORTUGAL FOR SPAIN.

IT is a rather striking fact, as Harrisse puts it, that we cannot place with an exact date any event in Columbus's Columbus's
life from August 7, 1473, when a document shows him obscure rec-<br>ord, 1473-<br>1487.
to have been in Savona, Italy, till he received at Cor-
doba, Spain, from the treasurer of the Catholic sovereigns, his
first gratuity on May 5, 1487, as is shown by the entry in the
books, "given this day 3,000 maravedis," about $18, "to Cris-
tobal Colomo, a stranger." The events of this period of about
fourteen years were those which made possible his later career.
The incidents connected with this time have become the shuttle-
cocks which have been driven backward and forward in their
chronological bearings, by all who have undertaken to study
the details of this part of Columbus's life. It is nearly as true
now as it was when Prescott wrote, that "the discrepancies
among the earliest authorities are such as to render hopeless
any attempt to settle with precision the chronology of Columbus's movements previous to his first voyage."

The motives which induced him to abandon Portugal, where
he had married, and where he had apparently found
not a little to reconcile him to his exile, are not ob- His motives<br>for leaving<br>Portugal.
scure ones as detailed in the ordinary accounts of his
life. All these narratives are in the main based, first, on the
*Historie* (1571) ; secondly, on the great historical work Chief
of Joam de Barros, pertaining to the discoveries of sources<br>of our
the Portuguese in the East Indies, first published in knowledge.
1552, and still holding probably the loftiest position in the historical literature of that country ; and, finally, on the lives of
João II., then monarch of Portugal, by Ruy de Pina and by
Vasconcellos. The latter borrowing in the main from the former, was exclusively used by Irving. Las Casas apparently
depended on Barros as well as on the *Historie*. It is neces-

sary to reconcile their statements, as well as it can be done, to get even an inductive view of the events concerned.

The treatment of the subject by Irving would make it certain that it was a new confidence in the ability to make long voyages, inspired by the improvements of the astrolabe as directed by Behaim, that first gave Columbus the assurance to ask for royal patronage of the maritime scheme which had been developing in his mind.

Just what constituted the acquaintance of Columbus with Columbus and Behaim. Behaim is not clearly established. Herrera speaks of them as friends. Humboldt thinks some intimacy between them may have existed, but finds no decisive proof of it. Behaim had spent much of his life in Lisbon and in the Azores, and there are some striking correspondences in their careers, if we accept the usual accounts. They were born and died in the same year. Each lived for a while on an Atlantic island, the Nuremberger at Fayal, and the Genoese at Porto Santo ; and each married the daughter of the governor of his respective island. They pursued their nautical studies at the same time in Lisbon, and the same physicians who reported to the Portuguese king upon Columbus's scheme of westward sailing were engaged with Behaim in perfecting the sea astrolabe.

The account of the audience with the king which we find in Columbus and the king of Portugal. the *Historie* is to the effect that Columbus finally succeeded in inducing João to believe in the practicability of a western passage to Asia ; but that the monarch could not be brought to assent to all the titular and pecuniary rewards which Columbus contended for as emoluments of success, and that a commission, to whom the monarch referred the project, pronounced the views of Columbus simply chimerical. Barros represents that the advances of Columbus were altogether too arrogant and fantastic ever to have gained the consideration of the king, who easily disposed of the Genoese's pretentious importunities by throwing the burden of denial upon a commission. This body consisted of the two physicians of the royal household, already mentioned, Roderigo and Josef, to whom was added Cazadilla, the Bishop of Ceuta.

Vasconcellos's addition to this story, which he derived almost entirely from Ruy de Pina, Resende, and Barros, is that there was subsequently another reference to a royal council, in which the subject was discussed in arguments, of which that historian preserves some reports. This discussion went farther than was perhaps intended, since Cazadilla proceeded to discourage all attempts at exploration even by the African route, as imperiling the safety of the state, because of the money which was required; and because it kept at too great a distance for an emergency a considerable force in ships and men. In fact the drift of the debate seems to have ignored the main projects as of little moment and as too visionary, and the energy of the hour was centered in a rallying speech made by the Count of Villa Real, who endeavored to save the interests of African exploration. The count's speech quite accomplished its purpose, if we can trust the reports, since it reassured the rather drooping energies of the king, and induced some active measures to reach the extremity of Africa.

In August, 1486, Bartholomew Diaz, the most eminent of a line of Portuguese navigators, had departed on the African route, with two consorts. As he neared the latitude of the looked-for Cape, he was driven south, Diaz's African voyage, 1486. and forced away from the land, by a storm. When he was enabled to return on his track he struck the coast, really to the eastward of the true cape, though he did not at the time know it. This was in May, 1487. His crew being unwilling to proceed farther, he finally turned westerly, and in due time discovered what he had done. The first passage of the Cape was thus made while sailing west, just as, possibly, the Passes the Cape. mariners of the Indian seas may have done. In December he was back in Lisbon with the exhilarating news, and it was probably conveyed to Columbus, who was then in Spain, by his brother Bartholomew, the companion of Diaz in this eventful voyage, as Las Casas discovered by an entry made by Bartholomew himself in a copy of D'Ailly's *Imago Mundi*. Thirty years before, as we have seen, Fra Mauro had prefigured the Cape in his map, but it was now to be put on the charts as a geographical discovery; and by 1490, or thereabouts, succeeding Portuguese navigators had pushed up the east coast of Africa to a point shown in a map preserved in the British Museum, but not far enough to connect with what was supposed with some certainty to be the limit reached during the voyages of the Arabian navigators, while sailing south from the Red Sea.   There was apparently not a clear conception in the minds of the Portuguese, at this time, just how far from the Cape the entrance of the Arabian waters really was.   It is possible that intelligence may have thus early come from the Indian

PORTUGUESE MAPPEMONDE, 1490.
[Sketched from the original MS. in the British Museum.]

Ocean, by way of the Mediterranean, that the Oriental sailors knew of the great African cape by approaching it from the east.   Such knowledge, if held to be visionary, was, however, established with some certainty in men's minds before Da

Gama actually effected the passage of the Cape. This confirmation had doubtless come through some missionaries of the Portuguese king, who in 1490 sent such a positive message from Cairo.

*Portuguese missionaries to Egypt.*

But while the new exertions along the African coast, thus inadvertently instigated by Columbus, were making, what was becoming of his own westward scheme?

The story goes that it was by the advice of Cazadilla that the Portuguese king lent himself to an unworthy device. This was a project to test the views of Columbus, and profit by them without paying him his price. An outline of his intended voyage had been secured from him in the investigation already mentioned. A caravel, under pretense of a voyage to the Cape de Verde Islands, was now dispatched to search for the Cipango of Marco Polo, in the position which Columbus had given it in his chart. The mercenary craft started out, and buffeted with head seas and angry winds long enough to emasculate what little courage the crew possessed. Without the prop of conviction they deserted their purpose and returned. Once in port, they began to berate the Genoese for his foolhardy scheme. In this way they sought to vindicate their own timidity. This disclosed to Columbus the trick which had been played upon him. Such is the story as the *Historie* tells it, and which has been adopted by Herrera and others.

*The Portuguese send out an expedition to forestall Columbus.*

At this point there is too much uncertainty respecting the movements of Columbus for even his credulous biographers to fill out the tale. It seems to be agreed that in the latter part of 1484 he left Portugal with a secrecy which was supposed to be necessary to escape the vigilance of the government spies. There is beside some reason for believing that it was also well for him to shun arrest for debts, which had been incurred in the distractions of his affairs.

*Columbus leaves Portugal, 1484.*

There is no other authority than Ramusio for believing with Muñoz that Columbus had already laid his project before the government of Genoa by letter, and that he now went to reënforce it in person. That power was sorely pressed with misfortunes at this time, and is said to have

*Supposed visit of Columbus to Genoa.*

declined to entertain his proposals. It may be the applicant was dismissed contemptuously, as is sometimes said. It is not, however, as Harrisse has pointed out, till we come down to Cassoni, in his *Annals of Genoa*, published in 1708, that we find a single Genoese authority crediting the story of this visit to Genoa. Harrisse, with his skeptical tendency, does not believe the statement.

Eagerness to fill the gaps in his itinerary has sometimes induced the supposition that Columbus made an equally unsuccessful offer to Venice; but the statement is not found except in modern writers, with no other citations to sustain it than the recollections of some one who had seen at some time in the archives a memorial to this effect made by Columbus. Some writers make him at this time also visit his father and provide for his comfort, — a belief not altogether consonant with the supposition of Columbus's escape from Portugal as a debtor.

Supposed visit to Venice.

Irving and the biographers in general find in the death of Columbus's wife a severing of the ties which bound him to Portugal; but if there is any truth in the tumultuous letter which Columbus wrote to Doña Juana de la Torre in 1500, he left behind him in Portugal, when he fled into Spain, a wife and children. If there is the necessary veracity in the *Historie*, this wife had died before he abandoned the country. That he had other children at this time than Diego is only known through this sad, ejaculatory epistle. If he left a wife in Portugal, as his own words aver, Harrisse seems justified in saying that he deserted her, and in the same letter Columbus himself says that he never saw her again.

The death of his wife.

Shown to be uncertain.

Ever since a physician of Palos, Garcia Fernandez, gave his testimony in the lawsuit through which, after Columbus's death, his son defended his titles against the Crown, the picturesque story of the convent of Rabida, and the appearance at its gate of a forlorn traveler accompanied by a little boy, and the supplication for bread and water for the child, has stood in the lives of Columbus as the opening scene of his career in Spain.

Convent of Rabida.

This Franciscan convent, dedicated to Santa Maria de Rabida, stood on a height within sight of the sea, very near the

town of Palos, and after having fallen into a ruin it was
restored by the Duke of Montpensier in 1855. A recent traveler has found this restoration "modernized, whitewashed, and
forlorn," while the refurnishing of the interior is described as
" paltry and vulgar," even in the cell of its friar, where the visitor now finds a portrait of Columbus and pictures of scenes
in his career.

This friar, Juan Perez de Marchena, was at the time of the
supposed visit of Columbus the prior of the convent, Friar Mar-
and being casually attracted by the scene at the gate, chena.
where the porter was refreshing the vagrant travelers, and by

PÈRE JUAN PEREZ DE MARCHENA.
[As given by Roselly de Lorgues.]

the foreign accent of the stranger, he entered into talk with the
elder of them and learned his name. Columbus also told him
that he was bound to Huelva to find the home of one Muliar,
a Spaniard who had married the youngest sister of his wife.
The story goes further that the friar was not uninformed in the
cosmographical lore of the time, had not been unobservant of
the maritime intelligence which had naturally been rife in the
neighboring seaport of Palos, and had kept watch of the recent

progress in geographical science. He was accordingly able to appreciate the interest which Columbus manifested in such subjects, as he unfolded his own notions of still greater discoveries which might be made at the west. Keeping the wanderer and his little child a few days, Marchena invited to the convent, to join with them in discussion, the most learned man whom the neighborhood afforded, the physician of Palos, — the very one from whose testimony our information comes. Their talks were not without reënforcements from the experiences of some of the mariners of that seaport, particularly one Pedro de Velasco, who told of manifestation of land which he had himself seen, without absolute contact, thirty years before, when his ship had been blown a long distance to the northwest of Ireland.

The friendship formed in the convent kept Columbus there amid congenial sympathizers, and it was not till some time in the winter of 1485–86, and when he heard that the Spanish sovereigns were at Cordoba, gathering a force to attack the Moors in

Columbus goes to Cordoba.

Granada, that, leaving behind his boy to be instructed in the convent, Columbus started for that city. He went not without confidence and elation, as he bore a letter of credentials which the friar had given him to a friend, Fernando de Talavera, the prior of the monastery of Prado, and confessor of Queen Isabella.

This story has almost always been placed in the opening of the career of Columbus in Spain. It has often in sympathizing hands pointed a moral in contrasting the abject condition of those days with the proud expectancy under which, some years later, he sailed out of the neighboring harbor of Palos, within eyeshot of the monks of Rabida. Irving, however, as he analyzed the reports of the famous trial already referred to, was

Doubts about the visits to Rabida.

quite sure that the events of two visits to Rabida had been unwittingly run into one in testimony given after so long an interval of years. It does indeed seem that we must either apply this evidence of 1513 and 1515 to a later visit, or else we must determine that there was great similarity in some of the incidents of the two visits.

The date of 1491, to which Harrisse pushes the incidents forward, depends in part on the evidence of one Rodriguez Cobezudo that in 1513 it was about twenty-two years since he had lent a mule to Juan Perez de Marchena, when he went to Santa

Fé from Rabida to interpose for Columbus. The testimony of Garcia Fernandez is that this visit of Marchena took place after Columbus had once been rebuffed at court, and the words of the witness indicate that it was on that visit when Juan Perez asked Columbus who he was and whence he came ; showing, perhaps, that it was the first time Perez had seen Columbus. Accordingly this, as well 'as the mule story, points to 1491. But that the circumstances of the visit which Garcia Fernandez recounts may have belonged to an earlier visit, in part confounded after fifteen years with a later one, may yet be not beyond a possibility. It is to be remembered that the *Historie* speaks of two visits, one later than that of 1484. It is not easy to see that all the testimony which Harrisse introduced to make the visit of 1491 the first and only visit of Columbus to the convent is sufficient to do more than render the case probable.

We determine the exact date of the entering of Columbus into the service of Spain to be January 20, 1486, from a record of his in his journal on shipboard under January 14, 1493, where he says that on the 20th of the same month he would have been in their Highnesses' service just seven years. We find almost as a matter of course other statements of his which give somewhat different dates by deduction. Two statements of Columbus agreeing would be a little suspicious. Certain payments on the part of the Crowns of Castile and Aragon do not seem to have begun, however, till the next year, or at least we have no earlier record of such than one on May 5, 1487, and from that date on they were made at not great intervals, till an interruption came, as will be later shown.

1486. Enters the service of Spain.

In Spain the Christoforo Colombo of Genoa chose to call himself Cristoval Colon, and the *Historie* tells us that he sought merely to make his descendants distinct of name from their remote kin. He argued that the Roman name was Colonus, which readily was transformed to a Spanish equivalent. Inasmuch as the Duke of Medina-Celi, who kept Columbus in his house for two years during the early years of his Spanish residence, calls him Colomo in 1493, and Oviedo calls him Colom, it is a question if he chose the form of Colon before he became famous by his voyage.

Changes his name to Colon.

The Genoese had been for a long period a privileged people The Genoese in Spain. in Spain, dating such acceptance back to the time of St. Ferdinand. Navarrete has instanced numerous confirmations of these early favors by successive monarchs down to the time of Columbus. But neither this prestige of his birthright nor the letter of Friar Perez had been sufficient to secure in the busy camp at Cordoba any recognition of this otherwise unheralded and humble suitor. The power of the sovereigns was overtaxed already in the engrossing preparations which the Court and army were making for a vigorous campaign against the Moors. The exigencies of the war carried the sovereigns, sometimes together and at other times apart, from point to point. Siege after siege was conducted, and Talavera, whose devotion had been counted upon by Columbus, had too much to occupy his attention, to give ear to propositions which at best he deemed chimerical.

We know in a vague way that while the Court was thus Columbus in Cordoba. withdrawn from Cordoba the disheartened wanderer remained in that city, supporting himself, according to Bernaldez, in drafting charts and in selling printed books, which Harrisse suspects may have been publications, such as were then current, containing calendars and astronomical predictions, like the *Lunarios* of Granollach and Andrès de Li.

It was probably at this time, too, that he made the acquaint- Makes acquaintances. ance of Alonso de Quintanilla, the comptroller of the finances of Castile. He attained some terms of friendship with Antonio Geraldini, the papal nuncio, and his brother, Alexander Geraldini, the tutor of the royal children. It is claimed that all these friends became interested in his projects, and were advocates of them.

We are told by Las Casas that Columbus at one time gath- Writes out the proofs of a western land. ered and placed in order all the varied manifestations, as he conceived them, of some such transatlantic region as his theory demanded; and it seems probable that this task was done during a period of weary waiting in Cordoba. We know nothing, however, of the manuscript except as Las Casas and the *Historie* have used its material, and through them some of the details have been gleaned in the preceding chapter.

These accessions of friends, aided doubtless by some such systemization of the knowledge to be brought to the question as this lost manuscript implies, opened the way to Mendoza. an acquaintance with Pedro Gonzales de Mendoza, Archbishop of Toledo and Grand Cardinal of Spain. This prelate, from the confidence which the sovereigns placed in him, was known in Martyr's phrase as "the third king of Spain," and it could but be seen by Columbus that his sympathies were essential to the success of plans so far reaching as his own. The cardinal was gracious in his intercourse, and by no means inaccessible to such a suitor as Columbus; but he was educated in the exclusive spirit of the prevailing theology, and he had a keen scent for anything that might be supposed heterodox. It proved necessary for the thought of a spherical earth to rest some time in his mind, till his ruminations could bring him to a perception of the truths of science.

According to the reports which Oviedo gives us, the seed which Columbus sowed, in his various talks with the cardinal, in due time germinated, and the constant mentor of Gets the ear the sovereigns was at last brought to prepare the of Ferdinand for way, so that Columbus could have a royal audience. Columbus. Thus it was that Columbus finally got the ear of Ferdinand, at Salamanca, whither the monarchs had come for a winter's sojourn after the turmoils of a summer's campaign against the Moors.

We cannot proceed farther in this narrative without understanding, in the light of all the early and late evidence Characters which we have, what kind of beings these sovereigns of the sovereigns of of Aragon and Castile were, with whom Columbus Spain. was to have so much intercourse in the years to come. Ferdinand and Isabella, the wearers of the crowns of Aragon and Castile, were linked in common interests, and their joint reign had augured a powerful, because united, Spain. The student of their characters, as he works among the documents of the time, cannot avoid the recognition of qualities little calculated to satisfy demands for nobleness and devotion which the world has learned to associate with royal obligations. It may be possibly too much to say that habitually, but not too much to assert that often, these Spanish monarchs were more ready at perfidy and deceit than even an allowance for the teachings of their time would permit. Often the student will find himself forced to grant that the queen was more culpable in these respects than the king. An anxious inquirer into the queen's ways is not quite sure that she was able to distinguish between her own interests and those of God. The documentary researches of Bergenroth have decidedly lowered her in the judgments of those who have studied that investigator's results. We need to plead the times for her, and we need to push the plea very far.

"Perhaps," says Helps, speaking of Isabella, "there is hardly any great personage whose name and authority are found in connection with so much that is strikingly evil, all of it done, or rather assented to, upon the highest and purest motives." To palliate on such grounds is to believe in the irresponsibility of motives, which should transcend times and occasions.

Isabella.

She is not, however, without loyal adulators of her own time and race.

We read in Oviedo of her splendid soul. Peter Martyr found commendations of ordinary humanity not enough for her. Those nearest her person spoke as admiringly. It is the fortune, however, of a historical student, who lies beyond the influence of personal favor, to read in archives her most secret professions, and to gauge the innermost wishes of a soul which was carefully posed before her contemporaries. It is mirrored to-day in a thousand revealing lenses that were not to be seen by her contemporaries. Irving and Prescott simply fall into the adulation of her servitors, and make her confessors responsible for her acquiescence in the expulsion of the Jews and in the horrors of the Inquisition.

The king, perhaps, was good enough for a king as such personages went in the fifteenth century; but his smiles and remorseless coldness were mixed as few could mix them, even in those days. If the Pope regarded him from Italy, that Holy Father called him pious. The modern student finds him a bigot. His subjects thought him great and glorious, but they did not see his dispatches, nor know his sometimes baleful domination in his cabinet. The French would not trust him. The English watched his ambition. The Moors knew him as their conqueror. The Jews fled before his evil eye.

Ferdinand.

The miserable saw him in his inquisitors. All this pleased the Pope, and the papal will made him in preferred phrase His Most Catholic Majesty, — a phrase that rings in diplomatic formalities to-day.

Every purpose upon which he had set his heart was apt to blind him to aught else, and at times very conveniently so. We may allow that it is precisely this single mind which makes a conspicuous name in history ; but conspicuousness and justness do not always march with a locked step.

He had, of course, virtues that shone when the sun shone. He could be equable. He knew how to work steadily, to eat moderately, and to dress simply. He was enterprising in his actions, as the Moors and heretics found out. He did not extort money; he only extorted agonized confessions. He said masses, and prayed equally well for God's benediction on evil as on good things. He made promises, and then got the papal dispensation to break them. He juggled in state policy as his mind changed, and he worked his craft very readily. Machiavelli would have liked this in him, and indeed he was a good scholar of an existing school, which counted the act of outwitting better than the arts of honesty ; and perhaps the world is not loftier in the purposes of statecraft to-day. He got people to admire him, but few to love him.

The result of an audience with the king was that the projects of Columbus were committed to Talavera, to be laid by him before such a body of wise men as the prior could gather in council. Las Casas says that the consideration of the plans was entrusted to " certain persons of the Court," and he enumerates Cardinal Mendoza, Diego de Deza, Alonso de Cardenas, and Juan Cabrero, the royal chamberlain. The meeting was seemingly held in the winter of 1486–87. The Catholic writers accuse Irving, and apparently with right, of an unwarranted assumption of the importance of what he calls the Council at Salamanca, and they find he has no authority for it, except a writer one hundred and twenty years after the event, who mentions the matter but incidentally. This source was Remesal's *Historia de Chyapa* (Madrid, 1619), an account of one of the Mexican provinces. There seems no reason to suppose that at best it was anything more than some informal conference

Columbus's views considered by Talavera and others.

At Salamanca.

of Talavera with a few councilors, and in no way associated with the prestige of the university at Salamanca. The registers of

UNIVERSITY OF SALAMANCA.
[*España*, p. 132.]

the university, which begin back of the assigned date for such Council, have been examined in vain for any reference to it.

The " Junta of Salamanca " has passed into history as a convocation of considerable extent and importance, and a representation of it is made to adorn one of the bas-reliefs of the Admiral's monument at Genoa. We have, however, absolutely

MONUMENT TO COLUMBUS ERECTED AT GENOA, 1862.

no documentary records of it. Of whatever moment it may have been, if the problem as Columbus would have presented it had been discussed, the reports, if preserved, could have thrown much light upon the relations which the cosmographical views of its principal character bore to the opinions then prevailing in learned circles of Spain. We know what the *Historie*, Bernaldez, and Las Casas tell us of Columbus's advocacy, but we must regret the loss of his own language and his own way of explaining himself to these learned men. Such a paper would serve a purpose of showing how, in this period of courageous and ardent insistence on a physical truth, he stood manfully for the light that was in him; and it would afford a needed foil to those pitiful aberrations of intellect which, in the years following, took possession of him, and which were so constantly reiterated with painful and maundering wailing.

Discarding, then, the array of argument which Irving borrows from Remesal, and barely associating a little conference, in which Columbus is a central figure, with that St. Stephen's convent whose wondrous petrifactions of creamy and reticulated stone still hold the admiring traveler, we must accept nothing more about its meetings than the scant testimony which has come down to us. It is pleasant to think how it was here that the active interest which Diego de Deza, a Dominican friar, finally took in the cause of Columbus may have had its beginning; but the extent of our positive knowledge regarding the meeting is the deposition of Rodriguez de Maldonado, who simply says that several learned men and mariners, hearing the arguments of Columbus, decided they could not be true, or at least a majority so decided, and that this testimony against Columbus had no effect to convince him of his errors. This is all that the "Junta of Salamanca" meant. A minority of unknown size favored the advocate.

Find favor with Deza.

When the spring of 1487 came, and the court departed to Cordoba, and began to make preparations for the campaign against Malaga, there was no hope that the considerations which had begun in the learned sessions at Salamanca would be followed up. Columbus seems to have journeyed after the Court in its migrations: sometimes lured by pittances doled out to him by the royal treasurer; sometimes getting pecuniary assistance from his new friend, Diego de Deza; selling now and then a map that he had made, it may be; and accepting hospitality

1487. The Court at Cordoba.

Malaga surrenders, 1487.

where he could get it, from such as Alonso de Quintanilla. In these wandering days, he was for a while, at least, in attendance on the Court, then surrounded with military parade, before the

SPAIN, 1482.
[From the *Ptolemy* of 1482.]

Moorish stronghold at Malaga. The town surrendered on August 18, 1487, and the Court then returned to Cordoba.

It was in the autumn of 1487, at Cordoba, that Columbus fell into such an intimacy as spousehood only can sanction with a person of good condition as to birth, but poor in the world's goods. Whether this relation had the sanction of the Church or not has been a subject of much inquiry and opinion. The class of French writers, who are aiming to secure the canonization of Columbus, have found it essential to clear the moral character of Columbus from every taint, and they confidently assert, and doubtless think they show, that nothing but conjugal right is manifest in this connection, — a question which the Church will in due time have to decide, if it ever brings itself to the recognition of the saintly character of the great discoverer. Even the ardent supporters of the cause of beatification are forced to admit that there is no record of such a marriage. No contemporary recognition of such a relation is evinced by any family ceremonies of baptism or the like, and there is no mention of a wife in all the transactions of the crowning endeavors of his life. As viceroy, at a later day, he constantly appears with no attendant vice-queen. She is absolutely out of sight until Columbus makes a significant reference to her in his last will, when he recommends this Beatrix Enriquez to his lawful son Diego; saying that she is a person to whom the testator had been under great obligations, and that his conscience is burdened respecting her, for a reason which he does not then think fitting to explain. This testamentary behest and acknowledgment, in connection with other manifestations, and the absence of proof to the contrary, has caused the belief to be general among his biographers, early and late, that the fruit of this intimacy, Ferdinand Columbus, was an illegitimate offspring. He was born, as near as can be made out, on the 15th of August, 1488. The mother very likely received for a while some consolation from her lover, but Columbus did not apparently carry her to Seville, when he went there himself; and the support which he gave her was not altogether regularly afforded, and was never of the quality which he asked Diego to grant to her when he died. She unquestionably survived the making of Diego's will in 1523, and then she fades into oblivion. Her son, Ferdinand, if he is the author of the *Historie*, makes no mention of a marriage to his mother, though he is careful to

*1487. Intimacy of Columbus with Beatrix Enriquez.*

*Ferdinand Columbus born, 1488.*

record the one which was indisputably legal, and whose fruit was Diego, the Admiral's successor. The lawful son was directed by Columbus, when starting on his third voyage, to pay to Beatrix ten thousand maravedis a year ; but he seems to have neglected to do so for the last three or four years of her life. Diego finally ordered these arrears to be paid to her heirs. Las Casas distinctly speaks of Ferdinand as a natural son, and Las Casas had the best of opportunities· for knowing whereof he wrote.

While all this suspense and amorous intrigue were perplexing the ardent theorist, he is supposed to have dispatched his brother Bartholomew to England to disclose his projects to Henry VII. Hakluyt, in his *Westerne Planting*, tells us that it " made much for the title of the kings of England " to the New World that Henry VII. gave a ready acceptance to the theory of Columbus as set forth somewhat tardily by his brother Bartholomew, when escaping from the detention of the pirates, he was at last able, on February 13, 1488, to offer in England his sea-card, embodying Christopher's theories, for the royal consideration.

Columbus sends his brother to England.

Relations of England to the views of Columbus.

William Castell, in his *Short Discovery of America*, says that Henry VII. " unhappily refused to be at any charge in the discovery, supposing the learned Columbus to build castles in the air." It is a common story that Henry finally brought himself to accede to the importunities of Bartholomew, but only at a late day, and after Christopher had effected his conquest of the Spanish Court. Columbus himself is credited with saying that Henry actually wrote him a letter of acceptance. This epistle was very likely a fruition of the new impulses to oceanic discovery which the presence, a little later, of the Venetian Cabots, was making current among the English sailors ; for John Cabot and his sons, one of whom, Sebastian, being at that time a youth of sixteen or seventeen, had, according to the best testimony, established a home in Bristol, not far from 1490.

The Cabots in England.

If the report of the Spanish envoy in England to his sovereigns is correct as to dates, it was near this time that the Bristol merchants were renewing their quests oceanward for the islands of Brazil and the Seven Cities. We have seen that these islands with others had for some time appeared on the conjectural charts of the Atlantic, and very likely they had appeared on the sea-card shown by Bartholomew Columbus to Henry VII. These efforts may perhaps have been in a measure instigated by that fact. At all events, any hazards of further western exploration could be met with greater heart if such stations of progress could be found in mid ocean. Of the report of all this which Bartholomew may have made to his brother we know absolutely nothing, and he seems not to have returned to Spain till after a sojourn in France which ended in 1494.

It was believed by Irving that Columbus, having opened a correspondence with the Portuguese king respecting a return to the service of that country, had received from that monarch an epistle, dated March 20, 1488, in which he was permitted to come back, with the offer of protection against any suit of civil or criminal nature, and that this had been declined. We are left to conjecture of what suits of either kind he could have been apprehensive.

Columbus invited back to Portugal.

Humboldt commends the sagacity of Navarrete in discerning that it was not so much the persuasion of Diego de Deza which kept Columbus at this time from accepting such royal offers, as the illicit connection which he had formed in Cordoba with Doña Beatrix Enriquez, who before the summer was over had given birth to a son.

On the other hand, that the permission was not neglected seems proved by a memorandum made by Columbus's own hand in a copy of Pierre d'Ailly's *Imago Mundi*, preserved in the Biblioteca Colombina at Seville, where, under date of December, 1488, " at Lisbon," he speaks of the return of Diaz from his voyage to the Cape of Good Hope. This proof is indeed subject to the qualification that Las Casas has considered the handwriting of the note to be that of Bartholomew Columbus, but Harrisse has no question of its identity with the chirography of Columbus. This last critic ventures the conjecture that it was in some way to settle the estate of his wife that Columbus at this time visited Portugal.

Columbus had ceased to receive the Spanish subsidies in June, 1488, or at least we know no record of any later largess. Ferdinand was born to him in Au-

Spanish subsidies withheld.

gust. It was very likely subsequent to this last event that Columbus crossed the Spanish frontier into Portugal, if Harrisse's view of his crossing at all be accepted. His stay was without doubt a short one, and from 1489 to 1492 there is every indication that he never left the Spanish kingdom.

We know on the testimony of a letter of Luis de la Cerda, the Duke of Medina-Celi, given in Navarrete, that for two years after the arrival of Columbus from Portugal he had been a guest under the duke's roof in Cogulludo, and it seems to Harrisse probable that this gracious help on the part of the duke was bestowed after the return to Spain. All that we know with certainty of its date is that it occurred before the first voyage, the duke himself mentioning it in a letter of March 19, 1493.

Duke of Medina-Celi harbors Columbus.

It was not till May, 1489, when the court was again at Cordoba, according to Diego Ortiz de Zuñiga, in his work on Seville, that the sovereigns were gracious enough to order Columbus to appear there, when they furnished him lodgings. They also, perhaps, at the same time, issued a general order, dated at Cordoba May 12, in which all cities and towns were directed to furnish suitable accommodations to Columbus and his attendants, inasmuch as he was journeying in the royal service.

1489. Columbus ordered to Cordoba.

The year 1489 was a hazardous but fruitful one. The sovereigns were pushing vigorously their conquest of the Moor. Isabella herself attended the army, and may have appeared in the beleaguering lines about Baza, in one of those suits of armor which are still shown to travelers. Zuñiga says that Columbus arrayed himself among the combatants, and was doubtless acquainted with the mission of two friars who had been guardians of the Holy Sepulchre at Jerusalem. These priests arrived during the siege, bringing a message from the Grand Soldan of Egypt, in which that potentate threatened to destroy all Christians within his grasp, unless the war against Granada should be stopped. The point of driving the Moors from Spain was too nearly reached for such a threat to be effective, and Isabella decreed the annual payment of a thousand ducats to support the faithful custodians of the Sepulchre, and sent a veil embroidered with her own hand to decorate the shrine. Irving traces to

Columbus at the siege of Baza.

Friars from the Holy Sepulchre.

this circumstance the impulse, which Columbus frequently in later days showed, to devote the anticipated wealth of the Indies to a crusade in Palestine, to recover and protect the Holy Sepulchre.

The campaign closed with the surrender on December 22 of the fortress of Baza, when Spain received from Muley Boabdil, the elder of the rival Moorish kings, all the territory which he claimed to have in his power. In February, 1490, Ferdinand and Isabella entered Seville in triumph, and a season of hilarity and splendor followed, signalized in the spring by the celebration with great jubilation of the marriage of the Princess Isabella with Don Alonzo, the heir to the crown of Portugal. These engrossing scenes were little suited to give Columbus a chance to press his projects on the Court. He soon found nothing could be done to get the farther attention of the monarchs till some respites occurred in the preparations for their final campaign against the younger Moorish king. It was at this time, as Irving and others have conjectured, that the consideration of the project of a western passage, which had been dropped when events moved the Court from Salamanca, was again taken up by such investigators as Talavera had summoned, and again the result was an adverse decision. This determination was communicated by Talavera himself to the sovereign, and it was accompanied by the opinion that it did not become great princes to engage in such chimerical undertakings.

*Boabdil surrenders, December 22, 1489.*

*Columbus's views again considered.*

It is supposed, however, that the decision was not reached without some reservation in the minds of certain of the reviewers, and that especially this was the case with Diego de Deza, who showed that the stress of the arguments advanced by Columbus had not been without result. This friar was tutor to Prince Juan, and it was not difficult for him to modify the emphatic denial of the judges. It was the pride of those who later erected the tombstone of Deza, in the cathedral at Seville, to inscribe upon it that he was the generous and faithful patron of Columbus. A temporizing policy was, therefore, adopted by the monarchs, and Columbus was informed that for the present the perils and expenses of the war called for an undivided attention, and that further consideration of his project must be deferred till the war was over. It was at Cordoba that this decision reached

*Deza impressed.*

*Delays.*

Columbus. In his eagerness of hope he suspected that the judgment had received some adverse color in passing through Tala-

CATHEDRAL OF SEVILLE.
[From Parcerisa and Quadrado's *España*.]

vera's mind, and so he hastened to Seville, but only to meet the same chilling repulse from the monarchs themselves. With dashed expectations he left the city.

Columbus goes to Seville; but is repelled.

feeling that the instrumentality of Talavera, as Peter Martyr
tells us, had turned the sovereigns against him.

CATHEDRAL OF CORDOBA.
[From Parcerisa and Quadrado's *España*.]

Seeks the
grandees of
Spain.
Columbus now sought to engage the attention of
some of the powerful grandees of Spain, who, though
subjects, were almost autocratic in their own regions,

serving the Crown not so much as vassals as sympathetic helpers in its wars. They were depended upon to recruit the armies from their own trains and dependents ; money came from their chests, provisions from their estates, and ships from their own marine ; their landed patrimonies, indeed, covered long stretches of the coast, whose harbors sheltered their considerable navies. Such were the dukes of Medina-Sidonia and Medina-Celi. Columbus found in them, however, the same wariness which he had experienced at the greater court. There was a willingness to listen ; they found some lures in the great hopes of Eastern wealth which animated Columbus, but in the end there was the same disappointment. One of them, the Duke of Medina-Celi, at last adroitly parried the importunities of Columbus, by averring that the project deserved the royal patronage rather than his meaner aid. He, however, told the suitor, if a farther application should be made to the Crown at some more opportune moment, he would labor with the queen in its behalf. The duke kept his word, and we get much of what we know of his interest in Columbus from the information given by one of the duke's household to Las Casas. This differs so far as to make the duke, perhaps as Harrisse thinks in the spring of 1491, actually fit out some caravels for the use of Columbus ; but when seeking a royal license, he was informed that the queen had determined to embark in the enterprise herself. Such a decision seems to carry this part of the story, at least, forward to a time when Columbus was summoned from Rabida.

A consultation which now took place at the convent of Rabida affords particulars which the historians have found difficulty, as already stated, in keeping distinct from those of an earlier visit, if there was such. Columbus, according to the usual story, visited the convent apparently in October or November, 1491, with the purpose of reclaiming his son Diego, and taking him to Cordoba, where he might be left with Ferdinand in the charge of the latter's mother. Columbus himself intended to pass to France, to see if a letter, which had been received from the king of France, might possibly open the way to the fulfillment of his great hopes. It is represented that it was this expressed intention of abandoning Spain which aroused the patriotism of Marchena, who undertook to prevent

*[marginal note: Medina-Sidonia and Medina-Celi.]*

*[marginal note: Columbus at Rabida.]*

the sacrifice.  We derive what we know of his method of pre-

Marchena encourages him.

vention from the testimony of Garcia Fernandez, the physician of Palos, who has been cited in respect to the alleged earlier visit.  This witness says that he was summoned to Rabida to confer with Columbus.  It is also made a part of the story that the head of a family of famous naviga- tors in Palos, Martin Alonso Pinzon, was likewise drawn into

Talks with Pinzon.

the little company assembled by the friar to consider the new situation.  Pinzon readily gave his adherence to the views of Columbus.  It is claimed, however, that the presence of Pinzon is disproved by documents showing him to have been in Rome at this time.

An alleged voyage of Jean Cousin, in 1488, two years and

Cousin's alleged voy- age, 1488,

more before this, from Dieppe to the coast of Brazil, is here brought in by certain French writers, like Es- tancelin and Gaffarel, as throwing some light on the intercourse of Columbus and Pinzon, later if not now.  It must be acknowledged that few other than French writers have cred- ited the voyage at all.  Major, who gave the story careful ex- amination, utterly discredits it.  It is a part of the story that one Pinzon, a Castilian, accompanied Cousin as a pilot, and this man is identified by these French writers as the navigator who is now represented as yielding a ready credence to the views of Columbus, and for the reason that he knew more than he openly professed.  They find in the later intercourse of Columbus and this Pinzon certain evidence of the estimation in which Colum- bus seemed to hold the practiced judgment, if not the know-

and Pinzon's supposed connection with it.

ledge, of Pinzon.  This they think conspicuous in the yielding which Columbus made to Pinzon's opinion during Columbus's first voyage, in changing his course to the southwest, which is taken to have been due to a know- ledge of Pinzon's former experience in passing those seas in 1488.  They trace to it the confidence of Pinzon in separating from the Admiral on the coast of Cuba, and in his seeking to anticipate Columbus by an earlier arrival at Palos, on the re- turn, as the reader will later learn.  Thus it is ingeniously claimed that the pilot of Cousin and colleague of Columbus were one and the same person.  It has hardly convinced other students than the French.  When the Pinzon of the " Pinta " at a later day was striving to discredit the leadership of Columbus, in the famous suit of the Admiral's heirs, he could hardly, for any reason which the French writers aver, have neglected so important a piece of evidence as the fact of the Cousin voyage and his connection with it, if there had been any truth in it. So we must be content, it is pretty clear, in charging Pinzon's conversion to the views of Columbus at Rabida upon the efficacy of Columbus's arguments. This Pinzon aids success of Columbus brought some substantial fruit Columbus, in the promise which Pinzon now made to bear the expenses of a renewed suit to Ferdinand and Isabella.

A conclusion to the deliberation of this little circle in the convent was soon reached. Columbus threw his cause into the hands of his friends, and agreed to rest quietly in the convent while they pressed his claims. Perez wrote a letter of supplication to the Queen, and it was dispatched by a respectable navigator of the neighborhood, Sebastian Rodriguez. He and Rodriguez goes to found the Queen in the city of Santa Fé, which had Santa Fé, grown up in the military surroundings before the city with a letter to the of Granada, whose siege the Spanish armies were then queen. pressing. The epistle was opportune, for it reënforced one which she had already received from the Duke of Medina-Celi, who had been faithful to his promise to Columbus, and who, judging from a letter which he wrote at a later day, March 19, 1493, took to himself not a little credit that he had thus been instrumental, as he thought, in preventing Columbus throwing himself into the service of France. The result was that the pilot took back to Rabida an intimation to Marchena that his presence would be welcome at Santa Fé. So mounting his mule, after midnight, fourteen days after Rodriguez Marchena had departed, the friar followed the pilot's tracks, follows. which took him through some of the regions already conquered from the Moors, and, reaching the Court, presented himself before the Queen. Perez is said to have found a seconder in Luis de Santangel, a fiscal officer of Aragon, and in the Marchioness of Moya, one of the ladies of the household. The friar is thought to have urged his petition so strongly that the Queen, who had all along been more open to the representa- The queen invites Co- tions of Columbus than Ferdinand had been, finally lumbus once determined to listen once more to the Genoese's ap- more. peals. Learning of the poor plight of Columbus, she ordered a gratuity to be sent to him, to restore his wardrobe and to furnish himself with the conveniences of the journey. Perez, having borne back the happy news, again returned to the Court, with Columbus under his protection. Thus once more buoyed in hope, and suitably arrayed for appearing at Court,

Columbus reaches Santa Fé, December, 1491.

Columbus, on his mule, early in December, 1491, rode into the camp at Santa Fé, where he was received and provided with lodgings by the accountant-general. This officer was one whom he had occasion happily to remember, Alonso de Quintanilla, through whose offices it was, in the end, that the Grand Cardinal of Spain, Mendoza, was at this time brought into sympathy with the Genoese aspirant.

Quintanilla and Mendoza.

Military events were still too imposing, however, for any immediate attention to his projects, and he looked on with admiration and a reserved expectancy, while the grand parade of the final submission of Boabdil the younger, the last of the Moorish kings, took place, and a long procession of the magnificence of Spain moved forward from the beleaguering camp to receive the keys of the Alhambra. Wars succeeding wars for nearly eight centuries had now come to an end. The Christian banner of Spain floated over the Moorish palace. The kingdom was alive in all its provinces. Congratulation and jubilation, with glitter and vauntings, pervaded the air.

Boabdil the younger submits.

The Moorish wars end.

Few observed the humble Genoese who stood waiting the sovereigns' pleasure during all this tumult of joy; but he was not forgotten. They remembered, as he did, the promise given him at Seville. The war was over, and the time was come.

Talavera and Columbus.

Talavera had by this time gone so far towards an appreciation of Columbus's views that Peter Martyr tells him, at a later day, that the project would not have succeeded without him. He was directed to confer with the expectant dreamer, and Cardinal Mendoza became prominent in the negotiations.

Columbus's position was thus changed. He had been a suitor. He was now sought. He had been persuaded from his purposed visit to France, in order that he might by his plans rehabilitate Spain with a new glory, complemental to her martial pride. This view as presented by Perez to Isabella had been accepted, and Columbus was summoned to present his case.

Here, when he seemed at last to be on the verge of success, the poor man, unused to good fortune, and mistaking its token, repeated the mistake which had driven him an outcast from Portugal. His arrogant spirit led him to magnify his importance before he had proved it; and he failed in the modesty which marks a conquering spirit.

The mistake of Columbus.

True science places no gratulations higher than those of its own conscience. Copernicus was at this moment delving into the secrets of nature like a nobleman of the universe. So he stands for all time in lofty contrast to the plebeian nature and sordid cravings of his contemporary.

When, at the very outset of the negotiations, Talavera found this uplifted suitor making demands that belonged rather to proved success than to a contingent one, there was little prospect of accommodation, unless one side or the other should abandon its position. If Columbus's own words count for anything, he was conscious of being a laughing-stock, while he was making claims for office and emoluments that would mortgage the power of a kingdom. A dramatic instinct has in many minds saved Columbus from the critical estimate of such presumption. Irving and the French canonizers dwell on what strikes them as constancy of purpose and loftiness of spirit. They marvel that poverty, neglect, ridicule, contumely, and disappointment had not dwarfed his spirit. This is the vulgar liking for the hero who is without heroism, and the martyr who makes a trade of it. The honest historian has another purpose. He tries to gauge pretense by wisdom. Columbus was indeed to succeed; but his success was an error in geography, and a failure in policy and in morals. The Crown was yet to succumb; but its submission was to entail miseries upon Columbus and his line, and a reproach upon Spain. The outcome to Columbus and to Spain is the direst comment of all.

His pretensions.

Columbus would not abate one jot of his pretensions, and an end was put to the negotiations. Making up his mind to carry his suit to France, he left Cordoba on his mule, in the beginning of February, 1492.

# CHAPTER IX.

## THE FINAL AGREEMENT AND THE FIRST VOYAGE, 1492.

COLUMBUS, a disheartened wanderer, with his back turned on the Spanish Court, his mule plodding the road to Cordoba, offered a sad picture to the few adherents whom he had left behind. They had grown to have his grasp of confidence, but lacked his spirit to clothe an experimental service with all the certainties of an accomplished fact.

*Columbus leaves the Court.*

The sight of the departing theorist abandoning the country, and going to seek countenance at rival courts, stirred the Spanish pride. He and his friends had, in mutual counsels, pictured the realms of the Indies made tributary to the Spanish fame. It was this conception of a chance so near fruition, and now vanishing, that moved Luis de Santangel and Alonso de Quintanilla to determine on one last effort. They immediately sought the Queen. In an audience the two advocates presented the case anew, appealing to the royal ambition, to the opportunity of spreading her holy religion, to the occasions of replenishing her treasure-chests, emptied by the war, and to every other impulse, whether of pride or patriotism. The trivial cost and risk were contrasted with the glowing possibilities. They repeated the offer of Columbus to share an eighth of the expense. They pictured her caravels, fitted out at a cost of not more than 3,000,000 crowns, bearing the banner of Spain to these regions of opulence. The vision, once fixed in the royal eye, spread under their warmth of description, into succeeding glimpses of increasing splendor. Finally the warmth and glory of an almost realized expectancy filled the Queen's cabinet.

*The Queen relents.*

The conquest was made. The royal companion, the Marchioness of Moya, saw and encouraged the kindling enthusiasm of Isabella; but a shade came over the Queen's face. The others knew it was the thought of Ferdinand's aloofness. The warrior of Aragon, with new conquests to regulate, with a treasury drained almost to the last penny, would have little heart for an undertaking in which his enthusiasm, if existing at all, had always been dull as compared with hers. She solved the difficulty in a flash. The voyage shall be the venture of Castile alone, and it shall be undertaken.

Orders were at once given for a messenger to overtake Columbus. A horseman came up with him at the bridge of Pinòs, two leagues from Granada. There was a moment's hesitancy, as thoughts of cruelly protracted and suspended feelings in the past came over him. His decision, however, was not stayed. He turned his mule, and journeyed back to the city. Columbus was sought once more, and in a way to give him the vantage which his imperious demands could easily use. Columbus brought back.

The interview with the Queen which followed removed all doubt of his complete ascendency. Ferdinand in turn yielded to the persuasions of his chamberlain, Juan Cabrero, and to the supplications of Isabella; but he succumbed without faith, if the story which is told of him in relation to the demand for similar concessions made twenty years later by Ponce de Leon is to be believed. "Ah," said Ferdinand, to the discoverer of Florida, " it is one thing to give a stretch of power when no one anticipates the exercise of it; but we have learned something since then; you will succeed, and it is another thing to give such power to you." This story goes a great way to explain the later efforts of the Crown to counteract the power which was, in the flush of excitement, unwittingly given to the new Admiral.

The ensuing days were devoted to the arrangement of details. The usual story, derived from the *Historie*, is that the Queen offered to pawn her jewels, as her treasury of Castile could hardly furnish the small sum required; but Harrisse is led to believe that the exigencies of the war had already required this sacrifice of the Queen, though the documentary evidence is wanting. Santangel, however, interposed. As treasurer of the ecclesiastical revenues in Aragon, he was able to show that while Isabella was foremost in promoting the enterprise, Ferdinand could join her in a loan from these coffers; and so it was that the necessary funds were, in reality, paid in The Queen's jewels.

the end from the revenues of Aragon. This is the common story, enlarged by later writers upon the narrative in Las Casas; but Harrisse finds no warrant for it, and judges the advance of funds to have been by Santangel from his private revenues, and in the interests of Castile only. And this seems to be proved by the invariable exclusion of Ferdinand's subjects from participating in the advantages of trade in the new lands, unless an exception was made for some signal service. This rule, indeed, prevailed, even after Ferdinand began to reign alone.

There is something quite as amusing as edifying in the osten-
Aims of the sible purposes of all this endeavor. To tap the re-
expedition. sources of the luxuriant East might be gratifying, but it was holy to conceive that the energies of the undertaking were going to fill the treasury out of which a new crusade for the rescue of the Holy Sepulchre could be sustained. The pearls and spices of the Orient, the gold and precious jewels of its mines, might conduce to the gorgeous and luxurious display of the throne, but there was a noble condescension in giving Co-
End of the lumbus a gracious letter to the Great Khan, and in
world ap- hoping to seduce his subjects to the sway of a religion
proaching. that allowed to the heathen no rights but conversion. There was at least a century and a half of such holy endeavors left for the ministrants of the church, as was believed, since the seven thousand years of the earth's duration was within one hundred and fifty-five years of its close, as the calculations of King Alonso showed. Columbus had been further drawn to these conclusions from his study of that conglomerating cardinal, Pierre d'Ailly, whose works, in a full edition, had been at this time only a few months in the book stalls. Humboldt has gone into an examination of the data to show that Columbus's calculation was singularly inexact; but the labor of verification seems hardly necessary, except as a curious study of absurdities. Columbus's career has too many such to detain us on any one.

On April 17, 1492, the King and Queen signed at Santa Fé
1492. April and delivered to Columbus a passport to all persons
17. Agree- in unknown parts, commending the Admiral to their
ment with
Columbus. friendship. This paper is preserved in Barcelona. On the same day the monarchs agreed to the conditions of a document which was drawn by the royal secretary, Juan de

Coloma, and is preserved among the papers of the Duke of Veragua. It was printed from that copy by Navarrete, and is again printed by Bergenroth as found at Barcelona. As formulated in English by Irving, its purport is as follows : —

1. That Columbus should have for himself during his life, and for his heirs and successors forever, the office of Admiral in all the lands and continents which he might discover or acquire in the ocean, with similar honors and prerogatives to those enjoyed by the high admiral of Castile in his district.

2. That he should be viceroy and governor-general over all the said lands and continents, with the privilege of nominating three candidates for the government of each island or province, one of whom should be selected by the sovereigns.

3. That he should be entitled to reserve for himself one tenth of all pearls, precious stones, gold, silver, spices, and all other articles of merchandises, in whatever manner found, bought, bartered, or gained within his admiralty, the costs being first deducted.

4. That he or his lieutenant should be the sole judge in all causes or disputes arising out of traffic between those countries and Spain, provided the high admiral of Castile had similar jurisdiction in his district.

5. That he might then and at all after times contribute an eighth part of the expense in fitting out vessels to sail on this enterprise, and receive an eighth part of the profits.

These capitulations were followed on the 30th of April by a commission which the sovereigns signed at Granada, in which it was further granted that the Admiral and his heirs should use the prefix Don.

*1492. April 30. Columbus allowed to use the prefix Don.*

It is supposed he now gave some heed to his domestic concerns. We know nothing, however, of any provision for the lonely Beatrix, but it is said that he placed his boy Ferdinand, then but four years of age, at school in Cordoba near his mother. He left his lawful son, Diego, well provided for through an appointment by the Queen, on May 8, which made him page to Prince Juan, the heir apparent.

*Arranges his domestic affairs.*

Columbus himself tells us that he then left Granada on the 12th of May, 1492, and went direct to Palos; stopping, however, on the way at Rabida, to exchange congratulations with its friar, Juan Perez, if indeed he did not lodge at the convent during his stay in the seaport.

*1492. May. Reaches Palos.*

Palos to-day consists of a double street of lowly, whitened

Palos described. houses, in a depression among the hills. The guides point out the ruins of a larger house, which was the home of the Pinzons. The Moorish mosque, converted into St. George's church in Columbus's day, still stands on the hill, just outside the village, with an image of St. George and the dragon over its high altar, just as Columbus saw it, while above the church are existing ruins of an old Moorish castle.

The story which Las Casas has told of the fitting out of the

Ships fitted out. vessels does not agree in some leading particulars with that which Navarrete holds to be more safely drawn from the documents which he has published. The fact seems to be that two of the vessels of Columbus were not constructed by the Duke of Medina-Sidonia, and later bought by the Queen, as Las Casas says ; but, it happening that the town of Palos, in consequence of some offense to the royal dignity, had been mulcted in the service of two armed caravels for twelve months, the opportunity was now taken by royal order, dated April 30, 1492, of assigning this service of crews and vessels to Columbus's fateful expedition.

The royal command had also provided that Columbus might

The Pinzons aid him. add a third vessel, which he did with the aid, it is supposed, of the Pinzons, though there is no documentary proof to show whence he acquired the necessary means. Las Casas and Herrera, however, favor the supposition, and it is of course sustained in the evidence adduced in the famous trial which was intended to magnify the service of the Pinzons. It was also directed that the seamen of the little fleet should receive the usual wages of those serving in armed vessels, and be paid four months in advance. All maritime towns were enjoined to furnish supplies at a reasonable price. All criminal processes against anybody engaged for the voyage were to be suspended, and this suspension was to last for two months after the return.

It was on the 23d of May that, accompanied by Juan Perez,

1492. May 23. Demands two ships of Palos. Columbus met the people of Palos assembled in the church of St. George, while a notary read the royal commands laid upon the town. It took a little time for the simple people to divine the full extent of such an order, — its consignment of fellow-creatures to the dreaded evils of the great unknown ocean. The reluctance to enter upon the undertaking proved so great, except among a few prisoners taken from the jails, that it became necessary to report the obstacle to the Court, when a new peremptory order was issued on June 20 to impress the vessels and crews. Juan de Peñalosa, an officer of the royal household, appeared in Palos to enforce this demand. Even such imperative measures availed little, and it was not till Martin Alonso Pinzon came forward, and either by an agreement to divide with Columbus the profits, or through some other understanding, — for the testimony on the point is doubtful, and Las Casas disbelieves any such division of profits, — exerted his influence, in which he was aided by his brother, also a navigator, Vicente Yañez Pinzon. There is a story traceable to a son of the elder Pinzon, who testified in the Columbus lawsuit that Martin Alonso had at one time become convinced of the existence of western lands from some documents and charts which he had seen at Rome. The story, like that of his companionship with Cousin, already referred to, has in it, however, many elements of suspicion.

*1492. June 20. Vessels and crews impressed.*

*The Pinzons.*

This help of the Pinzons proved opportune and did much to save the cause, for it had up to this time seemed impossible to get vessels or crews. The standing of these navigators as men and their promise to embark personally put a new complexion on the undertaking, and within a month the armament was made up. Harrisse has examined the evidence in the matter to see if there is any proof that the Pinzons contributed more than their personal influence, but there is no apparent ground for believing they did, unless they stood behind Columbus in his share of the expenses, which are computed at 500,000 maravedis, while those of the Queen, arranged through Santangel, are reckoned at 1,140,000 of that money. The fleet consisted, as Peter Martyr tells us, of two open caravels, " Nina " and " Pinta " — the latter, with its crew, being pressed into the service, — decked only at the extremities, where high prows and poops gave quarters for the crews and their officers. A large-decked vessel of the register known as a carack, and renamed by Columbus the " Santa Maria," which proved " a dull sailer and unfit for discovery," was taken by Columbus as his flagship. There is some confusion in the testimony relating to the name of this ship. The *Historie* alone calls her by this name. Las Casas simply styles her "The Captain." One of the pilots speaks of her as the "Mari Galante." Her owner was one Juan de la Cosa, apparently not the same person as the navigator and cosmographer later to be met, and he had command of her, while Pero Alonso Nino and Sancho Ruis served as pilots.

Captain G. V. Fox has made an estimate of her dimensions Character of from her reputed tonnage by the scale of that time, the ships. and thinks she was sixty-three feet over all in length, fifty-one feet along her keel, twenty feet beam, and ten and a half in depth.

The two Pinzons were assigned to the command of the other caravels, — Martin Alonso to the "Pinta," the larger of the two, with a third brother of his as pilot, and Vicente Yañez to the "Nina." Many obstacles and the natural repugnances of sailors to embark in so hazardous a service still delayed the preparations, but by the beginning of August the arrangements were complete, and a hundred and twenty persons, as Peter The crews. Martyr and Oviedo tell us, but perhaps the *Historie* and Las Casas are more correct in saying ninety in all, were ready to be committed to what many of them felt were most desperate fortunes. Duro has of late published in his *Colón y Pinzon* what purports to be a list of their names. It shows in Tallerte de Lajes a native of England who has been thought to be one named in his vernacular Arthur Lake ; and Guillemio Ires, called of Galway, has sometimes been fancied to have borne in his own land the name perhaps of Rice, Herries, or Harris. There was no lack of the formal assignments usual in such important undertakings. There was a notary to record the proceedings and a historian to array the story ; an interpreter to be prepared with Latin, Greek, Hebrew, Arabic, Coptic, and Armenian, in the hopes that one of these tongues might serve in intercourse with the great Asiatic potentates, and a metallurgist to pronounce upon precious ores. They were not without a physician and a surgeon. It does not appear if their hazards should require the last solemn rites that there was any priest to shrive them ; but Columbus determined to start with all the solemnity that a confession and the communion could impart, and this service was performed by Juan Perez, both for him and for his entire company.

The directions of the Crown also provided that Columbus should avoid the Guinea coast and all other posses- <small>Sailing directions from the Crown.</small> sions of the Portuguese, which seems to be little more than a striking manifestation of a certain kind of in- credulity respecting what Columbus, after all, meant by sailing west. Indeed, there was necessarily more or less vagueness in everybody's mind as to what a western passage would reveal, or how far a westerly course might of necessity be swung one way or the other.

The *Historie* tells us distinctly that Columbus hoped to find some intermediate land before reaching India, to be <small>Islands first to be sought.</small> used, as the modern phrase goes, as a sort of base of operations. This hope rested on the belief, then common, that there was more land than sea on the earth, and consequently that no wide stretch of ocean could exist without interlying lands.

There was, moreover, no confidence that such things as floating islands might not be encountered. Pliny and Seneca had described them, and Columbus was inclined to believe that St. Brandan and the Seven Cities, and such isles as the dwellers at the Azores had claimed to see in the offing, might be of this character.

There seems, in fact, to be ground for believing that Columbus thought his course to the Asiatic shores could hardly fail to bring him in view of other regions or islands lying in the western ocean. Muñoz holds that "the glory of such discoveries inflamed him still more, perhaps, than his chief design."

That a vast archipelago would be the first land encountered was not without confident believers. The Catalan <small>Asiatic archipelago.</small> map of 1374 had shown such islands in vast numbers, amounting to 7,548 in all; Marco Polo had made them 12,700, or was thought to do so; and Behaim was yet to cite the latter on his globe.

It was, indeed, at this very season that Behaim, having returned from Lisbon to his home in Nuremberg, had <small>Behaim's globe.</small> imparted to the burghers of that inland town those great cosmographical conceptions, which he was accustomed to hear discussed in the Atlantic seaports. Such views were exemplified in a large globe which Behaim had spent the summer in constructing in Nuremberg. It was made of pasteboard cov-

BEHAIM'S GLOBE, 1492.

*Note.* The curved sides of these cuts divide the Globe in the mid Atlantic.

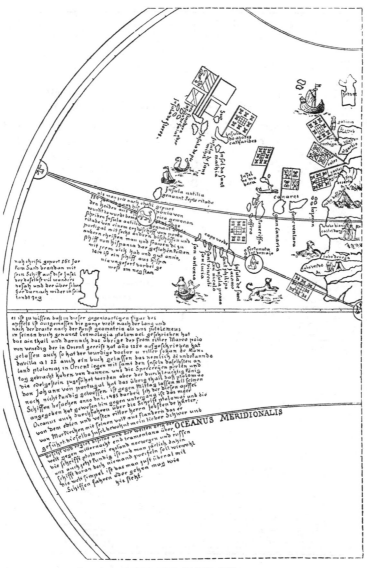

BEHAIM'S GLOBE, 1492.

[Taken from Ernest Mayer's *Die Hilfsmittel der Schiffahrtskunde* (Wein, 1879).]

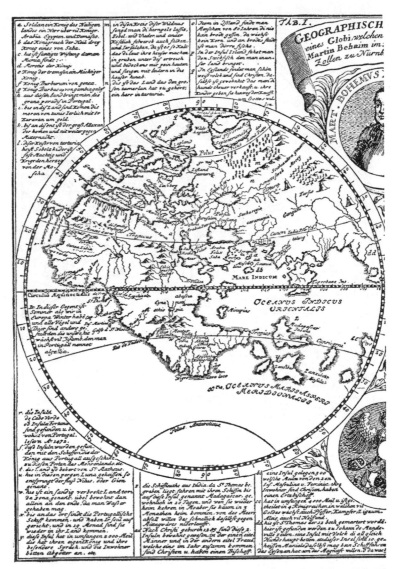

DOPPELMAYER'S ENGRAVING OF

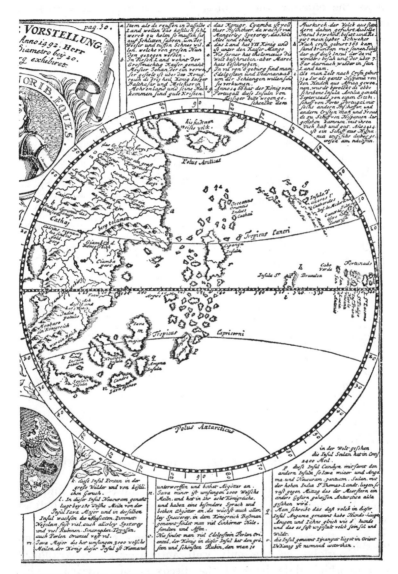

BEHAIM'S GLOBE, MUCH REDUCED.

ered with parchment, and is twenty-one inches in diameter. It shows the equator, the tropics, the polar circle, in a latitudinal way ; but the first meridian, passing through Madeira, is the only one of the longitudinal sectors which it represents.

THE ACTUAL AMERICA IN RELATION TO BEHAIM'S GEOGRAPHY.

Behaim had in this work the help of Holtzschner, and the globe has come down to our day, preserved in the town hall at Nuremberg, one of the sights and honors of that city. It shares Laon globe.          the credit, however, with another, called the Laon globe, as the only well-authenticated geographical spheres which date back of the discovery of America. This Laon globe is much smaller, being only six inches in diameter ; and though it is dated 1493, it is thought to have been made a few years earlier, — as D'Avezac thinks, in 1486.

Clements R. Markham, in a recent edition of Robert Hues' *Tractatus de Globis*, cites Nordenskiöld as considering Behaim's globe, without comparison, the most important geographical document since the atlas of Ptolemy, in A. D. 150. "He points out that it is the first which unreservedly adopts the existence of antipodes; the first which clearly shows that there is a passage from Europe to India; the first which attempts to deal with the discoveries of Marco Polo. It is an exact representation of geographical knowledge immediately previous to the first voyage of Columbus."

The Behaim globe has become familiar by many published drawings.

It has been claimed that Columbus probably took with him, on his voyage, the map which he had received from Toscanelli, with its delineation of the interjacent and island-studded ocean, which washed alike the shores of Europe and Asia, and that it was the subject of study by him and Pinzon at a time when Columbus refers in his journal to the use they made of a chart. Toscanelli's map.

That Toscanelli's map long survived the voyage is known, and Las Casas used it. Humboldt has not the same confidence which Sprengel had, that at this time it crossed the sea in the "Santa Maria;" and he is inclined rather to suppose that the details of Toscanelli's chart, added to all others which Columbus had gathered from the maps of Bianco and Benincasa — for it is not possible he could have seen the work of Behaim, unless indeed, in fragmentary preconceptions — must have served him better as laid down on a chart of his own drafting. There is good reason to suppose that, more than once, with the skill which he is known to have possessed, he must have made such charts, to enforce and demonstrate his belief, which, though in the main like that of Toscanelli, were in matters of distance quite different.

So, everything being ready, on the third of August, 1492, a half hour before sunrise, he unmoored his little fleet in the stream and, spreading his sails, the vessels passed out of the little river roadstead of Palos, gazed after, 1492, August 3, Columbus sails.
perhaps, in the increasing light, as the little crafts reached the ocean, by the friar of Rabida, from its distant promontory of rock.

The day was Friday, and the advocates of Columbus's canon-

On Friday. ization have not failed to see a purpose in its choice, as the day of our Redemption, and as that of the de- liverance of the Holy Sepulchre by Geoffrey de Bouillon, and

SHIPS OF COLUMBUS'S TIME.
(From Medina's *Arte de Navegar*, 1545.)

of the rendition of Granada, with the fall of the Moslem power in Spain. We must resort to the books of such advocates, if we would enliven the picture with a multitude of rites and devotional feelings that they gather in the meshes of the story of the departure. They supply to the embarkation a variety of detail that their holy purposes readily imagine, and place Columbus at last on his poop, with the standard of the Cross, the image of the Saviour nailed to the holy wood, waving in the early breezes that heralded the day. The embellishments may be pleasing, but they are not of the strictest authenticity.

SHIP, 1486.

In order that his performance of an embassy to the princes of the East might be duly chronicled, Columbus deter- Keeps a mined, as his journal says, to keep an account of the journal. voyage by the west, "by which course," he says, "unto the present time, we do not know, *for certain*, that any one has passed." It was his purpose to write down, as he proceeded, everything he saw and all that he did, and to make a chart of his discoveries, and to show the directions of his track.

Nothing occurred during those early August days to mar his

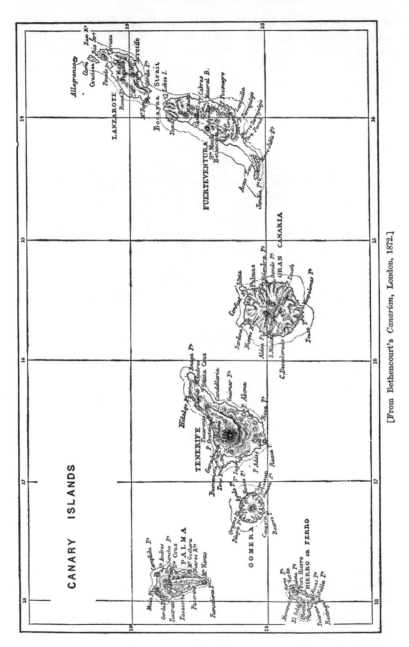

[From Bethencourt's *Canarian*, London, 1872.]

run to the Canaries, except the apprehension which he felt
that an accident, happening to the rudder of the " Pin- The "Pinta" disabled.
ta," — a steering gear now for some time in use, in
place of the old lateral paddles, — was a trick of two
men, her owners, Gomez Rascon and Christopher Quintero, to
impede a voyage in which they had no heart. The Admiral
knew the disposition of these men well enough not to be surprised at the mishap, but he tried to feel secure in the prompt
energy of Pinzon, who commanded the " Pinta."

As he passed (August 24–25, 1492) the peak of Teneriffe,
it was the time of an eruption, of which he makes bare Reaches the Canaries.
mention in his journal. It is to the corresponding
passages of the *Historie*, that we owe the somewhat sensational
stories of the terrors of the sailors, some of whom certainly must
long have been accustomed to like displays in the volcanoes of
the Mediterranean.

At the Gran Canaria the " Nina " was left to have her
lateen sails changed to square ones; and the " Pinta," it being
found impossible to find a better vessel to take her place, was
also left to be overhauled for her leaks, and to have her rudder again repaired, while Columbus visited Gomera, another
of the islands. The fleet was reunited at Gomera on September 2. Here he fell in with some residents of Ferro, the westernmost of the group, who repeated the old stories of land
occasionally seen from its heights, lying towards the setting
sun. Having taken on board wood, water, and provisions,
Columbus finally sailed from Gomera on the morning of Thurs-
day, September 6. He seems to have soon spoken 1492. September 6, leaves Gomera.
a vessel from Ferro, and from this he learned that
three Portuguese caravels were lying in wait for him
in the neighborhood of that island, with a purpose as he thought
of visiting in some way upon him, for having gone over to the
interests of Spain, the indignation of the Portuguese king. He
escaped encountering them.

Up to Sunday, September 9, they had experienced so much
calm weather, that their progress had been slow. This Sunday, September 9, 1492.
tediousness soon raised an apprehension in the mind
of Columbus that the voyage might prove too long
for the constancy of his men. He accordingly determined to
falsify his reckoning. This deceit was a large con- Falsifies his reckoning.
fession of his own timidity in dealing with his crew,

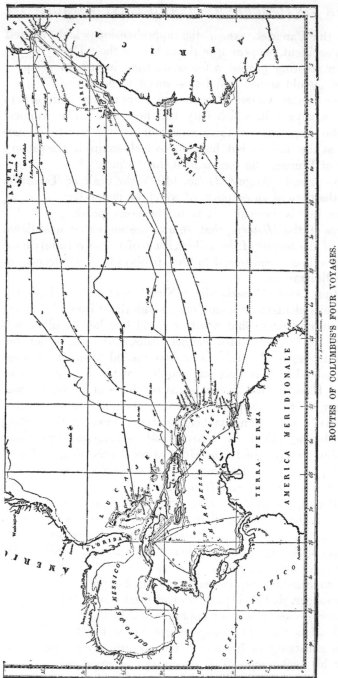

ROUTES OF COLUMBUS'S FOUR VOYAGES.

[Taken from the map in Blanchero's *La Tavola di Bronzo* (Geneva, 1857).]

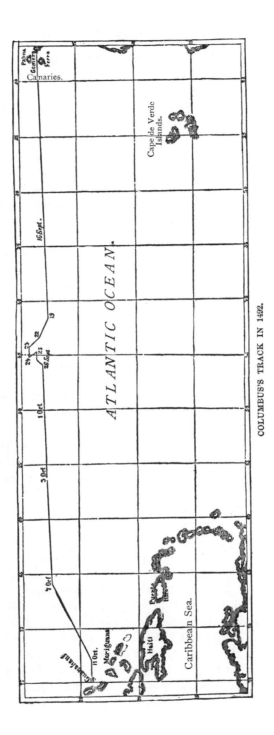

COLUMBUS'S TRACK IN 1492.

and it marked the beginning of a long struggle with deceived and mutinous subordinates, which forms so large a part of the record of his subsequent career.

The result of Monday's sail, which he knew to be sixty leagues, he noted as forty-eight, so that the distance from home might appear less than it was. He continued to practice this deceit.

The distances given by Columbus are those of dead reckoning beyond any question. Lieutenant Murdock, of the United States navy, who has commented on this voyage, makes his league the equivalent of three modern nautical miles, and his mile about three quarters of our present estimate for that distance. Navarrete says that Columbus reckoned in Italian miles, which are a quarter less than a Spanish mile. The Admiral had expected to make land after sailing about seven hundred leagues from Ferro ; and in ordering his vessels in case of separation to proceed westward, he warned them when they sailed that distance to come to the wind at night, and only to proceed by day.

His dead reckoning.

The log as at present understood in navigation had not yet been devised. Columbus depended in judging of his speed on the eye alone, basing his calculations on the passage of objects or bubbles past the ship, while the running out of his hour glasses afforded the multiple for long distances.

On Thursday, the 13th of September, he notes that the ships were encountering adverse currents. He was now three degrees west of Flores, and the needle of the compass pointed as it had never been observed before, directly to the true north. His observation of this fact marks a significant point in the history of navigation. The polarity of the magnet, an ancient possession of the Chinese, had been known perhaps for three hundred years, when this new spirit of discovery awoke in the fifteenth century. The Indian Ocean and its traditions were to impart, perhaps through the Arabs, perhaps through the returning Crusaders, a knowledge of the magnet to the dwellers on the shores of the Mediterranean, and to the hardier mariners who pushed beyond the Pillars of Hercules, so that the new route to that same Indian Ocean was made possible in the fifteenth century. The way was prepared for it

1492. September 13.

Reaches point of no variation of the needle.

Knowledge of the magnet.

gradually. The Catalans from the port of Barcelona pushed out into the great Sea of Darkness under the direction of their needles, as early at least as the twelfth century. The pilots of Genoa and Venice, the hardy Majorcans and the adventurous Moors, were followers of almost equal temerity.

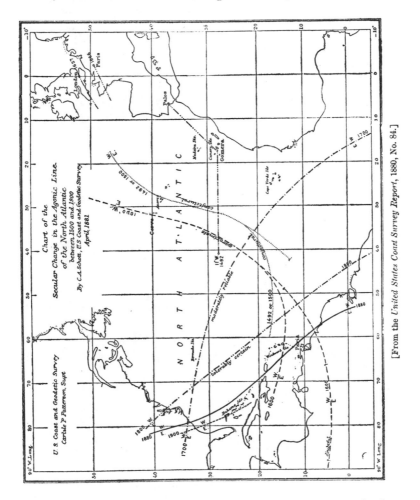

[From the *United States Coast Survey Report*, 1880, No. 84.]

A knowledge of the variation of the needle came more slowly to be known to the mariners of the Mediterranean. Variation of It had been observed by Peregrini as early as 1269, the needle. but that knowledge of it which rendered it greatly serviceable in voyages does not seem to be plainly indicated in any of the charts of these transition centuries, till we find it laid down on the maps of Andrea Bianco in 1436.

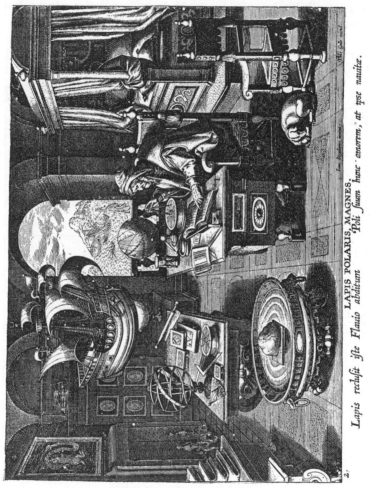

[From Hirth's *Bilderbuch*, vol. iii.]

It was no new thing then when Columbus, as he sailed westward, marked the variation, proceeding from the northeast more and more westerly; but it was a revelation when he came to a position where the magnetic north and the north star stood in conjunction, as they did on this 13th of September, 1492.

As he still moved westerly the magnetic line was found to move farther and farther away from the pole as it had before the 13th approached it. To an observer of Columbus's quick perceptions, there was a ready guess to possess his mind. This inference was that this line of no varia- tion was a meridian line, and that divergences from it east and west might have a regularity which would be found to furnish a method of ascertaining longitude far easier and surer than tables or water clocks. We know that four years later he tried to sail his ship on observations of this kind. The same idea seems to have occurred to Sebastian Cabot, when a little afterwards he approached and passed in a higher latitude, what he supposed to be the meridian of no variation. Humboldt is inclined to believe that the possibility of such a method of ascertaining longitude was that uncommunicable secret, which Sebastian Cabot many years later hinted at on his death-bed.

Columbus's misconception of the line of no variation.

Sebastian Cabot's observations of its help in determining longitude.

The claim was made near a century later by Livio Sanuto in his *Geographia*, published at Venice, in 1588, that Sebastian Cabot had been the first to observe this variation, and had explained it to Edward VI., and that he had on a chart placed the line of no variation at a point one hundred and ten miles west of the island of Flores in the Azores.

These observations of Columbus and Cabot were not wholly accepted during the sixteenth century. Robert Hues, in 1592, a hundred years later, tells us that Medina, the Span- ish grand pilot, was not disinclined to believe that mariners saw more in it than really existed and that they found it a convenient way to excuse their own blunders. Nonius was credited with saying that it simply meant that worn-out mag- nets were used, which had lost their power to point correctly to the pole. Others had contended that it was through insufficient application of the loadstone to the iron that it was so devious in its work.

Various views.

What was thought possible by the early navigators possessed the minds of all seamen in varying experiments for two cen- turies and a half. Though not reaching such satisfactory re- sults as were hoped for, the expectation did not prove so chimer- ical as was sometimes imagined when it was discovered that the lines of variation were neither parallel, nor straight, nor con-

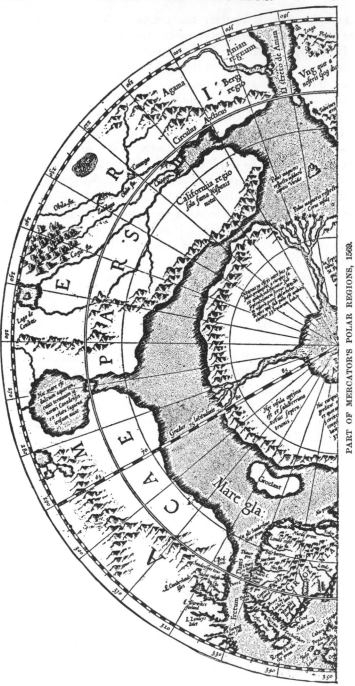

PART OF MERCATOR'S POLAR REGIONS, 1569.

[From R. Mercator's Atlas of 1595.]

stant. The line of no variation which Columbus found near the Azores has moved westward with erratic inclinations, Better understood. Carolina to Guiana. Science, beginning with its crude efforts at the hands of Alonzo de Santa Cruz, in 1530, has so mapped the surface of the globe with observations of its multifarious freaks of variation, and the changes are so slow, that a magnetic chart is not a bad guide to-day for ascertaining the longitude in any latitude for a few years neighboring to the date of its records. So science has come round in some measure to the dreams of Columbus and Cabot.

But this was not the only development which came from this ominous day in the mid Atlantic in that September Columbus of 1492. The fancy of Columbus was easily excited, remarks on and notions of a change of climate, and even aberra-changes of temperature tions of the stars were easily imagined by him amid and aberrations of stars. the strange phenomena of that untracked waste.

While Columbus was suspecting that the north star was somewhat willfully shifting from the magnetic pole, now to a distance of 5° and then of 10°, the calculations of modern astronomers have gauged the polar distance existing in 1492 at 3° 28', as against the 1° 20' of to-day. The confusion of Columbus was very like his confounding an old world with a new, inasmuch as he supposed it was the pole star and not the needle which was shifting.

He argued from what he saw, or thought he saw, that the line of no variation marked the beginning of a protuber-Imagines a ance of the earth, up which he ascended as he sailed protuberance on the westerly, and that this was the reason of the cooler earth. weather which he experienced. He never got over some notions of this kind, and believed he found confirmation of them in his later voyages.

Even as early as the reign of Edward III. of England, Nich olas of Lynn, a voyager to the northern seas, is thought The magto have definitely fixed the magnetic pole in the Arctic netic pole. regions, transmitting his views to Cnoyen, the master of the later Mercator, in respect to the four circumpolar islands, which in the sixteenth century made so constant a surrounding of the northern pole.

The next day (September 14), after these magnetic observa-
1492. September 14. tions, a water wagtail was seen from the " Nina," — a
bird which Columbus thought unaccustomed to fly
over twenty-five leagues from land, and the ships were now, according to their reckoning, not far from two hundred leagues
September 15. from the Canaries. On Saturday, they saw a distant
bolt of fire fall into the sea. On Sunday, they had a
drizzling rain, followed by pleasant weather, which reminded
September 16. Columbus of the nightingales, gladdening the climate
of Andalusia in April. They found around the ships
much green floatage of weeds, which led them to think some
islands must be near. Navarrete thinks there was some truth
in this, inasmuch as the charts of the early part of this century
represent breakers as having been seen in 1802, near the spot
where Columbus can be computed to have been at this time.
Columbus was in fact within that extensive *prairie* of floating
Sargasso Sea. seaweed which is known as the Sargasso Sea, whose
principal longitudinal axis is found in modern times
to lie along the parallel of 41° 30', and the best calculations
which can be made from the rather uncertain data of Columbus's journal seem to point to about the same position.

There is nothing in all these accounts, as we have them
abridged by Las Casas, to indicate any great surprise, and certainly nothing of the overwhelming fear which, the *Historie*
tells us, the sailors experienced when they found their ships
among these floating masses of weeds, raising apprehension of
a perpetual entanglement in their swashing folds.

The next day (September 17) the currents became favor-
1492. September 17. able, and the weeds still floated about them. The
variation of the needle now became so great that the
seamen were dismayed, as the journal says, and the observation
being repeated Columbus practiced another deceit and made it
appear that there had been really no variation, but only a shifting of the polar star ! The weeds were now judged to be river
weeds, and a live crab was found among them, — a sure sign of
near land, as Columbus believed, or affected to believe. They
killed a tunny and saw others. They again observed a water
wagtail, " which does not sleep at sea." Each ship pushed on
September 18. for the advance, for it was thought the goal was near.
The next day the " Pinta " shot ahead and saw

great flocks of birds towards the west. Columbus conceived
that the sea was growing fresher. Heavy clouds hung on the
northern horizon, a sure sign of land, it was supposed.

On the next day two pelicans came on board, and Columbus
records that these birds are not accustomed to go 1492. Sep-
twenty leagues from land. So he sounded with a line tember 19.
of two hundred fathoms to be sure he was not approaching
land; but no bottom was found. A drizzling rain also betokened land, which they could not stop to find, but would
search for on their return, as the journal says. The pilots now
compared their reckonings. Columbus said they were 400
leagues, while the " Pinta's " record showed 420, and the
" Nina's " 440.

On September 20, other pelicans came on board; and the
ships were again among the weeds. Columbus was de- 1492. Sep-
termined to ascertain if these indicated shoal water and tember 20.
sounded, but could not reach bottom. The men caught a bird
with feet like a gull; but they were convinced it was a river
bird. Then singing land-birds, as was fancied, hovered about
as it darkened, but they disappeared before morning. Then
a pelican was observed flying to the southwest, and as " these
birds sleep on shore, and go to sea in the morning," the men encouraged themselves with the belief that they could not be far
from land. The next day a whale could but be another indication of land; and the weeds covered the sea all about. On
Saturday, they steered west by northwest, and got September
clear of the weeds. This change of course so far to 22. Changes
the north, which had begun on the previous day, was his course.
occasioned by a head wind, and Columbus says that he welcomed it, because it had the effect of convincing the
sailors that westerly winds to return by were not im- Head wind.
possible. On Sunday (September 23), they found the wind still
varying; but they made more westering than before, — weeds,
crabs, and birds still about them. Now there was smooth water, which again depressed the seamen; then the sea September
arose, mysteriously, for there was no wind to cause 25.
it. They still kept their course westerly and continued it till
the night of September 25.

Columbus at this time conferred with Pinzon, as to a chart
which they carried, which showed some islands, near where they

now supposed the ships to be. That they had not seen land, they believed was either due to currents which had carried them too far north, or else their reckoning was not correct. At sunset Pinzon hailed the Admiral, and said he saw land, claiming the reward. The two crews were confident that such was the case, and under the lead of their commanders they all kneeled and repeated the *Gloria in Excelsis.* The land appeared to lie southwest, and everybody saw the apparition. Columbus changed the fleet's course to reach it; and as the vessels went on, in the smooth sea, the men had the heart, under their expectation, to bathe in its amber glories. On Wednesday, they were undeceived, and found that the clouds had played them a trick. On the 27th their course lay more directly west. So they went on, and still remarked upon all the birds they saw and weed-drift which they pierced. Some of the fowl they thought to be such as were common at the Cape de Verde Islands, and were not supposed to go far to sea. On the 30th September, they still observed the needles of their compasses to vary, but the journal records that it was the pole star which moved, and not the needle. On October 1, Columbus says they were 707 leagues from Ferro; but he had made his crew believe they were only 584. As they went on, little new for the next few days is recorded in the journal; but on October 3, they thought they saw among the weeds something like fruits. By the 6th, Pinzon began to urge a southwesterly course, in order to find the islands, which the signs seemed to indicate in that direction. Still the Admiral would not swerve from his purpose, and kept his course westerly. On Sunday, the "Nina" fired a bombard and hoisted a flag as a signal that she saw land, but it proved a delusion. Observing towards evening a flock of birds flying to the southwest, the Admiral yielded to Pinzon's belief, and shifted his course to follow the birds. He records as a further reason for it that it was by following the flight of birds that the Portuguese had been so successful in discovering islands in other seas.

Columbus now found himself two hundred miles and more farther than the three thousand miles west of Spain, where he

*Appearances of land.*

*Again changes his course.*

*September 26.*

*1492. September 27.*

*September 30.*

*October 1.*

*October 3.*

*October 6.*

*October 7.*

*Shifts his course to follow some birds.*

supposed Cipango to lie, and he was $25\frac{1}{2}°$ north of the equator, according to his astrolabe. The true distance of Ci- pango or Japan was sixty-eight hundred miles still <sub></sub>Cipango. farther, or beyond both North America and the Pacific. How much beyond that island, in its supposed geographical position, Columbus expected to find the Asiatic main we can only conjecture from the restorations which modern scholars have made of Toscanelli's map, which makes the island about 10° east of Asia, and from Behaim's globe, which makes it 20°. It should be borne in mind that the knowledge of its position came from Marco Polo, and he does not distinctly say how far it was from the Asiatic coast. In a general way, as to these distances from Spain to China, Toscanelli and Behaim agreed, and there is no reason to believe that the views of Columbus were in any noteworthy degree different.

In the trial, years afterwards, when the Fiscal contested the rights of Diego Colon, it was put in evidence by  Relations of one Vallejo, a seaman, that Pinzon was induced to  Pinzon to the change urge the direction to be changed to the southwest, be-  of course. cause he had in the preceding evening observed a flight of parrots in that direction, which could have only been seeking land. It was the main purpose of the evidence in this part of the trial to show that Pinzon had all along forced Columbus forward against his will.

How pregnant this change of course in the vessels of Columbus was has not escaped the observation of Humboldt and many others. A day or two further on his westerly way, and the Gulf Stream would, perhaps, insensibly have borne the little fleet up the Atlantic coast of the future United States, so that the banner of Castile might have been planted at Carolina.

On the 7th of October, Columbus was pretty nearly in latitude 25° 50′, — that of one of the Bahama Islands. Just where he was by longitude there is much more  October 7. doubt, probably between 65° and 66°. On the next day the land birds flying along the course of the ships seemed  October to confirm their hopes. On the 10th the journal re-  8-10. cords that the men began to lose patience ; but the Admiral reassured them by reminding them of the profits in store for them, and of the folly of seeking to return, when they had already gone so far.

It is possible that, in this entry, Columbus conceals the story
Story of a mutiny. which later came out in the recital of Oviedo, with
more detail than in the *Historie* and Las Casas, that
the rebellion of his crew was threatening enough to oblige him
to promise to turn back if land was not discovered in three
days. Most commentators, however, are inclined to think that
this story of a mutinous revolt was merely engrafted from hearsay or other source by Oviedo upon the more genuine recital,
and that the conspiracy to throw the Admiral into the sea has
no substantial basis in contemporary report. Irving, who has
a dramatic tendency throughout his whole account of the voyage
to heighten his recital with touches of the imagination, nevertheless allows this, and thinks that Oviedo was misled by listening
to a pilot, who was a personal enemy of the Admiral.

The elucidations of the voyage which were drawn out in the
famous suit of Diego with the Crown in 1513 and 1515, afford
no ground for any belief in this story of the mutiny and the
concession of Columbus to it.

It is not, however, difficult to conceive the recurrent fears of
his men and the incessant anxiety of Columbus to quiet them.
From what Peter Martyr tells us, — and he may have got it
directly from Columbus's lips, — the task was not an easy one
to preserve subordination and to instill confidence. He represents that Columbus was forced to resort in turn to argument,
persuasion, and enticements, and to picture the misfortunes of
the royal displeasure.

The next day, notwithstanding a heavier sea than they had
1492. October 11. before encountered, certain signs sufficed to lift them
out of their despondency. These were floating logs,
or pieces of wood, one of them apparently carved by hand, bits
of cane, a green rush, a stalk of rose berries, and other drifting
tokens.

Their southwesterly course had now brought them down to
1492. Octo-ber 11. Steer west. about the twenty-fourth parallel, when after sunset on
the 11th they shifted their course to due west, while
the crew of the Admiral's ship united, with more fervor
than usual, in the *Salve Regina*. At about ten o'clock Columbus,
Columbus sees a light. peering into the night, thought he saw — if we may
believe him — a moving light, and pointing out the
direction to Pero Gutierrez, this companion saw it too; but an-

other, Rodrigo Sanchez, situated apparently on another part of the vessel, was not able to see it. It was not brought to the attention of any others. The Admiral says that the light seemed to be moving up and down, and he claimed to have got other glimpses of its glimmer at a later moment. He ordered the *Salve* to be chanted, and directed a vigilant watch to be set on the forecastle. To sharpen their vision he promised a silken jacket, beside the income of ten thousand maravedis which the King and Queen had offered to the fortunate man who should first descry the coveted land.

This light has been the occasion of much comment, and nothing will ever, it is likely, be settled about it, further than that the Admiral, with an inconsiderate rivalry of a common sailor who later saw the actual land, and with an ungenerous assurance ill-befitting a commander, pocketed a reward which belonged to another. If Oviedo, with his prejudices, is to be believed, Columbus was not even the first who claimed to have seen this dubious light. There is a common story that the poor sailor, who was defrauded, later turned Mohammedan, and went to live among that juster people. There is a sort of retributive justice in the fact that the pension of the Crown was made a charge upon the shambles of Seville, and thence Columbus received it till he died.

Whether the light is to be considered a reality or a fiction will depend much on the theory each may hold regarding the position of the landfall. When Columbus claimed to have discovered it, he was twelve or fourteen leagues away from the island where, four hours later, land was indubitably found. Was the light on a canoe? Was it on some small, outlying island, as has been suggested? Was it a torch carried from hut to hut, as Herrera avers? Was it on either of the other vessels? Was it on the low island on which, the next morning, he landed? There was no elevation on that island sufficient to show even a strong light at a distance of ten leagues. Was it a fancy or a a deceit? No one can say. It is very difficult for Navarrete, and even for Irving, to rest satisfied with what, after all, may have been only an illusion of a fevered mind, making a record of the incident in the excitement of a wonderful hour, when his intelligence was not as circumspect as it might have been.

Four hours after the light was seen, at two o'clock in the

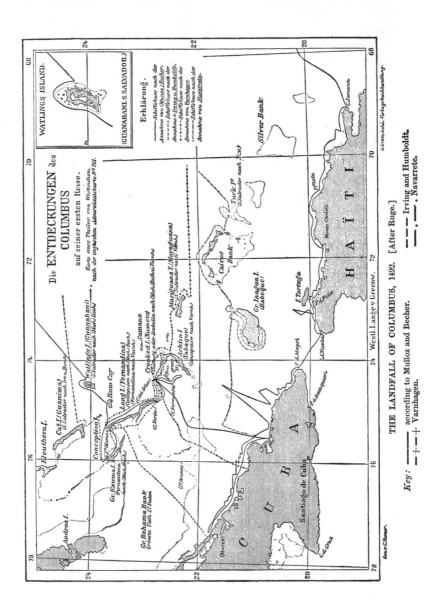

THE LANDFALL OF COLUMBUS, 1492. [After Ruge.]

*Key :* ———— according to Muñoz and Becher.  ———— Irving and Humboldt.
—+—+— +———+ .  ———·——· . Navarrete.

morning, when the moon, near its third quarter, was in the east, the "Pinta" keeping ahead, one of her sailors, Rodrigo de Triana, descried the land, two leagues away, <sub>1492, October 12, land discovered.</sub> and a gun communicated the joyful intelligence to the other ships. The fleet took in sail, and each vessel, under backed sheets, was pointed to the wind. Thus they waited for daybreak. It was a proud moment of painful suspense for

Columbus; and brimming hopes, perhaps fears of disappointment, must have accompanied that hour of wavering enchantment. It was Friday, October 12, of the old chronology, and the little fleet had been thirty-three days on its way from the Canaries, and we must add ten days more, to complete the period since they left Palos. The land before them was seen, as the day dawned, to be a small island, "called in the Indian tongue" Guanahani. Some <sub>Guanahani.</sub> naked natives were descried. The Admiral and the commanders of the other vessels prepared to land. Columbus took the royal standard and the others each a banner of the green cross, which bore the initials of the sovereign

COLUMBUS'S ARMOR.

with a cross between, a crown surmounting every letter. Thus, with the emblems of their power, and accompanied by Rodrigo de Escoveda and Rodrigo Sanchez and some seamen, the boat rowed to the shore. They immediately took formal possession of the land, and the notary recorded it.

The words of the prayer usually given as uttered by Columbus on taking possession of San Salvador, when he named the island, cannot be traced farther back <sub>Columbus lands and utters a prayer.</sub>

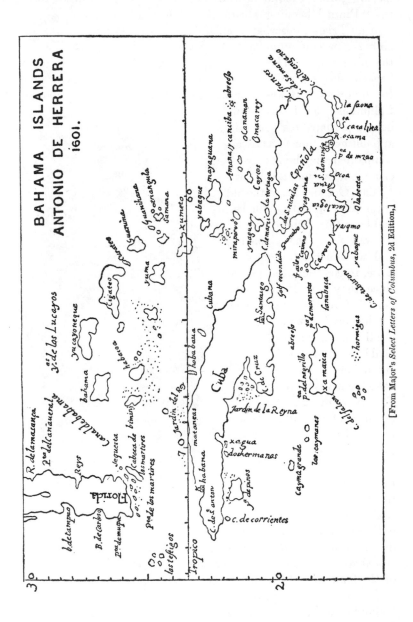

BAHAMA ISLANDS
ANTONIO DE HERRERA
1601.

[From Major's *Select Letters of Columbus*, 2d Edition.]

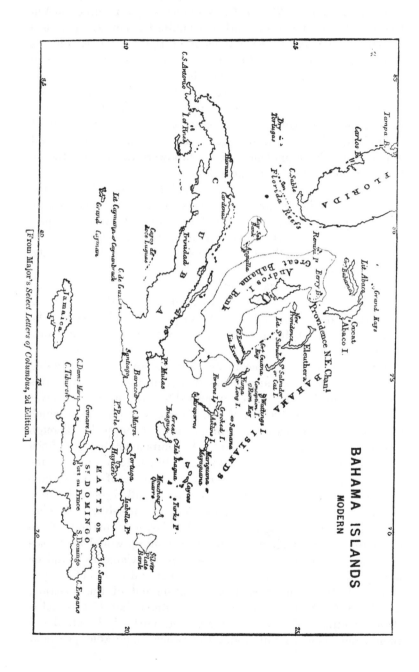

BAHAMA ISLANDS

MODERN

[From Major's *Select Letters of Columbus*, 2d Edition.]

than a collection of *Tablas Chronologicas*, got together at Valencia in 1689, by a Jesuit father, Claudio Clemente.   Harrisse finds no authority for the statement of the French canonizers that Columbus established a form of prayer which was long in vogue, for such occupations of new lands.

Las Casas, from whom we have the best account of the ceremonies of the landing, does not mention it; but we find pictured in his pages the grave impressiveness of the hour; the form of Columbus, with a crimson robe over his armor, central and grand ; and the humbleness of his followers in their contrition for the hours of their faint-heartedness.

Columbus now enters in his journal his impressions of the island and its inhabitants.   He says of the land that it bore

The island described. green trees, was watered by many streams, and produced divers fruits.   In another place he speaks of the island as flat, without lofty eminence, surrounded by reefs, with a lake in the interior.

The courses and distances of his sailing both before and on leaving the island, as well as this description, are the best means we have of identifying the spot of this portentous landfall.   The early maps may help in a subsidiary way, but with little precision.

There is just enough uncertainty and contradiction respecting

Identification of the landfall. the data and arguments applied in the solution of this question, to render it probable that men will never quite agree which of the Bahamas it was upon which these startled and exultant Europeans first stepped.   Though Las Casas reports the journal of Columbus unabridged for a period after the landfall, he unfortunately condenses it for some time previous.   There is apparently no chance of finding geographical conditions that in every respect will agree with this record of Columbus, and we must content ourselves with what offers the fewest disagreements.   An obvious method, if we could depend on Columbus's dead reckoning, would be to see for what island the actual distance from the Canaries would be nearest to his computed run ; but currents and errors of the eye necessarily throw this sort of computation out of the question, and Capt. G. A. Fox, who has tried it, finds that Cat Island is three hundred and seventeen, the Grand Turk six hundred and twenty-four nautical miles, and the other supposable points at intermediate distances out of the way as compared with his computation of the distance run by Columbus, three thousand four hundred and fifty-eight of such miles.

The reader will remember the Bahama group as a range of islands, islets, and rocks, said to be some three thou- The sand in number, running southeast from a point part Bahamas. way up the Florida coast, and approaching at the other end the coast of Hispaniola. In the latitude of the lower point of Florida, and five degrees east of it, is the isl- San Salva-dor, or Cat and of San Salvador or Cat Island, which is the most Island. northerly of those claimed to have been the landfall of Columbus. Proceeding down the group, we encounter Wat- Other ling's, Samana, Acklin (with the Plana Cays), Mari- islands. guana, and the Grand Turk, — all of which have their advocates. The three methods of identification which have been followed are, first, by plotting the outward track; identifica-second, by plotting the track between the landfall and tion. Cuba, both forward and backward; third, by applying the descriptions, particularly Columbus's, of the island first seen. In this last test, Harrisse prefers to apply the description of Las Casas, which is borrowed in part from that of the *Historie*, and he reconciles Columbus's apparent discrepancy when he says in one place that the island was " pretty large," and in another " small," by supposing that he may have applied these Acklin opposite terms, the lesser to the Plana Cays, as first Island. seen, and the other to the Crooked Group, or Acklin Island, lying just westerly, on which he may have landed. Harrisse is the only one who makes this identification; and he finds some confirmation in later maps, which show thereabout an island, Triango or Triangulo, a name said by Las Casas to have been applied to Guanahani at a later day. There is no known map earlier than 1540 bearing this alternative name of Triango.

San Salvador seems to have been the island selected by the earliest of modern inquirers, in the seventeenth and San eighteenth centuries, and it has had the support of Ir- Salvador. ving and Humboldt in later times. Captain Alexander Slidell Mackenzie of the United States navy worked out the problem for Irving. It is much larger than any of the other islands, and could hardly have been called by Columbus in any alternative way a " small " island, while it does not answer Columbus's description of being level, having on it an eminence of four hundred feet, and no interior lagoon, as his Guanahani demands. The French canonizers stand by the old traditions, and find it meet to say that "the English Protestants not finding the name San Salvador fine enough have substituted for it that of Cat, and in their hydrographical atlases the Island of the Holy Saviour is nobly called Cat Island."

The weight of modern testimony seems to favor Watling's
Watling's        island, and it so far answers to Columbus's description
Island.          that about one third of its interior is water, corresponding to his "large lagoon." Muñoz first suggested it in 1793; but the arguments in its favor were first spread out by Captain Becher of the royal navy in 1856, and he seems to have induced Oscar Peschel in 1858 to adopt the same views in his history of the range of modern discovery. Major, the map custodian of the British Museum, who had previously followed Navarrete in favoring the Grand Turk, again addressed himself to the problem in 1870, and fell into line with the adherents of Watling's. No other considerable advocacy of this island, if we except the testimony of Gerard Stein in 1883, in a book on voyages of discovery, appeared till Lieut. J. B. Murdoch, an officer of the American navy, made a very careful examination of the subject in the *Proceedings of the United States Naval Institute* in 1884, which is accepted by Charles A. Schott in the *Bulletin of the United States Coast Survey*. Murdoch was the first to plot in a backward way the track between Guanahani and Cuba, and he finds more points of resemblance in Columbus's description with Watling's than with any other. The latest adherent is the eminent geographer, Clements R. Markham, in the bulletin of the Italian Geographical Society in 1889. Perhaps no cartographical argument has been so effective as that of Major in comparing modern charts with the map of Herrera, in which the latter lays Guanahani down.

An elaborate attempt to identify Samana as the landfall was
Samana.          made by the late Capt. Gustavus Vasa Fox, in an appendix to the *Report of the United States Coast Survey* for 1880. Varnhagen, in 1864, selected Mariguana, and defended his choice in a paper. This island fails to satisfy
Grand Turk       the physical conditions in being without interior water.
Island.          Such a qualification, however, belongs to the Grand

Turk Island, which was advocated first by Navarrete in 1826, whose views have since been supported by George Gibbs, and for a while by Major.

It is rather curious to note that Caleb Cushing, who undertook to examine this question in the *North American Review,* under the guidance of Navarrete's theory, tried the same backward method which has been later applied to the problem, but with quite different results from those reached by more recent investigators. He says, " By setting out from Nipe [which is the point where Columbus struck Cuba] and proceeding in a retrograde direction along his course, we may surely trace his path, and shall be convinced that Guanahani is no other than Turk's Island."

# CHAPTER X.

WE learn that, after these ceremonies on the shore, the natives began fearlessly to gather about the strangers. Columbus, by causing red caps, strings of beads, and other trinkets to be distributed among them, made an easy conquest of their friendship. Later the men swam out to the ship to exchange their balls of thread, their javelins, and parrots for whatever they could get in return.

*The natives of Guanahani.*

The description which Columbus gives us in his journal of the appearance and condition of these new people is the earliest, of course, in our knowledge of them. His record is interesting for the effect which the creatures had upon him, and for the statement of their condition before the Spaniards had set an impress upon their unfortunate race.

They struck Columbus as, on the whole, a very poor people, going naked, and, judging from a single girl whom he saw, this nudity was the practice of the women. They all seemed young, not over thirty, well made, with fine shapes and faces. Their hair was coarse, and combed short over the forehead ; but hung long behind. The bodies of many were differently colored with pigments of many hues, though of some only the face, the eyes, or the nose were painted. Columbus was satisfied that they had no knowledge of edged weapons, because they grasped his sword by the blade and cut themselves. Their javelins were sticks pointed with fishbones. When he observed scars on their bodies, they managed to explain to him that enemies, whom the Admiral supposed to come from the continent, sometimes invaded their island, and that such wounds were received in defending themselves. They appeared to him to have no religion, which satisfied him that the task of converting them to Christianity would not be difficult. They learned readily to pronounce such words as were repeated to them.

On the next day after landing, Saturday, Columbus describes again the throng that came to the shore, and was struck with their broad foreheads. He deemed it a natural coincidence, being in the latitude of the Canaries, that the natives had the complexion prevalent among the natives of those islands. In this he anticipated the conclusions of the anthropologists, who have found in the skulls preserved in caves both in the Bahamas and in the Canaries, such striking similarities as have led to the supposition that ocean currents may have borne across the sea some of the old Guanche stock of the Canaries, itself very likely the remnant of the people of the European river-drift.

1492. October 13.

Affinities of the Lucayans.

Professor W. K. Brooks, of the Johns Hopkins University, who has recently published in the *Popular Science Monthly* (November, 1889) a study of the bones of the Lucayans as found in caves in the Bahamas, reports that these relics indicate a muscular, heavy people, about the size of the average European, with protuberant square jaws, sloping eyes, and very round skulls, but artificially flattened on the forehead, — a result singularly confirming Columbus's description of broader heads than he had ever seen.

" The Ceboynas," says a recent writer on these Indians, " gave us the hammock, and this one Lucayan word is their only monument," for a population larger than inhabits these islands to-day were in twelve years swept from the surface of the earth by a system devised by Columbus.

Hammocks.

The Admiral also describes their canoes, made in a wonderful manner of a single tree-trunk, and large enough to hold forty or forty-five men, though some were so small as to carry a single person only. Their oars are shaped like the wooden shovels with which bakers slip their loaves into ovens. If a canoe upsets, it is righted as they swim.

Canoes.

Columbus was attracted by bits of gold dangling at the nose of some among them. By signs he soon learned that a greater abundance of this metal could be found on an island to the south; but they seemed unable to direct him with any precision how to reach that island, or at least it was not easy so to interpret any of their signs. " Poor wretches ! " exclaims Helps, " if they had possessed the slightest gift of prophecy, they would have thrown these baubles into the deep-

Gold among them.

est sea." They pointed in all directions, but towards the east
as the way to other lands ; and implied that those enemies who
came from the northwest often passed to the south after gold.

Columbus traffics with them.
He found that broken dishes and bits of glass served
as well for traffic with them as more valuable articles,
and balls of threads of cotton, grown on the island,
seemed their most merchantable commodity.

With this rude foretaste, Columbus determined to push on
for the richer Cipango. On the next day he coasted
1492. October 14, sails towards Cipango.
along the island in his boats, discovering two or three
villages, where the inhabitants were friendly. They
seemed to think that the strangers had come from heaven, — at
least Columbus so interpreted their prostrations and uplifted
hands. Columbus, fearful of the reefs parallel to the shore,
kept outside of them, and as he moved along, saw a point of
land which a ditch might convert into an island. He thought
this would afford a good site for a fort, if there was need of one.

It was on this Sunday that Columbus, in what he thought
doubtless the spirit of the day in dealing with heathens,
1492. October 14.
gives us his first intimation of the desirability of using
force to make these poor creatures serve their new masters.
Columbus proposes to enslave the natives.
On returning to the ships and setting sail, he soon
found that he was in an archipelago. He had seized
some natives, who were now on board. These repeated to him the names of more than a hundred islands. He
describes those within sight as level, fertile, and populous, and
he determined to steer for what seemed the largest. He stood
1492. October 15.
off and on during the night of the 14th, and by noon
of the 15th he had reached this other island, which
he found at the easterly end to run five leagues north and south,
and to extend east and west a distance of ten leagues. Lured
by a still larger island farther west he pushed on, and skirting
the shore reached its western extremity. He cast anchor there
at sunset, and named the island Santa Maria de la Concepcion.
The natives on board told him that the people here wore gold
bracelets. Columbus thought this story might be a device of
his prisoners to obtain opportunities to escape. On the next
1492. October 16.
day, he repeated the forms of landing and taking possession. Two of the prisoners contrived to escape.
One of them jumped overboard and was rescued by a native

canoe. The Spaniards overtook the canoe, but not till its occupants had escaped. A single man, coming off in another canoe, was seized and taken on board ; but Columbus thought him a good messenger of amity, and loading him with presents, "not worth four maravedis," he put him ashore. Columbus watched the liberated savage, and judged from the wonder of the crowds which surrounded him that his ruse of friendship had been well played.

Another large island appeared westerly about nine leagues, famous for its gold ornaments, as his prisoners again declared. It is significant that in his journal, since he discovered the bits of gold at San Salvador, Columbus has not a word to say of reclaiming the benighted heathen ; but he constantly repeats his hope "with the help of our Lord," of finding gold. On the way thither he had picked up a second single man in a canoe, who had apparently followed him from San Salvador. He determined to bestow some favors upon him and let him go, as he had done with the other. Columbus sees a large island.

This new island, which he reached October 16, and called Fernandina, he found to be about twenty-eight leagues long, with a safer shore than the others. He anchored 1492. October 16. near a village, where the man whom he had set free had already come, bringing good reports of the stranger, and so the Spaniards got a kind reception. Great numbers of natives came off in canoes, to whom the men gave trinkets and molasses. He took on board some water, the natives assisting the crew. Getting an impression that the island contained a mine of gold, he resolved to follow the coast, and find Samaot, where the gold was said to be. Columbus thought he saw some improvement in the natives over those he had seen before, remarking upon the cotton cloth with which they partly covered their persons. He was surprised to find that distinct branches of the same tree bore different leaves. A single tree, as he says, will show as many as five or six varieties, not done by grafting, but a natural growth. He wondered at the brilliant fish, and found no land creatures but parrots and lizards, though a boy of the company told him that he had seen a snake. On Wednesday he started to sail around the island. In a little haven, where they tarried awhile, they first entered the native houses. They found everything in them neat, with nets extended between

posts, which they called *hamacs*, — a name soon adopted by
sailors for swinging-beds. The houses were shaped
like tents, with high chimneys, but not more than
twelve or fifteen together. Dogs were running about them,
but they could not bark. Columbus endeavored to buy a bit
of gold, cut or stamped, which was hanging from a man's
nose; but the savage refused his offers.

Hammocks.

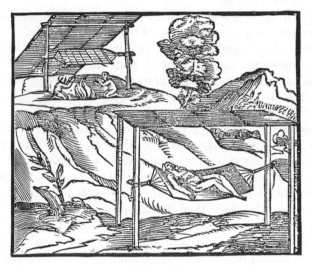

INDIAN BEDS.

The ships continued their course about the island, the weather
not altogether favorable; but on October 19 they
veered away to another island to the west of Fernandina, which Columbus named Isabella, after his Queen. This
he pronounced the most beautiful he had seen; and he remarks
on the interior region of it being higher than in the other
islands, and the source of streams. The breezes from the shore
brought him odors, and when he landed he became conscious
that his botanical knowledge did not aid him in selecting such
dyestuffs, medicines, and spices as would command high prices
in Spain. He saw a hideous reptile, and the canonizers, after
their amusing fashion, tell us that " to see and attack him were
the same thing for Columbus, for he considered it of importance to accustom Spanish intrepidity to such warfare." The

1492. Oc-
tober 19.

reptile proved inoffensive. The signs of his prisoners were interpreted to repeat here the welcome tale of gold. He To find gold Columbus's main object. understood them to refer to a king decked with gold. "I do not, however," he adds, "give much credit to these accounts, for I understand the natives but imperfectly." "I am proceeding solely in quest of gold and spices," he says 1492. October 21. again.

On Sunday they went ashore, and found a house from which the occupants had recently departed. The foliage was enchanting. Flocks of parrots obscured the sky. Specimens were gathered of wonderful trees. They killed a snake in a lake. They cajoled some timid natives with beads, and got their help in filling their water cask. They heard of a very large island named Colba, which had ships and sail- Cuba heard of. ors, as the natives were thought to say. They had little doubt that these stories referred to Cipango. They hoped the native king would bring them gold in the night; but this not happening, and being cheered by the accounts of Colba, they made up their minds that it would be a waste of time to search longer for this backward king, and so resolved to run for the big island. 1492. October 24. Isabella.

Starting from Isabella at midnight on October 24, and passing other smaller islands, they finally, on Sunday, October 26, entered a river near the easterly end of October 26. Cuba.

The track of Columbus from San Salvador to Cuba has been as variously disputed as the landfall; indeed, the divergent views of the landfall necessitate such later variations. Cuba.

They landed within the river's mouth, and discovered deserted houses, which from the implements within they supposed to be the houses of fishermen. Columbus observed that the grass grew down to the water's edge; and he reasoned therefrom that the sea could never be rough. He now observed mountains, and likened them to those of Sicily. He finally supposed his prisoners to affirm by their signs that the island was too large for a canoe to sail round it in twenty days. There were the old stories of gold; but the mention of pearls appears now for the first time in the journal, Pearls. which in this place, however, we have only in Las Casas's abridgment.

When the natives pointed to the interior and said, " Cuba-nacan," meaning, it is supposed, an inland region, Columbus imagined it was a reference to Kublai Khan; and the Cuban name of Mangon he was very ready to associate with the Mangi of Mandeville.

Columbus supposes himself at Mangi.

As he still coasted westerly he found river and village, and made more use of his prisoners than had before been possible. They seem by this time to have settled into an acquiescent spirit. He wondered in one place at statues which looked like women. He was not quite sure whether the natives kept them for the love of the beautiful, or for worship.

He found domesticated fowl; and saw a skull, which he supposed was a cow's, which was probably that of the sea-calf, a denizen of these waters. He thought the temperature cooler than in the other islands, and ascribed the change to the mountains. He observed on one of these eminences a protuberance that looked like a mosque. Such interpretation as the Spaniards could make of their prisoners' signs convinced them that if they sailed farther west they would find some potentate, and so they pushed on. Bad weather, however, delayed them, and they again opened communication with the natives. They could hear nothing of gold, but saw a silver trinket; and learned, as they thought, that news of their coming had been carried to the distant king. Columbus felt convinced that the people of these regions were banded enemies of the Great Khan, and that he had at last struck the continent of Cathay, and was skirting the shores of the Zartun and Quinsay of Marco Polo. Taking an observation, Columbus found himself to be in 21° north latitude, and as near as he could reckon, he was 1142 leagues west of Ferro. He really was 1105.

Columbus supposes himself on the coast of Cathay.

From Friday, November 2, to Monday, November 5, two Spaniards, whom Columbus had sent into the interior, accompanied by some Indians, had made their way unmolested in their search for a king. They had been entertained here and there with ceremony, and apparently worshiped as celestial comers. The evidences of the early Spanish voyagers give pretty constant testimony that the whites were supposed to have come from the skies. Columbus had given to his envoys samples of cinnamon, pepper, and other

1492. November 2-5.

Cuba explored.

spices, which were shown to the people. In reply, his messengers learned that such things grew to the southeast of them. Columbus later, in his first letter, speaks of cinnamon as one of the spices which they found, but it turned out to be the bark of a sort of laurel. Las Casas, in mentioning this expedition, says that the Spaniards found the natives smoking small tubes of dried leaves, filled with other leaves, which they called *tobacos*. Sir Arthur Helps aptly remarks on this Tobacco. trivial discovery by the Spaniards of a great financial resource of modern statesmen, since tobacco has in the end proved more productive to the Spanish crown than the gold which Columbus sought. The Spaniards found no large villages; but they perceived great stores of fine cotton of a long staple. They found the people eating what we must recognize as potatoes. Potatoes. The absence of gold gave Columbus an opportunity to wish more fervently than before for the conversion of some of these people.

While this party was absent, Columbus found a quiet beach, and careened his ships, one at a time. In melting his tar, the wood which he used gave out a powerful odor, and he pronounced it the mastic gum, which Europe had always got from Chios. As this work was going on, the Spaniards got from the natives, as best they could, many intimations of larger wealth and commerce to the southeast. Other strange stories One-eyed were told of men with one eye, and faces like dogs, faced men. and of cruel, bloodthirsty man-eaters, who fought to Cannibals. appease their appetite on the flesh of the slain.

It was not till the 12th of November that Columbus left this hospitable haven, at daybreak, in search of a place 1492. No-called Babeque, "where gold was collected at night vember 12. by torch-light upon the shore, and afterward ham- Babeque. mered into bars." He the more readily retraced his track, that the coast to the westward seemed to trend northerly, and he dreaded a colder climate. He must leave for another time the sight of men with tails, who inhabited a province in that direction, as he was informed.

Again the historian recognizes how a chance turned the Spaniards away from a greater goal. If Columbus had gone on westerly and discovered the insular character of Cuba, he might have sought the main of Mexico and Yucatan, and anticipated the wonders of the conquest of Córtez. He never was undeceived in believing that Cuba was the Asiatic main.

Columbus sailed back over his course with an inordinate idea of the riches of the country which he was leaving. He thought the people docile; that their simple belief in a God was easily to be enlarged into the true faith, whereby Spain might gain vassals and the church a people. He managed to entice on board, and took away, six men, seven women, and three children, condoning the act of kidnapping — the canonizers call it " retaining on board " — by a purpose to teach them the Spanish language, and open a readier avenue to their benighted souls. He allowed the men to have women to share their durance, as such ways, he says, had proved useful on the coast of Guinea.

Columbus captures some natives.

The Admiral says in his first letter, referring to his captives, " that we immediately understood each other, either by words or signs." This was his message to expectant Europe. His journal is far from conveying that impression.

The ships now steered east-by-south, passing mountainous lands, which on November 14 he tried to approach. After a while he discovered a harbor, which he could enter, and found it filled with lofty wooded islands, some pointed and some flat at the top. He was quite sure he had now got among the islands which are made to swarm on the Asiatic coast in the early accounts and maps. He now speaks of his practice in all his landings to set up and leave a cross. He observed, also, a promontory in the bay fit for a fortress, and caught a strange fish resembling a hog. He was at this time embayed in the King's Garden, as the archipelago is called.

1492. November 14.

Shortly after this, when they had been baffled in their courses, Martin Alonso Pinzon, incited, as the record says, by his cupidity to find the stores of gold to which some of his Indian captives had directed him, disregarded the Admiral's signals, and sailed away in the "Pinta." The flagship kept a light for him all night, at the mast-head; but in the morning the caravel was out of sight. The Admiral takes occasion in his journal to remark that this was not the first act of Pinzon's insubordination. On Friday, November 23, the vessels approached a headland, which the Indians called Bohio. The prisoners here began to manifest

Pinzon deserts.

1492. November 23.

fear, for it was a spot where the one-eyed people and the cannibals dwelt; but on Saturday, November 24, the 1492. November 24. ships were forced back into the gulf with the many islands, where Columbus found a desirable roadstead, which he had not before discovered.

On Sunday, exploring in a boat, he found in a stream "certain stones which shone with spots of a golden hue; 1492. November 25. and recollecting that gold was found in the river Tagus near the sea, he entertained no doubt that this was the metal, and directed that a collection of the stones should be made to carry to the King and Queen." It becomes noticeable, as Columbus goes on, that every new place surpasses all others; the atmosphere is better; the trees are more marvelous. He now found pines fit for masts, and secured some for the "Nina."

As he coasted the next day along what he believed to be a continental coast, he tried in his journal to account for the absence of towns in so beautiful a country. That there were inhabitants he knew, for he found traces of them on going ashore. He had discovered that all the natives had a great dread of a people whom they called Caniba or Canima, and he argued that the towns were kept back from the coast to avoid the chances of the maritime attacks of this fierce people. There was no doubt in the mind of Columbus that these inroads were conducted by subjects of the Great Khan.

While he was still stretching his course along this coast, observing its harbors, seeing more signs of habitation, and attempting to hold intercourse with the frightened natives, now anchoring in some haven, and now running up adjacent rivers in a galley, he found time to jot down in this journal for the future perusal of his sovereigns some of his suspicions, prophecies, and determinations. He complains of the difficulty of understanding his prisoners, and seems conscious of his frequent misconceptions of their meaning. He says he has lost confidence in them, and somewhat innocently imagines that they would escape if they could! Then he speaks of a determination to acquire their language, which he supposes to be the same through all the region. "In this way," he adds, "we can learn the riches of the country, and make endeavors to convert these people to our religion, for they are without even the faith of an idolater." He descants upon the salubrity of the air ; not one of his crew had had any illness, " except an old man, all his life a sufferer from the stone." There is at times a somewhat amusing innocence in his conclusions, as when finding a cake of wax in one of the houses, which Las Casas thinks was brought from Yucatan, he " was of the opinion that where wax was found there must be a great many other valuable commodities."

The ships were now detained in their harbor for several days, during which the men made excursions, and found a populous country ; they succeeded at times in getting into communication 1492. December 4. with the natives. Finally, on December 4, he left the Puerto Santo, as he called it, and coasting along easterly he reached the next day the extreme eastern end of what Leaves Cuba or Juana. we now know to be Cuba, or Juana as he had named it, after Prince Juan. Cruising about, he seems to have had an apprehension that the land he had been following might not after all be the main, for he appears to have looked around the southerly side of this end of Cuba and to have seen the southwesterly trend of its coast. He observed, the same day, Bohio. Española. land in the southeast, which his Indians called Bohio, and this was subsequently named Española. Las Casas explains that Columbus here mistook the Indian word meaning house for the name of the island, which was really in their tongue called Haiti. It is significant of the difficulty in identifying the bays and headlands of the journal, that at this point Las Casas puts on one side, and Navarrete on the opposite side, of the passage dividing Cuba from Española, one of the capes which Columbus indicates. Changing his course for this lofty island, he dispatched the " Nina " to search its shore and find a harbor. That night the Admiral's ship beat about, waiting for daylight. When it came, he took his observations of the coast, and espying an island separated by a wide channel Tortuga. from the other land, he named this island Tortuga. Finding his way into a harbor — the present St. Nicholas — he declares that a thousand caracks could sail about in it. Here he saw, as before, large canoes, and many natives, who fled on his approach. The Spaniards soon began as they went on to observe lofty and extensive mountains, " the whole country appearing like Castile." They saw another reminder of Spain as they were rowing about a harbor, which they entered, and which was opposite Tortuga, when a skate leaped into their boat, and the Admiral records it as a first instance in which they had seen a fish similar to those of the Spanish waters. He says, too, that he heard on the shore nightingales "and other Spanish birds," mistaking of course their identity. He saw myrtles and other trees "like those of Castile." There was another obvious reference to the old country in the name of Española, which he now bestowed upon the island. He could find few of the inhabitants, and conjectured that their towns were back from the coast. The men, however, captured a handsome young woman who wore a bit of gold at her nose ; and having bestowed upon her gifts, let her go. Soon after, the Admiral sent a party to a town of a thousand houses, thinking the luck of the woman would embolden the people to have a parley. The inhabitants fled in fear at first ; but growing bolder came in great crowds, and brought presents of parrots.

It was here that Columbus took his latitude and found it to be 17°, — while in fact it was 20°. The journal gives Columbus finds his latitude. numerous instances during all these explorations of the bestowing of names upon headlands and harbors, few of which have remained to this day. It was a common custom to make such use of a Saint's name on his natal day.

Dr. Shea in a paper which he published in 1876, in the first volume of the *American Catholic Quarterly,* has emphasized the help which the Roman nomenclature of Saints' Saints' names. days, given to rivers and headlands, affords to the geographical student in tracking the early explorers along the coasts of the New World. This method of tracing the progress of maritime discovery suggested itself early to Oviedo, and has been appealed to by Henry C. Murphy and other modern authorities on this subject.

Finally, on Friday, December 14, they sailed out of the harbor toward Tortuga. He found this island to be under 1492. December 14. extensive cultivation like a plain of Cordoba. The wind not holding for him to take the course which he wished to run, Columbus returned to his last harbor, the Puerto de la Concepcion. Again on Saturday he left it, and standing across to Tortuga once more, he went towards the shore Tortuga. and proceeded up a stream in his boats. The inhabitants fled as he approached, and burning fires in Tortuga as well as in Española seemed to be signals that the Spaniards were moving. During the night, proceeding along the channel between the two islands, the Admiral met and took on board a solitary Indian in his canoe. The usual gifts were put upon him, and when the ships anchored near a village, he was sent ashore with the customary effect. The beach soon swarmed with people, gathered with their king, and some came on board. The Spaniards got from them without difficulty the bits of gold which they wore at their ears and noses. One of the captive Indians who talked with the king told this " youth of twenty-one," that the Spaniards had come from heaven and were going

Babeque.        to Babeque to find gold; and the king told the Admiral's messenger, who delivered to him a present, that if he sailed in a certain course two days he would arrive there. This is the last we hear of Babeque, a place Columbus never found, at least under that name. Humboldt remarks that Columbus mentions the name of Babeque more than fourteen times in his journal, but it cannot certainly be identified with Española, as the *Historie* of 1571 declares it to be. D'Avezac has since shared Humboldt's view. Las Casas hesitatingly thought it might have referred to Jamaica.

Then the journal describes the country, saying that the land is lofty, but that the highest mountains are arable, and that the trees are so luxuriant that they become black rather than green. The journal further describes this new people as stout and courageous, very different from the timid islanders of other parts, and without religion. With his usual habit of contradiction, Columbus goes on immediately to speak of their pusillanimity, saying that three Spaniards were more than a match for a thousand of them. He prefigures their fate in calling them " well-fitted to be governed and set to work to till the land and do whatsoever is necessary."

It was on Monday, December 17, while lying off Española,

1492. December 17.        that the Spaniards got for the first time something more than rumor respecting the people of Caniba or the cannibals. These new evidences were certain arrows which

Cannibals.        the natives showed to them, and which they said had belonged to those man-eaters. They were pieces of cane, tipped with sticks which had been hardened by fire. " They were exhibited by two Indians who had lost some flesh from their bodies, eaten out by the cannibals. This the Admiral did not believe." It was now, too, that the Spaniards found gold in larger quantities than they had seen it before. They saw some beaten into thin plates. The cacique — here this word appears for the first time — cut a plate as big as his hand into pieces and bartered them, promising Cacique. to have more to exchange the next day. He gave the Spaniards to understand that there was more gold in Tortuga than in Española. It is to be remarked, also, in the Admiral's account, that while " Our Lord " is not recorded as indicating to him any method of converting the poor heathen, it was " Our Lord " who was now about to direct the Admiral to Babeque.

The next day, December 18, the Admiral lay at anchor, both because wind failed him, and because he would be 1492. December 18. able to see the gold which the cacique had promised to bring. It also gave him an opportunity to deck his ships and fire his guns in honor of the Annunciation of the Blessed Virgin.

In due time the king appeared, borne on a sort of litter by his men, and boarding the ship, that chieftain found Columbus at table in his cabin. The cacique was placed beside the Admiral, and similar viands and drinks were placed before him, of which he partook. Two of his dusky followers, sitting at his feet, followed their master in the act. Columbus, observing that the hangings of his bed had attracted the attention of the savage, gave them to him, and added to the present some amber beads from his own neck, some red shoes, and a flask of orange-flower water. " This day," says the record, " little gold was obtained ; but an old man indicated that at a distance of a hundred leagues or more were some islands, where much gold could be found, and in some it was so plentiful that it was collected and bolted with sieves, then melted and beaten into divers forms. One of the islands was said to be all gold, and the Admiral determined to go in the direction which this man pointed."

That night they tried in vain to stand out beyond Tortuga, but on the 20th of December, the record places the 1492. December 20. ships in a harbor between a little island, which Columbus called St. Thomas, and the main island. During the following day, December 21, he surveyed the roadstead, and St. Thomas Island. going about the region in his boats, he had a number of interviews with the natives, which ended with an interchange of gifts and courtesies.

On Saturday, December 22, they encountered some people, 1492. December 22. sent by a neighboring cacique, whom the Admiral's own Indians could not readily understand, the first of this kind mentioned in the journal. Writing in regard to a party which Columbus at this time sent to visit a large town not far off, he speaks of having his secretary accompany them, in order to repress the Spaniards' greediness, — an estimate of his followers which the Admiral had not before suffered himself to record, if we can trust the Las Casas manuscript. The results of this foray were three fat geese and some bits of gold. As he entered the adventure in his journal, he dwelt on the hope of gold being on the island in abundance, and if only the spot could be found, it might be got for little or nothing. " Our Lord, in whose hands are all things, be my help," he cries. " Our Lord, in his mercy, direct me where I may find the gold mine."

The Admiral now learns the name of another chief officer, Nitayno, whose precise position was not apparent, but Las Casas tells us later that this word was the title of one nearest Cibao. in rank to the cacique. When an Indian spoke of a place named Cibao, far to the east, where the king had banners made of plates of gold, the Admiral, in his eager confidence, had no hesitation in identifying it with Cipango and its gorgeous prince. It proved to be the place where in the end the best mines were found.

In speaking of the next day, Sunday, December 23, Las Casas 1492. December 23. tells us that Columbus was not in the habit of sailing on Sunday, not because he was superstitious, but because he was pious ; but that he did not omit the opportunity at this time of coursing the coast, " in order to display the symbols of Redemption."

Christmas found them in distress. The night before, everything looking favorable, and the vessel sailing along quietly, Columbus had gone to bed, being much in need of rest. The Columbus shipwrecked. helmsman put a boy at the tiller and went to sleep. The rest of the crew were not slow to do the same. The vessel was in this condition, with no one but the boy awake, when, carried out of her course by the current, she struck a sand bank. The cry of the boy awakened the Admiral, and he was the first to discover the danger of their situation. He ordered out a boat's crew to carry an anchor astern, but, bewildered or frightened, the men pulled for the "Nina." The crew of that caravel warned them off, to do their duty, and sent their own boat to assist. Help, however, availed nothing. The "Santa Maria" had careened, and her seams were opening. Her mast had been cut away, but she failed to right herself. The Admiral now abandoned her and rowed to the "Nina" with his men. Communicating with the cacique in the morning, that chieftain sent many canoes to assist in unloading the ship, so that in a short time everything of value was saved. This assistance gave occasion for mutual confidences between the Spaniards and the natives. "They are a loving, uncovetous people," he enters in his journal. One wonders, with the later experience of his new friends, if the cacique could have said as much in return. The Admiral began to be convinced that "the Lord had permitted the shipwreck in order that he might choose this place for a settlement." The canonizers go further and say, "the shipwreck made him an engineer."

Irving, whose heedless embellishments of the story of these times may amuse the pastime reader, but hardly satisfy the student, was not blind to the misfortunes of what Columbus at the time called the divine interposition. "This shipwreck," Irving says, "shackled and limited all Columbus's future discoveries. It linked his fortunes for the remainder of his life to this island, which was doomed to be to him a source of cares and troubles, to involve him in a thousand perplexities, and to becloud his declining years with humiliation and disappointment."

The saving of his stores and the loss of his ship had indeed already suggested what some of his men had asked for, that they might be left there, while the Admiral returned to Spain with the tidings of the discovery, if — as the uncomfortable thought sprung up in his mind — he had not already been anticipated by the recreant commander of the "Pinta." Accordingly Columbus ordered the construction of a fort, with tower and ditch, and arrangements were soon made to provide bread and wine for more than a year, beside seed for the next planting-time. The ship's long-boat could be

Fort built.

left; and a calker, carpenter, cooper, engineer, tailor, and sur- geon could be found among his company, to be of the party who were to remain and " search for the gold mine." He says that he expected they would collect a ton of gold in the interval of his absence; " for I have before protested to your High- nesses," he adds as he makes an entry for his sovereigns to read, " that the profits shall go to making a conquest of Jerusalem."

We know the names of those who agreed to stay on the island. Navarrete discovered the list in a proclama- tion made in 1507 to pay what was due them to their next of kin. This list gives forty names, though some accounts of the voyage say they numbered a few less. The company included the Irishman and Englishman already mentioned.

Garrison of La Navidad.

On the 27th of December, Columbus got the first tidings of the " Pinta " since she deserted him; and he sent a Spaniard, with Indians to handle the canoe, to a har- bor at the end of the island, where he supposed Pinzon's ship to be. Columbus was now perfecting his plans for the fort, and tried to make out if Guacanagari, the king, was not trying to conceal from him the situation of the mines. On Sunday, December 30, the Spanish and native leaders vied with each other in graciousness. The savage put his crown upon the Admiral. Columbus took off his necklace and scarlet cloak and placed them on the king. He clothed the savage's naked feet with buskins and decked the dusky hand with a sil- ver ring. On Monday, work was resumed in prepar- ing for their return to Spain, for, with the " Pinta " gone — for the canoe sent to find her had returned unsuccessful — and the " Nina " alone remaining, it was necessary to dimin- ish the risk attending the enterprise.

1492. De- cember 27.

December 30.

December 31.

On January 2, 1493, there was to be leave-taking of the cacique. To impart to him and to his people a dread of Spanish power, in the interests of those to be left, he made an exhibition of the force of his bombards, by sending a shot clean through the hull of the dismantled wreck. It is curi- ous to observe how Irving, with a somewhat cheap melodramatic instinct, makes this shot tear through a beautiful grove like a bolt from heaven !

1493. Janu- ary 2.

The king made some return by ordering an effigy of Colum- bus to be finished in gold, in ten days, — as at least so Columbus understood one of his Indians to announce the cacique's purpose.

Having commissioned Diego de Arana as commander and Pedro Gutierrez and Roderigo de Escoveda to act as his lieutenants of the fort and its thirty-nine men, Columbus now embarked, but not before he had addressed all sorts of good advice to those he was to leave behind, — advice that did no good, if the subsequent events are clearly divined. It was not, however, till Friday, January 4, 1493, that the wind permitted him to stand out of the harbor of the Villa de Navidad, as he had named the fort and settlement from the fact of his shipwreck there on the day of the nativity. Two days later they met the " Pinta," and Pinzon, her commander, soon boarded the Admiral to explain his absence, " saying he had left against his will." The Admiral doubted such professions ; but did not think it prudent to show active resentment, as Las Casas tells us. The fact apparently was that Pinzon had not found the gold he went in search of and so he had returned to meet his commander. He had been coasting the island for over twenty days, and had been seen by the natives, who made the report to the Admiral already mentioned. Some Indians whom he had taken captive were subsequently released by the Admiral, for the usual ulterior purpose. It is curious to observe how an act of kidnapping which emulated the Admiral's, if done by Pinzon, is called by the canonizers, " joining violence to rapine."

At this time Columbus records his first intelligence respecting an island, Yamaye, south of Cuba, which seems to have been Jamaica, where, as he learned, gold was to be found in grains of the size of beans, while in Española the grains were nearly the size of kernels of wheat. He was also informed of an island to the east, inhabited by women only. He also understood that the people of the continent to the south were clothed, and did not go naked like those of the islands.

Both vessels now having made a harbor, and the " Nina " beginning to leak, a day was spent in calking her seams. Columbus was not without apprehension that the two brothers, Martin Alonso Pinzon of the " Pinta," and Vicente Jañez Pinzon who had commanded the " Nina," might now with their adherents combine for mischief. He was accordingly all the more anxious

*Margin notes:*
1493. January 4.

January 6.

Jamaica.

to hasten his departure, without further following the coast of Española. Going up a river to replenish his water, he found on taking the casks on board that the crevices of the hoops had gathered fine bits of gold from the stream. This led him to count the neighboring streams, which he supposed might also contain gold.

It was not only gold which he saw. Three mermaids stood high out of the water, with not very comely faces to be sure, but similar to those of human beings; and he recalled having seen the like on the pepper coast in Guinea. The commentators suppose they may have been sea-calves indistinctly seen.

Columbus sees mermaids.

The two ships started once more on the 10th, sometimes lying to at night for fear of shoals, making and naming cape after cape. On the 12th, entering a harbor, Columbus discovered an Indian, whom he took for a Carib, as he had learned to call the cannibals which he so often heard of. His own Indians did not wholly understand this strange savage. When they sent him ashore the Spaniards found fifty-five Indians armed with bows and wooden swords. They were prevailed upon at first to hold communication; but soon showed a less friendly spirit, and Columbus for the first time records a fight, in which several of the natives were wounded. An island to the eastward was now supposed to be the Carib region, and he desired to capture some of its natives. Navarrete supposes that Porto Rico is here referred to. He also observed, as his vessels went easterly, that he was encountering some of the same sort of seaweed which he had sailed through when steering west, and it occurred to him that perhaps these islands stretched easterly, so as really to be not far distant from the Canaries. It may be observed that this propinquity of the new islands to those of the Atlantic, longer known, was not wholly eradicated from the maps till well into the earlier years of the sixteenth century.

1493. January 10. The ships sail for Spain.

January 12. Caribs.

They had secured some additional Indians near where they had had their fight, and one. of them now directed Columbus towards the island of the Caribs. The leaks of the vessels increasing and his crews desponding, Columbus soon thought it more prudent to shift his course for Spain direct, supposing at the same time that it would take him near Matinino, where the tribe of women lived. He had gotten the story somehow, very likely by a credulous adaptation of Marco Polo, that Caribs and the Caribs visited this island once a year and re- Amazons. claimed the male offspring, leaving the female young to keep up the tribe.

In following the Admiral along these coasts of Cuba and Española, no attempt has here been made to identify all his bays and rivers. Navarrete and the other commentators have done so, but not always with agreement.

On the 16th, they had their last look at a distant cape of Española, and were then in the broad ocean, with sea- 1493. January 16. weed and tunnies and pelicans to break its monotony. The "Pinta," having an unsound mast, lagged behind, and so the "Nina" had to slacken sail.

Columbus now followed a course which for a long time, owing to defects in the methods of ascertaining longitude, Homeward was the mariner's readiest recourse to reach his port. voyage. This was to run up his latitudes to that of his destination, and then follow the parallel till he sighted a familiar landmark.

By February 10, when they began to compare reckonings, Columbus placed his position in the latitude of Flores, 1493. February 10. while the others thought they were on a more southern course, and a hundred and fifty leagues nearer Spain. By the 12th it was apparent that a gale was coming on. The next day, February 13, the storm increased. During the fol- February 13. lowing night both vessels took in all sail and scudded before the wind. They lost sight of each other's lights, and never joined company. The "Pinta" with her weak mast was blown away to the north. The Admiral's ship could bear the gale better, but as his ballast was insufficient, he had A gale. to fill his water casks with sea-water. Sensible of their peril, his crew made vows, to be kept if they were saved. They drew lots to determine who should carry a wax taper of five pounds to St. Mary of Guadalupe, and the penance fell to the Admiral. A sailor by another lot was doomed to make a pilgrimage to St. Mary of Lorette in the papal territory. A third lot was drawn for a night watch at St. Clara de Mogues, and it fell upon Columbus. Then they all vowed to pay their devotions at the nearest church of Our Lady if only they got ashore alive.

There was one thought which more than another troubled Columbus at this moment, and this was that in case his ship foundered, the world might never know of his success, for he was apprehensive that the "Pinta" had already foundered. Not to alarm the crew, he kept from them the fact that a cask which they had seen him throw overboard contained an account of his voyage, written on parchment, rolled in a waxed cloth. He trusted to the chance of some one finding it. He placed a similar cask on the poop, to be washed off in case the ship went down. He does not mention this in the journal.

A narrative of his voyage thrown overboard.

After sunset on the 15th there were signs of clearing in the west, and the waves began to fall. The next morning at sunrise there was land ahead. Now came the test of their reckoning. Some thought it the rock of Cintra near Lisbon; others said Madeira; Columbus decided they were near the Azores. The land was soon made out to be an island; but a head wind thwarted them. Other land was next seen astern. While they were saying their *Salve* in the evening, some of the crew discerned a light to leeward, which might have been on the island first seen. Then later they saw another island, but night and the clouds obscured it too much to be recognized. The journal is blank for the 17th of February, except that under the next day, the 18th, Columbus records that after sunset of the 17th they sailed round an island to find an anchorage; but being unsuccessful in the search they beat out to sea again. In the morning of the 18th they stood in, discovered an anchorage, sent a boat ashore, and found it was St. Mary's of the Azores. Columbus was right!

1493. January 15.

January 16. Land seen.

At the Azores.

1493. February 18.

After sunset he received some provisions, which Juan de Casteñeda, the Portuguese governor of the island, had sent to him. Meanwhile three Spaniards whom Columbus sent ashore had failed to return, not a little to his disturbance, for he was aware that there might be among the Portuguese some jealousy of his success. To fulfill one of the vows made during the gale, he now sent one half his crew ashore in penitential garments to a hermitage near the shore, intending on their return to go himself with the other half. The record then reads: "The men being at their devotion, they were attacked by Casteñeda with horse and foot, and made prisoners." Not being able to see the hermitage from his anchorage, and not suspecting this event, but still anxious, he made sail and proceeded till he got a view of the spot. Now he saw the horsemen, and how presently they dismounted, and with arms in their hands, entering a boat, approached the ship. Then followed a parley, in which Columbus thought he discovered a purpose of the Portuguese to capture him, and they on their part discovered it to be not quite safe to board the Admiral. To enforce his dignity and authority as a representative of the sovereigns of Castile, he held up to the boats his commission with its royal insignia; and reminded them that his instructions had been to treat all Portuguese ships with respect, since a spirit of amity existed between the two Crowns. It behooved the Portuguese, as he told them, to be wary lest by any hostile act they brought upon themselves the indignation of those higher in authority. The lofty bearing of Casteñeda continuing, Columbus began to fear that hostilities might possibly have broken out between Spain and Portugal. So the interview ended with little satisfaction to either, and the Admiral returned to his old anchorage. The next day, to work off the lee shore, they sailed for St. Michael's, and the weather continuing stormy he found himself crippled in having but three experienced seamen among the crew which remained to him. So not seeing St. Michael's they again bore away, on Thursday the 21st, for St. Mary's, and again reached their former anchorage.  1493. February 21.

The storms of these latter days here induced Columbus in his journal to recall how placid the sea had been among those other new-found islands, and how likely it was the terrestial paradise was in that region, as theologians and learned philosophers had supposed. From these thoughts he was aroused by a boat from shore with a notary on board, and Columbus, after completing his entertainment of the visitors, was asked to show his royal commission. He records his belief that this was done to give the Portuguese an opportunity of retreating from their belligerent attitude. At all events it had that effect, and the Spaniards who had been restrained were at once released. It is surmised that the conduct of Casteñeda was in conformity with instructions from Lisbon, to detain Columbus should he find his way to any dependency of the Portuguese crown.

On Sunday, the 24th, the ship again put out to sea; on 1493. February 24. Wednesday, they encountered another gale; and on the following Sunday, they were again in such peril that they made new vows. At daylight the next day, some February 25. land which they had seen in the night, not without gloomy apprehension of being driven upon it, proved to be the rock of Cintra. The mouth of the Tagus was before Rock of Cintra seen. them, and the people of the adjacent town, observing the peril of the strange ship, offered prayers for its safety. The entrance of the river was safely made and the In the Tagus. multitude welcomed them. Up the Tagus they went to Rastelo, and anchored at about three o'clock in the afternoon. Here Columbus learned that the wintry roughness which he had recently experienced was but a part of the general severity of the season. From this place he dispatched a messenger to Spain to convey the news of his arrival to his Sends letter to the king of Portugal. sovereigns, and at the same time he sent a letter to the king of Portugal, then sojourning nine leagues away. He explained in it how he had asked the hospitality of a Portuguese port, because the Spanish sovereigns had directed him to do so, if he needed supplies. He further informed the king that he had come from the "Indies," which he had reached by sailing west. He hoped he would be allowed to bring his caravel to Lisbon, to be more secure; for rumors of a lading of gold might incite reckless persons, in so lonely a place as he then lay, to deeds of violence.

The *Historie* says that Columbus had determined beforehand Name of India. to call whatever land he should discover, India, because he thought India was a name to suggest riches, and to invite encouragement for his project.

While this letter to the Portuguese king was in transit, the attempt was made by certain officers of the Portuguese navy in the port of Rastelo to induce Columbus to leave his ship and give an account of himself; but he would make no compromise of the dignity of a Castilian admiral. When his resentment was known and his commission was shown, the Portuguese officers changed their policy to one of courtesy.

The next day, and on the one following, the news of his arrival being spread about, a vast multitude came in boats from all parts to see him and his Indians.

On the third day, a royal messenger brought an invitation from the king to come and visit the court, which Co- <sub>1493.</sub> lumbus, not without apprehension, accepted. The <sup>March 8.</sup> king's steward had been sent to accompany him and provide for his entertainment on the way. On the night of the following day, he reached Val do Paraiso, where the <sub>Columbus visits the king was. This spot was nine leagues from Lisbon,</sub> <sup>king.</sup> and it was supposed that his reception was not held in that city because a pest was raging there. A royal greeting was given to him. The king affected to believe that the voyage of Columbus was made to regions which the Portuguese had been allowed to occupy by a convention agreed upon with Spain in 1479. The Admiral undeceived him, and showed the king that his ships had not been near Guinea.

We have another account of this interview at Val do Paraiso, in the pages of the Portuguese historian, Barros, tinged, doubtless, with something of pique and prejudice, because the profit of the voyage had not been for the benefit of Portugal. That historian charges Columbus with extravagance, and even insolence, in his language to the king. He says that Columbus chided the monarch for the faithlessness that had lost him such an empire. He is represented as launching these rebukes so vehemently that the attending nobles were provoked to a degree which prompted whispers of assassination. That Columbus found his first harbor in the Tagus has given other of the older Portuguese writers, like Faria y Sousa, in his *Europa Portuguesa*, and Vasconcelles and Resende, in their lives of João II., occasion to represent that his entering it was not so much induced by stress of weather as to seek a triumph over the Portuguese king in the first flush of the news. It is also said that the resolution was formed by the king to avail himself of the knowledge of two Portuguese who were found among Columbus's men. With their aid he proposed to send an armed expedition to take possession of the new-found regions before Columbus could fit out a fleet for a second voyage. Francisco de Almeida was even selected, according to the report, to command this force. We hear, however, nothing more of it, and the Bull of Demarcation put an end to all such rivalries.

If, on the contrary, we may believe Columbus himself, in a letter which he subsequently wrote, he did not escape being suspected in Spain of having thus put himself in the power of the Portuguese in order to surrender the Indies to them.

Spending Sunday at court, Columbus departed on Monday, March 11, having first dispatched messages to the King and Queen of Spain. An escort of knights was provided for him, and taking the monastery of Villafranca on his way, he kissed the hand of the Portuguese queen, who was there lodging, and journeying on, arrived at his caravel on Tuesday night. The next day he put to sea, and on Thursday morning was off Cape St. Vincent. The next morning they were off the island of Saltes, and crossing bar with the flood, he anchored on March 15, 1493, not far from noon, where he had unmoored the "Santa Maria" over seven months before.

*1493. March 11. Columbus leaves the court.*

*Sails from the Tagus.*

*Reaches Palos, March 15, 1493.*

"I made the passage thither in seventy-one days," he says in his published letter; "and back in forty-eight, during thirteen of which number I was driven about by storms."

The "Pinta," which had parted company with the Admiral on the 14th of February, had been driven by the gale into Bayona, a port of Gallicia, in the northwest corner of Spain, whence Pinzon, its commander, had dispatched a messenger to give information of his arrival and of his intended visit to the Court. A royal order peremptorily stayed, however, his projected visit, and left the first announcement of the news to be proclaimed by Columbus himself. This is the story which later writers have borrowed from the *Historie.*

*The "Pinta's" experiences.*

Oviedo tells us that the "Pinta" put to sea again from the Gallician harbor, and entered the port of Palos on the same day with Columbus, but her commander, fearing arrest or other unpleasantness, kept himself concealed till Columbus had started for Barcelona. Not many days later Pinzon died in his own house in Palos. Las Casas would have us believe that his death arose from mortification at the displeasure of his sovereigns; but Harrisse points out that when Charles V. bestowed a coat-armor on the family, he recognized his merit as the discoverer of Española. There is little trustworthy information on the matter, and Muñoz, whose lack of knowledge prompts inferences on his part, represents that it was Pinzon's request to explain his desertion of Columbus, which was neglected by the Court, and impressed him with the royal displeasure.

*She reaches Palos.*

*Death of Pinzon.*

# CHAPTER XI.

COLUMBUS IN SPAIN AGAIN; MARCH TO SEPTEMBER, 1493.

PETER MARTYR tells us of the common ignorance and dread pervading the ordinary ranks of society, before and during the absence of Columbus, in respect to all that part of the earth's circumference which the sun looked upon beyond Gades, till it again cast its rays upon the Golden Chersonesus. During this absence from the known and habitable regions of the globe, that orb was thought to sweep over the ominous and foreboding Sea of Darkness. No one could tell how wide that sea was. The learned disagreed in their estimates. A conception, far under the actual condition, had played no small part in making the voyage of Columbus possible. Men possessed legends of its mysteries. Fables of its many islands were repeated ; but no one then living was credibly thought to have tested its glooms except by sailing a little beyond the outermost of the Azores.

It calls for no stretch of the imagination to picture the public sentiment in little Palos during the months of anxiety which many households had endured since that August morning, when in its dim light Columbus, the Pinzons, and all their companions had been wafted gently out to sea by the current and the breeze. The winter had been unusually savage and weird. The navigators to the Atlantic islands had reported rough passages, and the ocean had broken wildly for long intervals along the rocks and sands of the peninsular shores. It is a natural movement of the mind to wrap the absent in the gloom of the present hour ; and while Columbus had been passing along the gentle waters of the new archipelago, his actual experiences had been in strange contrast to the turmoil of the sea as it washed the European shores. He had indeed suffered on his return voyage the full tumultuousness of the elements, and we can hardly fail to recognize the disquiet of mind and falling of heart which those savage gales

Palos aroused at the return of Columbus.

must have given to the kin and friends of the untraceable wanderers.

The stories, then, which we have of the thanksgiving and jubilation of the people of Palos, when the "Nina" was descried passing the bar of the river, fall readily among the accepted truths of history. We can imagine how despondency vanished amid the acclaims of exultation ; how multitudes hung upon the words of strange revelations ; how the gaping populace wondered at the bedecked Indians ; and how throngs of people opened a way that Columbus might lead the votive procession to the church. The canonizers of course read between the lines of the records that it was to the Church of Rabida that Columbus with his men now betook themselves. It matters little.

There was much to mar the delight of some in the households. Comforting reports must be told of those who were left at La Navidad. No one had died, unless the gale had submerged the "Pinta" and her crew. She had not been seen since the "Nina" parted with her in the gale.

The story of her rescue has already been told. She entered the river before the rejoicings of the day were over, and relieved the remaining anxiety.

The Spanish Court was known to be at this time at Barcelona, the Catalan port on the Mediterranean. Columbus's first impulse was to proceed thither in his caravel ; but his recent hazards made him prudent, and so dispatching a messenger to the Court, he proceeded to Seville to wait their majesties' commands. Of the native prisoners which he had brought away, one had died at sea, three were too sick to follow him, and were left at Palos, while six accompanied him on his journey.

The Court at Barcelona.

The messenger with such startling news had sped quickly ; and Columbus did not wait long for a response to his letter. The document (March 30) showed that the event had made a deep impression on the Court. The new domain of the west dwarfed for a while the conquests from the Moors. There was great eagerness to complete the title, and gather its wealth. Columbus was accordingly instructed to set in motion at once measures for a new expedition, and then to appear at Court and explain to the monarchs what action on their part was needful. The demand was

1493. March 30. Columbus summoned to Court.

promptly answered; and having organized the necessary arrangements in Seville for the preparation of a fleet, he departed for Barcelona to make homage to his sovereigns. His Indians accompanied him. Porters bore his various wonders from the new islands. His story had preceded him, and town after town vied with each other in welcoming him, and passing him on to new amazements and honors.

By the middle of April he approached Barcelona, and was met by throngs of people, who conducted him into the city. His Indians, arrayed in effective if not accustomed ornament of gold, led the line. Bearers of all the marvels of the Indies followed, with their forty parrots and other strange birds of liveliest plumage, with the skins of unknown animals, with priceless plants that would now supplant the eastern spices, and with the precious ornaments of the dusky kings and princes whom he had met. Next, on horseback, came Columbus himself, conspicuous amid the mounted chivalry of Spain. Thus the procession marched on, through crowded streets, amid the shouts of lookers-on, to the alcazar of the Moorish kings in the Calle Ancha, at this time the residence of the Bishop of Urgil, where it is supposed Ferdinand and Isabella had caused their thrones to be set up, with a canopy of brocaded gold drooping about them. Here the monarchs awaited the coming of Columbus.

*1493. April. In Barcelona.*

*Received by the sovereigns.*

Ferdinand, as the accounts picture him, was a man whose moderate stature was helped by his erectness and robes to a decided dignity of carriage. His expression in the ruddy glow of his complexion, clearness of eye, and loftiness of brow, grew gracious in any pleasurable excitement. The Queen was a very suitable companion, grave and graceful in her demeanor. Her blue eyes and auburn tresses comported with her outwardly benign air, and one looked sharply to see anything of her firmness and courage in the prevailing sweetness of her manner. The heir apparent, Prince Juan, was seated by their side. The dignitaries of the Court were grouped about.

*King Ferdinand.*

*Queen Isabella.*

Las Casas tells us how commanding Columbus looked when he entered the room, surrounded by a brilliant company of cavaliers. When he approached the royal dais, both monarchs rose to receive him standing; and

*Columbus before the Court.*

when he stooped to kiss their hands, they gently and graciously lifted him, and made him sit as they did. They then asked to be told of what he had seen.

As Columbus proceeded in his narrative, he pointed out the visible objects of his speech, — the Indians, the birds, the skins, the barbaric ornaments, and the stores of gold. We are told of the prayer of the sovereigns at the close, in which all joined ; and of the chanted *Te Deum* from the choir of the royal chapel, which bore the thoughts of every one, says the narrator, on the wings of melody to celestial delights. This ceremony ended, Columbus was conducted like a royal guest to the lodgings which had been provided for him.

It has been a question if the details of this reception, which are put by Irving in imaginative fullness, and are commonly told on such a thread of incidents as have been related, are warranted by the scant accounts which are furnished us in the *Historie*, in Las Casas, and in Peter Martyr, particularly since the incident does not seem to have made enough of an impression at the time to have been noticed at all in the *Dietaria* of the city, a record of events embodying those of far inferior interest as we would now value them. Mr. George Sumner carefully scanned this record many years ago, and could find not the slightest reference to the festivities. He fancies that the incidents in the mind of the recorder may have lost their significance through an Aragonese jealousy of the supremacy of Leon and Castile.

It is certainly true that in Peter Martyr, the contemporary observer of this supposed pageantry, there is nothing to warrant the exuberance of later writers. Martyr simply says that Columbus was allowed to sit in the sovereigns' presence.

Whatever the fact as to details, it seems quite evident that this season at Barcelona made the only unalloyed days of happiness, freed of anxiety, which Columbus ever experienced. He was observed of all, and everybody was complacent to him. His will was apparently law to King and subject. Las Casas tells us that he passed among the admiring throngs with his face wreathed with smiles of content. An equal complacency of delight and expectation settled upon all with whom he talked of the wonders of the land which he had found. They dreamed as he did of entering into golden cities with their hundred bridges, that might cause new exultations, to which the present were as nothing. It was a fatal lure to the proud Spanish nature, and no one was doomed to expiate the folly of the delusion more poignantly than Columbus himself.

Now that India had been found by the west, as was believed, and Barcelona was very likely palpitating with the thought, the news spread in every direction. What were the discoveries of the Phœnicians to this? What questions of ethnology, language, species, migrations, phenomena of all sorts, in man and in the natural world, were pressing upon the mind, as the results were considered? Were not these parrots which Columbus had exhibited such as Pliny tells us are in Asia? Spread of the news.

The great event had fallen in the midst of geographical development, and was understood at last. Marco Polo and the others had told their marvels of the east. The navigators of Prince Henry had found new wonders on the sea. Regiomontanus, Behaim, and Toscanelli had not communed in vain with cosmographical problems. Even errors had been stepping-stones ; as when the belief in the easterly over-extension of Asia had pictured it near enough in the west to convince men that the hazard of the Sea of Darkness was not so great after all.

Spain was then the centre of much activity of mind. " I am here," records Peter Martyr, " at the source of this welcome intelligence from the new found lands, and as the historian of such events, I may hope to go down to posterity as their recorder." We must remember this profession when we try to account for his meagre record of the reception at Barcelona. Peter Martyr records the event.

That part of the letter of Peter Martyr, dated at Barcelona, on the ides of May, 1493, which conveyed to his correspondent the first tidings of Columbus's return, is in these words, as translated by Harrisse : " A certain Christopher Colonus, a Ligurian, returned from the antipodes. He had obtained for that purpose three ships from my sovereigns, with much difficulty, because the ideas which he expressed were considered extravagant. He came back and brought specimens of many precious things, especially gold, which those regions naturally produce." Martyr also tells us that when Pomponius Laetus got such news, he could scarcely refrain " from tears of joy at so unlooked-for an event." " What more delicious food for an ingenious mind ! " said Martyr to him in return. " To talk with people who have seen all this is elevating to the mind." The confidence of Martyr, however, in the belief of Columbus that the true Indies had been found was not marked. He speaks of the islands as adjacent to, and not themselves, the East.

Sebastian Cabot remembered the time when these marvelous tidings reached the court of Henry VII. in London, and he tells us that it was accounted a " thing more divine than human."

The news in England.

A letter which Columbus had written and early dispatched to Barcelona, nearly in duplicate, to the treasurers of the two crowns was promptly translated into Latin, and was sent to Italy to be issued in numerous editions, to be copied in turn by the Paris and Antwerp printers, and a little more sluggishly by those of Germany.

Columbus's first letter.

There is, however, singularly little commenting on these events that passed into print and has come down to us ; and we may well doubt if the effect on the public mind, beyond certain learned circles, was at all commensurate with what we may now imagine the recognition of so important an event ought to have been. Nordenskiöld, studying the cartography and literature of the early discoveries in America in his *Facsimile Atlas*, is forced to the conclusion that " scarcely any discovery of importance was ever received with so much indifference, even in circles where sufficient genius and statesmanship ought to have prevailed to appreciate the changes they foreshadowed in the development of the economical and political conditions of mankind."

Influence of the event.

It happened on June 19, 1493, but a few weeks after the Pope had made his first public recognition of the discovery, that the Spanish ambassador at ·the Papal Court, Bernardin de Carjaval, referred in an oration to " the unknown lands, lately found, lying towards the Indies ; " and at about the same time there was but a mere reference to the event in the *Los Tratados* of Doctor Alonso Ortis, published at Seville.

1493. June 19. Carjaval's oration.

While this strange bruit was thus spreading more or less, we get some glimpses of the personal life of Columbus during these days of his sojourn in Barcelona. We hear of him riding through the streets on horseback, on one side of the King, with Prince Juan on the other.

We find record of his being awarded the pension of thirty crowns, as the first discoverer of land, by virtue of the mysterious light, and Irving thinks that we may condone this theft from the brave sailor who unquestionably saw land the first, by remembering that " Columbus's whole ambition was involved." It seems to others that his whole character was involved.

We find him a guest at a banquet given by Cardinal Mendoza, and the well-known story of his making an egg stand upright, by chipping one end of it, is associated with this merriment of the table. An impertinent question of a shallow courtier had induced Columbus to show a table full of guests that it was easy enough to do anything when the way was pointed out. The story, except as belonging to a traditional stock of anecdotes, dating far back of Columbus, always ready for an application, has no authority earlier than Benzoni, and loses its point in the destruction of the end on which the aim was to make it stand. This has been so palpable to some of the repeaters of the story that they have supposed that the feat was accomplished, not by cracking the end of the egg, but by using a quick motion which broke the sack which holds the yolk, so that that weightier substance settled at one end, and balanced the egg in an upright position.

So passed the time with the new-made hero, in drinking, as Irving expresses it, " the honeyed draught of popularity before enmity and detraction had time to drug it with bitterness."

We find the sovereigns bestowing upon him, on the 20th of May, a coat of arms, which shows a castle and a lion in the upper quarters, and in those below, a group of golden islands in a sea of waves, on the one hand, and the arms to which his family had been entitled, on the other. Humboldt speaks of this archipelago as the first map of America, but he apparently knew only Oviedo's description of the arms, for the latter places the islands in a gulf formed by a mainland, and in this fashion they are grouped in a blazon of the arms which is preserved at the Ministry of Foreign Affairs at Paris — a duplicate being at Genoa. Harrisse says that this design is the original water-color, made under Columbus's eye in 1502. In this picture, — which is the earliest blazonry which has come down to us, — the other lower quarter has the five golden anchors on a blue ground, which it is claimed was ad-

THE ARMS OF COLUMBUS.
[From Oviedo's *Coronica*.]

judged to Columbus as the distinctive badge of an Admiral of Spain. The personal arms are relegated to a minor overlying shield at the lower point of the escutcheon. Oviedo also says that trees and other objects should be figured on the mainland.

The lion and castle of the original grant were simply re-minders of the arms of Leon and Castile; but Columbus seems, of his own motion, so far as Harrisse can discover, to have changed the blazonry of those objects in the drawing of 1502 to agree with those of the royal arms. It was by the same arrogant license, apparently, that he introduced later the continental shore of the archipelago; and Harrisse can find no record that the anchors were ever by any authority added to his blazon, nor that the professed family arms, borne in connection, had any warrant whatever.

The earliest engraved copy of the arms is in the *Historia General* of Oviedo in 1535, where a profile helmet supports a crest made of a globe topped by a cross. In Oviedo's *Coronica* of 1547, the helmet is shown in front view. There seems to have been some wide discrepancies in the heraldic excursions of these early writers. Las Casas, for instance, puts the golden lion in a silver field, — when heraldry abhors a conjunction of metals, as much as nature abhors a vacuum. The discussion of the family arms which were added by Columbus to the escutcheon made a significant part of the arguments in the suit, many years later, of Baldassare (Balthazar) Colombo to possess the Admiral's dignities ; and as Harrisse points out, the emblem of those Italian Colombos of any pretensions to nobility was invariably a dove of some kind, — a device quite distinct from those designated by Columbus. This assumption of family arms by Columbus is held by Harrisse to be simply a concession to the prejudices of his period, and to the exigencies of his new position.

The arms have been changed under the dukes of Veragua to show silver-capped waves in the sea, while a globe surmounted by a cross is placed in the midst of a gulf containing only five islands.

There is another later accompaniment of the arms, of which the origin has escaped all search. It is far more familiar than the escutcheon, on which it plays the part of a motto. His alleged It sometimes represents that Columbus found for the motto. allied crowns a new world, and at other times that he gave one to them.

> Por Castilla é por Leon
> Nuevo Mundo halló Colon.

> A Castilla, y a Leon
> Nuevo Mundo dió Colon.

Oviedo is the earliest to mention this distich in 1535. It is given in the *Historie*, not as a motto of the arms, but as an inscription placed by the king on the tomb of Columbus some years after his death. If this is true, it does away with the claims of Gomara that Columbus himself added it to his arms.

But diplomacy had its part to play in these events. As the Christian world at that time recognized the rights of the Holy Father to confirm any trespass on the possessions of the heathen, there was a prompt effort on the part of Ferdinand to bring the matter to the attention of the Pope. As early as 1438, bulls of Martin V. and Eugene IV. had permitted the Spaniards to sail west and the Portuguese south; and a confirmation of the same had been made by Pope Nicholas the Fifth. In 1479, the rival crowns of Portugal and Spain had agreed to respect their mutual rights under these papal decisions.

Diplomacy of the Bull of Demarcation.

The messengers whom Ferdinand sent to Rome were instructed to intimate that the actual possession which had been made in their behalf of these new regions did not require papal sanction, as they had met there no Christian occupants; but that as dutiful children of the church it would be grateful to receive such a benediction on their energies for the faith as a confirmatory bull would imply. Ferdinand had too much of wiliness in his own nature, and the practice of it was too much a part of the epoch, wholly to trust a man so notoriously perverse and obstinate as Alexander VI. was. Though Muñoz calls Alexander the friend of Ferdinand, and though the Pope was by birth an Aragonese, experience had shown that there was no certainty of his support in a matter affecting the interest of Spain.

A folio printed leaf in Gothic characters, of which the single copy sold in London in 1854 is said to be the only one known to bibliographers, made public to the world the famous Bull of Demarcation of Alexander VI., bearing date May 3, 1493. If one would believe Hakluyt, the Pope had been induced to do this act by his own option, rather than at the intercession of the Spanish monarchs. Under it, and a second bull of the day following, Spain was entitled to possess, " on condition of planting the Catholic

1493. May 3. The Bull issued.

POPE ALEXANDER VI.
[A bust in the Berlin Museum.]

faith," all lands not already occupied by Christian powers, west of a meridian drawn one hundred leagues west of the Azores and Cape de Verde Islands, evidently on the supposition that these two groups were in the same longitude, the fact being that the most westerly of the southern, and the most easterly of the northern, group possessed nearly the same meridian. Though Portugal was not mentioned in describing this line, it was understood that there was reserved to her the same privilege easterly.

There was not as yet any consideration given to the division which this great circle meridian was likely to make on the other side of the globe, where Portugal was yet to be most interested. The Cape of Good Hope had not then been doubled, and the present effect of the division was to confine the Portuguese to an exploration of the western African coast and to adjacent islands. It will be observed that in the placing of this line the magnetic phenomena which Columbus had observed on his recent voyage were not forgotten, if the coincidence can be so interpreted. Humboldt suggests that it can.

To make a physical limit serve a political one was an obvious
Line of no variation. recourse at a time when the line of no variation was thought to be unique and of a true north and south direction; but within a century the observers found three other lines, as Acosta tells us in his *Historia Natural de las Indias*, in 1589; and there proved to be a persistent migration of these lines, all little suited to terrestrial demarcations. Roselly de Lorgues and the canonizers, however, having given to Columbus the planning of the line in his cell at Rabida, think, with a surprising prescience on his part, and with a very convenient obliviousness on their part, that he had chosen " precisely the only point of our planet which science would choose in our day, — a mysterious demarcation made by its omnipotent Creator," in sovereign disregard, unfortunately, of the laws of his own universe!

Meanwhile there were movements in Portugal which Ferdinand had not failed to notice. An ambassador had
Suspicious movements in Portugal. come from its king, asking permission to buy certain articles of prohibited exportation for use on an African expedition which the Portuguese were fitting out. Ferdinand suspected that the true purpose of this armament was to seize

the new islands, under a pretense as dishonorable as that which covered the ostensible voyage to the Cape de Verde Islands, by whose exposure Columbus had been driven into Spain. The Spanish monarch was alert enough to get quite beforehand with his royal brother. Before the ambassador of which mention has been made had come to the Spanish Court, Ferdinand had dispatched Lope de Herrera to Lisbon, armed with a conciliatory and a denunciatory letter, to use one or the other, as he might find the conditions demanded. The Portuguese historian Resende tells us that João, in order to give a wrong scent, had openly bestowed largesses on some and had secretly suborned other members of Ferdinand's cabinet, so that he did not lack for knowledge of the Spanish intentions from the latter members. He and his ambassadors were accordingly found by Ferdinand to be inexplicably prepared at every new turn of the negotiations.

In this way João had been informed of the double mission of Herrera, and could avoid the issue with him, while he sent his own ambassadors to Spain, to promise that, pending their negotiations, no vessel should sail on any voyage of discovery for sixty days. They were also to propose that instead of the papal line, one should be drawn due west from the Canaries, giving all new discoveries north to the Spaniards, and all south to the Portuguese. This new move Ferdinand turned to his own advantage, for it gave him the opportunity to enter upon a course of diplomacy which he could extend long enough to allow Columbus to get off with a new armament. He then sent a fresh embassy, with instructions to move slowly and protract the discussion, but to resort, when compelled, to a proposition for arbitration. João was foiled and he knew it. " These ambassadors," he said, " have no feet to hurry and no head to propound." The Spanish game was the best played, and the Portuguese king grew fretful under it, and intimated sometimes a purpose to proceed to violence, but he was restrained by a better wisdom. We depend mainly upon the Portuguese historians for understanding these complications, and it is to be hoped that some time the archives of the Vatican may reveal the substance of these tripartite negotiations of the papal court and the two crowns.

Before Columbus had left Barcelona, a large gratuity had

been awarded to him by his sovereigns; an order had been issued commanding free lodgings to be given to him and his followers, wherever he went, and the original stipulations as to honors and authority, made by the sovereigns at Santa Fé, had been confirmed (May 28). A royal seal was now confided to his keeping, to be set to letters patent, and to commissions that it might be found necessary to issue. It might be used even in appointing a deputy, to act in the absence of Columbus. His appointments were to hold during the royal pleasure. His own power was defined at the same time, and in particular to hold command over the entire expedition, and to conduct its future government and explorations. He left Barcelona, after leavetakings, on May 28; and his instructions, as printed by Navarrete, were signed the next day. It is not unlikely they were based on suggestions of Columbus made in a letter, without date, which has recently been printed in the *Cartas de Indias* (1877). Early in June, he was in Seville, and soon after he was joined by Juan Rodriguez de Fonseca, archdeacon of Seville, who, as representative of the Crown, had been made the chief director of the preparations. It is claimed by Harrisse that this priest has been painted by the biographers of Columbus much blacker than he really was, on the strength of the objurgations which the *Historie* bestows upon him. Las Casas calls him worldly; and he deserves the epithet if a dominating career of thirty years in controlling the affairs of the Indies is any evidence of fitness in such matters. His position placed him where he had purposes to thwart as well as projects to foster, and the record of this age of discovery is not without many proofs of selfish and dishonorable motives, which Fonseca might be called upon to repress. That his discrimination was not always clear-sighted may be expected; that he was sometimes perfidious may be true, but he was dealing mainly with those who could be perfidious also. That he abused his authority might also go without dispute; but so did Columbus and the rest. In the game of diamond-cut-diamond, it is not always just to single out a single victim for condemnation, as is done by Irving and the canonizers.

It was while at Seville, engaged in this work of preparation,

1493. May. Honors of Columbus confirmed.

May 28. Columbus leaves Barcelona.

June. In Seville.

Fonseca.

that Fonseca sought to check the demands of Columbus as respects the number of his personal servitors. That these demands were immoderate, the character of Columbus, never cautious under incitement, warrants us in believing; and that the official guardian of the royal treasury should have views of his own is not to be wondered at. The story goes that the sovereigns forced Fonseca to yield, and that this was the offense of Columbus which could neither be forgotten nor forgiven by Fonseca, and for which severities were visited upon him and his heirs in the years to come. Irving is confident that Fonseca has escaped the condemnation which Spanish writers would willingly have put upon him, for fear of the ecclesiastical censors of the press.

The measures which were now taken in accordance with the instructions given to Columbus, already referred to, to regulate the commerce of the Indies, with a custom house at Cadiz and a corresponding one in Española under the control of the Admiral, ripened in time into what was known as the Council for the Indies. It had been early determined (May 23) to control all emigration to the new regions, and no one was allowed to trade thither except under license from the monarchs, Columbus, or Fonseca.

*Council for the Indies.*

A royal order had put all ships and appurtenances in the ports of Andalusia at the demand of Fonseca and Columbus, for a reasonable compensation, and compelled all persons required for the service to embark in it on suitable pay. Two thirds of the ecclesiastical tithes, the sequestered property of banished Jews, and other resources were set apart to meet these expenses, and the treasurer was authorized to contract a loan, if necessary. To eke out the resources, this last was resorted to, and 5,000,000 maravedis were borrowed from the Duke of Medina-Sidonia. All the transactions relating to the procuring and dispensing of moneys had been confided to a treasurer, Francisco Pinelo; with the aid of an accountant, Juan de Soria. Everything was hurriedly gathered for the armament, for it was of the utmost importance that the preparations should move faster than the watching diplomacy.

*New fleet equipped.*

Artillery which had been in use on shipboard for more than a century and a half was speedily amassed. The arquebuse, however, had not altogether been supplanted by the matchlock, and was yet preferred in some hands for its lightness. Military stores which had been left over from the Moorish war and were now housed in the Alhambra, at this time converted into an arsenal, were opportunely drawn upon.

The labor of an intermediary in much of this preparation fell upon Beradi and Vespucius. Juonato Beradi, a Florentine merchant then settled in Seville, and it is interesting to know that Americus Vespucius, then a mature man of two and forty, was engaged under Beradi in this work of preparation.

From the fact that certain horsemen and agriculturists were ordered to be in 1493. June 20. Seville on June 20, and to hold themselves in readiness to embark, it may be inferred that the sailing of some portion of the fleet may at that time have been expected at a date not much later.

The interest of Isabella in the new expedition was almost

**Der Pogner.**

Gut Armbroster kan machen ich/
Die Seulen zier ich fleissiglich/
Mit gwechs/schneweissem bein durchzogn/
Mit Hürnen oder Schälen pogn/
Darauff windfadn vnd ein Sännen/
Die nicht leichtlich ist zutrennen/
Darmit man gwiß zum Ziel mag schießn/
Der Kunst Syrus wir mit genießn.

X ij                    Der

CROSSBOW-MAKER.
[From Jost Amman's *Beschreibung*, 1586.]

wholly on its emotional and intellectual side. She had been greatly engrossed with the spiritual welfare of the In- Isabella's dians whom Columbus had taken to Barcelona. Their interest. baptism had taken place with great state and ceremony, the King, Queen, and Prince Juan officiating as sponsors. Indians bap-It was intended that they should reëmbark with the tized. new expedition. Prince Juan, however, picked out one of these Indians for his personal service, and when the fellow died, two years later, it was a source of gratification, as Herrera tells us, that at last one of his race had entered the gates of heaven! Only four of the six ever reached their native country. We know nothing of the fate of those left sick at Palos.

The Pope, to further all methods for the extension of the faith, had commissioned (June 24) a Benedictine Father Buil. monk, Bernardo Buil (Boyle), of Catalonia, to be his apostolic vicar in the new world, and this priest was to be ac-companied by eleven brothers of the order. The Queen in-trusted to them the sacred vessels and vestments from her own altar. The instructions which Columbus received were to deal lovingly with the poor natives. We shall see how faithful he was to the behest.

Isabella's musings were not, however, all so piously confined. She wrote to Columbus from Segovia in August, requiring him to make provisions for bringing back to Spain specimens of the peculiar birds of the new regions, as indications of untried climates and seasons.

Again, in writing to Columbus, September 5, she urged him not to rely wholly on his own great knowledge, but to Astronomy take such a skillful astronomer on his voyage as Fray and naviga-Antonio de Marchena, — the same whom Columbus tion. later spoke of as being one of the two persons who had never made him a laughing-stock. Muñoz says the office of astron-omer was not filled.

Dealing with the question of longitude was a matter in which there was at this time little insight, and no general agreement. Columbus, as we have seen, suspected the variation of the needle might afford the basis of a system ; but he grew to appre-hend, as he tells us in the narrative of his fourth voyage, that the astronomical method was the only infallible one, but whether his preference was for the opposition of planets, the occultations of stars, the changes in the moon's declination, or the comparisons of Jupiter's altitude with the lunar position, — all of which were in some form in vogue, — does not appear. The method by conveyance of time, so well known now in the use of chronometers, seems to have later been suggested by Alonso de Santa Cruz, — too late for the recognition of Columbus; but the instrumentality of water-clocks, sand-clocks, and other crude devices, like the timing of burning wicks, was too uncertain to obtain even transient sanction.

Der Vhrmacher.

Ich mache die reyſenden Vhr/
Gerecht vnd Glatt nach der Menſur/
Von hellem glaß vnd kleim Vhrſant/
Gut/daß ſie haben langen beſtandt/
Mach auch darzu Hültzen Geheuß/
Dareyn ich ſie fleiſſig beſchleuß/
Ferb die gheuß Grün/Graw/rot vñ blaw
Drinn man die Stund vnd vierteil hab.
                                    S üj  Der

THE CLOCK-MAKER.
[From Jost Amman's *Beschreibung*, Frankfort.]

The astrolabe, for all the improvements of Behaim, was still an awkward instrument for ascertaining latitude, especially on a rolling

Astrolabe.

or pitching ship, and we know that Vasco da Gama went on shore at the Cape de Verde Islands to take observations when the motion of the sea balked him on shipboard.

Whether the cross-staff or Jackstaff, a seaboard implement somewhat more convenient than the astrolabe, was known to Columbus is not very clear, — probably it was not; but the navigators that soon followed him found it more man- Cross-staff ageable on rolling ships than the older instruments. and Jackstaff. It was simply a stick, along which, after one end of it was placed at the eye, a scaled crossbar was pushed until its two ends touched, the lower, the horizon, and the upper, the heavenly body whose altitude was to be taken. A scale on the stick then showed, at the point where the bar was left, the degree of latitude.

The best of such aids, however, did not conduce to great accuracy, and the early maps, in comparison with modern, show sometimes several degrees of error in scaling from the equator. An error once committed was readily copied, and different cartographical records put in service by the professional map-makers came sometimes by a process of averages to show some sur- prising diversities, with positive errors of considerable Errors in extent. The island of Cuba, for instance, early found latitude. place in the charts seven and eight degrees too far north, with dependent islands in equally wrong positions.

As the preparations went on, a fleet of seventeen vessels, large and small, three of which were called transports, had, according to the best estimates, finally been put in readiness. Scillacio tells us that some of the smallest had been constructed of light draft, especially for exploring service. Horses and domestic animals of all kinds were at last gathered on board. Seventeen Every kind of seed and agricultural implement, stores vessels of commodities for barter with the Indians, and all the ready. appurtenances of active life were accumulated. Muñoz re- marks that it is evident that sugar cane, rice, and vines had not been discovered or noted by Columbus on his first voyage, or we would not have found them among the commodities provided for the second.

In making up the company of the adventurers, there was lit- tle need of active measures to induce recruits. Many Their com- an Hidalgo and cavalier took service at their own panies. cost. Galvano, who must have received the reports by tradi- tion, says that such was the " desire of travel that the men were ready to leap into the sea to swim, if it had been possible, into these new found parts." Traffic, adventure, luxury, feats of arms, — all were inducements that lured one individual or another. Some there were to make names for themselves in their new fields. Such was Alonso de Ojeda, a daring youth, expert in all activities, who had served his ambition in the Moorish wars, and had been particularly favored by the Duke of Medina-Celi, the friend of Columbus.

Ojeda.

We find others whose names we shall again encounter. The younger brother of Columbus, Diego Colon, had come to Spain, attracted by the success of Christopher. The father and uncle of Las Casas, from whose conversations with the Admiral that historian could profit in the future, Juan Ponce de Leon, the later discoverer of Florida, Juan de la Cosa, whose map is the first we have of the New World, and Dr. Chanca, a physician of Seville, who was pensioned by the Crown, and to whom we owe one of the narratives of the voyage, were also of the company.

Las Casas, Ponce de Leon, La Cosa, etc.

The thousand persons to which the expedition had at first been limited became, under the pressure of eager cavaliers, nearer 1,200, and this number was eventually increased by stowaways and other hangers-on, till the number embarked was not much short of 1,500. This is Oviedo's statement. Bernaldez and Peter Martyr make the number 1,200, or thereabouts. Perhaps these were the ordinary hands, and the 300 more were officers and the like, for the statements do not render it certain how the enumerations are made. So far as we know their names, but a single companion of Columbus in his first voyage was now with him. The twenty horsemen already mentioned are supposed to be the only mounted soldiers that embarked. Columbus says, in a letter addressed to their majesties, that " the number of colonists who desire to go thither amounts to two thousand," which would indicate that a large number were denied. The letter is undated, and may not be of a date near the sailing ; if it is, it probably indicates to some degree the number of persons who were denied embarkation. As the day approached for the departure there was some uneasiness over a report of a Portuguese caravel sailing westward from Madeira, and it was proposed to send some of the fleet in advance to overtake the vessel ; but after some diplomatic fence between Ferdi-

1,500 souls embark.

nand and João, the disquiet ended, or at least nothing was done on either side.

At one time Columbus had hoped to embark on the 15th of August; but it was six weeks later before everything was ready.

# CHAPTER XII.

## THE SECOND VOYAGE.

### 1493–1494.

THE last day in port was a season of solemnity and gratula-

The embar-<br>kation. tion. Coma, a Spaniard, who, if not an eyewitness, got his description from observers, thus describes the scene in a letter to Scillacio in Pavia: "The religious rites usual on such occasions were performed by the sailors; the last embraces were given; the ships were hung with brilliant cloths; streamers were wound in the rigging; and the royal standard flapped everywhere at the sterns of the vessels. The pipers and harpers held in mute astonishment the Nereids and even the Sirens with their sweet modulations. The shores reëchoed the clang of trumpets and the braying of clarions. The discharge of cannon rolled over the water. Some Venetian galleys chancing to enter the harbor joined in the jubilation, and the cheers of united nations went up with prayers for blessings on the venturing crews."

Night followed, calm or broken, restful or wearisome, as the

1493. Sep-<br>tember 25.<br>The fleet<br>sails. case might be, for one or another, and when the day dawned (September 25, 1493) the note of preparation was everywhere heard. It was the same on the three great caracks, on the lesser caravels, and on the light craft, which had been especially fitted for exploration. The eager and curious mass of beings which crowded their decks were certainly a motley show. There were cavalier and priest, hidalgo and artisan, soldier and sailor. The ambitious thoughts which animated them were as various as their habits. There were those of the adventurer, with no purpose whatever but pastime, be it easy or severe. There was the greed of the speculator, counting the values of trinkets against stores of gold.

There was the brooding of the administrators, with unsolved problems of new communities in their heads. There were ears that already caught the songs of salvation from native throats. There was Columbus himself, combining all ambitions in one, looking around this harbor of Cadiz studded with his lordly fleet, spreading its creaking sails, lifting its dripping anchors. It was his to contrast it with the scene at Palos a little over a year before. This needy Genoese vested with the viceroyalty of a new world was more of an adventurer than any. Columbus's He was a speculator who overstepped them all in au- character. dacious visions and golden expectancies. He was an administrator over a new government, untried and undivined. To his ears the hymns of the Church soared with a militant warning, dooming the heathen of the Indies, and appalling the Moslem hordes that imperiled the Holy Sepulchre.

Under the eye of this one commanding spirit, the vessels fell into a common course, and were wafted out upon the great ocean under the lead of the escorting galleys of the Venetians. The responsibility of the captain-general of the great armament had begun. He had been instructed to steer widely clear of the Portuguese coast, and he bore away in the lead directly to the southwest. On the seventh day (October 1) 1493. October 1. Canaries. they reached the Gran Canaria, where they tarried to repair a leaky ship. On the 5th they anchored at Gomera. Two days were required here to complete some parts of their equipment, for the islands had already become the centre of great industries and produced largely. " They have enterprising merchants who carry their commerce to many shores," wrote Coma to Scillacio.

There were wood and water to be taken on board. A variety of domestic animals, calves, goats, sheep, and swine ; some fowls, and the seed of many orchard and garden fruits, oranges, lemons, melons, and the like, were gathered from the inhabitants and stowed away in the remaining spaces of the ships.

On the 7th the fleet sailed, but it was not till the 13th that the gentle winds had taken them beyond Ferro and 1493. October 13. At sea. the unbounded sea was about the great Admiral. He bore away much more southerly than in his first voyage, so as to strike, if he could, the islands that were so constantly spoken of, the previous year, as lying southeasterly from Española.

His ultimate port was, of course, the harbor of La Navidad, and he had issued sealed instructions to all his commanders, to guide any one who should part company with the fleet. The winds were favorable, but the dull sailing of the Admiral's ship restrained the rest. In ten days they had overshot the longitude of the Sargossa Sea without seeing it, leaving its floating weeds to the north. In a few days more they experienced heavy St. Elmo's tempests. They gathered confidence from an old belief, when they saw St. Elmo waving his lambent flames about the upper rigging, while they greeted his presence with their prayers and songs.

"The fact is certain," says Coma, "that two lights shone through the darkness of the night on the topmast of the Admiral's ship. Forthwith the tempest began to abate, the sea to remit its fury, the waves their violence, and the surface of the waves became as smooth as polished marble." This sudden gale of four hours' duration came on St. Simon's eve.

The same authority represents that the protracted voyage had caused their water to run low, for the Admiral, confident of his nearness to land, and partly to reassure the timid, had caused it to be served unstintingly. "You might compare him to Moses," adds Coma, "encouraging the thirsty armies of the Israelites in the dry wastes of the wilderness."

On Saturday, November 2, the leaders compared reckonings. 1493. November 2. Some thought they had come 780 leagues from Ferro; others, 800. There were anxiety and weariness on board. The constant fatigue of bailing out the leaky ships had had its disheartening effect. Columbus, with a practiced eye, saw signs of land in the color of the water and the shifting winds, November 3. and he signaled every vessel to take in sail. It was a waiting night. The first light of Sunday glinted on the top of a lofty mountain ahead, descried by a watch at the Admiral's masthead. As the island was approached, the Admiral Dominica Island. named it, in remembrance of the holy day, Dominica. The usual service with the *Salve Regina* was chanted throughout the fleet, which moved on steadily, bringing island after island into view. Columbus could find no good anchorage Marigalante. at Dominica, and leaving one vessel to continue the search, he passed on to another island, which he named from his ship, Marigalante. Here he landed, set up the

GUADALOUPE, MARIE GALANTE, AND DOMINICA.
[From Henrique's *Les Colonies Françoises*, Paris, 1889.]

royal banner in token of possession of the group, — for he had
seen six islands, — and sought for inhabitants. He could find
none, nor any signs of occupation. There was nothing but a
tangle of wood in every direction, a sparkling mass of leafage,

trembling in luxurious beauty and giving off odors of spice. Some of the men tasted an unknown fruit, and suffered an immediate inflammation about the face, which it required remedies to assuage.   The next morning Columbus was attracted by the lofty volcanic peak of another island, and, sailing up to it, he could see cascades on the sides of this eminence.

1493. November 3. Guadaloupe.

" Among those who viewed this marvelous phenomena at a distance from the ships," says Coma, "it was at first a subject of dispute whether it were light reflected from masses of compact snow, or the broad surface of a smooth-worn road.   At last the opinion prevailed that it was a vast river."

Columbus remembered that he had promised the monks of Our Lady of Guadaloupe, in Estremadura, to place some token of them in this strange world, and so he gave this island the name of Guadaloupe.   Landing the next day, a week of wonders followed.

November 4.

The exploring parties found the first village abandoned; but this had been done so hastily that some young children had been left behind.   These they decked with hawks' bells, to win their returning parents.   One place showed a public square surrounded by rectangular houses, made of logs and intertwined branches, and thatched with palms.   They went through the houses and noted what they saw.   They observed at the entrance of one some serpents carved in wood.   They found netted hammocks, beside calabashes, pottery, and even skulls used for utensils of household service.   They discovered cloth made of cotton; bows and bone-tipped arrows, said sometimes to be pointed with human shin-bones; domesticated fowl very like geese; tame parrots; and pineapples, whose flavor enchanted them. They found what might possibly be relics of Europe, washed hither by the equatorial currents as they set from the African coasts, — an iron pot, as they thought it (we know this from the *Historie*), and the stern-timber of a vessel, which they could have less easily mistaken.   They found something to horrify them in human bones, the remains of a feast, as they were ready enough to believe, for they were seeking confirmation of the stories of cannibals which Columbus had heard on his first voyage.   They learned that boys were fattened like capons.

Cannibals.

[From Philoponus's *Nova Typis Transacta Navigatio.*]

The next day they captured a youth and some women, but the men eluded them. Columbus was now fully convinced that he had at last discovered the cannibals, and when it was found that one of his captains and eight men had not returned to their ship, he was under great apprehensions. He sent exploring parties into the woods. They hallooed and fired their arquebuses, but to no avail. As they threaded their way through the thickets, they came upon some villages, but the inhabitants fled, leaving their meals half cooked ; and they were convinced they saw human flesh on the spit and in the pots. While this party was absent, some women belonging to the neighboring islands, captives of this savage people, came off to the ships and sought protection. Columbus decked them with rings and bells, and forced them ashore, while they begged to remain. The islanders stripped off their ornaments, and allowed them to return for more. These women said that the chief of the island and most of the warriors were absent on a predatory expedition.

The party searching for the lost men returned without success, when Alonso de Ojeda offered to lead forty men into the interior for a more thorough search. This party was as unsuccessful as the other. Ojeda reported he had crossed twenty-six streams in going inland, and that the country was found everywhere abounding in odorous trees, strange and delicious fruits, and brilliant birds.

Ojeda's expedition.

While this second party was gone, the crews took aboard a supply of water, and on Ojeda's return Columbus resolved to proceed, and was on the point of sailing, when the absent men appeared on the shore and signaled to be taken off. They had got lost in a tangled and pathless forest, and all efforts to climb high enough in trees to see the stars and determine their course had been hopeless. Finally striking the sea, they had followed the shore till they opportunely espied the fleet. They brought with them some women and boys, but reported they had seen no men.

Among the accounts of these early experiences of the Spaniards with the native people, the story of cannibalism is a constant theme. To circulate such stories enhanced the wonder with which Europe was to be impressed. The cruelty of the custom was not altogether unwelcome to war-

Cannibals.

rant a retaliatory mercilessness. Historians have not wholly decided that this is enough to account for the most positive statements about man-eating tribes. Fears and prejudices might do much to raise such a belief, or at least to magnify the habits. Irving remarks that the preservation of parts of the human body, among the natives of Española, was looked upon as a votive service to ancestors, and it may have needed only prejudice to convert such a custom into cannibalism when found with the Caribs. The adventurousness of the nature Caribs. of this fierce people and their wanderings in wars naturally served to sharpen their intellects beyond the passive unobservance of the pacific tribes on which they preyed; so they became more readily, for this reason, the possessors of any passion or vice that the European instinct craved to fasten somewhere upon a strange people.

The contiguity of these two races, the fierce Carib and the timid tribes of the more northern islands, has long Caribs and puzzled the ethnologist. Irving indulged in some Lucayans. rambling notions of the origin of the Carib, derived from observations of the early students of the obscure relations of the American peoples. Larger inquiry and more scientific observation has since Irving's time been given to the subject, still without bringing the question to recognizable bearings. The craniology of the Caribs is scantily known, and there is much yet to be divulged. The race in its purity has long been extinct. Lucien de Rosny, in an anthropological study of the Antilles published by the French Society of Ethnology in 1886, has amassed considerable data for future deductions. It is a question with some modern examiners if the distinction between these insular peoples was not one of accident and surroundings rather than of blood.

When Columbus sailed from Guadaloupe on November 10, he steered northwest for Española, though his captives told him that the mainland lay to the south. He 1493. November 10. passed various islands, but did not cast anchor till the Columbus leaves Guadaloupe. 14th, when he reached the island named by him Santa Cruz, and found it still a region of Caribs. It was here the Spaniards had their first fight with this fierce people in trying to capture a canoe filled with them. The white men rammed and overturned the hollowed log ; but the Indians fought in the water so courageously that some of the Spanish bucklers were pierced with the native poisoned arrows, and one of the Spaniards, later, died of such a wound inflicted by one of the savage women. All the Caribs, however, were finally captured and placed in irons on board ship. One was so badly wounded that recovery was not thought possible, and he was thrown overboard. The fellow struck for the shore, and was killed by the Spanish arrows. The accounts describe their ferocious aspect, their coarse hair, their eyes circled with red paint, and the muscular parts of their limbs artificially extended by tight bands below and above.

Proceeding thence and passing a group of wild and craggy islets, which he named after St. Ursula and her Eleven Thousand Virgins, Columbus at last reached the island now called Porto Rico, which his captives pointed out to him as their home and the usual field of the Carib incursions. The island struck the strangers by its size, its beautiful woods and many harbors, in one of which, at its west end, they finally anchored. There was a village close by, which, by their accounts, was trim, and not without some pretensions to skill in laying out, with its seaside terraces. The inhabitants, however, had fled. Two days later, the fleet weighed anchor and steered for La Navidad.

It was the 22d of November when the explorers made a level shore, which they later discovered to be the eastern end of Española. They passed gently along the northern coast, and at an attractive spot sent a boat ashore with the body of the Biscayan sailor who had died of the poisoned arrow, while two of the light caravels hovered near the beach to protect the burying party. Coming to the spot where Columbus had had his armed conflict with the natives the year before, and where one of the Indians who had been baptized at Barcelona was taken, this fellow, loaded with presents and decked in person, was sent on shore for the influence he might exert on his people. This supposable neophyte does not again appear in history. Only one of these native converts now remained, and the accounts say that he lived faithfully with the Spaniards. Five of the seven who embarked had died on the voyage.

*Porto Rico.*

*1493. No-vember 22. Española.*

On the 25th, while the fleet was at anchor at Monte Christo, where Columbus had found gold in the river during his first voyage, the sailors discovered some decomposed 1493. November 25. bodies, one of them showing a beard, which raised apprehensions of the fate of the men left at La Navidad. The neighboring natives came aboard for traffic with so much readiness, however, that it did much to allay suspicion. It was the 27th when, after dark, Columbus cast anchor opposite the 1493. November 27. Off La Navidad. fort, about a league from land. It was too late to see anything more than the outline of the hills. Expecting a response from the fort, he fired two cannons; but there was no sound except the echoes. The Spaniards looked in vain for lights on the shore. The darkness was mysterious and painful. Before midnight a canoe was heard approaching, and a native twice asked for the Admiral. A boat was lowered from one of the vessels, and towed the canoe to the flag-ship. The natives were not willing to board her till Columbus himself appeared at the waist, and by the light of a lantern revealed his countenance to them. This reassured them. Their leader brought presents — some accounts say ewers of gold, others say masks ornamented with gold — from the cacique, Guacanagari, whose friendly assistance had been counted upon so much to befriend the little garrison at La Navidad.

These formalities over, Columbus inquired for Diego de Arana and his men. The young Lucayan, now Columbus's only interpreter, did the best he could with a dialect not his own to make a connected story out of the replies, which was in effect that sickness and dissension, together with the withdrawal of some to other parts of the island, had reduced the ranks of the garrison, when the fort as well as the neighboring village of Guacanagari was suddenly attacked by a mountain chieftain, Caonabo, who burned both fort and village. Those of the Spaniards who were not driven into the sea to perish had Its garrison killed. been put to death. In this fight the friendly cacique had been wounded. The visitors said that this chieftain's hurt had prevented his coming with them to greet the Admiral; but that he would come in the morning. Coma, in his account of this midnight interview, is not so explicit, and leaves the reader to infer that Columbus did not get quite so clear an apprehension of the fate of his colony.

When the dawn came, the harbor appeared desolate. Not a canoe was seen where so many sped about in the previous year. A boat was sent ashore, and found every sign that the fort had been sacked as well as destroyed. Fragments of clothing and bits of merchandise were scattered amid its blackened ruins. There were Indians lurking behind distant trees, but no one approached, and as the cacique had not kept the word which he had sent of coming himself in the morning, suspicions began to arise that the story of its destruction had not been honestly given. The new-comers passed a disturbed night with increasing mistrust, and the next morning Columbus landed and saw all for himself. He traveled farther away from the shore than those who landed on the preceding day, and gained some confirmation of the story in finding the village of the cacique a mass of blackened ruins. Cannon were again discharged, in the hopes that their reverberating echoes might reach the ears of those who were said to have abandoned the fort before the massacre. The well and ditch were cleaned out to see if any treasure had been cast into it, as Columbus had directed in case of disaster. Nothing was found, and this seemed to confirm the tale of the suddenness of the attack. Columbus and his men went still farther inland to a village; but its inmates had hurriedly fled, so that many articles of European make, stockings and a Moorish robe among them, had been left behind, spoils doubtless of the fort. Returning nearer the fort, they discovered the bodies of eleven men buried, with the grass growing above them, and enough remained of their clothing to show they were Europeans. This is Dr. Chanca's statement, who says the men had not been dead two months. Coma says that the bodies were unburied, and had lain for nearly three months in the open air; and that they were now given Christian burial.

Later in the day, a few of the natives were lured by friendly signs to come near enough to talk with the Lucayan interpreter. The story in much of its details was gradually drawn out, and Columbus finally possessed himself of a pretty clear conception of the course of the disastrous events. It was a tale of cruelty, avarice, and sensuality towards the natives on the part of the Spaniards, and of jealousy and brawls among themselves. No word of their governor had been sufficient to restrain their outbursts of passionate encounter, and no sense of insecurity could deter them from the most foolhardy risks while away from the fort's protection. Those who had been appointed to succeed Arana, if there were an occasion, revolted against him, and, being unsuccessful in overthrowing him, they went off with their adherents in search of the mines of Cibao. This carried them beyond the protection of Guacanagari, and into the territory of his enemy, Caonabo, a wandering Carib who had offered himself to the interior natives as their chieftain, and who had acquired a great ascendency in the island. This leader, who had learned of the dissensions among the Spaniards, was no sooner informed of the coming of these renegades within his reach than he caused them to be seized and killed. This emboldened him to join forces with another cacique, a neighbor of Guacanagari, and to attempt to drive the Spaniards from the island, since they had become a standing menace to his power, as he reasoned. The confederates marched stealthily, and stole into the vicinity of the fort in the night. Arana had but ten men within the stockade, and they kept no watch. Other Spaniards were quartered in the adjacent village. The onset was sudden and effective, and the dismal ruins of the fort and village were thought to confirm the story.

Other confirmations followed. A caravel was sent to explore easterly, and was soon boarded by two Indians from the shore, who invited the captain, Maldonado, to visit the cacique, who lay ill at a neighboring village. The captain went, and found Guacanagari laid up with a bandaged leg. The savage told a story which agreed with the one just related, and on its being repeated to Columbus, the Admiral himself, with an imposing train, went to see the cacique. Guacanagari seemed anxious, in repeating the story, to convince the Admiral of his own loyalty to the Spaniards, and pointed to his wounds and to those of some of his people as proof. There was the usual interchange of presents, hawks' bells for gold, and similar reckonings. Before leaving, Columbus asked to have his surgeon examine the wound, which the cacique said had been occasioned by a stone striking the leg. To get more light, the chieftain went out-of-doors, leaning upon the Admiral's arm. When the bandage was removed, there was no external sign of hurt; but the cacique winced if the flesh was touched. Father Boyle, who was in the Admiral's train, thought the wound a pretense, and the story fabricated to conceal the perfidy of the cacique, and urged Columbus to make an instant example of the traitor. The Admiral was not so confident as the priest, and at all events he thought a course of pacification and procrastination was the better policy. The interview did not end, according to Coma, without some strange manifestations on the part of the cacique, which led the Spaniards for a moment to fear that a trial of arms was to come. The chief was not indisposed to try his legs enough to return with the Admiral to his ship that very evening. Here he saw the Carib prisoners, and the accounts tell us how he shuddered at the sight of them. He wondered at the horses and other strange creatures which were shown to him. Coma tells us that the Indians thought that the horses were fed on human flesh. The women who had been rescued from the Caribs attracted, perhaps, even more the attention of the savage, and particularly a lofty creature among them, whom the Spaniards had named Doña Catalina. Guacanagari was observed to talk with her more confidingly than he did with the others.

Doña Catalina.

Father Boyle urged upon the Admiral that a duress similar to that of Catalina was none too good for the perfidious cacique, as the priest persisted in calling the savage, but Columbus hesitated. There was, however, little left of that mutual confidence which had characterized the relations of the Admiral and the chieftain during the trying days of the shipwreck, the year before. When the Admiral offered to hang a cross on the neck of his visitor, and the cacique understood it to be the Christian emblem, he shrank from the visible contact of a faith of which the past months had revealed its character. With this manifestation they parted, and the cacique was set ashore. Coma seems to unite the incidents of this interview on the ship with those of the meeting ashore.

There comes in here, according to the received accounts, a little passage of Indian intrigue and gallantry. A messenger appeared the next day to inquire when the Admiral sailed, and later another to barter gold. This last held some talk with the Indian women, and particularly with Catalina. About midnight a light appeared on the shore, and Catalina and her companions, while the ship's company, except a watch, were sleeping, let themselves down

The cacique and Catalina.

the vessel's side, and struck out for the shore. The watch discovered the escape, but not in time to prevent the women having a considerable start. Boats pursued, but the swimmers touched the beach first. Four of them, however, were caught, but Catalina and the others escaped.

When, the next morning, Columbus sent a demand for the fugitives, it was found that Guacanagari had moved his household and all his effects into the interior of the island. The story got its fitting climax in the suspicious minds of the Spaniards, when they supposed that the fugitive beauty was with him. Here was only a fresh instance of the savage's perfidy.

Columbus had before this made up his mind that the vicinity of his hapless fort was not a good site for the town which he intended to build. The ground was low, moist, and unhealthy. There were no building stones near at hand. There was need of haste in a decision. The men were weary of their confinement on shipboard. The horses and other animals suffered from a like restraint. Accordingly expeditions were sent to explore the coast, and it soon became evident that they must move beyond the limits of Guacanagari's territory, if they would find the conditions demanded. Melchior Maldonado, in command of one of these expeditions, had gone eastward until he coasted the country of another cacique. This chief at first showed hostility, but was won at last by amicable signs. From him they learned that Guacanagari had gone to the mountains. From another they got the story of the massacre of the fort, almost entirely accordant with what they had already discovered.

Not one of the reports from these minor explorations was satisfactory, and December 7, the entire fleet weighed anchor to proceed farther east. Stress of weather caused them to put into a harbor, which on examination seemed favorable for their building project. The roadstead was wide. A rocky point offered a site for a citadel. There were two rivers winding close by in an attractive country, and capable of running mills. Nature, as they saw it, was variegated and alluring. Flowers and fruits were in abundance. " Garden seeds came up in five days after they were sown," says Coma of their trial of the soil, "and the gardens were speedily clothed

*Columbus abandons La Navidad.*

*Isabella founded.*

in green, producing plentifully onions and pumpkins, radishes and beets." " Vegetables," wrote Dr. Chanca, " attain a more luxuriant growth here in eight days than they would in Spain in twenty." It was also learned that the gold mines of the

Cibao gold mines. Cibao mountains were inland from the spot, at no great distance.

The disembarkation began. Days of busy exertion followed. Horses, livestock, provisions, munitions, and the varied merchandise were the centre of a lively scene about their encampment. This they established near a sheet of water. Artificers, herdsmen, cavaliers, priests, laborers, and placemen made up the motley groups which were seen on all sides.

In later years, the Spaniards regulated all the formalities and prescribed with precision the proceedings in the laying out of towns in the New World, but Columbus had no such directions. The planting of a settlement was a novel and untried method. It was a natural thought to commemorate in the new Christian city the great patroness of his undertaking, and the settlement bore from the first the name of Isabella. His engineers laid out square and street. A site for the church was marked, another for a public storehouse, another for the house of the Admiral, — all of stone. The ruins of these three buildings are the most conspicuous relics in the present solitary waste. The great mass of tenements, which were stretched along the streets back from the public square, where the main edifice stood, were as hastily run up as possible, to cover in the colony. It was time enough for solider structures later to take their places. Parties were occupied in clearing fields and setting out orchards. There were landing piers to be made at the shore. So everybody tasked bodily strength in rival endeavors. The natural results followed in so incongruous a crowd. Those not accustomed to labor broke down from its hardships. The seekers for pleasure, not finding it in the common toil, rushed into excesses, and imperiled all. The little lake, so attractive to the inexperienced, was soon, with its night

Sickness in the colony. vapors, the source of disease. Few knew how to protect themselves from the insidious malaria. Discomfort induced discouragement, and the mental firmness so necessary in facing strange and exacting circumstances gave way. Forebodings added greater energy to the disease. It was not long before the colony was a camp of hospitals, about one half the people being incapacitated for labor. In the midst of all this downheartedness Columbus himself succumbed, Columbus and for some weeks was unable to direct the trying sick. state of affairs, except as he could do so in the intervals of his lassitude.

But as the weeks went on a better condition was apparent. Work took a more steady aspect. The ships had discharged their burdens. They lay ready for the return voyage.

Columbus had depended on the exertions of the little colony at La Navidad to amass a store of gold and other precious commodities with which to laden the returning vessels. He knew the disappointment which would arise if they should carry little else than the dismal tale of disaster. Nothing lay upon his mind more weightily than this mortification and mis-fortune. There was nothing to be done but to seek the mines of Cibao, for the chance of sending more encouraging reports. Gold had indeed been brought in to the settlement, but only scantily; and its quantity was not suited to make real the gorgeous dreams of the East with which Spain was too familiar.

Sends Ojeda to seek the Cibao mines.

So an expedition to Cibao was organized, and Ojeda was placed in command. The force assigned to him was but fifteen men in all, but each was well armed and courageous. They expected perils, for they had to invade the territory of Caonabo, the destroyer of La Navidad.

The march began early in January, 1494; perhaps just after they had celebrated their first solemn mass in a temporary chapel on January 6. For two days their progress was slow and toilsome, through forests without a sign of human life, for the savage denizens had moved back from the vicinity of the Spaniards. The men encamped, the second night, on the top of a mountain, and when the dawn broke they looked down on its further side over a broad valley, with its scattered villages. They boldly descended, and met nothing but hospitality from the villagers. Their course now lay towards and up the opposite slope of the valley. They pushed on without an obstacle. The rude inhabitants of the mountains were as friendly as those of the valley. They did not see nor did they hear anything of the great Caonabo. Every stream they

1494. January. First mass.

passed glittered with particles of gold in its sand.   The natives
had an expert way of separating the metal, and the Spaniards
flattered them for their skill.   Occasionally a nugget
was found.   Ojeda picked up a lump which weighed
nine ounces, and Peter Martyr looked upon it wonderingly
when it reached Spain.   If all this was found on the surface, what
must be the wealth in the bowels of these astounding mountains ?
The obvious answer was what Ojeda hastened back to make to
Columbus.   A similar story was got from a young cavalier, Gorvalan, who had been dispatched in another
direction with another force.   There was in all this the foundation of miracles for the glib tongue and lively imagination.
One of these exuberant stories reached Coma, and Scillacio
makes him say that "the most splendid thing of all (which I
should be ashamed to commit to writing, if I had not received
it from a trustworthy source) is that, a rock adjacent to a mountain being struck with a club, a large quantity of gold burst out,
and particles of gold of indescribable brightness glittered all
around the spot.   Ojeda was loaded down by means of this outburst."   It was stories like these which prepared the way for
the future reaction in Spain.

There was material now to give spirit to the dispatch to his
sovereigns, and Columbus sat down to write it.   It
has come down to us, and is printed in Navarrete's
collection, just as it was perused by the King and
Queen, who entered in the margins their comments and orders.
Columbus refers at the beginning to letters already written to
their Highnesses, and mentions others addressed to Father
Buele and to the treasurer, but they are not known.   Then,
speaking of the expeditions of Ojeda and Gorvalan, he begs
the sovereigns to satisfy themselves of the hopeful prospects
for gold by questioning Gorvalan, who was to return with the
ships.   He advises their Highnesses to return thanks to God
for all this.  Those personages write in the margin, "Their Highnesses return thanks to God !"  He then explains his embarrass-
ment from the sickness of his men, — the "greater part of all,"
as he adds, — and says that the Indians are very familiar, rambling about the settlement both day and night, necessitating a
constant watch.   As he makes excuses and gives his reasons for
not doing this or that, the compliant monarchs as constantly

Gold found.

Gorvalan's
expedition.

Columbus
writes to the
sovereigns.

write against the paragraphs, " He has done well." Columbus
says he is building stone bulwarks for defense, and when this
is done he shall provide for accumulating gold. " Exactly as
should be done," chime in the monarchs. He then asks for
fresh provisions to be sent to him, and tells how much they
have done in planting. " Fonseca has been ordered to send
further seeds," is the comment. He complains that the wine
casks had been badly coopered at Seville, and that the wine had
all run out, so that wine was their prime necessity. He urges
that calves, heifers, asses, working mares, be sent to them ;
and that above all, to prevent discouragement, the supplies
should arrive at Isabella by May, and that particularly medicines should come, as their stock was exhausted. He then refers to the cannibals whom he would send back, and asks that
they may be made acquainted with the true faith and taught
the Spanish tongue. " His suggestions are good," is the marginal royal comment.

Now comes the vital point of his dispatch. We want cattle, he says. They can be paid for in Carib slaves. Let yearly
caravels conduct this trade. It will be easy, with the Columbus
boats which are building, to capture a plenty of these proposes a
savages. Duties can be levied on these importa- slaves.
tions of slaves. On this point he urges a reply. The monarchs
see the fatality of the step, and, according to the marginal comment, suspend judgment and ask the Admiral's further thoughts.
" A more distinct suggestion for the establishment of a slave
trade was never proposed," is the modern comment of Arthur
Helps. Columbus then adds that he has bought for the use of
the colony certain of the vessels which brought them out, and
these would be retained at Isabella, and used in making further
discoveries. The comment is that Fonseca will pay the owners. He then intimates that more care should be exercised in
the selection of placemen sent to the colony, for the enterprise
had suffered already from unfitness in such matters. The monarchs promise amends. He complains that the Granada lancemen, who offered themselves in Seville mounted on fine horses,
had subsequently exchanged these animals to their own personal
advantage for inferior horses. He says the footmen made similar exchanges to fill their own pockets.

So, dating this memorial on January 30, 1494, the man who

was ambitious to become the first slave-driver of the New World

laid down his quill, praising God, as he asked his sovereigns to do. The poor creatures who wandered in and about among the cabins of the Spaniards were fast forming their own comments, which were quite as astute as those of the Admiral's royal masters. Holding up a piece of gold, the natives learned to say, — and Columbus had given them their first lesson in such philosophy, — " Behold

the Christians' God ! " Benzoni, the first traveler who came among them with his eyes open, and daring to record the truth, heard them say this. Intrusting his memorial to Antonio de Torres, and putting him in command of the

twelve ships that were to return to Spain, Columbus saw the fleet sail away on February 2, 1494. There would seem to have been committed to some one on the ships two other accounts of the results of this second voyage up to this time, which have come down to us. One of these is

a narrative by Dr. Chanca, the physician of the colony, whom Columbus, in his memorial to the monarchs, credits with doing good service in his profession at a sacrifice of the larger emoluments which the practice of it had brought to him in Seville. The narrative of Chanca had been sent by him to the cathedral chapter of Seville. The original is thought to be lost; but Navarrete used a transcript which belonged to a collection formed by Father Antonio de Aspa, a monk of the monastery of the Mejorada, where Columbus is known to have deposited some of his papers. Major has given us an English translation of it in his *Select Letters of Columbus.* Major's text will also be found in the late James Lenox's English version of the other account, which he gave to scholars in 1859.

There is a curious misconception in this last document, which represents that Columbus had reached these new regions by the African route of the Portuguese, — a confusion doubtless arising from the imperfect knowledge which the Italian translator,

Nicholas Scillacio, had of the current geographical developments. A Spaniard, Guglielmo Coma, seems to have written about the new discoveries in some letters, apparently revived in some way from somebody's personal observation, which Scillacio put into a Latin dress, and published at

Pavia, or possibly at Pisa. This little tract is of the utmost rarity, and Mr. Lenox, considering the suggestion of Ronchini, that the blunder of Scillacio may have caused the destruction of the edition, replies by calling attention to the fact that it is scarcely rarer than many other of the contemporary tracts of Columbus's voyage, about which there exists no such reason.

We get also some reports by Torres himself on the affairs of the colony in various letters of a Florentine merchant, Simone Verde, to whom he had communicated them. Verde's letters. These letters have been recently (1875) found in the archives of Florence, and have been made better known still later by Harrisse.

# CHAPTER XIII.

## THE SECOND VOYAGE, CONTINUED.

### 1494.

THE departure of the fleet madé conspicuous at last a threatening faction of those whose terms of service had prevented their taking passage in the ships. This organized discontent was the natural result of a depressing feeling that all the dreams of ease and plenty which had sustained them in their embarkation were but delusions. Life in Isabella had made many of them painfully conscious of the lack of that success and comfort which had been counted upon. The failure of what in these later days is known as the commissariat was not surprising. With all our modern experience in fitting out great expeditions, we know how often the fate of such enterprises is put in jeopardy by rascally contractors. Their arts, however, are not new ones. Fonseca was not so wary, Columbus was not so exacting, that such arts could not be practiced in Seville, as to-day in London and New York. This jobbery, added to the scant experience of honest endeavor, inevitably brought misfortune and suffering through spoiled provisions and wasted supplies.

The faction, taking advantage of this condition, had two persons for leaders, whose official position gave the body a vantage-ground. Bernal Diaz de Pisa was the comptroller of the colony, and his office permitted him to have an oversight of the Admiral's accounts. It is said that before this time he had put himself in antagonism to authority by questioning some of the doings of the Admiral. He began now to talk to the people of the Admiral's deceptive and exaggerating descriptions intended for effect in Spain, and no doubt represented them to be at least as false as they were. Diaz drew pictures that produced a prevailing gloom beyond what the facts warranted, for deceit is a game of varying extremes. He

*Life in Isabella.*

*Mutinous factions.*

was helped on by the assayer of the colony, Fermin Cado, who spoke as an authority on the poor quality of the gold, and on the Indian habit of amassing it in their families, so that the moderate extent of it which the natives had offered was not the accretions of a day, but the result of the labor of generations. With leaders acting in concert, it had been planned to seize the remaining ships, and to return to Spain. This done, the mutineers expected to justify their conduct by charges against the Admiral, and a statement of them had already been drawn up by Bernal Diaz. The mutiny, however, was discovered, and Columbus had the first of his many experiences in suppressing a revolt. Bernal Diaz was imprisoned on one of the ships, and was carried to Spain for trial. Other leaders were punished in one way and another. To prevent the chances of success in future schemes of revolt, all munitions and implements of war were placed together in one of the ships, under a supervision which Columbus thought he could trust. Their schemes discovered.

The prompt action of the Admiral had not been taken without some question of his authority, or at least it was held that he had been injudicious in the exercise of it. The event left a rankling passion among many of the colonists against what was called Columbus's vindictiveness and presumptuous zeal. With it all was the feeling that a foreigner was oppressing them, and was weaving about them the meshes of his arbitrary ambition.

Columbus now determined to go himself to the gold regions of the interior. He arranged that Diego, his brother, — another foreigner! — should have the command in his absence. Las Casas pictures for us this younger of the Colombos, and calls him gentle, unobtrusive, and kindly. He allows to him a priest's devotion, but does not consider him quite worldly enough in his dealings with men to secure himself against ungenerous wiles. Columbus goes to the gold mines. Diego Colon.

It was the 12th of March when Columbus set out on his march. He conducted a military contingent of about 400 well-armed men, including what lancers he could mount. In his train followed an array of workmen, miners, artificers, and porters, with their burdens of merchandise and 1494. March 12.

implements. A mass of the natives hovered about the procession.

Their progress was as martial as it could be made. Banners were flaunted. Drums and trumpets were sounded. Their armor was made to glisten. Crossing the low land, they came to a defile in the mountain. There was nothing before them but a tortuous native trail winding upward among the rocks and through tangled forest. It was ill suited for the passage of a heavily burdened force. Some of the younger cavaliers sprang to the front, and gathering around them woodmen and pioneers, they opened the way; and thus a road was constructed through the pass, the first made in the New World. This work of the proud cavaliers was called *El puerto de los Hidalgos.* The summit of the mountain afforded afresh the grateful view of the luxuriant valley which had delighted Ojeda, — royally rich as it was in every aspect, and deserving the name which Columbus now gave it of the Vega Real.

Columbus makes a road.

The Vega Real.

Here, on the summit of Santo Cerro, the tradition of the island goes that Columbus caused that cross to be erected which the traveler to-day looks upon in one of the side chapels of the cathedral at Santo Domingo. It stood long enough to perform many miracles, as the believers tell us, and was miraculously saved in an earthquake. De Lorgues does not dare to connect the actual erection with the holy trophy of the cathedral. Descending to the lowlands, the little army and its followers attracted the notice of the amazed natives by clangor and parade. This display was made more astounding whenever the horses were set to prancing, as they approached and passed a native hamlet. Las Casas tells us that the first horseman who dismounted was thought by the natives to have parceled out a single creature into convenient parts. The Indians, timid at first, were enticed by a show of trinkets, and played upon by the interpreters. Thus they gradually were won over to repay all kindnesses with food and drink, while they rendered many other kindly services. The army came to a large stream, and Columbus called it the River of Reeds. It was the same which, the year before, knowing it only where it emptied into the sea, he had called the River of Gold, because he had been struck with the shining particles

Erects a cross.

which he found among its sands. Here they encamped. The
men bathed. They found everything about them like the dales
of Paradise, if we may believe their rehearsals. The landscape
was very different from that which Bernal Diaz was to tell of,
if only once he got the ears of the Court in Seville.

The river was so wide and deep that the men could not ford
it, so they made rafts to take over everything but the horses.
These swam the current. Then the force passed on, but was
confronted at last by the rugged slopes of the Cibao   <sub>Cibao moun-</sub>
mountains. The soldiers clambered up the defile pain-   <sub>tains.</sub>
fully and slowly. The pioneers had done what they could to
smooth the way, but the ascent was wearying. They could occasionally turn from their toil to look back over this luxuriant
valley which they were leaving, and lose their vision in its vast
extent. Las Casas describes it as eighty leagues one way, and
twenty or thirty the other.

It was a scene of bewildering beauty that they left behind ;
it was one of sterile heights, scraggy pines, and rocky precipices
which they entered. The leaders computed that they were
eighteen leagues from Isabella, and as Columbus thought he saw
signs of gold, amber, lapis lazuli, copper, and one knows not
what else of wealth, all about him, he was content to establish
his fortified position hereabouts, without pushing farther. He
looked around, and found at the foot of one of the declivities
of the interior of this mountainous region a fertile plain, with
a running river, gurgling over beds of jasper and marble, and
in the midst of it a little eminence, which he could   <sub>Fort St.</sub>
easily fortify, as the river nearly surrounded it like a   <sub>Thomas.</sub>
natural ditch. Here he built his fort. Recent travelers say
that an overgrowth of trees now covers traces of its founda-
tions. The fortress was, as he believed, so near the gold that
one could see it with his eyes and touch it with his hands, and
so, as Las Casas tells us, he named it St. Thomas.

The Indians had already learned to recognize the Christian's
god. They found the golden deity in bits in the streams. They
took the idol tenderly to his militant people. For their part,
the poor natives much preferred rings and hawks' bells, and so
a basis of traffic was easily found. In this way Columbus got
some gold, but he more readily got stories of other spots, whither
the natives pointed vaguely, where nuggets, which would dwarf

all these bits, could be found. Columbus began to wonder why he never reached the best places.

The Spaniards soon got to know the region better. Juan de
Luxan, who had been sent out with a party to see
what he could find, reported that the region was moun-
tainous and in its upper parts sterile, to be sure, but that there were delicious valleys, and plenty of land to cultivate, and pas-turing enough for herds. When he came back with these re-ports, the men put a good deal of heart in the work which they were bestowing on the citadel of St. Thomas, so that it was soon done. Pedro Margarite was placed in command with fifty-six men, and then Columbus started to re-turn to Isabella.

*Country examined.*

*Columbus returns to Isabella.*

When the Admiral reached the valley, he met a train of sup-plies going forward to St. Thomas, and as there were difficulties of fording and other obstacles, he spent some time in examining the country and marking out lines of communication. This brought him into contact with the villages of the val-ley, and he grew better informed of the kind of peo-ple among whom his colonists were to live. He did not, how-ever, discern that under a usually pacific demeanor there was no lack of vigorous determination in this people, which it might not be so wise to irritate to the point of vengeance. He found, too, that they had a religion, perhaps prompting to some virtues he little suspected in his own, and that they jealously guarded their idols. He discovered that experience had given them no near acquaintance with the medicinal properties of the native herbs and trees. They associated myths with places, and would tell you that the sun and moon were but creatures of their isl-and which had escaped from one of their caverns, and that mankind had sprung from the crannies of their rocky places. The bounteousness of nature, causing little care for the future, had spread among them a love of hospitality, and Columbus found himself welcome everywhere, and continued to be so till he and his abused their privileges.

*Natives of the valley.*

On the 29th of March, Columbus was back in Isabella, to
find that the plantings of January were already yielding fruits, and the colony, in its agricultural aspects,
at least, was promising, for the small areas that had already been cultivated. But the tidings from the new fort in

*1494. March 29. Colum-bus in Isa-bella.*

the mountains which had just come in by messenger were not so
cheering, for it seemed to be the story of La Navidad repeated.
The license and exactions of the garrison had stirred up the
neighboring natives, and Pedro Margarite, in his message,
showed his anxiety lest Caonabo should be able to mass the
savages, exasperated by their wrongs, in an attack upon the
post. Columbus sent a small reinforcement to St. Thomas, and
dispatched a force to make a better road thither, in order to
facilitate any future operations.

The Admiral's more immediate attention was demanded by
the condition of Isabella. Intermittent fever and various other
disturbances incident to a new turning of a reeking soil were
making sad ravages in the colony. The work of Condition of
building suffered in consequence. The sick engrossed the town.
the attention of men withdrawn from their active labors, or
they were left to suffer from the want of such kindly aid. The
humidity of the climate and a prodigal waste had brought provisions so low that an allowance even of the unwholesome stock
which remained was made necessary. In order to provide
against impending famine, men were taken from the public
works and put to labor on a mill, in order that they might get
flour. No respect was paid to persons, and cavalier and priest
were forced into the common service. The Admiral was obliged
to meet the necessities by compulsory measures, for even an
obvious need did not prevent the indifferent from shirking, and
the priest and hidalgo from asserting their privileged rights.
Any authority that enforced sacrifice galled the proud spirits,
and the indignity of labor caused a mortification and despair
that soon thinned the ranks of the best blood of the colony.
Dying voices cursed the delusion which had brought them to
the New World, the victims, as they claimed, of the avarice
and deceit of a hated alien to their race.

Supineness in the commander would have brought everything
in the colony to a disastrous close. A steady progression of
some sort might be remedial. The Admiral's active mind determined on the diversion of further exploration with such a
force as could be equipped. He mustered a little Ojeda sent
army, consisting of 250 men armed with crossbows, to St.
Thomas.
100 with matchlocks, 16 mounted lancemen, and 20
officers. Ojeda was put at their head, with orders to lead them

to St. Thomas, which post he was to govern while Margarite
took the expeditionary party and scoured the country.   Navarrete has preserved for us the instructions which Columbus imparted.   They counseled a considerate regard for the natives,
who must, however, be made to furnish all necessaries at fair
prices.   Above all, every Spaniard must be prevented from en-
gaging in private trade, since the profits of such bartering were
reserved to the Crown, and it did not help Columbus in his dealings with the refractory colonists to have it known that a foreign interloper, like himself, shared this profit with the Crown.
Margarite was also told that he must capture, by force or stratagem, the cacique Caonabo and his brothers.

When Ojeda, who had started on April 9, reached the Vega
1494.          Real, he learned that three Spaniards, returning from
April 9.       St. Thomas, had been robbed by a party of Indians,
people of a neighboring cacique.   Ojeda seized the offenders,
the ears of one of whom he cut off, and then capturing the
cacique himself and some of his family, he sent the whole
party to Isabella.   Columbus took prompt revenge, or made
the show of doing so; but just as the sentence of execution was
to be inflicted, he yielded to the importunities of another cacique, and thought to keep by it his reputation for clemency.
Presently another horseman came in from St. Thomas, who, on
his way, had rescued, single-handed and with the aid of the terror which his animal inspired, another party of five Spaniards,
whom he had found in the hands of the same tribe.

Such easy conquests convinced Columbus that only proper
prudence was demanded to maintain the Spanish supremacy
with even a diminished force.   He had not forgotten the fears
of the Portuguese which were harassing the Spanish Court
when he left Seville, and, to anticipate them, he was anxious to
make a more thorough examination of Cuba, which was a part
of the neighboring main of Cathay, as he was ready to suppose.
He therefore commissioned a sort of junto to rule, while in
person he should conduct such an expedition by water.   His
Diego and    brother Diego was placed in command during his ab-
the junto.   sence, and he gave him for counselors, Father Boyle,
Pedro Fernandez Coronel, Alonso Sanchez Carvajal, and Juan
de Luxan.   He took three caravels, the smallest of his little
fleet, as better suited to explore, and left the two large ones
behind.

It was April 24 when Columbus sailed from Isabella, and at once he ran westerly. He stopped at his old fort, La Navidad, but found that Guacanagari avoided him, and no time could be lost in discovering why. On the 1494. April 24. Columbus sails for Cuba. 29th, he left Española behind and struck across to the Cuban shore. Here, following the southern side of that island, he anchored first in a harbor where there were preparations for a native feast; but the people fled when he landed, and the not overfed Spaniards enjoyed the repast that was abandoned. The Lucayan interpreter, who was of the party, managed after a while to allure a single Indian, more confident than the rest, to approach; and when this Cuban learned from one of a similar race the peaceful purposes of the Spaniards, he went and told others, and so in a little while Columbus was able to hold a parley with a considerable group. He caused reparation to be made for the food which his men had taken, and then exchanged farewells with the astounded folk.

On May 1, he raised anchor, and coasted still westerly, keeping near the shore. The country grew more populous. The amenities of his intercourse with the 1494. May 1. On the Cuban coast. feast-makers had doubtless been made known along the coast, and as a result he was easily kept supplied with fresh fruits by the natives. Their canoes constantly put off from the shore as the ships glided by. He next anchored in the harbor which was probably that known to-day as St. Jago de Cuba, where he received the same hospitality, and dispensed the same store of trinkets in return.

Here, as elsewhere along the route, the Lucayan had learned from the natives that a great island lay away to the south, which was the source of what gold they had. The informa- 1494. May 3. Steers for Jamaica. tion was too frequently repeated to be casual, and so, on May 3, Columbus boldly stood off shore, and brought his ships to a course due south.

It was not long before thin blue films appeared on the horizon. They deepened and grew into peaks. It was two days before the ships were near enough to their massive forms to see the signs of habitations everywhere scattered along the shore. The vessels stood in close to the land. A native flotilla hovered about, at first with menaces, but their occupants were soon won to friendliness by kindly signs. Not so, however, in the harbor, where, on the next day, he sought shelter and an opportunity to careen a leaky ship.  Here the shore swarmed

Natives of Jamaica.

with painted men, and some canoes with feathered warriors advanced to oppose a landing.  They hurled their javelins without effect, and filled the air with their screams and whoops.  Columbus then sent in his boats nearer the shore than his ships could go, and under cover of a discharge from his bombards a party landed, and with their cross-

A dog set upon them.

bows put the Indians to flight.  Bernaldez tells that a dog was let loose upon the savages, and this is the earliest mention of that canine warfare which the Spaniards later made so sanguinary.  Columbus now landed and took pos-

Santiago or Jamaica.

session of the island under the name of Santiago, but the name did not supplant the native Jamaica.  The warning lesson had its effect, and the next day some envoys of the cacique of the region made offers of amity, which were readily accepted.  For three days this friendly intercourse was kept up, with the customary exchange of gifts.  The Spaniards

Character of natives.

could but observe a marked difference in the character of this new people.  They were more martial and better sailors than any they had seen since they left the Carib islands. The enormous mahogany-trees of the islands furnished them with trunks, out of which they constructed the largest canoes. Columbus saw one which was ninety-six feet long and eight broad.  There was also in these people a degree of merriment such as the Spaniards had not noticed before, more docility and quick apprehension, and Peter Martyr gathered from those with whom he had talked that in almost all ways they seemed a manlier and experter race.  Their cloth, utensils, and implements were of a character not differing from others the explorers had seen, but of better handiwork.

As soon as he floated his ship, Columbus again stretched his course to the west, finding no further show of resistance.  The native dugout sallied forth to trade from every little inlet which was passed.  Finally, a youth came off and begged to be taken to the Spaniards' home, and the *Historie* tells us that it was not without a scene of distress that he bade his kinsfolk good-by, in spite of all their endeavors to reclaim him.  Columbus was struck with the courage and confidence of the youth, and ordered special kindnesses to be shown to him.  We hear nothing more of the lad.

Reaching now the extreme westerly end of Jamaica, and finding the wind setting right for Cuba, Columbus shifted his course thither, and bore away to the north. On the 18th of May, he was once more on its coast. The people were everywhere friendly. They told him that Cuba was an island, but of such extent that they had never seen the end of it. This did not convince Columbus that it was other than the mainland. So he went on towards the west, in full confidence that he would come to Cathay, or at least, such seemed his expectation. He presently rounded a point, and saw before him a large archipelago. He was now at that point where the Cabo de la Cruz on the south and this archipelago in the northwest embay a broad gulf. The islands seemed almost without number, and they studded the sea with verdant spots. He called them the Queen's Gardens. He could get better seaway by standing further south, and so pass beyond the islands; but suspecting that they were the very islands which lay in masses along the coast of Cathay, as Marco Polo and Mandeville had said, he was prompted to risk the intricacies of their navigation; so he clung to the shore, and felt that without doubt he was verging on the territories of the Great Khan. He began soon to apprehend his risks. The channels were devious. The shoals perplexed him. There was often no room to wear ship, and the boats had to tow the caravels at intervals to clearer water. They could not proceed at all without throwing the lead. The wind was capricious, and whirled round the compass with the sun. Sudden tempests threatened danger.

With all this anxiety, there was much to beguile. Every aspect of nature was like the descriptions of the East in the travelers' tales. The Spaniards looked for inhabitants, but none were to be seen. At last they espied a village on one of the islands, but on landing (May 22), not a soul could be found, — only the spoils of the sea which a fishing people would be likely to gather. Another day, they met a canoe from which some natives were fishing. The men came on board without trepidation and gave the Spaniards what fish they wanted. They had a wonderful way of catching fish. They used a live fish much as a falcon is used in catching its quarry. This fish would fasten itself to its prey by suckers growing about the head.

*[margin notes:]* Columbus returns to Cuba.

1494. May 18.

The Queen's Gardens.

The native fishermen let it out with a line attached to its tail, and pulled in both the catcher and the caught when the prey had been seized. These people also told the same story of the interminable extent westerly of the Cuban coast.

Columbus now passed out from among these islands and steered towards a mountainous region, where he again landed and opened intercourse with a pacific tribe on June 3. An old cacique repeated the same story of the illimitable land, and referred to the province of Mangon as lying farther west. This name was enough to rekindle the imagination of the Admiral. Was not Mangi the richest of the provinces that Sir John Mandeville had spoken of? He learned also that a people with tails lived there, just as that veracious narrator had described, and they wore long garments to conceal that appendage. What a sight a procession of these Asiatics would make in another reception at the Spanish Court!

1494. June 3.

Men with tails.

There was nothing now to impede the progress of the caravels, and on the vessels went in their westward course. Every day the crews got fresh fruits from the friendly canoes. They paid nothing for the balmy odors from the land. They next came to the Gulf of Xagua, and passing this they again sailed into shallow waters, whitened with the floating sand, which the waves kept in suspension. The course of the ships was tortuous among the bars, and they felt relieved when at last they found a place where their anchors would hold. To make sure that a way through this labyrinth could be found, Columbus sent his smallest caravel ahead, and then following her guidance, the little fleet, with great difficulty, and not without much danger at times, came out into clearer water. Later, he saw a deep bay on his right, and tacking across the opening he lay his course for some distant mountains. Here he anchored to replenish his water-casks. An archer straying into the forest came back on the run, saying that he had seen white-robed people. Here, then, thought Columbus, were the people who were concealing their tails! He sent out two parties to reconnoitre. They found nothing but a tangled wilderness. It has been suggested that the timorous and credulous archer had got half a sight of a flock of white cranes feeding in a savanna. Such is the interpretation of this story by

Gulf of Xagua.

White-robed men.

Irving, and Humboldt tells us there is enough in his experience with the habits of these birds to make it certain that the interpretation is warranted.

Still the Admiral went on westerly, opening communication occasionally with the shore, but to little advantage in gathering information, for the expedition had gone beyond the range of dialects where the Lucayan interpreter could be of service. The shore people continued to point west, and the most that could be made of their signs was that a powerful king reigned in that direction, and that he wore white robes. This is the story as Bernaldez gives it; and Columbus very likely thought it a premonition of Prester John. The coast still stretched to the setting sun, if Columbus divined the native signs aright, but no one could tell how far. The sea again became shallow, and the keels of the caravels stirred up the bottom. The accounts speak of wonderful crowds of tortoises covering the water, pigeons darkening the sky, and gaudy butterflies sweeping about in clouds. The shore was too low for habitation; but they saw smoke and other signs of life in the high lands of the interior. When the coast line began to trend to the southwest, — it was Marco Polo who said it would, — there could be little doubt that the Golden Chersonesus of the ancients, which we know to-day as the Malacca peninsula, must be beyond. *Columbus believes he sees the Golden Chersonesus,*

What next? was the thought which passed through the fevered brain of the Admiral. He had an answer in his mind, and it would make a new sensation for his poor colony at Isabella to hear of him in Spain. Passing the Golden Chersonesus, had he not the alternative of steering homeward by way of Ceylon and the Cape of Good Hope, and so astound the Portuguese more than he did when he entered the Tagus? *by which he would return to Spain.* Or, abandoning the Indian Ocean and entering the Red Sea, could he not proceed to its northern extremity, and there, deserting his ships, join a caravan passing through Jerusalem and Jaffa, and so embark again on the Mediterranean and sail into Barcelona, a more wonderful explorer than before?

These were the sublimating thoughts that now buoyed the Admiral, as he looked along the far-stretching coast, — or at least his friend Bernaldez got this impression from his intercourse with Columbus after his return to Spain.

If the compliant spirit of his crew had not been exhausted,
His crew rebel. he would perhaps have gone on, and would have been
forced by developments to a revision of his geographical faith.   His vessels, unfortunately, were strained in all their
seams.   Their leaks had spoiled his provisions.   Incessant labor had begun to tell upon the health of the crew.   They much
preferred the chances of a return to Isabella, with all its hazards, than a sight of Jaffa and the Mediterranean, with the untold dangers of getting there.

The Admiral, however, still pursued his course for a few
days more to a point, as Humboldt holds, opposite the St.
Philip Keys, when, finding the coast trending sharply to the
southwest, and his crew becoming clamorous, he determined to
go no farther.

It was now the 12th of June, 1494, and if we had nothing but
the *Historie* to guide us, we should be ignorant of the
1494.   June 12. He turns back. singular turn which affairs took.   Whoever wrote that
book had, by the time it was written, become conscious
that obliviousness was sometimes necessary to preserve the reputation of the Admiral.   The strange document which interests us, however, has not been lost, and we can read it in
Navarrete.

It is not difficult to understand the disquietude of Columbus's
mind.   He had determined to find Cathay as a counterpoise to
the troubled conditions at Isabella, both to assuage the gloomy
forebodings of the colonists and to reassure the public mind in
Spain, which might receive, as he knew, a shock by the reports
which Torres's fleet had carried to Europe.   He had been forced
by a mutinous crew to a determination to turn back, but his discontented companions might be complacent enough to express
an opinion, if not complacent enough to run farther hazards.
So Columbus committed himself to the last resort of deluded
minds, when dealing with geographical or historical problems,
— that of seeking to establish the truth by building monuments, placing inscriptions, and certifications under oath.   He
Enforces an oath upon his men caused the eighty men who constituted the crew of
his little squadron — and we find their name in Duro's
*Colón y Pinzón* — to swear before a notary that it
was possible to go from Cuba to Spain by land, across Asia.   It
was solemnly affirmed by this official that if any should swerve

from this belief, the miserable skeptic, if an officer, should be fined 10,000 maravedis ; and if a sailor, he should receive a hundred lashes and have his tongue pulled out. Such were the scarcely heroic measures that Columbus thought it necessary to employ if he would dispel any belief that all these islands of the Indies were but an ocean archipelago after all, and that the width of the unknown void between Europe and Asia, which he was so confident he had traversed, was yet undetermined. To make Cuba a continent by affidavit was easy ; to make it appear the identical kingdom of the Great Khan, he hoped would follow. During his first voyage, so far as he could make out an intelligible statement from what the natives indicated, he was of the opinion that Cuba was an island. It is to be feared that he had now reached a state of mind in which he did not dare to think it an island.

that Cuba is a continent.

If we believe the *Historie*, — or some passages in it, at least, — written, as we know, after the geography of the New World was fairly understood, and if we accept the evidence of the copyist, Herrera, Columbus never really supposed he was in Asia. If this is true, he took marvelous pains to deceive others by appearing to be deceived himself, as this notarial exhibition and his solemn asseveration to the Pope in 1502 show. The writers just cited say that he simply juggled the world by giving the name India to these regions, as better suited to allure emigration. Such testimony, if accepted, establishes the fraudulent character of these notarial proceedings. It is fair to say, however, that he wrote to Peter Martyr, just after the return of the caravels to Isabella, expressing a confident belief in his having come near to the region of the Ganges ; and divesting the testimony of all the jugglery with which others have invested it, there seems little doubt that in this belief, at least, Columbus was sincere.

On the next day, Columbus, standing to the southeast, reached a large island, the present Isle of Pines, which he called Evangelista. In endeavoring to skirt it on the south, he was entangled once more in a way that made him abandon the hope of a directer passage to Española that way, and to resolve to follow the coast back as he had come. He lost ten days in these uncertain efforts, which, with his provisions rap-

1494. June 13.

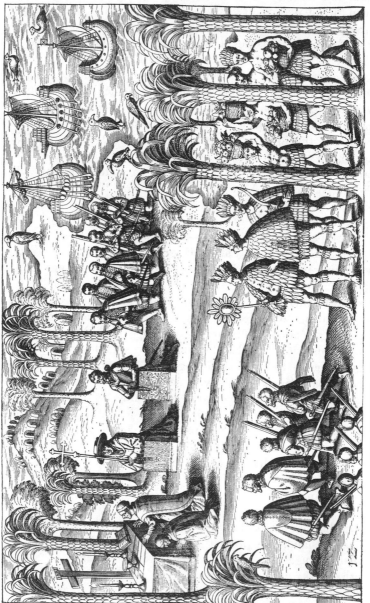

MASS ON SHORE.  [From Philoponus's *Nova Typis Transacta Navigatio.*]

idly diminishing, did not conduce to reassure his crew. On June 30, trying to follow the intricacies of the channels <sub>1494. June 30.</sub> which had perplexed him before, the Admiral's ship got a severe thump on the bottom, which for a while threatened disaster. She was pulled through, however, by main force, and after a while was speeding east in clear water. They had now sailed beyond those marshy reaches of the coast, where they were cut off from intercourse with the shore, and hoped soon to find a harbor, where food and rest might restore the strength of the crew. Their daily allowance had been reduced to a pound of mouldy bread and a swallow or two of wine. It was the <sub>1494.</sub> 7th of July when they anchored in an acceptable harbor. <sub>July 7.</sub>

Here they landed, and interchanged the customary pledges of amity with a cacique who presented himself on the shore. Men having been sent to cut down some trees, a large cross was made, and erected in a grove, and on this spot, with a crowd of natives looking on, the Spaniard celebrated high mass. A venerable Indian, who watched all the ceremonials with close attention, divining their religious nature, made known to the Admiral, through the Lucayan interpreter, something of the sustaining belief of his own people, in words that were impressive. Columbus's confidence in the incapacity of the native mind for such high conceptions as this poor Indian manifested received a grateful shock when the old man, grave in his manner and unconscious in his dignity, pictured the opposite rewards of the good and bad in another world. Then turning to the Admiral, he reminded him that wrong upon the unoffending was no passport to the blessings of the future. The historian who tells us this story, and recounts how it impressed the Admiral, does not say that its warnings troubled him much in the times to come, when the unoffending were grievously wronged. Perhaps there was something of this forgetful spirit in the taking of a young Indian away from his friends, as the chroniclers say he did, in this very harbor.

On July 16, Columbus left the harbor, and steering off shore to escape the intricate channels of the Queen's Gar- <sub>1494. July 16.</sub> dens which he was now re-approaching, he soon found searoom, and bore away toward Española. A gale coming on, the caravels were forced in shore, and discovered an <sub>1494. July 18.</sub> anchorage under Cabo de Cruz. Here they remained for three days, but the wind still blowing from the east, Columbus thought it a good opportunity to complete the circuit of On the coast Jamaica. He accordingly stood across towards that of Jamaica. island. He was a month in beating to the eastward along its southern coast, for the winds were very capricious. Every night he anchored under the land, and the natives supplied him with provisions. At one place, a cacique presented himself in much feathered finery, accompanied by his wife and relatives, with a retinue bedizened in the native fashion, and doing homage to the Admiral. It was shown how effective the Lucayan's pictures of Spanish glory and prowess had been, when the cacique proposed to put himself and all his train in the Admiral's charge for passage to the great country of the Spanish King. The offer was rather embarrassing to the Admiral, with his provisions running low, and his ships not of the largest. He relieved himself by promising to conform to the wishes of the cacique at a more opportune moment.

By the 19th of August, Columbus had passed the easternmost
1494. extremity of Jamaica, and on the next day he was
August 19. skirting the long peninsula which juts from the southwestern angle of Española. He was not, however, aware of
Española. his position till on the 23d a cacique came off to the
1494. caravels, and addressed Columbus by his title, with
August 23. some words of Castilian interlarded in his speech. It was now made clear that the ships had nearly reached their goal, and nothing was left but to follow the circuit of the island. It was no easy task to do so with a wornout crew and crazy ships. The little fleet was separated in a gale, and when
Columbus made the lofty rocky island which is now
Alto Velo. known as Alto Velo, resembling as it does in outline a tall ship under sail, he ran under its lee, and sent a boat ashore, with orders for the men to scale its heights, to learn if the missing caravels were anywhere to be seen. This endeavor was without result, but it was not long before the fleet was reunited. Further on, the Admiral learned from the natives that some of the Spaniards had been in that part of the island, coming from the other side. Finding thus through the native reports that all was quiet at Isabella, he landed nine men to push across the island and report his coming. Somewhat further to the east, a storm impending, he found a harbor, where

the weather forced him to remain for eight days. The Admiral's vessel had succeeded in entering a roadstead, but the others lay outside, buffeting the storm, — naturally a source of constant anxiety to him.

It was while in this suspense that Columbus took advantage of an eclipse of the moon, to ascertain his longitude. Columbus observes eclipse of the moon. His calculations made him five hours and a half west of Seville, — an hour and a quarter too much, making an error of eighteen degrees. This mistake was quite as likely owing to the rudeness of his method as to the pardonable errors of the lunar tables of Regiomontanus (Venice, 1492), then in use. These tables followed methods which had more or less controlled calculations from the time of Hipparchus.

The error of Columbus is not surprising. Even a century later, when Robert Hues published his treatise on the Molineaux globe (1592), the difficulties were in large part uncontrollable. " The most certain of all for this purpose," says this mathematician, " is confessed by all writers to be by eclipses of the moon. But now these eclipses happen but seldom, but are more seldom seen, yet most seldom and in very few places observed by the skillful artists in this science. So that there are but few longitudes of places designed out by this means. But this is an uncertain and ticklish way, and subject to many difficulties. Others have gone other ways to work, as, namely, by observing the space of the equinoctial hours betwixt the meridians of two places, which they conceive may be taken by the help of sundials, or clocks, or hourglasses, either with water or sand or the like. But all these conceits, long since devised, having been more strictly and accurately examined, have been disallowed and rejected by all learned men — at least those of riper judgments — as being altogether unable to perform that which is required of them. I shall not stand here to discover the errors and uncertainties of these instruments. Away with all such trifling, cheating rascals ! "

The weather moderating, Columbus stood out of the channel of Saona on September 24, and meeting the other caravels, which had weathered the storm, he still steered 1494. September 24. to the east. They reached the farthest end of Española opposite Porto Rico, and ran out to the island of Mona, in the channel between the two larger islands. Shortly after leaving

Mona, Columbus, worn with the anxieties of a five months' voyage, in which his nervous excitement and high hopes had sustained him wonderfully, began to feel the reaction. His near approach to Isabella accelerated this recoil, till his whole system suddenly succumbed. He lay in a stupor, knowing little, remembering nothing, his eyes dim and vitality oozing. Under other command, the little fleet sorrowfully, but gladly, entered the harbor of Isabella.

Columbus
reaches
Isabella.

Our most effective source for the history of this striking cruise is the work of Bernaldez, already referred to.

# CHAPTER XIV.

## THE SECOND VOYAGE, CONTINUED.

### 1494–1496.

IT was the 29th of September, 1494, when the " Nina," with the senseless Admiral on board, and her frail consorts stood into the harbor of Isabella. Taken ashore, the sick man found no restorative like the presence of his brother Bartholomew, who had reached Isabella during the Admiral's absence.

1494. September 29. Columbus in Isabella.

Several years had elapsed since the two congenial brothers had parted. We have seen that this brother

Finds Bartholomew Columbus there.

had probably been with Bartholomew Diaz when he discovered the African cape. It is supposed, from the inscriptions on it, that the map delivered by Bartholomew to Henry VII. had shown the results of Diaz's discoveries. This chart had been taken to England, when Bartholomew had gone thither, to engage the interest of Henry VII. in Columbus's behalf. There is some obscurity about the movements of Bartholomew at this time, but there is thought by some to be reason to believe that he finally got sufficient encouragement from that Tudor prince to start for

Bartholomew's career in England.

Spain with offers for his brother. The *Historie* tells us that the propositions of Bartholomew were speedily accepted by Henry, and this statement prevails in the earlier English writers, like Hakluyt and Bacon; but Oviedo says the scheme was derided, and Geraldini says it was declined. Bartholomew reached Paris just at the time when word had come there of Columbus's return from his first voyage. His kinship to the Admiral, and his own expositions of the geographical problem then attracting so much attention, drew him within the influence of the French court, and Charles VIII. is said to have furnished him the means — as Bartholomew was then low in purse

— to pursue his way to Spain. He was, however, too late to see the Admiral, who had already departed from Cadiz on this second voyage. Finding that it had been arranged for his brother's sons to be pages at Court, he sought them, and in company with them he presented himself before the Spanish monarchs at Valladolid. These sovereigns were about fitting out a supply fleet for Española, and Bartholomew was put in command of an advance section of it. Sailing from Cadiz on April 30, 1494, with three caravels, he reached Isabella on St. John's Day, after the Admiral had left for his western cruise.

In Spain.

If it was prudent for Columbus to bring another foreigner to his aid, he found in Bartholomew a fitter and more courageous spirit than Diego possessed. The Admiral was pretty sure now to have an active and fearless deputy, sterner, indeed, in his habitual bearing than Columbus, and with a hardihood both of spirit and body that fitted him for command. These qualities were not suited to pacify the haughty hidalgos, but they were merits which rendered him able to confront the discontent of all settlers, and gave him the temper to stand in no fear of them. He brought to the government of an illassorted community a good deal that the Admiral lacked. He was soberer in his imagination; not so prone to let his wishes figure the future; more practiced, if we may believe Las Casas, in the arts of composition, and able to speak and write much more directly and comprehensibly than his brother. He managed men better, and business proceeded more regularly under his control, and he contrived to save what was possible from the wreck of disorder into which his brother's unfitness for command had thrown the colony. This is the man whom Las Casas enables us to understand, through the traits of character which he depicts. Columbus was now to create this brother his representative, in certain ways, with the title of Adelantado.

His character.

Created Adelantado.

It was also no small satisfaction to the Admiral, in his present weakness, to learn of the well-being of his children, and of the continued favor with which he was held at Court, little anticipating the resentment of Ferdinand that an office of the rank of Adelantado should be created by any delegated authority. Columbus had pursued his recent explorations in some measure to forestall what he feared the Portuguese might be led to attempt in the same direction, for he had not been unaware of the disturbance in the court at Lisbon which the papal line of demarcation had created. He was glad now to learn from his brother that his own fleet had hardly got to sea from Cadiz, in September, 1493, when the Pope, by another bull on the 26th of that month, had declared that all countries of the eastern Indies which the Spaniards might find, in case they were not already in Christian hands, should be included in the grant made to Spain. This Bull of Extension, as it was called, was a new thorn in the side of Portugal, and time would reveal its effect. Alexander had resisted all importunities to recede from his position, taken in May.

Papal Bull of Extension.

Let us look now at what had happened in Española during the absence of Columbus ; but in the first place, we must mark out the native division of the island with whose history Columbus's career is so associated. Just back of Isabella, and about the Vega Real, whose bewildering beauties of grove and savanna have excited the admiration of modern visitors, lay the territory tributary to a cacique named Guarionex, which was bounded south by the Cibao gold mountains. South of these interior ridges and extending to the southern shore of the island lay the region (Maguana) of the most warlike of all the native princes, Caonabo, whose wife, Anacaona, was a sister of Behechio, who governed Xaragua, as the larger part of the southern coast, westward of Caonabo's domain, including the long southwestern peninsula, was called. The northeastern part of the island (Marien) was subject to Guacanagari, the cacique neighboring to La Navidad. The eastern end (Higuay) of the island was under the domination of a chief named Cotabanana.

Events in Española during the absence of Columbus.

It will be remembered that before starting for Cuba the Admiral had equipped an expedition, which, when it arrived at St. Thomas, was to be consigned to the charge of Pedro Margarite. This officer had instructions to explore the mountains of Cibao, and map out its resources. He was not to harass the natives by impositions, but he was to make them fear his power. It was also his business to avoid reducing the colony's supplies by making the natives support this exploring force.

If he could not get this support by fair means, he was to use foul means. Such instructions were hazardous enough; but

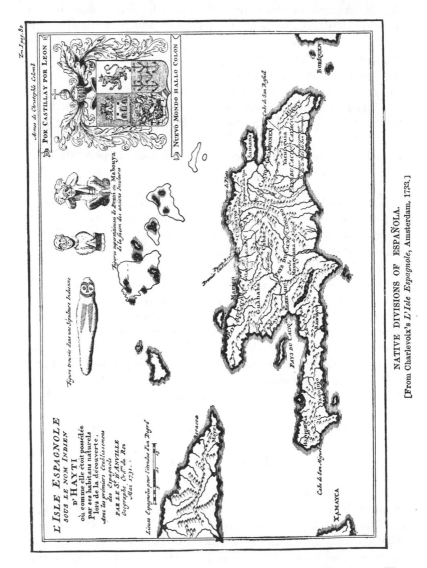

*L'ISLE ESPAGNOLE SOUS LE NOM INDIEN D'HAYTI* où comme elle étoit possédée par ses habitans naturels lors de la découverte, avec les premiers établissemens des Espagnols PAR LE S^r D'ANVILLE Géographe Ord^re du Roi Mai 1731.

Por Castillay por Leon

Armes de Christophe Colomb

Nuevo Mondo hallo Colon

NATIVE DIVISIONS OF ESPAÑOLA.
[From Charlevoix's *L'Isle Espagnole*, Amsterdam, 1733.]

Margarite was not the man to soften their application. He had even failed to grasp the spirit of the instructions which had been given by Columbus to ensnare Caonabo, which were

" as thoroughly base and treacherous as could well be imagined," says Helps, and the reader can see them in Navarrete.

This commander had spent his time mainly among the luxurious scenes of the Vega Real, despoiling its tribes of their provisions, and squandering the energies of his men in sensual diversions. The natives, who ought to have been his helpers, became irritated at his extortions and indignant at the invasion of their household happiness. The condition in the tribes which this riotous conduct had induced looked so threatening that Diego Columbus, as president of the council, wrote to Margarite in remonstrance, and reminded him of the Admiral's instructions to explore the mountains.

The haughty Spaniard, taking umbrage at what he deemed an interference with his independent command, readily lent himself to the faction inimical to Columbus. Factions. With his aid and with that of Father Boyle, a brother Catalonian, who had proved false to his office as a member of the ruling council and even finally disregardful of the royal wishes that he should remain in the colony, an uneasy party was soon banded together in Isabella. The modern French canonizers, in order to reconcile the choice by the Pope of this recusant priest, claim that his Holiness, or the king for him, confounded a Benedictine and Franciscan priest of the same name, and that the Benedictine was an unlucky changeling — perhaps even purposely — for the true monk of the Franciscans.

In the face of Diego, this cabal found little difficulty in planning to leave the island for Spain in the ships which had come with Bartholomew Columbus. Diego had no power to meet with compulsion the defiance of these mutineers, and was subjected to the sore mortification of seeing the rebels sail out of the harbor for Spain. There was left to Diego, however, some satisfaction in feeling that such dangerous ringleaders were gone ; but it was not unaccompanied with anxiety to know what effect their representations would have at Court. A like anxiety now became poignant in the Admiral's mind, on his return.

The stories which Diego and Bartholomew were compelled to tell Columbus of the sequel of this violent abandonment of the colony were sad ones. The license which Pedro Margarite had permitted became more extended, when the little armed force of the colony found itself without military restraint. It soon disbanded in large part, and lawless squads of soldiers were scattered throughout the country, wherever passion or avarice could find anything to prey upon. The long-suffering Indians soon reached the limits of endurance. A few acts of vengeance encouraged them to commit others, and everywhere small parties of the Spaniards were cut off as they wandered about for food and lustful conquests. The inhabitants of villages turned upon such stragglers as abused their hospitalities. Houses where they sheltered themselves were fired. Detached posts were besieged.

While this condition prevailed, Caonabo planned to surprise Fort St. Thomas. Ojeda, here in control with fifty men, commanded about the only remnant of the Spanish forces which acknowledged the discipline of a competent leader. The vigilant Ojeda did not fail to get intelligence of Caonabo's intentions. He made new vows to the Virgin, before an old Flemish picture of Our Lady which hung in his chamber in the fort, and which never failed to encourage him, wherever he tarried or wherever he strayed. Every man was under arms, and every eye was alert, when their commander, as great in spirit as he was diminutive in stature, marshaled his fifty men along his ramparts, as Caonabo with his horde of naked warriors advanced to surprise him. The outraged cacique was too late. No unclothed natives dared to come within range of the Spanish crossbows and arquebuses. Ojeda met every artful and stealthy approach by a sally that dropped the bravest of Caonabo's warriors.

The cacique next tried to starve the Spaniards out. His parties infested every path, and if a foraging force came out, or one of succor endeavored to get in, multitudes of the natives foiled the endeavor. Famine was impending in the fort. The procrastinations of the arts of beleaguering always help the white man behind his ramparts, when the savage is his enemy. The native force dwindled under the delays, and Caonabo at last abandoned the siege.

The native leader now gave himself to a larger enterprise. His spies told him of the weakened condition of Isabella, and he resolved to form a league of the principal caciques of the island to attack that settlement. Wherever the Spaniards had penetrated, they had turned the friendliest feelings into hatred, and in remote parts of the island the reports of the Spanish ravages served, almost as much as the experience of them, to embitter the savage. It was no small success for Caonabo to make the other caciques believe that the supernatural character of the Spaniards would not protect them if a combined attack should be arranged. He persuaded all of them but Guacanagari, for that earliest friend of Columbus remained firm in his devotion to the Spaniards. The Admiral's confidence in him had not been misplaced. He was subjected to attacks by the other chieftains, but his constancy survived them all. In these incursions of his neighbors, his wives were killed and captured, and among them the dauntless Catalina, as is affirmed ; but his zeal for his white neighbors did not abate.

When Guacanagari heard that Columbus had returned, he repaired to Isabella, and from this faithful ally ·the Admiral learned of the plans which were only waiting further developments for precipitate action. Columbus and Guacanagari.

Columbus, thus forewarned, was eager to break any confederacy of the Indians before it could gather strength. He had hardly a leader disengaged whom he could send on the warpath. It was scarcely politic to place Bartholomew in any such command over the few remaining Spanish cavaliers whose spirit was so necessary to any military adventure. He sent a party, however, to relieve a small garrison near the villages of Guatiguana, a tributary chief to the great cacique Guarionex; but the party resorted to the old excesses, and came near defeating the purposes of Columbus. Guatiguana was prevailed upon, however, to come to the Spanish settlement, and Columbus, to seal his agreement of amity with him, persuaded him to let the Lucayan interpreter marry his daughter. To this diplomatic arrangement the Admiral added the more powerful argument of a fort, called La Concepcion, which he later built where it could command the Vega Real. Fort Conception.

It was not long before four ships, with Antonio Torres in command, arrived from Spain, bringing a new store of provisions, another physician, and more medicines, and, what was much needed, artificers and numerous gardeners. There was some hope now that the soil could be made to do its part in the support of the colony. Torres's ships arrive.

To the Admiral came a letter, dated August 16, from Ferdinand and Isabella, giving him notice that all the difficulties with Portugal had been amicably adjusted. The court of Lisbon, finding that Pope Alexander was not inclined to recede from his position, and Spain not courting any difference that would lead to hostilities, both countries had easily been brought

1494. June 7. Treaty of Tordesillas. to an agreement, which was made at Tordesillas, June 7, 1494, to move the line of demarcation so much farther as to fall 370 leagues west of the Cape de Verde Islands. Each country then bound itself to respect its granted rights under the bull thus modified. The historical study of this diplomatic controversy over the papal division of the world is much embarrassed by the lack of documentary records of the correspondence carried on by Spain, Portugal, and the Pope.

This letter of August 16 must have been very gratifying to

The sovereign's letter to Columbus, Columbus. Their Majesties told him that one of the principal reasons of their rejoicing in his discoveries was that they felt it all due to his genius and perseverance, and that the events had justified his foreknowledge and their expectations. So now, in their desire to define the new line of demarcation, and in the hope that it might be found to run through some ocean island, where a monument could be erected, they turned to him for assistance, and they expected that if he could not return to assist in these final negotiations, he would dispatch to them some one who was competent to deal with the geographical problem.

Torres had also brought a general letter of counsel to the

and to the colonists. colonists, commanding them to obey all the wishes and to bow to the authority of the Admiral. Whatever his lack of responsibility, in some measure at least, for the undoubted commercial failure of the colony, its want of a product in any degree commensurate both with expectation and outlay could not fail, as he well understood, to have a strong effect both on the spirit of the people and on the constancy of his royal patrons, who might, under the urging of Margarite and his abettors, have already swerved from his support.

Reasons of this kind made it imperative that the newly arrived ships should be returned without delay, and with such reassuring messages and returns as could be furnished. The fleet departed on February 24, 1495. Himself still prostrate,

and needing his brother Bartholomew to act during this season of his incapacity, there was no one he could spare so 1495. February 24. The fleet returns to Spain well to meet the wishes of the sovereigns as his other brother. So armed with maps and instructions, and with the further mission of protecting the Admiral's interest at Court, Diego embarked in one of the caravels. All the gold which had been collected was consigned to Diego's care, but it was only a sorry show, after all. There had been a variety of new fruits and spices, and samples of baser metals gathered, and these helped to complete the lading. There was one resource left. He had intimated his readiness to avail himself of it in the communication of his views to the Carrying slaves. sovereigns, which Torres had already conveyed to them.
He now gave the plan the full force of an experiment, and packed into the little caravels full five hundred of the unhappy natives, to be sold as slaves. "The very ship," says Helps, " which brought that admirable reply from Ferdinand and Isabella to Columbus, begging him to seek some other way to Christianity than through slavery, even for wild man-devouring Caribs, should go back full of slaves taken from among the mild islanders of Hispaniola." The act was a long step in the miserable degradation which Columbus put upon those poor creatures whose existence he had made known to the world. Almost in the same breath, as in his letter to Santangel, he had suggested the future of a slave traffic out of that very existence. It is an obvious plea in his defense that the example of the church and of kings had made such heartless conduct a common resort to meet the financial burdens of conquest. The Portuguese had done it in Africa; the Spaniards had done it in Spain. The contemporary history of that age may be Columbus and slavery. said to ring with the wails and moans of such negro and Moorish victims. A Holy Religion had unblushingly been made the sponsor for such a crime. Theologians had proved that the Word of God could ordain misery in this world, if only the recompense came — or be supposed to come — in a passport to the Christian's heaven.

The merit which Columbus arrogated to himself was that he was superior to the cosmographical knowledge of his time. It was the merit of Las Casas that he threw upon the reeking passions of the enslaver the light of a religion that was above sophistry and purer than cupidity. The existence of Las Casas is the arraignment of Columbus.

It may be indeed asking too much of weak humanity to be good in all things, and therein rests the pitiful plea for Columbus, the originator of American slavery.

Events soon became ominous. A savage host began to gather in the Vega Real, and all that Columbus, now recovering his strength, could marshal in his defense was about two hundred foot and twenty horse, but they were cased in steel, and the natives were naked. In this respect, the fight was unequal, and the more so that the Spaniards were now able to take into the field a pack of twenty implacable bloodhounds. The bare bodies of the Indians had no protection against their insatiate thirst.

*Attacked by blood-hounds.*

It was the 27th of March, 1495, when Columbus, at the head of this little army, marched forth from Isabella, to confront a force of the natives, which, if we choose to believe the figures that are given by Las Casas, amounted to 100,000 men, massed under the command of Manicaotex. The whites climbed the Pass of the Hidalgos, where Columbus had opened the way the year before, and descended into that lovely valley, no longer a hospitable paradise. As they approached the hostile horde, details were sent to make the attacks various and simultaneous. The Indians were surprised at the flashes of the arquebuses from every quarter of the woody covert, and the clang of their enemies' drums and the bray of their trumpets drowned the savage yells. The native army had already begun to stagger in their wonder and perplexity, when Ojeda, seizing the opportune moment, dashed with his mounted lancemen right into the centre of the dusky mass. The bloodhounds rushed to their sanguinary work on his flanks. The task was soon done. The woods were filled with flying and shrieking savages. The league of the caciques was broken, and it was only left for the conquerors to gather up their prisoners. Guacanagari, who had followed the white army with a train of his subjects, looked on with the same wonder which struck the Indians who were beaten. There was no opportunity for him to fight at all. The rout had been complete. This notable conflict taking place on

*1495. March 27. Columbus marches,*

*and fights in the Vega Real.*

April 25, 1495, is a central point in a somewhat bewildering tangle of events, as our authorities relate them, so that it is not easy in all cases to establish their sequence. 1495. April 25.

The question of dealing with Caonabo was still the most important of all. It was solved by the cunning and dash of Ojeda. Presenting his plan to the Admiral, he was commanded to carry it out. Taking ten men whom he could trust, Ojeda boldly sought the village where Caonabo was quartered, and with as much intrepidity as cunning put himself in the power of that cacique. The chieftain was not without chivalry, and the confidence and audacity of Ojeda won him. Hospitality was extended, and the confidences of a mutual respect soon ensued. Ojeda proposed that Caonabo should accompany him to Isabella, to make a compact of friendship with the Viceroy. All then would be peaceful. Caonabo, who had often wondered at the talking of the great bell in the chapel at Isabella, as he had heard it when skulking about the settlement, eagerly sprang to the lure, when Ojeda promised that he should have the bell. Ojeda, congratulating himself on the success of his bait, was disconcerted when he found that the cacique intended that a large force of armed followers should make the visit with him. To prevent this, Ojeda resorted to a stratagem, which is related by Las Casas, who says it was often spoken of when that priest first came to the island, six years later. Muñoz was not brought to believe the tale ; but Helps sees no obstacle to giving it credence. Caonabo captured by Ojeda.

The Spaniards and the Indians were all on the march together, and had encamped by a river. Ojeda produced a set of burnished steel manacles, and told the cacique that they were ornaments such as the King of Spain wore on solemn occasions, and that he had been commanded to give them to the most distinguished native prince. He first proposed a bath in the river. The swim over, Caonabo was prevailed upon to be put behind Ojeda astride the same horse. Then the shining baubles were adjusted, apparently without exciting suspicion, amid the elation of the savage at his high seat upon the wondrous beast. A few sweeping gallops of the horse, guided by Ojeda, and followed by the other mounted spearmen, scattered the amazed crowd of the cacique's attendants. Then at a convenient gap in the circle

Ojeda spurred his steed, and the whole mounted party dashed into the forest and away. The party drew up only when they had got beyond pursuit, in order to bind the cacique faster in his seat. So in due time, this little cavalcade galloped into Isabella with its manacled prisoner.

The meeting of Columbus and his captive was one of very different emotions in the two, — the Admiral rejoicing that his most active foe was in his power, and the cacique abating nothing of the defiance which belonged to his freedom. Las Casas tells us that, as Caonabo lay in his shackles in an outer apartment of the Admiral's house, the people came and looked at him. He also relates that the bold Ojeda was the only one toward whom the prisoner manifested any respect, acknowledging in this way his admiration for his audacity. He would maintain only an indifferent haughtiness toward the Admiral, who had not, as he said, the courage to do himself what he left to the bravery of his lieutenant.

*Meets Columbus.*

Ojeda presently returned to his command at St. Thomas, only to find that a brother of Caonabo had gathered the Indians for an assault. Dauntless audacity again saved him. He had brought with him some new men, and so, leaving a garrison in the fort, he sallied forth with his horsemen and with as many foot as he could muster and attacked the approaching host. A charge of the glittering horse, with the flashing of sabres, broke the dusky line. The savages fled, leaving their commander a prisoner in Ojeda's hands.

*Ojeda attacks the Indians.*

Columbus followed up these triumphs by a march through the country. Every opposition needed scarce more than a dash of Ojeda's cavalry to break it. The Vega was once more quiet with a sullen submission. The confederated caciques all sued for peace, except Behechio, who ruled the southwestern corner of the island. The whites had not yet invaded his territory, and he retired morosely, taking with him his sister, Anacaona, the wife of the imprisoned Caonabo.

The battle and the succeeding collapse had settled the fate of the poor natives. The policy of subjecting men by violence to pay the tribute of their lives and property to Spanish cupidity was begun in earnest, and it was shortly after made to include the labor on the Spanish farms, which, under the names of repartimientos and encomiendas, de-

*Repartimientos and encomiendas.*

moralized the lives of master and slave. When prisoners were gathered in such numbers that to guard them was a burden, there could be but little delay in forcing the issue of the slave trade upon the Crown as a part of an established policy. To the mind of Columbus, there was now some chance of repelling the accusations of Margarite and Father Boyle by palpable returns of olive flesh and shining metal. A scheme of enforced contribution of gold was accordingly planned. Each native above the age of fourteen was required to pay every three months, into the Spanish coffers, his share of gold, measured by the capacity of a hawk's bell for the common person, and by that of a calabash for the cacique. In the regions distant from the gold deposits, cotton was accepted as a substitute, twenty-five pounds for each person. A copper medal was put on the neck of every Indian for each payment, and new exactions were levied upon those who failed to show the medals. The amount of this tribute was more than the poor natives could find, and Guarionex tried to have it commuted for grain; but the golden greed of Columbus was inexorable. He preferred to reduce the requirements rather than vary the kind. A half of a hawk's bell of gold was better than stores of grain. "It is a curious circumstance," says Irving, "that the miseries of the poor natives should thus be measured out, as it were, by the very baubles which first fascinated them."

To make this payment sure, it was necessary to establish other armed posts through the country; and there were speedily built that of Magdalena in the Vega, one called Esperanza in Cibao, another named Catalina, beside La Concepcion, which has already been mentioned. *Forts built.*

The change which ensued in the lives of the natives was pitiable. The labor of sifting the sands of the streams for gold, which they had heretofore made a mere pastime to secure bits to pound into ornaments, became a depressing task. To work fields under a tropical sun, where they had basked for sportive rest, converted their native joyousness into despair. They sang their grief in melancholy songs, as Peter Martyr tells us. Gradually they withdrew from their old haunts, and by hiding in the mountains, they sought to avoid the exactions, and to force the Spaniards, thus no longer supplied by native labor with food, to abandon their posts and re- *The natives debased.*

tire to Isabella, if not to leave the island. Scant fare for themselves and the misery of dank lurking-places were preferable to the heavy burdens of the taskmasters. They died in their retreats rather than return to their miserable labors. Even the long-tried friend of the Spaniards, Guacanagari, was made no exception. He and his people suffered every exaction with the

Guacanagari disappears.

rest of their countrymen. The cacique himself is said eventually to have buried himself in despair in the mountain fastnesses, and so passed from the sight of men.

The Spaniards were not so easily to be thwarted. They hunted the poor creatures like game, and, under the goading of lashes, such as survived were in time returned to their slavery. So thoroughly was every instinct of vengeance rooted out of the naturally timid nature of the Indians that a Spaniard might, as Las Casas tells us, march solemnly like an army through the most solitary parts of the island and receive tribute at every demand.

It is time to watch the effect of the representations of Margarite and Father Boyle at the Spanish Court. Columbus had

Columbus's interests in Spain.

been doubtless impelled, in these schemes of cruel exaction, by the fear of their influence, and with the hope of meeting their sneers at his ill success with substantial tribute to the Crown. The charges against Columbus and his policy and against his misrepresentation had all the immediate effect of accusations which are supported by one-sided witnesses. Every sentiment of jealousy and pride was played upon, and every circumstance of palliation and modification was ignored. The suspicious reservation which had more or less characterized the bearing of Ferdinand towards the transactions of the hero could become a background to the newer emotions. Fonseca and the comptroller Juan de Soria are charged with an easy acceptance of every insinuation against the Viceroy. The canonizers cannot execrate Fonseca enough. They make him alternately the creature and beguiler of the King. His subserviency, his trading in bishoprics, and his alleged hatred of Columbus are features of all their portraits of him.

The case against the Admiral was thus successfully argued. Testimony like that of the receiver of the Crown taxes in rebuttal of charges seemed to weigh little. Movements having been instituted at once (April 7, 1495) to succor the colony by the immediate dispatch of supplies, it was two days later agreed with Beradi — the same with whom Vespucius had been associated, as we have seen — to furnish twelve ships for Española. The resolution was then taken to send an agent to investigate the affairs of the colony. If he should find the Admiral still absent, — for the length of his cruise to Cuba had already, at that time, begun to excite apprehension of his safety, — this same agent was to superintend the distribution of the supplies which he was to take. At this juncture, in April, 1495, Torres, arriving with his fleet, reported the Admiral's safe return, and submitted the notarial document, in which Columbus had made it clear to his own satisfaction that the Golden Chersonesus was in sight. Whether that freak of geographical prescience threw about his expedition a temporary splendor, and again wakened the gratitude of the sovereigns, as Irving says it did, may be left to the imagination; but the fact remains that the sovereigns did not swerve from their purpose to send an Aguado sent inquisitor to the colony, and the same Juan Aguado to Española. who had come back with credentials from the Admiral himself was selected for the mission.

There were some recent orders of the Crown which Aguado was to break to the Admiral, from which Columbus could not fail to discover that the exclusiveness of his powers 1495. April was seriously impaired. On the 10th of April, 1495, 10. All Spaniards allowed to explore. it had been ordered that any native-born Spaniard lowed to explore. could invade the seas which had been sacredly apportioned to Columbus, that such navigator might discover what he could, and even settle, if he liked, in Española. This order was a ground of serious complaint by Columbus at a later day, for the reason that this license was availed of by unworthy interlopers. He declares that after the way had been shown even the very tailors turned explorers. It seems tolerably certain that this irresponsible voyaging, which continued till Columbus induced the monarchs to rescind the order in June, 1497, worked developments in the current cartography of the new regions which it is difficult to trace to their distinct sources. Gomara intimates that during this period there were Nameless nameless voyagers, of whose exploits we have no voyagers. record by which to identify them, and Navarrete and Humboldt find evidences of explorations which cannot otherwise be accounted for.

How far this condition of affairs was brought about by the
Enemies of
Columbus.
importunities of the enemies of Columbus is not clear. The surviving Pinzons are said to have been in part those who influenced the monarchs, but doubtless a share of profits, which the Crown required from all such private speculation, was quite as strong an incentive as any importunities of eager mariners. The burdens of the official expeditions were onerous for an exhausted treasury, and any resource to replenish its coffers was not very narrowly scrutinized in the light of the pledges which Columbus had exacted from a Crown that was beginning to understand the impolicy of such concessions.

There was also at this time a passage of words between Fon-
Fonseca
and Diego
Colon.
seca and Diego Colon that was not without irritating elements. The Admiral's brother had brought some gold with him, which he claimed as his own. Fonseca withheld it, but in the end obeyed the sovereign's order and released it. It was no time to add to the complications of the Crown's relations with the distant Viceroy.

Aguado bore a royal letter, which commanded Columbus to
Royal let-
ter to Co-
lumbus.
reduce the dependents of the colony to five hundred, as a necessary retrenchment. There had previously been a thousand. Directions were also given to control the apportionment of rations. A new metallurgist and master-miner, Pablo Belvis, was sent out, and extraordinary privileges in the working of the mines were given to him. Muñoz says that he introduced there the quicksilver process of separating the gold from the sand. A number of new priests were collected to take the place of those who had returned, or who desired to come back.

Such were the companions and instructions that Aguado was commissioned to bear to Columbus. There was still another movement in the policy of the Crown that offered the Viceroy little ground for reassurance. The prisoners which he had sent by the ships raised a serious question. It was determined that
Columbus
and slavery.
any transaction looking to the making slaves of them had not been authorized; but the desire of Columbus so to treat them had at first been met by a royal order directing their sale in the marts of Andalusia. A few days later, under

the influence of Isabella, this order had been suspended, till an inquiry could be made into the cause of the capture of the Indians, and until the theologians could decide upon the justifiableness of such a sale. If we may believe Bernaldez, who pictures their misery, they were subsequently sold in Seville. Muñoz, however, says that he could not find that the trouble which harassed the theologians was ever decided. Such hesitancy was calculated to present a cruel dilemma to the Viceroy, since the only way in which the clamor of the Court for gold could be promptly appeased came near being prohibited by what Columbus must have called the misapplied mercy of the Queen. He failed to see, as Muñoz suggests, why vassals of the Crown, entering upon acts of resistance, should not be subjected to every sort of cruelty. Humboldt wonders at any hesitancy when the grand inquisitor, Torquemada, was burning heretics so fiercely at this time that such expiations of the poor Moors and Jews numbered 8,800 between 1481 and 1498!

Aguado, with four caravels, and Diego Columbus accompanying him, having sailed from Cadiz late in August, 1495, reached the harbor of Isabella some time in October. The new commissioner found the Admiral absent, occupied with affairs in other parts of the island. Aguado soon made known his authority. It was embraced in a brief missive, dated April 9, 1495, and as Irving translates it, it read: "Cavaliers, esquires, and other persons, who by our orders are in the Indies, we send to you Juan Aguado, our groom of the chambers, who will speak to you on our part. We command you to give him faith and credit." The efficacy of such an order depended on the royal purpose that was behind it, and on the will of the commissioner, which might or might not conform to that purpose. It has been a plea of Irving and others that Aguado, elated by a transient authority, transcended the intentions of the monarchs. It is not easy to find a definite determination of such a question. It appears that when the instrument was proclaimed by trumpet, the general opinion did not interpret the order as a suspension of the Viceroy's powers. The Adelantado, who was governing in Columbus's absence, saw the new commissioner order arrests, countermand directions, and in various ways assume the functions of a governor. Bartholomew was in no condition to do more than mildly remon-

*1495. October. Aguado at Isabella.*

strate. It was clearly not safe for him to provoke the great body of the discontented colonists, who professed now to find a champion sent to them by royal order.

Columbus heard of Aguado's arrival, and at once returned to Isabella. Aguado, who had started to find him with an escort of horse, missed him on the road, and this delayed their meet-
Meets Co-
lumbus.
ing a little. When the conference came, Columbus, with a dignified and courteous air, bowed to a superior authority. It has passed into history that Aguado was disappointed at this quiet submission, and had hoped for an altercation, which might warrant some peremptory force. It is also said that later he endeavored to make it appear how Columbus had not been so complacent as was becoming.

It was soon apparent that this displacement of the Admiral was restoring even the natives to hope, and their caciques were not slow in presenting complaints, not certainly without reason, to the ascendant power, and against the merciless extortions of the Admiral.

The budget of accusations which Aguado had accumulated
Accuses
Columbus.
was now full enough, and he ordered the vessels to make ready to carry him back to Spain. The situation for Columbus was a serious one. He had in all this trial experienced the results of the intrigues of Margarite and Father Boyle. He knew of the damaging persuasiveness of the Pinzons. He had not much to expect from the advocacy of Diego. There was nothing for him to do but to face in person the charges as reënforced by Aguado. He resolved to return in the ships. " It is not one of the least singular traits in his history," says Irving, " that after having been so many years in persuading mankind that there was a new world to be discovered, he had almost an equal trouble in proving to them the advantage of the discovery." He himself never did prove it.

The ships were ready. They lay at anchor in the roadstead.
Ships
wrecked in
the harbor.
A cloud of vapor and dust was seen in the east. It was borne headlong before a hurricane such as the Spaniards had never seen, and the natives could not remember its equal. It cut a track through the forests. It lashed the sea until its expanse seethed and writhed and sent its harried waters tossing in a seeming fright. The uplifted surges broke the natural barriers and started inland. The

ships shuddered at their anchorage; cables snapped; three caravels sunk, and the rest were dashed on the beach. The tumult lasted for three hours, and then the sun shone upon the havoc.

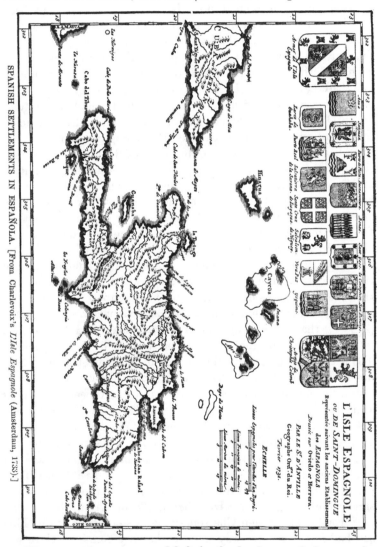

SPANISH SETTLEMENTS IN ESPAÑOLA. [From Charlevoix's *L'Isle Espagnole* (Amsterdam, 1733).]

There was but one vessel left in the harbor, and she was shattered. It was the "Nina," which had borne Columbus in his western cruise. As soon as the little colony recovered its senses, men were set to work repairing the solitary caravel, and con-structing another out of the remnants of the wrecks.

While this was going on, a young Spaniard, Miguel Diaz by name, presented himself in Isabella. He had been in the service of the Adelantado, and was not unrecognized. He was one who had some time before wounded another Spaniard in a duel, and, supposing that the wound was mortal, he had, with a few friends, fled into the woods and wandered away till he came to the banks of the Ozema, a river on the southern coast of the island, at the mouth of which the city of Santo Domingo now stands. Here, as he said, he had attracted the attention of a female cacique, there reigning, and had become her lover. She confided to him the fact that there were rich gold mines in her territory, and to make him more content in her company, she suggested that perhaps the Admiral, if he knew of the mines, would abandon the low site of Isabella, and find a better one on the Ozema. Acting on this suggestion, Diaz, with some guides, returned to the neighborhood of Isabella, and lingered in concealment till he learned that his antagonist had survived his wound. Then, making bold, he entered the town, as we have seen. His story was a welcome one, and the Adelantado was dispatched with a force to verify the adventurer's statement. In due time, the party returned, and reported that at a river named Hayna they had found such stores of gold that Cibao was poor in comparison. The explorers had seen the metal in all the streams; they observed it in the hillsides. They had discovered two deep excavations, which looked as if the mines had been worked at some time by a more enterprising people, since of these great holes the natives could give no account. Once more the Admiral's imagination was fired. He felt sure that he had come upon the Ophir of Solomon. These ancient mines must have yielded the gold which covered the great Temple. Had the Admiral not discovered already the course of the ships which sought it? Did they not come from the Persian gulf, round the Golden Chersonesus, and so easterly, as he himself had in the reverse way tracked the very course? Here was a new splendor for the Court of Spain. If the name of India was redolent of spices, that of Ophir could but be resplendent with gold! That was a message worth taking to Europe.

The two caravels were now ready. The Adelantado was left in command, with Diego to succeed in case of his death. Francisco Roldan was commissioned as chief magistrate, and the Fathers Juan Berzognon and Roman Pane remained behind to pursue missionary labors among the natives. Instructions were left that the valley of the Ozema should be occupied, and a fort built in it. Diaz, with his queenly Catalina, had become important.

There was a motley company of about two hundred and fifty persons, largely discontents and vagabonds, crowded into the two ships. Columbus was in one, and Aguado in the other. So they started on their adventurous and wearying voyage on March 10, 1496. They carried about thirty Indians in confinement, and among them the manacled Caonabo, with some of his relatives. Columbus told Bernaldez that he took the chieftain over to impress him with Spanish power, and that he intended to send him back and release him in the end. His release came otherwise. There is some disagreement of testimony on the point, some alleging that he was drowned during the hurricane in the harbor, but the better opinion seems to be that he died on the voyage, of a broken spirit. At any rate, he never reached Spain, and we hear of him only once while on shipboard.

*1496. March 10. Columbus and Aguado sail for Spain, carrying Caonabo.*

We have seen that on his return voyage in 1492 Columbus had pushed north before turning east. It does not appear how much he had learned of the experience of Torres's easterly passages. Perhaps it was only to make a new trial that he now steered directly east. He met the trade winds and the calms of the tropics, and had been almost a month at sea when, on April 6, he found himself still neighboring to the islands of the Caribs. His crew needed rest and provisions, and he bore away to seek them. He anchored for a while at Marigalante, and then passed on to Guadaloupe.

*1496. April 6.*

He had some difficulty in landing, as a wild, screaming mass of natives was gathered on the beach in a hostile manner. A discharge of the Spanish arquebuses cleared the way, and later a party scouring the woods captured some of the courageous women of the tribe. These were all released, however, except a strong, powerful woman, who, with a daughter, refused to be left, for the reason, as the story goes,

*At Guadaloupe.*

that she had conceived a passion for Caonabo. By the 20th, the ships again set sail; but the same easterly trades baffled them, and another month was passed without much progress.

1496. June.

By the beginning of June, provisions were so reduced that there were fears of famine, and it began to be considered whe.her the voyagers might not emulate the Caribs and eat the Indians. Columbus interfered, on the plea that the poor crea- tures were Christian enough to be protected from such a fate ; but as it turned out, they were not Christian enough to be saved from the slave-block in Andalu.ia. The alert senses of Colum- bus had convinced him that land could not be far distant, and he was confirmed in this by his reckoning. These opinions of Columbus were questioned, however, and it was not at all clear in the minds of some, even of the experienced pilots who were on board, that they were so near the latitude of Cape St. Vin- cent as the Admiral affirmed. Some of these navigators put the ships as far north as the Bay of Biscay, others even as far as the English Channel. Columbus one night ordered sail to be taken in. They were too near the land to proceed. In the

1496. June 11. Cadiz.

morning, they saw land in the neighborhood of Cape St. Vincent. On June 11, they entered the harbor of Cadiz.

# CHAPTER XV.

IN SPAIN, 1496–1498.

### DA GAMA, VESPUCIUS, CABOT.

" THE wretched men crawled forth," as Irving tells us of their debarkation, " emaciated by the diseases of the <sub>1496. Co-</sub> colony and the hardships of the voyage, who carried <sub>lumbus ar-<br>rives at</sub> in their yellow countenances, says an old writer, a <sub>Cadiz,</sub> mockery of that gold which had been the object of their search, and who had nothing to relate of the New World but tales of sickness, poverty, and disappointment." This is the key to the contrasts in the present reception of the adventurers with that which greeted Columbus on his return to Palos.

When Columbus landed at Cadiz, he was clothed with the robe and girdled with the cord of the Franciscans. His face was unshaven. Whether this was in penance, or an assumption of piety to serve as a lure, is not clear. Oviedo says it was to express his humility ; and his humbled pride needed some such expression.

He found in the harbor three caravels just about starting for Española with tardy supplies. It had been intended to send some in January ; but the ships which started with them suffered wreck on the neighboring coasts. He had only to ask Pedro Alonso Niño, the commander of this little fleet, for his dispatches, to find the condition of feeling which he was to encounter in Spain. They gave him a sense, more than and learns ever before, of the urgent necessity of making the the condition of the colony tributary to the treasury of the Crown. It was public mind. clear that discord and unproductiveness were not much longer to be endured. So he wrote a letter to the Adelantado, which was to go by the ships, urging expedition in quieting the life of the colonists, and in bringing the resources of the island under such control that it could be made to yield a steady flow of treasure. To this end, the new mines of Hayna must be further explored, and the working of them started with diligence.

1496. June 17. Columbus writes to Bartholomew. A port of shipment should be found in their neighborhood, he adds. With such instructions to Bartholomew, the caravels sailed on June 17, 1496. It must have been with some trepidation that Columbus forwarded to the Court the tidings of his arrival. If the two dispatches which he sent could have been preserved, we might better understand his mental condition.

As soon as the messages of Columbus reached their Majesties, Invited to Court. then at Almazan, they sent, July 12, 1496, a letter inviting him to Court, and reassuring him in his despondency by expressions of kindness. So he started to join the Court in a somewhat better frame of mind. He led some of his bedecked Indians in his train, not forgetting " in the towns " to make a cacique among them wear conspicuously a golden necklace.

Bernaldez tells us that it was in this wily fashion that Columbus made his journey into the country of Castile, — " the which collar," that writer adds, " I have seen and held in these hands ; " and he goes on to describe the other precious ornaments of the natives, which Columbus took care that the gaping crowds should see on this wandering mission.

It is one of the anachronisms of the *Historie* of 1571 that it places the Court at this time at Burgos, and makes it there to celebrate the marriage of the crown prince with Margaret of Austria. The author of that book speaks of seeing the festivities himself, then in attendance as a page upon Don Juan. It was a singular lapse of memory in Ferdinand Columbus — if this statement is his — to make two events like the arrival of his father at Court, with all the incidental parade as described in the book, and the ceremonies of that wedding festival identical in time. The wedding was in fact nine months later, in April, 1497.

Columbus's reception, wherever it was, seems to have been Received by the sovereigns. gracious, and he made the most of the amenities of the occasion to picture, in his old exaggerating way, the wealth of the Ophir mines. He was encouraged by the effect which his enthusiasm had produced to ask to be supplied with another fleet, partly to send additional supplies to Española, but mainly to enable him to dis-  Makes new demands.

cover that continental land farther south, of which he had so constantly heard reports.

It was easy for the monarchs to give fair promises, and quite as easy to forget them, for a while at least, in the busy scenes which their political ambitions were producing. Belligerent relations with France necessitated a vigilant watch about the Pyrenees. There were fleets to be maintained to resist, both in the Mediterranean and on the Atlantic coast, attacks which might unexpectedly fall. An imposing armada was preparing to go to Flanders to carry thither the Princess Juana to her espousal with Philip of Austria. The same fleet was to bring back Philip's sister Margaret to become the bride of Prince Juan, in those ceremonials to which reference has already been made.

These events were too engrossing for the monarchs to give much attention to the wishes of Columbus, and it was not till the autumn of 1496 that an appropriation was made to equip another little squadron for him. The hopes it raised were soon dashed, for having some occasion 1496. Autumn. A new expedition ordered. to need money promptly, at a crisis of the contest which the King was waging with France, the money which had been intended for Columbus was diverted to the new exigency. What was worse in the eyes of Columbus, it was to be paid out of some gold which it was supposed that Niño had brought back from the mines of Hayna. This officer on arriving at Cadiz had sent to the Court some boastful messages about his golden lading, which were not confirmed when in December the sober dispatch of the Adelantado, which Niño had kept back, came to be read. The nearest approach to gold which the caravels brought was another crowd of dusky slaves, and the dispatches of Bartholomew pictured the colony in the same conditions of destitution as before. There was no stimulant in such reports either for the Admiral or for the Court, and the New World was again dismissed from the minds of all, or consigned to their derision.

When the spring months of 1497 arrived, there were new hopes. The wedding of Prince Juan at Burgos was over, and the Queen was left more at liberty to think of her patronage of the new discoveries. The King was growing more and more apathetic, and some of 1497. Spring. Columbus's rights reaffirmed.

the leading spirits of the Court were inimical, either actively or reservedly. By the Queen's influence, the old rights bestowed upon Columbus were reaffirmed (April 23, 1497), and he was offered a large landed estate in Española, with a new territorial title; but he was wise enough to see that to accept it would complicate his affairs beyond their present entanglement. He was solicitous, however, to remove some of his present pecuniary embarrassments, and it was arranged that he should be relieved

New powers. from bearing an eighth of the cost of the ventures of the last three years, and that he should surrender all rights to the profits; while for the three years to come he

FERDINAND OF ARAGON.
[From an ancient medallion given in Buckingham Smith's *Coleccion.*]

should have an eighth of the gross income, and a further tenth of the net proceeds. Later, the original agreement was to be restored. His brother Bartholomew was created Adelantado, giving thus the royal sanction to the earlier act of the Admiral. In the letters patent made out previous to Columbus's second voyage, the Crown distinctly reserved the right to grant other licenses, and invested Fonseca with the power to do so, allowing to Columbus nothing more than one eighth of the tonnage; and in the ordinance of June 2, 1497, in which they now revoked all previous licenses, the revocation was confined to such things as were repugnant to the rights of Columbus. It was also agreed that the Crown should

BARTHOLOMEW COLUMBUS.
[From Barcia's *Herrera*.]

maintain for him a body of three hundred and thirty gentlemen, soldiers, and helpers, to accompany him on his new expedition, and this number could be increased, if the profits of the colony warranted the expenditure. Power was given to him to grant land to such as would cultivate the soil for four years; but all brazil-wood and metals were to be reserved for the Crown.

All this seemed to indicate that the complaints which had been made against the oppressive sternness of the Admiral's rule had not as yet broken down the barriers of the Queen's protection.  Indeed, we find up to this time no record of any serious question at Court of his authority, and Irving thinks nothing indicates any symptom of the royal discontent except the reiterated injunctions, in the orders given to him respecting the natives and the colonists, that leniency should govern his conduct so far as was safe.

Permission being given to him to entail his estates, he marked out in a testamentary document (February 22, 1498) the succession of his heirs, — male heirs, with Ferdinand's rights protected, if Diego's line ran out ; then male heirs of his brothers ; and if all male heirs failed, then the estates were to descend by the female line.  The title Admiral was made the paramount honor, and to be the perpetual distinction of his representatives.  The entail was to furnish forever a tenth of its revenues to charitable uses.  Genoa was placed particularly under the patronage of his succeeding representatives, with injunctions always to do that city service, as far as the interests of the Church and the Spanish Crown would permit.  Investments were to be made from time to time in the bank of St. George at Genoa, to accumulate against the opportune moment when the recovery of the Holy Sepulchre seemed feasible, either to help to that end any state expedition or to fit out a private one.  He enjoined upon his heirs a constant, unwavering devotion to the Papal Church and to the Spanish Crown.  At every season of confession, his representative was commanded to lay open his heart to the confessor, who must be prompted by a perusal of the will to ask the crucial questions.

*1498.  February 22.  Makes a will.*

It was in the same document that Columbus prescribed the signature of his representatives in succeeding generations, following a formula which he always used himself.

*Columbus's signature.*

.S.

.S. A. S.

X. M. Y.

χβο FERENS.

The interpretation of this has been various : *Servus Supplex Altissimi Salvatoris, Christus, Maria, Yoseph, Christo ferens,* is one solution; *Servidor sus Altezas sacras, Christo, Maria Ysabel,* is another; and these are not all.

The complacency of the Queen was soothing; her appointment of his son Ferdinand as her page (February 18, 1498) was gratifying, but it could not wholly compensate Columbus for the condition of the public mind, of which he was in every way forcibly reminded. There were both the whisper of detraction spreading abroad, and the outspoken objurgation. The physical debility of his returned companions was made a strong contrast to his reiterated stories of Paradise. Fortunes wrecked, labor wasted, and lives lost had found but a pitiable compensation in a few cargoes of miserable slaves. The people had heard of his enchanting landscapes, but they had found his aloes and mastic of no value. Hidalgoes said there was nothing of the luxury they had been told to expect. ·The gorgeous cities of the Great Khan had not been found. Such were the kind of taunts to which he was subjected.

*Unpopularity of Columbus.*

Columbus, during this period of his sojourn in Spain, spent a considerable interval under the roof of Andres Bernaldez, and we get in his history of the Spanish kings the advantage of the talks which the two friends had together.

*His sojourn with Bernaldez.*

The Admiral is known to have left with Bernaldez various documents which were given to him in the presence of Juan de Fonseca. From the way in which Bernaldez speaks of these papers, they would seem to have been accounts of the voyage of Columbus then already made, and it was upon these documents that Bernaldez says he based his own narratives.

This ecclesiastic had known Columbus at an earlier day, when the Genoese was a vender of books in Andalusia, as he says; in characterizing him, he calls his friend in another place a man of an ingenious turn, but not of much learning, and he leaves one to infer that the book-vender was not much suspected of great familiarity with his wares.

*Bernaldez's opinions.*

We get as clearly from Bernaldez as from any other source the measure of the disappointment which the public shared as respects the conspicuous failure of these voyages of Columbus in their pecuniary relations.

The results are summed up by that historian to show that the cost of the voyages had been so great and the returns so small that it came to be believed that there was in the new regions no gold to speak of.    Taking the first voyage, — and the second was hardly better, considering the larger opportunities, — Harrisse has collated, for instance, all the references to what gold Columbus may have gathered ; and though there are some contradictory reports, the weight of testimony seems to confine the amount to an inconsiderable sum, which consisted in the main of personal ornaments.    There are legends of the gold brought to Spain from this voyage being used to gild palaces and churches, to make altar ornaments for the cathedral at Toledo, to serve as gifts of homage to the Pope, but we may safely say that no reputable authority supports any such statements.

Scant returns of gold.

Notwithstanding this seeming royal content of which the signs have been given, there was, by virtue of a discontented and irritated public sentiment, a course open to Columbus in these efforts to fit out his new expedition which was far from easy.    There was so much disinclination in the merchants to furnish ships that it required a royal order to seize them before the small fleet could be gathered.

The enlistments to man the ships and make up the contingent destined for the colony were more difficult still. The alacrity with which everybody bounded to the summons on his second voyage had entirely gone, and it was only by the foolish device which Columbus decided upon of opening the doors of the prisons and of giving pardon to criminals at large, that he was enabled to help on the registration of his company.

Difficulties in fitting out the new expedition.

Criminals enlisted.

Finding that all went slowly, and knowing that the colony at Española must be suffering from want of supplies, the Queen was induced to order two caravels of the fleet to sail at once, early in 1498, under the command of Pedro Fernandez Coronel.    This was only possible because the Queen took some money which she had laid aside as a part of a dower which was intended for her daughter Isabella, then betrothed to Emmanuel, the King of Portugal.

1498.  Two caravels sail.

So much was gratifying ; but the main object of the new expedition was to make new discoveries, and there were many harassing delays yet in store for Columbus before he could depart with the rest of his fleet. These delays, as we shall see, enabled another people, under the lead of another Italian, to precede him and make the first discovery of the mainland. The Queen was cordial, but an affliction came to distract her, in the death of Prince Juan. Fonseca, who was now in charge of the fitting out of the caravels, seems to have lacked heart in the enterprise; but it serves the purpose of Colum- Fonseca's lack of heart. bus's adulatory biographers to give that agent of the Crown the character of a determined enemy of Columbus.

Even the prisons did not disgorge their vermin, as he had wished, and his company gathered very slowly, and never became full. Las Casas tells us that troubles followed him even to the dock. The accountant of Fonseca, one Ximeno de Breviesca, got into an altercation with the Admiral, who knocked him down and exhibited other marks of pas- Columbus's altercation with Fonseca's accountant. sion. Las Casas further tells us that this violence, through the representations of it which Fonseca made, produced a greater effect on the monarchs than all the allegations of the Admiral's cruelty and vindictiveness which his accusers from Española had constantly brought forward, and that it was the immediate cause of the change of royal sentiment towards him, which soon afterwards appeared. Columbus seems to have discovered the mistake he had made very promptly, and wrote to the monarchs to counteract its effect. It was therefore with this new anxiety upon his mind that he for the third time committed himself to his career of adventure and exploration. The canonizers would have it that their sainted hero found it necessary to prove by his energy in personal violence that age had not impaired his manhood for the trials before him!

Before following Columbus on this voyage, the reader must take a glance at the conditions of discovery elsewhere, for these other events were intimately connected with the significance of Columbus's own voyagings.

The problem which the Portuguese had undertaken to solve was, as has been seen, the passage to India by the Da Gama's passage of the African cape. Stormy Cape of Africa. Even before Columbus had sailed on his first voyage, word had come in 1490 to encourage King João II. His emissaries in Cairo had learned from the Arab sailors that the passage of the cape was practicable on the side of the Indian Ocean. The success of his Spanish rivals under Columbus in due time encouraged the Portuguese king still more, or at least piqued him to new efforts.

Vasco da Gama was finally put in command of a fleet specially equipped. It was now some years since his pilot, Pero de Alemquer, had carried Diaz well off the cape. On Sunday, July 8, 1497, Da Gama sailed from below Lisbon, and on November 22 he passed with full sheets the formidable cape. It was not, however, till December 17 that he reached the point where Diaz had turned back. His further progress does not concern us here. Suffice it to say that he cast an-

VASCO DA GAMA.
[From Stanley's *Da Gama*.]

chor at Calicut May 20, 1498, and India was reached
*Reaches Calicut May 20, 1498.* ten days before Columbus started a third time to verify his own beliefs, but really to find them errors.

Towards the end of August, or perhaps early in September, of the next year (1499), Da Gama arrived at Lisbon on his return voyage, anticipated, indeed, by one of his caravels, which, separated from the commander in April or May, had pushed ahead and reached home on the 10th of July. Portugal at once resounded with jubilation. The fleet had returned crippled with disabled crews, and half the vessels had disappeared; but the solution of a great problem had been reached.

The voyage of Da Gama, opening a trade eagerly pursued and eagerly met, offered, as we shall see, a great contrast to the small immediate results which came from the futile efforts of Columbus to find a western way to the same regions.

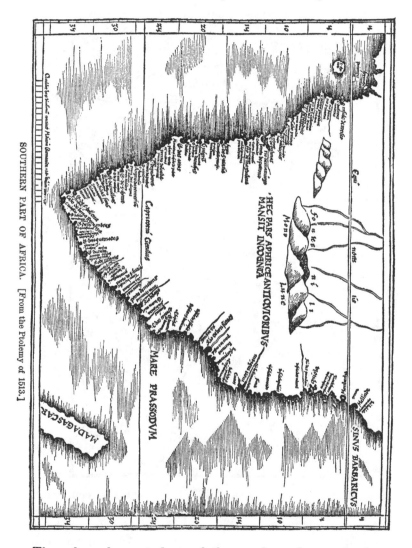

SOUTHERN PART OF AFRICA. [From the Ptolemy of 1513.]

There have been students of these early explorers who have contended that, while Columbus was harassed in Spain with

these delays in preparing for his third voyage, the Florentine
Vespucius, whom we have encountered already as

helping Berardi in the equipment of Columbus's
fleets, had, in a voyage of which we have some con-

EARLIEST REPRESENTATION OF SOUTH AMERICAN NATIVES, 1497–1504.
[From Stevens's reproduction in his *American Bibliographer*.]

fused chronology, already in 1497 discovered and coursed the
northern shores of the mainland south of the Caribbean Sea.

Bernaldez tells us that, during the interval between the second and third voyages of Columbus, the Admiral "accorded
permission to other captains to make discoveries at the west,
who went and discovered various islands." Whether we can

connect this statement with any such voyage as is now to be considered is a matter of dispute.

This question of the first discovery of the mainland of South America, — we shall see that North America's mainland had already been discovered, — whether by Columbus or Vespucius, is one which has long vexed the historian and still does perplex him, though the general consensus of opinion at the present day is in favor of Columbus, while pursuing the voyage through which we are soon to follow him. The question is much complicated by the uncertainties and confusion of the narratives which are our only guides. The discovery, if not claimed by Vespucius, has been vigorously claimed for him. Its particulars are also made a part of the doubt which has clouded the recitals concerning the voyage of Pinzon and Solis to the Honduras coast, which are usually placed later; but by Oviedo and Gomara this voyage is said to have preceded that of Columbus.

The claim for Vespucius is at the best but an enforced method of clarifying the published texts concerning the voyages, in the hopes of finding something like consistency in their dates. Any commentator who undertakes to get at the truth must necessarily give himself up to some sort of conjecture, not only as respects the varied inconsistencies of the narrative, but also as regards the manifold blunders of the printer of the little book which records the voyages. Muñoz had it in mind, it is understood, to prove that Vespucius could not have been on the coast at the date of his alleged discovery; but in the opinions of some the documents do not prove all that Muñoz, Navarrete, and Humboldt have claimed, while the advocacy of Varnhagen in favor of Vespucius does not allow that writer to see what he apparently does not desire to see. The most, perhaps, that we can say is that the proof against the view of Varnhagen, who is in favor of such a voyage in 1497, is not wholly substantiated. The fact seems to be, so far as can be made out, that Vespucius passed from one commander's employ to another's, at a date when Ojeda, in 1499, had not completed his voyage, and when Pinzon started. So supposing a return to Spain in order for Vespucius to restart with Pinzon, it is also supposable that the year 1499 itself may have seen him under two different leaders. If this is the correct view, it

*Who discovered South America?*

*Claimed for Vespucius.*

of course carries forward the date to a time later than the discovery of the mainland by Columbus. It is nothing but plausible conjecture, after all; but something of the nature of conjecture is necessary to dissipate the confusion. The belief of this sharing of service is the best working hypothesis yet devised upon the question.

If Vespucius was thus with Pinzon, and this latter navigator did, as Oviedo claims, precede Columbus to the mainland, there is no proof of it to prevent a marked difference of opinion among all the writers, in that some ignore the Florentine navigator entirely, and others confidently construct the story of his discovery, which has in turn taken root and been widely believed.

A voyage of 1497 does not find mention in any of the contemporary Portuguese chroniclers. This absence of reference is serious evidence against it. It seems to be certain that within twenty years of their publication, there were doubts raised of the veracity of the narratives attributed to Vespucius, and Sebastian Cabot tells us in 1505 that he does not believe them in respect to this one voyage at any rate, and Las Casas is about as well convinced as Cabot was that the story was unfounded. Las Casas's papers passed probably to Herrera, who, under the influence of them, it would seem, formulated a distinct allegation that Vespucius had falsified the dates, converting 1499 into 1497. To destroy all the claims associated with Pinzon and Solis, Herrera carried their voyage forward to 1506. It was in 1601 that this historian made these points, and so far as he regulated the opinions of Europe for a century and a half, including those of England as derived through Robertson, Vespucius lived in the world's regard with a clouded reputation. The attempt of Bandini in the middle of the last century to lift the shadow was not very fortunate, but better success followed later, when Canovai delivered an address which then and afterwards, when it was reinforced by other publications of his, was something like a gage thrown to the old-time defamatory spirit. This denunciatory view was vigorously worked, with Navarrete's help, by Santarem in the *Coleccion* of that Spanish scholar, whence Irving in turn got his opinions. Santarem professed to have made most extensive examinations of Portuguese and French manuscripts without finding a trace of the Florentine.

*Alleged voyage of 1497.*

Undaunted by all such negative testimony, the Portuguese Varnhagen, as early as 1839, began a series of publications aimed at rehabilitating the fame of Vespucius, against the views of all the later writers, Humboldt, Navarrete, Santarem, and the rest. Humboldt claimed to adduce evidence to show that Vespucius was all the while in Europe. Varnhagen finally brought himself to the belief that in this disputed voyage of 1497 Vespucius, acting under the orders of Vicente Yañez Pinzon and Juan Diaz de Solis, really reached the main at Honduras, whence he followed the curvatures of the coast northerly till he reached the capes of Chesapeake. Thence he steered easterly, passed the Bermudas, and arrived at Seville. If this is so, he circumnavigated the archipelago of the Antilles, and disproved the continental connection of Cuba. Varnhagen even goes so far as to maintain that Vespucius had not been deceived into supposing the coast was that of Asia, but that he divined the truth. Varnhagen stands, however, alone in this estimate of the evidence.

Valentini, in our day, has even supposed that the incomplete Cuba of the Ruysch map of 1508 was really the Yucatan shore, which Vespucius had skirted.

The claim which some French zealots in maritime discovery have attempted to sustain, of Norman adventurers being on the Brazil coast in 1497-98, is hardly worth consideration.

We turn now to other problems. The Bull of Demarcation was far from being acceptable as an ultimate decision in England, and the spirit of her people towards it is well shown in the *Westerne Planting* of Hakluyt. This chronicler mistrusts that its "certain secret causes" — which words he had found in the papal bull, probably by using an inaccurate version — were no other than "the feare and jelousie that King Henry of England, with whom Bartholomew Columbus had been to deal in this enterprise, and who even now was ready to send him into Spain to call his brother Christopher to England, should put a foot into this action;" and so the Pope, "fearing that either the King of Portugal might be reconciled to Columbus, or that he might be drawn into England, thought secretly by his unlawful division to defraud England and Portugal of that benefit." So England and Portugal had something like a common cause, and the record of how they worked that cause is told in the stories of Cabot first, and of Cortereal later. We will examine at this point the Cabot story only.

Bristol had long been the seat of the English commerce with Iceland, and one of the commodities received in return for English goods was the stockfish, which Cabot was to recognize on the Newfoundland banks. These stories of the codfish noticed by Cabot recalled in the mind of Galvano in 1555,
Newfound-land fish-eries.
and again more forcibly to Hakluyt a half century later, when Germany was now found to be not far from the latitude of Baccalaos, that there was a tale of some strange men, in the time of Frederick Barbarossa (A. D. 1153), being driven to Lubec in a canoe.

It is by no means beyond possibility that the Basque and other fishermen of Europe may have already strayed to these fishing grounds of Newfoundland, at some period anterior to this voyage of Cabot, and even traces of their frequenting the coast in Bradore Bay have been pointed out, but without convincing as yet the careful student.

A Venetian named Zuan Caboto, settling in England, and thenceforward calling himself John Cabot, being a
John Cabot.
man of experience in travel, and having seen at one time at Mecca the caravans returning from the east, was impressed, as Columbus had been, with a belief in the roundness of the earth. It is not unlikely that this belief had taken for him a compelling nature from the stories which had come to England of the successful voyage of the Spaniards. Indeed, Ramusio distinctly tells us that it was the bruit of Columbus's first voyage which gave to Cabot "a great flame of desire to attempt some notable thing."

When Cabot had received for himself and his three sons — one of whom was Sebastian Cabot — a patent (March
1496. March 5. Cabot's patent.
5, 1496) from Henry VII. to discover and trade with unknown countries beyond the seas, the envoy of Ferdinand and Isabella at the English court was promptly instructed to protest against any infringement of the rights of Spain
1497. May. Cabot sails.
in the western regions. Whether this protest was accountable for the delay in sailing, or not, does not appear, for Cabot did not set sail from Bristol till May, 1497.

It is inferred from what Beneventanus says in his *Ptolemy* of 1508 that Ruysch, who gives us the earliest engraved map of Cabot's discoveries, was a companion of Cabot in this initial voyage. When that editor says that he learned from Ruysch of his experiences in sailing from the south of England to a point in 53 degrees of north latitude, and thence due west, it may be referred to such participancy in this expedition from Bristol. We know from a conversation which is reported in Ramusio — unless there is some mistake in it — that Cabot apprehended the nature of what we call great circle sailing, and claimed that his course to the northwest would open India by a shorter route than the westerly run of Columbus.

*Ruysch with Cabot.*

When Cabot had ventured westerly 700 leagues, he found land, June 24, 1497. There has been some confidence at different times, early and late, that the date of this first Cabot voyage was in reality three years before this. The belief arose from the date of 1494 being given in what seem to have been early copies of a map ascribed to Sebastian Cabot, whence the date 1494 was copied by Hakluyt in 1589, though eleven years later he changed it to 1497. It is sufficient to say that few of the critics of our day, except D'Avezac, hold to this date of 1494. Major supposes that the map of 1544, now in the Paris library and ascribed to Cabot, was a re-drawn draft from the lost Spanish original, in which the date in Roman letters, VII, may have been so carelessly made in joining the arms of the V that it was read IIII; and some such inference was apparently in the mind of Henry Stevens when he published his little tract on Sebastian Cabot in 1870.

*1497. June 24. Cabot sees land.*

*Date of the voyage, 1494 or 1497?*

The country which Cabot thus first saw was supposed by him to be a part of Asia, and to be occupied, though no inhabitants were seen.

Cabot was for over three hundred years considered as having made his landfall on the coast of Labrador, or at least we find no record that the legend of the map of 1544, placing it at Cape Breton, had impressed itself authoritatively upon the minds of Cabot's contemporaries and successors. Biddle and Humboldt, in the early part of the present century, accepted the Labrador landfall with little question. So it happened that when, in 1843, the Cabot mappemonde of 1544

*Cabot's landfall.*

was discovered, and it was found to place the landfall at the island of Cape Breton, a certain definiteness, where there had been so much vagueness, afforded the student some relief; but as the novelty of the sensation wore off, confidence was again lost, inasmuch as the various uncertainties of the document give much ground for the rejection of all parts of its testimony at variance with better vouched beliefs. It is quite possible that more satisfactory proofs can be adduced of another region for the landfall, but none such have yet been presented to scholars.

It is commonly held now that, sighting land at Cape Breton, Cabot coursed northerly, passed the present Prince Edward Island, and then sailed out of the Strait of Belle Isle, — or at least this is as reasonable a route to make out of the scant record as any, though there is nothing like a commonly received opinion on his track. There is some ground for thinking that he could not have entered the Gulf of St. Lawrence at all. He landed nowhere and saw no inhabitants. If he struck the mainland, it was probably the coasts of New Brunswick or Labrador bordering on the Gulf of St. Lawrence. The two islands which he observed on his right may have been headlands of Newfoundland, seeming to be isolated.

He reached Bristol in August, having been absent about three months. Raimondo de Soncino, under date of the 24th of that month, wrote to Italy of Cabot's return, and a fortnight earlier (August 10) we find record of a gratuity of ten pounds given to Cabot in recognition of this service. It proved to be an expedition which was to create a greater sensation of its kind than the English had before known. Bristol had nurtured for some years a race of hardy seamen. They had risked the dangers of the great unknown ocean in efforts to find the fabulous island of Brazil, and they had pushed adventurously westward at times, but always to return without success. The intercourse of England with the northern nations and with Iceland may have given them tidings of Greenland; but there is no reason to believe that they ever supposed that country to be other than an extended peninsula of Europe, enfolding the North Atlantic. Cabot's telling of a new land, his supposing it the empire of the Great Khan, his tales of the wonderful fishing ground thereabouts, where the water was so dense with fish that his vessels were

1497. August. Cabot returns.

impeded, and his expectation of finding the land of spices if he went southward from the region of his landfall, were all stories calculated to incite wonder and speculation. It was not strange, then, that England found she had her new sea-hero, as Spain had hers in Columbus ; that the king gave him money <small>Cabot in</small> and a pension ; and that, conscious of a certain dig- <small>England.</small> nity, Cabot went about the city, drawing the attention of the curious by reason of the fine silks in which he arrayed himself.

Cabot had no sooner returned than Pedro de Ayala, the Spanish envoy in London, again entered a protest, and gave notice to the English king that the land which had <small>Spain jealous</small> been discovered belonged to his master. There is <small>of England.</small> some evidence that Spain kept close watch on the country at the north through succeeding years, and even intended settlement.

This Spanish ambassador wrote home from London, July 25, 1498, that after his first voyage, Cabot had been in <small>Cabot in</small> Seville and Lisbon. This renders somewhat probable <small>Seville ?</small> the suspicion that he may have had conferences with La Cosa and Columbus.

That John Cabot, on returning from his first voyage, produced a chart which he had made, and that on this and on a solid globe, also of his construction, he had laid down what he considered to be the region he had reached, now admit <small>Cabot's</small> of no doubt. Foreign residents at the English court <small>charts.</small> reported such facts to the courts of Italy and of Spain. In the map of La Cosa (1500), we find what is considered a reflex of this Cabot chart, in the words running along a stretch of the northeast coast of Asia, which announce the waters adjacent as those visited by the English, and a neighboring headland as the Cape of the English. Even La Cosa's use of the Cabot map was lost sight of before long, and this record of La Cosa remained unknown till Humboldt discovered the map in Paris, in 1832, in the library of Baron Walckenaer, whence it passed in 1853 into the royal museum at Madrid. The views of Cabot respecting this region seem to have been soon obscured by the more current charts showing the voyages of the Cortereals, when the Cape of the English readily disappeared in the "Cabo de Portogesi," a forerunner, very likely, of what we know to-day as Cape Race.

Such an appetizing tale as that of the first Cabot expedition

was not likely to rest without a sequel. On the 3d of February, 1497–98, nearly four months before Columbus
sailed on his third voyage, the English king granted
a new patent to John Cabot, giving him the right to
man six ships if he could, and in May he was at sea.

1497-98.
February.
The second
Cabot voy-
age.

Though his sons were not mentioned in the patent, it is supposed that Sebastian Cabot accompanied his father. One vessel
putting back to Ireland, five others went on, carrying John
Cabot westward somewhere and to oblivion, for we never hear
of him again. Stevens ventures the suggestion that John Cabot
may have died on the voyage of 1498, whereby Sebastian came
into command, and so into a prominence in his own recollections
of the voyage, which may account for the obscuration of his
father's participancy in the enterprise. One of the ships would
seem to have been commanded by Lanslot Thirkill, of London.

What we know of this second voyage are mentions in later
years, vague in character, and apparently traceable to what
Sebastian had said of it, and not always clearly, for there is an
evident commingling of events of this and of the earlier voyage.
We get what we know mainly from Peter Martyr, who tells
us that Cabot called the region Baccalaos, and from Ramusio,
who reports at second hand Sebastian's account, made forty
years after the event. From such indefinite sources we can
make out that the little fleet steered northwesterly, and got into
water packed with ice, and found itself in a latitude where
there was little night. Thence turning south they ran down to
36° north latitude. The crews landed here and there, and saw
people dressed in skins, who used copper implements. When
they reached England we do not know, but it was after October, 1498.

The question of this voyage having extended down the Atlantic seaboard of the present United States to the region
of Florida, as has been urged, seems to be set at rest

Extent of
this voyage.

in Stevens's opinion, from the fact that, had Cabot gone so far,
he would scarcely have acquiesced in the claims of Ponce de
Leon, Ayllon, and Gomez to have first tracked parts of this
coast, when Sebastian Cabot as pilot major of Spain (1518),
and as president of the Congress of Badajoz (1524), had to
adjudicate on such pretensions. There are some objections to
this view, in that the results of *unofficial* explorers as shown in

the Portuguese map of Cantino — if that proposition is tenable — and the rival English discoverers, of whom Cabot had been one, might easily have been held to be beyond the Spanish jurisdiction. It is not difficult to demonstrate in these matters the Spanish constant unrecognition of other national explorations.

It has also sometimes been held that the wild character of the coast along which Cabot sailed must have convinced him that he was bordering some continental region intervening between him and the true coast of Asia; that with the " great displeasure " he had felt in finding the land running north, Cabot, in fact, must have comprehended the geographical problem of America long before it was comprehended by the Spaniards. The testimony of the La Cosa and Ruysch maps is not favorable to such a belief.

It seems pretty certain that the success of the Cabot voyage in any worldly gain was not sufficient to move the English again for a long period. Still, the political effect was to raise a claim for England to a region not then known to be a new continent, but of an appreciable acquisition, and England never afterwards failed to rest her rights upon this claim of discovery; and even her successors, the American people, have not been without cause to rest valuable privileges upon the same. The geographical effect was seen in the earliest map which we possess of the new lands as discovered by Spain and England, the great oxhide map of Juan de la Cosa, the companion of Columbus on his second voyage, and the cartographer of his discoveries, which has already been mentioned, and of which a further description will be given later.

Why is it that we know no more of these voyages of the Cabots? There seems to be some ground for the suspicion that the " maps and discourses " which Sebastian Cabot left behind him in the hands of William Worthington may have fallen, through the subornation by Spain of the latter, into the hands of the rivals of England at a period just after the publication (1582) of Hakluyt's *Divers Voyages*, wherein the possession of them by Worthington was made known; at least, Biddle has advanced such a theory, and it has some support in what may be conjectured of the history of the famous Cabot map of 1544, only brought to light three hun-

*England rests her claim on it.*

*Scant knowledge of the Cabot voyages.*

dred years later. Here was a map evidently based in part on such information as was known in Spain. It was engraved, as seems likely, though purporting to be the work of Cabot, in the Low Countries, and was issued without name of pub-

The Cabot mappe-monde. lisher or place, as if to elude responsibility. Notwithstanding it was an engraved map, implying many copies, it entirely disappeared, and would not have been known to exist except that there are references to such a map as having hung in the gallery at Whitehall, as used by Ortelius before 1570, and as noted by Sanuto in 1588. So thorough a suppression would seem to imply an effort on the part of the Spanish authorities to prevent the world's profiting by the publication of maritime knowledge which in some clandestine way had escaped from the Spanish hydrographical office. That this suppression was in effect nearly successful may be inferred from the fact that but a single copy of the map has come down to us, the one now in the great library at Paris, which was found in Germany by Von Martius in 1843.

There has been a good deal done of late years — beginning with Biddle's *Sebastian Cabot* in 1831, a noteworthy

Writers on Cabot. book, showing how much the critical spirit can do to unravel confusion, and ending with the chapter on Cabot by the late Dr. Charles Deane in the *Narrative and Critical History of America*, and with the *Jean et Sébastien Cabot* of Harrisse (Paris, 1882) — to clear up the great obscurity regarding the two voyages of John Cabot in 1497 and 1498, an obscurity so dense that for two hundred years after the events there was no suspicion among writers that there had been more than a single voyage. It would appear that this obscurity had mainly arisen from the way in which Sebastian Cabot himself spoke of his explorations, or rather from the way in which he is reported to have spoken.

# CHAPTER XVI.

## THE THIRD VOYAGE.

### 1498–1500.

In following the events of the third voyage, we have to depend mainly on two letters written by Columbus himself. One is addressed to the Spanish monarchs, and is preserved in a copy made by Las Casas. What Peter Martyr tells us seems to have been borrowed from this letter. The other is addressed to the " nurse " of Prince Juan, of which there are copies in the Columbus Custodia at Genoa, and in the Muñoz collection of the Royal Academy of History at Madrid. They are both printed in Navarrete and elsewhere, and Major in his *Select Letters of Columbus* gives English versions.

There are also some evidences that the account of this voyage given in the *Itinerarium Portugalensium* was based on Columbus's journal, which Las Casas is known to have had, and to have used in his *Historia*, adding thereto some details which he got from a recital by Bernaldo de Ibarra, one of Columbus's companions, — indeed, his secretary. The map which accompanied these accounts by Columbus is lost. We only know its existence through the use of it made by Ojeda and others.

Las Casas interspersed among the details which he recorded from Columbus's journal some particulars which he got from Alonso de Vallejo. One of the pilots, Hernan Perez Matheos, enabled Oviedo to add still something more to the other sources; and then we have additional light from the mouths of various witnesses in the Columbus lawsuit. There is a little at second hand, but of small importance, in a letter of Simon Verde printed by Harrisse.

Before setting sail, Columbus prepared some directions for his
Columbus's son Diego, of which we have only recently had notes,
son Diego. such appearing in the bulletin of the Italian Geographical Society for December, 1889. He commands in these injunctions that Diego shall have an affectionate regard for the mother of his half-brother Ferdinand, adds some rules for the guidance of his bearing towards his sovereigns and his fellow-men, and recommends him to resort to Father Gaspar Gorricio whenever he might feel in need of advice.

Columbus lifted anchor in the port of San Lucar de Barrameda on May 30, 1498. He was physically far from
1498. May being in a good condition for so adventurous an under-
30. Colum-
bus sails. taking. He had hoped, he says to his sovereigns, " to find repose in Spain; whereas on the contrary I have experienced nothing but opposition and vexation." His six vessels stood off to the southwest, to avoid a French — some say a Portuguese — fleet which was said to be cruising near Cape St. Vincent. His plan was a definite one, to keep in a southerly course till he reached the equatorial regions, and then to proceed west. By this course, he hoped to strike in that direction the continental mass of which he had intimation both from the reports of the natives in Española and from the trend which he had found in his last voyage the Cuban coast to have. Herrera tells us that the Portuguese king professed to have some knowledge of a continent in this direction, and we may con-
Rumors of a nect it, if we choose, with the stories respecting Be-
southern
continent. haim and others, who had already sailed thitherward, as some reports go; but it is hard to comprehend that any belief of that kind was other than a guess at a compensating scheme of geography beyond the Atlantic, to correspond with the balance of Africa against Europe in the eastern hemisphere. It is barely possible, though there is no positive evidence of it, that the reports from England of the Cabot discoveries at the north may have given a hint of like prolongation to the south. But a more impelling instinct was the prevalent one of his time, which accompanied what Michelet calls that terrible malady breaking out in this age of Europe, the hunger and thirst for gold and other precious things, and which associated the possession of them with the warmer regions of the globe.

"To the south," said Peter Martyr. "He who would find riches must avoid the cold north!"

Navarrete preserves a letter which was written to Columbus by Jayme Ferrer, a lapidary of distinction. This jeweler confirmed the prevalent notion, and said that in all his intercourse with distant marts, whence Europe derived its gold and jewels, he had learned from their vendors how such objects of commerce usually came in greatest abundance from near the equator, while black races were those that predominated near such sources. Therefore, as Ferrer told Columbus, steer south and find a black race, if you would get at such opulent abundance. The Admiral remembered he had heard in Española of blacks that had come from the south to that island in the past, and he had taken to Spain some of the metal which had been given to him as of the kind with which their javelins had been pointed. The Spanish assayers had found it a composition of gold, copper, and silver.

So it was with expectations like these that Columbus now worked his way south. He touched for wood and water at Porto Santo and Madeira, and thence proceeded to Gomera. Here, on June 16, he found a French cruiser with two Spanish prizes, but the three ships eluded his grasp and got to sea. He sent three caravels in pursuit, and the Spanish prisoners rising on the crew of one of the prizes, she was easily captured and brought into port.

The Spanish fleet sailed again on June 21. The Admiral had detailed three of his ships to proceed direct to Española to find the new port on its southern side near the mines of Hayna. Their respective captains were to command the little squadron successively a week at a time. These men were: Alonso Sanchez de Carvajal, a man of good reputation; Pedro de Arona, a brother of Beatrix de Henriquez, who had borne Ferdinand to the Admiral; and Juan Antonio Colombo, a Genoese and distant kinsman of the Admiral.

Parting with these vessels off Ferro, Columbus, with the three others, — one of which, the flagship, being decked, of a hundred tons burthen, and requiring three fathoms of water, — steered for the Cape de Verde Islands. His stay here was not inspiring. A depressing climate of vapor and an arid landscape told upon his health and upon that of his crew. Encountering difficulties in getting fresh pro-

*Jayme Ferrer.*

*Columbus steers southerly.*

*1498. June 16. At Gomera.*

*Sends three ships direct to Española.*

*Columbus at the Cape de Verde Islands.*

visions and cattle, he sailed again on July 5, standing to the southwest.   Calms and the currents among the islands baffled him, however, and it was the 7th before the high peak of Del

1498.  July 15.   Fuego sank astern.   By the 15th of July he had reached the latitude of 5° north.   He was now within the verge of the equatorial calms.   The air soon burned every-thing distressingly ; the rigging oozed with the running tar ;

Calms and torrid heats.   the seams of the vessels opened ; provisions grew putrid, and the wine casks shrank and leaked.   The fiery ordeal called for all the constancy of the crew, and the Admiral himself needed all the fortitude he could command to bear a brave face amid the twinges of gout which were prostrat-ing him.   He changed his course to see if he could not run out of the intolerable heat, and after a tedious interval, with no cessation of the humid and enervating air, the ships gradually drew into a fresher atmosphere.   A breeze rippled the water, and the sun shone the more refreshing for its clearness.   He now steered due west, hoping to find land before his water and provisions failed.   He did not discover land as soon as he ex-

1498.  July 31. Trinidad seen.   pected, and so bore away to the north, thinking to see some of the Carib Islands.   On July 31 relief came, none too soon, for their water was nearly exhausted. A mariner, about midday, peering about from the masthead, saw three peaks just rising above the horizon.   The cry of land was like a benison.   The *Salve Regina* was intoned in every part of the ship.   Columbus now headed the fleet for the land. As the ships went on and the three peaks grew into a triple mountain, he gave the island the name of Trinidad, a reminder in its peak of the Trinity, which he had determined at the start to commemorate by bestowing that appellation on the first land he saw.   He coasted the shore of this island for some distance before he could find a harbor to careen his ships and replenish

August 1.   his water casks.   On August 1 he anchored to get water, and was surprised at the fresh luxuriance of the country.   He could see habitations in the interior, but no-where along the shore were any signs of occupation.   His men, while filling the casks, discovered footprints and other traces of human life, but those who made them kept out of sight.

He was now on the southern side of the island, and in that channel which separates Trinidad from the low country about

the mouths of the Orinoco. Before long he could see the opposite coast stretching away for twenty leagues, but he First sees
did not suspect it to be other than an island, which the South American
he named La Isla Santa. coast.

It was indeed strange but not surprising that Columbus found
an island of a new continent, and supposed it the mainland of
the Old World, as happened during his earlier voyages; and
equally striking it was that now when he had actually seen the
mainland of a new world he did not know it.

By the 2d of August the Admiral had approached that narrow channel where the southwest corner of Trinidad 1498. Au-
comes nearest to the mainland, and here he anchored. gust 2.
A large canoe, containing five and twenty Indians, put off towards his ships, but finally its occupants lay upon their paddles
a bowshot away. Columbus describes them as comely in shape,
naked but for breech-cloths, and wearing variegated scarfs about
their heads. They were lighter in skin than any Indians he had
seen before. This fact was not very promising in view of the
belief that precious products would be found in a country inhabited by blacks. The men had bucklers, too, a defense he
had never seen before among these new tribes. He tried to
lure them on board by showing trinkets, and by improvising
some music and dances among his crew. The last expedient
was evidently looked upon as a challenge, and was met by a
flight of arrows. Two crossbows were discharged in return, and
the canoe fled. The natives seemed to have less fear of the
smaller caravels, and approached near enough for the captain
of one of them to throw some presents to them, a cap, and a
mantle, and the like; but when the Indians saw that a boat was
sent to the Admiral's ship, they again fled.

While here at anchor, the crew were permitted to go ashore
and refresh themselves. They found much delight in the cool
air of the morning and evening, coming after their experiences
of the torrid suffocation of the calm latitudes. Nature had
appeared to them never so fresh.

Columbus grew uneasy in his insecure anchorage, for he had
discovered as yet no roadstead. He saw the current flowing
by with a strength that alarmed him. The waters seemed to
tumble in commotion as they were jammed together in the narrow pass before him. It was his first experience of that

African current which, setting across the ocean, plunges here-
The Gulf abouts into the Caribbean Sea, and, sweeping around
Stream. the great gulf, passes north in what we know as the
Gulf Stream.   Columbus was as yet ignorant, too, of the great
masses of water which the many mouths of the Orinoco discharge along this shore; and when at night a great roaring
billow of water came across the channel, — very likely an unusual volume of the river water poured out of a sudden, — and
he found his own ship lifting at her anchor and one of his caravels snapping her cable, he felt himself in the face of new dangers, and of forces of nature to which he was not accustomed.
To a seaman's senses not used to such phenomena, the situation
of the ships was alarming.   Before him was the surging flow
of the current through the narrow pass, which he had already
Boca del named the Mouth of the Serpent (Boca del Sierpe).
Sierpe. To attempt its passage was almost foolhardy.   To return along the coast stemming such a current seemed nearly impossible.   He then sent his boats to examine the pass, and they
found more water than was supposed, and on the assurances of
the pilot, and the wind favoring, he headed his ships for the
boiling eddies, passed safely through, and soon reached the
placid water beyond.   The shore of Trinidad stretched northerly, and he turned to follow it, but somebody getting a taste of
the water found it to be fresh.   Here was a new surprise.   He
Gulf of had not yet comprehended that he was within a land-
Paria. locked gulf, where the rush of the Orinoco sweetens
the tide throughout.   As he approached the northwestern limit
of Trinidad, he found that a lofty cape jutted out opposite a
similar headland to the west, and that between them lay a
second surging channel, beset with rocks and seeming to be
more dangerous than the last.   So he gave it a more ferocious
Boca del name, the Mouth of the Dragon (Boca del Drago).
Drago. To follow the opposite coast presented an alternative
that did not require so much risk, and, still ignorant of the way
in which his fleet was embayed in this marvelous water, he ran
across on Sunday, August 5, to the opposite shore.   He now
coasted it to find a better opening to the north, for he had supposed this slender peninsula to be another island.   The water
grew fresher as he went on.   The shore attracted him, with its
harbors and salubrious, restful air, but he was anxious to get

into the open sea. He saw no inhabitants. The liveliest creatures which he observed were the chattering monkeys. At
length, the country becoming more level, he ran into the mouth

GULF OF PARIA.

of a river and cast anchor. It was perhaps here that the
Spaniards first set foot on the continent. The accounts are
somewhat confused, and need some license in reconciling them.
They had, possibly, landed earlier.

A canoe with three natives now came out to the caravel near-est shore. The Spanish captain secured the men by a clever trick. After a parley, he gave them to understand he would go on shore in their boat, and jumping violently on its gunwale, he overturned it. The occupants were easily captured in the water. Being taken on board the flagship, the inevitable hawks' bells captivated them, and they were set on shore to delight their fellows. Other parleys and interchanges of gifts fol-lowed. Columbus now ascertained, as well as he could by signs,

Paria.

that the word "Paria," which he heard, was the name of the country. The Indians pointed westerly, and indicated that men were much more numerous that way. The Spaniards were struck with the tall stature of the men, and noted the absence of braids in their hair. It was curious to see them smell of everything that was new to them, — a piece of brass, for instance. It seemed to be their sense of inquiry and recognition. It is not certain if Columbus participated in this intercourse on shore. He was suffering from a severe eruption of the eyes, and one of the witnesses said that the formal tak-ing possession of the country was done by deputy on that ac-count. This statement is contradicted by others.

As he went on, the country became even more attractive, with its limpid streams, its open and luxuriant woods, its clambering vines, all enlivened with the flitting of brilliant birds. So he

The natives.

called the place The Gardens. The natives appeared to him to partake of the excellence of the country. They were, as he thought, manlier in bearing, shapelier in frame, with greater intelligence in their eyes, than any he had earlier discovered. Their arts were evidently superior to anything he had yet seen. Their canoes were handier, lighter, and had covered pavilions in the waist. There were strings of pearls upon the women which raised in the Spaniards an increased sense of cupidity. The men found oysters clinging to the boughs that drooped along the shore. Columbus recalled how he had read in Pliny of the habit of the pearl oyster to open the mouth to catch the dew, which was converted within into pearls. The people were as hospitable as they were gracious, and gave the strangers feasts as they passed from cabin to cabin. They pointed beyond the hills, and signified that another coast lay there, where a greater store of pearls could be found.

To leave this paradise was necessary, and on August 10 the ships went further on, soon to find the water growing still fresher and more shallow. At last, thinking it 1498. August 10. dangerous to push his flagship into such shoals, Columbus sent his lightest caravel ahead, and waited her coming back. On the next day she returned, and reported that there was an inner bay beyond the islands which were seen, into which large volumes of fresh water poured, as if a huge continent were drained. Here were conditions for examination under more favorable circumstances, and on August 11 Columbus turned his prow toward the Dragon's Mouth. His stewards declared the provisions growing bad, and even the large stores intended for the colony were beginning to spoil. It was necessary to reach his destination. Columbus's own health was sinking. His gout had little cessation. His eyes had almost closed with a weariness that he had before experienced on the Cuban cruise, and he could but think of the way in which he had been taken prostrate into Isabella on returning from that expedition.

Near the Dragon's Mouth he found a harbor in which to prepare for the passage of the tumultuous strait. There seemed no escape from the trial. The passage lay before him, wide enough in itself, but two islands parted its currents and forced the boiling waters into narrower confines. Columbus studied their motion, and finally made up his mind that the turmoil of the waters might after all come from the meeting of the tide and the fresh currents seeking the open sea, and not from rocks or shoals. At all events, the passage must be made. The wind veering round to the right quarter, he set sail and entered the boisterous currents. As long as the wind Passes the Boca del Drago. lasted there was a good chance of keeping his steering way. Unfortunately, the wind died away, and so he trusted to luck and the sweeping currents. They carried him safely beyond. Once without, he was brought within sight of two islands to the northeast. They were apparently those we to-day call Tobago and Grenada. It was now the 15th of August, and Tobago and Grenada. Columbus turned westward to track the coast. He came to the islands of Cubagua and Margarita, and surprised some native canoes fishing for pearls. His crews soon got into parley with the natives, and breaking up some Valentia Cubagua and Margarita. ware into bits, the Spaniards bartered them so successfully that they secured three pounds, as Columbus tells us, of the coveted

Pearls.          jewels.  He had satisfied himself that here was a new
field for the wealth which could alone restore his credit
in Spain; but he could not tarry.  As he wore ship, he left
behind a mountainous reach of the coast that stretched westerly,
and he would fain think that India lay that way, as it had from
Cuba.  At that island and here, he had touched, as he thought,
the confines of Asia, two protuberant peninsulas, or perhaps
masses of the continent, separated by a strait, which possibly
lay ahead of him.

There was much that had been novel in all these experiences.
Columbus felt that the New World was throwing wider open
the gates of its sublime secrets.  Lying on his couch, almost

Columbus's
geographical
delusions.          helpless from the cruel agonies of the gout, and sight-
less from the malady of his eyes, the active mind of
the Admiral worked at the old problems anew.  We
know it all from the letter which a few weeks later he drafted
for the perusal of his sovereigns, and from his reports to Peter
Martyr, which that chronicler has preserved for us.  We know
from this letter that his thoughts were still dwelling on the
Mount Sopora of Solomon, " which mountain your Highnesses
now possess in the island of Española," — a convenient step-
ping-stone to other credulous fancies, as we shall see.  The
sweetness and volume of the water which had met him in the
Gulf of Paria were significant to him of a great watershed behind.  He reverted to the statement in Esdras of the vast pre-
ponderance on the globe of land, six parts to one of water, and
thought he saw a confirmation of it in the immense flow that
argued a corresponding expansion of land.  He recalled all that
he recollected of Aristotle and the other sages.  He went back
to his experiences in mid-ocean, when he was startled at the coincidence of the needle and the pole star.  He remembered how
he had found all the conditions of temperature and the other
physical aspects to be changed as he passed that line, and it
seemed as if he was sweeping into regions more ethereal.  He
had found the same difference when he passed, a few weeks
before, out of the baleful heats of the tropical calms.  He grew
to think that this line of no variation of magnetism with corresponding marvels of nature marked but the beginning of a new
section of the earth that no one had dreamed of.  St. Augus-

tine, St. Basil, and St. Ambrose had placed the Garden of Eden
far in the Old World's east, apart from the common vicinage of
men, high up above the baser parts of the earth, in a region

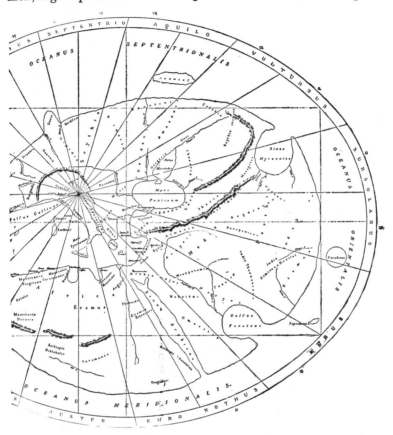

PRE-COLUMBIAN MAPPEMONDE, PRESERVED AT RAVENNA, RESTORED BY GRA-
VIER AFTER D'AVEZAC IN *BULLETIN DE LA SOCIÉTÉ NORMANDE*, 1888.

bathed in the purest ether, and so high that the deluge had not
reached it. All the stories of the Middle Ages, absorbed in the
speculative philosophy of his own time, had pointed to the distant east as the seat of Paradise, and was he not now coming to
it by the western passage? If the scant riches of the soil could
not restore the enthusiasm which his earlier discoveries aroused
in the dull spirits of Europe, would not a glimpse of the ecstatic
pleasures of Eden open their eyes anew? He had endeavored

to make his contemporaries feel that the earth was round, and he had proved it, as he thought, by almost touching, in a westward passage, the Golden Chersonesus.  It is significant that the later *Historie* of 1571 omits this vagary of Paradise.  The world had moved, and geographical discovery had made some records in the interim, awkward for the biographer of Columbus.

There was a newer belief linked with this hope of Paradise.  Paradise found.  All this wondrous life and salubrity which Columbus saw and felt, if it had not been able to restore his health, could only come from his progress up a swelling apex of the earth, which buttressed the Garden of Eden.  It was clear to his mind that instead of being round the earth was pear-shaped, and that this great eminence, up which he had been going, was constantly lifting him into purer air.  The great fountain which watered the spacious garden of the early race had discharged its currents down these ethereal slopes, and sweetened all this gulf that had held him so close within its embaying girth.  If such were the wonders of these outposts of the celestial life, what must be the products to be seen as one journeyed up, along the courses of such celestial streams ?  As he steered for Española, he found the currents still helped him, or he imagined they did.  Was it not that he was slipping easily down this wonderful declivity ?

That he had again discovered the mainland he was convinced by such speculations.  He had no conception of the physical truth.  The vagaries of his time found in him the creature of their most rampant hallucinations.  This aberration was a potent cause in depriving him of the chance to place his own name on this goal of his ambition.  It accounts much for the greater impression which Americus Vespucius, with his clearer instincts, was soon to make on the expectant and learned world.  The voyage of that Florentine merchant, one of those trespassers that Columbus complained of, was, before the Admiral should see Spain again, to instigate the publication of a narrative, which took from its true discoverer the rightful baptism of the world he had unwittingly found.  The wild imaginings of Columbus, gathered from every resource of the superstitious past, moulded by him into beliefs that appealed but little to the soberer intelligence of his time, made known in tumultuous writings, and presently to be expressed with every symptom of mental wandering in more elaborate treatises, offered to his time an obvious contrast to the steadier head of Vespucius. The latter's far more graphic description gained for him, as we shall see, the position of a recognized authority. While Columbus was puzzling over the aberration of the pole star and misshaping the earth, Vespucius was comprehending the law of gravitation upon our floating sphere, and ultimately representing it in the diagram which illustrated his narrative. We shall need to return on a later page to these causes which led to the naming of America.

Columbus and Vespucius.

For four days Columbus had sailed away to the northwest, coming to the wind every night as a precaution, before he sighted Española on August 19, being then, as he made out, about fifty leagues west of the spot where he supposed the port had been established for the mines of Hayna. He thought that he had been steering nearer that point, but the currents had probably carried him unconsciously west by night, as they were at that moment doing with the relief ships that he had parted with off Ferro. As Columbus speculated on this steady flow of waters with that keenness of observation upon natural phenomena which attracted the admiration of Humboldt, and which is really striking, if we separate it from his turbulent fancies, he accounted by its attrition for the predominating shape of the islands which he had seen, which had their greatest length in the direction of the current. He knew that its force would, perhaps, long delay him in his efforts to work eastward, and so he opened communication with the shore in hopes to find a messenger by whom to dispatch a letter to the Adelantado. This was easily done, and the letter reached its destination, whereupon Bartholomew started out in a caravel to meet the little fleet. It was with some misgiving that Columbus resumed his course, for he had seen a crossbow in the hands of a native. It was not an article of commerce, and it might signify another disaster like that of La Navidad. He was accordingly relieved when he shortly afterwards saw a Spanish caravel approaching, and, hailing the vessel, found that the Adelantado had come to greet him.

1498. August 19. Columbus sees Española.

His observations of nature.

Meets the Adelantado.

There was much interchange of news and thought to occupy the two in their first conference ; and Columbus's anxiety to know the condition of the colony elicited a wearisome story, little calculated to make any better record in Spain than the reports of his own rule in the island.

The chief points of it were these : Bartholomew had early carried out the Admiral's behests to occupy the Hayna country. He had built there a fortress which he had named St. Cristoval, but the workmen, finding particles of gold in the stones and sands which they used, had nicknamed it the Golden Tower. While this was doing, there was difficulty in supporting the workmen. Provisions were scarce, and the Indians were not inclined to part with what they had. The Adelantado could go to the Vega and exact the quarterly tribute under compulsion; but that hardly sufficed to keep famine from the door at St. Cristoval. Nothing had as yet been done to plant the ground near the fort, nor had herds been moved there. The settlement of Isabella was too far away for support. Meanwhile Niño had arrived with his caravels, but he had not brought all the expected help, for the passage had spoiled much of the lading. It was by Niño that Bartholomew received that dispatch from his brother which he had written in the harbor of Cadiz when, on his arrival from his second voyage, he had discerned the condition of public opinion. It was at this time, too, that he repeated to Bartholomew the decision of the theologians, that to be taken in war, or to be guilty of slaying any of their Majesties' liege subjects, was quite enough to render the Indians fit subjects for the slave-block. The Admiral's directions, therefore, were to be sure that this test kept up the supply of slaves; and as there was nobody to dispute the judgment of his deputy, Niño had taken back to Spain those three hundred, which were, as we have seen, so readily converted into reputed gold on his arrival.

*Events in Española during the absence of Columbus.*

*Santo Domingo founded.*

*Columbus and slavery.*

Bartholomew had selected the site for a new town near the mouth of the Ozema, convenient for the shipment of the Hayna treasure, and, naming it at first the New Isabella, it soon received the more permanent appellation of Santo Domingo, which it still bears.

*Santo Domingo named.*

Bartholomew had a pleasing story to tell of the way in which he had brought Behechio and his province of Xaragua into subjection. This territory was the region westward Xaragua from about the point where Columbus had touched the conquered. island a few days before. Anacaona, the wife of Caonabo, — now indeed his widow, — had taken refuge with Be- hechio, her brother, after the fall of her husband. Behechio and Anacaona. She is represented as a woman of fine appearance, and more delicate and susceptible in her thoughts than was usual among her people; and perhaps Bartholomew told his brother what has since been surmised by Spanish writers, that she had managed to get word to him of her friendly sentiments for celestial visitors. Bartholomew found, as he was marching thither with such forces as he could spare for the expedition, that the cacique who met him in battle array was easily disposed, for some reason or other, perhaps through Anacaona's influence, to dismiss his armed warriors, and to escort his visitor through his country with great parade of hospitality. When they reached the cacique's chief town, a sort of fête was prepared in the Adelantado's honor, and a mock battle, not without sacrifice of life, was fought for his delectation. Peter Martyr tells us that when the comely young Indian maidens advanced with their palm branches and saluted the Adelantado, it seemed as if the beautiful dryads of the olden tales had slipped out of the vernal woods. Then Anacaona appeared on a litter, with no apparel but garlands, the most beautiful dryad of them all. Everybody feasted, and Bartholomew, to ingratiate himself with his host, eat and praised their rarest delicacy, the guana lizard, which had been offered to them many times before, but which they never as yet had tasted. It became after this a fashion with the Spaniards to dote on lizard flesh. Everything within the next two or three days served to cement this new friendship, when the Adelantado put it to a test, as indeed had been his purpose from the beginning. He told the cacique of the great power of his master and of the Spanish sovereigns; of their gracious regard for all their distant subjects, and of the poor recompense of a tribute which was expected for their protection. "Gold!" exclaimed the cacique, "we have no gold here." "Oh, whatever you have, cotton, hemp, cassava bread, — anything will be acceptable." So the details were arranged. The cacique was gratified at being let off so easy, and the Spaniards went their way.

This and the subsequent visit of Bartholomew to Xaragua to receive the tribute were about the only cheery incidents in the dreary retrospect to which the Admiral listened. The rest was trouble and despair. A line of military posts had been built connecting the two Spanish settlements, and the manning of them, with their dependent villages, enabled the Adelantado to scatter a part of the too numerous colony at Isabella, so that it might be relieved of so many mouths to feed. This done, Native conspiracy. there was a conspiracy of the natives to be crushed. Two of the priests had made some converts in the Vega, and had built a chapel for the use of the neophytes. One of the Spaniards had outraged a wife of the cacique. Either for this cause, or for the audacious propagandism of the priests, some natives broke into the Spanish chapel, destroyed its shrine, and buried some of its holy vessels in a field. Plants grew up there in the form of a cross, say the veracious narrators. This, nevertheless, did not satisfy the Spaniards. They seized such Indians as they considered to have been engaged in the desecration, and gave them the fire and fagots, as they would have done to Moor or Jew. The horrible punishment aroused the cacique Guarionex with a new fury. He leagued the neighboring caciques into a conspiracy. Their combined forces were threatening Fort Conception when the Adelantado arrived with succor. By an adroit movement, Bartholomew ensnared by night every one of the leaders in their villages, and executed two of them. The others he ostentatiously pardoned, and he could tell Columbus of the great renown he got for his clemency.

There was nothing in all the bad tidings which Bartholomew Roldan's revolt. had to rehearse quite so disheartening as the revolt of Roldan, the chief judge of the island, — a man who had been lifted from obscurity to a position of such importance that Columbus had placed the administration of justice in his hands. The reports of the unpopularity of Columbus in Spain, and the growing antipathy in Isabella to the rule of Bartholomew as a foreigner, had served to consolidate the growing number of the discontented, and Roldan saw the opportunity of easily raising himself in the popular estimate by organizing the latent spirit of rebellion. It was even planned to assassinate the Adelantado, under cover of a tumult, which was to be raised at an execution ordered by him; but as the Adelantado had pardoned the offender, the occasion slipped by. Bartholomew's absence in Xaragua gave another opportunity. He had sent back from that country a caravel loaded with cotton, as a tribute, and Diego, then in command at Isabella, after unlading the vessel, drew her up on the beach. The story was busily circulated that this act was done simply to prevent any one seizing the ship and carrying to Spain intelligence of the misery to which the rule of the Columbuses was subjecting the people. The populace made an issue on that act, and asked that the vessel be sent to Cadiz for supplies. Diego objected, and to divert the minds of the rebellious, as well as to remove Roldan from their counsels, he sent him with a force into the Vega, to overawe some caciques who had been dilatory in their tribute. This mission, however, only helped Roldan to consolidate his faction, and gave him the chance to encourage the caciques to join resistance.

Roldan had seventy well-armed men in his party when he returned to Isabella to confront Bartholomew, who had by this time got back from Xaragua. The Adelantado was not so easily frightened as Roldan had hoped, and finding it not safe to risk an open revolt, this mutinous leader withdrew to the Vega with the expectation of surprising Fort Conception. That post, however, as well as an outlying fortified house, was under loyal command, and Roldan was for a while thwarted. Bartholomew was not at all sure of any of the principal Spaniards, but how far the disaffection had gone he was unable to determine. Although he knew that certain leading men were friendly to Roldan, he was not prepared to be passive. His safety depended on resolution, and so he marched at once to the Vega. Roldan was in the neighborhood, and was invited to a parley. It led to nothing. The mutineers, making up their minds to fly to the delightful pleasures of Xaragua, suddenly marched back to Isabella, plundered the arsenal and storehouses, and tried to launch the caravel. The vessel was too firmly imbedded to move, and Roldan was forced to undertake the journey to Xaragua by land. To leave the Adelantado behind was a sure way to bring an enemy in his rear, and he accordingly thought it safer to reduce the garrison at Conception, and per-

The mutineers in the Vega Real.

At Isabella.

haps capture the Adelantado. This movement failed; but it resulted in Roldan's ingratiating himself with the tributary caciques, and intercepting the garrison's supplies. It was at this juncture, when everything looked desperate for Bartholomew, shut up in the Vega fort, that news reached him of the arrival (February 3, 1498) at the new port of Santo Domingo

Coronel arrives. of the advance section of the Admiral's fleet, sent thither, as we have seen, by the Queen's assiduity, under the command of Pedro Fernandez Coronel.

Bartholomew could tell the Admiral of the good effect which the intelligence received through Coronel had on the colony. His own title of Adelantado, it was learned, was legitimated by the act of the sovereigns; and Columbus himself had been powerful enough to secure confirmation of his old honors, and to obtain new pledges for the future. The mutineers soon saw that the aspects of their revolt were changed. They could not, it would seem, place that dependence on the unpopularity of the Admiral at Court which had been a good part of their encouragement.

Proceeding to Santo Domingo, Bartholomew proclaimed his

Bartholomew's new honors. new honors, and, anxious to pacificate the island before the arrival of Columbus, he dispatched Coronel to communicate with Roldan, who had sulkily followed the Adelantado in his march from the Vega. Roldan refused all intercourse, and, shielding himself behind a pass in the mountains, he warned off the pacificator. He would yield to no one but the Admiral.

There was nothing for the Adelantado to do but to outlaw the

The rebels go to Xaragua. rebels, who, in turn, sped away to what Irving calls the "soft witcheries" of the Xaragua dryads. The archrebel was thus well out of the way for a time; but his influence still worked among the Indians of the Vega, and Bartholomew had not long left Conception before the garrison was made aware of a native conspiracy to surprise it.

Word was sent to Santo Domingo, and the Adelantado was

Guarionex's revolt. promptly on the march for relief. Guarionex, who had headed the revolt again, fled to the mountains of Ciguay, where a mountain cacique, Mayobanex, the same who had conducted the attack on the Spaniards at the Gulf of Samana during the first voyage, received the fugitive chief of the valley.

It was into these mountain fastnesses that the Adelantado now pursued the fugitives, with a force of ninety foot, a few horse, and some auxiliary Indians. He boldly thridded the defiles, and crossed the streams, under the showers of lances and arrows. As the native hordes fled before him, he fired their villages in the hope of forcing the Ciguayans to surrender their guest; but the mountain leaders could not be prevailed upon to wrong the rights of hospitality. When no longer able to resist in arms, Mayobanex and Guarionex fled to the hills.

The Adelantado now sent all of his men back to the Vega to look after the crops, except about thirty, and with these he scoured the region. He would not have had success by mere persistency, but he got it by artifice and treachery. Both Mayobanex and Guarionex were betrayed in their hiding-places and captured. Clemency was shown to their families and adherents, and they were released; but both caciques remained in their bonds as hostages for the maintenance of the quiet which was now at last in some measure secured.

Such was the condition of affairs when Columbus arrived and heard the story of these two troubled years and more during which he had been absent. 1498. August 30. Columbus arrives.

It was the 30th of August when Columbus and his brother landed at Santo Domingo. There had not been much to encourage the Admiral in this story of the antecedent events. No portrayal of riot, dissolution, rapine, intrigue, and idleness could surpass what he saw and heard of the bedraggled and impoverished settlement at Isabella. The stores which he had brought would be helpful in restoring confidence and health; but it was a source of anxiety to him that nothing had been heard of the three caravels from which he had parted off Ferro.

These vessels appeared not long afterwards, bringing a new perplexity. Forced by currents which their crews did not understand, they had been carried westerly, and had wandered about in the unknown seas in search of Española. A few days before reaching Santo Domingo, the ships had anchored off the territory of Behechio, where Roldan and his followers already were. The mutineers observed the approach of the caravels, not quite sure of their character, thinking possibly that they had been dispatched against their band; Roldan and the belated ships.

but Roldan boldly went on board, and, ascertaining their condition, he had the address to represent that he was stationed in that region to collect the tribute, and was in need of stores, arms, and munitions. The commander of the vessel at once sent on shore what he demanded; and while this was going on, Roldan's men ingratiated themselves with the company on board the caravels, and readily enlisted a part of them in the revolt. The new-comers, being some of the emancipated convicts which Columbus had so unwisely registered among his crews, were not difficult to entice to a life of pleasure. By the time Roldan had secured his supplies and was ready to announce his true character, it was not certain how far the captains of the vessels could trust their crews. The chief of these commanders undertook, when the worst was known, to bring the revolters back to their loyalty; but he argued in vain. The wind being easterly, and to work up against it to Santo Domingo being a slow process, it was decided that one of the captains, Colombo, should conduct about forty armed men by land to the new town. When he landed them, the insidious work of the mutineers became apparent. Only eight of his party stood to his command, and over forty marched over to the rebels, each with his arms. The overland march was necessarily given up, and the three caravels, to prevent further desertions, hoisted sail and departed. Carvajal remained behind to urge Roldan to duty; but the most he could do was to exact a promise that he would submit to the Admiral if pardoned, but not to the Adelantado.

The report which Carvajal made to Columbus, when shortly afterwards he joined his companions in Santo Domingo, coming by land, was not very assuring. Columbus was too conscious of the prevalence of discontent, and he had been made painfully aware of the uncertainty of convict loyalty. He then made up his mind that all such men were a menace, and that 1498. September 12. they were best got rid of. Accordingly he announced that five ships were ready to sail for Spain and would take any who should desire to go, and that the passage would be free.

Learning from Carvajal that Roldan was likely soon to lead his men near Fort Conception, Columbus notified Miguel Ballester, its commander, to be on his guard. He also directed him to seek an interview with the rebel leader, in order to lure him back to duty by offer of pardon from the Admiral. As soon as Ballester heard of Roldan's arrival in the neighborhood, he went out to meet him. Roldan, however, was in no mood to succumb. His force had grown, and some of the leading Spaniards had been drawn towards him. So he defied the Admiral in his speeches, and sent him word that if he had any further communications to make to him they should be sent by Carvajal, for he would treat with no other. Columbus, on receiving this message, and not knowing how far the conspiracy had extended among those about him, ordered out the military force of the settlement. There were not more than seventy men to respond ; nor did he feel much confidence in half of these. There being little chance of any turn of affairs for the better with which he could regale the sovereigns, Columbus ordered the waiting ships to sail, and on October 18 they put to sea.

Roldan and Ballester.

1498. October 18. The ships sail for Spain.

The ships carried two letters which Columbus had written to the monarchs. In the one he spoke of his new discoveries, and of the views which had developed in his mind from the new phenomena, as has already been represented, and promised that the Adelantado should soon be dispatched with three caravels to make further explorations. In the other he repeated the story of events since he had landed at Santo Domingo. He urged that Roldan might be recalled to Spain for examination, or that he might be committed to the custody of Carvajal and Ballester to determine the foundation of his grievances. At the same time he requested that a further license be given, to last two years, for the capture and transmission of slaves. It was not unlikely that the case of Roldan and his abettors was represented with equal confidence in other letters, for there were many hands among the passengers to which they could be confided.

Columbus and slavery.

The ships gone, the Admiral gave himself to the difficult task of pacificating the colony. The vigorous rule of the Adelantado had made enemies who were to be propitiated, though Las Casas tells us that the rule had been strict no farther than that it had been necessarily imperative in emergencies. Columbus wrote on October 20 an expostulatory letter to Roldan. To send it by Carvajal, as was necessary, if Roldan was to receive it, would be to

Columbus seeks to quiet the colony.

1498. October 20.

intrust negotiations to a person who was already committed in some sort to the rebel's plan, or at least some of the Admiral's leading councilors believed such to be the case, apparently too hastily. Columbus did not share that distrust, and Carvajal was sent. This letter crossed one from the leading rebels, in which they demanded from Columbus release from his service, and expressed their determination to maintain independence.

When Carvajal reached Bonao, where the rebels were gathered, — and Ballester had accompanied him, — their joint persuasions had some effect on Roldan and others, principal rebels; but the followers, as a mass, objected to the leaders entering into any conference except under a written guaranty of safety for them and those that should accompany them. This message was accordingly returned to Columbus, and Ballester at the same time wrote to him that the revolt was fast making head; that the garrisons were disaffected, and losing by desertion; and that the common people could not be trusted to stand by the Admiral if it came to war. He advised, therefore, a speedy reconciliation or agreement of some sort. The guaranty was sent, and Roldan soon presented himself to the Admiral. The demands of the rebel and the prerogatives of the Admiral were, it proved, too widely apart for any accommodation. So Roldan, having possessed himself of the state of feeling in Santo Domingo, returned to his followers, promising to submit definite terms in writing. These were sent under date of November 6, 1498, with a demand for an answer before the 11th. The terms were inadmissible. To disarm charges of exaction, Columbus made public proclamation of a readiness to grant pardon to all who should return to allegiance within thirty days, and to such he would give free transportation to Spain. Carvajal carried this paper to Roldan, and was accompanied by Columbus's major-domo, Diego de Salamanca, in the hopes that the two might yet arrange some terms, mutually acceptable.

*Conferences with Roldan.*

*1498. November 6. Roldan's terms.*

The messenger found Roldan advanced from Bonao, and besieging Ballester in Conception. The revolt had gone too far, apparently, to be stayed, but the persuasion of the mediators at last prevailed, and terms were arranged. These provided full pardon and certificates of good conduct; free passage from Xaragua, to which point two caravels should be sent; the full complement of slaves which other returning colonists had; liberty for such as had them to take their native wives, and restoration

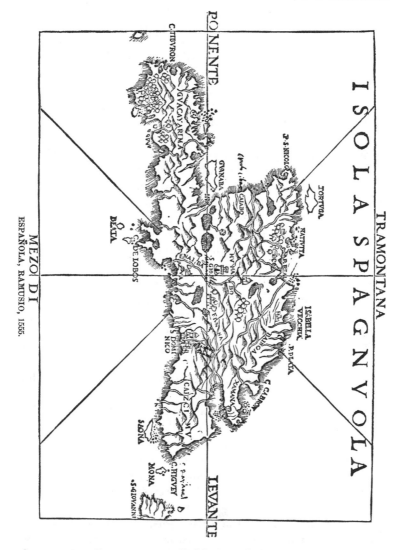

of sequestered property. Roldan and his companions signed this agreement on November 16, and agreed to wait eight days for the signature of the Admiral. Columbus signed it on the 21st, and further granted

Columbus agrees to them.

indulgences of one kind or another to such as chose to remain in Española.

Under the agreement, the ships were to be ready in fifty days, but Columbus, in the disorganized state of the colony, found it impossible to avoid delays, and his self-congratulations that he had got rid of the turbulent horde were far from warranted. While under this impression, and absent with the Adelantado, inspecting the posts throughout the island, and deciding how best he could restore the regularities of life and business, the arrangements which he had made for carrying out the agreement with Roldan had sorely miscarried. Nearly double the time assigned to the preparation of the caravels had elapsed, when the vessels at last left Santo Domingo for Xaragua. A storm disabling one of them, there were still further delays; and when all were ready, the procrastination in their outfit offered new grounds for dispute, and it was found necessary to revise the agreement. Carvajal was still the mediator. Roldan met the Admiral on a caravel, which had sailed toward Xaragua. The terms which Roldan now proposed were that he should be permitted to send some of his friends, fifteen in number, if he desired so many, to Spain; that those who remained should have grants of land; that proclamation should be made of the baseless character of the charges against him and his accomplices; and that he himself should be restored to his office of Alcalde Mayor. Columbus, who had received a letter from Fonseca in the mean while, showing that there was little chance of relief from Spain, saw the hopelessness of his situation, and sufficiently humbled himself to accept the terms. When they were submitted to the body of the mutineers, this assembly added another clause giving them the right to enforce the agreement by compulsion in case the Admiral failed to carry it out. This, also, was agreed to in despair; while the Admiral endeavored to relieve the mortification of the act by inserting a clause enforcing obedience to the commands of the sovereigns, of himself, and of his regularly appointed justices. This agreement was ratified at Santo Domingo, September 28, 1499.

It was not a pleasant task for Columbus to brook the presence of Roldan and his victorious faction in Santo Domingo. The reinstated alcalde had no occasion to be very com-

*Delays in carrying out the agreement.*

*New agreement.*

*Signed September 28, 1499.*

*Roldan reinstated.*

plaisant after he had seen the Admiral cringe before him. Columbus endeavored, in making the grants of lands, to separate the restored rebels as much as he could, in order to avoid the risks of other mutinous combinations. He agreed with the caciques that they should be relieved from the ordinary tribute of treasure if they would furnish these new grantees with laborers for their farms. Thus at the hands of Columbus arose the beginning of that system of *repartimientos*, with all its miseries for the poor natives, which ended in their extermination. The apologists of Columbus consider that the exigencies of his situation forced him into these fiendish enactments, and that he is not to be held responsible for them as of his free will. They forget the expressions of his first letter to Santangel, which prefigured all the misery which fell upon myriads of these poor creatures. The record, unfortunately, shows that it was Columbus who invariably led opinion in all these oppressions, and not he who followed it. His artfulness never sprang to a new device so exultingly as when it was a method of increasing the revenue at the cost of the natives. When we read, in the letter written to his sovereigns during this absence, of his always impressing on the natives, in his intercourse with them, "the courtesy and nobleness of all Christians," we shudder at the hollowness of the profession.

The personal demands of Roldan under the capitulation were also to be met. They included restoration of lands which he called his own, new lands to be granted, the stocking of them from the public herds; and Columbus met them, at least, until the grants should be confirmed at Court. This was not all. Roldan visited Bonao, and made one of his late lieutenants an assistant alcalde, — an assumption of the power of appointment at which Columbus was offended, as some tell us; but if the *Historie* is to be depended on, the appointment invited no unfavorable comment from Columbus. When it was found that this new officer was building a structure ostensibly for farm purposes, but of a character more like a fortress, suitable for some new mutiny to rally in, Columbus at last rose on his dignity and forbade it.

In October, 1499, the Admiral dispatched two caravels to Spain. It did not seem safe for him to embark in them, though he felt his presence was needed

*[margin notes:] Repartimientos. Columbus and slavery. Roldan's demands. 1499. October. Caravels sent to Spain.*

at Court to counteract the mischief of his enemies and Roldan's friends. Some of the latter went in the ships. The most he could do was to trust his cause to Miguel Ballester and Garcia de Barrantes, who embarked as his representatives. They bore his letters to the monarchs. In these he enumerated the compulsions under which he had signed the capitulation with Roldan, and begged their Majesties to treat it as given under coercion, and to bring the rebels to trial. He then mentioned what other assistants he needed in governing the colony, such as a learned judge and some discreet councilors. He ended with asking that his son, Diego, might be spared from Court to assist him.

*Columbus sends Ballester to support his cause in Spain.*

While Columbus was making these requests, he was ignorant of the way in which the Spanish Court had already made serious trespasses upon his prerogatives as Admiral of the Indies. He had said in his letter to the sovereigns, " Your Majesties will determine on what is to be done," in consequence of these new discoveries at Paria. He was soon to become painfully conscious of what was done. The real hero of Columbus's second voyage, Alonso de Ojeda, comes again on the scene. He was in Spain when the accounts which Columbus had transmitted to Court of his discoveries about the Gulf of Paria reached Seville. Such glowing descriptions fired his ambition, and learning from Columbus's other letters and from the reports by those who had returned of the critical condition of affairs in Española, he anticipated the truth when he supposed that the Admiral could not so smother the disquiet of his colony as to venture to leave it for further explorations. He saw, too, the maps which Columbus had sent back and the pearls which he had gathered. He acknowledged all this in a deposition taken at Santo Domingo in 1513. So he proposed to Fonseca that he might be allowed to undertake a private voyage, and profit, for himself and for the Crown, by the resources of the country, inasmuch as it must be a long time before Columbus himself could do so. Fonseca readily commended the plan and gave him a license, stipulating that he should avoid any Portuguese possession and any lands that Columbus had discovered before 1495. It was the purpose, by giving this date, to throw open the Paria region.

*Royal infringements of Columbus's privileges.*

*1499. Ojeda's voyage.*

The ships were fitted out at Seville in the early part of 1499, and some men, famous in these years, made part of the company which sailed on them. There was Americus Ves- <sub>Vespucius</sub> pucius, who was seemingly now for the first time to <sup>with Ojeda.</sup> embark for the New World, since it is likely that out of this very expedition the alleged voyage of his in 1497 has been made to appear by some perversion of chronology. There was <sub>Juan de la</sub> Juan de la Cosa, a famous hydrographer, who was the <sup>Cosa.</sup> companion of Columbus in his second Cuban cruise. Irving says that he was with Columbus in his first voyage; but it is thought that it was another of the same name who appears in the registers of that expedition. Several of those who had returned from Española after the Paria cruise of Columbus were also enlisted, and among them Bartholomew Roldan, the pilot of that earlier fleet. The expedition of Ojeda <sub>1499. May 20. Ojeda sails.</sub> sailed May 20, 1499. They made land 200 leagues east of the Orinoco, and then, guided by Columbus's charts, the ships followed his track through the Serpent's and the Dragon's Mouths. Thence passing Margarita, they sailed on towards the mountains which Columbus had seen, and finally entered a gulf, where they saw some pile dwellings of the natives. They accordingly named the basin Venezuela, in reference to <sub>At Venezuela.</sub> the great sea-built city of the Adriatic. It is noteworthy that Ojeda, in reporting to their Majesties an account of this voyage, says that he met in this neighborhood some English vessels, an expedition which may have been instigated by Cabot's success. It is to be observed, at the same time, that this is the only authority which we have for such an early visit of the English to this vicinity, and the statement is not credited by Biddle, Helps, and other recent writers. Ojeda turned eastward not long after, having run short of provisions. He then approached the prohibited Española, and hoped to elude notice while foraging at its western end.

It was while here that Ojeda's caravels were seen and tidings of their presence were transmitted to Santo Domingo. Ignorance of what he had to deal with in these intruders <sub>1499. September 5. Ojeda touches at Española.</sub> was one of the reasons which made it out of the question for Columbus to return to Spain in the ships which he had dispatched in October. Ojeda had appeared on the coast on September 5, 1499, and as succeeding reports came to Columbus, it was divulged that Ojeda was in command, and that he was cutting dyewoods thereabouts.

Now was the time to heal the dissensions of Roldan, and to give him a chance to recover his reputation. So the Admiral selected his late bitter enemy to manage the expedition which he thought it necessary to dispatch to the spot.

Columbus sends Roldan to warn Ojeda off.

Roldan sailed in command of two caravels on September 29, and, approaching unobserved the place where Ojeda's ships were at anchor, he landed with twenty-five men, and sent out scouts. They soon reported that Ojeda was some distance away from his ships at an Indian village, making cassava bread. Ojeda heard of the approach, but not in time to prevent Roldan getting between him and his ships. The intruder met him boldly, said he was on an exploring expedition, and had put in for supplies, and that if Roldan would come on board his ships, he would show his license signed by Fonseca. When Roldan went on board, he saw the document. He also learned from those he talked with in the ships — and there were among them some whom he knew, and some who had been in Española — that the Admiral's name was in disgrace at Court, and there was imminent danger of his being deprived of his command at Española. Moreover, the Queen, who had befriended him against all others, was ill beyond recovery. Ojeda promising to sail round to Santo Domingo and explain his conduct to the Admiral, Roldan left him, and carried back the intelligence to Columbus.

The Viceroy waited patiently for Ojeda's vessels to appear, and to hear the explanation of what he deemed a flagrant violation of his rights. Ojeda, having got rid of Roldan, had accomplished all that he intended by the promise. When he set sail, it was to pass round the coast easterly to the shore of Xaragua, where he anchored, and opened communication with the Spanish settlers, remnants of Roldan's party, who had not been quite satisfied to find their reinstated leader acting as an emissary of Columbus. Ojeda, with impetuous sympathy, listened to their complaints, and had agreed to be their leader in marching to Santo Domingo to demand some redresses, when Roldan, sent by Columbus to watch him, once more appeared. Ojeda declined a conference, and kept on his ship. Roldan had harbored a deserter from one of Ojeda's fleet, and as he refused to give him up, Ojeda watched his opportunity and seized two of Roldan's men to hold as hostages. So the two wary adventurers watched each other for an advantage. After a while, Ojeda, in his ships, stood down the coast. Roldan followed along the shore. Coming up to where the ships were anchored, Roldan induced Ojeda to send a boat ashore, when, by an artifice, he captured the boat and its crew. This game of stratagems ended with an agreement on Ojeda's part to leave the island, while Roldan restored the captive boat. The prisoners were exchanged. Ojeda bore off shore, and though Roldan heard of his landing again at a distant point, he was gone when the pursuers reached the spot. Las Casas says that Ojeda made for some islands, where he completed his lading of 1500. June. slaves, and set sail for Spain, arriving at Cadiz in Ojeda reaches June, 1500. Cadiz.

While Columbus was congratulating himself on being well rid of this dangerous visitor, he was not at all aware of the uncontrollable eagerness which the joyous reports of pearls had engendered in the adventurous spirits of the Spanish seaports. Among such impatient sailors was the pilot, Pedro Niño's voyage to the Alonso Niño, who had accompanied Columbus on his age to the first voyage, and had also but recently returned from pearl coast. the Paria coast, having been likewise with the Admiral on his third voyage. He found Fonseca as willing, if only the Crown could have its share, as Ojeda had found him, and just as forgetful of the vested rights of Columbus. So the license was granted only a few days after that given to Ojeda, and of similar import. Niño, being a poor man, sought the aid Guerra aids of Luis Guerra in fitting out a small caravel of only him. fifty tons ;· and in consideration of this assistance, Guerra's brother, Cristoval, was placed in command, with a crew, all told, of thirty-three souls. They sailed from Palos early in June, 1499, and were only fifteen days behind Ojeda on the coast. They had some encounters and some festivities with the natives ; but they studiously attended to their main object of bartering for pearls, and when they reached Spain on their return in April, 1500, and laid out the shares for the Crown, for Guerra, and for the crew, of the rich stores of pearls which they had gathered, men said, " Here at last is one voyage to the new islands from which some adequate return is got." And so the first commensurate product of the Indies, instead of saving the credit of Columbus, filled the pockets of an interloping adventurer.

But a more considerable undertaking of the same illegitimate character was that of Vicente Yañez Pinzon, the com-
V. Y. Pin-
zon's voy-
age.
panion of Columbus on his first voyage. Leaguing with him a number of the seamen of the Admiral, including some of his pilots on his last voyage, Pinzon fitted out at Palos four caravels, which sailed near the beginning of December, 1499, not far from the time when Columbus
1499. De-
cember.
was thinking, because of the flight of Ojeda, that an end was at last coming to these intrusions within his prescribed seas. Pinzon was not so much influenced by greed as by something of that spirit which had led him to embark with Columbus in 1492, the genuine eagerness of the explorer. He was destined to do what Columbus had been prevented from doing by the intense heat and by the demoralized condition of his crew, — strike the New World in the equatorial latitudes. So he stood boldly southwest, and crossed the equator,
Pinzon
crosses the
equator.
the first to do it west of the line of demarcation. Here were new constellations as well as a new continent for the transatlantic discoverer. The north star had sunk out of sight. Thus it was that the southern heavens brought
The south-
ern sky.
a new difficulty to navigation, as well as unwonted stellar groups to the curious observer. The sailor of the northern seas had long been accustomed to the fixity of the polar star in making his observations for latitude. The southern heavens were without any conspicuous star in the neighborhood of the pole: and in order to determine such questions, the star at the foot of the Southern Cross was soon selected, but it necessitated an allowance of 30° in all observations.

It was on January 20, 1500, or thereabouts, that Pinzon saw a
1500. Janu-
ary 20. Sees
Cape Conso-
lation.
cape which he called Consolation, and which very likely was the modern Cape St. Augustine, — though the identification is not established to the satisfaction of all, — which would make Pinzon the first European to see the most easterly limit of the great southern continent. A belief like this requires us, necessarily, to reject Varnhagen's view that as

early as the previous June (1499) Ojeda had made his landfall just as far to the east. Pinzon took possession of <sub>Coasts</sub>
the country, and then, sailing north, passed the mouth <sup>north.</sup>
of the Amazon, and found that even out of sight of land he could
replenish his water-casks from the flow of fresh waters, which
the great river poured into the ocean. It did not occur to his
practical mind, as it had under similar circumstances to Columbus, that he was drinking the waters of Paradise!

Reaching the Gulf of Paria, Pinzon passed out into the Caribbean Sea, and touched at Española in the latter part
of June, 1500. Proceeding thence to the Lucayan <sub>1500. June.</sub> Pinzon at
Islands, two of his caravels were swallowed up in a <sub>Española.</sub>
gale, and the other two disabled. The remaining ships crossed
to Española to refit, whence sailing once more, they <sub>Reaches</sub>
reached Palos in September, 1500. <sub>Palos, Sep-<br>tember,<br>1500.</sub>

Meanwhile, following Pinzon, Diego de Lepe, sailing also
from Palos with two caravels in January, 1500, tracked <sub>1500. Jan-</sub>
the coast from below Cape St. Augustine northward. <sub>uary. Diego<br>de Lepe's</sub>
He was the first to double this cape, as he showed in <sub>voyage.</sub>
the map which he made for Fonseca, and doing so he saw the
coast stretching ahead to the southwest. From this time South
America presents on the charts this established trend of the
coast. Humboldt thinks that Diego touched at Española before
returning to Spain in June, 1500.

We must now return to the further exploration of the Portuguese by the African route, for we have reached a <sub>Portuguese</sub>
period when, by accident and because of the revised <sub>explorations<br>by the Afri-</sub>
line of demarcation, the Portuguese pursuing that <sub>can route.</sub>
route acquired at the same time a right on the American coast
which they have since maintained in Brazil, as against what
seems to have been a little earlier discovery of that coast by
Pinzon, in the voyage already mentioned.

In the year following the return to Lisbon of Da Gama with
the marvelous story of the African route to India, the Portuguese government were prompted naturally enough to establish
more firmly their commercial relations with Calicut. They accordingly fitted out three ships to make trial once more of the
voyage. The command was given to Pedro Alvarez Cabral, and

there were placed under him Diaz, who had first rounded the stormy cape, and Coelho, who had accompanied Da Gama. The expedition sailed on March 9, 1500. Leaving the

1500. March 9.

Cape de Verde Islands, Cabral shaped his course more westerly than Da Gama had done, but for what reason is not satisfactorily ascertained. Perhaps it was to avoid the calms off the coast of Guinea; perhaps to avoid breasting a storm; and indeed it may have been only to see if any land lay thitherward easterly of the great line of demarcation. Whatever the motive, the fleet was brought on April 22 opposite an emi-

Cabral discovers the Brazil coast.

nence, which received then the name of Monte Pascoal, and is to-day, as then it became by right of discovery, within the Portuguese limits of South America, the Land of the True Cross, as he named it, Vera Cruz; later, however, to be changed to Santa Cruz. The coast was examined,

1500. May 1.

and in the bay of Porto Seguro, on May 1, formal possession of the country was taken for the crown of Portugal. Cabral sent a caravel back with the news, expressed in a letter drawn up by Pedro Vaz de Caminha. This letter, which is dated on the day possession was taken, was first made known by Muñoz, who discovered it in the archives at Lisbon. It was not till July 29 that the Portuguese king, in a letter which is printed by Navarrete, notified the Spanish monarchs of Cabral's discovery, and this letter was printed in Rome, October 23, 1500.

It seems to have been the apprehension of the Portuguese, if we may trust this letter, that the new coast lay directly in the route to the Cape of Good Hope, though on the right hand.

Leaving two banished criminals to seek their chances of life in the country, and to ascertain its products, Cabral set sail on May 22, and proceeded to the Cape of Good Hope. Fearful gales were encountered and four vessels were lost, and his sub-

Cabral at Calicut, September 13, 1500.

ordinate, Diaz, found an ocean grave off the stormy cape of his own finding. But Calicut was at last reached, September 13.

There is a day or two difference in the dates assigned by different authorities for this discovery of Cabral. Ra-

Date of Cabral's discovery.

musio, quoting a pilot of the fleet fourteen months after the event, says April 24, and leading Portuguese historians have followed him ; but the letter which Cabral sent back to Portugal, as already related, says April 22. The question would be a trifling one, as Humboldt suggests, His landfall. except that it bears upon the question of just where this fortuitous landfall was made, involving estimates of distance sailed before Cabral entered the harbor of Porto Seguro. It is probable that this was at a point a hundred and seventy leagues south of the spot reached earlier (January, 1500) by Pinzon and De Lepe. Yet on this point there are some differences of opinion, which are recapitulated by Humboldt.

The most impartial critics, however, agree with Humboldt in giving Pinzon the lead, if not to the extent of the Cabral and forty-eight days before Cabral left Lisbon, as Hum- Pinzon. boldt contends.

If Barros is correct in his deductions, it was not known on board of Cabral's fleet that Columbus had already discovered in the Paria region what he supposed an extension of the Asiatic main. The first conclusion of the Portuguese naturally was that they had stumbled either on a new group of islands, or perhaps on some outlying members of the group of the Antilles. Of course nothing was known at the time of the discoveries of Pinzon and Lepe.

It has often been remarked that if Columbus had not sailed in 1492, Cabral would have revealed America in 1500. It is a striking fact that the Portuguese had pursued their quest for India with an intelligence and prescience which geographical truth confirmed. The Spaniards went their way in The results error, and it took them nearly thirty years to find a of the African route that could bring them where they could defend route. at the antipodes their rights under the Bull of Demarcation. Columbus sought India and found America without knowing it. Cabral, bound for the Cape of Good Hope, stumbled upon Brazil, and preëmpted the share of Portugal in the New World as Da Gama has already secured it in Asia. Thus the African route revealed both Cathay and America.

For these voyages commingling with those of Columbus along the spaces of the Caribbean Sea, we get the best in- The Colum- formation, all things considered, from the testimonies bus law- suit. of the participants in them, which were rendered in the famous lawsuit which the Crown waged against the heirs of

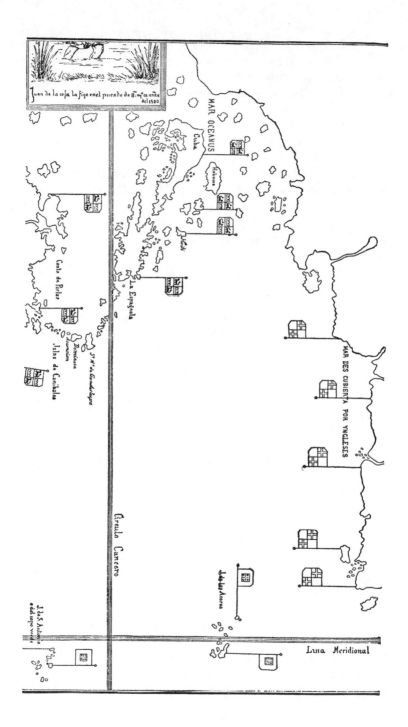

Juan de la cosa la fizo enel puerto de S.ta m.a en año del 1500

MAR OCEANUS

Cuba

Habana

Jamaica

La Española

MAR DES CUBIERTA POR YNGLESES

Costa de Perlas

Dominica

S.ta M.a de Guadalupe

Islas de Canibales

Circulo Cancero

J. de los Azores

Luna Meridional

J. de S. Antonio
del cabo verde

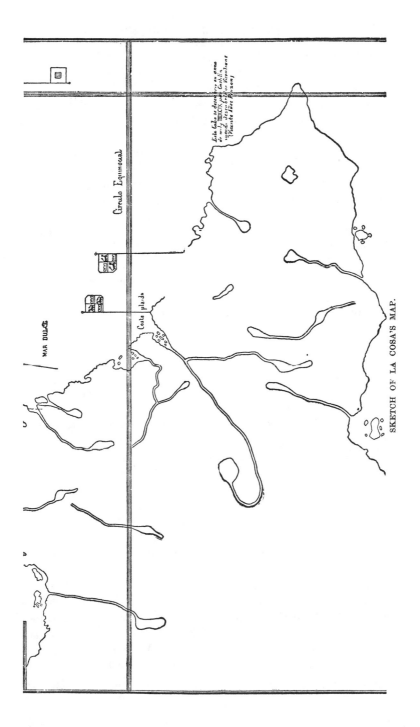

Cırculo Equinocal

MAR DULCE

Costa pla da

Esta cabo se descubrieron en anno de mil ×CCCCX por Castilla siendo descobridor Vincente Yañes Pinzon

SKETCH OF LA COSA'S MAP.

Columbus.   The well-known map of Juan de la Cosa posts us
best on the cartographical results of these same voyages up to the summer of 1500.

La Cosa was, as Las Casas called him, the best of the pilots
then living, and there is a story of his arrogating to himself a
superiority to Columbus, even.

As La Cosa returned to Spain with Ojeda in June, 1500,
and sailed again in October with Bastidas, this famous map
was apparently made in that interval, since it purports in an
inscription to have been drafted in 1500.   In posting the geographical knowledge which he had acquired up to that date, La
Cosa drew upon his own experiences in the voyages which he
had already made with Columbus (1493–96), and with Ojeda
(1499–1500).   It is to be regretted that we have from his
pencil no later draft, for his experience in these seas was long
and intimate, since he accompanied Bastidas in 1500–2, led expeditions of his own in 1504–6 and 1507–8, and went again
with Ojeda in 1509.

La Cosa, indeed, does not seem to have improved his map on
any subsequent date, and that he puts down Cape St. Augustine so accurately is another proof of that headland being seen
by Pinzon or Lepe in 1500, and that news of its discovery had
reached the map-makers.

The objections to La Cosa's map as a source of historical information have been that (1) he gives an incorrect
shape to Cuba, and makes it an island eight years before Ocampo sailed around it; and that (2) he gives
an unrecognizable coast northward from where the Gulf of
Mexico should be.   Henry Stevens, in his *Historical and Geographical Notes*, undertakes to answer these objections.

First, Stevens reverts to the belief of La Cosa that he did
not imagine Cuba to be an island, because no one ever
knew of an island 335 leagues long, as Columbus and
he, sailing along its southern side, had found it to be, taking the
distance they had gone rather than the true limits.   Stevens
depends much on the belief of Columbus that the bay of islands
which he fancied himself within, when he turned back, was the
Gulf of Ganges, — supposing that Peter Martyr quoted Columbus, when he wrote to that effect in August, 1495.   If Varnhagen is correct in his routes of Vespucius, that navigator, in

1497, making the circuit of the Gulf of Mexico, had established the insularity of Cuba. Few modern scholars, it is fair to say, accept Varnhagen's theories. It became a question, after Humboldt had made the La Cosa chart public in 1833, how its maker had got the information of the insularity of Cuba. Humboldt

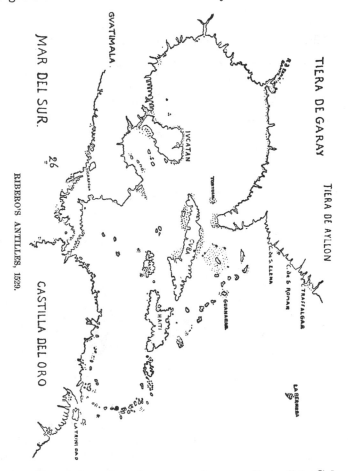

was convinced that though a "complacent witness" to Columbus's ridiculous notarial transaction during his second voyage, La Cosa had dared to tell the truth, even at the small risk of having his tongue pulled out.

The Admiral's belief, bolstered after his own fashion by suborning his crew, was far from being accepted by all.

Peter Martyr not long afterward voiced the hesitancy which was growing. It was beginning to be believed that the earth was larger than Columbus thought, and that his discoveries had not taken him as far as Cathay. Every new report veered the vane on this old gossiper's steeple, and he went on believing one day and disbelieving the next.

We may perhaps question now if the official promulgation of the Cuban circumnavigation by Sebastian Ocampo in 1508 was

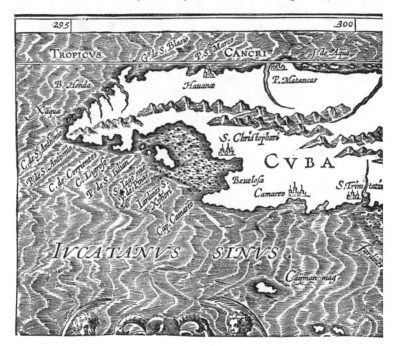

much more than the Spanish acknowledgment of its insularity, when they could no longer deny it. Henry Stevens has claimed to put La Cosa's island of Cuba in accord with Columbus, or at least partly so. He finds this western limit of Cuba on the La Cosa map drawn with "a dash of green paint," which he holds to be a color used to define unknown coasts. He studied the map in Jomard's colored facsimile, and trusted it, not having examined the original to this end, — though he had apparently seen it in the Paris auction-room in 1853, when, as a com-

petitor, he had run up the price which the Spanish government
paid for it. He says that the same green emblem of unknown
lands is also placed upon the coast of Asia, where a peninsular
Cuba would have joined it. He seems to forget that he should
have found, to support his theory, a gap rather than a supposable coast, and should rather have pointed to the vignette of
St. Christopher as affording that gap.

Ruysch in 1507 marked in his map this unknown western

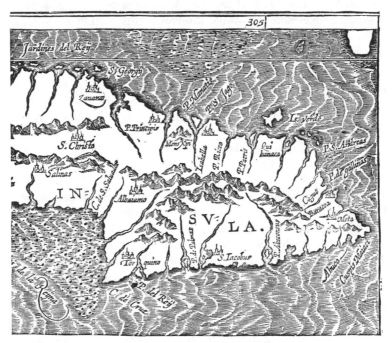

CUBA.

limit with a conventional scroll, while he made his north coast
not unlike. the Asiatic coast of Mauro (1457) and Behaim
(1492), and with no gap. Stevens also interprets the St. Dié
map of 1508–13 as showing this peninsular Cuba in what is
there placed as the main, with a duplicated insular Cuba in
what is called Isabella. The warrant for this supposition is
the transfer under disguises of the La Cosa and Ruysch names
of their Cuba to the continental coast of the St. Dié map,
leaving the " Isabella " entirely devoid of names.

Stevens ventures the opinion that La Cosa may have been on the first voyage of Columbus as well as on the second, and his reason for this is that the north coast of Cuba, which Columbus then coasted, is so correctly drawn; but this opinion ignores the probability, indeed the certainty, that this approximate accuracy could just as well be reached by copying from Columbus's map of that first voyage.

It should be borne in mind, however, that Varnhagen, who had faith in the 1497 voyage of Vespucius as having settled the insular character of Cuba, interprets this St. Dié map quite differently, as showing a rudimentary Gulf of Mexico and the Mississippi mouth instead of the Gulf of Ganges.

Second, Stevens grasps the obvious interpretation that La Cosa simply drew in for this northern coast that of Asia as he conceived it. This hardly needs elucidation. But his opinion is not so well grounded that the northern part of this Asiatic coast, where La Cosa intended to improve on the notions which had come from Marco Polo and the rest, is simply the *northern* coast of the Gulf of St. Lawrence as laid down by the explorations of Cabot. If it be taken as giving from Cabot's recitals the trend of the coasts found by him, it seems to show that that navigator knew nothing of the southern entrance of that gulf. This adds further to the uncertainty of what is called the Cabot mappemonde of 1544. That La Cosa intended the coasts of the Cabots' discoveries to belong to inland waters Stevens thinks is implied by the sea thereabouts being called *Mar* instead of *Mar oceanus.* It is difficult to see the force of these supplemental views of Stevens, and to look upon the drawing of La Cosa in this northern region as other than Asia modified vaguely by the salient points of the outer coast lines as glimpsed by Cabot.

*La Cosa's coast of Asia.*

If the Spanish envoy in England carried out his intention of sending a copy of Cabot's chart to Spain, it could hardly have escaped falling into the hands of La Cosa. We have already mentioned the chance of John Cabot having visited the peninsula in the interval between his two voyages.

*Columbus and the Cabot voyages.*

The chief ground for believing that Columbus ever heard of the voyages of the Cabots — for there is no plain statement that he did — is that we know how La Cosa had knowledge of them; and that upon his map the vignette of St. Christopher bearing the infant Christ may possibly have been, as it has sometimes been held to be, a direct reference to La Cosa's commander, who may be supposed in that case to have been acquainted with the compliment paid him, and consequently with the map's record of the Cabots.

Whether La Cosa understood the natives better than Columbus, or whether he had information of which we have no record, it is certain that within two years rumor or fact brought it to the knowledge of the Portuguese that the westerly end of Cuba lay contiguous to a continental shore, stretching to the north, in much the position of the eastern seaboard of the United States. This is manifest from the Cantino The Cantino map. map, which was sent from Lisbon to Italy before November, 1502, and which prefigured the so-called Admiral's map of the Ptolemy of 1513. There will be occasion to discuss later the over-confident dictum of Stevens that this supposed North American coast was simply a duplicated Cuba, turned north and south, and stretching from a warm region, as the Spaniards knew it, well up into the frozen north. Cosa's map seems to have exerted little or no influence on the earliest printed maps of the New World, and in this it differs from the Cantino map.

We know not what unexpected developments may further have sprung from obscure and furtive explorations, which were now beginning to be common, and of which the record Minor expeditions. is often nothing more than an inference. Stories of gold and pearls were great incentives. The age was full of a spirit of private adventure. The voyages of Ojeda, Niño, and Pinzon were but the more conspicuous.

# CHAPTER XVII.

## THE DEGRADATION AND DISHEARTENMENT OF COLUMBUS.

### 1500.

COLUMBUS, writing to the Spanish sovereigns from Española, said, in reference to the lifelong opposition which he had encountered: —

"May it please the Lord to forgive those who have calumniated and still calumniate this excellent enterprise of mine, and oppose and have opposed its advancement, without considering how much glory and greatness will accrue from it to your Highnesses throughout all the world. They cannot state anything in disparagement of it except its expense, and that I have not immediately sent back the ships loaded with gold."

*Opponents of Columbus.*

Was this an honest statement? Columbus knew perfectly well that there had been much else than disappointment at the scant pecuniary returns. He knew that there was a widespread dissatisfaction at his personal mismanagement of the colony; at his alleged arrogance and cupidity as a foreigner; at his nepotism; at his inordinate exaltation of promise, and at his errant faith that brooked no dispute. He knew also that his enthusiasm had captivated the Queen, and that as long as she could be held captive he could appeal to her not in vain. If there had been any honesty in the Queen's professions in respect to the selling of slaves, he knew that he had outraged them. Even when he was writing this letter, it came over him that there was a fearful hazard for him both in the persistency of this denunciation of others against him and in the heedless arrogance of such perverseness on his own part.

*Charges against Columbus.*

"I know," he says, "that water dropping on a stone will at length make a hole." We shall see before long that foreboding cavity.

The defection of Roldan turned so completely into servility is but one of the strange contrasts of the wonderful course of vicissitudes in the life of Columbus. There presently came a new trial for him and for Roldan. A young well-born Spaniard, Fernando de Guevara, had appeared in Espa-ñola recently, and by his dissolute life he had created such scandals in Santo Domingo that Columbus had ordered him to leave the island. He had been sent to Xaragua to embark in one of Ojeda's ships; but that adventurer had left the coast when the outlaw reached the port. While waiting another opportunity to embark, Guevara was kept in that part of the island under Roldan's eye. This implied no such restraint as to deny him access to the society of Anacaona, with whose daughter, Higuamota, who seems to have inherited something of her mother's commanding beauty and mental qualities, he fell in love, and found his passion requited. He sought companionship also with one of the lieutenants of Roldan, who had been a leader in his late revolt, Adrian de Moxica, then living not far away, who had for him the additional attachment of kinship, for the two were cousins. Las Casas tells us that Roldan had himself a passion for the young Indian beauty, and it may have been for this as well as for his desire to obey the Admiral that he commanded the young cavalier to go to a more distant province. The ardent lover had sought to prepare his way for a speedy marriage by trying to procure a priest to baptize the maiden. This caused more urgent commands from Roldan, which were ostentatiously obeyed, only to be eluded by a clandestine return, when he was screened with some associates in the house of Anacaona. This queenly woman seems to have favored his suit with her daughter. He was once more ordered away, when he began to bear himself defiantly, but soon changed his method to suppliancy. Roldan was appeased by this. Guevara, however, only made it the cloak for revenge, and with some of his friends formed a plot to kill Roldan. This leaked out, and the youth and his accomplices were arrested and sent to Santo Domingo. This action aroused Roldan's old confederate, Moxica, and, indignant at the way in which the renegade rebel had dared to turn upon his former associates, Moxica resolved upon revenge. To carry it out he started

on a tour through the country where the late mutineers were settled, and readily engaged their sympathies. Among

Moxica's
plot.

those who joined in his plot was Pedro Riquelme,
whom Roldan had made assistant alcalde. The old spirit of
revolt was rampant. The confederates were ready for any
excess, either upon Roldan or upon the Admiral. Columbus
was at Conception in the midst of the aroused district, when a
deserter from the plotters informed him of their plan. With a
small party the Admiral at once sped in the night to the un-

Moxica
taken.

guarded quarters of the leaders, and Moxica and several of his chief advisers were suddenly captured and
carried to the fort. The execution of the ringleader was at
once ordered. Impatient at the way in which the condemned
man dallied in his confessions to a priest, Columbus ordered him
pushed headlong from the battlements. The French canonists
screen Columbus for this act by making Roldan the perpetrator
of it. The other confederates were ironed in confinement at
Conception, except Riquelme, who was taken later and conveyed
to Santo Domingo.

The revolt was thus summarily crushed. Those who had
escaped fled to Xaragua, whither the Adelantado and Roldan
pursued them without mercy.

Columbus had perhaps never got his colony under better control than existed after this vigorous exhibition of his

Columbus
and his col-
ony.

authority. Such a show of prompt and audacious
energy was needed to restore the moral supremacy
which his recusancy under the threats of Roldan had lost. The
fair weather was not to last long.

Early in the morning of August 23, 1500, two caravels were
descried off the harbor of Santo Domingo. The Ad-

1500. Au-
gust 23. Bo-
badilla ar-
rives.

miral's brother Diego was in authority, Columbus
being still at Conception, and Bartholomew absent
with Roldan. Diego sent out a canoe to learn the purpose of
the visitors. It returned, and brought word that a commissioner was come to inquire into the late rebellion of Roldan.
Diego's messengers had at the same time informed the new-
comer of the most recent defection of Moxica, and that there
were still other executions to take place, particularly those of
Riquelme and Guevara, who were confined in the town. As

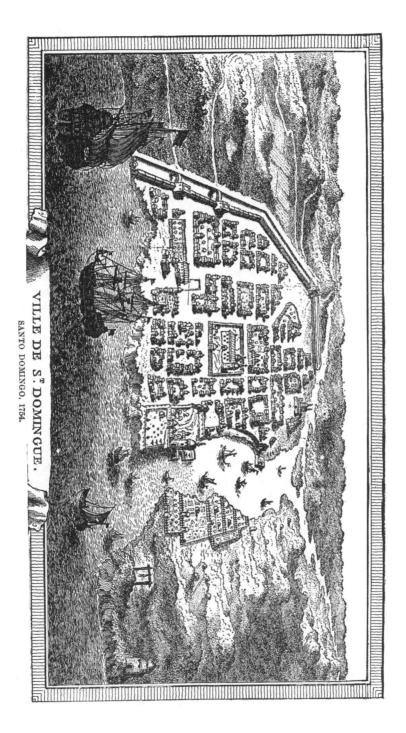

VILLE DE S.ᵀ DOMINGUE.

SANTO DOMINGO, 1754.

the ships entered the river, the gibbets on either bank, with their dangling Spaniards, showed the commissioner that there were other troublous times to inquire into than those named in his warrant. While the commissioner remained on board his ship, receiving the court of those who early sought to propitiate him, and while he was getting his first information of the condition of the island, mainly from those who had something to gain by the excess of their denunciations, it is necessary to go back a little in time, and ascertain who this important personage was, and what was the mission on which he had been sent.

The arrangements for sending him had been made slowly. They were even outlined when Ojeda had started on his voyage, for he had, in his interviews with Roldan, blindly indicated that some astonishment of this sort was in store. Evidently Fonseca had not allowed Ojeda to depart without some intimations.

*Growth of the royal dissatisfaction with Columbus.*

Notwithstanding Columbus professed to believe that nothing but the lack of pecuniary return for the great outlays of his expeditions could be alleged against them, he was well aware, and he had constantly acted as if well aware, of the great array of accusations which had been made against him in Spain, with a principal purpose of undermining the indulgent regard of the Queen for him. He had known it with sorrow during his last visit to Spain, and had found, as we have seen, that he could not secure men to accompany him and put themselves under his control unless he unshackled criminals in the jails. He little thought that such utter disregard of the morals and self-respect of those whom he had settled in the New World would, by a sort of retributive justice, open the way, however unjustly, to put the displaced gyves on himself, amid the exultant feelings of these same criminals. Such reiterated criminations were like the water-drops that wear the stone, and he had, as we have noted, felt the certainty of direful results.

*Charges against Columbus.*

How much the disappointment at the lack of gold had to do with increasing the force of these charges, it is not difficult to imagine. Columbus was certainly not responsible for that; but he was responsible for the inordinate growth of the belief in the profuse wealth of the new-found Indies. His constantly

repeated stories of the wonderful richness of the region had done
their work.  His professions of a purpose to enrich the   His exagger-
world with noble benefactions, and to spend his treas-   ations of the
wealth of
ure on the recovery of the Holy Sepulchre, were the   the Indies.
vain boastings of a man who thought thereby to enroll his
name among the benefactors of the Church.  He did not per-
ceive that the populace would wonder whence these   Columbus
resources were to come, unless it was by defrauding   deceives the
Crown.
the Crown of its share, and by amassing gold while
t. y could not get any.  There is something ludicrous in the
excuse which he later gave for concealing from the sovereigns
his accumulation of pearls.  He felt it sufficient to say that
he thought he would wait till he could make as good a show
of gold !  There were some things that even fifteenth-century
Christians held to be more sacred than wresting Jerusalem
from the Moslem, and these were money in hand when they
had earned it, and food to eat when their misfortunes had beg-
gared their lives.  It was not an uncalled-for strain on their
loyalty to the Crown, when the notion prevailed that the sovereigns and their favorite were gathering riches out of their
despair.  There was little to be wondered at, in the crowd of
these hungry and debilitated victims, wandering about the
courts of the Alhambra, under the royal windows, and   Columbus's
clamoring for their pay.  There was nothing to be   sons hooted
at in the
surprised at in the hootings that followed the Ad-   Alhambra.
miral's sons, pages of the Queen, if they passed within sight
of these embittered throngs.

It was quite evident that Ferdinand, who had never warmed
to the Admiral's enthusiasm, had long been conscious that in
the exclusive and extended powers which had been   Ferdinand's
given to Columbus a serious administrative blunder   confessed
blunder.
had been made.  He said as much at a later day to
Ponce de Leon.

The Queen had been faithful, but the recurrent charges had
given of late a wrench to her constancy.  Was it not certain
that something must be wrong, or these accusations would not go
on increasing ?  Had not the great discoverer fulfilled his mission when he unveiled a new world ?  Was it quite sure that
the ability to govern it went along with the genius to find it ?
These were the questions which Isabella began to put to her-

self. She was not a person to hesitate at anything, when con-

viction came. She had shown this in the treatment of the Jews, of the Moors, and of other heretics. The conviction that Columbus was not equal to his trust was now coming to her. The news of the serious outbreak of

Roldan's conspiracy brought the matter to a test, and in the spring of 1499 the purpose to send out some one with almost unlimited powers for any emergency was decided upon. Still the details were not worked out, and there were occurrences in the internal and external affairs of Spain that required the prior attention of the sovereigns. Very likely the news of Columbus's success in finding a new source of wealth in the pearls of Paria may have had something to do with the delay. When the ships which carried to Spain a crowd of Roldan's followers arrived, the question took a fresh interest. Columbus's friends, Ballester and Barrantes,

now found their testimony could make little headway against the crowd of embittered witnesses on the other side. Isabella, besides, was forced to see in the slaves that Columbus had sent by the same ships something of an obstinate opposition to her own wishes. Las Casas tells us that so great was the Queen's displeasure that it was only the remembrance of Columbus's services that saved him from prompt disgrace. To be sure, the slaves had been sent in part by virtue of the capitulation which Columbus had made with the rebels, but should the Viceroy of the Indies be forced to such capitulations? Had he kept the colony in a condition worthy of her queenly patronage, when it could be reported to her that the daughters of caciques were found among these natives bearing their hybrid babes? "What authority had my viceroy to give my vassals to such ends?" she asked.

There were two things in recent letters of Columbus which

damaged his cause just at this juncture. One was his petition for a new lease of the slave trade. This Isabella answered by ordering all slaves which he had sent home to be sought out and returned. Her agents found a

few. The other was the request of Columbus for a judge to examine the dispute between himself and Roldan. This Ferdinand answered by appointing the commissioner whose arrival at Santo Domingo we have chronicled. He was Francisco de Bobadilla, an officer of the royal household.

Before disclosing what Bobadilla did in Santo Domingo, it is best to try to find out what he was expected to do.

There is no person connected with the career of Columbus — hardly excepting Fonseca — more generally defamed than this man, who was, nevertheless, if we may believe His charac-Oviedo, a very honest and a very religious man. The ter. historians of Columbus need to mete out to Bobadilla what very few have done, the same measure of palliation which they are more willing to bestow on Columbus. With this parallel justice, it may be that he will not bear with discredit a comparison with Columbus himself, in all that makes a man's actions excusable under provocation and responsibility. An indecency of haste may come from an excess of zeal quite as well as from an unbridled virulence.

It may be in some ways a question if the conditions this man was sent to correct were the result of the weakness or inadaptability of Columbus, or merely the outcome of circumstances, enough beyond his control to allow of excuses. There is, however, no question that the Spanish government had duties to perform towards itself and its subjects which made it properly disinclined to jeopardize the interests which accompany such duties.

Bobadilla was, to be sure, invested with dangerous powers, but not with more dangerous ones than Columbus Bobadilla's himself had possessed. When two such personations powers. of unbridled authority come in antagonism, the possessor of the greater authority is sure to confirm himself by commensurate exactions upon the other. Bobadilla's commission was an implied warrant to that end. He might have been more prudent of his own state, and should have remembered that a trust of the nature of that with which he was invested was sure to be made accountable to those who imparted to him the power, and perhaps at a time when they chose to abandon their own instructions. He ought to have known that such an abandonment comes very easy to all governments in emergencies. He might have been more considerate of the man whom Spain had so recently flattered. He should not have forgotten, if almost everybody else had, that the Admiral had given a new world to Spain.

He should not have been unmindful, if almost every one else was, that this new world was a delusion now, but might dissolve into a beatific vision. But all this was rather more than human nature was capable of in an age like that. It is to be said of Bobadilla that when he summoned Columbus to Santo Domingo and prejudged him guilty, he had shown no more disregard of a rival power, which he was sent to regulate, than Columbus had manifested for a deluded colony, when he selfishly infected it with the poison of the prisons. It must not, indeed, be forgotten that the strongest support of the new envoy came from the very elements of vice which Columbus had implanted in

Columbus and the criminals. the island. He grew to understand this, and later he was forced to give a condemnation of his own act when he urged the sending of such as are honorably known, " that the country may be peopled with honest men."

Las Casas tells us of Bobadilla that his probity and disinterestedness were such that no one could attack them. If it be left for posterity to decide between the word of Las Casas and Columbus, in estimates of virtue and honesty, there is no question of the result. When Bobadilla was selected to be sent to

Bobadilla's character. Española, there was every reason to choose the most upright of persons. There was every reason, also, to instruct him with a care that should consider every probable attendant circumstance. After this was done, the discretion of the man was to determine all. We can read in the records the formal instructions ; but there were beside, as is expressly stated, verbal directions which can only be surmised. Bobadilla was accused of exceeding the wishes of the Queen. Are we sure

Did he exceed his powers? that he did ? It is no sign of it that the monarchs subsequently found it politic to disclaim the act of their agent. Such a desertion of a subordinate was not unusual in those times, nor indeed would it be now.

If Isabella, " for the love of Christ and the Virgin Mary," could depopulate towns, as she said she did, by the ravages of the inquisition, and fill her coffers by the attendant sequestrations, it is not difficult to conceive that, with a similar and convenient conviction of duty, she would give no narrow range to her vindictiveness and religious zeal when she came to deal with an Admiral whom she had created, and who was not very deferential to her wishes.

A synopsis of the powers confided to Bobadilla in writing needs to be presented. They begin with a letter of March 21, 1499, referring to reports of the Roldan insurrection, and directing him, if on inquiry he finds any persons culpable, to arrest them and sequestrate their effects, and to call upon the Admiral for assistance in carrying out these orders. Two months later, May 21, a circular letter was framed and addressed to the magistrates of the islands, which seems to have been intended to accredit Bobadilla to them, if the Admiral should be no longer in command. This order gave notice to these magistrates of the full powers which had been given to Bobadilla in civil and criminal jurisdiction. Another order of the same date, addressed to the " Admiral of the ocean sea," orders him to surrender all royal property, whether forts, arms, or otherwise, into Bobadilla's hands, — evidently intended to have an accompanying effect with the other. Of a date five days later another letter addressed to the Admiral reads to this effect : —

Bobadilla's powers.

" We have directed Francisco de Bobadilla, the bearer of this, to tell you for us of certain things to be mentioned by him. We ask you to give faith and credence to what he says, and to obey him. May 26, 1499."

This is an explicit avowal on the sovereigns' part of having given verbal orders. In addition to these instructions, a royal order required the commissioner to ascertain what was due from the Crown for unpaid salaries, and to compel the Admiral to join in liquidating such obligations so far as he was bound for them, " that there may be no more complaints." If one may believe Columbus's own statements as made in his subsequent letter to the nurse of Prince Juan, it had been neglect, and not inability, on his part which had allowed these arrears to accrue. Bobadilla was also furnished with blanks signed by the sovereigns, to be used to further their purposes in any way and at his discretion. With these extraordinary documents, and possessed of such verbal and confidential directions as we may imagine rather than prove, Bobadilla had sailed in July, 1500, more than a year after the letters were dated. His two caravels brought back to Española a number of natives, who were in charge of some Franciscan friars.

His verbal orders.

1500. July. Bobadilla leaves Spain.

We left Bobadilla on board his ship, receiving court from all

Bobadilla lands at Santo Domingo.
who desired thus early to get his ear. It was not till the next day that he landed, attended by a guard of twenty-five men, when he proceeded to the church to mass.

This over, the crowd gathered before the church. Bobadilla ordered a herald to read his original commission of March 21,

His demands.
1499, and then he demanded of the acting governor, Diego, who was present, that Guevara, Riquelme, and the other prisoners should be delivered to him, together with all the evidence in their cases, and that the accusers and magistrates should appear before him. Diego referred him to the Admiral as alone having power in such matters, and asked for a copy of the document just read to send to Columbus. This Bobadilla declined to give, and retired, intimating, however, that there were reserved powers which he had, before which even the Admiral must bow.

The peremptoriness of this movement was, it would seem, uncalled for, and there could have been little misfortune in waiting the coming of the Admiral, compared with the natural results of such sudden overturning of established authority in the absence of the holder of it. Urgency may not, nevertheless, have been without its claims. It was desirable to stay the intended executions; and we know not what exaggerations had already filled the ears of Bobadilla. At this time there would seem to have been the occasion to deliver the letter to Columbus which had commanded his obedience to the verbal instructions of the sovereigns; and such a delivery might have turned the current of these hurrying events, for Columbus had shown, in the case of Agueda, that he was graciously inclined to authority. Instead of this, however, Bobadilla, the next day, again appeared at mass, and caused his other commissions to be read, which in effect made him supersede the Admiral. This superiority Diego and his councilors still unadvisedly declined to recognize. The other mandates were read in succession; and the gradual rise to power, which the documents seemed to imply, as the progress of the investigations demanded support, was thus reached at a bound. This is the view of the case which has been taken by Columbus's biographers, as naturally drawn from the succession of the powers which were given to Bobadilla. It is merely an inference, and we know not the directions for their proclamations, which had been verbally imparted to Bobadilla. It is this uncertainty which surrounds the case with doubt. It is apparent that the reading of these papers had begun to impress the rabble, if not those in authority. That order which commanded the payment of arrears of salaries had a very gratifying effect on those who had suffered from delays. Nothing, however, moved the representatives of the Viceroy, who would not believe that anything could surpass his long-conceded authority.

There is nothing strange in the excitement of an officer who finds his undoubted supremacy thus obstinately spurned, and we must trace to such excitement the somewhat overstrained conduct which made a show of carrying by assault the fortress in which Guevara and the other prisoners were confined. Miguel Diaz, who commanded the fort, — the same who had disclosed the Hayna mines, — when summoned to surrender had referred Bobadilla to the Admiral from whom his orders came, and asked for copies of the letters patent and orders, for more considerate attention. It was hardly to be expected that Bobadilla was to be beguiled by any such device, when he had a force of armed men at his back, aided by his crew and the aroused rabble, and when there was nothing before him but a weak citadel with few defenders. There was nothing to withstand the somewhat ridiculous shock of the assault but a few frail bars, and no need of the scaling ladders which were ostentatiously set up. Diaz and one companion, with sword in hand, stood passively representing the outraged dignity of command. Bobadilla was victorious, and the manacled Guevara and the rest passed over to new and less stringent keepers.

Bobadilla was now in possession of every channel of authority. He domiciled himself in the house of Columbus, took possession of all his effects, including his papers, making no distinction between public and private ones, and used what money he could find to pay the debts of the Admiral as they were presented to him. This proceeding was well calculated to increase his popularity, and it was still more enhanced when he proclaimed liberty to all to gather gold for twenty years, with only the payment of one seventh instead of a third to the Crown.

Bobadilla assaults the fort.

Bobadilla in full possession.

Let us turn to Columbus himself.  The reports which
reached him at Fort Conception did not at first con-

vey to him an adequate notion of what he was to encounter.  He associated the proceedings with such
unwarranted acts as Ojeda's and Pinzon's in coming with
their ships within his prescribed dominion.  The greater audacity, however, alarmed him, and the threats which Bobadilla
had made of sending him to Spain in irons, and the known
success of his usurpation within the town, were little calculated
to make Columbus confident in the temporary character of the
outburst.  He moved his quarters to Bonao to be nearer the
confusion, and here he met an officer bearing to him a copy of
the letters under which the government had been assumed by
Bobadilla.  Still the one addressed to Columbus, commanding
him to acquiesce, was held back.  It showed palpably that
Bobadilla conceived he had passed beyond the judicial aim of
his commission.  Columbus, on his part, was loath to reach
that conclusion, and tried to gain time.  He wrote to Bobadilla
an exculpating and temporizing letter, saying that he was about
to leave for Spain, when everything would pass regularly
into Bobadilla's control.  He sent other letters, calculated to
create delays, to the Franciscans who had come with

him.  He had himself affiliated with that order, and
perhaps thought his influence might not be unheeded.
He got no replies, and perhaps never knew what the spirit of
these friars was.  They evidently reflected the kind of testimony which Bobadilla had been accumulating.  We find
somewhat later, in a report of one of them, Nicholas Glass-
berger, — who speaks of the 1,500 natives whom they had
made haste to baptize in Santo Domingo, — some of the cruel
insinuations which were rife, when he speaks of "a certain
admiral, captain, and chief, who had ill treated these natives,
taking their goods and wives, and capturing their virgin daughters, and had been sent to Spain in chains."

Columbus as yet could hardly have looked forward to any
such indignity as manacles on his limbs.  Nor did he probably
suspect that Bobadilla was using the signed blanks, entrusted
to him by the sovereigns, to engage the interests of Roldan and
other deputies of the Viceroy scattered through the island.
Columbus, in these uncertainties, caused it to be known that

he considered his perpetual powers still unrevoked, if indeed they were revocable at all. This state of his mind was rudely jarred by receiving a little later, at the hands of Francisco Velasquez, the deputy treasurer, and of Juan de Trasierra, one of the Franciscans, the letter addressed to him by the sovereigns, commanding him to respect what Bobadilla should tell him. Here was tangible authority; and when it was accompanied by a summons from Bobadilla to appear before him, he hesitated no longer, and, with the little state befitting his disgrace, proceeded at once to Santo Domingo.

Bobadilla sends the sovereigns' letter to Columbus.

The Admiral's brother Diego had already been confined in irons on one of the caravels; and Bobadilla, affecting to believe, as Irving holds, that Columbus would not come in any compliant mood, made a bustle of armed preparation. There was, however, no such intention on Columbus's part, nor had been, since the royal mandate of implicit obedience had been received. He came as quietly as the circumstances would permit, and when the new governor heard he was within his grasp, his orders to seize him and throw him into prison were promptly executed (August 23, 1500). In the southeastern part of the town, the tower still stands, with little signs of decay, which then received the dejected Admiral, and from its summit all approaching vessels are signaled to-day. Las Casas tells us of the shameless and graceless cook, one of Columbus's own household, who riveted the fetters. "I knew the fellow," says that historian, "and I think his name was Espinosa."

Columbus approaches Santo Domingo.

1500. August 23. Columbus is imprisoned in chains.

While the Adelantado was at large with an armed force, Bobadilla was not altogether secure in his triumph. He demanded of Columbus to write to his brother and counsel him to come in and surrender. This Columbus did, assuring the Adelantado of their safety in trusting to the later justice of the Crown. Bartholomew obeyed, as the best authorities say, though Peter Martyr mentions a rumor that he came in no accommodating spirit, and was captured while in advance of his force. It is certain he also was placed in irons, and confined on one of the caravels. It was Bobadilla's purpose to keep the leaders apart, so there could be no concert of action, and even to prevent their seeing any one who could inform them of the progress of the inquest, which was at once begun. It seems evident that Bobadilla, either of his own impulse or in accordance with secret instructions, was acting with a secrecy and precipitancy which would have been justifiable in the presence of armed sedition, but was uncalled for with no organized opposition to embarrass him. Columbus at a later day tells us that he was denied ample clothing, even, and was otherwise ill treated. He says, too, he had no statement of charges given to him. It is a later story, started by Charlevoix, that such accusations were presented to him in writing, and met by him in the same method.

Charges against Columbus.

The trial was certainly a remarkable procedure, except we consider it simply an *ex parte* process for indictment only, as indeed it really was. Irving lays stress on the reversal by Bobadilla of the natural order of his acts, amounting, in fact, to prejudging a person he was sent to examine. He also thinks that the governor was hurried to his conclusions' in order to make up a show of necessity for his precipitate action. It has something of that look. " The rebels he had been sent to judge became, by this singular perversion of rule," says Irving, " necessary and cherished evidences to criminate those against whom they had rebelled." This is the mistake of the apologists for Columbus. Bobadilla seems to have been sent to judge between two parties, and not to assume that only one was culpable. Even Irving suspects the true conditions. He allows that Bobadilla would not have dared to go to this length, had he not felt assured that " certain things," as the mandate to Columbus expressed it, would not be displeasing to the king.

The charges against the Admiral had been stock ones for years, and we have encountered them more than once in the progress of this narrative. They are rehearsed at length in the documents given by Navarrete, and are repeated and summarized by Peter Martyr. It is perhaps true that there was some novelty in the asseveration that Columbus's recent refusal to have some Indians baptized was simply because it deprived him of selling them as slaves. This accusation, considering Columbus's relations to the slave trade which he had created, is as little to be wondered at as any.

Las Casas tells us how indignant Isabella had been with his presumptuous way of dealing with what she called her subjects, and by a royal order of June 20, 1500, she had ordered, as we have seen, the return in Bobadilla's fleet of nineteen of the slaves who had been sold. There was no better way of commending Bobadilla's action to the Queen, apparently, than by making the most of Columbus's unfortunate relations to the slave trade.

Columbus and slavery.

As the accusations were piled up, Bobadilla saw the inquest leading, in his mind, to but one conclusion, the unnatural character of the Viceroy and his unfitness for command, — a phrase not far from the truth, but hardly requiring the extraordinary proceedings which had brought the governor to a recognition of it. There is little question that the public sentiment of the colony, so far at least as it dare manifest itself, commended the governor. Columbus in his dungeon might not see this with his own eyes, but if the reports are true, his ears carried it to his spirit, for howls and taunts against him came from beyond the walls, as the expression of the hordes which felt relieved by his fate. Columbus himself confessed that Bobadilla had " succeeded to the full " in making him hated of the people. All this was matter to brood upon in his loneliness. He magnified slight hints. He more than suspected he was doomed to a violent fate. When Alonso de Villejo, who was to conduct him to Spain, in charge of the returning ships, came to the dungeon, Columbus saw for the first time some recognition of his unfortunate condition. Las Casas, in recounting the interview, says that Villejo was " an hidalgo of honorable character and my particular friend," and he doubtless got his account of what took place from that important participant.

" Villejo," said the prisoner, " whither do you take me ? "

" To embark on the ship, your excellency."

" To embark, Villejo ? Is that the truth ? "

" It is true," said the captain.

For the first time the poor Admiral felt that he yet might see Spain and her sovereigns.

The caravels set sail in October, 1500, and soon passed out of earshot of the hootings that were sent after the miserable prisoners. The new keepers of Columbus were not of the same sort as those who cast such farewell taunts. If the *Historie* is to be believed, Bobadilla had ordered the chains to be kept on throughout the voyage,

1500. October. Columbus sent to Spain.

since, as the writer of that book grimly suggests, Columbus might at any time swim back, if not secured. Villejo was kind. So was the master of the caravel, Andreas Martin. They suggested that they could remove the manacles during the voyage; but the Admiral, with that cherished constancy which persons feel, not always wisely, in such predicaments, thinking to magnify martyrdom, refused. " No," he said ; " my sovereigns ordered me to submit, and Bobadilla has chained me. I

His chains.

will wear these irons until by royal order they are removed, and I shall keep them as relics and memorials of my services."

The relations of Columbus and Bobadilla bring before us the most startling of the many combinations of events in the history of a career which is sadder, perhaps, notwithstanding its glory,

Degradation of Columbus.

than any other mortal presents in profane history. The degradation of such a man appeals more forcibly to human sympathy than almost any other event in the record of humanity. That sympathy has obscured the im-

His letter to the nurse of Prince Juan analyzed.

port of his degradation, and that mournful explanation of the events, which, either on his voyage or shortly after his return, Columbus wrote and sent to the nurse of Prince Juan, has long worked upon the sensibilities of a world tender for his misfortunes. We cannot indeed read this letter without compassion, nor can we read it dispassionately without perceiving that the feelings of the man who wrote it had been despoiled of a judicial temper by his errors as well as by his miseries. His statements of the case are wholly one-sided. He never sees what it pains him to see. He forgets everything that an enemy would remember. He finds it difficult to tell the truth, and trusts to iterated professions to be taken for truths. He claims to have no conception why he was imprisoned, when he knew perfectly well, as he says himself, that he had endeavored to create an opposition to constituted authority " by verbal and written declarations ; " and he reiterates this statement after he had bowed to royal commands

Charges against Columbus.

that were as explicit as his own treatment of them had been recalcitrant. Indeed, he puts himself in the rather ridiculous posture of answering a long series of charges, of which at the same time he professes to be ignorant.

In the course of this letter, Columbus set up a claim that he had been seriously misjudged in trying to measure his accountability by the laws that govern established governments rather than by those which grant indulgences to the conqueror of a numerous and warlike nation. The position is curiously inconsistent with his professed intentions, as the sole ruler of a colony, to be just in the eyes of God and men. The Crown had given him its authority to establish precisely what he claims had not been established, a government of laws kindly disposed to protect both Spaniard and native, and yet he did not understand why his doings were called in question. He had boasted repeatedly how far from warlike and dangerous the natives were, so that a score of Spaniards could put seven thousand to rout, as he was eager to report in one case. The chief of the accusations against him did not pertain to his malfeasance in regard to the natives, but towards the Spaniards themselves, and it was begging the question to consider his companions a conquered nation. If there were no established government as respects them, he would be the last to admit it; and if it were proved against him, there was no one so responsible for the absence of it as himself. Again he says: " I ought to be judged by cavaliers who have gained victories themselves, — by gentlemen, and not by lawyers." The fact was that the case had been judged by hidalgoes without number, and to his disgrace, and it was taken from them to give him the protection of the law, such as it was; and, as he himself acknowledges, there is in the Indies " neither civil right nor judgment seat." As he was the source of all the bulwarks of life and liberty in these same Indies, he thus acknowledges the deficiencies of his own protective agencies. There is something childishly immature in the proposition which he advances that he should be judged by persons in his own pay.

It is of course necessary to allow the writer of this letter all the palliation that a man in his distressed and disordered condition might claim. Columbus had in Palliation. fact been perceptibly drifting into a state of delusion and aberration of mind ever since the sustaining power of a great cause had been lifted from him. From the moment when he turned his mule back at the instance of Isabella's message, the lofty purpose had degenerated to a besetting cupidity, in which he made even the Divinity a constant abettor. In this same letter he tells of a vision of the previous Christmas, when the Lord confronted him miraculously, and reminded him of his vow to amass treasure enough in seven years to undertake his crusade to Jerusalem. This visible Godhead then comforted him with the assurance that his divine power would see that it came to pass. " The seven years you were to await have not yet passed. Trust in me and all will be right." It is easy to point to numerous such instances in Columbus's career, and the canonizers do not neglect to do so, as evincing the sublime confidence of the devoted servant of the Lord ; but one can hardly put out of mind the concomitants of all such confidence. The most that we can allow is the unaccountableness of a much-vexed conscience.

# CHAPTER XVIII.

## 1500–1502.

IT was in October, 1500, after a voyage of less discomfort than usual, that the ships of Villejo, carrying his manacled prisoners, entered the harbor of Cadiz. If Bobadilla had precipitately prejudged his chief prisoner, public sentiment, when it became known that Columbus had arrived in chains, was not less headlong in its sympathetic revulsion. Bobadilla would at this moment have stood a small chance for a dispassionate examination. The discoverer of the New World coming back from it a degraded prisoner was a discordant spectacle in the public mind, filled with recollections of those days of the first return to Palos, when a new range had been given to man's conceptions of the physical world. This common outburst of indignation showed, as many times before and since, how the world's sense of justice has in it more of spirit than of steady discernment. The hectic flush was sure to pass, — as it did.

*1500. October. Columbus reaches Cadiz.*

*Public sympathy at his degradation.*

It was while on his voyage, or shortly after his return, that Columbus wrote the letter to the lady of the Court usually spoken of as the nurse of Prince Juan, which has been already considered. Before the proceedings of the inquest which Bobadilla had forwarded by the ship were sent to the Court, then in the Alhambra, Columbus, with the connivance of Martin, the captain of his caravel, had got this exculpatory letter off by a special messenger. The lady to whom it was addressed was, it will be remembered, Doña Juana de la Torre, an intimate companion of the Queen, with whom the Admiral's two sons, as pages of the Queen, had been for some months in daily relations. The text of this letter has long been known. Las Casas copied it in his *Historia*.

*Columbus's letter to the nurse of Prince Juan.*

Navarrete gives it from another copy, but corrected by the text preserved at Genoa; while Harrisse tells us that the text in Paris contains an important passage not in that at Genoa.

While its ejaculatory arguments are not well calculated to impose on the sober historian, there was enough of fervor laid against its background of distressing humility to work on the sympathies of its recipient, and of the Queen, to whom it was early and naturally revealed. "I have now reached that point that there is no man so vile, but thinks it his right to insult me," was the language, almost at its opening, which met their eyes. The further reading of the letter brought up a picture of the manacled Admiral. Very likely the rumor of the rising indignation spreading from Cadiz to Seville, and from Seville elsewhere, as well as the letters of the alcalde of Cadiz, into whose hands Columbus had been delivered, and of Villejo, who had had him in custody, added to the tumult of sensations mutually shared in that little circle of the monarchs and the Doña Juana. If we take the prompt action of the sovereigns in ordering the immediate release of Columbus, their letter of sympathy at the baseness of his treatment, the two thousand ducats put at his disposal to prepare for a visit to the Court, and the cordial royal summons for him to come, — if all these be taken at their apparent value, the candid observer finds himself growing distrustful of Bobadilla's justification through his secret instructions. As the observer goes on in the story and notes the sequel, he is more inclined to believe that the sovereigns, borne on the rising tide of indignant sympathy, had defended themselves at the expense of their commissioner. We may never know the truth.

The sovereigns order Columbus to be released.

That was a striking scene when Columbus, delivered from his irons on the 17th of December, 1500, held his first interview with the Spanish monarchs. Oviedo was an eyewitness of it; but we find more of its accompaniments in the story as told by Herrera than in the scant narrative of the *Historie*. Humboldt fancies that it was the Admiral's son who wrote it. The author of that book had no heart to record at much length the professions of regret on the part of the King, since they were not easily reconcilable with what, in that writer's judgment, would have been the honorable reception of Bobadilla and Roldan, had they

1500. December 17. Columbus at Court.

escaped the fate of the tempests which later overwhelmed them. When the first warmth of Columbus's reception had subsided, there would have been no reason to suspect that those absent servants of the Crown would have been denied a suitable welcome.

Herrera tells us of the touching character of this interview of December 17; how the Queen burst into tears, and the emotional Admiral cast himself on the ground at her feet. When Columbus could speak, he began to recall the reasons for which he had been imprisoned, and rehearsed them with humble and exculpatory professions. He forgot that in the letter which so excited their sympathy he had denied that he knew any such reasons, and the sovereigns forgot it too. The meeting had awakened the tenderer parts of their natures, and their hearts went out to him. They made verbal promises of largesses and professions of restitution, but Harrisse could find no written expressions of this kind, till in the instructions of March 14, 1502, when they expressed their directions for his guidance during his next voyage. The Admiral grew confident, as of old, in their presence. He had always reached a coign of vantage in his personal intercourse with the Queen. He had evidently not lost that power. He began to picture his return to Santo Domingo with the triumph that he now enjoyed. It was a hollow hope. He was never again to be Viceroy of the Indies.

The disorders in Española were but a part of the reasons why it was now decided to suspend the patented rights of the Admiral, if not permanently to deny the further exercise of them. We have seen how the government had committed itself to other discoveries, profiting, as it did, by the maps which Columbus had sent back to Spain. These discoveries were a new source of tribute which could not be neglected. Rival nations too were alert, and ships of the Portuguese and of the English had been found prowling about within the unquestioned limits allowed to Spain by the new treaty line of Tordesillas. At the north and at the south these same powers were pushing their search, to see if perchance portions of the new regions could not be found to project so far east as to bring them on the Portuguese side of that same line. Portugal had already claimed that Cabral had found such territory

*Columbus suspended from power.*

*Other explorers in American waters.*

*Portuguese claims.*

under the equator and south of it.   An eastward projection of
Brazil at the south, twenty degrees and more, is very common
in the contemporary Portuguese maps.

On the 13th of May, 1501, a new Portuguese fleet of three
ships, under the command of Gonçalo Coelho, sailed
from Lisbon to develop the coast of the southern
Vera Cruz, as South America was now called, and to
see if a way could be found through it to the Moluccas.   In
June, the fleet, while at the Cape de Verde Islands, met Cabral
with his vessels on their return from India.   Here it was that
Cabral's interpreter, Gasparo, communicated the particulars
of Cabral's discovery to Vespucius, who was, as seems pretty
clear, though by no means certain, on board this outward-bound
fleet.   A letter exists, brought to light by Count
Baldelli Boni, not, however, in the hand of Vespucius,
in which the writer, under date of June 4, gave the
results of his note-takings with Cabral to Pier Francisco de
Medici.   Varnhagen is in some doubt about the genuineness of
this document.   Indeed, the historian, if he weighs all the testimony that has been adduced for and against the participancy
of Vespucius in this voyage, can hardly be quite sure that the
Florentine was aboard at all, and Santarem is confident he was
not.   Navarrete thinks he was perhaps there in some subordinate capacity.   Humboldt is staggered at the profession of Vespucius in still keeping the Great Bear above the horizon at 32°
south, since it is lost after reaching 26°.

With all this doubt, we have got to make something out of
another letter, which in the published copy purports to have
been written in 1503 about this voyage by Vespucius himself,
and from it we learn that his ship had struck the coast at Cape
St. Roque, on August 17, 1501.   The discoverers reached and
named Cape St. Augustine on August 28.   On November 1,
they were at Bahia.   By the 3d of April, 1502, they had
reached the latitude of 52° south, when, driven off the coast in
a severe gale, they made apparently the island of Georgia,
whence they stood over to Africa, and reached Lisbon on September, 7, 1502.   By what name Vespucius called this South
American coast we do not know, for his original Italian text is
lost, but the *Mundus Novus* of the Latin paraphrase or version
raised a feeling of expectancy that something new had really

*1501. May 13. Coelho's voyage.*

*Was Vespu-
cius on this
voyage?*

# Mundus Nouus

¶ De natura et moribus z ceteris id gnis gētᵹ
que i nouo mūdo opeła z impēsis sereniſſimi
portugallie regis superioribus ānis inuento

Albericus vesputius Laurētio petri de medicis Salutē plurimā dicit
Uperiorib⁹ diebus satis ample tibi ſcripſi de reditu meo ab no
uis illis regionib⁹ quas z claſſe. z impenſis. z mandato iſtius
sereniſſimi portugallie regis pquesuimus z iuenimus quaſcᵹ
nouū mundū appellare licet Quādo apud maiores noſtros nulla de ip
ſis fuerit habita cognitio z audientib⁹ ōnib⁹ ſit nouiſſima res. Ec̄m hec
opinionē noſtroᵹ antiquoᵹ excedit. cū illoᵹ maior pars dicat vltra line
am equinoctialē. z versus meridiem nō eſſe ᵽtinentē. sed mare tm̄ quod
atlanticū vocaē z ſi qui eoꝝ ᵽtinentē ibi eſſe affirmauerūt eā eſſe terram
habitabilē multis rōnib⁹ negauerūt Sed hanc eoꝝ opinionē eſſe falſaᵹ
z veritati oīo ᵽtrariam:hec mea vltima nauigatio declarauit:cū in ᵽti
bus illis meridianis:ᵽtinentē inueuerim frequētioꝛib⁹ populis. z aīa
lib⁹ habitatā. ᵹ noſtram Europam seu Aſiam vel Africā. z ū sup aerē
magis ᵽatum z amenū. ᵹm qualis alia regione a nob! cognita prout
inferius intelliges. vbrsuccincte tantū reꝝ capita ſcribemus. et res dig
niores annotatioue. z memoria que a me vel viſe. vel audite in hoc nouo
mundo fuere. vt infra patebit.

Roſpero curſu quartodecimo mēſis Maḣ Milleſimo ᵹngen
teſimo optimo receſſimus ab Olyſippo mādāte ᵽ ſato rege cū
trib⁹ nauib⁹ ad inquirendas nouas regiones bⁱ⁹ auſtrū Ui
ginti menſib⁹ ᵽtinenter nauigauimus ad meridiē Cuius nauigatōis oꝛ
do talis eſt Nauigatio noſtra fuit ᵽ insulas fortunatas. ſic olim dictas
nūc aſit appellātur insule magne canarie. que sunt in tercio climate. z in
ᵹſinib⁹ habitatio occidentis I nde ᵽ oceanū totū littus africū. z ᵽtē ethi
opie ᵽcurruimus vſqᵹ ad promontoꝛiū ethiopū. ſic a ᵽtholomeo dictū qꝺ
nūc a noſtris appellat Caput viride. z ab ethiopibus Beſeghice. z regio
illa mandinga gradib⁹ quattuordecim vltra torridam zonam a linea e
quinoctiali verſus Septētrionē ᵹ a nigris gētib⁹. z populis habitatur
Ibi reſumptis virib⁹. z neceſſarijs noſtre nauigationi ertuiimus ancho
ras z erpandimus vela ventis. z noſtrū iter ᵽ vaſtiſſimū oceanū dirige
tes versus antarcticum ᵽarſuper ᵽoccidentē inflerimus ᵽ ventum. qui
Uulturnus dicē. z adiequa receſſimus a dicto promontoꝛio duū men
ſium. z triū dierū ſpacio nauigauimus antecᵹ vlla terra nob! appareret
In ea aſit marie vaſtitate quid paſſi fuerimus ᵹ naufragi pericula. z cᵹ
coꝛpis incōmoda ſuſtinuerimus ᵹbuſcᵹ arietatib⁹ aīmi laboꝛauimus.
eſtimationi eoꝝ relinquo. qui multarū rerū experientia optane noꝛūt
ᵹꝺ ſit incerta querere. aᵹ an ſi ſint ignoꝛantes inueſtigare. z vt vno vbo
vniuerſa pſtringam ſcies qꝺ ex dich⁹ ſeraginta septem quib⁹ nauigaui
mus ᵽtinuos Quadꝛagita quatuoꝛ habuim⁹ cū pluuia. tonitruis z co
ruſcationib⁹. ita obſcuros. vt neqᵹ ſolem in die neqᵹ ſerenum cełū in octe

MUNDUS NOVUS, first page.

been found, distinct from the spicy East. Varnhagen is convinced that Vespucius, different from Columbus, had
awakened to the conception of an absolutely new
quarter of the earth. There is little ground for the
belief, however, in its full extent and confidence. The little
tract had in it the elements of popularity, and in 1504 and 1505
the German and French presses gave it currency in several editions in the Latin tongue, whence it was turned into Italian,
German, and Dutch, spreading through Europe the fame of
Vespucius. We trace to this voyage the origin of the nomenclature of the coast of the South American continent which then
grew up, and is represented in the earlier maps, like that of
Lorenz Fries, for instance, in 1504.

A letter dated August 12, 1507, preserved in Tritemius's
*Epistolarum familiarum libri duo* (1536), has been thought to
refer to a printed map which showed the discoveries
of Vespucius down to 10° south. This map is unknown, apparently, as the particulars given concerning it do not agree with the map of Ruysch, the only one, so
far as known, to antedate that epistle. It is possibly the missing map which Waldseemüller is thought to have first made,
and which became the prototype of the recognized Waldseemüller map of the Ptolemy of 1513, and was possibly the one
from which the Cantino map, yet to be described, was
perfected in other parts than those of the Cortereal
discoveries. This anterior map may have been merely
an early state of the plate, and Lelewel gives reasons for believing that early impressions of this map were in the market in
1507.

Thus while Columbus was nurturing his deferred hopes, neglected and poor, and awaiting what after all was but
a tantalizing revival of royal interest, the rival Portuguese, acting most probably under the influences of
Columbus's own countryman, this Florentine, were stretching
farther towards the true western route to the Moluccas than the
Admiral had any conception of. Vespucius was also at the
same time unwittingly asserting claims which should in the end
rob the Great Discoverer of the meed of bestowing his name on
the new continent which he had just as unwittingly discovered.
The contrast is of the same strange impressiveness which

marks so many of the improbable turns in the career of Columbus.

Meanwhile, what was going on in the north, where Portugal was pushing her discoveries in the region already explored by Cabot? The Spaniards had been dilatory here. The monarchs, May 6, 1500, while they were distracted with the reports of the disquietude of Española, had *1500. Spanish purposes at the north.* turned their attention in this direction, and had thought of sending ships into the seas which "Sebastian Cabot had discovered." They had done nothing, however, though Navarrete finds that explorations thitherward, under **Juan Dornelos** and **Ojeda**, had been planned.

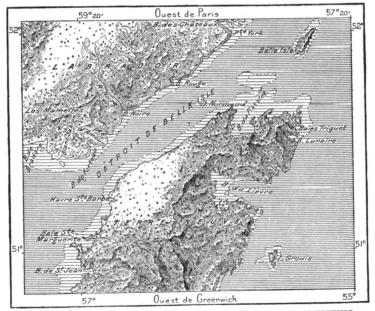

STRAITS OF BELLE ISLE, SHOWING SITE OF EARLY NORMAN FISHING STATION AT BRADORE. [After Reclus's *L'Amerique.*]

If we may believe some of the accounts of explorations this way on the part of the Bretons and Normans, they had founded a settlement called Brest on the Labra- *Bretons and Normans at the north.* dor coast, just within the Straits of Belle Isle, on a bay now called Bradore, as early as 1500. It is said that traces

*Quittance écrite et signee par Gaspar*
*Corte-Real, à Lisbonne, le 21 avril 1501*

**MS. OF GASPAR CORTEREAL.**
[From Harrisse's *Cortereal, Postscriptum*, 1883.]

of their houses can be still seen there. But there is no definite contemporary record of their exploits. We have such records of the Portuguese movements, though not through Spanish sources. Unaccountably, Peter Martyr, who kept himself alert for all such impressions, makes no reference to any Portuguese voyages; and it is only when we come down to Gomara (1551) that we find a Spanish writer reverting to the narratives. In doing so, Gomara makes, at the same time, some confusion in the chronology.

Portugal had missed a great opportunity in discrediting Columbus, but she had succeeded in finding one in Da Gama. She was now in wait for a chance to mate her southern route with a western, or rather with a northern, — at any rate, with one which would give her some warrant for efforts not openly in violation of the negotiations which had followed upon the Bull of Demarcation. Opportunely, word came to Lisbon of the successes of the Cabot voyages, and there was the probability of islands and interjacent passages at the north very like the geographical configuration which the Spaniards had found farther south. To appearances, Cabot had met with such land on the Portuguese side of the division line of the treaty of Tordesillas. Cortereal voyages.

King Emanuel had a vassal in Gaspar Cortereal, who at this time was a man about fifty years old, and he had already in years past conducted explorations oceanward, though we have no definite knowledge of their results. It has been conjectured that Columbus may have known him; but there is nothing to make this certain. At any rate, there was little in the surroundings of Columbus at Española, when he was subjected to chains in the summer of 1500, to remind him of any northern rivalry, though the visits of Ojeda and Pinzon to that island were foreboding. It was just at that time that Cortereal sailed away from Portugal to the northwest. He discovered the Terra do Labrador, which he named apparently because he thought its natives would increase very handily the slave labor of Portugal. To follow up this quest, Gaspar sailed again with three ships, May 15, 1501, which is the date given by Damian de Goes. Harrisse is not so sure, but finds that Gaspar was still in port April 21, 1501. Cortereal ran a course a little more to the west, and 1500. Gaspar Cortereal. 1501. Gaspar Cortereal again.

came to a coast, two thousand miles away, as was reckoned, and skirted it without finding any end. He decided from the volume of its rivers, that it was probably a continental area. The voyagers found in the hands of some natives whom they saw a broken sword and two silver earrings, evidently of Italian

*Quittance écrite et signée par Miguel*
*Corte-Real, à Malaga, le 7 août 1501.*

MS. OF MIGUEL CORTEREAL.
[From Harrisse's *Cortereal, Postscriptum.*]

make. The natural inference is that they had fallen among tribes which Cabot had encountered on his second voyage, if indeed these relics did not represent earlier visitors. Cortereal also found in a high latitude a country which he called *Terra Verde.* Two of the vessels returned safely, bringing home some of the natives, and the capture of such, to make good the name bestowed during the previous voyage, seems to have been the principal aim of the explorers. The third ship, with Gaspar on board, was never afterwards heard of.

It so happened that Pasqualigo, the Venetian ambassador in

Lisbon, made record of the return of the first of these vessels, in a letter which he wrote from Lisbon, October 19, 1501; and it is from this, which made part of the well-known *Paesi novamente retrovati* (Vicenza, 1507), that we derive what little knowledge we have of these voyages. The reports have fortunately been supplemented by Harrisse in a dispatch dated October 17, 1501, which he has produced from the archives of Modena, in which one Alberto Cantino tells how he heard the captain of the vessel which arrived second tell the story to the king. This dispatch to the Duke of Ferrara was followed by a map showing the new discoveries. This cartographical record had been known for some years before it was reproduced by Harrisse on a large scale. It is apparent from this that the discoverers believed, or feigned to believe, that the new-found regions lay westward from Ireland half-way to the American coasts. The evidence that they feigned to believe rather than that they knew these lands to be east of their limitary line may not be found; but it was probably some such doubt of their honesty which induced Robert Thorne, of Bristol, to speak of the purpose which the Portuguese had in falsifying their maps. Nor were the frauds confined to maps. Translations were distorted and narratives perverted. Biddle, in his *Life of Cabot*, points out a marked instance of this, where the simple language of Pasqualigo is· twisted so as to convey the impression of a long acquaintance of the natives with Italian commodities, as proving that the Italians had formerly visited the region, — a hint which Biddle supposed the Zeni narrative at a later date was contrived to sustain, so as to deceive many writers. We shall soon revert to this Cantino map.

*Original sources on the Cortereal voyages.*

*Portuguese habit of concealing information.*

The voyage which Miguel Cortereal is known to have undertaken in the summer of 1501, which has been connected with this series of northwest voyages, is held by Harrisse, in his revised opinions, not to have been to the New World at all, but to have been conducted against the Grand Turk, and Cortereal returned from it on November 4, 1501.

*1501. Miguel Cortereal.*

To search for the missing Gaspar Cortereal, Miguel, on May 10, 1502, again sailed to the northwest with two or three ships. They found the same coast as before, searched it without success, and returned again with-

*1502. Miguel Cortereal again.*

out a leader; for Miguel's ship missed the others at a rendez-
vous and was never again heard of.

The endeavors of the Portuguese in this direction did not
end here; and the region thus brought by them to the attention of the cartographer soon acquired in their maps the name
Terre des        of *Terre des Cortereal*, or *Terra dos Corte reals*, or,
Cortereal.      as Latinized by Sylvanus, *Regalis Domus*.   There is
little, however, to connect these earliest ventures with later history, except perhaps that from their experiences it is that a
Straits of      vague cartographical conception of the fabled Straits
Anian.         of Anian confronts us in many of the maps of the
latter half of the sixteenth century.   No one has made it quite
sure whence the appellation or even the idea of such a strait
came.  By some it has been thought to have grown out of Marco
Polo's Ania, which was conceived to be in the north.  By Navarrete, Humboldt, and others it has been made to grow in some
way out of these Cortereal voyages, and Humboldt supposes that
the entrance to Hudson Bay, under 60° north latitude, was
thought at that time to lead to some sort of a transcontinental
passage, going it is hardly known where.   The name does not
seem at first to have been magnified into all its later associations
of a kingdom, or "regnum" of Anian, as the Latin nomenclature then had it.   Its great city of Quivira did not appear
till some time after the middle of the sixteenth century, and
then it was not always quite certain to the cosmographical mind
whether all this magnificence might not better be placed on the
Asiatic side of such a strait.   This imaginary channel was
made for a long period to run along the parallels of latitudes
somewhere in the northern regions of the New World, after
America had begun generally to have its independent existence
recognized, south of the Arctic regions at least.   The next stage
of the belief violently changed the course of the straits across
the parallels, prefiguring the later discovered Bering's Straits;
and this is made prominent in maps of Zalterius (1566) and
Mercator (1569), and in the maps of those who copied these
masters.

It took thirty years for the Cortereal discoveries to work
Spanish        their way into the conceptions of the Spanish map-
maps.         makers.   Whether this dilatory belief came from lack
of information, obliviousness, or simply from an heroic persist-

ence in ignoring what was not their boast, is a question to be decided through an estimate of the Spanish character. There seems, however, to have been interest enough on the part of a single Italian noble to seek information at once, as we see from the Cantino map ; but the knowledge was not, nevertheless,

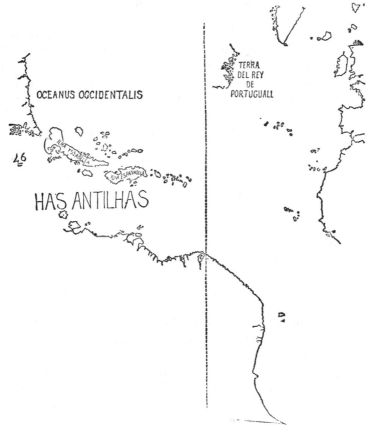

THE CANTINO MAP.

apparently a matter of such interest but it could escape Ruysch in 1508. Not till Sylvanus issued his edition of Maps of the Ptolemy, in 1511, did any signs of these Cortereal Cortereal discoveries. expeditions appear on an engraved map.

Only a few years have passed since students of these carto-graphical fields were first allowed free study of this The Cantino Cantino map. It is, after La Cosa, the most inter- map. 1502.

esting of all the early maps of the American coast as its configuration had grown to be comprehended in the ten years which
followed the first voyage of Columbus.

There are three special points of interest in this chart.   The
The Corte-
real discov-
eries east of
the line of
demarca-
tion. first is the evident purpose of the maker, when sending
it (1502) to his correspondent in Italy, to render it
clear that the coasts which the Portuguese had tracked
in the northwest Atlantic were sufficiently protuberant towards the rising sun to throw them on the Portuguese side
of the revised line of demarcation.   It is by no means certain,
however, in doing so, that they pretended their discoveries to
have been other than neighboring to Asia, since a peninsula
north of these regions is called a " point of Asia."   The ordinary belief of geographers at that time was that our modern
Greenland was an extension of northern Europe.   So it does
Terra Verde. not seem altogether certain that the *Terra Verde* of
Cortereal can be held to be identical with its name-
sake of the Sagas.

The second point of interest is what seems to be the connection between this map and those which had emanated
Columbus
and the Can-
tino map in
the Paria
region. from the results of the Columbus voyages, directly
or indirectly.   Columbus had made a chart of his
track through the Gulf of Paria, and had sent it to
Spain, and Ojeda had coursed the same region by it.   We
know from a letter of Angelo Trivigiano, the secretary of the
Venetian ambassador in Spain, dated at Granada, August 21,
1501, and addressed to Domenico Malipiero, that at that
time Columbus, who had ingratiated himself with the writer of
Columbus
in want. the letter, was living without money, in great want,
and out of favor with the sovereigns.   This letter-
writer then speaks of his intercession with Peter Martyr to
have copies of his narrative of the voyages of Columbus made,
and of his pleading with Columbus himself to have transcripts
of his own letters to his sovereigns given to him, as well as a
map of the new discoveries from the Admiral's own charts,
which he then had with him in Granada.

There are three letters of Trivigiano, but the originals are
not known.   Foscarini in 1752 used them in his *Della Lette-
ratura veneziana*, as found in the library of Jacopo Soranzo ;
but both these originals and Foscarini's copies have eluded the

search of Harrisse, who gives them as printed or abstracted by Zurla.

What we have is not supposed to be the entire text, and we may well regret the loss of the rest. Trivigiano says of the map that he expected it to be extremely well executed on a large scale, giving ample details of the country which had been discovered. He refers to the delays incident to sending to Palos to have it made, because persons capable of such work could only be found there.

No such copy as that made for Malipiero is now known. Harrisse thinks that if it is ever discovered·it will be very like the Cantino map, with the Cortereal discoveries left out. This same commentator also points out that there are certainly indications in the Cantino map that the maker of it, in drafting the region about the Gulf of Paria at least, worked either from Columbus's map or from some copy of it, for his information seems to be more correct than that which La Cosa followed.

The third point of interest in this Cantino map, and one which has given rise to opposing views, respects that coast which is drawn in it north of the completed Cuba, and which at first glance is taken with little ques- *What is the coast north of Cuba?* tion for the Atlantic coast of the United States from Florida up. Is it such? Did the cartographers of that time have anything more than conjecture by which to run such a coast line?

A letter of Pasqualigo, dated at Lisbon, October 18, 1501, and found by Von Ranke at Venice in the diary of Marino Sanuto, — a running record of events, which begins in 1496, — has been interpreted by Humboldt as signifying that at this time it was known among the Portuguese observers of the maritime reports that a continental stretch of coast connected the Spanish discoveries in the Antilles with those of the Portuguese at the north. Harrisse questions this interpretation, and considers that what Humboldt thinks knowledge was simply a tentative conjecture. If this knowledge is represented in the Cantino map, there is certainly too great remoteness in the regions of the Cortereal discoveries to form such a connection. It is of course possible that the map is a falsification in this respect, to make the line of demarcation serve the Portuguese interests, and such falsification is by no means improbable.

It will be remembered that the La Cosa map showed no hesitancy in placing the Antilles on the coast of Asia, and put the region of the Cabot landfall on the coast of Cathay. Consequently, the difference between the La Cosa and the Cantino The Cantino maps for this region north of Cuba is phenomenal. and La Cosa In these two or three years (1500–1502), something maps at va-riance. had come to pass which seemed to raise the suspicion that this northern continental line might possibly not be Asiatic after all, or at least it might not have the trend or contour which had before been given it on the Asiatic theory. It is an interesting question from whom this information could have come. Was this coast in the Cantino map indeed not North American, but the coast of Yucatan, misplaced, as one conjecture has been? But this involves a recognition of some voyage on the Yucatan coast of which we have no record. Was it the result of one of the voyages of Vespucius, and was Varnhagen right in tracking that navigator up the east Florida shore? Was it drawn by some unauthorized Spanish mariners, who were — we know Columbus complained of such — invading his vested rights, or perhaps by some of those to whom he was finally induced to concede the privilege of exploration? Was it found by some English explorer who answers the description of Ojeda in 1501, when he complains that people of this nation had been in these regions some years before? Was it the discovery of some of those against whom a royal prohibition of discovery was issued by the Catholic kings, September 3, 1501? Was it anything more than the result of some vague information from the Lucayan Indians, aided by a sprinkling of supposable names, respecting a land called Bimini lying there Bimini. away? Eight or nine years later, Peter Martyr, in the map which he published in 1511, seems to have thought so, and certain stories of a fountain of youth in regions lying in that direction were already prevalent, as Martyr also shows us. The fact seems to be that we have no Spanish map between the making of La Cosa's in 1500 and this one of Peter Martyr in 1511, to indicate any Spanish acquaintance with such a northern coast.

This map of 1511, if it is honest enough to show what the Peter Mar-tyr's map. 1511. Spanish government knew of Florida, is indicative of but the vaguest information, and its divulgence of that coast may, in Brevoort's opinion, account for the rarity of the chart, in view of the determination of Spain to keep control as far as she could of all cartographical records of what her explorers found òut.

It is evident, if we accept the theory of this Cantino map showing the coast of the United States, that we have in it a delineation nearer the source by several years than those which modern students have longer known in the Waldseemüller map of 1508, the Stobnicza map of 1512, the Reisch map of 1515, and the so-called Admiral's map of 1513, — all which arose, it is very clear, from much the same source as this of Cantino. What is that source ? There are some things that seem to indicate that this source was the description of Portuguese rather than of other seamen. This belief falls in with what we know of the cordial relations of Portugal and Duke René, under whose auspices Waldseemüller at least worked. Thus it would seem that while Spain was impeding cartographical knowledge through the rest of Europe, Portugal was so assiduously helping it that for many years the Ptolemies and other central and southern European publications were making known the cosmographical ideas which originated in Portugal.

It has been already said that Humboldt in his *Examen Critique* (iv. 262) refers to a letter which indicates that in October, 1501, the Portuguese had already learned, or it may be only conjectured, that the coast from the region of the Antilles ran uninterruptedly north till it united with the snowy shores of the northern discoveries. This, then, seems to indicate that it was a Portuguese source that supplied conjecture, if not fact, to the maker of the Cantino map. Harrisse's solution of this matter, as also mentioned already, is that the letter found by Von Ranke and the letter which we know Pasqualigo sent to Venice about the Cortereal voyages were one and the same, and that it was rather conjecture than fact that the Portuguese possessed at this time.

The obvious difficulty in the cartographical problem for the Portuguese was, as has been said, to make it appear that they were not disregarding the agreement at Tordesillas while they were securing a region for sovereignty. We have already said that this accounts for the extreme eastern position found in the Cantino and the cognate maps of the Newfoundland region, which, as thus drawn, it was not easy to connect with the coast line of eastern Florida. Hence the open sea-gap which exists between them in the maps, while the evidence of the descriptions would make the coast line continuous.

We have thus suggested possible solutions of this continental shore above Florida. It must be confessed that the truth is far from patent, and we must yet wait perhaps a long time before we discover, if indeed we ever do, to whom this mapping of the coast, as shown in the Cantino map, was due.

There are evidences other than those of this Cantino map
Was the Florida coast known? that the Portuguese were in this Floridian region in the early years of the sixteenth century, and Lelewel tried to work out their discoveries from scattered data, in a conjectural map, which he marks 1501–1504, and which resembles the Ptolemy map of 1513. The bringing forward of the Cantino map confirms much of the supposed cartography.

There is one theory which to some minds gives a very easy solution of this problem, without requiring belief in any knowledge, clandestine or public, of such a land.

Brevoort in his *Verrazano* had already been inclined to the view later emphasized by Stevens in his *Schöner*, and reiterated by Coote in his editorial revision of that posthumous work.

Stevens is content to allow Ocampo, in 1508, to have been the earliest probable discoverer of this coast, and Ponce de Leon as the original attested finder in 1513.

The Stevens theory is that this seeming Florida arose from a
This Cantino coast a duplicated Cuba. Portuguese misconception of the first two voyages of Columbus, by which two regions were thought to have been coasted instead of different sides of the same, and that what others consider an early premonition of Florida and the upper coasts was simply a duplicated Cuba, to make good the Portuguese conception. It is not explained how so strange a misconception of very palpable truths could have arisen, or how a coast trending north and south so far could have been confounded with one stretching at right angles to such a course for so short a distance.

Stevens traces the influence of his " bogus Cuba " in a long series of maps based on Portuguese notions, in which he names those of Waldseemüller (1513), Stobnicza (1512), Schöner (1515, 1520), Reisch (1515), Bordone (1528), Solinus (1520), Friess (1522), and Grynæus (1532 — made probably earlier), as opposed to the Spanish and more truthful view, which is expressed by Ruysch (1507–8) and Peter Martyr, (1511).

It is a proposition not to be dismissed lightly nor accepted triumphantly on our present knowledge. We must wait for further developments.

The fancy that this coast was Asia and that Cuba was Asia might, indeed, have led to the transfer to it at one time of the names which Columbus had placed along the north coast of his supposed peninsular Cuba; but that proves a misplacement of the names, and not a creation of the coast. For a while this continental land was backed up on the maps against a meridian scale, which hid the secret of its western limits, and left it a possible segment of Asia. Then it stood out alone with a north and southwestern line, but with Asia beyond, just as if it were no part of it, and this delineation was common even while there was a division of geographical belief as to North America and Asia being one.

The fact that Cuba, in the drafting of the La Cosa and Cantino maps, is represented as an island has at times Cuba an island. been held to signify that the views of Columbus respecting its peninsular rather than its insular character were not wholly shared by his contemporaries. That foolish act by which, under penalty, the Admiral forced his crew to swear that it was a part of the main might well imply that he expected his assertions would be far from acceptable to other cosmographers. If Varnhagen's opinion as to the track of Vespucius in his voyage of 1497, following the contour of the Gulf of Mexico, be accepted as knowledge of the time, the insularity of Cuba was necessarily proved even at that early day; but it is the opinion of Henry Stevens, as has been already shown, that the green outline of the western parts of Cuba in La Cosa's chart was only the conventional way of expressing an uncertain coast. Consequently it did not imply insularity. If it is to be supposed that the Portuguese had a similar method of expressing uncertainties of coast, they did not employ it in the Cantino map, and Cuba in 1502 is unmistakably an island. It is, moreover, sufficiently like the Cuba of La Cosa to show it was drawn from one and the same prototype. If the maker of the Cantino map followed La Cosa, or a copy of La Cosa, or the material from which La Cosa worked, there is no proof that he ever suspected the peninsularity of Cuba.

Columbus, in his hours of neglect, and amid his unheeded pleas for recognition, during these two grewsome years in Spain, may never have comprehended in their full significance these active efforts of the Portuguese to anticipate his own hopes of a western passage beyond the Golden Chersonesus; but the doings of Mendoza, Cristobal Guerra, and other fellow-subjects of Spain were not wholly unknown to him.

Columbus looking on at other explorations.

In October, 1500, and before Columbus knew just what his reception in Spain was going to be, Rodrigo de Bastidas, accompanied by La Cosa and Vasco Nuñez Balboa, sailed from Cadiz on an expedition that had for its object to secure to the Crown one quarter of the profits, and to make an examination of the coast line beyond the bay of Venezuela, in order that it might be made sure that no channel to an open sea lay beyond. The two caravels followed the shore to Nombre de Dios, and at the narrowest part of the isthmus, without suspecting their nearness to the longed-for sea, the navigators turned back. Finding their vessels unseaworthy, for the worms had riddled their bottoms, they sought a harbor in Española, near which their vessels foundered after they had saved a part of their lading. A little later, this gave Bobadilla a chance to arrest the commander for illicit trade with the natives. This transaction was nothing more, apparently, than the barter of trinkets for provisions, as he was leading his men across the island to the settlements.

1500. October. Bastidas's expedition.

It was while with Bastidas, in 1501–2, that La Cosa reports seeing the Portuguese prowling about the Caribbean and Mexican waters, seeking for a passage to Calicut. It was while on a mission of remonstrance to Lisbon that La Cosa was later arrested and imprisoned, and remained till August, 1504, a prisoner in Portugal.

Portuguese and English in these regions.

We have seen that in 1499 Ojeda had met or heard of English vessels on the coast of Terra Firma, or professed that he had. The Spanish government, suspecting they were but precursors of others who might attempt to occupy the coast, determined on thwarting such purposes, if possible, by anticipating occupation. Ojeda was given the power to lead thither a colony, if he could do it without cost to the Crown, which reserved a due share of his profits. He obtained the assistance of Juan de Vegara and Garcia de Ocampo, and with this back-ing he sailed with four ships from Cadiz in January, 1502, while Columbus was preparing his own little fleet for his last voyage. It was a venture, however, that came to naught. The natives, under ample provocation, proved hos-tile, food was lacking, the leaders quarreled, and the partners of Ojeda, combining, overpowered (May, 1502) their leader, and sent him a prisoner to Española, where he arrived in Septem-ber, 1502.

1502. Jan-uary. Oje-da's voyage.

There has never been any clear definition as to who these Englishmen were, or what was their project, during these earliest years of the sixteenth century. There is evidence that Henry VII. about this time author-ized some ventures in which his countrymen were joint sharers with the Portuguese, but we know nothing further of the regions visited than that the Privy Purse expenses show how some Bristol men received a gratuity for having been at the "Newefounde Launde." There is also a vague notion to be formed from an old entry that Sebastian Cabot himself again visited this region in 1503, and brought home three of the natives, — to say nothing of additional even vaguer suspicions of other ventures of the English at this time.

English in the West Indies.

In enumerating the ocean movements that were now going on, some intimation has been given of the tiresome expectancy of something better which was intermittently beguiling the spirits of Columbus during the eighteen months that he remained in Spain. It is necessary to trace his unhappy life in some detail, though the particulars are not abundant.

Ferdinand had not been unobservant of all these expedition-ary movements, and they were quite as threatening to the Spanish supremacy in the New World as his own personal defection was to the dejected Admiral. It had become very clear that by tying his own hands, as he had in the compact which Columbus was urging to have ob-served, the King had allowed opportunities to pass by which he could profit through the newly aroused enthusiasm of the sea-

Columbus's life in Spain. 1500-1502.

ports.　We have seen that he had, nevertheless, through Fonseca sanctioned the expeditions of Ojeda, Pinzon, and others, and had notably in that of Niño got large profits for the exchequer. He had done this in defiance of the vested rights of Columbus, and there is little doubt that to bring Columbus into disgrace by the loss of his Admiral's power served in part to open the field of discovery more as Ferdinand wished.　With the Viceroy

Ferdinand<br>allows other<br>expeditions.

dethroned and become a waiting suitor, there was little to stay Ferdinand's ambition in sending out other explorers.　His experience had taught him to allow no stipulations on which explorers could found exorbitant demands upon the booty and profit of the ventures.　Anybody could sail westward now, and there was no longer the courage of conviction required to face an unknown sea and find an opposite shore.　Columbus, who had shown the way, was now easily cast off as a useless pilot.

It was not difficult for the King to frame excuses when Columbus urged his reinstatement.　There was no use in sending back an unpopular viceroy before the people of the colony had been quieted.　Give them time.　It might be seasonable enough to send to them their old master when they had forgotten their misfortunes under him.　Perhaps a better man than Bobadilla could be found to still the commotions, and if so he might be sent.　In the face of all this and the King's determination, Columbus could do nothing but acquiesce, and so he gradually made up his mind to bide his time once more.　It was not a new discipline for him.

It was clear from the intelligence which was reaching Spain that Bobadilla would have to be superseded.　Freed

Bobadilla's<br>rule in<br>Española.

from the restraints which had created so much complaint during the rule of Columbus, and even courted with offers of indulgence, the miserable colony at Española readily degenerated from bad to worse.　The new governor had hoped to find that a lack of constraint would do for the people what an excess of it had failed to do.　He erred in his judgment, and let the colony slip beyond his control.　Licentiousness was everywhere.　The only exaction he required was the tribute of gold.　He reduced the proportion which must be surrendered to the Crown from a third to an eleventh, but he so apportioned the labor of the natives to the colonists that the yield of gold grew rapidly, and became more with the tax an eleventh than it had been when it was a third. This inhuman degradation of the poor natives had become an organized misery when, a little later, Las Casas arrived in the colony, and he depicts the baleful contrasts of the Indians and their attractive island. Gold was potent, but it was not potent enough to keep Bobadilla in his place. The representations of the agony of life among the natives were so harrowing that it was decided to send a new governor at once.

The person selected was Nicholas de Ovando, a man of whom Las Casas, who went out with him, gives a high character for justice, sobriety, and graciousness. Perhaps he deserved it. The sympathizers with Columbus *Ovando sent to Española.* find it hard to believe such praise. Ovando was commissioned as governor over all the continental and insular domains, then acquired or thereafter to be added to the Crown in the New World. He was to have his capital at Santo Domingo. He was deputed, with about as much authority as Bobadilla had had, to correct abuses and punish delinquents, and was to take one third of all gold so far stored up, and one half of what was yet to be gathered. He was to monopolize all trade for the Crown. He was to segregate the colonists as much as possible in settlements. No supplies were to be allowed to the people unless they got them through the royal factor. New efforts were to be made through some Franciscans, who accompanied Ovando, to convert the Indians. The natives were to be made to work in the mines as hired servants, paid by the Crown.

It had already become evident that such labor as the mining of gold required was too exhausting for the natives, and the death-rate among them was such that eyes were already opened to the danger of extermination. By a sophistry which suited a sixteenth-century Christian, the existence of this poor race was to be prolonged by introducing the negro race from Africa, to take the heavier burden of the toil, because *Negro slaves to be introduced.* it was believed they would die more slowly under the trial. So it was royally ordered that slaves, born of Africans, in Spain, might be carried to Española. The promise of Columbus's letter to Sanchez was beginning to prove delusive. It was going to require the degradation of two races instead of one. That was all!

To assuage the smart of all this forcible deprivation of his

1501. Co-
lumbus's
property
restored.
power, Columbus was apprised that under a royal order of September 27, 1501, Ovando would see to the restitution of any property of his which Bobadilla had appropriated, and that the Admiral was to be allowed to

His factor.
send a factor in the fleet to look after his interests under the articles which divided the gold and treasure between him and the Crown. To this office of factor Columbus appointed Alonso Sanchez de Carvajal.

The pomp and circumstance of the fleet were like a biting

Ovando's
fleet.
sarcasm to the poor Admiral. One might expect he could have no high opinions of its pilots, for we find him writing to the sovereigns, on February 6, a letter laying before them certain observations on the art of navigation, in which he says: " There will be many who will desire to sail to the discovered islands ; and if the way is known those who have had experience of it may safest traverse it." Perhaps he meant to imply that better pilots were more important than much parade. He in his most favored time had never been fitted out with a fleet of thirty sail, so many of them large ships. He had never carried out so many cavaliers, nor so large a proportion of such persons of rank, as made a shining part of the 2,500 souls now embarked. He could contrast his Franciscan gown and girdle of rope with Ovando's brilliant silks and brocades which the sovereigns authorized him to wear. There was more state in the new governor's bodyguard of twenty-two esquires, mounted and foot, than Columbus had ever dreamed of in Santo Domingo. Instead of vile convicts there were respectable married men with their families, the guaranty of honorable living. So that when the fleet went to sea, Febru-

1502. Feb-
ruary 3. It
sails.
ary 13, 1502, there were hopes that a right method of founding a colony on family life had at last found favor.

The vessels very soon encountered a gale, in which one

1502. April.
Reaches
Santo Do-
mingo.
ship foundered, and from the deck-loads which were thrown over from the rest and floated to the shore it was for a long time apprehended that the fleet had suffered much more severely. A single ship was all that failed finally to reach Santo Domingo about the middle of April, 1502.

Let us turn now to Columbus himself. He had not failed, as we have said, to reach something like mental quiet in the conviction that he could expect nothing but neglect for the present. So his active mind engaged in those visionary and speculative trains of thought wherein, when his body was weary and his spirits harried, he was prone to find relief.

He set himself to the composition of a maundering and erratic paper, which, under the title of *Libros de las proficias*, is preserved in the Biblioteca Colombina at Seville. The manuscript, however, is not in the handwriting of Columbus, and no one has thought it worth while to print the whole of it. *Columbus's Libros de las proficias.*

In it there is evidence of his study, with the assistance of a Carthusian friar, of the Bible and of the early fathers of the Church, and it shows, as his letter to Juan's nurse had shown, how he had at last worked himself into the belief that all his early arguments for the westward passage were vain; that he had simply been impelled by something that he had not then suspected; and that his was but a predestined mission to make good what he imagined was the prophecy of Isaiah in the Apocalypse. This having been done, there was *Isaiah's prophecy.* something yet left to be accomplished before the anticipated eclipse of all earthly things came on, and that was the conquest of the Holy Land, for which he was the appointed leader. He addressed this driveling exposition, together with an urgent appeal for the undertaking of the crusade, to Ferdinand and Isabella, but without convincing them that such a self-appointed instrument of God was quite worthy of their employment. *Conquest of the Holy Land.*

The great catastrophe of the world's end was, as Columbus calculated, about 155 years away. He based his estimate upon an opinion of St. Augustine that the world would endure for 7,000 years; and upon King Alfonso's reckoning that nearly 5,344 years had passed when Christ appeared. The 1,501 years since made the sum 6,845, leaving out of the 7,000 the 155 years of his belief. *End of the world.*

He also fancied, or professed to believe, in a letter which he subsequently wrote to the Pope, that the present deprivation of his titles and rights was the work of Satan, who came to see that the success of Columbus in the Indies *Defeated by Satan.*

would be only a preparation for the Admiral's long-vaunted recovery of the Holy Land. The Spanish government meanwhile knew, and they had reason to know, that their denial of his prerogatives had quite as much to do with other things as with a legion of diabolical powers. Unfortunately for Columbus, neither they nor the Pope were inclined to act on any interpretation of fate that did not include a civil policy of justice and prosperity.

These visions of Columbus were harmless, and served to beguile him with pious whimsies. But the mood did not last. He
His geographical whimsies. next turned to his old geographical problems. The Portuguese were searching north and south for the passage that would lead to some indefinite land of spices, and afford a new way to reach the trade with Calicut and the Moluccas, which at this time, by the African route, was pouring wealth into the Portuguese treasury in splendid contrast to the scant return from the Spanish Indies. He harbored a belief that a better passage might yet be found beyond the Caribbean Sea. La Cosa, in placing that vignette of St. Christopher and the infant Christ athwart the supposed juncture of Asia and
Would seek a passage westerly through the Caribbean Sea. South America, had eluded the question, not solved it. Columbus would now go and attack the problem on the spot. His expectation to find a desired opening in that direction was based on physical phenomena, but in fact on only partial knowledge of them. He had been aware of the strong currents which set westward through the Caribbean Sea, and he had found them still flowing west when he had reached the limit of his exploration of the southern coast of Cuba. Bastidas, who had just pushed farther west on the main coast, had turned back while the currents were still flowing on, along what seemed an endless coast beyond. Bastidas did not arrive in Spain till some months after Columbus had sailed, for he was detained a prisoner in Española at this time. Some tidings of his experiences may have reached Spain, however, or the Admiral may not have got his confirmation of these views
Columbus misunderstands the currents. till he found that voyager at Santo Domingo, later. Columbus had believed Cuba to be another main, confining this onward waste of waters to the south of it. It was clear to him that such currents must find an outlet to the west, and if found, such a passage would carry him on to

the sea that washed the Golden Chersonesus. He indeed died without knowing the truth. This same current, deflected about Honduras and Yucatan, sweeps by a northerly circuit round the great Gulf of Mexico, and, passing out by the Cape of Florida, flows northward in what we now call the Gulf Stream.  Gulf Stream.

There is nothing in all the efforts of the canonizers more absurdly puerile than De Lorgues's version of the way in which Columbus came to believe in this strait. He had a vision, and saw it! The only difficulty in the matter was that the poor Admiral was so ecstatic in his hallucination that he mistook the narrowness of an isthmus for the narrowness of a strait!

The proposition of such a search was not inopportune in the eyes of Ferdinand. There were those about the Court who thought it unwise to give further employment to a man who was degraded from his honors; but to the King it was a convenient way of removing a persistent and active-minded complainant from the vicinity of the Court, to send him on some quest or other, and no one could tell but there was some truth in his new views. It was worth while to let him try. So once again, by the royal permission, Columbus set himself to work equipping a little fleet. It was the autumn of 1501 when he appeared in Seville with the sovereign's commands. He varied his work of preparing the ships with spending some part of his time on his treatise on the prophecies, while a friar named Gaspar Gorricio helped him in the labor. Early in 1502 he had got it into shape to present to the sovereigns, and in February he wrote the letter to Pope Alexander VII. which has already been mentioned.  A convenient relief to Ferdinand to send Columbus on such a search.  1501. Columbus prepares to equip his ships.  1502. February. Columbus writes to the Pope.

As the preparations went on, he began to think of Española, and how he might perhaps be allowed to touch there; but orders were given to him forbidding it on the outward passage, though suffering it on the return, for it was hoped by that time that the disorders of the island would be suppressed. It was arranged that the Adelantado and his own son Ferdinand should accompany him, and some interpreters learned in Arabic were put on board, in case his success put him in contact with the people of the Great Khan.  Forbidden to touch at Española.

The suspension of his rights lay heavily on his mind, and early in March, 1502, he ventured to refer to the subject once more in a letter to the sovereigns. They replied, March 14, in some instructions which they sent from Valencia de Torre, advising him to keep his mind at ease, and leave such things to the care of his son Diego. They assured him that in due time the proper restitution of all would be made, and that he must abide the time.

He had already taken steps to secure a perpetuity of the record of his honors and deeds, if nothing else could be permanent. It was at Seville, January 5, 1502, that Columbus, appearing before a notary in his own house, attested that series of documents respecting his titles and prerogatives which are so religiously preserved at Genoa. These papers, as we have seen, were copies which Columbus had lately secured from the documents in the Spanish Admiralty, among which he was careful to include the revocation of June 2, 1497, of the licenses which, much to Columbus's annoyance, had been granted in 1495, to allow others than himself to explore in the new regions. We may not wonder at this, but we can hardly conjecture why a transaction of his which had caused as much as anything his wrongs, mortification, and the loss of his dignities should have been as assiduously preserved. These are the royal orders which enabled Columbus, at his request, to fill up his colony with unshackled convicts. This he might as well have let the world forget. The royal order requiring Bobadilla or his successor to restore all the sequestered property of Columbus, and the new declaration of his rights, he might well have been anxious to preserve.

There was one other act to be done which lay upon his mind, now that the time of sailing approached. He wished to make provision that his heirs should be able to confer some favor on his native city, and he directed that investments should be made for that purpose in the Bank of St. George at Genoa. He then notified the managers of that bank of his intention in a letter which is so characteristic of his moods of dementation that it is here copied as Harrisse translates it : —

*margin notes:*
1502. January 5. Columbus's care to preserve his titles, etc.

Columbus and the Bank of St. George.

HIGH NOBLE LORDS : — Although the body walks about here, the heart is constantly over there. Our Lord has conferred on me the greatest favor to any one since David. The results of my undertaking already appear, and would shine greatly were they not concealed by the blindness of the government. I am going again to the Indies under the auspices of the Holy Trinity, soon to return; and since I am mortal, I leave it with my son Diego that you receive every year, forever, one tenth of the entire revenue, such as it may be, for the purpose of reducing the tax upon corn, wine, and other provisions. If that tenth amounts to something, collect it. If not, take at least the will for the deed. I beg of you to entertain regard for the son I have recommended to you. Nicolo de Oderigo knows more about my own affairs than I do myself, and I have sent him the transcripts of any privileges and letters for safe-keeping. I should be glad if you could see them. My lords, the King and Queen endeavor to honor me more than ever. May the Holy Trinity preserve your noble persons and increase your most magnificent House. Done in Sevilla, on the second day of April, 1502.

The chief Admiral of the ocean, Viceroy and Governor-General of the islands and continent of Asia and the Indies, of my lords, the King and Queen, their Captain-General of the sea, and of their Council.

S.

.S.A.S.

X M Y

χῥο FERENS.

The letter was handed by Columbus to a Genoese banker, then in Spain, Francisco de Rivarolla, who forwarded it to Oderigo; but as this ambassador was then on his way to Spain, Harrisse conjectures that he did not receive the letter till his return to Genoa, for the reply of the bank is dated December 8, 1502, long after Columbus had sailed. This response was addressed to Diego, and inclosed a letter to the Admiral. The great affection and good will of Columbus towards " his first country " gratified them inexpressibly, as they said to the son; and to the father they acknowledged the act of his intentions to be " as great and extraordinary as that

1502. December 8. The bank's reply.

which has been recorded about any man in the world, considering that by your own skill, energy, and prudence, you have discovered such a considerable portion of this earth and sphere of the lower world, which during so many years past and centuries had remained unknown to its inhabitants."

The letter of Columbus to the bank remained on the files of that institution — a single sheet of paper, written on one side only, and pierced in the centre for the thread of the file — undiscovered till the archivist of the bank, attracted by the indorsement, M D II, EPLA D. ADMIRATI DON XROPHORI COLUMBI, identified it in 1829, when, at the request of the authorities of Genoa, it was transferred to the keeping of its archivists. It is to be seen at the city hall, to-day, placed between two glass plates, so that either side of the paper can be read.

# CHAPTER XIX.

## THE FOURTH VOYAGE.

### 1502–1504.

THEIR Majesties, in March, 1502, were evidently disturbed at Columbus's delays in sailing, since such detentions brought to them nothing but the Admiral's continued importunities. They now instructed him to sail without the least delay. Nevertheless, Columbus, who had given out, as Trivigiano reports, that he expected his discoveries on this voyage to be more surprising and helpful than any yet made, his purpose being, in fact, to circumnavigate the globe, did not sail from Cadiz till May 9 or 11, 1502, — the accounts vary. He had four caravels, from fifty to seventy tons each, and they carried in all not over one hundred and fifty men.

Apparently not forgetting the Admiral's convenient reservation respecting the pearls in his third voyage, their Majesties in their instructions particularly enjoined upon him that all gold and other precious commodities which he might find should be committed at once to the keeping of François de Porras, who was sent with him to the end that the sovereigns might have trustworthy evidence in his accounts of the amount received. Equally mindful of earlier defections, their further instructions also forbade the taking of any slaves.

Years had begun to rest heavily on the frame of Columbus. His constitution had been strained by long exposures, and his spirits had little elasticity left. Hope, to be sure, had not altogether departed from his ardent nature ; but it was a hope that had experienced many reverses, and its pinions were clipped. There was still in him no lack of mental vitality ; but his reason had lost equipoise, and his discernment was clouded with illusory visions.

There was the utmost desire at this time on the part of their Majesties that no rupture should break the friendly relations which were sustained with the Portuguese court, and it had been arranged that, in case Columbus should fall in with any Portuguese fleet, there should be the most civil interchange of courtesies.  The Spanish monarchs had also given orders, since word had come of the Moors besieging a Portuguese post on the African coast, that Columbus should first go thither and afford the garrison relief.

It was found, on reaching that African harbor on the 15th,
Columbus stops on the African coast. that the Moors had departed.  So, with no longer delay than to exchange civilities, he lifted anchor on the same day and put to sea.  It was while he was at the Canaries, May 20–25, taking in wood and water, that Columbus
1502. May. At the Canaries. wrote to his devoted Gorricio a letter, which Navarrete preserves.  " Now my voyage will be made in the name of the Holy Trinity," he says, " and I hope for success."

There is little to note on the voyage, which had been a prosperous one, and on June 15 he reached Martinino
1502. June 15. Reaches Martinico. (Martinico).  He himself professes to have been but twenty days between Cadiz and Martinino, but the statement seems to have been confused, with his usual inaccuracy.  He thence pushed leisurely along over much the same track which he had pursued on his second voyage, till he steered finally for Santo Domingo.

It will be recollected that the royal orders issued to him before leaving Spain were so far at variance with Columbus's wishes that he was denied the satisfaction of touching at Española.
Determines to go to Española. There can be little question as to the wisdom of an injunction which the Admiral now determined to disregard.  His excuse was that his principal caravel was a poor sailer, and he thought he could commit no mistake in insuring greater success for his voyage by exchanging at that port this vessel for a better one.  He forgot his own treatment of Ojeda when he drove that adventurer from the island, where, to provision a vessel whose crew was starving, Ojeda dared to trench on his government.  When we view this pretense for thrusting himself upon an unwilling community in the light of his unusually quick and prosperous voyage and his failure to

make any mention of his vessel's defects when he wrote from the Canaries, we can hardly avoid the conclusion that his determination to call at Española was suddenly taken. His whole conduct in the matter looks like an obstinate purpose to carry his own point against the royal commands, just as he had tried to carry it against the injunctions respecting the making of slaves. We must remember this when we come to consider the later neglect on the part of the King. We must remember, also, the considerate language with which the sovereigns had conveyed this injunction : " It is not fit that you should lose so much time ; it is much fitter that you should go another way ; though if it appears necessary, and God is willing, you may stay there a little while on your return."

Roselly de Lorgues, with his customary disingenuousness, merely says that Columbus came to Santo Domingo, to deliver letters with which he was charged, and to exchange one of his caravels.

It was the 29th of June when the little fleet of Columbus arrived off the port. He sent in one of his command- ers to ask permission to shelter his ships, and the privilege of negotiating for another caravel, since, as he says, " one of his ships had become unseaworthy and could no longer carry sail." His request came to Ovando, who was now in command. This governor had left Spain in February, only a month before Columbus received his final in- structions, and there can be little doubt that he had learned from Fonseca that those instructions would enjoin Columbus not to complicate in any way Ovando's assumption of command by ap- proaching his capital. Las Casas seems to imply this. How- ever it may be, Ovando was amply qualified by his own instruc- tions to do what he thought the circumstances required. Co- lumbus represented that a storm was coming on, or rather the *Historie* tells us that he did. It is to be remarked that Colum- bus himself makes no such statement. At all events, word was sent back to Columbus by his boat that he could not enter the harbor. Irving calls this an " ungracious refusal," and it turned out that later events have op- portunely afforded the apologists for the Admiral the occasion to point a moral to his advantage, particularly since Columbus, if we may believe the doubtful story, confident of his prognosti-

1502. June 29. Columbus arrives off Santo Domingo.

Columbus forbidden to enter the harbor.

cations, had again sent word that the fleet lying in the harbor, ready to sail, would go out at great peril in view of an impending storm. It seems to be quite uncertain if at the time his crew had any knowledge of his reasons for nearing Española, or of his being denied admittance to the port. At least Porras, from the way he describes the events, leaves one to make such an inference.

This fleet in the harbor was that which had brought Ovando,

Ovando's fleet. and was now laden for the return. There was on board of it, as Columbus might have learned from his messengers, the man of all men whom he most hated, Bobadilla,

Bobadilla, Roldan, and others on the fleet. who had gracefully yielded the power to Ovando two months before, and of whom Las Casas, who was then fresh in his inquisitive seeking after knowledge respecting the Indies and on the spot, could not find that any one spoke ill. On the same ship was Columbus's old rebellious and tergiversating companion, Roldan, whose conduct had been in these two months examined, and who was now to be sent to Spain for further investigations. There was also embarked, but in chains, the unfortunate cacique of the Vega, Guarionex, to be made a show of in Seville. The lading of the ships was the most wonderful for wealth that had ever been sent from the island. There was the gold which Bobadilla had collected, including a remarkable nugget which an Indian woman had picked up in a brook, and a large quantity which Roldan and his friends were taking on their own account, as the profit of

Columbus's factor had placed his gold on one of the ships. their separate enterprises. Carvajal, whom Columbus had sent out with Ovando as his factor, to look after his pecuniary interests under the provisions which the royal commands had made, had also placed in one of the caravels four thousand pieces of the same precious metal, the result of the settlement of Ovando with Bobadilla, and the accretions of the Admiral's share of the Crown's profits.

Undismayed by the warnings of Columbus, this fleet at once

Ovando's fleet puts to sea and is wrecked; put to sea, the Admiral's little caravels having meanwhile crept under the shore at a distance to find such shelter as they could. The larger fleet stood homeward, and was scarcely off the easterly end of Española when a furious hurricane burst upon it. The ship which carried Bobadilla, Roldan, and Guarionex succumbed and went down.

Others foundered later. Some of the vessels managed to return to Santo Domingo in a shattered condition. A single caravel, it is usually stated, survived the shock, so that it alone could proceed on the voyage; and if the testimony is to be believed, this was the weakest of them all, but she carried the gold of Columbus. Among the caravels which put back to Santo Domingo for repairs was one on which Bastidas was going to Spain for trial. This one arrived at Cadiz in September, 1502.

but ship with Columbus's gold is saved.

The ships of Columbus had weathered the gale. That of the Admiral, by keeping close in to land, had fared best. The others, seeking sea-room, had suffered more. They lost sight of each other, however, during the height of the gale; but when it was over, they met together at Port Hermoso, at the westerly end of the island. The gale is a picture over which the glow of a retributive justice, under the favoring dispensation of chance, is so easily thrown by sympathetic writers that the effusions of the sentimentalists have got to stand at last for historic verity. De Lorgues does not lose the opportunity to make the most of it.

Columbus's ships weather the gale.

Columbus, having lingered about the island to repair his ships and refresh his crews, and also to avoid a second storm, did not finally get away till July 14, when he steered directly for Terra Firma. The currents perplexed him, and, as there was little wind, he was swept west further than he expected. He first touched at some islands near Jamaica. Thence he proceeded west a quarter southwest, for four days, without seeing land, as Porras tells us, when, bewildered, he turned to the northwest, and then north. But finding himself (July 24) in the archipelago near Cuba, which on his second voyage he had called The Gardens, he soon after getting a fair wind (July 27) stood southwest, and on July 30 made a small island, off the northern coast of Honduras, called Guanaja by the natives, and Isla de Pinos by himself. He was now in sight of the mountains of the mainland. The natives struck him as of a physical type different from all others whom he had seen. A large canoe, eight feet beam, and of great length, though made of a single log, approached with still stranger people in it. They had apparently come from a region further north;

1502. July 14. Columbus sails away.

July 30. At Guanaja.

Meets a strange canoe.

and under a canopy in the waist of the canoe sat a cacique with his dependents. The boat was propelled by five and twenty men with paddles. It carried various articles to convince Columbus that he had found a people more advanced in arts than those of the regions earlier discovered. They had with them copper implements, including hatchets, bells, and the like. He saw something like a crucible in which metal had been melted. Their wooden swords were jagged with sharp flints, their clothes were carefully made, their utensils were polished and handy. Columbus traded off some trinkets for such specimens as he wanted. If he now had gone in the direction from which this marvelous canoe had come, he might have thus early opened the wondrous world of Yucatan and Mexico, and closed his career with more marvels yet. His beatific visions, which he supposed were leading him under the will of the Deity, led him, however, south. The delusive strait was there. He found an old man among the Indians, whom he kept as a guide, since the savage could draw a sort of chart of the coast. He dismissed the rest with presents, after he had wrested from them what he wanted. Approaching the mainland, near the present Cape of Honduras, the Adelantado landed on Sunday, August 14, and mass was celebrated in a grove near the beach. Again, on the 17th, Bartholomew landed some distance eastward of the first spot, and here, by a river (Rio de la Posesion, now Rio Tinto), he planted the Castilian banner and formally took possession of the country. The Indians were friendly, and there was an interchange of provisions and trinkets. The natives were tattooed, and they had other customs, such as the wearing of cotton jackets, and the distending of their ears by rings, which were new to the Spaniards.

On the Honduras coast.

Tracking the coast still eastward, Columbus struggled against the current, apparently without reasoning that he might be thus sailing away from the strait, so engrossed was he with the thought that such a channel must be looked for farther south. His visions had not helped him to comprehend the sweep of waters that would disprove his mock oaths of the Cuban coast. So he wore ship constantly against the tempest and current, and crawled with bewildered expectation along the shore. All this tacking tore his sails, racked his caravels, and wore out his seamen. The men were in despair, and confessed

Seeking a strait.

one another. Some made vows of penance, if their lives were
preserved. Columbus was himself wrenched with the Columbus
gout, and from a sort of pavilion, which covered his oppressed
couch on the quarter deck, he kept a good eye on all with the gout.

CARTE DES PROVINCES DE NICARAGUA ET COSTA RICA

Pour l'Histoire Generale des Voyages
Par M. B. Ing. de la Marine.
1754.

MOSQUITOS

NICARAGUA

COSTA RICA

BELLIN'S HONDURAS.

they encountered. "The distress of my son," he says, "grieved
me to the soul, and the more when I considered his tender age;

for he was but thirteen years old, and he enduring so much toil for so long a time." "My brother," he adds further, "was in the ship that was in the worst condition and the most exposed to danger; and my grief on this account was the greater that I brought him with me against his will."

It was no easy work to make the seventy leagues from Cape Honduras to Cape Gracios à Dios, and the bestowal of this name denoted his thankfulness to God, when, after forty days of this strenuous endeavor, his caravels were at last able to

1502. September. Cape Gracios à Dios. round the cape, on September 12 (or 14). A seaboard stretching away to the south lay open before him, — now known as the Mosquito Coast. The current which sets west so persistently here splits and sends a branch down this coast. So with a "fair wind and tide," as he says, they followed its varied scenery of crag and lowland for more than sixty leagues, till they discovered a great flow of water coming out of a river. It seemed to offer an opportunity to replenish their casks and get some store of wood. On the 16th of September, they anchored, and sent their boats to explore. A meeting of the tide and the river's flow raised later a tumultuous sea at the bar, just as the boats were coming out. The men were unable to surmount the difficulty, and

Loses a boat's crew. one of the boats was lost, with all on board. Columbus recorded their misfortune in the name which he gave to the river, El Rio del Desastre. Still coasting onward, on September 25 they came to an alluring roadstead between

1502. September 25. The Garden. an island and the main, where there was everything to enchant that verdure and fragrance could produce. He named the spot The Garden (La Huerta). Here, at anchor, they had enough to occupy them for a day or two in restoring the damage of the tempest, and in drying their stores, which had been drenched by the unceasing downpour of the clouds. The natives watched them from the shore, and made a show of their weapons. The Spaniards remaining inactive, the savages grew more confident of the pacific intent of their visitors, and soon began swimming off to the caravels. Columbus tried the effect of largesses, refusing to barter, and made gifts of the Spanish baubles. Such gratuities, however, created distrust, and every trinket was returned. Two young girls had been sent on board as hostages, while the

Spaniards were on shore getting water; but even they were stripped of their Spanish finery when restored to their friends, and every bit of it was returned to the givers. There seem to be discordant statements by Columbus and in the *Historie* respecting these young women, and Columbus gives them a worse character than his chronicler. When the Adelantado went ashore with a notary, and this official displayed his paper and inkhorn, it seemed to strike the wondering natives as a spell. They fled, and returned with something like a censer, from which they scattered the smoke as if to disperse all baleful spirits. Character of the natives.

These unaccustomed traits of the natives worked on the superstitions of the Spaniards. They began to fancy they had got within an atmosphere of sorceries, and Columbus, thinking of the two Indian maiden hostages, was certain there was a spell of witchcraft about them, and he never quite freed his mind of this necromantic ghost.

The old Indian whom Columbus had taken for a guide when first he touched the coast, having been set ashore at Cape Gracios à Dios, enriched with presents, Columbus now seized seven of this new tribe, and selecting two of the most intelligent as other guides, he let the rest go. The seizure was greatly resented by the tribe, and they sent emissaries to negotiate for the release of the captives, but to no effect.

Departing on October 5 from the region which the natives called Cariari, and where the fame of Columbus is still preserved in the Bahia del Almirante, the explorers soon found the coast trending once more towards the east. They were tracking what is now known as the shore of Costa Rica. They soon entered the large and island-studded Caribaro Bay. Here the Spaniards were delighted to find the natives wearing plates of gold as ornaments. They tried to traffic for them, but the Indians were loath to part with their treasures. The natives intimated that there was much more of this metal farther on at a place called Veragua. So the ships sailed on, October 17, and reached that coast. The Spaniards came to a river; but the natives sent defiance to them in the blasts of their conch-shells, while they shook at them their lances. Entering the tide, they splashed the water towards their enemies, in token of contempt. Colum-

1502. October. Cariari.

Gold sought at Veragua.

BELLINI'S VERAGUA.

bus's Indian guides soon pacified them, and a round of barter
followed, by which seventeen of their gold disks were secured for
three hawks' bells. The intercourse ended, however, in a little
hostile bout, during which the Spanish crossbows and lombards
soon brought the savages to obedience.

Still the caravels went on. The same scene of startled natives,
in defiant attitude, soon soothed by the trinkets was repeated
everywhere. In one place the Spaniards found what they had
never seen before, a wall laid of stone and lime, and Columbus
began to think of the civilized East again. Coast peoples are
always barbarous, as he says; but it is the inland people who are
rich. As he passed along this coast of Veragua, as the name has
got to be written, though his notary at the time caught the Indian
pronunciation as Cobraba, his interpreters pointed out its villages, and the chief one of all; and when they had passed on
a little farther they told him he was sailing beyond the gold
country. Columbus was not sure but they were trying to induce him to open communication again with the shore, to offer
chances for their escape. The seeker of the strait could not
stop for gold. His vision led him on to that marvelous land of
Ciguare, of which these successive native tribes told
him, situated ten days inland, and where the people    Ciguare.
reveled in gold, sailed in ships, and conducted commerce in
spices and other precious commodities. The women there were
decked, so they said, with corals and pearls. " I should be
content," he says, " if a tithe of this which I hear is true."
He even fancied, from all he could understand of their signs
and language, that these Ciguare people were as terrible in war
as the Spaniards, and rode on beasts. " They also say that the
sea surrounds Ciguare, and that ten days' journey from thence
is the river Ganges." Humboldt seems to think that in all
this Columbus got a conception of that great western ocean
which was lying so much nearer to him than he supposed. It
may be doubted if it was quite so clear to Columbus as Humboldt thinks; but there is good reason to believe that Columbus
imagined this wonderful region of Ciguare was half-way to the
Ganges. If, as his canonizers fondly suppose, he had   At the
not mistaken in his visions an isthmus for a strait, he   isthmus.
might have been prompted to cross the slender barrier which
now separated him from his goal.

On the 2d of November, the ships again anchored in a spacious harbor, so beautiful in its groves and fruits, and with such deep water close to the shore, that Columbus gave it the name of Puerto Bello (Porto Bello), — an appellation which has never left it. It rained for seven days while they lay here, doing nothing but trading a little with the natives for provisions. The Indians offered no gold, and hardly any was seen. Starting once more, the Spaniards came in sight of the cape known since as Nombre de Dios, but they were thwarted for a while in their attempts to pass it. They soon found a harbor, where they stayed till November 23; then going on again, they secured anchorage in a basin so small that the caravels were placed almost beside the shore. Columbus was kept here by the weather for nine days. The basking alligators reminded him of the crocodiles of the Nile. The natives were uncommonly gentle and gracious, and provisions were plenty. The ease with which the seamen could steal ashore at night began to be demoralizing, leading to indignities at the native houses. The savage temper was at last aroused, and the Spanish revelries were brought to an end by an attack on the ships. It ceased, as usual, after a few discharges of the ships' guns.

Columbus had not yet found any deflection of that current which sweeps in this region towards the Gulf of Mexico. He had struggled against its powerful flow in every stage of his progress along the coast. Whether this had brought him to believe that his vision of a strait was delusive does not appear. Whether he really knew that he had actually joined his own explorations, going east, to those which Bastidas had made from the west is equally unknown, though it is possible he may have got an intimation of celestial and winged monsters from the natives. If he comprehended it, he saw that there could be no strait, this way at least. Bastidas, as we have seen, was on board Bobadilla's fleet when Columbus lay off Santo Domingo. There is a chance that Columbus's messenger who went ashore may have seen him and his charts, and may have communicated some notes of the maps to the Admiral. Some of the companions of Bastidas on his voyage had reached Spain before Columbus sailed, and there may have been some knowledge imparted in that way. If Columbus knew the truth, he did not disclose it.

*[Marginal notes:]* 1502. November 2. / Porto Bello. / Nombre de Dios. / Bastidas's exploration of this coast.

Porras, possibly at a later day, seems to have been better informed, or at least he imparts more in his narrative than Columbus does. He says he saw in the people of these parts many of the traits of those of the pearl coast at Paria, and that the maps, which they possessed, showed that it was to this point that the explorations of Ojeda and Bastidas had been pushed.

There were other things that might readily have made him turn back, as well as this despair of finding a strait. Columbus His crew were dissatisfied with leaving the gold of turns back. Veragua. His ships were badly bored by the worms, and they had become, from this cause and by reason of the heavy weather which had so mercilessly followed them, more and more unseaworthy. So on December 5, 1502, when he 1502. December 5. passed out of the little harbor of El Retrete, he began a backward course. Pretty soon the wind, which had all along faced him from the east, blew strongly from the west, checking him as much going backward as it had in his onward course. It seemed as if the elements were turned against him. The gale was making sport of him, as it veered in all directions. It was indeed a Coast of Contrasts (La Costa de los Contrastes), as Columbus called it. The lightning streaked the skies continually. The thunder was appalling. For nine days the little ships, strained at every seam, leaking at A gale. every point where the tropical sea worm had pierced them, writhed in a struggle of death. At one time a gigantic waterspout formed within sight. The sea surged around its base. The clouds stooped to give it force. It came staggering and lunging towards the fragile barks. The crews exorcised the watery spirit by repeating the Gospel of St. John the Evangelist, and the crazy column passed on the other side of them.

Added to their peril through it all were the horrors of an impending famine. Their biscuit were revolting because of the worms. They caught sharks for food.

At last, on December 17, the fleet reunited, — for they had, during the gales, lost sight of each other, — and entered 1502. December 17. a harbor, where they found the native cabins built in the tree tops, to be out of the way of griffins, or some other beasts. After further buffeting of the tempests, they finally Bethlehem made a harbor on the coast of Veragua, in a river River. which Columbus named Santa Maria de Belen (Bethlehem),

it being Epiphany Day; and here at last they anchored two of
the caravels on January 9, and the other two on the 10th
(1503). Columbus had been nearly a month in passing thirty
leagues of coast. The Indians were at first quieted in the
usual way, and some gold was obtained by barter. The Spaniards had not been here long, however, when they
found themselves (January 24, 1503) in as much
danger by the sudden swelling of the river as they had been
at sea. It was evidently occasioned by continued falls of rain
in distant mountains, which they could see. The caravels were
knocked about like cockboats. The Admiral's ship snapped
a mast. "It rained without ceasing," says the Admiral, recording his miseries, "until the 14th of February;" and during the continuance of the storm the Adelantado was sent on
a boat expedition to ascend the Veragua River, three miles
along the coast, where he was to search for mines. The party
proceeded on February 6 as far as they could in the boats,
and then, leaving part of the men for a guard, and taking
guides, which the Quibian — that being the name, as he says,
which they gave to the lord of the country — had provided,
they reached a country where the soil to their eyes seemed full
of particles of gold. Columbus says that he afterwards learned
that it was a device of the crafty Quibian to conduct them
to the mines of a rival chief, while his own were richer and
nearer, all of which, nevertheless, did not escape the
keen Spanish scent for gold. Bartholomew made
other excursions along the coast; but nowhere did it
seem to him that gold was as plenty as at Veragua.

Columbus now reverted to his old fancies. He remembered
that Josephus has described the getting of gold for the Temple
of Jerusalem from the Golden Chersonesus, and was not this
the very spot? "Josephus thinks that this gold of the Chronicles and the Book of Kings was found in the Aurea,"
he says. "If it were so, I contend that these mines
of the Aurea are identical with those of Veragua. David in
his will left 3,000 quintals of Indian gold to Solomon, to assist
in building the Temple, and according to Josephus it came
from these lands." He had seen, as he says, more promise of
gold here in two days than in Española in four years. It was
very easy now to dwarf his Ophir at Hayna! Those other

1503. Jan-
uary 24.

Bartholo-
mew seeks
the mines.

Mines of
Aurea.

riches were left to those who had wronged him. The pearls of the Paria coast might be the game of the common adventurer. Here was the princely domain of the divinely led discoverer, who was rewarded at last!

A plan was soon made of founding a settlement to hold the region and gain information, while Columbus returned to Spain for supplies. Eighty men were to stay. They began to build houses. They divided the stock of provisions and munitions, and transferred that intended for the colony to one of the caravels, which was to be left with them. Particular pains were taken to propitiate the natives by presents, and the Quibian was regaled with delicacies and gifts. When this was done, it was found that a dry season had come on, and there was not water enough on the bar to float the returning caravels.

Meanwhile the Quibian had formed a league to exterminate the intruders. Columbus sent a brave fellow, Diego Mendez, to see what he could learn. He found a force of savages advancing to the attack; but this single Spaniard disconcerted them, and they put off the plan. Again, with but a single companion, one Rodrigo de Escobar, Mendez boldly went into the Quibian's village, and came back alive to tell the Admiral of all the preparations for war which he had seen, or which were inferred at least. The news excited the quick spirits of the Adelantado, and, following a plan of Mendez, he at once started (March 30) with an armed force. He came with such celerity to the cacique's village that the savages were not prepared for their intrusion, and by a rapid artifice he surrounded the lodge of the Quibian, and captured him with fifty of his followers. The Adelantado sent him, bound hand and foot, and under escort, down the river, in charge of Juan Sanchez, who rather resented any intimation of the Adelantado to be careful of his prisoner. As the boat neared the mouth of the river, her commander yielded to the Quibian's importunities to loosen his bonds, when the chief, watching his opportunity, slipped overboard and dove to the bottom. The night was dark, and he was not seen when he came to the surface, and was not pursued. The other prisoners were delivered to the Admiral. The Adelantado meanwhile had sacked the cacique's cabin, and brought away its golden treasures.

*Columbus seeks to make a settlement.*

*Diego Mendez's exploits.*

*The Quibian taken,*

*but escapes.*

Columbus, confident that the Quibian had been drowned, and that the chastisement which had been given his tribe was a wholesome lesson, began again to arrange for his departure. As the river had risen a little, he succeeded in getting his lightened caravels over the bar, and anchored them outside, where their lading was again put on board. To offer some last injunctions and to get water, Columbus, on April 6, sent a boat, in command of Diego Tristan, to the Adelantado, who was to be left in command. When the boat got in, Tristan found the settlement in great peril. The Quibian, who had reached the shore in safety after his adventure, had quickly organized an attacking party, and had fallen upon the settlement. The savages were fast getting their revenge, for the unequal contest had lasted nearly three hours, when the Adelantado and Mendez, rallying a small force, rushed so impetuously upon them that, with the aid of a fierce bloodhound, the native host was scattered in a trice. Only one Spaniard had been killed and eight wounded, including the Adelantado; but the rout of the Indians was complete.

1503.
April 6.

The settlement attacked.

It was while these scenes were going on that Tristan arrived in his boat opposite the settlement. He dallied till the affair was ended, and then proceeded up the river to get some water. Those on shore warned him of the danger of ambuscade; but he persisted. When he had got well beyond the support of the settlement, his boat was beset with a shower of javelins from the overhanging banks on both sides, while a cloud of canoes attacked him front and rear. But a single Spaniard escaped by diving, and brought the tale of disaster to his countrymen.

Tristan murdered.

The condition of the settlement was now alarming. The Indians, encouraged by their success in overcoming the boat, once more gathered to attack the little group of " encroaching Spaniards," as Columbus could but call them. The houses which sheltered them were so near the thick forest that the savages approached them on all sides under shelter. The woods rang with their yells and with the blasts of their conch-shells. The Spaniards got, in their panic, beyond the control of the Adelantado. They prepared to take the caravel and leave the river; but it was found she would not float over the bar. They then sought to send a boat to the Admiral, lying outside, to prevent his sailing without them ; but the current and tide commingling made such a commotion on the bar that no boat could live in the sea. The bodies of Tristan and his men came floating down stream, with carrion crows perched upon them at their ghastly feast. It seemed as if nature visited them with premonitions. At last the Adelantado brought a sufficient number of men into such a steady mood that they finally constructed out of whatever they could get some sort of a breastwork near the shore, where the ground was open. Here they could use their matchlocks and have a clear sweep about them. They placed behind this bulwark two small falconets, and prepared to defend themselves. They were in this condition for four days. Their provisions, however, began to run short, and every Spaniard who dared to forage was sure to be cut off. Their ammunition, too, was not abundant.

Meanwhile Columbus was in a similar state of anxiety. "The Admiral was suffering from a severe fever," he says, "and worn with fatigue." His ships were lying at anchor outside the bar, with the risk of being obliged to put to sea at any moment, to work off a lee shore. Tristan's prolonged absence harassed him. Another incident was not less ominous. The companions of the Quibian were confined on board in the forecastle ; and it was the intention to take them to Spain as hostages, as it was felt they would be, for the colony left behind. Those in charge of them had become careless about securing the hatchway, and one night they failed to chain it, trusting probably to the watchfulness of certain sailors who slept upon the hatch. The savages, finding a footing upon some ballast which they piled up beneath, suddenly threw off the cover, casting the sleeping sailors violently aside, and before the guard could be called the greater part of the prisoners had jumped into the sea and escaped. Such as were secured were thrust back, but the next morning it was found that they all had strangled themselves.

After such manifestations of ferocious determination, Columbus began to be further alarmed for the safety of his brother's companions and of Tristan's. For days a tossing surf had made an impassable barrier between him and the shore. He had but one boat, and he did not dare to risk it in an attempt

*Columbus at anchor outside the bar.*

to land. Finally, his Sevillian pilot, Pedro Ledesma, offered

Ledesma's exploit. to brave the dangers by swimming, if the boat would take him close to the surf. The trial was made; the man committed himself to the surf, and by his strength and skill so surmounted wave after wave that he at length reached stiller water, and was seen to mount the shore. In due time he was again seen on the beach, and plunging in once more, was equally successful in passing the raging waters, and was picked up by the boat. He had a sad tale to tell the Admiral. It was a story of insubordination, a powerless Adelantado, and a frantic eagerness to escape somehow. Ledesma said that the men were preparing canoes to come off to the ships, since their caravel was unable to pass the bar.

There was long consideration in these hours of disheartenment; but the end of it was a decision to rescue the colony and abandon the coast. The winds never ceased to be high, and

Resolve to abandon the region. Columbus's ships, in their weakened condition, were only kept afloat by care and vigilance. The loss of the boat's crew threw greater burdens and strains upon those who were left. It was impossible while the surf lasted to send in his only boat, and quite as impossible for the fragile canoes of his colony to brave the dangers of the bar in coming out. There was nothing for Columbus to do but to hold to his anchor as long as he could, and wait.

Our pity for the man is sometimes likely to unfit us to judge his own record. Let us try to believe what he says of himself, and watch him in his delirium. "Groaning with exhaustion," he says, "I fell asleep in the highest part of the ship, and

Columbus in delirium hears a voice. heard a compassionate voice address me." It bade him be of good cheer, and take courage in the service of God! What the God of all had done for Moses and David would be done for him! As we read the long report of this divine utterance, as Columbus is careful to record it, we learn that the Creator was aware of his servant's name resounding marvelously throughout the earth. We find, however, that the divine belief curiously reflected the confidence of Columbus that it was India, and not America, that had been revealed. "Remember David," said the Voice, "how he was a shepherd, and was made a king. Remember Abraham, how he was a hundred when he begat Isaac, and that there is youth still for the aged." Columbus adds that when the Voice chided him he wept for his errors, and that he heard it all as in a trance.

The obvious interpretation of all this is either that by the record Columbus intended a fable to impress the sovereigns, for whom he was writing, or that he was so moved to hallucinations that he believed what he wrote. The hero worship of Irving decides the question easily. "Such an idea," says Irving, referring to the argument of deceit, and forgetting the Admiral's partiality for such practices, "is inconsistent with the character of Columbus. In recalling a dream, one is unconsciously apt to give it a little coherency." Irving's plea is that it was a mere dream, which was mistaken by Columbus, in his feverish excitement, for a revelation. "The artless manner," adds that biographer, "in which he mingles the rhapsodies and dreams of his imagination with simple facts and sound practical observations, pouring them forth with a kind of Scriptural solemnity and poetry of language, is one of the most striking illustrations of a character richly compounded of extraordinary and apparently contradictory elements." We may perhaps ask, Was Irving's hero a deceiver, or was he mad? The chances seem to be that the whole vision was simply the product of one of those fits of aberration which in these later years were no strangers to Columbus's existence. His mind was not infrequently, amid disappointments and distractions, in no fit condition to ward off hallucination.

Humboldt speaks of Columbus's letter describing this vision as showing the disordered mind of a proud soul weighed down with dead hopes. He has no fear that the strange mixture of force and weakness, of pride and touching humility, which accompanies these secret contortions will ever impress the world with other feelings than those of commiseration.

It is a hard thing for any one, seeking to do justice to the agonies of such spirits, to measure them in the calmness of better days. "Let those who are accustomed to slander and aspersion ask, while they sit in security at home, Why dost thou not do so and so under such circumstances?" says Columbus himself. It is far easier to let one's self loose into the vortex and be tossed with sympathy. But if four centuries have done anything for us, they ought to have cleared the air of its mirages. What is pitiable may not be noble.

The Voice was, of course, associated in Columbus's mind with the good weather which followed. During this a raft was made of two canoes lashed together beneath a platform, and, using this for ferrying, all the stores were floated off safely to the ships, so that in the end nothing was left behind but the decaying and stranded caravel. This labor was done under the direction of Diego Mendez, whom the Admiral rewarded by kissing him on the cheek, and by giving him command of Tristan's caravel, which was the Admiral's flagship.

The colony embark.

It is a strange commentary on the career and fame of Columbus that the name of this disastrous coast should represent him to this day in the title of his descendant, the Duke of Veragua. Never a man turned the prow of his ship from scenes which he would sooner forget, with more sorrow and relief, than Columbus, in the latter days of April, 1503, with his enfeebled crews and his crazy hulks, stood away, as he thought, for Española. And yet three months later, and almost in the same breath with which he had rehearsed these miseries, with that obliviousness which so often caught his errant mind, he wrote to his sovereigns that "there is not in the world a country, whose inhabitants are more timid; added to which there is a good harbor, a beautiful river, and the whole place is capable of being easily put into a state of defense. Your people that may come here, if they should wish to become masters of the products of other lands, will have to take them by force, or retire empty-handed. In this country they will simply have to trust their persons in the hands of a savage." The man was mad.

1503. April. Columbus sails away.

It was easterly that Columbus steered when his ships swung round to their destined course. It was not without fear and even indignation that his crews saw what they thought a purpose to sail directly for Spain in the sorry plight of the ships. Mendez, indeed, who commanded the Admiral's own ship, says "they thought to reach Spain." The Admiral, however, seems to have had two purposes. He intended to run eastward far enough to allow for the currents, when he should finally head for Santo Domingo. He intended also to disguise as much as he could the route back, for fear that others would avail themselves of his crew's knowledge to rediscover these golden coasts. He remembered how the companions of his Paria voyage had led other expeditions to that region of pearls. He is said also to have taken from his crew all their memoranda of the voyage, so that there would be no such aid available to guide others. " None of them can explain whither I went, nor whence I came," he says. " They do not know the way to return thither."

By the time he reached Puerto Bello, one of his caravels had become so weakened by the boring worms that he had At Puerto to abandon her and crowd his men into the two re- Bello. maining vessels. His crews became clamorous when he reached the Gulf of Darien, where he thought it prudent to At the Gulf abandon his easterly course and steer to the north. of Darien. It was now May 1. He hugged the wind to overcome the currents, but when he sighted some islands to the westward of Española, on the 10th, it was evident that the cur- 1503. May rents had been bearing him westerly all the while. 10. They were still drifting him westerly, when he found himself, on May 30, among the islands on the Cuban coast May 30. On which he had called The Gardens. " I had reached," the Cuban coast. he says in his old delusion, " the province of Mago, which is contiguous to that of Cathay." Here the ships anchored to give the men refreshment. The labor of keeping the vessels free from water had been excessive, and in a secure roadstead it could now be carried on with some respite of toil, if the weather would only hold good. This was not to be, however. A gale ensued in which they lost their anchors. The two caravels, moreover, sustained serious damage by collision. All the anchors of the Admiral's ship had gone but one, and though that held, the cable nearly wore asunder. After six days of this stormy weather, he dared at last to crawl along the coast. Fortunately, he got some native provisions at one place, which enabled him to feed his famished men. The currents and adverse winds, however, proved too much for the power of his ships to work to windward. They were all the while in danger of foundering. " With three pumps and the use of pots and kettles," he says, " we could scarcely clear the water that came into the ship, there being no remedy but this for the mischief done by the ship worm." He 1503. June reluctantly, therefore, bore away for Jamaica, where, 23. Reaches Jamaica. on June 23, he put into Puerto Buono (Dry Harbor). Finding neither water nor food here, he went on the next day to Port San Gloria, known in later days as Don Christopher's Cove. Here he found it necessary, a little later (July 23 and 1503. July, August 12), to run his sinking ships, one after the August. His ships stranded. other, aground, but he managed to place them side by side, so that they could be lashed together. They soon filled with the tide. Cabins were built on the forecastles and sterns to live in, and bulwarks of defense were reared as best they could be along the vessels' waists. Columbus now took the strictest precautions to prevent his men wandering ashore, for it was of the utmost importance that no indignity should be offered the natives while they were in such hazardous and almost defenseless straits.

It became at once a serious question how to feed his men. Whatever scant provisions remained on board the stranded caravels were spoiled. His immediate savage neighbors supplied them with cassava bread and other food for a while, but they had no reserved stores to draw upon, and these sources were soon exhausted.

Diego Mendez now offered, with three men, carrying goods Mendez seeks food for the company. to barter, to make a circuit of the island, so that he could reach different caciques, with whom he could bargain for the preparation and carriage of food to the Spaniards. As he concluded his successive impromptu agreements with cacique after cacique, he sent a man back loaded with what he could carry, to acquaint the Admiral, and let him prepare for a further exchange of trinkets. Finally, Mendez, left without a companion, still went on, getting some Indian porters to help him from place to place. In this way he reached the eastern end of the island, where he ingratiated himself with a powerful cacique, and was soon on excellent terms with him. From this chieftain he got a canoe with natives to paddle, and loading it with provisions, he skirted westerly along the coast, until he reached the Spaniards' harbor. His mission bade fair to have accomplished its purpose, and provisions came in plentifully for a while under the arrangements which he had made.

Columbus's next thought was to get word, if possible, to Ovando, at Española, so that the governor could send a vessel to rescue them. Columbus proposed to Mendez that he should attempt the passage with the canoe in which he had returned from his expedition. Mendez pictured the risks of going forty leagues in these treacherous seas in a frail canoe, and intimated that the Admiral had better make trial of the courage of the whole company first. He said that if no one else offered to go he would shame them by his courage, as he had more than once done before. So the company were assembled, and Columbus made public the proposition. Every one hung back from the hazards, and Mendez won his new triumph, as he had supposed he would. He then set to work fitting the canoe for the voyage. He put a keel to her. He built up her sides so that she could better ward off the seas, and rigged a mast and sail. She was soon loaded with the necessary provisions for himself, one other Spaniard, and the six Indians who were to ply the paddles.

Mendez prepares to go to Española.

The Admiral, while the preparations were making, drew up a letter to his sovereigns, which it was intended that Mendez, after arranging with Ovando for the rescue, should bear himself to Spain by the first opportunity. At least it is the reasonable assumption of Humboldt that this is the letter which has come down to us dated July 7, 1503.

1503. July 7. Letter of Columbus to the sovereigns.

It is not known that this epistle was printed at the time, though manuscript copies seem to have circulated. An Italian version of it was, however, printed at Venice a year before Columbus died. The original Spanish text was not known to scholars till Navarrete, having discovered in the king's library at Madrid an early transcript of it, printed it in the first volume of his *Coleccion*. It is the document usually referred to, from the title of Morelli's reprint (1810) of the Italian text, as the *Lettera rarissima di Cristoforo Colombo*.

*Lattera rarissima.*

This letter is even more than his treatise on the prophets a sorrowful index of his wandering reason. In parts it is the merest jumble of hurrying thoughts, with no plan or steady purpose in view. It is in places well calculated to arouse the deepest pity. It was, of course, avowedly written at a venture, inasmuch as the chance of its reaching the hands of his sovereigns was a very small one. "I send this letter," he says, "by means of and by the hands of Indians; it will be a miracle if it reaches its destination."

He not only goes back over the adventures of the present expedition, in a recital which has been not infrequently quoted in previous pages, but he reverts gloomily to the more distant past. He lingers on the discouragements of his first years in Spain. "Every one to whom the enterprise was mentioned," he says of those days, "treated it as ridiculous, but now there is not a man, down to the very tailors, who does not beg to be allowed to become a discoverer." He remembers the neglect which followed upon the first flush of indignation when he returned to Spain in chains. "The twenty years' service through which I have passed with so much toil and danger have profited me nothing, and at this very day I do not possess a roof in Spain that I can call my own. If I wish to eat or sleep I have nowhere to go but to a low tavern, and most times lack wherewith to pay the bill. Another anxiety wrings my very heart-strings, when I think of my son Diego, whom I have left an orphan in Spain, stripped of the house and property which is due to him on my account, although I had looked upon it as a certainty that your Majesties, as just and grateful princes, would restore it to him in all respects with increase."

"I was twenty-eight years old," he says again, "when I came into your Highnesses' services, and now I have not a hair upon me that is not gray, my body is infirm, and all that was left to me, as well as to my brother, has been taken away and sold, even to the frock that I wore, to my great dishonor."

And then, referring to his present condition, he adds : "Solitary in my trouble, sick, and in daily expectation of death, I am surrounded by millions of hostile savages, full of cruelty. Weep for me, whoever has charity, truth, and justice!"

He next works over in his mind the old geographical problems. He recalls his calculation of an eclipse in 1494, when he supposed, in his error, that he had "sailed twenty-four degrees westward in nine hours." He recalls the stories that he had heard on the Veragua coast, and thinks that he had known it all before from books. Marinus had come near the truth, he gives out, and the Portuguese have proved that the Indies in Ethiopia is, as Marinus had said, four and twenty degrees from the equinoctial line. "The world is but small," he sums up; "out of seven divisions of it, the dry part occupies six, and the seventh is entirely covered by water. I say that the world is not so large as vulgar opinion makes it, and that one degree from the equinoctial line measures fifty-six miles and two thirds, and this may be proved to a nicety."

And then, in his thoughts, he turns back to his quest for gold, just as he had done in action at Darien, when in despair he gave up the search for a strait. It was gold, to his mind, that could draw souls from purgatory. He Columbus on gold. exclaims: "Gold is the most precious of all commodities. Gold constitutes treasure, and he who possesses it has all he needs in this world, as also the means of rescuing souls from purgatory, and restoring them to the enjoyment of paradise."

Then his hopes swell with the vision of that wealth which he thought he had found, and would yet return to. He alone had the clues to it, which he had concealed from others. "I can safely assert that to my mind my people returning to Spain are the bearers of the best news that ever was carried to Spain. . . . I had certainly foreseen how things would be. I think more of this opening for commerce than of all that has been done in the Indies. This is not a child to be left to the care of a stepmother."

These were some of the thoughts, in large part tumultuous, incoherent, dispirited, harrowing, weakening, and sad, penned within sound of the noise of Mendez's preparations, and disclosing an exultant and bewildered being, singularly compounded.

This script was committed to Mendez, beside one addressed to Ovando, and another to his friend in Spain, Father Gorricio, to whom he imparts some of the same frantic expectations. "If my voyage will turn out as favorable to my health," he says, "and to the tranquillity of my house, as it is likely to be for the glory of my royal masters, I shall live long."

Mendez started bravely. He worked along the coast of the island towards its eastern end; not without peril, Mendez starts. however, both from the sea and from the Indians. Finally, his party fell captives to a startled cacique; but while the savages were disputing over a division of the spoils, Mendez succeeded in slipping back to the canoe, and, putting off alone, paddled it back to the stranded ships.

Another trial was made at once, with larger preparation. A second canoe was added to the expedition, and the charge of

this was given to Bartholomew Fiesco, a Genoese, who had
Mendez starts again. commanded one of the caravels. The daring adventurers started again with an armed party under the Adelantado following them along the shore.

The land and boat forces reached the end of the island without molestation, and then, bidding each other farewell, the canoes headed boldly away from land, and were soon lost to the sight of the Adelantado in the deepening twilight. The land party returned to the Admiral without adventure. There was little now for the poor company to do but to await the return of Fiesco, who had been directed to come back at once and satisfy the Admiral that Mendez had safely accomplished his mission.

Many days passed, and straining eyes were directed along the shore to catch a glimpse of Fiesco's canoe; but it came not. There was not much left to allay fear or stifle disheartenment. The cramped quarters of the tenements on the hulks, the bad food which the men were forced to depend upon, and the vain watchings soon produced murmurs of discontent, which it needed but the captious spirit of a leader to convert into the turmoil of revolt. Such a gatherer of sedition soon appeared.
The revolt of Porras. There were in the company two brothers, Francisco de Porras, who had commanded one of the vessels, and Diego de Porras, who had, as we have seen, been joined to the expedition to check off the Admiral's accounts of treasures acquired. The very espionage of his office was an offense to the Admiral. It was through the caballing of these two men that the alien spirits of the colony found in one of them at last a determined actor. It is not easy to discover how far the accusations against the Admiral, which these men now began to· dwell upon, were generally believed. It served the leaders' purposes to have it appear that Columbus was in reality banished from Spain, and had no intention of returning thither till Mendez and Fiesco had succeeded in making favor for him at Court; and that it was upon such a mission that these lieutenants had been sent. It was therefore necessary, if those who were thus cruelly confined in Jamaica wished to escape a lingering death, to put on a bold front, and demand to be led away to Española in such canoes as could be got of the Indians.

It was on the 2d of January, 1504, that, with a crowd of

sympathizers watching within easy call, Francisco de Porras suddenly presented himself in the cabin of the weary and bedridden Admiral. An altercation ensued, in which the Admiral, propped in his couch, endeavored to assuage the bursting violence of his accuser, and to bring him to a sense of the patient duty which the conditions demanded. It was one of the times when desperate straits seemed to restore the manhood of Columbus. It was, however, of little use. The crisis was not one that, in the present temper of the mutineers, could be avoided. Porras, finding that the Admiral could not be swayed, called out in a loud voice, "I am for Castile! Those who will may come with me!" This signal was expected, and a shout rang in the air among those who were awaiting it. It aroused Columbus from his couch, and he staggered into sight; but his presence caused no cessation of the tumult. Some of his loyal companions, fearing violence, took him back to his bed. The Adelantado braced himself with his lance for an encounter, and was pacified only by the persuasions of the Admiral's friends. They loyally said, "Let the mutineers go. We will remain." The angry faction seized ten canoes, which the Admiral had secured from the Indians, and putting in them what they could get, they embarked for their perilous voyage. Some others who had not joined in their plot being allured by the flattering hope of release, there were forty-eight in all, and the little flotilla, amid the mingled execrations and murmurs of despair among the weak and the downcast who stayed behind, paddled out of that fateful harbor.

*1504. January 2. Demands of Porras.*

*The flotilla of Porras sails.*

The greater part of all who were vigorous had now gone. There were a few strong souls, with some vitality left in them, among the small company which remained to the Admiral; but the most of them were sorry objects, with dejected minds and bodies more or less prostrate from disease and privation. The conviction soon settled upon this deserted community that nothing could save them but a brotherly and confident determination to help one another, and to arouse to the utmost whatever of cheer and good will was latent in their spirits. They could hardly have met an attack of the natives, and they knew it. This made them more considerate in their treatment of their neighbors, and the supply of provisions which they could get from those who visited the ship was plentiful for a while. But the habits of the savages were not to accumulate much beyond present needs, and when the baubles which the Spaniards could distribute began to lose their strange attractiveness, the incentive was gone to induce exertion, and supplies were brought in less and less frequently. It was soon found that hawks' bells had diminished in value. It took several to appease the native cupidity where one had formerly done it.

There was another difficulty. There were failures on the part of the more distant villages to send in their customary contributions, and it soon came to be known that Porras and his crew, instead of having left the island, were wandering about, exacting provisions and committing indignities against the inhabitants wherever they went.

Porras's men still on the island.

It seems that the ten canoes had followed the coast to the nearest point to Española, at the eastern end of the island, and here, waiting for a calm sea, and securing some Indians to paddle, the mutineers had finally pushed off for their voyage. The boats had scarcely gone four leagues from land, when the wind rose and the sea began to alarm them. So they turned back. The men were little used to the management of the canoes, and they soon found themselves in great peril. It seemed necessary to lighten the canoes, which were now taking in water to a dangerous extent. They threw over much of their provisions; but this was not enough. They then sacrificed one after another the natives. If these resisted, a swoop of the sword ended their miseries. Once in the water, the poor Indians began to seize the gunwales; but the sword chopped off their hands. So all but a few of them, who were absolutely necessary to manage the canoes, were thrown into the sea. Such were the perils through which the mutineers passed in reaching the land.

His voyage a failure.

A long month was now passed waiting for another calm sea; but when they tempted it once more, it rose as before, and they again sought the land. All hope of success was now abandoned. From that time Porras and his band gave themselves up to a lawless, wandering life, during which they created new jealousies among the tribes. As we have seen, by their exactions they began at last to tap the distant sources of supplies for the Admiral and his loyal adherents.

Columbus now resorted to an expedient characteristic of the ingenious fertility of his mind. His astronomical tables enabled him to expect the approach of a lunar eclipse (February 29, 1504), and finding it close at hand he hastily summoned some of the neighboring caciques. 1504. February 29. Eclipse of the moon. He told them that the God of the Spaniards was displeased at their neglect to feed his people, and that He was about to manifest that displeasure by withdrawing the moon and leaving them to such baleful influences as they had provoked. When night fell and the shadow began to steal over the moon, a long howl of horror arose, and promises of supplies were made by the stricken caciques. They hurled themselves for protection at the feet of the Admiral. Columbus retired for an ostensible communion with this potent Spirit, and just as the hour came for the shadow to withdraw he appeared, and announced that their contrition had appeased the Deity, and a sign would be given of his content. Gradually the moon passed out of the shadow, and when in the clear heavens the luminary was again swimming unobstructed in her light, the work of astonishment had been done. After that, Columbus was never much in fear of famine.

It is time now to see how much more successful Mendez and Fiesco had been than Porras and his crew. They had accomplished the voyage to Española, it is true, but under such perils and sufferings that Fiesco could not induce a crew sufficient to man the canoe to return with him to the Admiral. The canoe voyage of Mendez. The passage had been made under the most violent conditions of tropical heat and unprotected endurance. Their supply of water had given out, and the tortures of thirst came on. They looked out for the little island of Navasa, which lay in their track, where they thought At Navasa Island. that in the crevices of the rocks they might find some water. They looked in vain. The day when they had hoped to see it passed, and night came on. One of the Indians died, and was dropped overboard. Others lay panting and exhausted in the bottom of the canoes. Mendez sat watching a glimmer of light in the eastern horizon that betokened the coming of the moon.

Presently a faint glisten of the real orb grew into a segment. He could see the water line as the illumination increased. There was a black stretch of something jagging the lower edge of the segment. It was land! Navasa had been found. By morning they had reached the island. Water was discovered among the rocks; but some drank too freely, and paid the penalty of their lives. Mussels were picked up along the shore; they built a fire and boiled them. All day long they gazed

They see Española. longingly on the distant mountains of Española, which were in full sight. Refreshed by the day's rest, they embarked again at nightfall, and on the following day arrived at Cape Tiburon, the southwestern peninsula of Española, hav-

Mendez lands at Española. ing been four days on the voyage from Jamaica. They landed among hospitable natives, and having waited two days to recuperate, Mendez took some savages in a canoe, and started to go along the coast to Santo Domingo, one hundred and thirty leagues distant. He had gone nearly two thirds of the distance when, communicating with the shore, he learned that Ovando was not in Santo Domingo, but at Xaragua. So Mendez abandoned his canoe, and started alone through the forests to seek the governor.

Ovando received him cordially, but made excuses for not

Ovando delays sending relief to Columbus. sending relief to Columbus at once. He was himself occupied with the wars which he was conducting against the natives. There was no ship in Santo Domingo of sufficient burden to be dispatched for such a rescue. So excuse after excuse, and promises of attention unfulfilled, kept Mendez in the camp of Ovando for seven months. The governor always had reasons for denying him permission to go to Santo Domingo, where Mendez had hopes of procuring a vessel. This procrastinating conduct has naturally given rise to the suspicion that Ovando was not over-anxious to deliver Columbus from his perils; and there can be little question that for the Admiral to have sunk into oblivion and leave no trace would have relieved both the governor and his royal master of some embarrassments.

At length Ovando consented to the departure of Mendez to Santo Domingo. There was a fleet of caravels expected there, and Mendez was anxious to see if he could not procure one of them on the Admiral's own account to undertake the voyage of rescue. His importunities became so pressing that Ovando at last consented to his starting for that port, seventy leagues distant.

No sooner was Mendez gone than Ovando determined to ascertain the condition of the party at Jamaica without helping them, and so he dispatched a caravel to reconnoitre. He purposely sent a small craft, that there might be no excuse for attempting to bring off the company; and to prevent seizure of the vessel by Columbus, her commander was instructed to lie off the harbor, and only send in a boat, to communicate with no one but Columbus; and he was particularly enjoined to avoid being enticed on board the stranded caravels. The command of this little craft of espionage was given to one of Columbus's enemies, Diego de Escobar, who had been active as Roldan's lieutenant in his revolt.

Ovando sends Escobar to observe Columbus.

When the vessel appeared off the harbor where Columbus was, eight months had passed since Mendez and Fiesco had departed. All hopes of hearing of them had been abandoned. A rumor had come in from the natives that a vessel, bottom upwards, had been seen near the island, drifting with the current. It is said to have been a story started by Porras that its effect might be distressing to Columbus's adherents. It seems to have had the effect to hasten further discontent in that stricken band, and a new revolt was almost ready to make itself known when Escobar's tiny caravel was descried standing in towards shore.

The vessel was seen to lie to, when a boat soon left her side. As it came within hailing, the figure of Escobar was recognized. Columbus knew that he had once condemned the man to death. Bobadilla had pardoned him. The boat bumped against the side of one of the stranded caravels; the crew brought it sidewise against the hulk, when a letter for the Admiral was handed up. Columbus's men made ready to receive a cask of wine and side of bacon, which Escobar's companions lifted on board. All at once a quick motion pushed the boat from the hulks, and Escobar stopped her when she had got out of reach. He now addressed Columbus, and gave him the assurances of Ovando's regret that he had no suitable vessel to send to him, but that he hoped before long to have such. He added that if

Columbus desired to reply to Ovando's letter, he would wait a brief interval for him to prepare an answer.

The Admiral hastily made his reply in as courteous terms as possible, commending the purposes of Mendez and Fiesco to the governor's kind attention, and closed with saying that he reposed full confidence in Ovando's expressed intention to rescue his people, and that he would stay on the wrecks in patience till the ships came. Escobar received the letter, and returned to his caravel, which at once disappeared in the falling gloom of night.

Columbus was not without apprehension that Escobar had come simply to make sure that the Admiral and his company still survived, and Las Casas, who was then at Santo Domingo, seems to have been of the opinion that Ovando had at this time no purpose to do more. The selection of Escobar to carry a kindly message gave certainly a dubious ostentation to all expressions of friendly interest. The transaction may possibly admit of other interpretations. Ovando may reasonably have desired that Columbus and his faithful adherents should not abide long in Española, as in the absence of vessels returning to Spain the Admiral might be obliged to do. There were rumors that Columbus, indignant at the wrongs which he felt he had received at the hands of his sovereigns, had determined to hold his new discoveries for Genoa, and the Admiral had referred to such reports in his recent letter to the Spanish monarchs. Such reports easily put Ovando on his guard, and he may have desired time to get instructions from Spain. At all events, it was very palpable that Ovando was cautious and perhaps inhuman, and Columbus was to be left till Escobar's report should decide what action was best.

Columbus endeavored to make use of the letter which Escobar had brought from Ovando to win Porras and his vagabonds back to loyalty and duty. He dispatched messengers to their camp to say that Ovando had notified him of his purpose to send a vessel to take them off the island. The Admiral was ready to promise forgiveness and forgetfulness, if the mutineers would come in and submit to the requirements of the orderly life of his people. He accompanied the message with a part of the bacon which Escobar had delivered as a present from the governor. The lure, however, was

Columbus communicates with Porras.

not effective. Porras met the ambassadors, and declined the proffers. He said his followers were quite content with the freedom of the island. The fact seemed to be that the mutineers were not quite sure of the Admiral's sincerity, and feared to put themselves in his power. They were ready to come in when the vessels came, if transportation would be allowed them so that their band should not be divided; and until then they would cause the Admiral's party no trouble, unless Columbus refused to share with them his stores and trinkets, which they must have, peacefully or forcibly, since they had lost all their supplies in the gales which had driven them back.

It was evident that Porras and his company were not reduced to such straits that they could be reasoned with, and the messengers returned.

The author of the *Historie*, and others who follow his statements, represent that the body of the mutineers was far from being as arrogant as their leaders, was much more tractable in spirit, and was inclined to catch at the chance of rescue. The leaders labored with the men to keep them steady in their revolt. Porras and his abettors did what they could to picture the cruelties of the Admiral, and even accused him of necromancy in summoning the ghost of a caravel by which to make his people believe that Escobar had really been there. Then, to give some activity to their courage, the whole body of the mutineers was led towards the harbor on pretense of capturing stores. The Adelantado went out to meet them with fifty armed followers, the best he could collect from the wearied companions of the Admiral. Porras refused all offers of conference, and led his band to the attack. There was a plan laid among them that six of the stoutest should attack the Adelantado simultaneously, thinking that if their leader should be overpowered the rest would flee. The Adelantado's courage rose with the exigency, as it was wont to do. He swung his sword with vigor, and one after another the assailants fell. At last Porras struck him such a blow that the Adelantado's buckler was cleft and his hand wounded. The blow was too powerful for the giver of it. His sword remained wedged in the buckler, affording his enemy a chance to close, while an attempt was made to extricate the weapon. Others came to the loyal leader's assistance, and Porras was secured and bound.

*Bartholomew and his men confront the Porras mutineers.*

This turned the current of the fight. The rebels, seeing their
Porras<br>taken. leader a prisoner, fled in confusion, leaving the field
to the party of the Adelantado. The fight had been
a fierce one. They found among the rebel dead Juan San-
Sanchez<br>killed. chez, who had let slip the captured Quibian, and
among the wounded Pedro Ledesma, who had braved
Ledesma<br>wounded. the breakers at Veragua. Las Casas, who knew the
latter at a later day, deriving some help from him in
telling the story of these eventful months, speaks of the many
and fearful wounds which he bore in evidence of his rebellion and courage, and of the sturdy activity of his assailants.
We owe also to Ledesma and to some of his companions,
who, with himself, were witnesses in the later lawsuit of Diego
Colon with the Crown, certain details which the principal narrators fail to give us.

A charm had seemed throughout the conflict to protect the
Admiral's friends. None were killed outright, and but one
other beside their leader was wounded. This man, the Admiral's steward, subsequently died.

The victors returned to the ships with their prisoners; and
in the midst of the gratulations which followed on the
1504. March<br>20. The<br>rebels pro-<br>pose to<br>submit. next day, March 20, 1504, the fugitives sent in an
address to the Admiral, begging to be pardoned and
received back to his care and fortunes. They acknowledged their errors in the most abject professions, and called
upon Heaven to show no mercy, and upon man to know no
sympathy, in dealing retribution, if they failed in their fidelity
thereafter. The proposition of surrender was not without em-
barrassment. The Admiral was fearful of the trial of their
constancy when they might gather about him with all the
chances of further cabaling. He also knew that his provisions were fast running out. Accordingly, in accepting their
surrender, he placed them under officers whom he could trust,
and supplying them with articles of barter, he let them wander about the island under suitable discipline, hoping that they
would find food where they could. He promised, however, to
recall them when the expected ships arrived.

It was not long they had to wait. One day two ships were
seen standing in towards the harbor. One of them proved to be
a caravel which Mendez had bought on the Admiral's account,

out of a fleet of three, just then arrived from Spain, and had victualed for the occasion. Having seen it depart from Santo Domingo, Mendez, in the other ships of this opportune fleet, sailed directly for Spain, to carry out the further instructions of the Admiral.

Ships come to rescue them.

The other of the approaching ships was in command of Diego de Salcedo, the Admiral's factor, and had been dispatched by Ovando. Las Casas tells us that the governor was really forced to this action by public sentiment, which had grown in consequence of the stories of the trials of Columbus which Mendez had told. It is said that even the priests did not hesitate to point a moral in their pulpits with the governor's dilatory sympathy.

Finally, on June 28, everything was ready for departure, and Columbus turned away from the scene of so much trouble. "Columbus informed me afterwards, in Spain," says Mendez, recording the events, "that in no part of his life did he ever experience so joyful a day, for he had never hoped to have left that place alive." Four years later, under authority from the Admiral's son Diego, the town of Sevilla Nueva, later known as Sevilla d' Oro, was founded on the very spot.

1504. June 28. Columbus leaves Jamaica.

The Admiral now committed himself once more to the treacherous currents and adverse winds of these seas. We have seen that Mendez urged his canoe across the gap between Jamaica and the nearest point of Española in four days; but it took the ships of Columbus about seven weeks to reach the haven of Santo Domingo. There was much time during this long and vexatious voyage for Columbus to learn from Salcedo the direful history of the colony which had been wrested from him, and which even under the enlarged powers of Ovando had not been without manifold tribulations. We must rehearse rapidly the occurrences, as Columbus heard of them. He could have got but the scantiest inkling of what had happened during the earliest months of Ovando's rule, when he applied by messenger, in vain, for admission to the harbor, now more than two years ago. The historian of this period must depend mainly upon Las Casas, who had come out with Ovando, and we must sketch an outline of the tale, as Columbus heard it, from that

Events at Española during the absence of Columbus.

Ovando's rule.

writer's *Historia.* It was the old sad story of misguided aspirants for wealth in their first experiences with the hazards and toils of mining, — much labor, disappointed hopes, failing provisions, no gold, sickness, disgust, and a desponding return of the toilers from the scene of their infatuation. It took but eight days for the crowds from Ovando's fleet, who trudged off manfully to the mountains on their landing, to come trooping back, dispirited and diseased.

Columbus could hardly have listened to what was said of suffering among the natives during these two years of his ab-
Columbus and slavery. sence without a vivid consciousness of the baleful system which he had introduced when he assigned crowds of the poor Indians to be put to inhuman tasks by Roldan's crew. The institution of this kind of distribution of labor had grown naturally, but it had become so appalling under Bobadilla that, when Ovando was sent out, he was instructed to put an end to it. It was not long before the governor had to confront the exasperated throngs coming back from the mines, dejected and empty-handed. It was apparent that nothing of the expected revenue to the Crown was likely to be produced from half the yield of metal when there was no yield at all. So, to induce greater industry, Ovando reduced the share of the Crown to a third, and next to a fifth, but without success. It was too apparent that the Spaniards would not persist in labors which brought them so little. At a period when Columbus was flattering himself that he was laying claim to far richer gold fields at Veragua, Ovando was devising a renewal of the Admiral's old slave-driving methods to make the mines of Hayna yield what they could. He sent messages to the sovereigns informing them that their kindness to the natives was really inconsiderate ; that the poor creatures, released from labor, were giving themselves up to mischief ; and that, to make good Christians of them, there was needed the appetizing effect of healthful work upon the native soul. The appeal and the frugal returns to the treasury were quite sufficient to gain the sovereigns to Ovando's views ; and while bewailing any cruelty to the poor
1503. December 20. Forced labor of the natives. natives, and expressing hopes for their spiritual relief, their Majesties were not averse, as they said (December 20, 1503), to these Indians being made to labor as much as was needful to their health. This

was sufficient. The fatal system of Columbus was revived with increased enormities. Six or eight months of unremitting labor, with insufficient food, were cruelly exacted of every native. They were torn from their families, carried to distant parts of the island, kept to their work by the lash, and, if they dared to escape, almost surely recaptured, to work out their period under the burden of chains. At last, when they were dismissed till their labor was again required, Las Casas tells us that the passage through the island of these miserable creatures could be traced by their fallen and decaying bodies. This was a story that, if Columbus possessed any of the tendernesses that glowed in the heart of Las Casas, could not have been a pleasant one for his contemplation.

There was another story to which Columbus may have listened. It is very likely that Salcedo may have got all the particulars from Diego Mendez, who was a witness of the foul deeds which had indeed occurred during those seven months when Ovando, then on an expedition in Xaragua, kept that messenger of Columbus waiting his pleasure. Anacaona, the sister of Behechio, had succeeded to that cacique in the rule of Xaragua. The licentious conduct and the capricious demands of the Spaniards settled in this region had increased the natural distrust and indignation of the Indians, and some signs of discontent which they manifested had been recounted to Ovando as indications of a revolt which it was necessary to nip in the bud. So the governor had marched into the country with three hundred foot and seventy horse. The chieftainess, Anacaona, came forth to meet him with much native parade, and gave all the honor which her savage ceremonials could signify to her distinguished guest. She lodged him as well as she could, and caused many games to be played for his divertisement. In return, Ovando prepared a tournament calculated to raise the expectation of his simple hosts, and horseman and foot came to the lists in full armor and adornment for the heralded show. On a signal from Ovando, the innocent parade was converted in an instant into a fanatical onslaught. The assembled caciques were hedged about with armed men, and all were burned in their cabins. The general populace were transfixed and trampled by the charging mounted spearmen, and only those who could elude the obsti-

*Anacaona treacherously treated.*

*The Indians slaughtered.*

nate and headlong dashes of the cavalry escaped. Anacaona was seized and conveyed in chains to Santo Domingo, where, with the merest pretense of a trial for conspiracy, she was soon hanged.

And this was the pacification of Xaragua. That of Higuey,
the most eastern of the provinces, and which had not

Xaragua and Higuey overrun. yet acknowledged the sway of the Spaniards, followed, with the same resorts to cruelty. A cacique of this region had been slain by a fierce Spanish dog which had been set upon him. This impelled some of the natives living on the coast to seize a canoe having eight Spaniards in it, and to

Esquibel's campaign. slaughter them; whereupon Juan de Esquibel was sent with four hundred men on a campaign against Cotabanama, the chief cacique of Higuey. The invaders met more heroism in the defenders of this country than they had been accustomed to, but the Spanish armor and weapons enabled Esquibel to raid through the land with almost constant success. The Indians at last sued for peace, and agreed to furnish a tribute of provisions. Esquibel built a small fortress, and putting some men in it, he returned to Santo Domingo; not, however, until he had received Cotabanama in his camp. The Spanish leader brought back to Ovando a story of the splendid physical power of this native chief, whose stature, proportions, and strength excited the admiration of the Spaniards.

The peace was not of long duration. The reckless habits of the garrison had once more aroused the courage of the Indians, and some of the latest occurrences which Salcedo could tell of as

New revolt in Higuey. having been reported at Santo Domingo just before his sailing for Jamaica were the events of a new revolt in Higuey.

Such were the stories which Columbus may have listened to during the tedious voyage which was now, on August 3,

1504. August 3. Columbus at Beata. approaching an end. On that day his ships sailed under the lea of the little island of Beata, which lies midway of the southern coast of Española. Here he landed a messenger, and ordered him to convey a letter to Ovando, warning the governor of his approach. Salcedo had told Columbus that the governor was not without apprehension that his coming might raise some factious disturbances among the people, and in this letter the Admiral sought to disabuse

Ovando's mind of such suspicions, and to express his own purpose to avoid every act of irritation which might possibly embarrass the administration of the island. The letter dispatched, Columbus again set sail, and on August 15 his ship entered the harbor of Santo Domingo. Ovando received him with every outward token of respect, and lodged him in his own house. 1504. August 15. At Santo Domingo. Columbus, however, never believed that this officious kindness was other than a cloak to Ovando's dislike, if not hatred. There was no little popular sympathy for the misfortunes which Columbus had experienced, but his relations with the governor were not such as to lighten the anxieties of his sojourn. It is known that Cortes was at this time only recently arrived at Santo Domingo; but we can only conjecture what may have been his interest in Columbus's recitals.

There soon arose questions of jurisdiction. Ovando ordered the release of Porras, and arranged for sending him to Spain for trial. The governor also attempted to interfere with the Admiral's control of his own crew, on the ground that his commission gave him command over all the regions of the new islands and the main. Columbus cited the instructions, which gave him power to rule and judge his own followers. Ovando did not push his claims to extremities, but the irritation never subsided; and Columbus seems to have lost no opportunity, if we may judge from his later letters, to pick up every scandalous story and tale of maladministration of which he could learn, and which could be charged against Columbus and Ovando. Ovando in later appeals to the sovereigns for a restitution of his own rights. The Admiral also inquired into his pecuniary interests in the island, and found, as he thought, that Ovando had obstructed his factor in the gathering of his share. Indeed, there may have been some truth in this; for Carvajal, Columbus's first factor, had complained of such acts to the sovereigns, which elicited an admonishment from them to Ovando.

Such money as Columbus could now collect he used in refitting the ship which had brought him from Jamaica, and he put her under the order of the Adelantado. Securing also another caravel for his own conveyance, he embarked on her with his son, and on September 12 both ships started on their homeward voyage. They were scarcely at sea, when the ship

which bore the Admiral lost her mast in a gale. He transferred himself and his immediate dependents to the

1504. September 12.<br>Columbus<br>sails for<br>Spain.

other vessel, and sent the disabled caravel back to
Santo Domingo. His solitary vessel now went forward, amid all the adversities that seemed to cling
inevitably to this last of Columbus's expeditions. Tempest
after tempest pursued him. The masts were sprung, and again

1504. November 7.<br>Reaches San<br>Lucar.

sprung; and in a forlorn and disabled condition the
little hapless bark finally entered the port of San
Lucar on November 7, 1504. He had been absent
from Spain for two years and a half.

# CHAPTER XX.

## COLUMBUS'S LAST YEARS.—DEATH AND CHARACTER.

### 1504–1506.

FROM San Lucar, Columbus, a sick man in search of quiet and rest, was conveyed to Seville. Unhappily, there was neither repose nor peace of mind in store for him. He remained in that city till May, 1505, broken in spirits and almost helpless of limb. Fortunately, we can trace his varying mental moods during these few months in a series of letters, most of which are addressed by him to his son Diego, then closely attached to the Court. These writings have fortunately come down to us, and they constitute the only series of Columbus's letters which we have, showing the habits of his mind consecutively for a confined period, so that we get a close watch upon his thoughts. They are the wails of a neglected soul, and the cries of one whose hope is cruelly deferred. They have in their entirety a good deal of that haphazard jerkiness tiresome to read, and not easily made evident in abstract. They are, however, not so deficient in mental equipoise as, for instance, the letter sent from Jamaica. This is perhaps owing to the one absorbing burden of them, his hope of recovering possession of his suspended authority.

He writes on November 21, 1504, a fortnight after his landing at San Lucar, telling his son how he has engaged his old friend, the Dominican Deza, now the Bishop of Palencia, to intercede with the sovereigns, that justice may be done to him with respect to his income, the payment of which Ovando had all along, as he contends, obstructed at Española. He tries to argue that if their Highnesses but knew it, they would, in ordering restitution to him, increase their own share. He hopes they have no doubt that his zeal for their interests has been quite as much as he could manifest if he had par-

adise to gain, and hopes they will remember, respecting any
errors he may have committed, that the Lord of all judges such
things by the intention rather than by the outcome.   He seems
to have a suspicion that Porras, now at liberty and about the
Court, might be insidiously at work to his old commander's dis-
advantage, and he represents that neither Porras nor his brother
had been suitable persons for their offices, and that what had
been done respecting them would be approved on inquiry.
" Their revolt," he says, " surprised me, considering all that I
had done for them, as much as the sun would have alarmed me
if it had shot shadows instead of light." He complains of
Ovando's taking the prisoners, who had been companions of
Porras, from his hands, and that, made free, they had even dared
to present themselves at Court.   " I have written," he adds,
" to their Highnesses about it, and I have told them that it
can't be possible that they would tolerate such an offense."
He says further that he has written to the royal treasurer, begging him to come to no decision of the representations of such
detractors until the other side could be heard, and he adds that
he has sent to the treasurer a copy of the oath which the mutineers sent in after Porras had been taken.   " Recall to all
these people," he writes to his son, " my infirmities, and the
recompense due to me for my services."

Diego was naturally, from his residence at Court, a convenient medium to bring all Columbus's wishes to the notice of
those about the sovereigns.   The Admiral writes to Diego again
that he hopes their Highnesses will see to the paying of his
men who had come home.   " They are poor, and have been
gone three years," he says.   " They bring home evidences of
the greatest of expectations in the new gold fields of Veragua ; "
and then he advises his son to bring this fact to the attention
of all who are concerned, and to urge the colonizing of the new
country as the best way to profit from its gold mines.   For
a while he harbored the hope that he might at once go on to
the Court, and a litter which had served in the obsequies of
Cardinal Mendoza was put at his disposal ; but this plan was
soon given up.

A week later, having in the interim received a letter of the
15th, from Diego, Columbus writes again, under date
of November 28.   In this epistle he speaks of the

1504. No-
vember 28.

severity of his disease, which keeps him in Seville, from which, however, he hopes to depart the coming week, and of his disappointment that the sovereigns had not replied to his inquiries. He sends his love to Diego Mendez, hoping that his friend's zeal and love of truth will enable him to overcome the deceits and intrigues of Porras.

Columbus was not at this time aware that the impending death of the Queen had something to do with the delays in his own affairs at Court. Two days (November 26) before the Admiral wrote this note, Isabella had died, worn out by her labors, and depressed by the afflictions which she had experienced in her domestic circle. She was an unlovely woman at the best, an obstructor of Christian charity, but in her wiles she had allured Columbus to a belief in her countenance of him. The conventional estimate of her character, which is enforced in the rather cloying descriptions of Prescott, is such as her flatterers drew in her own times; but the revelations of historical research hardly confirm it. It was with her much as with Columbus, — she was too largely a creature of her own age to be solely judged by the criteria of all ages, as lofty characters can be.

1504. November 26. Queen Isabella dies.

Isabella's character.

The loss of her influence on the king removed, as it proved, even the chance of a flattering delusiveness in the hopes of Columbus. As the compiler of the *Historie* expresses it, "Columbus had always enjoyed her favor and protection, while the King had always been indifferent, or rather inimical." She had indeed, during the Admiral's absence on his last voyage, manifested some new appreciation of his services, which cost her little, however, when she made his eldest son one of her bodyguard and naturalized his brother Diego, to fit him for ecclesiastical preferment.

On December 1, ignorant of the sad occurrences at Court, Columbus writes again, chiding Diego that he had not in his dutifulness written to his poor father. "You ought to know," he says, "that I have no pleasure now but in a letter from you." Columbus by this time had become, by the constant arrival of couriers, aware of the anxiety at Court over the Queen's health, and he prays that the Holy Trinity will restore her to health, to the end that all that has been begun may be happily finished. He reiterates what he

1504. December 1.

had previously written about the increasing severity of his malady, his inability to travel, his want of money, and how he had used all he could get in Española to bring home his poor companions. He commends anew to Diego his brother Ferdinand, and speaks of this younger son's character as beyond his years. " Ten brothers would not be too many for you," he adds; "in good as in bad fortune, I have never found better friends than my brothers."

Nothing troubles him more than the delays in hearing from Court. A rumor had reached him that it was intended to send some bishops to the Indies, and that the Bishop of Palencia was charged with the matter. He begs Diego to say to the bishop that it was worth while, in the interests of all, to confer with the Admiral first. In explaining why he does not write to Diego Mendez, he says that he is obliged to write by night, since by day his hands are weak and painful. He adds that the vessel which put back to Santo Domingo had arrived, bringing the papers in Porras's case, the result of the inquest which had been taken at Jamaica, so that he could now be able to present an indictment to the Council of the Indies. His indignation is aroused at the mention of it. " What can be so foul and brutal! If their Highnesses pass it by, who is going again to lead men upon their service!"

Two days later (December 3), he writes again to Diego about the neglect which he is experiencing from him and from others at Court. " Everybody except myself is receiving letters," he says. He incloses a memoir expressing what he thought it was necessary to do in the present conjunction of his affairs. This document opens with calling upon Diego zealously to pray to God for the soul of the Queen. " One must believe she is now clothed with a sainted glory, no longer regretting the bitterness and weariness of this life." The King, he adds, " deserves all our sympathy and devotion." He then informs Diego that he has directed his brother, his uncle, and Carvajal to add all their importunities to his son's, and to the written prayers which he himself has sent, that consideration should be given to the affairs of the Indies. Nothing, he says, can be more urgent than to remedy the abuses there. In all this he curiously takes on the tone of his own accusers a few years before. He represents that pecuniary

1504. December 3.

returns from Española are delayed; that the governor is detested by all; that a suitable person sent there could restore harmony in less than three months; and that other fortresses, which are much needed, should be built, " all of which I can do in his Highness's service," he exclaims, " and any other, not having my personal interests at stake, could not do it so well!" Then he repeats how, immediately after his arrival at San Lucar, he had written to the King a very long letter, advising action in the matter, to which no reply had been returned.

It was during Columbus's absence on this last voyage that, by an ordinance made at Alcalá, January 20, 1503, the famous *Casa de Contratacion* was established, with authority over the affairs of the Indies, having the power to grant licenses, to dispatch fleets, to dispose of the results of trade or exploration, and to exercise certain judicial prerogatives. This council was to consist of a treasurer, a factor, and a comptroller, to whom two persons learned in the law were given as advisers. Alexander VI. had already, by a bull of November 16, 1501, authorized the payment to the constituted Spanish officials of all the tithes of the colonies, which went a long way in giving Spain ecclesiastical supremacy in the Indies, in addition to her political control.

1503. January 20. The *Casa de Contratacion* established.

It was to this council that Columbus refers, when he says he had told the gentlemen of the *Contratacion* that they ought to abide by the verbal and written orders which the King had given, and that, above all, they should watch lest people should sail to the Indies without permission. He reminded them of the sorry character of the people already in the New World, and of the way in which treasure was stored there without protection.

Ten days later (December 13), he writes again to Diego, recurring to his bitter memories of Ovando, charging him with diverting the revenues, and with bearing himself so haughtily that no one dared remonstrate. " Everybody says that I have as much as 11,000 or 12,000 castellanos in Española, and I have not received a quarter. Since I came away he must have received 5,000." He then urges Diego to sue the King for a mandatory letter to be sent to Ovando, forcing immediate payment. " Carvajal knows very well that this ought to be done. Show him this letter," he adds. Then re-

1504. December 13.

ferring to his denied rights, and to the best way to make the King sensible of his earlier promises, he next advises Diego to lessen his expenses; to treat his uncle with the respect which is due to him; and to bear himself towards his younger brother as an older brother should. "You have no other brother," he says; "and thank God this one is all you could desire. He was born with a good nature." Then he reverts to the Queen's death. "People tell me," he writes, "that on her death-bed she expressed a wish that my possession of the Indies should be restored to me."

A week later (December 21), he once more bewails the way in which he is left without tidings. He recounts the exertions he had made to send money to his advocates at Court, and tells Diego how he must somehow continue to get on as best he can till their Highnesses are content to give them back their power. He repeats that to bring his companions home from Santo Domingo he had spent twelve hundred castellanos, and that he had represented to the King the royal indebtedness for this, but it produced no reimbursement. He asks Diego to find out if the Queen, "now with God, no doubt," had spoken of him in her will; and perhaps the Bishop of Palencia, "who was the cause of their Majesties' acquiring the Indies, and of my returning to the Court when I had departed," or the chamberlain of the King could find this out. Columbus may have lived to learn that the only item of the Queen's will in which he could possibly have been in mind was the one in which she showed that she was aroused to the enormities which Columbus had imposed on the Indians, and which had come to such results that, as Las Casas says, it had been endeavored to keep the knowledge of it from the Queen's ears. She earnestly enjoined upon her successors a change of attitude towards the poor Indians.

Columbus further says that the Pope had complained that no account of his voyage had been sent to Rome, and that accordingly he had prepared one, and he desired Diego to read it, and to let the King and the bishop also peruse it before it was forwarded to Rome. It is possible that the Adelantado was dispatched with the letter. The canonizers say that the mission to Rome had also a secret purpose, which was to counteract the schemes of Fonseca to create

*1504. December 21.*

*Columbus writes to the Pope.*

bishoprics in Española, and that the advice of Columbus in the end prevailed over the "cunning of diplomacy."

There had been some time before, owing to the difficulty which had been experienced in mounting the royal cavalry, an order promulgated forbidding the use of mules in travel, since it was thought that the preference for this animal had brought about the deterioration and scarcity of horses. It was to this injunction that Columbus now referred when he asked Diego to get a dispensation from the King to allow him to enjoy the easier seat of a mule when he should venture on his journey towards the Court, which, with this help, he hoped to be able to begin within a few weeks. Such an order was in due time issued on February 23, 1505.

1505. February 23. Columbus allowed to ride a mule.

On December 29, Columbus wrote again. The letter was full of the same pitiful suspense. He had received no letters. He could but repeat the old story of the letters of credit which he had sent and which had not been acknowledged. No one of his people had been paid, he said, neither the faithful nor the mutineers. "They are all poor. They are going to Court," he adds, "to press their claims. Aid them in it." He excepts, however, from the kind interest of his friends two fellows who had been with him on his last voyage, one Camacho and Master Bernal, the latter the physician of the flagship. Bernal was the instigator of the revolt of Porras, he says, "and I pardoned him at the prayer of my brother."

1504. December 29.

It will be remembered that, previous to starting on his last voyage, Columbus had written to the Bank of St. George in Genoa, proposing a gift of a tenth of his income for the benefit of his native town. The letter was long in reaching its destination, but a reply was duly sent through his son Diego. It never reached Columbus, and this apparent spurning of his gift by Genoa caused not a small part of his present disgust with the world.

Columbus and the Bank of St. George.

On December 27, 1504, he wrote to Nicolo Oderigo, reminding him of the letter, and complaining that while he had expected to be met on his return by some confidential agent of the bank, he had not even had a letter in response. "It was uncourteous in these gentlemen of St. George not to have favored me with an answer." The intention was, in fact, far from being unappreciated, and at a later day the

1504. December 27.

promise became so far magnified as to be regarded as an actual gift, in which the Genoese were not without pride. The purpose never, however, had a fulfillment.

On January 4, 1505, the Admiral wrote to his friend Father
1505. January 4. Gorricio, telling him that Diego Mendez had arrived from the Court, and asking the friar to encase in wax the documentary privileges of the Admiral which had been intrusted to him, and to send them to him. "My disease grows better day by day," he adds.

On January 18, 1505, he again wrote. The epistle was in
1505. January 18. some small degree cheery. He had heard at last from Diego. "Zamora the courier has arrived, and I have looked with great delight upon thy letter, thy uncle's, thy brother's, and Carvajal's." Diego Mendez, he says, sets out in three or four days with an order for payment. He refers with some playfulness, even, to Fonseca, who had just been raised to the bishopric of Placentia, and had not yet returned from Flanders to take possession of the seat. "If the Bishop of Placentia has arrived, or when he comes, tell him how much pleased I am at his elevation; and that when I come to Court I shall depend on lodging with his Grace, whether he wishes it or not, that we may renew our old fraternal bonds." His biographers have been in some little uncertainty whether he really meant here Fonseca or his old friend Deza, who had just left that bishopric vacant for the higher post of Archbishop of Seville. A strict application of dates makes the reference to Fonseca. One may imagine, however, that Columbus was not accurately informed. It is indeed hard to understand the pleasantry, if Fonseca was the bitter enemy of Columbus that he is pictured by Irving.

Some ships from Española had put into the Tagus. "They have not arrived here from Lisbon," he adds. "They bring much gold, but none for me."

We next find Columbus in close communion with a contemporary with whose fame his own is sadly conjoined. Some ac-
Conference with Vespucius. count of the events of the voyage which Vespucius had made along the coast of South America with Coelho, from which he had returned to Lisbon in September, 1502, has been given on an earlier page. Those events and his descriptions had already brought the name of Vespu-

cius into prominence throughout Europe, but hardly before he had started on another voyage in the spring or early summer of 1503, just at the time when Columbus was endeavoring to work his way from the Veragua coast to Española. The authorities are not quite agreed whether it was on May 10, 1503, or a month later, on June 10, that the little Portuguese fleet in which Vespucius sailed left the Tagus, to find a way, if possible, to the Moluccas somewhere along the same great coast. This expedition had started under the command of Coelho, but meeting with mishaps, by which the fleet was separated, Vespucius, with his own vessel, joined later by another with which he fell in, proceeded to Bahia, where a factory for storing Brazil-wood was erected; thence, after a stay there, they sailed for Lisbon, arriving there after an absence of seventy-seven days, on June 18, 1504. It was later, on September 4, that Vespucius wrote, or rather dated, that account of his voyage which was to work such marvels, as we shall see, in the reputation of himself and of Columbus. There is no reason to suppose that Columbus ever knew of this letter of September 4, so subversive as it turned out of his just fame; nor, judging from the account of their interview which Columbus records, is there any reason to suppose that Vespucius himself had any conception of the work which that fateful letter was already accomplishing, and to which reference will be made later.

*Vespucius's account of his voyage.*

On February 5, 1505, Columbus wrote to Diego: " Within two days I have talked with Americus Vespucius, who will bear this to you, and who is summoned to Court on matters of navigation. He has always manifested a disposition to be friendly to me. Fortune has not always favored him, and in this he is not different from many others. His ventures have not always been as successful as he would wish. He left me full of the kindliest purposes towards me, and will do anything for me which is in his power. I hardly knew what to tell him would be helpful in him to do for me, because I did not know what purpose there was in calling him to Court. Find out what he can do, and he will do it; only let it be so managed that he will not be suspected of rendering me aid. I have told him all that it is possible to tell him as to my own affairs, including what I have done and what recompense I

*1505. February 5.*

have had. Show this letter to the Adelantado, so that he may advise how Vespucius can be made serviceable to us."

We soon after this find Vespucius installed as an agent of the Spanish government, naturalized on April 24 as a Castilian, and occupied at the seaports in superintending the fitting out of ships for the Indies, with an annual salary of thirty thousand maravedis. We can find no trace of any assistance that he afforded the cause of Columbus.

*1505. April 24. Vespucius naturalized.*

Meanwhile events were taking place which Columbus might well perhaps have arrested, could he have got the royal ear. An order had been sent in February to Española to sell the effects of Columbus, and in April other property of the Admiral had been seized to satisfy his creditors.

*Columbus's effects sold.*

In May, 1505, Columbus, with the friendly care of his brother Bartholomew, set out on his journey to Segovia, where the Court then was. This is the statement of Las Casas, but Harrisse can find no evidence of his being near the Court till August, when, on the 25th, he attested, as will appear, his will before a notary. The change bringing him into the presence of his royal master only made his mortification more poignant. His personal suit to the King was quite as ineffective as his letters had been. The sovereign was outwardly beneficent, and inwardly uncompliant. The Admiral's recitals respecting his last voyage, both of promised wealth and of saddened toil, made little impression. Las Casas suspects that the insinuations of Porras had preoccupied the royal mind. To rid himself of the importunities of Columbus, the King proposed an arbiter, and readily consented to the choice which Columbus made of his old friend Deza, now Archbishop of Seville; but Columbus was too immovably fixed upon his own rights to consent that more than the question of revenue should be considered by such an arbiter. His recorded privileges and the pledged word of the sovereign were not matters to be reconsidered. Such was not, however, the opinion of the King. He evaded the point in his talk with bland countenance, and did nothing in his acts beyond referring the question anew to a body of counselors convened to determine the fulfillment of the Queen's will. They did nothing quite as easily as the King. Las Casas tells us that the King was only

*1505. May. Columbus goes to Segovia.*

*August 25. Attests his will.*

*Columbus and Ferdinand.*

restrained by motives of outward decency from a public rejection of all the binding obligations towards the Admiral into which he had entered jointly with the Queen.

Columbus found in all this nothing to comfort a sick and desponding man, and sank in despair upon his couch. He roused enough to have a will drafted August 25, which confirmed a testament made in 1502, before starting on his last voyage. His disease renewed its attacks. An old wound had reopened. From a bed of pain he began again his written appeals. He now gave up all hopes for himself, but he pleaded for his son, that upon him the honors which he himself had so laboriously won should be bestowed. Diego at the same time, in seconding the petition, promised, if the reinstatement took place, that he would count those among his counselors whom the royal will should designate. Nothing of protest or appeal came opportunely to the determined King. "The more he was petitioned," says Las Casas, "the more bland he was in avoiding any conclusion. He hoped by exhausting the patience of the Admiral to induce him to accept some estates in Castile in lieu of such powers in the Indies. Columbus rejected all such intimations with indignation. He would have nothing but his bonded rights. "I have done all that I can do," he said in a pitiful, despairing letter to Deza. "I must leave the issue to God. He has always sustained me in extremities."

*1505. August 25. His will.*

*Columbus pleads for his son.*

*Rejects offers of estates.*

"It argued," says Prescott, in commenting on this, "less knowledge of character than the King usually showed, that he should have thought the man who had broken off all negotiations on the threshold of a dubious enterprise, rather than abate one tittle of his demands, would consent to such abatement, when the success of that enterprise was so gloriously established."

The Admiral was, during this part of his suit, apparently at Salamanca, for Mendez speaks of him as being there confined to his bed with the gout, while he himself was doing all he could to press his master's claims to have Diego recognized in his rights. In return for this service, Mendez asked to be appointed principal Alguazil of Española for life, and he says the Admiral acknow-

*Columbus at Salamanca.*

*Mendez and Columbus.*

ledged that such an appointment was but a trifling remuneration for his great services, but the requital never came.

There broke a glimmer of hope. The death of the Queen had left the throne of Castile to her daughter Juana, the wife of Philip of Austria, and they had arrived from Flanders to be installed in their inheritance. Columbus, who had followed
Columbus unable to leave Valladolid to greet Philip and Juana.
the Court from Segovia to Salamanca, thence to Valladolid, was now unable to move further in his decrepitude, and sent the Adelantado to propitiate the daughter of Isabella, with the trust that something of her mother's sympathy might be vouchsafed to his entreaties. Bartholomew never saw his brother again, and was not privileged to communicate to him the gracious hopes which the benignity of his reception raised.

A year had passed since the Admiral had come to the neighborhood of the Court, wherever it was, and nothing had been accomplished in respect to his personal interests. Indeed, little touching the Indies at all seems to have been done. There had
Negroes sent to Española.
been trial made of sending negro slaves to Española as indicating that the native bondage needed reinforcement; but Ovando had reported that the experiment was a failure, since the negroes only mixed with the Indians and taught them bad habits. Ferdinando cared little for this, and at Segovia, September 15, 1505, he notified Ovando that he should send some more negroes. Whether Columbus was aware of this change in the methods of extracting gold from the soil we cannot find.

As soon as Bartholomew had started on his mission the malady of Columbus increased. He became conscious that the time had come to make his final dispositions. It was on May
1506. May 4. Codicil to his will.
4, 1506, according to the common story, that he signed a codicil to his will on a blank page in a breviary which had been given to him, as he says, by Alexander VI., and which had "comforted him in his battles, his captivities, and his misfortunes." This document has been accepted by some of the commentators as genuine; Harrisse and others are convinced of its apocryphal character. It was not found till 1779. It is a strange document, if authentic. It holds that such dignities as were his under the Spanish Crown, acknowledged or not, were his of right to alienate from the

Spanish throne. It was, if anything, a mere act of bravado, as if to flout at the authority which could dare deprive him of his possessions. He provides for the descent of his honors in the male line, and that failing, he bequeaths them to the republic of Genoa! It was a gauge of hostile demands on Spain which no one but a madman would imagine that Genoa would accept if she could. He bestowed on his native city, in the same reckless way, the means to erect a hospital, and designated that such resources should come from his Italian estates, whatever they were. Certainly the easiest way to dispose of the paper is to consider it a fraud. If such, it was devised by some one who entered into the spirit of the Admiral's madness, and made the most of rumors that had been afloat respecting Columbus's purposes to benefit Genoa at the expense of Spain.

*Thought to be spurious.*

About a fortnight later (May 19), he ratified an undoubted will, which had been drafted by his own hand the year before at Segovia, and executed it with the customary formalities. Its testamentary provisions were not unnatural. He made Diego his heir, and his entailed property was, in default of heirs to Diego, to pass to his illegitimate son Ferdinand, and from him, in like default, to his own brother, the Adelantado, and his male descendants ; and all such failing, to the female lines in a similar succession. He enjoined upon his representatives, of whatever generation, to serve the Spanish King with fidelity. Upon Diego, and upon later heads of the family, he imposed the duty of relieving all distressed relatives and others in poverty. He imposed on his lawful son the appointment of some one of his lineage to live constantly in Genoa, to maintain the family dignity. He directed him to grant due allowances to his brother and uncle ; and when the estates yielded the means, to erect a chapel in the Vega of Española, where masses might be said daily for the repose of the souls of himself and of his nearest relatives. He made the furthering of the crusade to recover the Holy Sepulchre equally contingent upon the increase of his income. He also directed Diego to provide for the maintenance of Donna Beatrix Enriquez, the mother of Ferdinand, as " a person to whom I am under great obligations," and "let this be done for the discharge of my conscience, for it weighs heavy on my soul, —

*1506. May 19. Ratified his will.*

the reasons for which I am not here permitted to give;" and this was a behest that Diego, in his own will, acknowledges his failure to observe during the last years of the lady's life. Then, in a codicil, Columbus enumerates sundry little bequests to other persons to whom he was indebted, and whose kindness he wished to remember. He was honest enough to add that his bequests were imaginary unless his rights were acknowledged. "Hitherto I neither have had, nor have I now, any positive income." He failed to express any wish respecting the spot of his interment. The documents were committed at once to a notary, from whose archives a copy was obtained in 1524 by his son Diego, and this copy exists to-day among the family papers in the hands of the Duke of Veragua.

This making of a will was almost his last act. On the next 1506. May 20. Columbus dies. day he partook of the sacrament, and uttering, "Into thy hands, O Lord, I commit my spirit," he gasped his last. It was on the 20th of May, 1506, — by some circumstances we might rather say May 21, — in the city

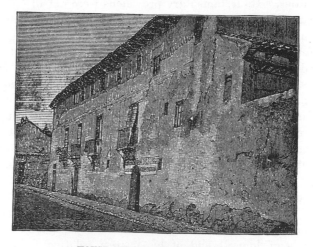

HOUSE WHERE COLUMBUS DIED.

[From Ruge's *Geschichte des Zeitalters der Entdeckungen.*]

of Valladolid, that this singular, hopeful, despondent, melancholy life came to its end. He died at the house No. 7 Calle de Colon, which is still shown to travelers.

There was a small circle of relatives and friends who

mourned. The tale of his departure came like a sough of wind to a few others, who had seen no way to alleviate a misery that merited their sympathy. The King could have but found it a relief from the indiscretion of his early promises. The world at large thought no more of the mournful pro- His death cession which bore that wayworn body to the grave unnoticed. than it did of any poor creature journeying on his bier to the potter's field.

It is hard to conceive how the fame of a man over whose acts in 1493 learned men cried for joy, and by whose deeds the adventurous spirit had been stirred in every seaport of western Europe, should have so completely passed into oblivion that a professed chronicler like Peter Martyr, busy tattler as he was, should take no notice of his illness and death. There have come down to us five long letters full of news and gossip, which Martyr wrote from Valladolid at this very time, with not a word in them of the man he had so often commemorated. Fracanzio da Montalboddo, publishing in 1507 some correction of his early voyages, had not heard of Columbus's death; nor had Madrignano in dating his Latin rendering of the same book in 1508. It was not till twenty-seven days after the death-bed scene that the briefest notice was made in passing, in an official document of the town, to the effect that " the said Admiral is dead ! "

It is not even certain where the body was first placed, though it is usually affirmed to have been deposited in the Franciscan convent in Valladolid. Nor is there any His burial. evidence to support another equally prevalent story that King Ferdinand had ordered the removal of the remains to Seville seven years later, when a monument was built bearing the often-quoted distich, —

À CASTILLA Y À LEON
NUEVO MUNDO DIÓ COLON, —

it being pretty evident that such an inscription was never thought of till Castellanos suggested it in his *Elegias* in 1588. If Diego's will in 1509 can be interpreted on this matter, it seems pretty sure that within three years (1509) after the death of Columbus, instead of seven, his coffin had been conveyed to Seville and placed inside the convent His coffin carried to Seville. of Las Cuevas, in the vault of the Carthusians, where the bodies of his son Diego and brother Bartholomew were in due time to rest beside his own. Here the remains were undisturbed till 1536, when the records of the convent affirm that they were given up for transportation, though the royal order is given as of June 2, 1537. From that date till 1549 there is room for conjecture as to their abiding-place.

It was during this interval that his family were seeking to carry out what was supposed to be the wish of the Admiral to rest finally in the island of Española. From 1537 to 1540 the government are known to have issued three different orders respecting the removal of the remains, and it is conjectured the transference was actually made in 1541, shortly after the completion of the cathedral at Santo Domingo. If any record was made at the time to designate the spot of the reëntombment in that edifice, it is not now known, and it was not till 1676 that somebody placed an entry in its records that the burial had been made on the right of the altar. A few years later (1683), the recollections of aged people are quoted to substantiate such a statement. We find no other notice till a century afterwards, when, on the occasion of some repairs, a stone vault, supposed in the traditions to be that which held the remains, was found on " the gospel side " of the chancel, while another on " the epistle side " was thought to contain the remains of Bartholomew Columbus. This was the suspected situation of the graves when the treaty of Basle, in 1795, gave the Santo Domingo end of the island to France, and the Spanish authorities, acting in concert with the Duke of Veragua, as the representative of the family of Columbus, determined on the removal of the remains to Havana. It is a question which has been raised since 1877 whether the body of Columbus was the one then removed, and over which so much parade was made during the transportation and reinterment in Cuba. There has been a controversy on the point, in which the Bishop of Santo Domingo and his adherents have claimed that the remains of Columbus are still in their charge, while it was those of his son Diego which had been removed. The Academy of History at Madrid have denied this, and in a long report to the Spanish government have asserted that there was no mistake in the transfer, and that the additional casket found was that of Christopher Colon, the

*(margin note:)* 1541. Removed to Santo Domingo.

*(margin note:)* Remains removed to Havana.

CATHEDRAL AT SANTO DOMINGO.

grandson. It was represented, moreover, that those features of the inscription on the lately found leaden box which seemed to indicate it as the casket of the first Admiral of the Indies had Question of the identity of his remains. been fraudulently added or altered. The question has probably been thrown into the category of doubt, though the case as presented in favor of Santo Domingo has some recognizably weak points, which the advocates of the other side have made the most of, and to the satisfaction perhaps of the more careful inquirers. The controversial literature on the subject is considerable. The repairs of 1877 in the Santo Domingo cathedral revealed the empty vault from which the transported body had been taken; but they showed also the occupied vault of the grandson Luis, and another in which was a leaden case which bore the inscriptions which are in dispute.

It is the statement of the *Historie* that Columbus preserved Alleged burial of his chains with him. the chains in which he had come home from his third voyage, and that he had them buried with him, or intended to do so. The story is often repeated, but it has no other authority than the somewhat dubious one of that book; and it finds no confirmation in Las Casas, Peter Martyr, Bernaldez, or Oviedo.

Humboldt says that he made futile inquiry of those who had assisted in the reinterment at Havana, if there were any trace of these fetters or of oxide of iron in the coffin. In the accounts of the recent discovery of remains at Santo Domingo, it is said that there was equally no trace of fetters in the casket.

The age of Columbus is almost without a parallel, presenting The age of Columbus. perhaps the most striking appearances since the star shone upon Bethlehem. It saw Martin Luther burn the Pope's bull, and assert a new kind of independence. It added Erasmus to the broadeners of life. Ancient art was revivified in the discovery of its most significant remains. Modern art stood confessed in Da Vinci, Michael Angelo, Titian, Raphael, Holbein, and Dürer. Copernicus found in the skies a wonderful development without great telescopic help. The route of the Portuguese by the African cape and the voyage of Columbus opened new worlds to thought and commerce. They made the earth seem to man, north and south, east and west, as

STATUE OF COLUMBUS AT SANTO DOMINGO.

man never before had imagined it. It looked as if mercantile endeavor was to be constrained by no bounds. Articles of trade were multiplied amazingly. Every movement was not only new and broad, but it was rapid beyond conception. It was more like the remodeling of Japan, which we have seen in our day, than anything that had been earlier known.

The long sway of the Moors was disintegrating. The Arab domination in science and seamanship was yielding to the Western genius. The Turks had in the boyhood (1453) of Columbus consummated their last great triumph in the capture of Constantinople, thus placing a barrier to Christian commerce with the East. This conquest drove out the learned Christians of the East, who had drunk of the Arab erudition, and they fled with their stores of learning to the western lands, coming back to the heirs of the Romans with the spirit which Rome in the past had sent to the East.

But what Christian Europe was losing in the East Portugal and Prince Henry were gaining for her in the great and forbidding western waste of waters and along its African shores. As the hot tide of Mahometan invasion rolled over the Bosphorus, the burning equatorial zone was pierced from the north along the coasts of the Black Continent.

Italy, seeing her maritime power drop away as the naval supremacy of the Atlantic seaboard rose, was forced to send her experienced navigators to the oceanic ports, to maintain the supremacy of her name and genius in Cadamosto, Columbus, Vespucius, Cabot, and Verrazano. Those cosmographical views which had come down the ages, at times obscured, then for a while patent, and of which the traces had lurked in the minds of learned men by an almost continuous sequence for many centuries, at last possessed by inheritance the mind of Columbus. By reading, by conference with others, by noting phenomena, and by reasoning, in the light of all these, upon the problem of a western passage to India, obvious as it was if once the sphericity of the earth be acknowledged, he gradually grew to be confident in himself and trustful in his agency with others. He was far from being alone in his beliefs, nor was his age anything more than a reflection of long periods of like belief. There was simply needed a man with courage and constancy in his convic-

*Italian discoverers.*

*His growing belief in the western passage.*

tions, so that the theory could be demonstrated. This age produced him. Enthusiasm and the contagion of palpable though shadowy truths gave Columbus, after much tribulation, the countenance in high quarters that enabled him to reach success, deceptive though it was. It would have been well for his memory if he had died when his master work was done. With his great aim certified by its results, though they were far from being what he thought, he was unfortunately left in the end to be laid bare on trial, a common mortal after all, the creature of buffeting circumstances, and a weakling in every ele- Deficiencies ment of command. His imagination had availed him of character. in his upward course when a serene habit in his waiting days could obscure his defects. Later, the problems he encountered were those that required an eye to command, with tact to persuade and skill to coerce, and he had none of them.

The man who becomes the conspicuous developer of any great world-movement is usually the embodiment of the ripened aspirations of his time. Such was Columbus. It is the forerunner, the man who has little countenance in his age, who points the way for some hazardous after-soul to pursue. Such was Roger Bacon, the English Franciscan. It was Bacon's Roger Ba- lot to direct into proper channels the new surging of con and the experimental sciences which was induced by the Columbus. revived study of Aristotle, and was carrying dismay into the strongholds of Platonism. Standing out from the background of Arab regenerating learning, the name of Roger Bacon, linked often with that of Albertus Magnus, stood for the best knowledge and insight of the thirteenth century. Bacon it was who gave that tendency to thought which, seized by Cardinal Pierre d'Ailly, and incorporated by him in his *Imago Mundi* Pierre d'Ail- (1410), became the link between Bacon and Colum- ly's *Imago* bus. Humboldt has indeed expressed his belief that *Mundi.* this encyclopædic Survey of the World exercised a more important influence upon the discovery of America than even the prompting which Columbus got from his correspondence with Toscanelli. How well Columbus pored over the pages of the *Imago Mundi* we know from the annotations of his own copy, which is still preserved in the Biblioteca Colombina. It seems likely that Columbus got directly from this book most that he knew of those passages in Aristotle, Strabo, and Seneca which speak of the Asiatic shores as lying opposite to Hispania. There is some evidence that this book was his companion even on his voyages, and Humboldt points out how he translates a passage from it, word for word, when in 1498 he embodied it in a letter which he wrote to his sovereigns from Española.

If we take the pains, as Humboldt did, to examine the writings of Columbus, to ascertain the sources which he cited, we find what appears to be a broad acquaintance with books. It is to be remembered, however, that the Admiral quoted usually at second hand, and that he got his acquaintance with classic authors, at least, mainly through this *Imago Mundi* of Pierre d'Ailly. Humboldt, in making his list of Columbus's authors, omits the references to the Scriptures and to the Church fathers, "in whom," as he says, "Columbus was singularly versed," and then gives the following catalogue : —

His acquaintance with the elder writers.

Aristotle ; Julius Cæsar ; Strabo ; Seneca ; Pliny ; Ptolemy ; Solinus ; Julius Capitolinus ; Alfrazano ; Avenruyz ; Rabbi Samuel de Israel ; Isidore, Bishop of Seville ; the Venerable Bede ; Strabus, Abbé of Reichenau ; Duns Scotus ; François Mayronis ; Abbé Joachim de Calabre ; Sacrobosco, being in fact the English mathematician Holywood ; Nicholas de Lyra, the Norman Franciscan ; King Alfonso the Wise, and his Moorish scribes ; Cardinal Pierre d'Ailly ; Gerson, Chancellor of the University of Paris ; Pope Pius II., otherwise known as Æneas Sylvius Piccolomini ; Regiomontanus, as the Latinized name of Johann Müller of Königsberg is given, though Columbus does not really name him ; Paolo Toscanelli, the Florentine physician ; and Nicolas de Conti, of whom he had heard through Toscanelli, perhaps.

Humboldt can find no evidence that Columbus had read the travels of Marco Polo, and does not discover why Navarrete holds that he had, though Polo's stories must have permeated much that Columbus read ; nor does he understand why Irving says that Columbus took Marco Polo's book on his first voyage.

We see often in the world's history a simultaneousness in the regeneration of thought. Here and there a seer works on in ignorance of some obscure brother elsewhere. Rumor and circulating manuscripts bring them into sympathy. They grow by the correlation. It is just this correspondence that confronts us in Columbus and Toscanelli, and it is not quite, but almost, perceptible that this wise Floren- Columbus and Tosca-nelli. tine doctor was the first, despite Humboldt's theory, to plant in the mind of Columbus his aspirations for the truths of geography. It is meet that Columbus should not be mentioned without the accompanying name of Toscanelli. It was the Genoese's different fortune that he could attempt as a seaman a practical demonstration of his fellow Italian's views.

Many a twin movement of the world's groping spirit thus seeks the light. Progress naturally pushes on parallel lines. Commerce thrusts her intercourse to remotest regions, while the Church yearns for new souls to convert, and peers longingly into the dim spaces that skirt the world's geography. Navigators improve their methods, and learned men in the arts supply them with exacter instruments. The widespread manifestations of all this new life at last crystallize, and Gama and Columbus appear, the reflex of every development.

Thus the discovery of Columbus came in the ripeness of time. No one of the anterior accidents, suggesting a western land, granting that there was some measure of Opportune-ness of his discoveries. fact in all of them, had come to a world prepared to think on their developments. Vinland was practically forgotten, wherever it may have been. The tales of Fousang had never a listener in Europe. Madoc was as unknown as Elidacthon. While the new Indies were not in their turn to be forgotten, their discoverer was to bury himself in a world of conjecture. The superlatives of Columbus soon spent their influence. The pioneer was lost sight of in the new currents of thought which he had started. Not of least interest among them was the cognizance of new races of men, and new revelations in the animal and physical kingdoms, while the question of their origins pressed very soon on the theological and scientific sense of the age.

No man craves more than Columbus to be judged with all the palliations demanded of a difference of his own Not above his age. age and ours. No child of any age ever did less to improve his contemporaries, and few ever did more to prepare

the way for such improvements.   The age created him and the
Claims for age left him.   There is no more conspicuous example
palliation. in history of a man showing the path and losing it.

It is by no means sure, with all our boast of benevolent progress, that atrocities not much short of those which we ascribe
to Columbus and his compeers may not at any time disgrace
the coming as they have blackened the past years of the nineteenth century.   This fact gives us the right to judge the infirmities of man in any age from the high vantage-ground of
the best emotions of all the centuries.   In the application of
such perennial justice Columbus must inevitably suffer.   The
degradation of the times ceases to be an excuse when the man
to be judged stands on the pinnacle of the ages.   The biographer cannot forget, indeed, that Columbus is a portrait set in
the surroundings of his times ; but it is equally his duty at the
same time to judge the paths which he trod by the scale of an
eternal nobleness.

The very domination of this man in the history of two hemispheres warrants us in estimating him by an austere sense
of occasions lost and of opportunities embraced.   The really
great man is superior to his age, and anticipates its future ;
not as a sudden apparition, but as the embodiment of a long
growth of ideas of which he is the inheritor and the capable
Test of his exemplar.   Humboldt makes this personal domina-
character. tion of two kinds.   The one comes from the direct
influence of character ; the other from the creation of an idea,
which, freed from personality, works its controlling mission
by changing the face of things.   It is of this last description
that Humboldt makes the domination of Columbus.   It is
Not a crea- extremely doubtful if any instance can be found of
tor of ideas. a great idea changing the world's history, which has
been created by any single man.   None such was created by
Columbus.   There are always forerunners whose agency is
postponed because the times are not propitious.   A masterful
thought has often a long pedigree, starting from a remote antiquity, but it will be dormant till it is environed by the circumstances suited to fructify it.   This was just the destiny of
the intuition which began with Aristotle and came down to Columbus.   To make his first voyage partook of foolhardiness, as
many a looker-on reasonably declared.   It was none the less

foolhardy when it was done. If he had reached the opulent and powerful kings of the Orient, his little cockboats and their brave souls might have fared hard for their intrusion. His blunder in geography very likely saved him from annihilation.

The character of Columbus has been variously drawn, almost always with a violent projection of the limner's own personality. We find Prescott contending that "whatever the defects of Columbus's mental constitution, the finger of the historian will find it difficult to point to a single blemish in his moral character." It is certainly difficult to point to a more flagrant disregard of truth than when we find Prescott further saying, "Whether we contemplate his character in its public or private relations, in all its features it wears the same noble aspects. It was in perfect harmony with the grandeur of his plans, and with results more stupendous than those which Heaven has permitted any other mortal to achieve." It is very striking to find Prescott, after thus speaking of his private as well as public character, and forgetting the remorse of Columbus for the social wrongs he had committed, append in a footnote to this very passage a reference to his "illegitimate" son. It seems to mark an obdurate purpose to disguise the truth. This is also nowhere more patent than in the palliating hero-worship of Irving, with his constant effort to save a world's exemplar for the world's admiration, and more for the world's sake than for Columbus's.

*His character differently drawn.*

*Prescott.*

*Irving.*

Irving at one time berates the biographer who lets "pernicious erudition" destroy a world's exemplar; and at another time he does not know that he is criticising himself when he says that "he who paints a great man merely in great and heroic traits, though he may produce a fine picture, will never present a faithful portrait." The commendation which he bestows upon Herrera is for precisely what militates against the highest aims of history, since he praises that Spanish historian's disregard of judicial fairness.

In the being which Irving makes stand for the historic Columbus, his skill in softened expression induced Humboldt to suppose that Irving's avoidance of exaggeration gave a force to his eulogy, but there was little need to exaggerate merits, if defects were blurred.

The learned German adds, in the opening of the third volume of his *Examen Critique*, his own sense of the impressiveness of Columbus. That impressiveness stands confessed; but it is like a gyrating storm that knows no law but the vagrancy of destruction.

Humboldt.

One need not look long to discover the secret of Humboldt's estimate of Columbus. Without having that grasp of the picturesque which appeals so effectively to the popular mind in the letters of Vespucius, the Admiral was certainly not destitute of keen observation of nature, but unfortunately this quality was not infrequently prostituted to ignoble purposes. To a student of Humboldt's proclivities, these traits of observation touched closely his sympathy. He speaks in his *Cosmos* of the development of this exact scrutiny in manifold directions, notwithstanding Columbus's previous ignorance of natural history, and tells us that this capacity for noting natural phenomena arose from his contact with such. It would have been better for the fame of Columbus if he had kept this scientific survey in its purity. It was simply, for instance, a vitiated desire to astound that made him mingle theological and physical theories about the land of Paradise. Such jugglery was promptly weighed in Spain and Italy by Peter Martyr and others as the wild, disjointed effusions of an overwrought mind, and "the reflex of a false erudition," as Humboldt expresses it. It was palpably by another effort, of a like kind, that he seized upon the views of the fathers of the Church that the earthly Paradise lay in the extreme Orient, and he was quite as audacious when he exacted the oath on the Cuban coast, to make it appear by it that he had really reached the outermost parts of Asia.

Humboldt seeks to explain this errant habit by calling it " the sudden movement of his ardent and passionate soul; the disarrangement of ideas which were the effect of an incoherent method and of the extreme rapidity of his reading; while all was increased by his misfortunes and religious mysticism." Such an explanation hardly relieves the subject of it from blunter imputations. This urgency for some responsive wonderment at every experience appears constantly in the journal of Columbus's first voyage, as, for instance, when he makes every harbor exceed in beauty the last he had seen. This was the commonplace exaggeration which in our day is confined to the calls of speculating land companies. The fact was that Humboldt transferred to his hero something of the superlative love of nature that he himself had experienced in the same regions; but there was all the difference between him and Columbus that there is between a genuine love of nature and a commercial use of it. Whenever Columbus could divert his mind from a purpose to make the Indies a paying investment, we find some signs of an insight that shows either observation of his own or the garnering of it from others, as, for example, when he remarks on the decrease of rain in the Canaries and the Azores which followed upon the felling of trees, and when he conjectures that the elongated shape of the islands of the Antilles on the lines of the parallels was due to the strength of the equatorial current.

Observations of nature.

Since Irving, Prescott, and Humboldt did their work, there has sprung up the unreasoning and ecstatic French school under the lead of Roselly de Lorgues, who seek to ascribe to Columbus all the virtues of a saint.

Roselly de Lorgues and his school.

" Columbus had no defect of character and no worldly quality," they say. The antiquarian and searching spirit of Harrisse, and of those writers who have mainly been led into the closest study of the events of the life of Columbus, has not done so much to mould opinion as regards the estimate in which the Admiral should be held as to eliminate confusing statements and put in order corroborating facts. The reaction from the laudation of the canonizers has not produced any writer of consideration to array such derogatory estimates as effectually as a plain recital of established facts would do it. Hubert Bancroft, in the incidental mention which he makes of Columbus, has touched his character not inaptly, and with a consistent recognition of its infirmities. Even Prescott, who verges constantly on the ecstatic elements of the adulatory biographer, is forced to entertain at times " a suspicion of a temporary alienation of mind," and in regard to the letter which Columbus wrote from Jamaica to the sovereigns, is obliged to recognize " sober narrative and sound reasoning strangely blended with crazy dreams and doleful lamentations." " Vagaries like these," he adds, " which came occasionally like clouds over his soul to shut out the light of reason, cannot fail

Harrisse.

to fill the mind of the reader, as they doubtless did those of the sovereigns, with mingled sentiments of wonder and compassion." An unstinted denunciatory purpose, much weakened by an inconsiderate rush of disdain, characterizes an American writer, Aaron Goodrich, in his *Life of the so-called Christopher Columbus* (New York, 1875); but the critic's temper is too peevish and his opinions are too unreservedly biased to make his results of any value.

Aaron Goodrich.

The mental hallucinations of Columbus, so patent in his last years, were not beyond recognition at a much earlier age, and those who would get the true import of his character must trace these sorrowful manifestations to their beginnings, and distinguish accurately between Columbus when his purpose was lofty and unselfish and himself again when he became mercenary and erratic. So much does the verdict of history lodge occasionally more in the narrator of events than in the character of them that, in Humboldt's balancing of the baser with the nobler symptoms of Columbus's nature, he does not find even the most degraded of his actions other than powerful in will, and sometimes, at least, clear in intelligence. There were certainly curiously transparent, but transient gleams of wisdom to the last. Humboldt further says that the faith of Columbus soothed his dreary and weary adversities by the charm of ascetic reveries. So a handsome euphuism tries to save his fame from harsher epithets.

Humboldt.

It was a faith, says the same delineator, which justified at need, under the pretext of a religious object, the employment of deceit and the excess of a despotic power; a tenderer form, doubtless, of the vulgar expression that the end sanctifies the means. It is not, however, within the practice of the better historical criticism of our day to let such elegant wariness beguile the reader's mind. If the different, not to say more advanced, condition of the critical mind is to be of avail to a new age through the advantage gained from all the ages, it is in precisely this emancipation from the trammels of traditionary bondage that the historian asserts his own, and dispels the glamour of a conventionalized hero-worship.

Dr. Shea, our most distinguished Catholic scholar, who has dealt with the character of Columbus, says: " He accomplished less than some adventurers with poor

Dr. J. G. Shea.

equipped vessels. He seems to have succeeded in attaching but few men to him who adhered loyally to his cause. Those under him were constantly rebellious and mutinous; those over him found him impracticable. To array all these as enemies, inspired by a satanic hostility to a great servant of God, is to ask too much for our belief ; " and yet this is precisely what Irving by constant modifications, and De Lorgues in a monstrous degree, feel themselves justified in doing.

There is nothing in Columbus's career that these French canonizers do not find convertible to their purpose, The French whether it be his wild vow to raise 4,000 horse and canonizers. 50,000 foot in seven years, wherewith to snatch the Holy Sepulchre from the infidel, or the most commonplace of his canting ejaculations. That Columbus was a devout Catholic, according to the Catholicism of his epoch, does not admit of question, but when tried by any test that finds the perennial in holy acts, Columbus fails to bear the examination. He had nothing of the generous and noble spirit of a conjoint lover of man and of God, as the higher spirits of all times have developed it. There was no all-loving Deity in his conception. His Lord was one in whose name it was convenient to practice enormities. He shared this subterfuge with Isabella and the rest. We need to think on what Las Casas could be among his contemporaries, if we hesitate to apply the conceptions of an everlasting humanity.

The mines which Columbus went to seek were hard to find. The people he went to save to Christ were easy to exterminate. He mourned bitterly that his own efforts were ill requited. He had no pity for the misery of others, except they be his dependents and co-sharers of his purposes. He found a policy worth commemorating in slitting the noses and tearing off the ears of a naked heathen. He vindicates his excess by impressing upon the world that a man setting out to conquer the Indies must not be judged by the amenities of life which belong to a quiet rule in established countries. Yet, with a chance to establish a humane life among peoples ready to be moulded to good purposes, he sought from the very first to organize among them the inherited evils of " established countries." He Converts talked a great deal about making converts of the poor and slaves. souls, while the very first sight which he had of them prompted him to consign them to the slave-mart, just as if the first step to Christianize was the step which unmans.

The first vicar apostolic sent to teach the faith in Santo Domingo returned to Spain, no longer able to remain, powerless, in sight of the cruelties practiced by Columbus. Isabella prevented the selling of the natives as slaves in Spain, when Columbus had dispatched thither five shiploads. Las Casas tells us that in 1494–96 Columbus was generally hated in Española for his odiousness and injustice, and that the Admiral's policy with the natives killed a third of them in those two years. The Franciscans, when they arrived at the island, found the colonists exuberant that they had been relieved of the rule which Columbus had instituted; and the Benedictines and Dominicans added their testimony to the same effect.

The very first words, as has been said, that he used, in conveying to expectant Europe the wonders of his discovery, suggested a scheme of enslaving the strange people. He had already made the voyage that of a kidnapper, by entrapping nine of the unsuspecting natives.

*He urges enslaving the natives from the first.*

On his second voyage he sent home a vessel-load of slaves, on the pretense of converting them, but his sovereigns intimated to him that it would cost less to convert them in their own homes. Then he thought of the righteous alternative of sending some to Spain to be sold to buy provisions to support those who would convert others in their homes. The monarchs were perhaps dazed at this sophistry; and Columbus again sent home four vessels laden with reeking cargoes of flesh. When he returned to Spain, in 1496, to circumvent his enemies, he once more sought in his turn, and by his reasoning, to cheat the devil of heathen souls by sending other cargoes. At last the line was drawn. It was not to save their souls, but to punish them for daring to war against the Spaniards, that they should be made to endure such horrors.

It is to Columbus, also, that we trace the beginning of that monstrous guilt which Spanish law sanctioned under the name of *repartimientos*, and by which to every colonist, and even to the vilest, absolute power was given over as many natives as his means and rank entitled him to hold. Las Casas tells us that Ferdinand could hardly have had a conception of the enormities of the system. If so, it was because he winked out of sight the testimony of observers, while he listened to the tales prompted of greed, rapine, and cruelty. The value of the system to force heathen out of hell, and at the same time to replenish his treasury, was the side of it presented to Ferdinand's mind by such as had access to his person. In 1501, we find the Dominicans entering their protest, and by this Ferdinand was moved to take the counsel of men learned in the law and in what passed in those days for Christian ethics. This court of appeal approved these necessary efforts, as was claimed, to increase those who were new to the faith, and to reward those who supported it.

Peter Martyr expressed the comforting sentiments of the age: " National right and that of the Church concede personal liberty to man. State policy, however, demurs. Custom repels the idea. Long experience shows that slavery is necessary to prevent those returning to their idolatry and error whom the Church has once gained." All professed servants of the Church, with a few exceptions like Las Casas, ranged themselves with Columbus on the side of such specious thoughts ; and Las Casas, in recognizing this fact, asks what we could expect of an old sailor and fighter like Columbus, when the wisest and most respectable of the priesthood backed him in his views. It was indeed the misery of Columbus to miss the opportunity of being wiser than his fellows, the occasion always sought by a commanding spirit, and it was offered to him almost as to no other.

There was no restraining the evil. The cupidity of the colonists overcame all obstacles. The Queen was beguiled into giving equivocal instructions to Ovando, who succeeded Progress of to Bobadilla, and out of them by interpretation grew slavery in the West Indies. an increase of the monstrous evil. In 1503, every atrocity had reached a legal recognition. Labor was forced ; the slaves were carried whither the colonists willed ; and for eight months at least in every year, families were at pleasure disrupted without mercy. One feels some satisfaction in seeing Columbus himself at last, in a letter to Diego, December 1, 1504, shudder at the atrocities of Ovando. When one sees the utter annihilation of the whole race of the Antilles, a thing clearly assured at the date of the death of Columbus, one wishes that that dismal death-bed in Valladolid could have had its gloom illumined by a consciousness that the hand which lifted the banner of Spain and of Christ at San Salvador had done something to stay the misery which cupidity and perverted piety had put in course. When a man seeks to find and parades reasons for committing a crime, it is to stifle his conscience. Columbus passed years in doing it.

Back of Isabella in this spasmodic interest in the Indians
Talavera. was the celebrated Archbishop of Granada, Fernando de Talavera, whom we have earlier known as the prior of Prado. He had been since 1478 the confessor of the Queen, and when the time came for sending missionaries to the Antilles it was natural that they were of the order of St. Jerome, of which Talavera was himself a member. Columbus, through a policy which induced him to make as apparent as possible his
The Francis- mingling of interests with the Church, had before this
cans. adopted the garb of the Franciscans, and this order was the second in time to be seen in Española in 1502. They were the least tolerant of the leading orders, and had already shown a disposition to harass the Indians, and were known to treat haughtily the Queen's intercessions for the poor souls. It was not till after the death of Columbus that the Dominicans, coming in 1510, reinforced the kindly spirit of the priests of St. Jerome. Still later they too abandoned their humanity.

The downfall of Columbus began when he wrested from the reluctant monarchs what he called his privileges, and when he insisted upon riches as the accompaniment of such state and consequence as those privileges might entail. The terms were granted, so far as the King was concerned, simply to put a stop to importunities, for he never anticipated being called upon to confirm them. The insistency of Columbus in this respect is in strange contrast to the satisfaction which the captains of Prince Henry, Da Gama and the rest, were content to find in
Columbus's the unpolluted triumphs of science. The mercenary
mercenary Columbus was forced to the utterance of Solomon:
impulses. " I looked upon the labor that I had labored to do, and behold all was vanity and vexation of spirit." The Preacher never had a better example. Columbus was wont to say that gold gave the soul its flight to paradise. Perhaps he
His praise of referred to the masses which could be bought, or to
gold. the alms which could propitiate Heaven. He might

better have remembered the words of warning given to Baruch: "Seekest thou great things for thyself? Seek them not. For, saith the Lord, thy life will I give unto them for a prey in all places whither thou goest." And a prey in all places he became.

Humboldt seeks to palliate this cupidity by making him the conscious inheritor of the pecuniary chances which every free son of Genoa expected to find within his grasp by commercial enterprise. Such prominence was sought because it carried with it power and influence in the republic.

If Columbus had found riches in the New World as easily as he anticipated, it is possible that such affluence would have moulded his character in other ways for good or for evil. He soon found himself confronting a difficult task, to satisfy with insufficient means a craving which his exaggerations had established. This led him to spare no device, at whatever sacrifice of the natives, to produce the coveted gold, and it was an ingenious mockery that induced him to deck his captives with golden chains and parade them through the Spanish towns.

After Da Gama had opened the route to Cathay by the Cape of Good Hope, and Columbus had, as he supposed, touched the eastern confines of the same country, the wonder- <sup>Nicolas de</sup> ful stories of Asiatic glories told by Nicolas de Conti <sup>Conti.</sup> were translated, by order of King Emanuel (in 1500), into Portuguese. It is no wonder that the interest in the development of 1492 soon waned when the world began to compare the descriptions of the region beyond the Ganges, as made known by Marco Polo, and so recently by Conti, and the apparent confirmation of them established by the Portuguese, with the meagre resources which Columbus had associated <sup>The world's</sup> with the same country, in all that he could say about <sup>disgust.</sup> the Antilles or bring from them. An adventurous voyage across the Sea of Darkness begat little satisfaction, if all there was to show for it consisted of men with tails or a single eye, or races of Amazons and cannibals.

When we view the character of Columbus in its influence upon the minds of men, we find some strange anomalies. Before his passion was tainted with the ambition of wealth and its consequence, and while he was urging the acceptance of his views for their own sake, it is very evident that he impressed others in a way that never happened after he had secured his privileges. It is after this turning-point of his life that we begin to see his falsities and indiscretions, or at least to find record of them. The incident of the moving light in the night before his first landfall is a striking instance of his daring disregard of all the qualities that help a commander in his dominance over his men. It needs little discrimination to discern the utter deceitfulness of that pretense. A noble desire to win the loftiest honors of the discovery did not satisfy a mean, insatiable greed. He blunted every sentiment of generosity when he deprived a poor sailor of his pecuniary reward. That there was no actual light to be seen is apparent from the distance that the discoverers sailed before they saw land, since if the light had been ahead they would not have gone on, and if it had been abeam they would not have left it. The evidence is that of himself and a thrall, and he kept it secret at the time. The author of the *Historie* sees the difficulty, and attempts to vaporize the whole story by saying that the light was spiritual, and not physical. Navarrete passes it by as a thing necessary, for the fame of Columbus, to be ignored.

*Columbus's lack of generosity.*

A second instance of Columbus's luckless impotence, at a time when an honorable man would have relied upon his character, was the attempt to make it appear that he had reached the coast of Asia by imposing an oath on his men to that effect, in penalty of having their tongues wrenched out if they recanted. One can hardly conceive a more debasing exercise of power.

*His enforced oath at Cuba.*

His insistence upon territorial power was the serious mistake of his life. He thought, in making an agreement with his sovereigns to become a viceroy, that he was securing an honor ; he was in truth pledging his happiness and beggaring his life. He sought to attain that which the fates had unfitted him for, and the Spanish monarchs, in an evil day, which was in due time their regret, submitted to his hallucinated dictation. No man ever evinced less capacity for ruling a colony.

*His ambition of territorial power.*

The most sorrowful of all the phases of Columbus's character is that hapless collapse, when he abandoned all faith in the natural world, and his premonitions

*His professed inspiration.*

of it, and threw himself headlong into the vortex of what he called inspiration.

Everything in his scientific argument had been logical. It produced the reliance which comes of wisdom. It was a manly show of an incisive reason. If he had rested here his claims for honor, he would have ranked with the great seers of the universe, with Copernicus and the rest. His successful suit with the Spanish sovereigns turned his head, and his degradation began when he debased a noble purpose to the level of mercenary claims. He relied, during his first voyage, more on chicanery in controlling his crew than upon the dignity of his aim and the natural command inherent in a lofty spirit. This deceit was the beginning of his decadence, which ended in a sad self-aggrandizement, when he felt himself no longer an instrument of intuition to probe the secrets of the earth, but a possessor of miraculous inspiration. The man who had been self-contained became a thrall to a fevered hallucination.

The earnest mental study which had sustained his inquisitive spirit through long years of dealings with the great physical problems of the earth was forgotten. He hopelessly began to accredit to Divinity the measure of his own fallibility. "God made me," he says, "the messenger of the new heaven and the new earth, of which He spoke in the Apocalypse by St. John, after having spoken of it by the mouth of Isaiah, and He showed me the spot where to find it." He no longer thought it the views of Aristotle which guided him. The Greek might be pardoned for his ignorance of the intervening America. It was mere sacrilege to impute such ignorance to the Divine wisdom.

There is no excuse but the plea of insanity. He naturally lost his friends with losing his manly devotion to a Lost his cause. I do not find the beginning of this sur- friends. render of his manhood earlier than in the will which he signed February 22, 1498, when he credits the Holy Trinity with having inspired him with the idea that one could go to the Indies by passing westward.

In his letter to the nurse of Don Juan, he says that the prophecy of Isaiah in the Apocalypse had found its interpreter in him, the messenger to disclose a new part of the world. "Human reason," he wrote in the *Proficias*, "mathematics, and maps have served me in no wise. What I have accomplished is simply the fulfillment of the prophecy of David."

We have seen a pitiable man meet a pitiable death. Hardly His pitiable a name in profane history is more august than his. death. Hardly another character in the world's record has made so little of its opportunities. His discovery was a blunder; his blunder was a new world; the New World is his monument! Its discoverer might have been its father; he proved to be its despoiler. He might have given its young days such a benignity as the world likes to associate with a maker; he left it a legacy of devastation and crime. He might have been an unselfish promoter of geographical science; he proved a rabid seeker for gold and a viceroyalty. He might have won converts to the fold of Christ by the kindness of his spirit; he gained the execrations of the good angels. He might, like Las Casas, have rebuked the fiendishness of his contemporaries; he set them an example of perverted belief. The triumph of Barcelona led down to the ignominy of Valladolid, with every step in the degradation palpable and resultant.

# CHAPTER XXI.

## THE DESCENT OF COLUMBUS'S HONORS.

COLUMBUS had left behind him, as the natural guardians of his name and honors, the following relatives: his His kinsfolk. brother Bartholomew, who in December, 1508, had issue of an illegitimate daughter, his only child so far as known; his brother Diego, who, as a priest, was precluded from having lawful issue; his son Diego, now become the first inheritor of his honors; his natural son, Ferdinand, the most considerable in intellectual habit of all Columbus's immediate kin.

The descent of his titles depended in the first instance on such a marriage as Diego might contract. Within a His son Diego. year or two Diego had had by different women two bastard children, Francisco and Cristoval, shut off from heirship by the manner of their birth. Diego was at this time not far from four and twenty years of age.

Ten or twelve days after Diego succeeded to his inheritance, Philip the Handsome, now sharing the throne of Castile as husband of Juana, daughter of Isabella, ordered that what was due to Columbus should be paid to his successor. This order reached Española in June, 1506, but was not obeyed promptly; and when Ferdinand of Aragon returned from Italy in August, 1507, and succeeded to the Castilian throne, he repeated the order on August 24.

It would seem that in due time Diego was in receipt of 450,000 ounces of gold annually from the four foun- Diego's income. dries in Española. This, with whatever else there may have been, was by no means satisfactory to the young aspirant, and he began to press Ferdinand for a restitution of his inherited honors and powers with all the perti- Diego presses for a restitution of Columbus's honors. nacity which had characterized his father's urgency. Upon the return of Ferdinand from Naples, Diego determined to push the matter to an issue, but Ferdinand still evaded it. Diego now asked, according to Las Casas and Herrera, to be allowed to bring a suit against the Crown before the Council of the Indies, and the King yielded to the request, confident, very likely, in his ability to control the verdict in the public interests. The suit at once began (1508), and

1508. Suit against the Crown. continued for several years before all was accomplished, and in December of that same year (1508), we find Diego empowering an attorney of the Duke of Alva to represent his case.

The defense of the Crown was that a transmission of the viceroyalty to the Admiral's son was against public policy, and at variance with a law of 1480, which forbade any judicial office under the Crown being held in perpetuity. It was further argued in the Crown's behalf that Columbus had not been the chief instrument of the first discovery and had not discovered the mainland, but that other voyagers had anticipated him. In response to all allegations, Diego rested his case on the contracts of the Crown with his father, which assured him the powers he asked for. Further than this, the Crown had already recognized, he claimed, a part of the contract in its orders of June 2, 1506, and August 24, 1507, whereby the revenues due under the contracts had been restored to him. It was also charged by the defense that Columbus had been relieved of his powers because he had abused them, and the answer to this was that the sovereigns' letter of 1502 had acknowledged that Bobadilla acted without authority. A number of navigators in the western seas were put on the stand to rebut the allegation of existing knowledge of the coast before the voyages of Columbus, particularly in substantiating the priority of the voyage of Columbus to the coast of Paria, and the evidence was sufficient to show that all the alleged claims were simply perverted notions of the really later voyage of Ojeda in 1499. It is from the testimony at this time, as given in Navarrete, that the biographers of Columbus derive considerable information, not otherwise attainable, respecting the voyages of Columbus, — testimony, however, which the historian is obliged to weigh with caution in many respects.

The case was promptly disposed of in Diego's favor, but not

Diego wins. without suspicions of the Crown's influence to that end. The suit is, indeed, one of the puzzles in the history of Columbus and his fame. If it was a suit to secure a verdict against the Crown in order to protect the Crown's rights under the bull of demarcation, we can understand why much that would have helped the position of the fiscal was not brought forward. If it was what it purported to be, an effort to relieve the Crown of obligations fastened upon it under misconceptions or deceits, we may well marvel at such omission of evidence.

It was left for the King to act on the decision for restitution. This might have been by his studied procrastination indefinitely delayed but for a shrewd movement on the part of Diego, who opportunely aspired to the hand of Doña Maria de Toledo, the daughter of Fernando de Toledo. This nobleman was brother of the Duke of Alva, one of the proudest grandees of Spain, and he was also cousin of Ferdinand, the King. The alliance, soon effected, brought the young suitor a powerful friend in his uncle, and the bride's family *Diego marries Maria de Toledo.* were not averse to a connection with the heir to the viceroyalty of the Indies, now that it was confirmed by the Council of the Indies. Harrisse cannot find that the promised dower ever came with the wife; but, on the contrary, Diego seems to have become the financial agent of his wife's family. A demand for the royal acquiescence in the orders of the Council could now be more easily made, and Ferdinand readily conceded all but the title of Viceroy. Diego waived that for the time, and he was accordingly accredited as governor of Española, in the place of Ovando. *Diego waives his right to the title of Viceroy.*

Isabella had indeed, while on her death-bed, importuned the King to recall Ovando, because of the appalling stories of his cruelty to the Indians. Ferdinand had found that the governor's vigilance conduced to heavy remittances of gold, and had shown no eagerness to carry out the Queen's wishes. He had even ordered Ovando to begin that transference of the poor Lucayan Indians from their own islands to work in the Española mines which soon resulted in the depopulation of the Bahamas. Now that he was forced to withdraw Ovando he made it as agreeable for him as possible, *Ovando recalled.* and in the end there was no lack of commendation of his administration. Indeed, as Spaniards went in those days, Ovando was good enough to gain the love of Las Casas, "except for some errors of moral blindness."

It was on May 3, 1509, that Ferdinand gave Diego his in-
1509. June
9. Diego
sails for
Española. structions; and on June 9, the new governor with
his noble wife sailed from San Lucar. There went
with Diego, beside a large number of noble Spaniards who introduced, as Oviedo says, an infusion of the best
Spanish blood into the colony, his brother Ferdinand, who
was specially charged, as Oviedo further tells us, to found
monasteries and churches. His two uncles also accompanied
him. Bartholomew had gone to Rome after Columbus's death,
with the intention of inducing Pope Julius II. to urge upon the
King a new voyage of discovery; and Harrisse thinks that this
is proved by some memoranda attached to an account of the
coasts of Veragua, which it is supposed that Bartholomew gave
at this time to a canon of the Lateran, which is now preserved
in the Megliavecchian library, and has been printed by Harrisse in his *Bibliotheca Americana Vetustissima.* It was perhaps on this visit that the Adelantado took to Rome that map
of Columbus's voyage to those coasts which it is usually said
was carried there in 1505, when he may possibly have borne
thither the letter of Columbus to the Pope.

The position which Bartholomew now went with Diego to assume, that of the Chief Alguazil of Santo Domingo, caused
much complaint from Diego Mendez, who claimed the credit of
Bartholo-
mew Colum-
bus, and Di-
ego Mendez. bringing about the restitution of Diego's power, and
who had, as he says, been promised both by Columbus
and by his son this office as recompense for his many
services.

The fleet arrived at its destination July 10, 1509. The wife
1509. July
10. Diego
reaches his
government. of the governor had taken a retinue, which for splendor had never before been equaled in the New World,
and it enabled her to maintain a kind of viceregal
state in the little capital. It all helped Diego to begin his rule
with no inconsiderable consequence. There was needed something of such attraction to beguile the spirits of the settlers, for,
as Benzoni learned years afterwards, when he visited the region,
the coming of the son of Columbus had not failed to engender
jealousies, which attached to the imposition of another foreigner upon the colony.

The King was determined that Diego's rule should be confined to Española, and, much to the governor's annoyance, he

parceled out the coasts which Columbus had tracked near the Isthmus of Panama into two governments, and installed Ojeda in command of the eastern one, which was called New Andalusia, while the one beyond the Gulf of Uraba, which included Veragua, he gave to Diego de Nicuessa, and called it Castilla del Oro.

Ojeda and Nicuessa.

IVLIVS II PAPA SAVONENSIS LIGVR.

POPE JULIUS II.

This action of the King, as well as his effort to put Porto Rico under an independent governor, incited new ex- postulations from Diego, and served to make his rule

Porto Rico.

in the island quite as uncomfortable as its management had been to his father. There also grew up the same discourage-

Faction of Passamonte. ment from faction. The King's treasurer, Miguel Passamonte, became the head of the rebellious party, not without suspicion that he was prompted to much denunciations in his confidential communications with the King. Reports of Diego's misdeeds and ambitions, threatening the royal power even, were assiduously conveyed to the King. The sovereign devised a sort of corrective, as he thought, of this, by institut-

1511. October 5. Audiencia. ing later, October 5, 1511, a court of appeals, or *Audiencia*, to which the aggrieved colonists could go in their defense against oppression or extortion. Its natural effect was to undermine the governor's authority and to weaken his influence. He found himself thwarted in all efforts to relieve the Indians of their burdens, as nothing of that sort could be done without disturbing the revenues of leading colonists. There was no great inducement to undo measures by which no one profited in receipts more than himself, and the cruel devastation of the native population ran on as it had done. He certainly did not show himself averse to continuing the system of *repartimientos* for the benefit of himself and his friends.

Diego, who had been for a while in Spain, returned in 1512 to Española, and later new orders were sent out by the King, and these included commands to reduce the labor of the Indians one third, to import negro slaves from Guinea as a measure of further relief to the natives, and to brand Carib slaves, so as to protect other Indians from harsh treatment intended for the Caribs alone.

Diego was again in Spain in 1513, and the attempts of Ojeda and Nicuessa having failed, later orders in 1514 so far reinstated Diego in his viceregal power as to permit him to send his

Bartholomew Columbus died. uncle Bartholomew to take possession of the Veragua coast. But the life of the Adelantado was drawing to a close, and his death soon occurring nothing was done.

Affairs had come to such a pass that Diego again felt it necessary to repair to Court to counteract his enemies' intrigues, and once more getting permission from the King, he sailed for

1515. Diego in Spain. Spain, April 9, 1515, leaving the Vice-Queen with a council in authority.

Diego found the King open and kindly, and not averse to acknowledging the merits of his government. He again pressed his bonded rights with the old fervency. " I would bestow them willingly on you," said the King ; " but I cannot do so without

CHARLES THE FIFTH.

intrusting them also to your son and to his successors." " Is it just," said Diego, " that I should suffer for a son which I may never have ? " Las Casas tells us that Diego repeated this colloquy to him.

The King found it reasonable to question if Columbus had really sailed along all the coasts in which Diego claimed a share, and ordered an examination of the matter to be made. While these claims were in abeyance, the King died, January 23, 1516.

*1516. January 23. Ferdinand died.*

This event much retarded the settlement of the difficulties. Cardinal Ximenes, who held power for a while, was not willing to act, and nothing was done for four years, during part of which period Diego was certainly in Española. We know also that he was present at the convocation of Barcelona, presided over by the Emperor, when Las Casas made his urgent appeals for the Indians and pictured their hardships. Finally, in 1520, when Charles V. was about to embark for Flanders, Diego was in a position to advance to the Emperor so large a sum as ten thousand ducats, which was, as it appears, about a fifth of his annual income from Española at this time. This financial succor seemed to open the way for the Emperor to dismiss all charges against Diego, and to reinstate him in qualified authority as Viceroy over the Indies.

*Diego again in Española.*

*1520. Diego in Spain.*

*Diego partially reinstated.*

This seeming restitution was not without a disagreeable accompaniment in the appointment of a supervisor to reside at his viceregal court and report on the Viceroy's doings. In September, 1520, Diego sailed once more for his government, and on November 14 we find him in Santo Domingo, and shortly afterwards engaged in the construction of a lordly palace, which he was to occupy, and which is seen there to-day. The substantialness of its structure gave rise to rumors that he was preparing a fortress for ulterior aims.

*1520. September. Diego returns to Española.*

Diego soon found that various administrative measures had not gone well in his absence. Commanders of some of the provinces had exceeded their powers, and it became necessary to supersede them. This made them enemies as a matter of course. The raising of sugar-cane had rapidly developed under the imported African labor, and the revenues now came for the most part from the plantations rather than from the mines. The negroes so increased that it was not long before some of them dared to rise in revolt, but the mischief was stopped by a rapid swoop of armed horsemen. The

*Negro slaves increase.*

RUINS OF DIEGO COLON'S HOUSE.

jealousies and revengeful accusations of Diego's enemies were not so easily quelled, and before long he was summoned to Spain to render an account of his doings, for Lucas Vasquez de Ayllon had presented charges against him.   On September 16, 1523, Diego embarked, and landed at St. Lucar November 5.   He presented himself before the Emperor at Vittoria in January, 1524, and reviewed his conduct.   This he succeeded in doing in a manner to disarm his foes; and this success encouraged him to press anew for his inherited rights.   The demand ended in the

1523. Diego in Spain. questions in dispute being referred to a board; and Diego for two years followed the Court in its migrations, to be in attendance on the sessions of this commission.   His

1526. February 23. Diego dies. health gave way under the strain, so that, with everything still unsettled, he died at Montalvan, February 23, 1526, having survived his father for twenty troublous years.   His remains were laid in the monastery of Las Cuevas by the side of Columbus.   Being later conveyed to the cathedral at Santo Domingo, they were, if one may credit the quite unproved statements of the priests of the cathedral, mistaken for those of his father, and taken to Havana in 1795.

The Vice-Queen and her family were still in Santo Domingo,

His family. and her children were seven in number, four daughters and three sons.   The descent of the honors came eventually to the descendants of one of these daughters, Isabel, who married George of Portugal, Count of Gelves.   Of the

Luis Colon succeeds. three sons, Luis succeeded his father, and was in turn succeeded by Diego, a son of Luis's brother Cristoval.

The Vice-Queen, after making an ineffectual attempt to colonize Veragua, in which she was thwarted by the royal *Audiencia* at Española, returned to Spain in 1529.   Her son Luis, the heir, was still a child, having been born in 1521 or 1522.   For fourteen years his mother pressed his claims upon the Emperor, Charles V., and she was during a part of the time in such distress that she borrowed money of Ferdinand Columbus and pledged her jewels.   She lived till 1549, and died at Santo Domingo.

Early in 1536 the Cardinal Garcia de Loyasa, in behalf of

1536.  The Crown's compromise with Luis. the Council of the Indies, rendered a decision in which he and Ferdinand Columbus had acted as arbiters, which was confirmed by the Emperor in September of the same year. This was that, upon the abandonment by Luis of all claims upon the revenues of the Indies, of the title of Viceroy, and of the right to appoint the officers of the New World, he should be given the island of Jamaica in fief, a perpetual annuity of ten thousand ducats, and the title of Duke of Veragua, with an estate twenty-five leagues square in that province, to support the title and functions of Admiral of the Indies. In 1540 Luis returned to Española with the title of Captain-General, and in 1542 married at Santo Domingo, much against his mother's wish, Maria de Orozco, who later lived in Honduras and married another. While she was still living, Luis again espoused at Santo Domingo Maria de Mosquera. In 1551 he returned to Spain.

Duke of Veragua.

1540. Luis in Española.

Whatever remained of the rights which Columbus had sought to transmit to his heirs had already been modified to their detriment by Charles, under decrees in 1540, 1541, and 1542 ; and when Charles was succeeded by Philip II., early in 1556, one of the first acts of the latter was to force Luis to abandon his fief of Veragua and to throw up his power as Admiral. The Council of the Indies took cognizance of the case in July, 1556, and on September 28 following, Philip II., at Ghent, recompensed the grandson of Columbus, for his submission to the inevitable, by decreeing to Luis the honorary title of Admiral of the Indies and Duke of Veragua, with an income of seven thousand ducats. So in fifty years the dreams of Columbus for territorial magnificence came to naught, and the confident injunctions of his will were dissipated in the air.

Columbus's privileges gradually abridged.

1556. All Columbus's territorial rights abandoned.

Immediately after this, Luis furtively married, while his other wives were still living, Ana de Castro Ossorio. The authorities found in these polygamous acts a convenient opportunity to get another troublesome Colon out of the way, and arrested Luis in 1559. He was held in prison for nearly five years, and when in 1563 judgment was got against him, he was sentenced to ten years of exile, half of which was to be passed in Oran, in Africa. While his appeal was pending, his scandalous life added crime to crime, and finally, in November, 1565, his sentence being confirmed, he was conducted to Oran, and there he died February 3, 1572.

Luis a polygamist.

1572. Luis dies.

# THE COLUMBUS PEDIGREE.

NOTE. Dotted lines mark illegitimate descents; the dash-and-dot lines mark pretended descents. The heavy face numerals show the successful holders of the honors of Columbus. The lines *a a*, *b b*, and *c c* join respectively.

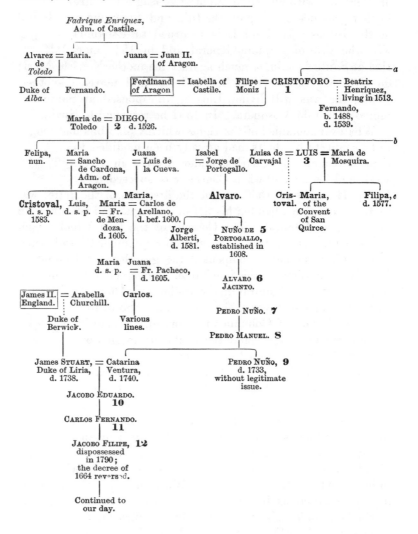

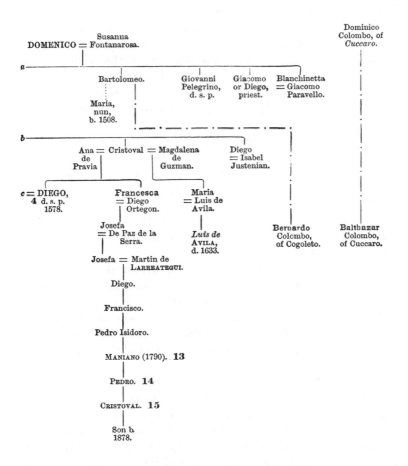

DOMENICO = Susanna Fontanarosa.

Dominico Colombo, of *Cuccaro.*

*a*

Bartolomeo.

Maria, nun, b. 1508.

Giovanni Pelegrino, d. s. p.

Giacomo or Diego, priest.

Blanchinetta = Giacomo Paravello.

*b*

Ana de Pravia = Cristoval = Magdalena de Guzman.

Diego = Isabel Justenian.

*c* = DIEGO, 4 d. s. p. 1578.

Francesca = Diego Ortegon.

Maria = Luis de Avila.

Josefa = De Paz de la Serra.

*Luis de* AVILA, d. 1633.

Bernardo Colombo, of Cogoleto.

Balthazar Colombo, of Cuccaro.

Josefa = Martin de LARREATEGUI.

Diego.

Francisco.

Pedro Isidoro.

MANIANO (1790). **13**

PEDRO. **14**

CRISTOVAL. **15**

Son b. 1878.

Luis left two illegitimate children, one a son; but his lawful heirs were adjudged to be the children of Maria de Mosquera, two daughters, one a nun and the other Filipa. This last presented a claim for the titles in opposition to the demands of Diego, the nephew of her father. She declared this cousin to be the natural, and not the lawful, son of Luis's brother. It was easy enough to forget such imputations in coming to the final conclusion, when Filipa and Diego took each other in marriage (May 15, 1573) to compose their differences, the husband becoming Duke of Veragua. Filipa died in November, 1577, and her husband January 27, 1578. As they had no children, the male line of Columbus became extinct seventy years after his death.

*His heirs.*

*His daughter marries her cousin Diego, the male heir.*

*Columbus's male line extinct.*

The lawsuit which followed for the settlement of the succession was a famous one. It lasted thirty years. The claimants were at first eight in number, but they were reduced to five by deaths during the progress of the trials.

*The long lawsuit and its many contestants.*

The first was Francesca, own sister of Diego, the late Duke. Her claim was rejected; but five generations later the dignities returned to her descendants.

The second was the representative of Maria, the daughter of Luis, and sister-in-law of Diego. The claim made by her heir, the convent of San Quirce, was discarded.

The third was Cristoval, the bastard son of Luis, who claimed to be the fruit of a marriage of Luis, concluded while he was in prison accused of polygamy. Cristoval died in 1601, before the cause was decided.

The fourth was Alvaro de Portogallo, Count of Gelves, a son of Isabel, the sister of Luis. He had unsuccessfully claimed the titles when Luis died, in 1572, and again put forth his claims in 1578, when Diego died, but he himself died, pending a decision, in 1581. His son, Jorge Alberto, inherited his rights, but died in 1589, before a decision was reached, when his younger brother, Nuño de Portogallo, became the claimant, and his rights were established by the tribunal in 1608, when he became Duke of Veragua. His enjoyment of the title was not without unrest, but the attempts to dispossess him failed.

The fifth was Cristoval de Cardona, Admiral of Aragon, son

of Maria, elder sister of Luis. This claimant died in 1583, while his claim, having once been allowed, was held in abeyance by an appeal of his rivals. His sister, Maria, was then adjudged inheritor of the honors, but she died in 1605, before the final decree.

The sixth was Maria de la Cueva, daughter of Juana, sister of Luis, who died before December, 1600, while her daughter died in 1605, leaving Carlos Pacheco a claimant, whose rights were disallowed.

The seventh was Balthazar Colombo, a descendant of a Domenico Colombo, who was, according to the claim, the same Domenico who was the father of Columbus. His genealogical record was not accepted.

The eighth was Bernardo Colombo, who claimed to be a descendant of Bartholomew Columbus, the Adelantado, a claim not made good.

These last two contestants rested their title in part on the fact that their ancestors had always borne the name of Colombo, and this was required by Columbus to belong to the inheritors of his honors. The lineal ancestors of the other claimants had borne the names of Cardona, Portogallo, or Avila.

From Nuño de Portogallo the titles descended to his son Alvaro Jacinto, and then to the latter's son, Pedro Nuño de Portogallo succeeds, and the line later changes. Nuño. His rights were contested by Luis de Avila (grandson of Cristoval, brother of Luis Colon), who tried in 1620 to reverse the verdict of 1608, and it was not till 1664 that Pedro Nuño defeated his adversaries. He was succeeded by his son, Pedro Manuel, and he by his son, Pedro Nuño, who died in 1733, when this male line became extinct.

The titles were now illegally assumed by Pedro Nuño's sister, Catarina Ventura, who by marriage gave them to her husband, James Fitz-James Stuart, son of the famous Duke of Berwick, and by inheritance in his own right, Duke of Liria. When he died, in 1738, the titles passed to his son, Jacobo Eduardo; thence to the latter's son, Carlos Fernando, who transmitted them to his son, Jacobo Filipe. This last was obliged, by a verdict in 1790, which reversed the decree of 1664, to yield the titles to the line of Francesca, sister of Diego, the fourth holder of them. This Francesca married Diego Ortegon, and their grandchild, Josefa, married Martin Larreategui, whose great-great-grandson, Mariano (by decrees 1790–96), became Duke of Veragua, from whom the title descended to his son, Pedro, and then to his grandson, Cristoval, the present Duke, born in 1837, whose heir, the next Duke, was born in 1878. The value of the titles is said to-day to represent about eight or ten thousand dollars, and this income is chargeable upon the revenues of Cuba and Porto Rico.

In concluding this rapid sketch of the descent of the blood and honors of Columbus, two striking thoughts are presented. The Larreateguis are a Basque family. The blood of Columbus, the Genoese, now mingles with that of the hardiest race of navigators of western Europe, and of whom it may be expected that if ever earlier contact of Europe with the New World is proved, these Basques will be found the forerunners of Columbus. The blood of the supposed discoverer of the western passage to Asia flows with that of the earliest stock which is left to us of that Oriental wave of population which inundated Europe, in the far-away times when the races which make our modern Christian histories were being disposed in valleys and on the coasts of what was then the Western World.

# APPENDIX.

———◆———

## THE GEOGRAPHICAL RESULTS.

THERE was a struggling effort of the geographical sense of the world for thirty years and more after the death of Columbus, before the fact began to be grasped that a great continent was in- <sup>Progress of</sup> terposed as a substantial and independent barrier in the discovery. track to India.  It took nearly a half century more before men generally recognized that fact, and then in most cases it was accepted with the reservation of a possible Asiatic connection at the extreme north. It was something more than two hundred and twenty years from the death of Columbus before that severance at the north was incontestably established by the voyage of Bering, and a hundred and thirty years longer before at last the contour of the northern coast of the continent was established by the proof of the long-sought northwest passage in 1850.  We must now, to complete the story of the influence of Columbus, rehearse somewhat concisely the narrative of this progressive outcome of that wonderful voyage of 1492.  The spirit of western discovery, which Columbus imparted, was of long continuance.

"If we wish to make ourselves thoroughly acquainted," says Dr. Kohl, " with the history of discovery in the New World, we must not only follow the navigators on their ships, but we must look into the cabinets of princes and into the counting-houses of merchants, and likewise watch the scholars in their speculative studies." There was no rallying point for the scholar of cosmography <sup>The influence of Ptolemy and his</sup> in those early days of discovery like the text and influence <sup>career.</sup> of Ptolemy.

We know little of this ancient geographer beyond the fact of his living in the early portion of the second century, and mainly at Alexandria, the fittest home of a geographer at that time, since this Egyptian city was peerless for commerce and learning.  Here he could do best what he advises all geographers to do, consult the journals of travelers, and get information of eclipses, as the same phenomena were

observed at different places; such, for instance, as that of the moon
noted at Arbela in the fifth, and seen at Carthage in the second hour.

The precision of Ptolemy was covered out of sight by graphic
fancies among the cosmographers of succeeding ages, till about the beginning of the fourteenth century Italy and the western Mediterranean islands began to produce those atlases of sea-charts, which have
come down to us under the name of "portolanos;" and still
later a new impetus was given to geographical study by the
manuscripts of Ptolemy, with his maps, which began to be common in

PTOLEMY.
[From Reusner's *Icones.*]

western Europe in the beginning of the fifteenth century, largely
through the influence of communications with the Byzantine peoples.

The portolanos, however, never lost their importance. Nordenskiöld
says that, from the great number of them still extant in Italy, we may
deduce that they had a greater circulation during the sixteenth cen-

tury than printed cartographical works. About five hundred of these
sea-charts are known in Italian libraries, and the greater proportion of
them are of Italian origin.

It is a composite Latin text, brought into final shape by Jacobus
Angelus not far from 1400–1410, which was the basis of the early
printed editions of Ptolemy. This version was for a while circulated in
manuscript, sometimes with copies of the maps of the Old World having a Latinized nomenclature; and the public libraries of Europe contain here and there specimens of these early copies, one of which it is
thought was known to Pierre d'Ailly. It is a question if Angelus
supplied the maps which accompanied these early manuscripts, and
which got into the Bologna edition of 1462 (wrongly dated for 1472),
and into the metrical version of Berlingièri. These maps, whether
always the same in the early manuscripts or not, were later superseded
by a new set of maps made by a German cartographer, Nicolaus Donis,
which he added to a revision of Angelus's Latin text. Latin text of
These later maps were close copies of the original Greek Ptolemy.

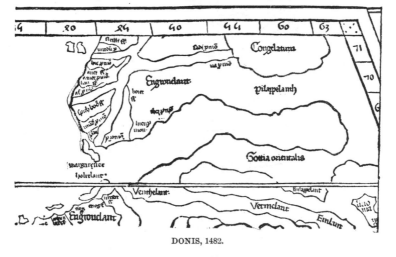

DONIS, 1482.

maps, and were accompanied by others of a similar workmanship,
which represented better knowledge than the Greeks had. In 1478
these Donis maps were first engraved on copper, and were The Donis
used in the later editions of 1490, and slightly corrected maps.
in those of 1507 and 1508. The engravers were Schweinheim and
Buckinck, and their work, following copies of it in the edition of
1490, has been admirably reproduced in *The Facsimile Atlas* of
Nordenskiöld (Stockholm, 1889).

Meanwhile, editions of the text of Angelus had been issued at

Ulm in 1482, and giving additions in 1486, with woodcut maps, the same in both issues on a different projection, assigned to Dominus Nicolaus Germanus, who had, according to Nordenskiöld, completed the manuscript fifteen years earlier. It is significant, perhaps, of the slowness with which the bruit of Portuguese discoveries to the south had traveled that there is in the maps of Africa no extension of Ptolemy's knowledge. But if they are deficient in the south, they are
Greenland  remarkable in the north for showing the coming America
in maps.   in a delineation of Greenland, which, as we have already pointed out, was no new object in the manuscript portolanos, even as far back as the early part of the same century.

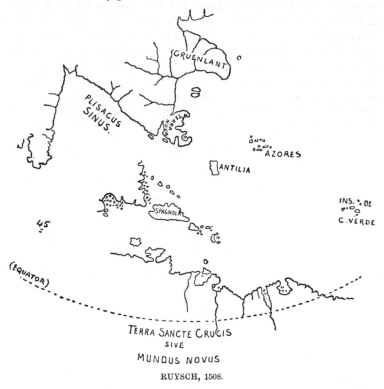

RUYSCH, 1508.

Two years after the death of Columbus, we find in the edition of 1508, and sometimes in the edition of 1507, — there is no difference between the two issues except in the title-page, — the first engraved map which has particular reference to the new geographical developments of the age.

This Ruysch map shows the African coast discoveries of the Portuguese, with the discoveries of Marco Polo towards the east. In connection with the latter, the same material which Behaim had used in his globe seems to have been equally accessible to Ruysch. The latter's map has a legend on the sea between Iceland and Greenland, saying that an island situated there was burnt up in 1456. This statement has been connected by some with another contained in the Sagas, that from an island in this channel both Greenland and Iceland could be seen.

1507-8. The Ruysch map.

We also learn from another legend that Portuguese vessels had pushed down the South American coast to 50° south latitude, and the historians of these early voyages have been unable to say who the pioneers were who have left us so early a description of Brazil.

It is inferred from a reference of Beneventanus, in his Ptolemy, respecting this map, that some aid had been derived from a map made by one of the Columbuses, and a statement that Bartholomew Columbus, in Rome in 1505, gave a map of the new discoveries to a canon of San Giovanni di Laterano has been thought to refer to such a map, which would, if it could be established, closely connect the Ruysch map with Columbus. It is also supposed to have some relation to Cabot, since a voyage which Ruysch made to the new regions westward from England may have been, and probably was, with that navigator. In this case, the reference to that part of the coast of Asia which the English discovered may record Ruysch's personal experiences. If these things can be considered as reasonably established, it gives great interest to this map of Ruysch, and connects Columbus not only with the earliest manuscript map, La Cosa of 1500, but also with the earliest engraved map of the New World, as Ruysch's map was.

Columbus and the Ruysch map.

In speaking of the Ruysch map, Henry Stevens thinks that the cartographer laid down the central archipelago of America from the printed letter of Columbus, because it was the only account in print in 1507; but why restrict the sources of information to those in print, when La Cosa's map might have been copied, or the material which La Cosa employed might have been used by others, and when the Cantino map is a familiar copy of Portuguese originals, all of which might well have been known in the varied circles with which Ruysch is seen by his map to have been familiar?

Sources of the Ruysch map.

While it is a fact that central and northern Europe got its cartographical knowledge of the New World almost wholly from Portugal, owing, perhaps, to the exertions of Spain to preserve their explorers' secrets, we do not, at the same time, find a single engraved Portuguese map of the early years of this period of discovery.

Portuguese geography and maps.

A large map, to show the Portuguese discoveries during years then

Portuguese portolano.

recent, was probably made for King Emanuel, and it has come down to us, being preserved now at Munich.   This chart wholly omits the Spanish work of exploration, and records only the coasts coursed by Cabral in the south, and by the Cortereals in the north.   We have a further and similar record in the chart of Pedro

Pedro Reinel.

Reinel, which could not have been made far from the same time, and which introduces to us the same prominent cape which in La Cosa's map had been called the English cape as "Cavo

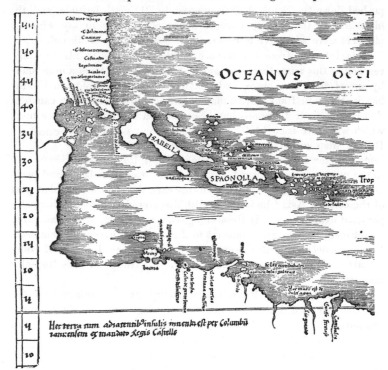

THE SO-CALLED ADMIRAL'S MAP.

Razo," a name preserved to us to-day in the Cape Race of Newfound-land.

There is abundant evidence of the non-communicative policy of Spain.   This secretiveness was understood at the time Robert Thorne,

Spain and Portugal conceal their geo- graphical secrets.

in 1527, complained, as well as Sir Humphrey Gilbert in his *Discoverie*, that a similar injunction was later laid by Por-tugal.   In Veitia Linage's *Norte* we read of the cabinets in which these maps were preserved, and how the Spanish pilot major and royal cosmographer alone kept the keys. There exists a document by which one of the companions of Magellan was put under a penalty of two thousand ducats not to disclose the route he traversed in that famous voyage. We know how Columbus endeavored to conceal the route of his final voyage, in which he reached the coast of Veragua.

MÜNSTER, 1532.

In the two maps of nearly equal date, being the earliest engraved charts which we have, the Ruysch map of 1508 and the so-called Admiral's map of 1507 (1513), the question of a strait leading to the Asiatic seas, which Columbus had spent so much energy in trying to find during his last voyage, is treated differently. We have seen that La Cosa confessed his uncertain knowledge by covering

A strait to India.

# Globus mundi

## Declaratio siue descriptio mundi

et totius orbis terrarum,globulo rotundo comparati vt spera soli
da,Qua cuiuis etia mediocriter docto ad oculu videre licet an
tipodes esse,quoꝝ pedes nostris oppositi sunt,Et qualiter in vna
quaꝗ orbis parte homines vitam agere queunt salutare,sole sin
gula terre loca illustrante:que tamen terra in vacuo aere pendere
videtur:solo dei nutu sustetata,alijsꝗ permultis de quarta orbis
terrarum parte nuperab Americo reperta,

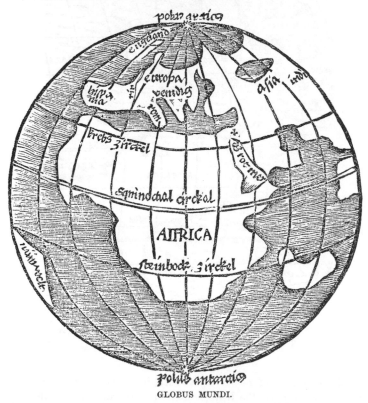

GLOBUS MUNDI.

the place with a vignette. In the Ruysch map there is left the possibility of such a passage ; in the other there is none, for the main shore is
that of Asia itself, whose coast line uninterruptedly connects with that
of South America. The belief in such a strait in due time was fixed,

# ℭ A treatyſe of
the newe *India*, with other new
founde landes and Jlandes, aſwell
eaſtwarde as weſtwarde, as they
are knowen and found in theſe oure
dayes, after the deſcription of Se-
baſtian Munſter in his boke of vni-
uerſall Coſmographie: wherin the
diligent reader may ſee the good
ſucceſſe and rewarde of noble
and honeſte enterpryſes,
by the which, not only world-,
ly ryches are obtayned,
but alſo God is glo-
rified, & the Chri-
ſtian faythen-
larged.
Tranſlated out of Latin into Engliſhe. By
Rycharde Eden.

℁ Præter ſpem ſub ſpæ.

EDEN.

and lingered even beyond the time when Cortes showed there was no ground for it. We find it in Schöner's globes, in the Tross gores, and even so late as 1532, in the belated map of Münster.

The map of the *Globus Mundi* (Strassburg, 1509) has some significance as being the earliest issued north of the Alps, recording both the Portuguese and Spanish discoveries; though it merely gives the projecting angle of the South American coast as representing the developments of the west.

Earliest map to show America made north of the Alps.

It is doubtful if any reference to the new discoveries had appeared in English literature before Alexander Barclay produced in 1509 a translation of Brant's *Ship of Fools,* and for a few years there were only chance references which made no impression on the literary instincts of the time.　It was not till after the middle of the century, in 1553, that Richard Eden, translating a section of Sebastian Münster's *Cosmographia,* published it in London as a *Treatyse of the newe India,* and English-reading people first saw a considerable account of what the rest of Europe had been doing in contrast with the English maritime apathy.　Two years later (1555), Eden, drawing this time upon Peter Martyr, did much in his *Decades of the Newe World* to enlarge the English conceptions.

English references to America.

Richard Eden.

But the most striking and significant of all the literary movements which grew out of the new oceanic developments was that which gave a name to the New World, and has left a continent, which Columbus unwittingly found, the monument of another's fame.

The naming of America.

It was in September, 1504, that Vespucius, remembering an old schoolmate in Florence, Piero Soderini, who was then the perpetual Gonfalonière of that city, took what it is supposed he had written out at length concerning his experiences in the New World, and made an abstract of it in Italian.　Dating this on the 4th of that month, he dispatched it to Italy. It is a question whether the original of this abridged text of Vespucius is now known, though Varnhagen, with a confidence few scholars have shared, has claimed such authenticity for a text which he has printed.

1504. September. Letter of Vespucius.

It concerns us chiefly to know that somehow a copy of this condensed narrative of Vespucius came into the hands of his fellow-townsman, Fra Giovanni Giocondo, then in Paris at work as an architect constructing a bridge over the Seine.　It is to be allowed that R. H. Major, in tracing the origin of the French text, assumes something to complete his story, and that this precise genesis of the narrative which was received by Duke René of Lorraine is open to some question.　The supposition that a young Alsatian, then in Paris, Mathias Ringmann, had been a friend of Giocondo, and had been the bearer of this new version to René, is likewise a conjecture.　Whether Ringmann was such a messenger or not matters little, but the time was fast approaching when this young man was to be associated with a proposition made in the little village of St. Dié, in the Vosges, which was one of those obscure but far-reaching mental premonitions so often affecting the world's history, without the backing of great names or great events.　This almost unknown place was within the domain of this same Duke René, a wise man, who

St. Dié.

liked scholars and scholarly tomes. His patronage had fostered there a small college and a printing-press. There had been grouped around these agencies a number of learned men, or those

Duke René.

VESPUCIUS.

ambitious of knowledge. Scholars in other parts of Europe, when they heard of this little coterie, wondered how its members had congregated there. One Walter Lud, or Gualterus Ludovicus, as they liked to Latinize his name, a dependent and secretary of Duke René, was now a man not much under sixty, and he had been the grouper and manager of this body of scholars. There had lately been brought to join them this same Mathias Ringmann, who came from Paris with all the learning that he had tried to imbibe under the tutoring of Dr. John Faber. If we believe the story as Major has worked it out, Ringmann had come to this sparse community with all the fervor for the exploits of Vespucius which he got in the French capital from associating with that Florentine's admirer, the architect Giocondo.

Coming to St. Dié, Ringmann had been made a professor of Latin, and with the usual nominal alternation had become known as Philesius ; and as such he appears a little later in connection with a Latin version of the French of Giocondo, which was soon made by another of the St. Dié scholars, a canon of the cathedral there, Jean Bassin de Sandacourt. Still another young man, Walter Waldseemüller, had not long before been made a teacher of geography in the college, and his name, as was the wont, had been classicized into Hylacomylus.

There have now been brought before the reader all the actors in this little St. Dié drama, upon which we, as Americans, must gaze back through the centuries as upon the baptismal scene of a continent.

The Duke had emphasized the cosmographical studies of the age by this appointment of an energetic young student of geography, who

Waldseemüller.

seems to have had a deft hand at map-making. Waldseemüller had some hand, at least, in fashioning a map of the new discoveries at the west, and the Duke had caused the map to be engraved, and we find a stray note of sales of it singly as early as 1507, though it was not till 1513 that it fairly got before the world in the Ptolemy of that year. Waldseemüller had also developed out of these studies a little cosmographical treatise, which the college press was set to work upon, and to swell it to the dignity of a book, thin as it still was, the diminutive quarto was made to include Bassin's Latin version of the Vespucius narrative, set out with some Latin verses by

Cosmographiæ Introductio.

Ringmann. The little book called *Cosmographiæ Introductio* was brought out at this obscure college press in St Dié, in April and August, 1507. There were some varieties in each of these issues, while that part which constituted the Vespucius narrative was further issued in a separate publication.

It was in this form that Vespucius's narrative was for the first time, unless Varnhagen's judgment to the contrary is superior to all others, brought before the world. The most significant quality of the little book, however, was the proposition which Waldseemüller, with his anonymous views on cosmography, advanced in the introductory parts. It is assumed by writers on the subject that it was not Waldseemüller alone who was responsible for the plan there given to name that part of the New World which Americus Vespucius had described after the voyager who had so graphically told his experiences on its shores. The plan, it is supposed, met with the approval of, or was the outcome

# COSMOGRAPHIAE
# INTRODVCTIO
# CVM QVIBVS
# DAM GEOME
# TRIAE
# AC
# ASTRONO
# MIAE PRINCIPIIS AD
# EAM REM NECESSARIIS

Infuper quattuor Americi
Vefpucij nauigationes.

Vniuerfalis Cofmographiæ defcriptio tam
in folido ῷplano/ eis etiam infertis
quæ Ptholomꝫo ignota a nu
peris reperta funt.

# DISTHYCON

Cum deus aftra regat/& terræ climata Cæfar
Nec tellus/nec eis fydera maius habent.

TITLE OF THE COSMOGRAPHIÆ INTRODUCTIO.

of the counsels of, this little band of St. Dié scholars collectively. It is not the belief of students generally that this coterie, any more than Vespucius himself, ever imagined that the new regions were really disjoined from the Asiatic main, though Varnhagen contends that Vespucius knew they were. One thing is certainly true: that there was no intention to apply the name which was now proposed to anything more than the continental mass of the Brazilian shore which Vespucius had coasted, and which was looked upon as a distinct region from the islands which Columbus had traversed. It had come to be believed that the archipelago of Columbus was far from the paradise of luxury and wealth that his extravagant terms called for, and which the descriptions of Marco Polo had led the world to expect, supposing the regions of the overland and oceanic discoverers to be the same. Further than this, a new expectation had been aroused by the reports which had come to Europe of the vaster proportions and of the brilliant paroquets — for such trivial aspects gave emphasis — of the more southern regions. It was an instance of the eagerness with which deluded minds, to atone for their first disappointment, grasp at the *Mundus Novus.* chances of a newer satisfaction. This was the hope which was entertained of this *Mundus Novus* of Vespucius, — not a new world in the sense of a new continent.

The Española and its neighboring regions of Columbus, and the Baccalaos of Cabot and Cortereal, clothed in imagination with the descriptions of Marco Polo, were nothing but the Old World approached from the east instead of from the west. It was different with the *Mundus Novus* of Vespucius. Here was in reality a new life and habitation, doubtless connected, but how it was not known, with the great eastern world of the merchants. It corresponded with nothing, so far as understood, in the Asiatic chorography. It was ready for a new name, and it was alone associated with the man who had, in the autumn of 1502, so described it, and from no one else could its name be so acceptably taken. Europe and Asia were geographically contiguous, and so might be Asia and the new "America."

The sudden eclipse which the name of Columbus underwent, as the *Eclipse of Columbus's name.* fame of Vespucius ran through the popular mind, was no unusual thing in the vicissitudes of reputations. Factitious prominence is gained without great difficulty by one or for one, if popular issues of the press are worked in his interest, and if a great variety of favoring circumstances unite in giving currency to rumors and reports which tend to invest him with exclusive interest. The curious public willingly lends itself to any end that taxes nothing but its credulity and good nature.

We have associated with Vespucius just the elements of such a suc- *Fame of Vespucius.* cess, while the fame of Columbus was waning to the death, namely : a stretch of continental coast, promising something more than the scattered trifles of an insalubrious archipelago ; a new southern heavens, offering other glimpses of immensity ; descriptions that were calculated to replace in new variety and mystery the stale stories of Cipango and Cathay: the busy yearnings of a group of young and ardent spirits, having all the apparatus of a press to apply to the making of a public sentiment; and the enthusiasm of narrators who sought to season their marvels of discovery with new delights and honors.

The hold which Vespucius had seized upon the imagination of Europe, and which doubtless served to give him prominence in the popular appreciation, as it has served many a ready and picturesque writer since, was that glowing redundancy of description, both of the earth and the southern constellations, which forms so conspicuous a feature of his narratives. It was the later voyage of Vespucius, and not his alleged voyage of 1497, which raised, as Humboldt has pointed out, the great interest which his name suggested.

Just what the notion prevailing at the time was of the respective exploits of Columbus and Vespucius is easily gathered from a letter dated May 20, 1506, which appears in a *Dyalogus Johannis Stamler de diversarum gencium sectis, et mundi regionibus*, published in 1508. In this treatise a reference is made to the letters of Columbus (1493) and Vespucius (1503) as concerning an insular and continental space respectively. It speaks of " Cristofer Colom, the discoverer of *new islands*, and of Albericus Vespucius concerning the new discovered *world*, to both of whom our age is most largely indebted." It will be remembered that an early misnaming of Vespucius by calling him Albericus instead of Americus, which took place in one of the early editions of his narrative, remained for some time to confuse the copiers of them. Columbus and Vespucius.

If we may judge from a diagram which Vespucius gives of a globe with two standing men on it ninety degrees apart, each dropping a line to the centre of the earth, this navigator had grasped, together with the idea of the sphericity of the globe, the essential conditions of gravitation. There could be no up-hill sailing when the zenith was always overhead. Curiously enough, the supposition of Columbus, when as he sailed on his third voyage he found the air grow colder, was that he was actually sailing up-hill, ascending a protuberance of the earth which was like the stem end of a pear, with the crowning region of the earthly paradise atop of all! Such contrasts show the lesser navigator to be the greater physicist, and they go not a small way in accounting for the levelness of head which gained the suffrages of the wise. Vespucius on gravitation.

When Duke René, upon whom so much had depended in the little community at St. Dié, died, in 1508, the geographical printing schemes of Waldseemüller and his fellows received a 1508. Duke René died.

severe reverse, and for a few years we hear nothing more of the edition of Ptolemy which had been planned.  The next year (1509),
Waldseemüller, now putting his name to his little treatise, was forced,

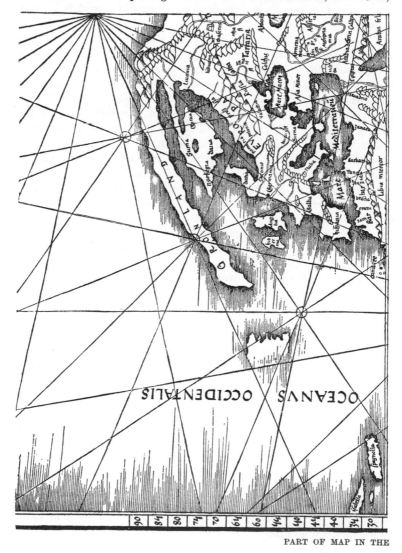

PART OF MAP IN THE

because of the failure of the college press, to go to Strassburg to have
a new edition of it printed (1509).  The proposals for naming the
continental discoveries of Vespucius seem not in the interim to have

excited any question, and so they are repeated. We look in vain in the copy of this edition which Ferdinand Columbus bought at Venice in July, 1521, and which is preserved at Seville, for any marginal pro-

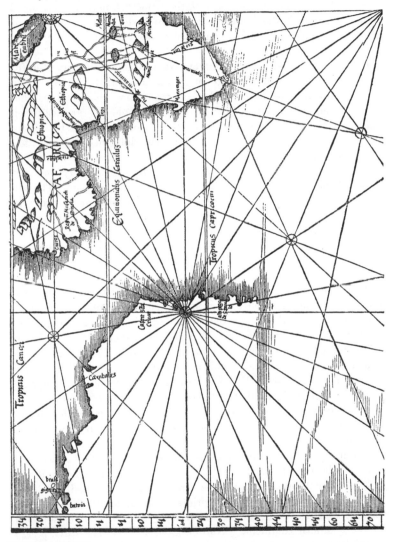

PTOLEMY OF 1513.

test. The author of the *Historie*, how far soever Ferdinand may have been responsible for that book, is equally reticent. There was indeed no reason why he should take any exception. The fitness of the

appellation was accepted as in no way invalidating the claim of Columbus to discoveries farther to the north ; and in another little tract,
1509. *Glo-*   printed at the same time at Grüniger's Strassburg press, the
*bus Mundi.*   anonymous *Globus Mundi*, the name " America " is adopted
in the text, though the small bit of the new coast shown in its map is
called by a translation of Vespucius's own designation merely " *Newe
Welt.*"

The Ptolemy scheme bore fruit at last, and at Strassburg, also, for
          here the edition whose maps are associated with the name
1513. The   of Waldseemüller, and whose text shows some of the influ-
Strassburg
Ptolemy.   ence of a Greek manuscript of the old geographer which
Ringmann had earlier brought from Italy, came out in 1513.  Here
was a chance, in a book far more sure to have influence than the little
anonymous tract of 1507, to impress the new name America upon
the world of scholars and observers, and the opportunity was not
seized.  It is not easy to divine the cause of such an omission.  The edition has two maps which show this Vespucian continent in precisely
the same way, though but one of them shows also to its full extent
the region of Columbus's explorations.  On one of these maps the
southern regions have no designation whatever, and on the other, the
" Admiral's map," there is a legend stretched across it, assigning the
discovery of the region to Columbus.

We do not know, in all the contemporary literature which has come
down to us, that up to 1513 there had been any rebuke at the ignorance or temerity which appeared in its large bearing to be depriving
Columbus of a rightful honor.  That in 1509 Waldseemüller should
have enforced the credit given to Vespucius, and in 1513 revoked it in
favor of Columbus, seems to indicate qualms of conscience of which
we have no other trace.  Perhaps, indeed, this reversion of sympathy
is of itself an evidence that Waldseemüller had less to do with the
edition than has been supposed.  It is too much to assert that Waldseemüller repented of his haste, but the facts in one light would indicate it.

Like many such headlong projects, however, the purpose had passed
The name   beyond the control of its promoters.  The euphony, if not
America be-
gins to be   the fitness, of the name America had attracted attention,
accepted.   and there are several printed and manuscript globes and
maps in existence which at an early date adopted that designation
for the southern continent.  Nordenskiöld (*Facsimile Atlas*, p. 42)
quotes from the commentaries of the German Coclæus, contained in
the *Meteorologia Aristotelis* of Jacobus Faber (Nuremberg, 1512)
a passage referring to the " Nova Americi terra."  To complicate
matters still more, within a few years after this an undated edition of

Waldseemüller's tract appeared at Lyons, — perhaps without his participation, — which was always found, down to 1881, without a map, though the copies known were very few; but in that year a copy with a map was discovered, now owned by an American collector, in which

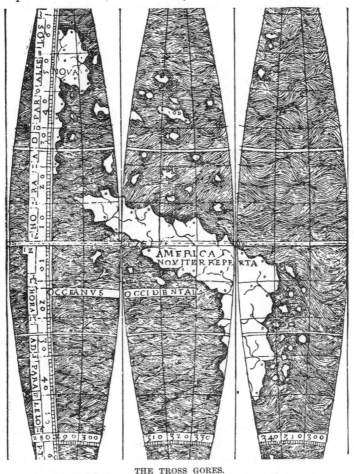

THE TROSS GORES.

the proposition of the text is enforced with the name America on the representation of South America. A section of this map is here given as the Tross Gores. In the present condition of our knowledge of the matter, it was thus at a date somewhere about 1516–17 that the name appeared first in any printed map, unless, indeed, we allow a somewhat earlier date to two globes in the Haus-lab collection at Vienna. On the date of these last objects there is,

1516–17.
First in a map.

however, much difference of opinion, and one of them has been depicted and discussed in the *Mittheilungen* of the Geographische
Gesellschaft (1886, p. 364) of Vienna. Here, as in the descriptive
texts, it must be clearly kept in mind, however, that no one at this
date thought of applying the name to more than the land which Ves-

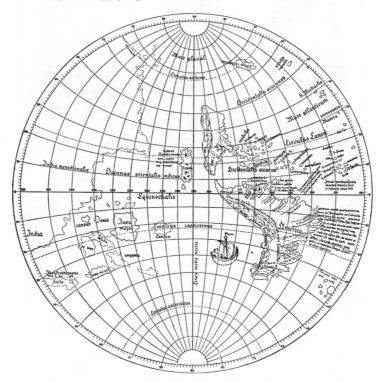

THE HAUSLAB GLOBE.

pucius had found stretching south beyond the equator on the east side
of South America, and which Balboa had shown to have a similar
trend on the west. The islands and region to the north, which Columbus and Cabot had been the pioneers in discovering, still remained
a mystery in their relations to Asia, and there was yet a long time to
elapse before the truth should be manifest to all, that a similar expanse of ocean lay westerly at the north, as was shown by Balboa to
extend in the same direction at the south.

This Vespucian baptism of South America now easily worked its
way to general recognition. It is found in a contemporary set of
gores which Nordenskiöld has of late brought to light, and was soon

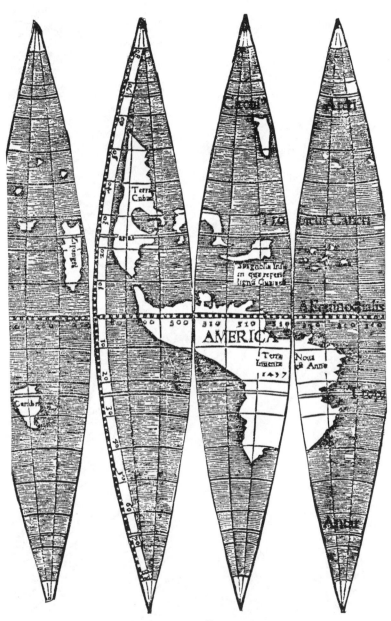

THE NORDENSKIÖLD GORES.

APIANUS, 1520.

adopted by the Nuremberg globe-maker, Schöner (1515, etc.) ; by
Vadianus at Vienna, when editing Pomponius Mela (1515) ; by Apian
on a map used in an edition of Solinus, edited by Camers (1520) ;

SCHÖNER GLOBE, 1515.

and by Lorenz Friess, who had been of Duke René's coterie and a
correspondent of Vespucius, on a map introduced into the
Grüniger Ptolemy, published at Strassburg (1522), which
also reproduced the Waldseemüller map of 1513. This is
the earliest of the Ptolemies in which we find the name accepted on
its maps.

1522. The
name first in
a Ptolemy.

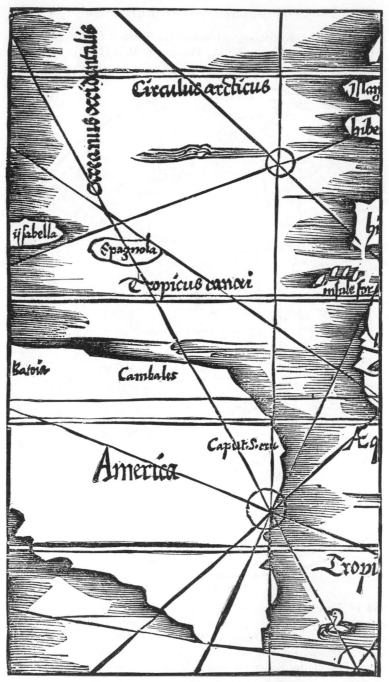

FRIESS (*Frisius*), IN THE PTOLEMY OF 1522.

There is one significant fact concerning the conflict of the Crown with the heirs of Columbus, which followed upon the Admiral's death, and in which the advocates of the government sought to prove that the claim of Columbus to have discovered the continental shore about the Gulf of Paria in 1498 was not to be sustained in view of visits by others at an earlier date. This significant fact is that Vespucius is not once mentioned during the litigation. It is of course possible, and perhaps probable, that it was for the interests of both parties to keep out of view a servant of Portugal trenching upon what was believed to be Spanish territories. The same impulse could hardly have influenced Ferdinand Columbus in the silent acquiescence which, as a contemporary informs us, was his attitude towards the action of the St. Dié professors. There seems little doubt of his acceptance of a view, then undoubtedly common, that there was no conflict of the claims of the respective navigators, because their different fields of exploration had not brought such claims in juxtaposition.

Following, however, upon the assertion of Waldseemüller, that Vespucius had " found " this continental tract needing a name, there grew up a belief in some quarters, and deducible from the very obscure chronology of his narrative, which formulated itself in a statement that Vespucius had really been the first to set foot on any part of this extended main. It was here that very soon the jealousy of those who had the good name of Columbus in their keeping began to manifest itself, and some time after *Who first landed on the southern main?* 1527, — if we accept that year as the date of his beginning work on the *Historie*, — Las Casas, who had had some intimate relations with Columbus, tells us that the report was rife of Vespucius himself being privy to such pretensions. Unless Las Casas, or the reporters to whom he referred, had material of which no one now has knowledge, it is certain that there is no evidence connecting Vespucius with the St. Dié proposition, and it is equally certain that evidence fails to establish beyond doubt the publication of any map bearing the name America while Vespucius lived. He had been made pilot major of Spain March 22, 1508, and had died February 22, 1512. We have no chart made by Vespucius himself, though it is known that in 1518 such a chart was in the possession of Ferdinand, brother of Charles the Fifth. The recovery of this chart would doubtless render a signal service in illuminating this and other questions of early *Vespucius's maps.* American cartography. It might show us how far, if at all, Vespucius " sinfully failed towards the Admiral," as Las Casas reports of him, and adds : " If Vespucius purposely gave currency to this belief of his first setting foot on the main, *Vespucius not privy to the naming.* it was a great wickedness ; and if it was not done intentionally, it looks like it." With all this predisposition, however, towards an implication of Vespucius, Las Casas was cautious enough to consider that, after all, it may have been the St. Dié coterie who were alone responsible for starting the rumor.

It is very clear that in Spain there had been no recognition of the name "America," nor was it ever officially recognized by the Spanish government. Las Casas understood that it had been applied by "foreigners," who had, as he says, "called America what ought to be called Columba." Just what date should attach to this protest of Las Casas is not determinable. If it was later than the gore-map of Mercator in 1541, which was the first, so far as is known, to apply the name to both North and South America, there is certainly good reason for the disquietude of Las Casas. If it was before that, it was because, with the progress of discovery, it had become more and more clear that all parts of the new regions were component parts of an absolutely new continent, upon which the name of the first discoverer of any part of it, main or insular, ought to have been bestowed. That it should be left to "foreign writers," as Las Casas said, to give a name representing a rival interest to a world that Spanish enterprise had made known was no less an indignity to Spain than to her great though adopted Admiral.

It happens that the suggestion which sprang up in the Vosges worked steadily onward through the whole of central Europe. That it had so successful a propagation is owing, beyond a doubt, as much to the exclusive spirit of the Spanish government in keeping to itself its hydrographical progress as to any other cause. We have seen how the name spread through Germany and Austria. It was taken up by Stobnicza in Poland in 1512, in a Cracow introduction to Ptolemy; and many other of the geographical writers of central and southern Europe adopted the designation. The *New Interlude*, published in England in 1519, had used it, and towards the middle of the century the fame of Vespucius had occupied England, so far as Sir Thomas More and William Cunningham represent it, to the almost total obscuration of Columbus.

It was but a question of time when Vespucius would be charged with promoting his own glory by borrowing the plumes of Columbus. Whether Las Casas, in what has been quoted, initiated such accusations or not, the account of that writer was in manuscript and could have had but small currency.

The first accusation in print, so far as has been discovered, came from the German geographer, Johann Schöner, who, having already in his earlier globes adopted the name America, now in a tract called

*Marginal notes:*

"America" not used in Spain.

1541. Mercator first applied the name to both North and South America.

Spread of the name in central Europe.

*Opusculum Geographicum*, which he printed at Nuremberg in 1533, openly charged Vespucius with attaching his own name to a region of India Superior. Two years later, Servetus, while he repeated in his Ptolemy of 1535 the earlier maps bearing the name America, entered in his text a protest against its use by alleging distinctly that Columbus was earlier than Vespucius in finding the new main. 1533. Schö-<br>ner accuses<br>Vespucius<br>of participa-<br>tion in the<br>injustice.

Within a little more than a year from the death of Vespucius, and while the maps assigned to Waldseemüller were pressed on the attention of scholars, the integralness of the great southern continent, to which a name commemorating Americus had been given, was made manifest, or at least probable, by the discovery of Balboa.

Let us now see how the course of discovery was finding record during these early years of the sixteenth century in respect to the great but unsuspected barrier which actually interposed in the way of those who sought Asia over against Spain. A barrier<br>suspected.

In the north, the discoveries of the English under Cabot, and of the Portuguese under the Cortereals, soon led the Normans and Bretons from Dieppe and Saint Malo to follow in the wake of such predecessors. As early as 1504 the fishermen of these latter peoples seem to have been on the northern coasts, and we owe to them the name of Cape Breton, which is thought to be the oldest French name in our American geography. It is the "Gran Capitano" of Ramusio who credits the Bretons with these early visits at the north, though we get no positive cartographical record of such visits till 1520, in a map which is given by Kunstmann in his *Atlas*. Discoveries<br>in the north. 1504. Nor-<br>mans and<br>Bretons.

Again, in 1505, some Portuguese appear to have been on the Newfoundland coast under the royal patronage of Henry VII. of England, and by 1506 the Portuguese fishermen were regular frequenters of the Newfoundland banks. We find in the old maps Portuguese names somewhat widely scattered on the neighboring coast lines, for the frequenting of the region by the fishermen of that nation continued well towards the close of the century. 1505. Por-<br>tuguese.

There are also stories of one Velasco, a Spaniard, visiting the St. Lawrence in 1506, and Juan de Agramonte in 1511 entered into an agreement with the Spanish King to pursue discovery in these parts more actively, but we have no definite knowledge of results. 1506. Span-<br>iards.

The death of Ferdinand, January 23, 1516, would seem to have put a stop to a voyage which had already been planned for Spain by Sebastian Cabot, to find a northwest passage ; but the next year (1517)

Cabot, in behalf of England, had sailed to Hudson's Strait, and thence
north to 67° 30′, finding "no night there," and observing
extraordinary variations of the compass. Somewhat later
there are the very doubtful claims of the Portuguese to explorations under Fagundes about the Gulf of St. Lawrence
in 1521.

1517. Sebas-
tian Cabot.

1521. Portu-
guese.

By 1506 also there is something like certainty respecting the Normans, and under the influence of a notable Dieppese, Jean
Ango, we soon meet a class of adventurous mariners tempt-
ing distant and marvelous seas. We read of Pierre Cri-
gnon, and Thomas Aubert, both of Dieppe, Jean Denys of Honfleur,
and Jean Parmentier, all of whom have come down to us through the
pages of Ramusio. It is of Jean Denys in 1506, and of Thomas Aubert a little later, that we find the fullest recitals. To Denys there
has been ascribed a mysterious chart of the Gulf of St. Lawrence ; but if the copy which is preserved represents it, there
can be no hesitation in discarding it as a much later cartographical
record. The original is said to have been found in the archives of the
ministry of war in Paris so late as 1854, but no such map is found there
now. The copy which was made for the Canadian archives is at Ot-
tawa, and I have been favored by the authorities there with a tracing
of it. No one of authority will be inclined to dispute the judgment of
Harrisse that it is apocryphal. We are accordingly left in uncertainty
just how far at this time the contour of the Golfo Quadrago, as the
Gulf of St. Lawrence was called, was made out. Aubert is said to
have brought to France seven of the natives of the region in 1509.
Ten years or more later (1519, etc.), the Baron de Léry is
thought to have attempted a French settlement thereabouts,
of which perhaps the only traces were some European cattle, the descendants of his small herd landed there in 1528, which were found on
Sable Island many years later.

1506. An-
go's cap-
tains.

Denys's
map.

1518. Léry.

We know from Herrera that in 1526 Nicholas Don, a Breton, was
fishing off Baccalaos, and Rut tells us that in 1527 Norman and Breton vessels were pulling fish on the shores of
Newfoundland. Such mentions mark the early French knowledge of
these northern coasts, but there is little in it all to show any contribution to geographical developments.

1526. Nich-
olas Don.

Before this, however, the first serious attempt of which we have
incontrovertible evidence was made to connect these discoveries in the north with those of the Spanish in the Antilles. As early as 1511 the map given by Peter Martyr
had shown that, from the native reports or otherwise, a
notion had arisen of lands lying north of Cuba. In 1512
Ponce de Leon was seeking a commission to authorize him

Attempts to
connect the
northern
discoveries
with those of
the Spanish.

1511. Peter
Martyr's
map.

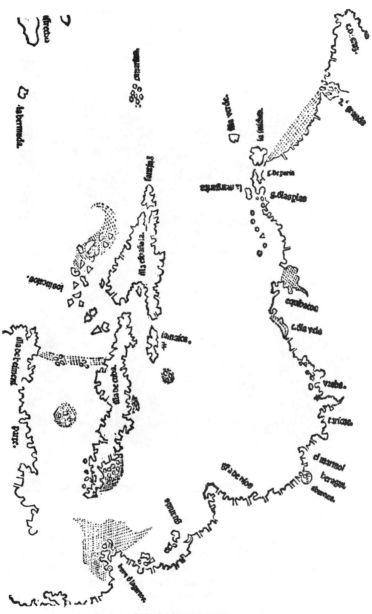

PETER MARTYR, 1511.

to go and see what this reported land was like, with its fountain of
1512. Ponce youth.  He got it February 23, 1512, when Ferdinand com-
de Leon.    missioned him " to find and settle the island of Bimini," if
none had already been there, or if Portugal had not already acquired

PONCE DE LEON.
[From Barcia's *Herrera*.]

possession in any part that he sought.  Delays in preparation post-
1513.     poned the actual departure of his expedition from Porto
March.    Rico till March, 1513.  On the 23d of that month, Easter
Sunday, he struck the mainland somewhere opposite the Bahamas, and
          named the country Florida, from the day of the calendar.
Florida.  He tracked the coast northward to a little above 30° north
latitude.  Then he retraced his way, and rounding the southern cape,

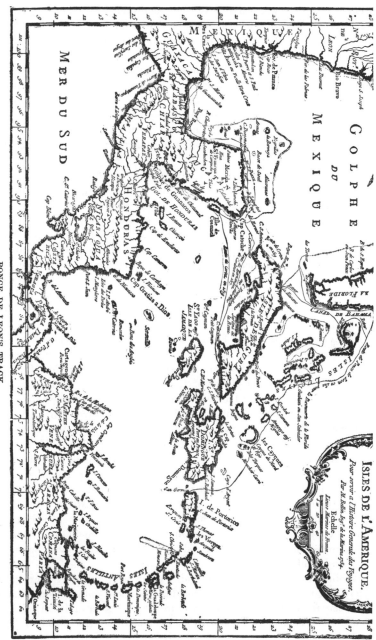

PONCE DE LEON'S TRACK.

went well up the western side of the peninsula. Whether any stray explorers had been before along this shore may be a question. Private Spanish or Portuguese adventurers, or even Englishmen, had not been unknown in neighboring waters some years earlier, as we have evidence. We find certainly in this voyage of Ponce de Leon for the first time an unmistakable official undertaking, which we might expect would soon have produced its cartographical record. The interdicts of the Council of the Indies were, however, too powerful, and the old lines of the Cantino map still lingered in the maps for some years, though by 1520 the Floridian peninsula began to take recognizable shape in certain Spanish maps.

Just what stood for Bimini in the reports of this expedition is not clear; but there seems to have been a vague notion of its not being the same as Florida, for when Ponce de Leon got a new patent in September, 1514, he was authorized to settle both "islands," Bimini and Florida, and Diego Colon as viceroy was directed to help on the expedition. Seven years, however, passed in delays, so that it was not till 1521 that he attempted to make a settlement, but just at what point is not known. Sickness and loss in encounters with the Indians soon discouraged him, and he returned to Cuba to die of an arrow wound received in one of the forays of the natives.

It was still a question if Florida connected with any adjacent lands. Several minor expeditions had added something to the stretch of coast, but the main problem still stood unsolved. In 1519 Pineda had made the circuit of the northern shores of the Gulf of Mexico, and at the river Panuco he had been challenged by Cortes as trenching on his government. Turning again eastward, Pineda found the mouth of the river named by him Del Espiritu Santo, which passes with many modern students as the first indication in history of the great Mississippi, while others trace the first signs of that river to Cabeça de Vaca in 1528, or to the passage higher up its current by De Soto in 1541. Believing it at first the long-looked-for strait to pass to the Indies, Pineda entered it, only to be satisfied that it must gather the watershed of a continent, which in this part was now named Amichel. It seemed accordingly certain that no passage to the west was to be found in this part of the gulf, and that Florida must be more than an island.

While these explorations were going on in the gulf, others were conducted on the Atlantic side of Florida. If the Pompey Stone which has been found in New York State, to the confusion of historical students, be accepted as genuine, it is evidence that the Spaniard had in 1520 penetrated from some point on the coast to that region. In

1520 we get demonstrable proof, when Lucas Vasquez de Ayllon sent a caravel under Gordillo, which joined company on the way with another vessel bound on a slave-hunting expedition, and the two, proceeding northward, sighted the main coast at a river which they found to be in thirty-three and a half degrees of north latitude, on the South Carolina coast.  They returned without further exploration.  Ayllon, without great success, attempted further explorations in 1525 ; but in 1526 he went again with greater preparations, and made his landfall a little farther north, near the mouth of the Wateree River, which he called the Jordan, and sailed on to the Chesapeake,

1520.
Ayllon.

THE AYLLON MAP.

where, with the help of negro slaves, then first introduced into this region, he began the building of a town at or near the spot where the English in the next century founded Jamestown ; or at least this is the conjecture of Dr. Shea.  Here Ayllon died of a pestilential fever October 18, 1526, when the disheartened colonists, one hundred and fifty out of the original five hundred, returned to Santo Domingo.

Spaniards in Virginia.

While these unfortunate experiences were in progress, Estevan Gomez, sent by the Spanish government, after the close of the conference at Badajos, to make sure that there was no passage to the Moluccas anywhere along this Atlantic coast, started in the autumn of 1524, if the data we have admit of that conclusion as to the time, from Corunna, in the north of Spain.  He proceeded at once, as Charles V. had directed him, to the Baccalaos region, striking the mainland possibly at Labrador, and then turned south, carefully examining all inlets.  We have no authoritative narrative sanctioned by his name, or by that of any one accompanying the expedition ; nor has the map which Alonso Chaves made to con-

1524.
Gomez.

Chaves's map.

form to what was reported by Gomez been preserved, but the essential features of the exploration are apparently embodied in the great map of Ribero (1529), and we have sundry stray references in the later chroniclers. From all this it would seem that Gomez followed the coast southward to the point of Florida, and made it certain to most minds that no such passage to India existed, though there was a lingering suspicion that the Gulf of St. Lawrence had not been sufficiently explored.

1529. Ribero's map.

Let us turn now to the southern shores of the Caribbean Sea. New efforts at colonizing here were undertaken in 1508-9. By this time the coast had been pretty carefully made out as far as Honduras, largely through the explorations of Ojeda and Juan de la Cosa. The scheme was a dual one, and introduces us to two new designations of the regions separated by that indentation of the coast known as the Gulf of Uraba. Here Ojeda and Nicuessa were sent to organize governments, and rule their respective provinces of Nueva Andalusia and Castilla del Oro for the period of four years. Mention has already been made of this in the preceding chapter. They delayed getting to their governments, quarreled for a while about their bounds on each other, fought the natives with desperation but not with much profit, lost La Cosa in one of the encounters, and were thwarted in their purpose of holding Jamaica as a granary and in getting settlers from Española by the alertness of Diego Colon, who preferred to be tributary to no one.

Shores of the Caribbean Sea.

Ojeda and Nicuessa.

All this had driven Ojeda to great stress in the little colony of San Sebastian which he had founded. He attempted to return for aid to Española, and was wrecked on the voyage. This caused him to miss his lieutenant Enciso, who was on his way to him with recruits. So Ojeda passes out of history, except so far as he tells his story in the testimony he gave in the suit of the heirs of Columbus in 1513-15.

New heroes were coming on. A certain Pizarro had been left in command by Ojeda, — not many years afterwards to be heard of. One Vasco Nuñez de Balboa, a poor and debt-burdened fugitive, was on board of Enciso's ship, and had wit enough to suggest that a region like San Sebastian, inhabited by tribes which used poisoned arrows, was not the place for a colony struggling for existence and dependent on foraging. So they removed the remnants of the colony, which Enciso had turned back as they were escaping, to the other side of the bay, and in this way the new settlement came within the jurisdiction of Nicuessa, whom a combination soon deposed and shipped to sea, never to be heard of. It was in these commotions that Vasco Nuñez de Balboa brought himself into a prominence that

Pizarro.

ended in his being commissioned by Diego Colon as governor of the
new colony.   He had, meanwhile, got more knowledge of a great sea
at the westward than Columbus had acquired on the coast of Veragua

*El  Adelantado BASCO NUÑES de
xeres que descubrió la mar del Sur.*

BALBOA.   [From Barcia's *Herrera.*]

in 1503.   Balboa rightly divined that its discovery, if he could effect
it, would serve him a good purpose in quieting any jealousies of his
rule, of which he was beginning to observe symptoms.   So on the 1st
of September, 1513, he set out in the direction which the natives had
indicated, and by the 24th he had reached a mountain from the top

of which his guides told him he would behold the sea. On the 25th his party ascended, himself in front, and it was not long before he stood gazing upon the distant ocean, the first of Europeans to discern the long-coveted sea. Down the other slope the Spaniards went. The path was a difficult one, and it was three days before one of his advanced squads reached the beach. Not till the next day, the 29th, did Vasco Nuñez himself join those in advance, when, striding into the tide, he took possession of the sea and its bordering lands in the name of his sovereigns. It was on Saint Miguel's Day, and the Bay of Saint Miguel marks the spot to-day. Towards the end of January, 1514, he was again with the colony at Antigua del Darien. Thence, in March, he dispatched a messenger to Spain with news of the great discovery.

*1513. Balboa and the South Sea.*

This courier did not reach Europe till after a new expedition had been dispatched under Pedrarias, and with him went a number of followers, who did in due time their part in thridding and designating these new paths of exploration. We recognize among them Hernando de Soto, Bernal Diaz, the chronicler of the exploits of Cortes, and Oviedo, the historian. It was from April till June, 1514, that Pedrarias was on his way, and it was not long before the new governor with his imposing array of strength brought the recusant Balboa to trial, out of which he emerged burdened with heavy fines. The new governor planned at once to reap the fruits of Balboa's discovery. An expedition was sent along his track, which embarked on the new sea and gathered spoils where it could. Pedrarias soon grew jealous of Balboa, for it was not without justice that the state of the augmented colony was held to compare unfavorably with the conditions which Balboa had maintained during his rule. But constancy was never of much prevalence in these days, and Balboa's chains, lately imposed, were stricken off to give him charge of an exploration of the sea which he had discovered. Once here, Balboa planned new conquests and a new independency. Pedrarias, hearing of it through a false friend of Balboa, enticed the latter into his neighborhood, and a trial was soon set on foot, which ended in the execution of Balboa and his abettors. This was in 1517.

*Pedrarias.*

*1517. Balboa executed.*

It was not long before Pedrarias removed his capital to Panama, and in 1519 and during the few following years his captains pushed their explorations northerly along the shores of the South Sea, as the new ocean had been at once called.

As early as 1515 Pizarro and Morales had wandered down the coast southward to a region called Biru by the natives, and this was as far as adventure had carried any Spaniard, dur-

*1515. Biru.*

ing the ten years since Balboa's discovery. They had learned here of a rich region farther on, and it got to be spoken of by the same name, or by a perversion of it, as Peru. In this interval the town 1519. Pana-
of Panama had been founded (1519), and Pizarro and ma founded.
Almagro, with the priest Luque, were among those to whom allotments were made.

It was by these three associates, in 1524 and 1526, that the expeditions were organized which led to the exploration of the
coasts of Peru and the conquest of the region. The equa- Peru.
tor was crossed in 1526; in 1527 they reached 9° south. It was not till 1535 that, in the progress of events, a knowledge of the coast was extended south to the neighborhood of Lima, which was founded in that year. In the autumn of 1535, Almagro started south
to make conquest of Chili, and the bay of Valparaiso was Chili.
occupied in September, 1536. Eight years later, in 1544, explorations were pushed south to 41°. It was only in 1557 that expeditions reached the archipelago of Chiloe, and the whole coast of
South America on the Pacific was made out with some de- Chiloe.
tail down to the region which Magellan had skirted, as will be shortly shown.

It will be remembered that in 1503 Columbus had struck the coast of Honduras west of Cape Gracias à Dios. He learned then of lands to the northwest from some Indians whom he met in a canoe, but his eagerness to find the strait of his dreams led him south. It was fourteen years before the promise of that canoe was revealed.
1508.
In 1508 Ocampo had found the western extremity of Cuba, Ocampo
and made the oath of Columbus ridiculous. and Cuba.

In 1517 a slave-hunting expedition, having steered towards the west from Cuba, discovered the shores of Yucatan; and the next 1517. Yu-
year (1518) the real exploration of that region began when catan.
Juan de Grijalva, a nephew of the governor of Cuba, led thither an expedition which explored the coast of Yucatan and Mexico.

When Grijalva returned to Cuba in 1518, it was to find an expedition already planned to follow up his discoveries, and Her- 1518.
nando Cortes, who had been in the New World since 1504, Cortes.
had been chosen to lead it, with instructions to make further explorations of the coast, — a purpose very soon to become obscured in other objects. He sailed on the 17th of November, and stopped along the coast of Cuba for recruits, so it was not till February 18,
1519, that he sunk the shores of Cuba behind him, and in 1519.
March he was skirting the Yucatan shore and sailed on to San Juan de Uloa. In due time, forgetting his instructions, and caring for other

conquests than those of discovery, he began his march inland. The story of the conquest of Mexico does not help us in the aim now in view, and we leave it untold.

EL CAPITAN JUAN
de GRIJALVA de
Cuellar

GRIJALVA. [From Barcia's *Herrera.*]

It was not long after this conquest before belated apostles of the belief of Columbus appeared, urging that the capital of Montezuma was in reality the Quinsay of Marco Polo, with its great commercial interests, as was maintained by Schöner in his *Opusculum Geographicum* in 1533.

Quinsay.

We have seen how Pineda's expedition to the northern parts of the Gulf of Mexico in 1519 had improved the knowledge of that shore, and we have a map embodying these explorations, which was sent to Spain in 1520 by Garay, then governor of

1520.
Garay.

Jamaica. It was now pretty clear that the blank spaces of earlier maps, leaving it uncertain if there was a passage westerly somewhere in the northwest corner of the gulf, should be

Gulf of Mexico.

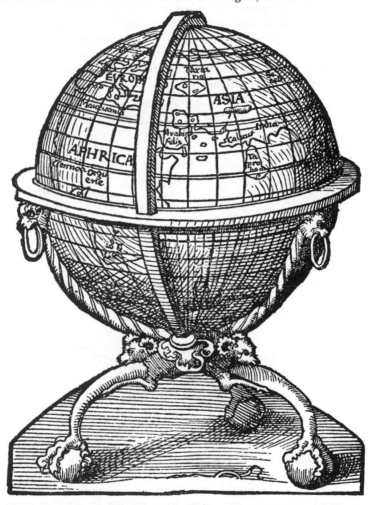

GLOBE GIVEN IN SCHÖNER'S *OPUSCULUM GEOGRAPHICUM*, 1533.

filled compactly. Still, a belief that such a passage existed somewhere in the western contour of the gulf was not readily abandoned. Cortes, when he sent to Spain his sketch of the gulf, which was published there in 1524, was dwelling on the hope that some such channel existed near Yucatan, and his insular

1524. Cortes's Gulf of Mexico.

delineation of that peninsula, with a shadowy strait at its base, was eagerly grasped by the cartographers. Such a severance finds a place in the map of Maiollo of 1527, which is preserved in the Ambrosian library at Milan. Grijalva, some years earlier, had been

Yucatan as an island.

sent, as we have seen, to sail round Yucatan; and though there are various theories about the origin of that name, it seems likely enough that the tendency to give it an insular form arose from a misconception of the Indian appellation. At all events, the island of Yucatan lingered long in the early maps.

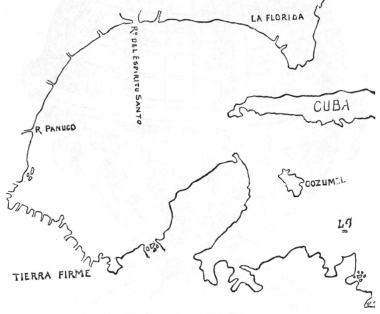

GULF OF MEXICO, 1520.

In 1523 Cortes had sent expeditions up the Pacific, and one up the

1523.
Cortes.

Atlantic side of North America, to find the wished-for passage; but in vain.

Meanwhile, important movements were making by the Portuguese

Spanish and Portuguese rivalries.

beyond that great sea of the south which Balboa had discovered. These movements were little suspected by the Spaniards till the development of them brought into contact these two great oceanic rivals.

The Portuguese, year after year, had extended farther and farther their conquests by the African route. Arabia, India, Malacca, Sumatra, fell under their sway, and their course was still eastward, until in 1511 the coveted land of spices, the clove and the nutmeg, was reached in the Molucca Islands. This progress of the Portuguese had been watched with a jealous eye by Spain. It was a question if, in passing to these islands, the Portuguese had not crossed the line of demarcation as carried to the antipodes. If they had, territory neighboring to the Spanish American discoveries had been

1511. Moluccas.

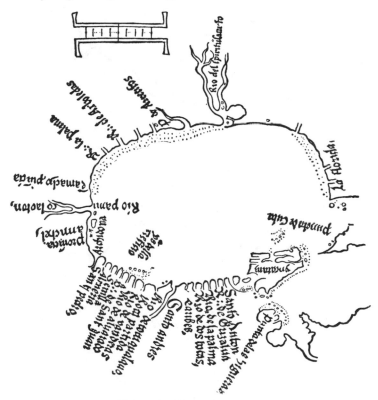

GULF OF MEXICO, BY CORTES.

appropriated by that rival power wholly unconfronted. This was simply because the Spanish navigators had not as yet succeeded in finding a passage through the opposing barrier of what they were beginning to suspect was after all an intervening land. Meanwhile, Columbus and all since his day having failed to find such a passage by way of the Caribbean Sea, and no one yet discovering any at the north, nothing was left but to seek it at the south. This was the only chance of contesting with the Portuguese the rights which occupation was establishing for them at the Moluccas.

A western passage sought at the south.

On the 29th of June, 1508, a new expedition left San Lucar under
Pinzon and Solis. They made their landfall near Cape St.
Augustine, and, passing south along the coast of what had
now come to be commonly called Brazil, they traversed the
opening of the broad estuary of the La Plata without knowing it, and

1508. Pin-<br>
zon and<br>
Solis.

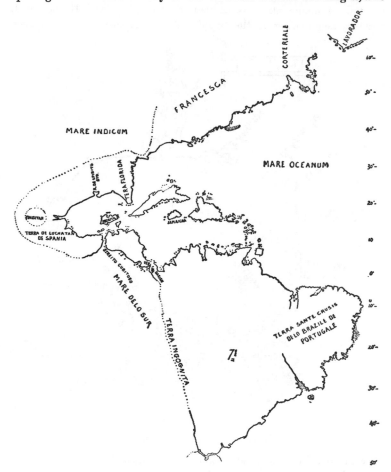

MAIOLLO MAP, 1527.

went five degrees beyond (40° south latitude) without finding the
sought-for passage.

There is some reason to suppose that as early as 1511 the Portuguese had become in some degree familiar with the coast
about Rio de Janeiro, and there is a story of one Juan de
Braza settling near this striking bay at this early day. It

1511. Portu-<br>
guese at Rio<br>
de Janeiro.

was during the same year (1511) that Ferdinand Columbus prepared his *Colon de Concordia,* and in this he maintained the theory of a passage to be found somewhere beyond the point towards the south which the explorers had thus far reached.

*Ferdinand Columbus and the western passage.*

DE COSTA'S DRAWING FROM THE LENOX GLOBE.

A few years later (1516) the Spanish King sent Juan Diaz de Solis to search anew for a passage. He found the La Plata, and for a while hoped he had discovered the looked-for strait. Magellan, who had taken some umbrage during his Portuguese service, came finally to the Spanish King, and, on the plea that the Moluc-

*1516. Solis.*

cas fell within the Spanish range under the line of demarcation, suggested an expedition to occupy them.   He professed to be able
to reach them by a strait which he could find somewhere to
the south of the La Plata.   It has long been a question if Magellan's

1519.   Ma-
gellan

SCHÖNER'S GLOBE, 1520.

anticipation was based simply on a conjecture that, as Africa had been
found to end in a southern point, America would likewise be discovered
to have a similar southern cape.   It has also been a question if Magellan actually had any tidings from earlier voyages to afford a ground

for believing in such a geographical fact. It is possible that other early discoverers had been less careful than Solis, and had been misled by the broad estuary of the La Plata to think that it was really an interoceanic passage. Some such intelligence would seem to have instigated the conditions portrayed in one early map, but the general notion of cartographers at the time terminates the known coast at Cape

MAGELLAN.

Frio, near Rio de Janeiro, as is seen to be the case in the Ptolemy map of 1513. There is a story, originating with Pigafetta, his historian, that Magellan had seen a map of Martin Behaim, showing a southern cape; but if this map existed, it revealed probably nothing more than a conjectural termination, as shown in the Lenox and earliest Schöner globes of 1515 and 1520. Still, Wieser and Nordenskiöld are far from being confident that some definite knowledge of such a cape had not been attained, probably, as it is thought, from private commercial voyage of which we may have a record in the *Newe Zei-*

*tung* and in the *Luculentissima Descriptio*. It is to be feared that the fact, whatever it may have been, must remain shadowy.

Magellan's fleet was ready in August, 1519. His preparation had been watched with jealousy by Portugal, and it was even hinted that if the expedition sailed a matrimonial alliance of Spain and Portugal which was contemplated must be broken off. Magellan was appealed to by the Portuguese ambassador to abandon his purpose, as one likely to embroil the two countries. The stubborn navigator was not to be persuaded, and the Spanish King made him governor of all countries he might discover on the " back side " of the New World.

In the late days of 1519, Magellan touched the coast at Rio de Janeiro, where, remaining awhile, he enjoyed the fruits of its equable climate. Then, passing on, he crossed the mouth of the La Plata, and soon found that he had reached a colder climate and was sailing along a different coast. The verdure which had followed the warm currents from the equatorial north gave way to the concomitants of an icy flow from the Antarctic regions which made the landscape sterile. So on he went along this inhospitable region, seeking the expected strait. His search in every inlet was so faithful that he neared the southern goal but slowly. The sternness of winter caught his little barks in a harbor near 50° south latitude, and his Spanish crews, restless under the command of a Portuguese, revolted. The rebels were soon more numerous than the faithful. The position was more threatening than any Columbus had encountered, but the Portuguese had a hardy courage and majesty of command that the Genoese never could summon. Magellan confronted the rebels so boldly that they soon quailed. He was in unquestioned command of his own vessels from that time forward. The fate of the conquered rioters, Juan de Carthagena and Sanchez de la Reina, cast on the inhospitable shore of Patagonia in expiation of their offense, is in strong contrast to the easy victory which Columbus too often yielded to those who questioned his authority. The story of Magellan's pushing his fleet southward and through the strait with a reluctant crew is that of one of the royally courageous acts of the age of discovery.

On October 21, 1520, the ships entered the longed-for strait, and on the 28th of November they sailed into the new sea; then stretching their course nearly north, keeping well in sight of the coast till the Chiloe Archipelago was passed, the ships steered west of Juan Fernandez without seeing it, and subsequently gradually turned their prows towards the west.

1520, October. Magellan enters the strait.

It is not necessary for our present purpose to follow the incidents of the rest of this wondrous voyage, — the reaching the Ladrones and the Asiatic islands, Magellan's own life sacrificed, all his ships but one

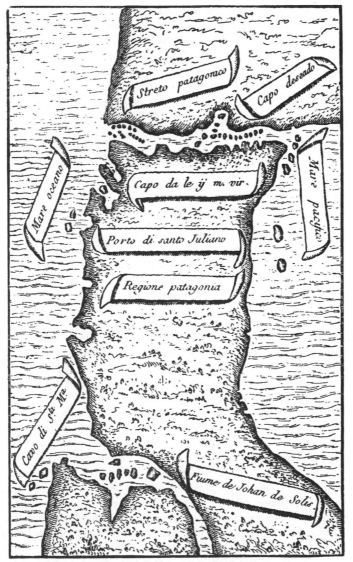

MAGELLAN'S STRAITS BY PIZAFETTA.

[The north is at the bottom.]

abandoned or lost, the passing of the Cape of Good Hope by the " Victoria," and her arrival on September 6, 1522, under Del Cano, at the Spanish harbor from which the fleet had sailed.  The Emperor bestowed

*The western way discovered.*

on this lucky first of circumnavigators the proud motto, inscribed on a globe, " Primus circumdedisti me."  The Spaniards' western way to the Moluccas was now disclosed.

The South Sea of Balboa, as soon as Magellan had established its

*Pacific Ocean.*

extension farther south, took from Magellan's company the name Pacific, though the original name which Balboa had

MAGELLAN'S STRAIT.

applied to it did not entirely go out of vogue for a long time in those portions contiguous to the waters bounding the isthmus and its adjacent lands.

For a long time after it was known that South America was severed,

*North America and Asia held to be one.*

as Magellan proved, from Asia, the belief was still commonly held that North America and Asia were one and continuous.  While no one ventures to suspect that Columbus had any prescience of these later developments, there are those like Varnhagen who claim a distinct insight for Vespucius ; but it is by no means clear, in the passages which are cited, that Vespucius thought the continental mass of South America more distinct from Asia than Columbus did, when the volume of water poured out by the Orinoco convinced the Admiral that he was skirting a continent, and not an island.  .That Columbus thought to place there the region of the Biblical paradise shows that its continental features did not dissociate it from Asia.  The New World of Vespucius was established by his own testimony as hardly more than a new part of Asia.

In 1525 Loyasa was sent to make further examination of Magellan's

*1525. Loyasa.*

Strait.  It was at this time that one of his ships, commanded by Francisco de Hoces, was driven south in February, 1526, and discovered Cape Horn, rendering the insular character of Tierra del Fuego all but certain. The fact was kept secret, and the map-makers were not generally made aware of this terminal cape till Drake saw it, fifty-two years later. De Hoces discovers Cape Horn. It was not till 1615–17 that Schouten and Lemaire made clear the eastern ·limits of Tierra del Fuego when they discovered the passage between that island and Staten Island, and during the same interval Schouten doubled Cape Horn for the first time. It was in 1618–19 that the observations of Nodal first gave the easterly bend to the southern extremity of the continent.

The last stretch of the main coast of South America to be made out was that on the Pacific side from the point where Magellan turned away from it up to the bounds of Peru, where Pizarro and his followers had mapped it. This trend of the coast began to be understood about 1535 ; but it was some years before its details got into maps. The final definition of it came from Camargo's 1535. Chili. voyage in 1540, and was first embodied with something like accuracy in Juan Freire's map of 1546, and was later helped by explorations from the north. But this proximate precision gave way in 1569 to a protuberant angle of the Chili coast, as drawn by Mercator, which in turn lingered on the chart till the next century.

We need now to turn from these records of the voyagers to see what impression their discoveries had been making upon the cartographers and geographers of Europe. Cartographical views.

Bernardus Sylvanus Ebolensis, in a new edition of Ptolemy which was issued at Venice in 1511, paid great attention to the changes necessary to make Ptolemy's descriptions correspond to later explorations in the Old World, but less attention to the more important developments of the New World. Sylvanus's Ptolemy. 1511. Nordenskiöld thinks that this condition of Sylvanus's mind shows how little had been the impression yet made at Venice by the discoveries of Columbus and Da Gama. The maps of this Ptolemy are woodcuts, with type let in for the names, which are printed in red, in contrast with the black impressed from the block.

Sylvanus's map is the second engraved map showing the new discoveries, and the earliest of the heart-shaped projections. It has in "Regalis Domus" the earliest allusion to the Cortereal voyage in a printed map. Sylvanus follows Ruysch in making Greenland a part of Asia. The rude map gores of about the same date which Nordenskiöld has brought to the attention of scholars, and which he considers to have been made at Ingolstadt, agree mainly with this map of Sylvanus, and in respect to the western world both of these Nordenskiöld gores.

maps, as well as the Schöner globe of 1515, seem to have been based on much the same material.

We find in 1512, where we might least expect it, one of the most remarkable of the early maps, which was made for an introduction 1512. Stob- to Ptolemy, published at this date at Cracow, in Poland, nicza map. by Stobnicza. This cartographer was the earliest to in-

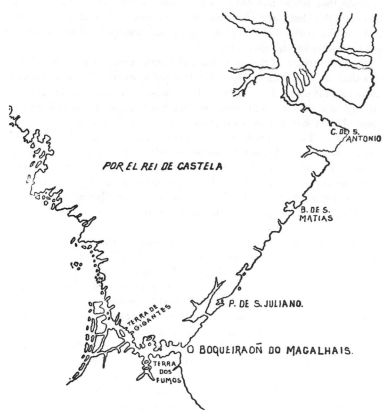

POR EL REI DE CASTELA

C. DE S. ANTONIO

B. DE S. MATIAS

P. DE S. JULIANO.

TERRA DE GIGANTES

O BOQUEIRAOÑ DO MAGALHAIS.

TERRA DOS FUMOS

FREIRE'S MAP, 1546.

troduce into the plane delineation of the globe the now palpable division of its surface into an eastern and western hemisphere. His map, for some reason, is rarely found in the book to which it belongs. Nordenskiöld says he has examined many copies of the book in the libraries of Scandinavia, Russia, and Poland, without finding a copy with it; but it is found in other copies in the great libraries at Vienna and Munich. He thinks the map may have been excluded

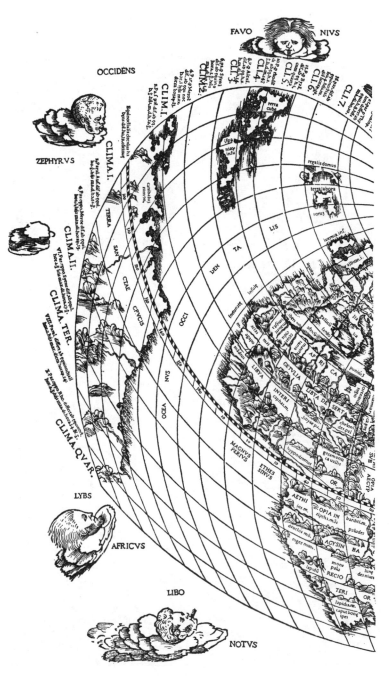

SYLVANUS'S PTOLEMY OF 1511.

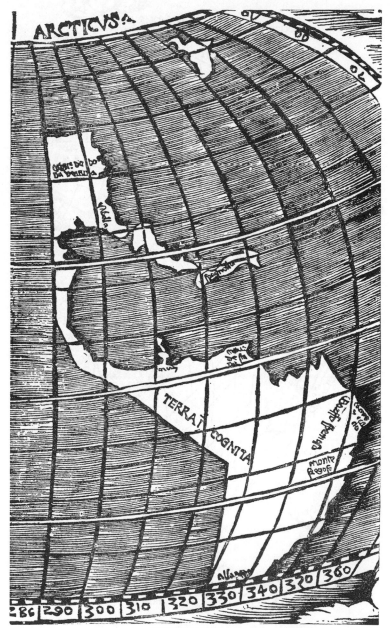

STOBNICZA'S MAP.

from most of the editions because of its rudeness, or " on account of its being contrary to the old doctrines of the Church." Its importance in the growth of the ideas respecting the new discoveries in the western hemisphere is, however, very great, since for the first time it gives a north and south continent connected by an isthmus, and represents as never before in an engraved map the western hemisphere as an entirety. This is remarkable, as it was published a year before Balboa made his discovery of the Pacific Ocean. It is not difficult to see the truth of Nordenskiöld's statement that the map divides the waters of the globe into two almost equal oceans, " communicating only in the extreme south and in the extreme north," but the south communication which is unmistakable is by the Cape of Good Hope. The extremity of South America is not reached because of the marginal scale, and because of the same scale it is not apparent that there is any connection between the Pacific and Indian oceans, and for similar reasons connection is not always clear at the north. There must have been information at hand to the maker of this map of which modern scholars can find no other trace, or else there was a wild speculative spirit which directed the pencil in some singular though crude correspondence to actual fact. This is apparent in its straight conjectural lines on the west coast of South America, which prefigure the discoveries following upon the enterprise of Balboa and the voyage of Magellan.

If Stobnicza, apparently, had not dared to carry the southern extremity of South America to a point, there had been no such hesitancy in the makers of two globes of about the same date, — the little copper sphere picked up by Richard M. Hunt, the architect, in an old shop in Paris, and now in the Lenox Library in New York, and the rude sketch, giving quartered hemispheres separated on the line of the equator, which is preserved in the cabinet of Queen Victoria, at Windsor, among the papers of Leonardo da Vinci. This little draft has a singular interest both from its association with so great a name as Da Vinci's, and because it bears at what is, perhaps, the earliest date to be connected with such cartographical use the name America lettered on the South American continent. Major has contended for its being the work of Da Vinci himself, but Nordenskiöld demurs. This Swedish geographer is rather inclined to think it the work of a not very well informed copier working on some Portuguese prototype.

It is worthy of remark that, in the same year with the discovery of the South Sea by Balboa, an edition of Ptolemy made popular a map which had indeed been cut in its first state as early as 1507, but which still preserved the contiguity of the Antilles to the region of the Ganges and its three mouths. This was the well-known " Admiral's

map," usually associated with the name of Waldseemüller, and if this
same cartographer, as Franz Wieser conjectures, is respon-

1507–13.
Admiral's
map.

sible for the map in Reisch's *Margarita philosophica*
(1515), a sort of cyclopædia, he had in the interim awaked
to the significance of the discovery of Balboa, for the Ganges has dis-

1515.
Reisch's
map.

appeared, and Cipango is made to lie in an ocean beyond
the continental Zoana Mela (America), which has an unde-
fined western limit, as it had already been depicted in the
Stobnicza map of 1512.

THE ALLEGED DA VINCI SKETCH.
[*Combination.*]

It was in this Strassburg Ptolemy of 1513 that Ringmann, who had
been concerned in inventing the name of America, revised the Latin
of Angelus, using a Greek manuscript of Ptolemy for the purpose.

First mod-
ern atlas.

Nordenskiöld speaks of this edition as the first modern atlas
of the world, extended so as to give in two of its maps —
that known as the "Admiral's map," and another of Africa — the
results following upon the discoveries of Columbus and Da Gama.
This "Admiral's map," which has been so often associated with Columbus, is hardly a fair representation of the knowledge that Columbus had attained, and seems rather to be the embodiment of the discoveries of many, as the description of it, indeed, would leave us to

infer; while the other American chart of the volume is clearly of Portuguese rather than of Spanish origin, as may be inferred by the lavish display of the coast connected with the descriptions by Vespu-

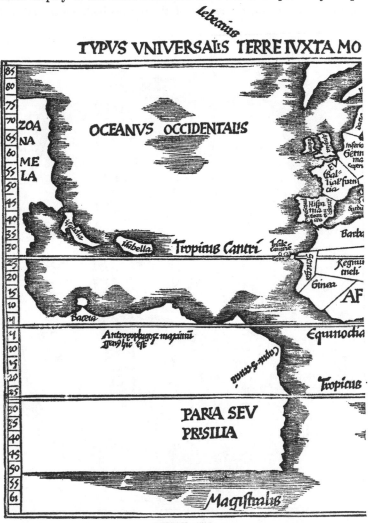

REISCH, 1515.

cius. On the other hand, nothing but the islands of Española and Cuba stand in it for the explorations of Columbus. Both of these maps are given elsewhere in this Appendix.

We could hardly expect, indeed, to find in these maps of the Ptolemy of 1513 the results of Balboa's discovery at the isthmus; but that the maps were left to do service in the edition of 1520 indicates that the discovery of the South Sea had by no means unsettled the public mind as to the Asiatic connection of the regions both north and south

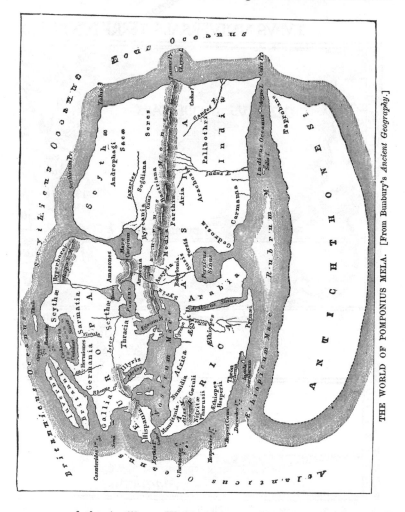

THE WORLD OF POMPONIUS MELA.   [From Bunbury's *Ancient Geography*.]

Asiatic con-
nection of
North
America.

of the Antilles. Within the next few years several maps indicate the enduring strength of this conviction. A Portuguese portolano of 1516–20, in the Royal Library at Munich, shows Moslem flags on the coasts of Venezuela and Nicaragua. A map of Ayllon's discoveries on the Atlantic coast in 1520, preserved in the British Museum, has a Chinaman and an elephant delineated on the empty spaces of the continent. Still, geographical opinions had become divided, and the independent continental masses of Stobnicza were having some ready advocates.

## IOACHIMVS VADIANVS MEDI.
### cus;& Poëta.

*Phœbi cultor eram:medicæ ftudiofus & artis,*
*Ac melicæ: Galli Conful in vrbe br*

### M; D. LI.

VADIANUS.

There was at this time a circle of geographers working at Vienna, reëditing the ancient cosmographers, and bringing them into relations with the new results of discovery. Two of these

Vienna geographers.

early writers thus attracting attention were Pomponius Mela, whose
Pomponius Mela. *Cosmographia* dated back to the first century, and Solinus,
Solinus. whose *Polyhistor* was of the third.   The Mela fell to the
care of Johann Camers, who published it as *De Situ Orbis*
at Vienna in 1512, at the press of Singrein ; and this was followed in
1518 by another issue, taken in hand by Joachim Watt, better known
Vadianus. under the Latinized name of Vadianus, who had been born
in Switzerland, and who was one of the earlier helpers in
popularizing the name of America.   The Solinus, the care of which

APIANUS.   [From Reusner's *Icones.*]

was undertaken by Camers, the teacher of Watt, was produced under
these new auspices at the same time.   Two years later (1520) both of
1520. these old writers attained new currency while issued to-
Apianus. gether and accompanied by a map of Apianus, — as the
German Bienewitz classicized his name, — in which further iteration

was given to the name of America by attaching it to the southern continent of the west.

In this map Apianus, in 1520, was combining views of the western hemisphere, which had within the few antecedent years found advocacy among a new school of cartographers. These students represented the northern and southern continents as independent entities, disconnected at the isthmus, where Columbus had hoped to find his strait. This is shown in the earliest of the Schöner globes, the three copies of which known to us are preserved, one at Frankfort and two at Weimar. It is in the *Luculentissima Descriptio*, which was written to accompany this Schöner globe of 1515, where we find that statement already referred to, which chronicles, as Wieser thinks, an earlier voyage than Magellan's to the southern strait, which separated the " America " of Vespucius from that great Antarctic continent which did not entirely disappear from our maps till after the voyage of Cook.

A strait at the Isthmus of Panama.

1515. Schöner.

Antarctic continent.

It is a striking instance of careless contemporary observation, which the student of this early cartography has often to confront, that while Reisch, in his popular cyclopædia of the *Margarita Philosophica* which he published first in 1503, gave not the slightest intimation of the• discoveries of Columbus, he did not much improve matters in 1515, when he ignored the discoveries of Balboa, and reproduced in the main the so-called " Admiral's map " of the Ptolemy of 1513. It is to be observed, however, that Reisch was in this reproduced map of 1515 the first of map-makers to offer in the word " Prisilia " on the coast of Vespucius the prototype of the modern Brazil. It will be remembered that Cabral had supposed it an island, and had named it the Isla de Santa Cruz. The change of name induced a pious Portuguese to believe it an instigation of the devil to supplant the remembrance of the holy and sacred wood of the great martyr by the worldly wood, which was commonly used to give a red color to cloth!

1515. Reisch.

Brazil.

In 1519, in the *Suma de Geographia* of Fernandez d'Enciso, published later at Seville, in 1530, we have the experience of one of Ojeda's companions in 1509. This little folio, now a scarce book, is of interest as first formulating for practical use some of the new theories of seamanship as developed under the long voyages at this time becoming common. It has also a marked interest as being the earliest book of the Spanish press which had given consideration at any length to the new possessions of Spain.

Theories of seamanship.

We again find a similar indisposition to keep abreast of discovery, so perplexing to later scholars, in the new-cast edition of Ptolemy in

1522, which contains the well-known map of Laurentius Frisius. It

1522.
Frisius.

is called by Nordenskiöld, in subjecting it to analysis in his *Facsimile Atlas*, " an original work, but bad beyond all criticism, as well from a geographical as from a xylographical point of view." One sees, indeed, in the maps of this edition, no knowledge of the increase of geographical knowledge during later years. We observe, too, that they go back to Behaim's interpretation of Marco

SCHÖNER.

Polo's India, for the eastern shores of Asia. The publisher, Thomas Ancuparius, seems never to have heard of Columbus, or at least fails to mention him, while he awards the discovery of the New World to Vespucius. The maps, reduced in the main from those of the edition of 1513, were repeated in those of 1525, 1535, and 1541, without change and from the same blocks.

The results of the voyage of Magellan and Del Cano promptly

attained a more authentic record than usually fell to the lot of these early ocean experiences.

The company which reached Spain in the " Victoria " went at once to Valladolid to report to the Emperor, and while there a pupil and secretary of Peter Martyr, then at Court, Maximilianus Transylvanus by name, got from these men the particulars of their discoveries, and, writing them out in Latin, he sent the missive to his father, the Archbishop of Salzburg, — the young man was a natural son of this prelate, — and in some way the narrative got into print at Cologne and Rome in 1523. 1523. Magellan's voyage described.

Schöner printed in 1523 a little tract, *De nuper . . . repertis insulis ac regionibus* to elucidate a globe which he had at that time constructed. It was published at Timiripæ, as the imprint reads, which has been identified by Coote as the Grecized form of the name of a small village not far from Bamberg, where Schöner was at that time a parochial vicar. When a new set of engraved gores were first brought to light by Ludwig Rosenthal, in Munich, in 1885, they were considered by Wieser, who published an account of them in 1888, as the lost globe of Schöner. Stevens, in a posthumous book on *Johann Schöner*, expressed a similar belief. This was a view which Stevens's editor, C. H. Coote, accepted. The opinion, however, is open to question, and Nordenskiöld finds that the Rosenthal gores have nothing to do with the lost globe of Schöner, and puts them much later, as having been printed at Nuremberg about 1540. 1523. Schöner. Rosenthal gores.

The voyage of Magellan had reopened the controversy of Spain with Portugal, stayed but not settled by the treaty of Tordesillas. Estevan Gomez, a recusant captain of Magellan's fleet, who had deserted him just as he was entering the straits, had arrived in Spain May 6, 1521, and had his own way for some time in making representation of the foolhardiness of Magellan's undertaking. Political aspects of Magellan's voyage. Gomez.

On March 27, 1523, Gomez received a concession from the Emperor to go on a small armed vessel for a year's cruise in the northwest, to make farther search for a passage, but he was not to trespass on any Portuguese possession. The disputes between Portugal and Spain intensifying, Gomez's voyage was in the mean time put off for a while.

Gomara tells us that, in the opinion of his time, the Spaniards had gained the Moluccas, at the conference at Tordesillas, by yielding to the demands of the Portuguese, so that what Portugal gained in Brazil and Newfoundland she lost in Asia and adjacent parts. The Portuguese historian, Osorius, viewed Dispute over the Moluccas.

it differently; he counted in the American gain for his country, but he denied the Spanish rights at the antipodes. So the longitude of the Moluccas became a sharp political dispute, which there was an at-

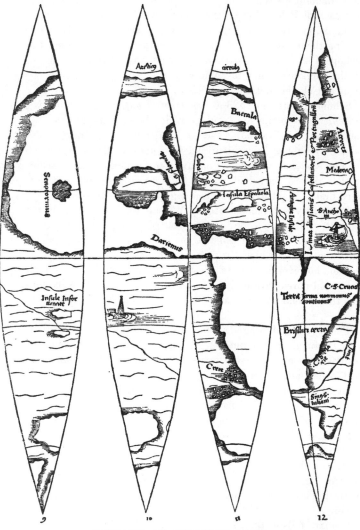

ROSENTHAL OR NUREMBERG GORES.

Congress at Badajos.

tempt to settle in 1524 in a congress of the two nations that was convened alternately at Badajos and Elvas, situated on opposite sides of the Caya, a stream which separates the two countries.

Ferdinand Columbus, by a decree of February 19, 1524, had been made one of the arbiters. After two months of wrangling, each side stood stiff in its own opinions, and it was found best to break up the congress. Following upon the dissolution of this body, the Spanish government was impelled to make the management of the Indies more effective than it had been under the commissions Council of the Indies. which had existed, and on August 18, 1524, the Council of the Indies was reorganized in more permanent form.

An immediate result of the interchange of views at Badajos was a renewal of the Gomez project, to examine more carefully the eastern coast of what is now the United States, in the hopes of yet discovering a western passage. Of that voyage, which is first mentioned in the *Sumario* of Oviedo in 1526, and of the failure of its chief Gomez's voyage. aim, enough has already been said in the early part of this appendix.

It has been supposed by Harrisse that the results of this voyage were embodied in the earliest printed Spanish map which we have showing lines of latitude and longitude, — that found in a joint edition of Martyr and Oviedo (1534), and which is only known in a copy now in the Lenox Library.

The purpose which followed upon the congress of Badajos, to penetrate the Atlantic coast line and find a passage to the western sea, was communicated to Cortes, then in Mexico, some time before the date of his fourth letter, October 15, 1524. The news found him already convinced of the desirableness of establishing a port on the great sea of the west, and he selected Zucatula as a station for the fleets which he undertook to build.

Other projects delayed the preparations which were planned, and it was not till September 3, 1526, that Cortes signified to the 1526. Cortes sends ships to the Moluccas. Emperor his readiness to send his ships to the Moluccas. After a brief experimental trip up the coast from Zucatula, three of his vessels were finally dispatched, in October, 1527, on a disastrous voyage to those islands, where the purpose was to confront the Portuguese pretensions. It so happened, meanwhile, that Charles V. needed money for his projects in Italy, and he called Ferdinand Columbus to Court to consult with him about a sale of his rights in the Moluccas to Portugal. Ferdinand made a report, which has not come down to us, but a decision to sell was reached, and the Portuguese King agreed to the price of purchase on June 20, The Moluccas sold to Portugal. 1530. Thus the Moluccas, which had been so long the goal of Spanish ambition, pass out of view in connection with American discovery.

There is some ground for the suspicion, if not belief, that the Portuguese from the Moluccas had before this pushed eastward across the Pacific, and had even struck the western verge of that continent which separated them from the Spanish explorers on the Atlantic side.

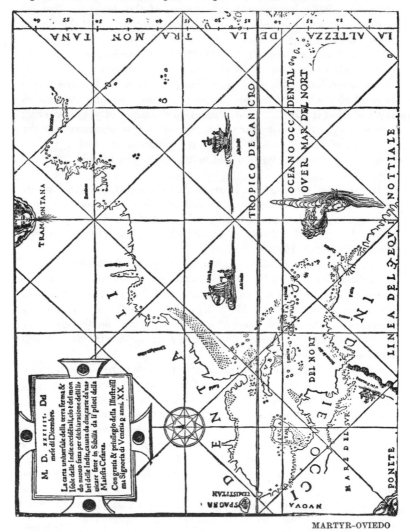

MARTYR-OVIEDO

We come next to some further developments on the eastern coast of North America. A certain French corsair, known from his Florentine birth as Juan Florin, had become a terror by preying on the Spanish commerce in the Indies. In January, 1524,

North
America,
east coast.

he was on his way, under the name of Verrazano, in the expedition which has given him fame, and has supplied not a little ground for contention, and even for total distrust of the    Verrazano.

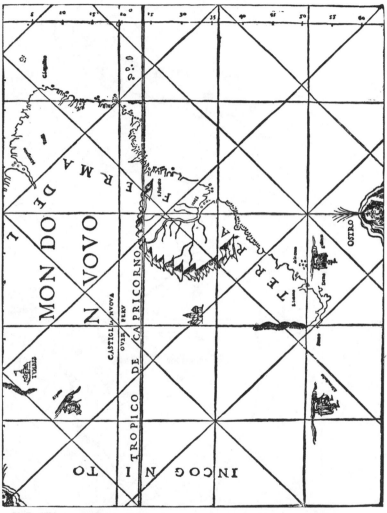

MAP, 1534.

voyage as a fact. He struck the coast of North Carolina, turned south, but, finding no harbor, retraced his course, and, making several landings farther north, finally entered, as it would seem from his description, the harbor of New York. The only point that he names

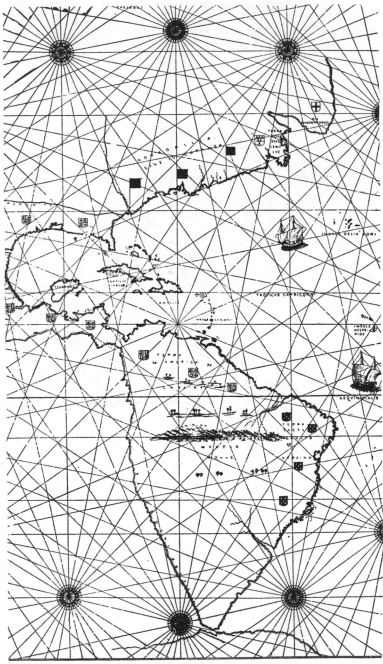

THE VERRAZANO MAP.

is a triangular island which he saw as he went still farther to the east, and which has been supposed to be Block Island, or possibly Martha's Vineyard. At all events, the name Luisa which he gave to it after the mother of Francis I. clung to an island in this neighborhood in the maps for some time longer. So he went on, and, if his landings have been rightly identified, he touched at Newport, then at some place evidently near Portsmouth in New Hampshire, and then, skirting the islands of the Maine coast, he reached the country which he recognized as that where the Bretons had been. He now ended what he considered the exploration of seven hundred leagues of an unknown

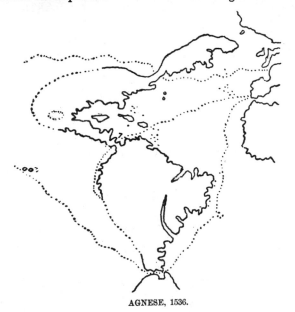

AGNESE, 1536.

land, and bore away for France, reaching Dieppe in July, whence, on the 9th, he wrote the letter to the King which is the source of our information. Attempts have been made, especially by the late Henry C. Murphy, to prove this letter a forgery, but in the opinion of most scholars without success.

Fortunately for the student, Hieronimo. da Verrazano made, in 1529, a map, still preserved in the college of the Propaganda at Rome, in which the discoveries of his brother, Giovanni, are laid down. In this the name of Nova Gallia supplants that of Francesca, which had been used in the map of Maiollo (1527), supposed, also, to have some relation to the Verrazano voyage.

The most distinguishing feature of the Verrazano map is a great

MÜNSTER.

1540.

inland expanse of water, which was taken to be a part of some western ocean, and which remained for a long while in some form or other in the maps. It was made to approach so near the Atlantic that at one point there was nothing but a slender isthmus connecting the discoveries of the north with the country of Ponce de Leon and Ayllon at the south.

It is in the *Sumario* (1526) of Oviedo that we get the first idea of this sea of Verrazano, as Brevoort contends, and we see it in the Maiollo map of the next year, called "Mare Indicum," as if it were an indentation of the great western ocean of Balboa. It was a favorite fancy of Baptista Agnese, in the series of portolanos associated with his name during the middle of the century, and in which he usually indicated supposable ocean routes to Asia. As time went on, the idea was so far modified that this indentation took the shape of a loop of the Arctic seas, or of that stretch of water which at the north connected the Atlantic and Pacific, as shown in the Münster map in the Ptolemy of 1540, — a map apparently based on the portolanos of Agnese, — though the older form of the sea seems to be adopted in the globe of Ulpius (1542). This idea of a Carolinian isthmus prevailed for some years, and may have grown out of a misconception of the Carolina sounds, though it is sometimes carried far enough north, as in the Lok map of 1582, to seem as if Buzzard's Bay were in some way thought to stretch westerly into its depths. The last trace of this mysterious inner ocean, so far as I have discovered, is in a map made by one of Ralegh's colonists in 1585, and preserved among the drawings of John White in the De Bry collection of the British Museum, and brought to light by Dr. Edward Eggleston. This drawing makes for the only time that I have observed it, an actual channel at "Port Royal," leading to this oceanic expanse, which

*The sea of Verrazano.*

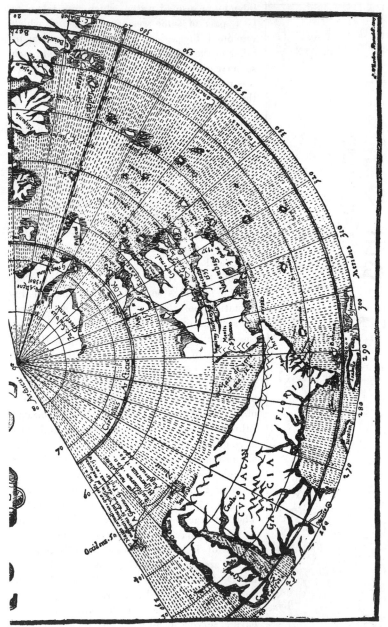

MICHAEL LOK, 1582.

was later interpreted as an inland lake. Thus it was that this geographical blunder lived more or less constantly in a succession of maps for about sixty years, until sometimes it vanished in a large lake in Carolina, or in the north it dwindled until it began to take a new lease of life in an incipient Hudson's Bay, as in the great Lake of Tadenac, figured in the Molineaux map of 1600, and in the Lago Dagolesme in the Botero map of 1603.

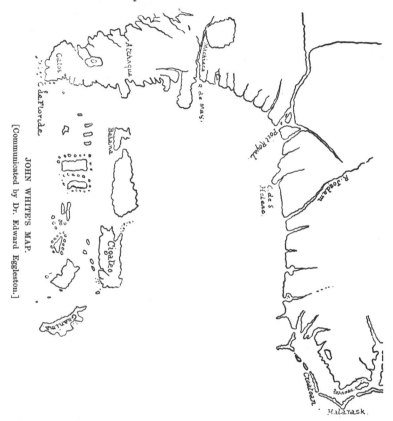

It was apparently during the voyage of Verrazano that an Indian name which was understood as " Aranbega " was picked up along the northern coasts as designating the region, and which a little later was reported by others as " Norumbega," and so passed into the mysterious and fabled nomenclature of the coast with a good deal of the unstableness that attended the fabulous islands of the Atlantic in the fancy of the geographers of the Middle Ages. As a definition of territory it gradually grew to have a more and more restricted

Norumbega.

Terra florida

Noua terra labora torum dicta

terra hec ab Anglis prin fuit inuenta

Scotia

OCEA
NVS
OCCIDEN
TALIS

Grando

Hispania Aragonu

Insuleca narie

O PICVS CANCRI

B.

Douarnen

Insaleca bouerde

Johanes

Cadulonga

A
Gine

aua noua

Dariou

ra Austr
ale?

CSTIALIS

Terrafirma

C·S·Augustin

CORN

ICVS CAPRI

R·S·christo
phori

Ps·Iuhan

um orien

Stridtum omnium
sanctorum

**ROBERT THORNE, 1527.**

application, coming down mainly after a while to the limits of the later New England, and at last finding, as Dr. Dee (1580), Molineaux (1600), and Champlain (1604) understood it, a home on the Penobscot. Still the region it represented contracted and expanded in people's notions, and on maps the name seemed to have a license to wander.

During this period the English also were up and down the coast, but they contributed little to our geographical knowledge. Slave- The English catching on the coast of Guinea, and lucrative sales of the on the coast. human plunder in the Spanish West Indies and neighboring regions, seem to have taken William Hawkins and others of his William countrymen to these coasts not infrequently between 1525 Hawkins. and 1540.

There is some reason to believe that John Rut, an Englishman, may have explored the northeast coasts of the present United John Rut. States in 1527, a proposition, however, open to argument, as the counter reasonings of Dr. Kohl and Dr. De Costa show. It is certain that at this time Robert Thorne, an English merchant living in Seville, was gaining what knowledge he could to promote English enterprise in the north, and there has come down to us the map which in 1527 he gave to the English ambassador in Spain, Edward Leigh, to be transmitted to Henry VIII.

It was in 1526 when the Spanish authorities thought that the time was fitting for making a sort of register of the progress of Progress of discovery and of the attendant cartographical advances. maritime Nordenskiöld says that "from the beginning of the print- art. ing of maps the graduations of latitude and longitude were marked down in most printed maps, at least in the margin;" the most conspicuous example of omitting these being, perhaps, in the work of Sebastian Münster, at a period a little later than the one we have now reached.

In 1503 Reisch for the first time settled upon something like the modern methods of indicating latitude and longitude in the Latitude map which he annexed to his *Margarita philosophica* at and longi- Freiburg, though so far as climatic lines could stand for tude. latitudinal notions, Pierre d'Ailly had set an example of scaling the zones from the equator in his map of 1410. The Spaniards, however, did not fall into the method of Reisch, so far as published maps are concerned, till long afterwards (1534).

Up to the time when the Strassburg Ptolemy was issued, in 1513, the chief activity in map-making had been in Italy. The Italian cartographers of that country got what they could from maps.

Spain, but the main dependence was on Portuguese sources, though the rivals of Spain were not always free in imparting the knowledge of their hydrographical offices, since we find Robert Thorne, in 1527, charging the Portuguese with having falsified their records. It is worthy of remark that no official map of the Indies was published in Spain till 1790.

SEBASTIAN MÜNSTER.
[From Reusner's *Icones*, 1590.]

After 1513, and so on to the middle of the century, it was to the
Cartographi-
cal activity
north of the
Alps.
north of the Alps that the cosmographical students turned for the latest light upon all oceanic movements. The question of longitude was the serious one which both navigators and map-makers encountered. The cartographers were trying all
Map pro-
jections.
sorts of experiments in representing the converging meridians on a plane surface, so as not to distort the geography, and in order to afford some manifest method for the guidance of ships.

These experiments resulted, as Nordenskiöld counts, in something like twenty different projections being devised before 1600. For the seaman the difficulty was no less burdensome in trying to place his ship at sea, or to map the contours of the coasts he was following. The navigator's main dependence was the course he was steering and an estimate of his progress. He made such allowance as he could for his drift in the currents. We have seen how the imperfection of his instruments and the defects of his lunar tables misled Colum- Lunar observations. bus egregiously in the attempts which he made to define the longitude of the Antilles. He placed Española at 70° west of Seville, and La Cosa came near him in counting it about 68°, so far as one can interpret his map. The Dutch at this time were beginning to grasp the idea of a chronometer, which was the de- Chronometers. vice finally to prove the most satisfactory in these efforts.

Reinerus Gemma of Friesland, known better as Gemma Frisius, began to make the Dutch nautical views better known when he suggested, a few years later, the carrying of time in running off the longitudes, and something of his impress on the epoch was shown in the stand which a pupil, Mercator, took in geographical science. The *Spieghel der Zeevaardt* of Lucas Wagenaer, in 1584 (Leyden), was Earliest sea-atlas. the first sea-atlas ever printed, and showed again the Dutch advance.

There were also other requirements of sea service that were not forgotten, among which was a knowledge of prevalent winds and ocean currents, and this was so satisfactorily acquired that the return voyage from the Antilles came, within thirty years after Columbus, to be made with remarkable ease. Oviedo tells us that in 1525 two caravels were but twenty-five days in passing from San Domingo to the river of Seville.

Two of the duties imposed by the Spanish government upon the Casa de la Contratacion, soon after the discovery of the New World, were to patronize invention to the end of discovering a process for making fresh water out of salt, and to improve ships' pumps, — the last a conception not to take effective shape till Ribero, the royal cosmographer, secured a royal pension for such an invention in 1526.

It was in the midst of these developments, both of the practical parts of seamanship and of the progress of oceanic discovery, that in 1526 there was held at Seville a convention of pilots and Congress of pilots at Seville. cosmographers, called by royal order, to consolidate and correlate all the cartographical data which had accumulated up to that time respecting the new discoveries.

Ferdinand Columbus was at this time in Seville, engaged in com-

pleting a house and library for himself, and in planting the park about
Ferdinand    them with trees brought from the New World, a single one
Columbus.    of which, a West Indian sapodilla, was still standing in
1871.    It was in this house that the convention sat, and Ferdinand

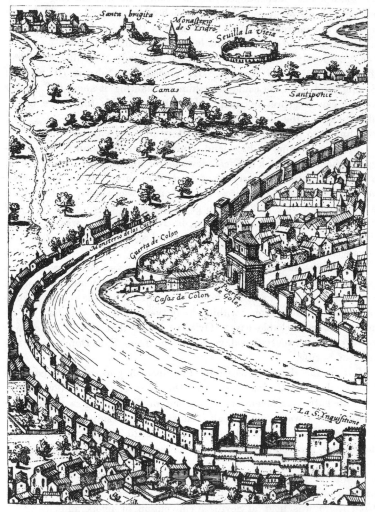

HOUSE AND LIBRARY OF FERDINAND COLUMBUS.

Columbus presided over it, while the examinations of the pilots were
conducted by Diego Ribero and Alonso de Chaves.

There have come down to us two monumental maps, the outgrowth of this convention. One of these is dated at Seville, in 1527, purporting to be the work of the royal cosmographer, and has been usually known by the name of Ferdinand Columbus; and the other, dated 1529, is known to have been made by Diego Ribero, also a royal cosmographer. These maps closely resemble each other.

1527–29. Maps.

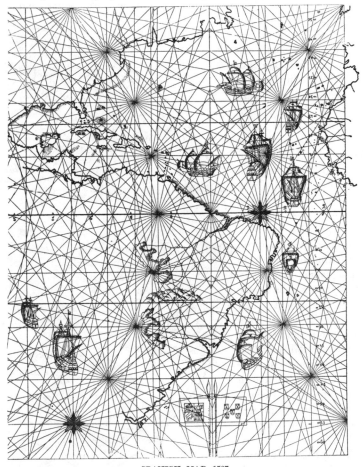

SPANISH MAP, 1527.

[After sketch in E. Mayer's *Die Entwicklung der Seekarten* (Wien, 1877).]

The Weimar chart of 1527, which Kohl, Stevens, and others have assigned to Ferdinand Columbus, has been ascribed by Harrisse to Nuño Garcia de Toreno, but by Coote, in editing Stevens on *Schöner*, it is assigned to Ribero, as a precursor of his undoubted production of 1529.

We have seen how, succeeding to the belief of Columbus that the new regions were Asia, there had grown up, a few years after his death, in spite of his audacious notarial act at Cuba, a strong presumption

Idea of a new continent spreading.

among geographical students that a new continent had been found. We have seen this conception taking form with more or less uncertainty as to its western confines immediately upon, and even anticipating, the discovery of the actual South Sea by Balboa, and can follow it down in the maps or globes of Stobnicza and Da Vinci, in that known as the Lenox globe, in those called the Tross and Nordenskiöld gores, the Schöner and Hauslab globes, the Ptolemy map of 1513, and in those of Reisch, Apianus, Laurentius Frisius, Maiollo, Bordone, Homem, and Münster, — not to name some others. In twenty years it had come to be a prevalent belief, and men's minds were turned to a consideration of the possibility of this revealed continent having been, after all, known to the ancients, as Glareanus, quoting Virgil, was the earliest to assert in 1527.

About 1525 there came a partial reaction, as if the discovery of Balboa had been pushed too far in its supposed results.

THE NANCY

Reaction in the monk Franciscus.

We find this taking form in 1526, in an identification of North America with eastern Asia in a map ascribed to the monk Franciscus, while South America is laid down as a continental island, separated from India by a strait only. The strait is soon succeeded by an isthmus, and in this way we get a solution of the problem which had some currency for half a century or more.

Orontius Finæus was one of these later compromisers in cartography, in a map which he is supposed to have made in 1531, but which appeared the next year in the *Novus Orbis* Orontius Finæus.

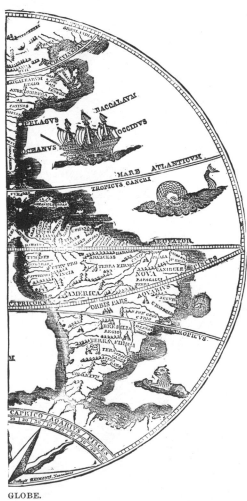

GLOBE.

(1532) of Simon Grynæus, and was used in some later publications also. We find in this map, about the Gulf of Mexico, the names which Cortes had applied in his map of 1520 mingled with those of the Asiatic coast of Marco Polo. We annex a sketch of this map as reduced by Brevoort to Mercator's projection. A map very similar to this and of about the same date is preserved in the British Museum among the Sloane manuscripts, and the same bold solution of the difficulty is found in the Nancy globe of about 1540, and in the globe of Gaspar Vopel of 1543.

There is a good instance of the instability of geographical knowledge at this time in the conversion of Johann Schöner from a belief in an Johann Schöner. insular North America, to which he had clung in his globes of 1515 and 1520, to a position which he took in 1533, in his *Opusculum Geographicum*, where he maintains that the city of Mexico is the Quinsay of Marco Polo.

ORONTIUS FINÆUS, 1532.

[After Cimelinus's Copperplate of 1566.]

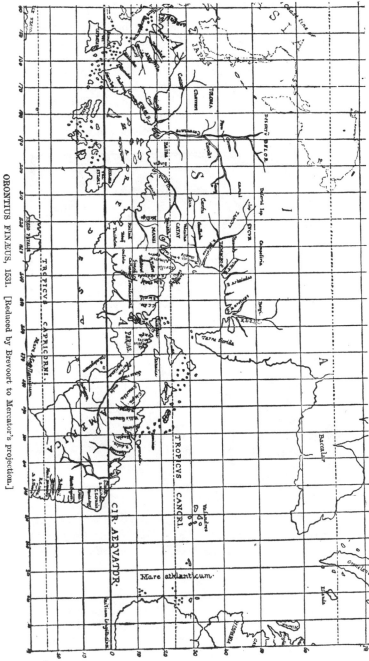

ORONTIUS FINÆUS, 1531. [Reduced by Brevoort to Mercator's projection.]

Previous to Cortes's departure for Spain in 1528, he had, as we have seen, dispatched vessels from Tehuantepec to the Moluccas, but

The Pacific explored.

nothing was done to explore the Pacific coast northward till his return to Mexico.   In the spring or early summer of 1532 he sent Hurtado de Mendoza up the coast ; but little success attending the exploration, Cortes himself proceeded to Tehuantepec and constructed other vessels, which sailed in October, 1533.   A gale drove them to the west, and when they succeeded in working back and

CORTES.

making the coast, they found themselves well up what proved to be

California.

the California peninsula.   They now coasted south and developed its shape, which was further brought out in detail by an expedition led by Cortes himself in 1535, and by a later one sent by him under Francisco de Ulloa in 1539.   Cortes had supposed

the peninsula an island, but this expedition of 1539 demonstrated the
fact that no passage to the outer sea existed at the head of the gulf,
which these earliest navigators had called the Sea of Cortes. The
conqueror of Mexico had now made his last expedition on the Pacific,
and his name was not destined to be long connected with this new
field of discovery, unless, indeed, it was a prompting of Cortes —
hardly proved, however — which attached to this peninsular region
the euphonious name of California, and which, after an interval when
the gulf was called the Red Sea, was applied to that water also. The
views of Ulloa were confirmed in part, at least, by Castillo in 1540,
who has left us a map of the gulf.

CASTILLO'S CALIFORNIA.

The outer coast of the peninsula as far north as 28° 30' had been
established in 1533. It was ten years later, in 1543, that Cabrillo,
making his landfall in the neighborhood of 33°, just within the south-

ern bounds of the present State of California, coasted up to Cape Mendocino, and perhaps to 44°, or nearly, to that spot, in the present State of Oregon. If Cabrillo, who had died January 3, 1543, did not himself go so high, the credit belongs to Ferrelo, his chief pilot

Late in 1542 Mendoza sent an expedition under Ruy Lopez de Villalobos, across the Pacific, and if a map of Juan Freire, made in 1546, is an indication of his route, he seems to have gone higher up the coast than any previous explorer.

While this development of the northwest coast of North America The Atlantic was going on, there were other discoverers still endeavor-
coast of
North ing on the Atlantic side to connect the waters of the two
America. oceans.

In April, 1534, Jacques Cartier, a jovial and roistering fellow, as
1534. Father Jouon des Longrais, his latest biographer, makes
Cartier. him out (*Jacques Cartier*, Paris, 1888), and who had led the roving life of a corsair in the recent wars of France, was now turning his energy to solve the great problem of this western passage. He sailed from St. Malo, and for the first time laid open, by an official examination, the inner spaces of the St. Lawrence Gulf, which might have been, indeed, and probably were, known earlier to the hardy Breton and Norman fishermen. We are deficient in a knowledge of the early frequenting of these coasts because the charts of such fishermen, and of those who visited the region for trade in peltries, have not come down to us, though Kohl thinks there is some likelihood of such records being preserved in a portolano of the British Museum.

The track of Cartier about the Gulf of St. Lawrence has caused some discussion and difference of opinion in the publications of Kohl, De Costa, Laverdière, and W. F. Ganong, the latter writer claiming, in a careful paper in the *Transactions* of the Royal Society of Canada for 1889, that in the correct interpretation of Cartier's first voyage we find a key to the cartography of the gulf for almost a century.

The Rotz map of 1542 seems to be the earliest map which we know to show a knowledge of Cartier's first voyage. The Henri II. map of 1542 still more develops his work of exploration.

The chance of further discovery in this direction induced the French king once more to commission Cartier, October 30, 1534, and early in 1535 his little fleet sailed, and by August, after some discouragements, not lessened when he found the water freshening, he began to ascend the St. Lawrence River, reaching the site of Montreal. No map by Cartier himself is preserved, though it is known that he made such. Thenceforward the cartography of this northeastern region showed the St. Lawrence Gulf in a better development of the earlier so-called Square Gulf and of the great river of Canada. It is of record that Francis I., in commissioning Cartier, considered that he was dispatching him to ascend an Asiatic river, and the name of Lachine even to-day is preserved as evidence of the belief which Cartier entertained that he was within the bounds of China.

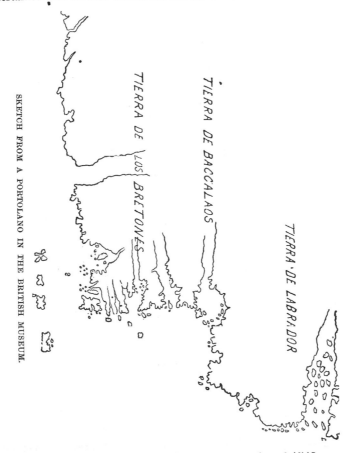

SKETCH FROM A PORTOLANO IN THE BRITISH MUSEUM.

TIERRA DE LOS BRETONES

TIERRA DE BACCALAOS

TIERRA·DE LABRADOR

John Rotz's *Boke of Idiography* — a manuscript of 1542, preserved in the British Museum — shows, in his drawing of the region about the Gulf of St. Lawrence, certain signs, as Kohl thinks, of having had access to the charts of Cartier, and Harrisse traces in them the combined influence of the Portuguese and Dieppe navigators.

John Rotz's map.

The Cartier voyages seem to have made little impression outside of France, and we find for some years few traces of his discoveries in the portolanos of Italy and in the maps of the rest of Europe. It was only when the expedition of Roberval, in 1540–41, excited attention that the rest of Europe seemed to recognize these French efforts.

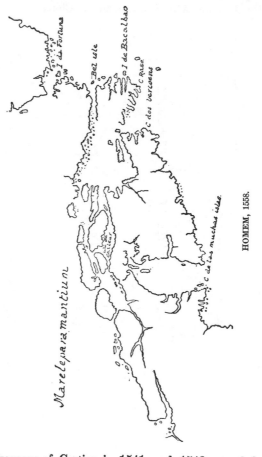

The later voyages of Cartier, in 1541 and 1543, revealed nothing
Cartier's<br>later<br>voyages.
more of general geographical interest. Indeed, the hope of a western passage in this direction had been abandoned in effect after Cartier's second voyage, although the pilot Allefonsce, who accompanied a later expedition, had been
Allefonsce.
detailed to explore the Labrador coast to that end, and had been turned back by ice. After this he seems to have gone south into a great bay, under 42°, the end of which he did not reach. This may have been the large expanse partly shut in by Cape Sable (Nova

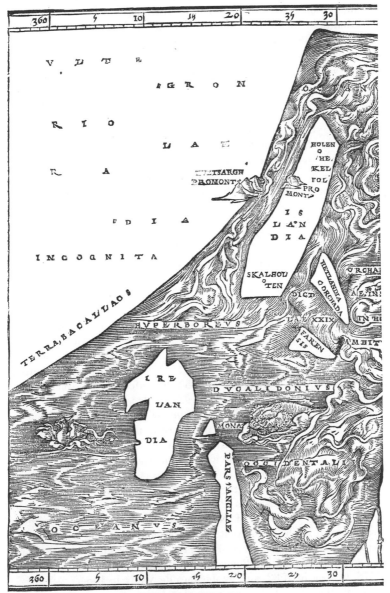

ZIEGLER'S SCHONDIA.

Scotia) and Cape Cod, now called in the coast survey charts the Gulf of Maine; or perhaps it may conform, taking into account his registered latitude, to the inner bight of it called Massachusetts Bay. At all events, Allefonsce believed himself on coasts contiguous to Tartary, through which he had hopes to find access to the more hospitable orient (occident) farther south. He apparently had something of the same notion regarding the westerly stretch of water which he found below Cape Cod, extending he knew not where, along the inclosure of the present Long Island Sound.

In the years both before and after the middle of the century, French vessels were on this coast in considerable numbers for purposes of trade or for protecting French interests, but we know nothing of any accessions to geographical knowledge which they made.

Allefonsce speaks of the Saguenay as widening, when he went up,

RUSCELLI, 1544.

till it seemed to be an arm of the sea, and "I think the same," he adds, "runs into the Sea of Cathay;" and so he draws it on one of his maps, — an idea made more general in the map of Homem in 1558, where the St. Lawrence really becomes a channel, locked by islands, bordering an Arctic Sea. Ramusio, in 1553, has inferred from such reports as he could get of Cartier's explorations, that his track had lain in channels bounded by islands, and a similar view had already been expressed in a portolano of 1536, preserved in the Bodleian, which Kohl associates with Homem or Agnese. The oceanic expansion of the Saguenay is preserved as late as the Molineaux map of 1600.

It is to the work of Allefonsce that we probably owe another confusion of this northern cartography in the sixteenth century. What River of Norumbega. we now know as Penobscot Bay and River was called by him the River of Norumbega, and he seems to have given some ground for believing that this river connected the waters of the Atlantic with the great river of Canada, just as we find it later shown upon Gastaldi's map in Ramusio, by Ruscelli in 1561, by Martines in 1578, by Lok in 1582, and by Jacques de Vaulx in 1584.

While this idea of the north was developing, there came in another that made the peninsular Greenland of the ante-Columbian maps grow into a link of land connecting Europe with the Americo-Asiatic main, so that one might in truth perambulate the globe Greenland connects Europe and America. dryshod. We find this conception in the maps of the Bavarian Ziegler (1532), and in the Italians Ruscelli (1544) and

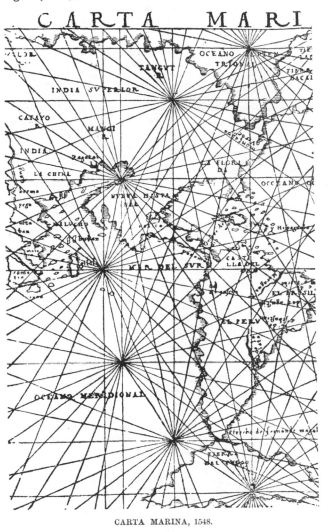

CARTA MARINA, 1548.

Gastaldi (1548), — the last two represented in the Ptolemies of those years published in Italy. But these Italian cosmographers were by no means constant in their belief, as Ruscelli showed in his Ptolemy of 1561, and Gastaldi in his Ramusio map of 1550.

*CHRISTOPHER COLUMBUS.*

As the Pacific explorations were stretched northward from Mexico,
and the peninsula of California was brought into promi-
Asia and
America
joined in the
higher lati-
tudes.
nence, there remained for some time a suspicion that the
western ocean made a great northerly bend, so as to sever
North America from Asia except along the higher latitudes.

MYRITIUS, 1590.

We find this northerly extension of the Pacific in a map of copper preserved in the Carter-Brown library, which seems to have been the
work of a Florentine goldsmith somewhere about 1535 ; in the Carta
Marina of Gastaldi in 1548 ; and it even exists in maps of a later date,

like that of Paolo de Furlani (1560) and that of Myritius (1587). This map of Myritius, which appeared in his *Opusculum Geographicum*, published at Ingolstadt in 1590, is the work of, perhaps, the last of

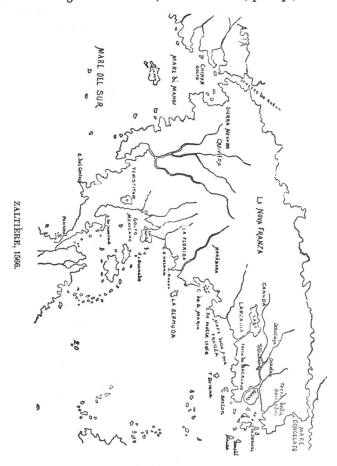

the geographers who did not leave more or less doubt about the connection of North America with Asia. So it took about a full century for the entanglement of the coasts of Asia and America, which Columbus had imagined, to be practically eradicated from the maps. Not that there were not doubters, even very early, but the faith in a new continent grew slowly and had many set-backs; nor did the Asiatic connection fade entirely out, as among the possibilities of geography, for considerably more than a century yet to come. The uncertainties of the higher latitudes

Entanglement of the American and Asiatic coasts.

kept knowledge in suspense, and even the English settlers on the northerly coasts of the United States were not quite sure. Thomas Morton, the chronicler of a colony on the Massachusetts shores, felt it necessary, so late as 1636, to make a reservation that possibly the mainland of America bordered on the land of the Tartars. In-

PORCACCHI, 1572.

deed, no one could say positively, though much was conjectured, that there was not a terrestrial connection in the extreme northwest,

1728.
Bering.
under arctic latitudes, till Bering in 1728, two hundred and thirty-six years after Columbus offered his prayer at San Salvador, passed from the Pacific into the polar waters. This became the solution of the fabled straits of Anian, an inheritance from the very earliest days of northern exploration, which, after the

middle of the sixteenth century, was revived in the maps of Martines, Zaltière, Mercator, Porcacchi, Furlani, and Wytfliet, prefiguring the channel which Bering passed. Much in the same way as the southern apex of South America was a vision in men's minds long before Magellan found his way to the Pacific.

But we have anticipated a little. Coincident with the efforts of Cartier to discover this northern passage we mark other navigators working at the same problem. The Spaniard Alonso de Chaves made a chart of this eastern coast in 1536 ; but we only know of its existence from the description of it written by Oviedo in 1537. In the earliest map which we have from the hand of Gerard Mercator, and of which the only copy known was discovered some years ago by the late James Carson Brevoort, of New York, we find the northern passage well defined in 1538, and a broad channel separating the western coast of America from a parallel coast of Asia, — a kind of delineation which is followed in some globe-gores of about 1540, which Nordenskiöld thinks may have been the work of George Hartmann, of Nuremberg. This map is evidently based on Portuguese information, and that Swedish scholar finds no ground for associating it with the lost globe of Schöner, as Stevens has done. A facsimile of part of it has already been given.

1536. Choves.

1538. Mercator.

1540. Hartmann gores.

Sebastian Münster, in his maps in the Ptolemy of 1540–45, makes a clear seaway to the Moluccas somewhere in the latitude of the Strait of Belle Isle. Münster was in many ways antiquated in his notions. He often resorted to the old device of the Middle Ages by supplying the place of geographical details with figures of savages and monsters.

1540–45. Münster.

We come now to two significant maps in the early history of American cartography.

Columbus had been dead five and thirty years when a natural result grew out of those circumstances which conspired to name the largest part of the new discoveries after a secondary pathfinder. We have seen that there seemed at first no injustice in the name of America being applied to a region in the main external to the range of Columbus's own explorations, and how it took nearly a half century before public opinion, as expressed in the protest of Schöner in 1533, recognized the injustice of using another's name. Whether that protest was prompted by a tendency, already shown, to give the name to the whole western hemisphere is not clear ; but certainly within eight years such a general application was publicly made, when Mercator, in drafting in 1541 some gores for a globe, divided the

name AME—RICA so that it covered both North and South Amer-
1541.     ica, and qualified its application by a legend which says
Mercator.     that the continent is " called to-day by many, New India."
Thus a name that in the beginning was given to a part in distinction

MERCATOR'S

merely and without any reference to the entire field of the new explorations, was now become, by implication, an injustice to the great first
discoverer of all. The mischief, aided by accident and by a not unac-

countable evolution, was not to be undone, and, in the singular muta-
tions of fate, a people inhabiting a region of which neither Columbus
nor Vespucius had any conception are now distinctively known in the
world's history as Americans.

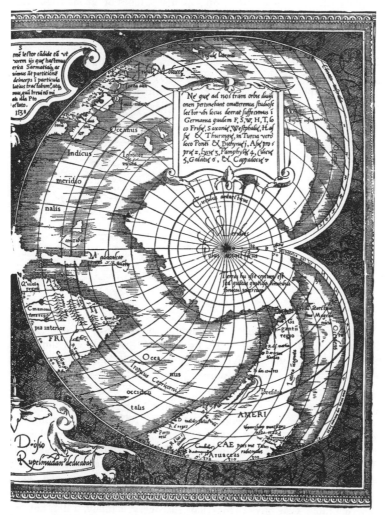

GLOBE OF 1538.

These 1541 gores of Mercator were first made known to scholars a
few years ago, when the Belgian government issued a facsimile edition of the only copy then known, which the Royal Library at Brus-

sels had just acquired; but since there have been two other copies brought to light,— one at St. Nicholas in Belgium, and the other in the Imperial library at Vienna.

There are some indications on Spanish globes of about 1540, and

Henry II. map.     in the Desceliers or Henry II. map of 1546, that the Spanish government had sent explorers to the region of Canada not long after Cartier's earliest explorations, and it is significant that the earliest published map to show these Cartier discoveries is the

1544. Cabot map.     other of the two maps already referred to, namely, the Cabot mappemonde of 1544, which has been supposed a Spanish cartographical waif.  Early publications of southern and middle Europe showed little recognition of the same knowledge.

MÜNSTER, 1545.

The Cabot map has been an enigma to scholars ever since it was discovered in Germany, in 1843, by Von Martius.  It was deposited the next year in the great library at Paris.  It is a large elliptical world-map, struck from an engraved plate, and it bears sundry elucidating inscriptions, some of which must needs have come from Sebastian Cabot, others seem hardly to merit his authorship, and one acknowledges him as the maker of the map.  There is, accordingly, a composite character to the production, not easily to be analyzed so as to show the credible and the incredible by clear lines of demarcation. We learn from it how it proclaimed for the first time the real agency of John Cabot in the discovery of North America, confirmed when Hakluyt, in 1582, printed the patent from Henry VII.  There is an unaccountable year given for that discovery, namely, 1494, but we seem to get the true date when Michael Lok, in 1582, puts down "J. Cabot, 1497," against Cape Breton in his map of that year.  As this last map appeared in Hakluyt's *Divers Voyages*, and as Hakluyt tells us of the existence of Cabot's maps and of his seeing them, we may

AME

BACCALEARUM
REGIO

INS.CORTEREALIS

HISPANIA MAJOR
CAPTA ANNO
1530

ANGOLA

ESPIRITO SANTO

R. DEL

FLORIDA

NEPTAPOLIS

BARMUDA
SIVE
GARCA

CORBO
FLORES

GRACIOSA

FAIALO VEL PICO

TERCERA
S. MIG

S. MA

ACORES IN

PORTUS
MADERA

GUANAO

HISPANIA
NOVA

CUBA

JUCATANA

COSUMELLA

JAMAICA

NAPR
NOVA
HISPANIA

CAMERCANE
INSULE

INS FORTU

NUNC CAN.

HESPERIDES
INS DE ANT

N

TRINITATIS INS

PARIA

B. PAI

PERU
NOVA CASTILIA

C S CR

C S AU

COSCO

RICA
A MULTIS HODIE NOVA
INDIA DICTA

MARE PACIFICUM

74

FRETUM PATHAGONICUM
SIVE MAGELLANICUM

MERCATOR, 1541. [Sketched from his gores.]

FROM THE SEBASTIAN CABOT MAPPEMONDE, 1544.

presume that we have in this date of 1497 an authoritative statement. We learn also from this map of 1544 that the land first seen was the point of the island now called Cape Breton. Without the aid of this map, Biddle, who wrote before its discovery, had contended for Labrador as the landfall.

We know, on the testimony of Robert Thorne in 1527, if from no other source, that it was a settled policy of the Spanish government to allow no one but proper cartographical designers to make its maps, "for that peradventure it would not sound well to them that a stranger should know or discover their secrets." Scarcity of Spanish printed maps. This doubtless accounts for the fact that, in the two hundred maps mentioned by Ortelius in 1570 as used by him in compiling his atlas, not one was published in Spain; and every bibliographer knows that not a single edition of Ptolemy, the best known channel of communicating geographical knowledge in this age of discovery, bears a Spanish imprint. The two general maps of America during the sixteenth century, which Dr. Kohl could trace to Spanish presses, were that of Medina in 1545 and that of Gomara in 1554, and these were not of a scale to be of any service in navigating.

There seem to be insuperable objections to considering that Sebastian Cabot had direct influence in the production of the map now under consideration. It is full of a lack of knowledge which it is not possible to ascribe to him. That it is based upon some drafts of Cabot is most probably true; but they Cabot's connection with the map of 1544. are clearly drafts, confused and in some ways perverted, and eked out by whatever could be picked up from other sources.

That the Cabot map was issued in more than one edition is inferred partly from the fact that the legends which Chytræus quotes from it differ somewhat from those now in the copy preserved in Paris; and indeed Harrisse finds reason to suppose that there may have been four different editions. That in some form or other it was better known in England than elsewhere is deduced from certain relations sustained with that country on the part of those who have mentioned the map, — Livio Sanuto, Ortelius, Sir Humphrey Gilbert, Richard Willes, Hakluyt, and Purchas.

Whoever its author and whatever its minor defects, this so-called Cabot map of 1544 may reasonably be accepted as the earliest really honest, unimaginative exhibition of the American continent which had been made. There was in it no attempt to fancy a northwest passage; no confidence in the marine or terrestrial actuality of the region now known to be covered by the north Pacific; no certainty about the entire western coast line of South America, though this might have been decided upon if the maker of the map had been posted to date

for that region. The maker of it further showed nothing of that presumption, which soon became prevalent, of making Tierra del Fuego
merely but one of the various promontories of an immense Antarctic
continent, which later stood in the planispheres of Ortelius and Wytfliet.

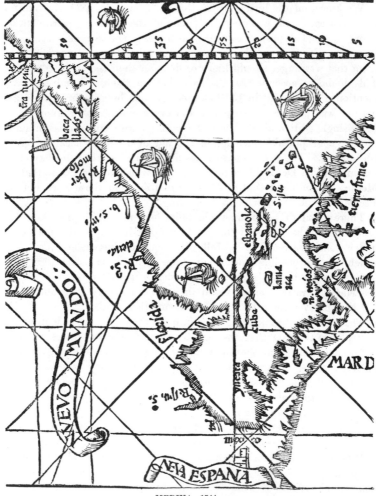

MEDINA, 1544.

This map of Cabot was the last of the principal cartographical monuments made north of the Alps in this early half of the sixteenth century. The centre of geographical study was now
transferred to Italy, where it had begun with the opening of

Geographi-
cal study
transferred
to Italy.

the interest in oceanic discovery.   For the next score years and more
we must look mainly to Venice for the newer development.

In the Venice Ptolemy of 1548, we have for the first time a *series*
of maps of the New World by Gastaldi, which were simply enlarged

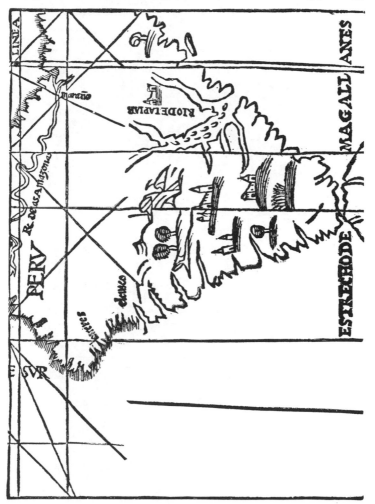

MEDINA, 1544.

by Ruscelli in the edition of 1561, except in a few instances, 1548, Gas-
where new details were added, like the making of Yucatan  taldi.
a peninsula instead of the island which Gastaldi had drawn.   They
were repeated in the edition of 1562.

Meanwhile the most popular sea manuals of this period were Spanish ; but they studiously avoided throwing much light on
Sea manuals. the new geography.

WYTFLIET, 1597.

That of Martin Cortes was the first to suggest a magnetic pole as
distinct from the terrestrial pole. Its rival, the *Arte de Navegar* of
Pedro de Medina, published at Valladolid in 1545, never reached the
same degree of popularity, nor did it deserve to, for his notions were
in some respects erratic.

The English in their theories of navigation had long depended on the teachings of the Spaniards, and Eden had translated the chief Spanish manual in his *Arte of Navigation* of 1561.

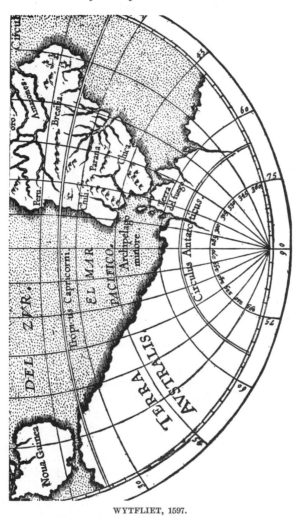

WYTFLIET, 1597.

A great advance was possible now, for a new principle had been devised, and an estimate of the progress of a ship was no longer dependent on visual observation. The log had made it possible to put dead reckoning on a pretty firm basis. This was the <sup>Ship's log.</sup> great new feature of the *Regiment of the Sea*, which the Englishman,

William Bourne, published in 1573; and sixteen years later, in 1589, another Englishman, Blunderville, made popularly known the new instrument for taking meridian altitudes at sea, the cross-staff, which had very early superseded the astrolabe on shipboard.

The inclination or dip of the needle, showing by its increase an approach to a magnetic pole, was not scaled till 1576, when Robert Norman made his observations, and it is not without some service to-day in that combination of phenomena of which Columbus noted the earliest traces in his first voyage of 1492.

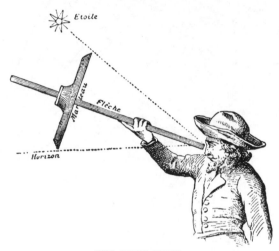

THE CROSS-STAFF.

It is significant how large a part in the cardinal discoveries of the fifteenth and sixteenth centuries was taken by Italian navigators, seamen, shipwrights, mathematicians, and merchants, whether in Portugal or Spain, France or England. It is curious, too, to observe how, when the theoretical work and confirmatory explorations were finished, and the commercial spirit succeeded to that of science, England embarked with her adventurous spirit. The death of Queen Mary in 1558 was the signal for English exertion, and that exertion became ominous to all Europe in the reign of Elizabeth, accompanied by an intellectual movement, typified in Bacon and Shakespeare, similar to that which stirred the age of Columbus and the Italian renaissance.

*Italian discoverers.*

*English discoverers.*

John Hawkins and African marauders of his English kind were selling negro slaves in Española in 1562 and subsequent years, and from them we get our first English accounts of the Florida coast, which on their return voyages they skirted.

*John Hawkins.*

America had at this time been abandoned for a long while to Spain and France, and the latter power had only entered into competition with Charles V., when Francis I., as we have seen, had sent out Verrazano in 1521 to take possession of the north Atlantic coasts. Out of this grew upon the maps the designation of New France, New which was attached to the main portion of the North Amer- France. ican continent. And this French claim is recognized in the maps, painted about 1562, on the walls of the geographical gallery in the Vatican. So the French stole upon the possession of Spain in the West Indies ; and the English followed in their wake, when the death of Mary rendered it easier for the English to smother their inherited antipathy to France. This done, the English in due time joined the French in efforts to gain an ascendency over Spain in the Indies, to compensate for the loss of such power in Italy. The Span- Spanish settlements fail iards, though they had attempted to make settlements along at the north. the Chesapeake at different times between 1566 and 1573, never succeeded in making any impression on the history of this northern region.

The cartography of the north was at this period subject to two new influences ; and both of them make large demands upon the credulity of scholarship in these latter days.

Attempts have been made to trace some portion of the development of the coasts of the northeastern parts of the United States André to the publications of a mendacious monk, André Thevet. Thevet. He had been sent out to the French colony of Rio de Janeiro in 1555, where he remained prostrated with illness till he was able to reëmbark for France, January 31, 1556. In 1558 he published his *Singularitez de la France Antarctique*, a descriptive and conglomerate work, patched together from all such sources as he could pillage, professing to follow more or less his experiences on this voyage. He says nothing in it of his tracking along the east coast of the present United States. Seeking notoriety and prestige for his country, he pretends, however, in his *Cosmographie* published in 1575, to recount the experiences of the same voyage, and now he professes to have followed this same eastern coast to the region of Norumbega. Well-equipped scholars find no occasion to believe that these later statements were other than boldly conceived falsehoods, which he had endeavored to make plausible by the commingling of what he could filch from the narratives of others.

It was at this time also (1558) that there was published at Venice the strange and riddle-like narrative which purports to give the experiences of the brothers Zeni in the north Atlantic waters in the four-

The Zeni story.  teenth century.   The publication came at a time when, with the transfer of cartographical interest from over the Alps to the home of its earliest growth, the countrymen of Columbus were seeking to reinstate their credit as explorers, which during the fifteenth

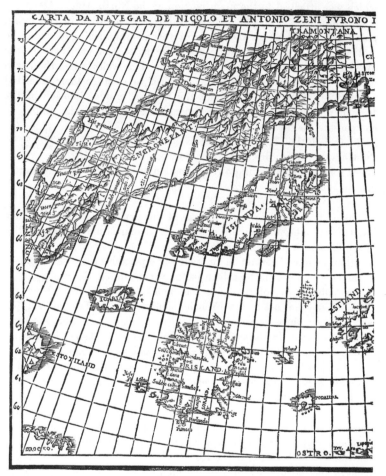

THE ZENI MAP.

century and the early part of the sixteenth they had lost to the peoples of the Iberian peninsula.   Anything, therefore, which could empha- size their claims was a welcome solace.   This accounts both for the bringing forward at this time of the long-concealed Zeni narrative, — granting its genuineness, — and for the influence which its accompanying map had upon contemporary cartography. This map professed to be based upon the discoveries made by the Zeni brothers, and upon the knowledge acquired by them at the north in the fourteenth century. It accordingly indicated the existence of countries called Estotiland and Drogeo, lying to the west, which it was now easy to identify with the Baccalaos of the Cabots, and with the New France of the later French.

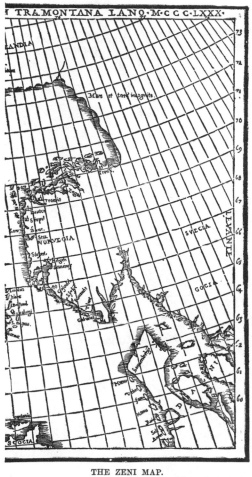

THE ZENI MAP.

"If this remarkable map," says Nordenskiöld, "had not received extensive circulation under the sanction of Ptolemy's name," The Zeni map. for it was copied in the edition of 1561 of that geographer, "it would probably h a v e been soon forgotten. During nearly a whole century it had exercised an influence on the mapping of the northern countries t o which there are few parallels to be found in the history of cartography." It is Nordenskiöld's further opinion that the Zeni map was drawn from an old map of the north made in the thirteenth century, from which the map found in the Warsaw Codex of Ptolemy of 1467 was also drawn. He further infers that some changes and additions were imposed to make it correspond with the text of the Zeni narrative.

The year 1569 is marked by a stride in cartographical science, of which we have not yet outgrown the necessity.

The plotting of courses and distances, as practiced by the early explorers, was subject to all the errors which necessarily accompany the lack of well-established principles, in representing the curved surface of the globe on a plane chart.

**1569. Mercator's projection.**

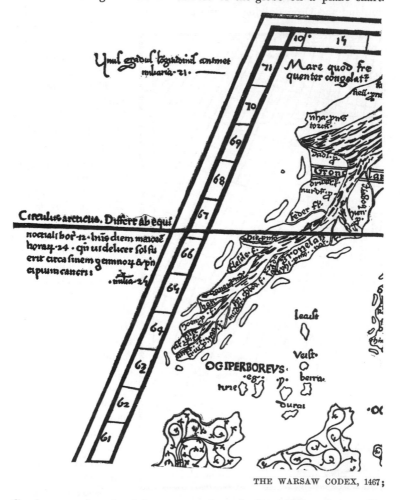

THE WARSAW CODEX, 1467;

Cumbrous and rude globes were made to do duty as best they could ; but they were ill adapted to use at sea. Nordenskiöld (*Facsimile Atlas*, p. 22) has pointed out that Pirckheimer, in the Ptolemy of 1525, had seemingly anticipated the theory which Mercator now with some sort of prevision developed into a principle, which was applied in his great plane chart of 1569. The principle, however, was not definite

enough in his mind for the clear exposition of formulæ, and he seems
not to have attempted to do more than rough-hew the idea. The hint
was a good one, and it was left for the Englishman Edward Wright to
put its principles into a formulated problem in 1599, a century and

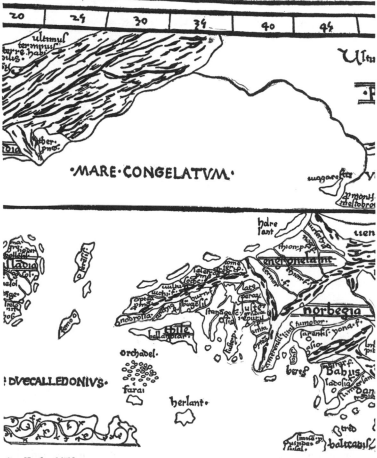

after Nordenskiöld.

more after Columbus had dared to track the ocean by following latitudinal lines in the simplest manner.

It has been supposed that Wright had the fashioning of the large
map which, on this same Mercator projection, Hakluyt had included
in his *Principall Navigations* in 1599. Hondius had also adopted
a like method in his *mappemonde* of the same year.

In 1570 the publication of the great atlas of Abraham Ortelius
showed that the centre of map-making had again passed
from Italy, and had found a lodgment in the Netherlands.
The *Theatrum* of Ortelius was the signal for the downfall
of the Ptolemy series as the leading exemplar of geographical ideas.

1570. The
*Theatrum* of
Ortelius.

MERCATOR, 1569.

The editions of that old cartographer, with their newer revisions, never
again attained the influence with which they had been invested since
the invention of printing. This influence had been so great that Nordenskiöld finds that between 1520 and 1550 the Ptolemy
maps had been five times as numerous as any other. They
had now passed away; and it is curious to observe that Ortelius seems
to have been ignorant of some of the typical maps anterior to his
time, and which we now look to in tracing the history of American
cartography, like those of Ruysch, Stobnicza, Agnese, Apianus, Vadianus, and Girava.

Decline of
Ptolemy.

It has already been mentioned that when Ortelius published his *Theatrum*, and gave a list of ninety-nine makers of maps whom he had consulted, not a solitary one of Spanish make was to be found among them. It shows how effectually the Council of the Indies had concealed the cartographical records of their office.

Ortelius.

MERCATOR.

It was eighty years since the English under John Cabot had undertaken a voyage of discovery in the New World. The interval passed not without preparation for new efforts, which had for a time, however, been extended to the northwest rather than to the northeast. In 1548 Sebastian Cabot had returned to his native land to assume the first place in her maritime world. His influence in directing, and that of Richard Eden in informing, the English mind prepared the way for the advent of Frobisher, the younger Hawkins, and Drake.

1577. English explorations.

1548. Sebastian Cabot.

Frobisher's voyage of 1576 was the true beginning of the arctic search for a northwest passage, all earlier efforts having been in lower latitudes.   He had sought, by leaving Greenland

1576.  Frobisher.

ORTELIUS.

on the right, to pass north of the great American barrier, and thus reach the land of spices.  He congratulated himself on having found the long-desired strait, when, naming it for himself, he returned to

England. Frobisher attempted to add to these earlier discoveries by a voyage the next year, 1577, but he made exploration secondary to mining for gold, and not much was done. A

1577-78.
Frobisher.

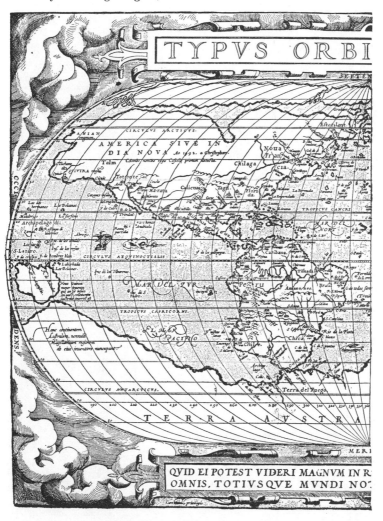

TYPVS ORBI

QVID EI POTEST VIDERI MAGNVM IN R
OMNIS, TOTIVSQVE MVNDI NO

ORTELIUS, 1570.

third voyage in 1578 brought him into Hudson's Straits, which he entered with the hope of finding it the channel to Cathay. But in all his voyages Frobisher only crossed the threshold of the arctic north.

It was one of the results of Frobisher's voyages that they served to implant in the minds of the cartographers of the northern waters the notions of the Zeni geography, and aided to

SEBASTIAN CABOT.

give those notions a new lease of favor. It is conjectured that Frobisher had the Zeni map with him, or its counterpart in one of the re-

cent Ptolemies. This map had placed the point of Greenland under
66° instead of 61°, and under the last latitude this map had shown
the southern coast of its insular Frisland. Therefore, when Frobisher
saw land under 61°, which was in fact Greenland, he supposed it to
be Frisland, and thus the maps after him became confused. A like

FROBISHER.

mischance befell Davis, a little later. When this navigator found
Greenland in 61°, he supposed it an island south of Greenland, which
he called "Desolation," and the fancy grew up that Frobisher's route
must have gone north of this island and between it and Greenland, and
so we have in later maps this other misplacement of discoveries.

While Frobisher was absent, Drake developed his great 1577. Fran-
scheme of following in the southerly track of Magellan.    cis Drake.

Four years before (1573), being at Panama, he had seen from a tree-top the great Pacific, and had resolved to be the first of the English to furrow its depths. In 1577, starting on his great voyage of circum-navigation, he soon added a new stretch of the Pacific coast to the better knowledge of the world. When he returned to England, he proved to be the first commander who had taken his ship, the " Peli-can," later called the " Golden Hind " wholly round the globe, for Ma-gellan had died on the way. Passing through Magellan's Strait and Drake sees Cape Horn. entering the Pacific, Drake's ship was separated from its companions and driven south. It was then he saw the Cape

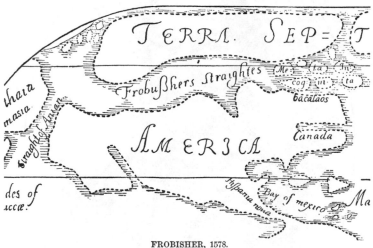

FROBISHER, 1578.

Horn of a later Dutch navigator, and proved the non-existence of that neighboring antarctic continent, which was still persistently to cling to the maps. Bereft of his other ships, which the storm had driven apart, Drake, during the early months of 1579, made havoc among the Span-ish galleons which were on the South American coasts.

In March, 1579, surfeited with plunder, he started north from the coast of Mexico, to find a passage to the Atlantic in the upper lati-tudes.

In June he had reached 42° north, though some have supposed that In the north Pacific. he went several degrees higher. He had met, however, a rigorous season, and his ropes crackled with the ice. The change was such a contrast to the allurements of his experiences farther to the south that he gave up his search for the strait that would carry him, as he had hoped, to the Atlantic, and, turning south, he reached a bay somewhere in the neighborhood of San Francisco,

where he tarried for a while. Having placed the name of **New Al-**
**bion** on the upper California coast, and fearing to run the hazards of
the southern seas, where his plundering had made the Spaniards alert,

FRANCIS DRAKE.

he sailed westerly, and, rounding the Cape of Good Hope, reached
England in due time, and was acknowledged to be the earliest of English circumnavigators.

It is one of the results of Drake's explorations in 1579–80 that
we get in subsequent maps a more northerly trend to the California
coast.

Shortly after this, a great confusion in the maps of this Pacific region
Confusion in the Pacific coast cartography. came in.    From what it arose is not very apparent, except that absence of direct knowledge in geography opens a wide field for discursiveness.    The Michael Lok map of 1582 indicates this uncertainty.   It seemed to be the notion that the Arctic Sea was one and the same with that of Verrazano; also, that it came down to about the latitude of Puget Sound, and that the Gulf of California stretched nearly up to meet it.

Francisco Gali. Francisco Gali, a Spanish commander, returning to Acapulco from China in 1583, tried the experiment of steering northward to about 38°, when he turned west and sighted the American coast in that latitude.    At this point he steered south, and showed the practicability of following this circuitous route with less time than was required to buffet the easterly trades by a direct eastern passage. His experiment established one other fact, namely, the great width of water separating the two continents in those upper latitudes ; for he had
Proves the great width of the Pacific. found it to be 1200 leagues across instead of there being a narrow strait, as the theorizing geographers had supposed. Gali seems also to have shown that the distance south from Cape Mendocino to the point of the California peninsula was not more than half as great as the maps had made it.   His voyage was a significant source of enlightenment to the cartographers.

Eastern coast of North America. To return to the eastern coasts.   An English vessel under Simon Ferdinando spent a short season in 1579 somewhere about the Gulf of Maine, and was followed the next year by
1579. The English on the coast. another under John Walker, and in 1593 by still a third under Richard Strong.
For eighty years England might have rested her claim to North America on the discoveries of the Cabots ; but Queen Elizabeth first gave prominence to these pretensions when she granted to Sir Humphrey Gilbert in 1578 the right to make a settlement somewhere in these more northerly regions.    Gilbert's first voyage accomplished nothing, and there was an interdict to prevent a second, since England might have use for daring seamen nearer home.   "First," says Robert Hues, " Sir Humphrey Gilbert, with great courage and forces, attempted to make discovery of those parts of America which were
Sir Humphrey Gilbert. yet unknown to the Spaniards; but the success was not answerable."   The effort was not renewed till 1583, when Gilbert took possession of Newfoundland and attempted to make settlements farther south ; but disaster followed him, and his ship foundered off the Azores on his return voyage.

It was at this time that Sir Walter Ralegh came into prominence in pushing English colonization in America.  He had been <sub>Sir Walter</sub> associated with his half-brother, Gilbert, in the earlier move- <sub>Ralegh.</sub> ments, but now he was alone.   In 1584 he got his new charter, partly

GILBERT'S MAP, 1576.

by reason of the urgency of Hakluyt in his *Westerne Planting.*  Ralegh had his eye upon a more southern coast than Gilbert had aimed for, — upon one better fitted to develop self-dependent colonization. He knew that north of what was called Florida the Spaniards had but scantily tracked the country, and that they probably maintained no settlements.  Therefore to reach a region somewhere south of the

Chesapeake was the aim of the first company sent out under Ralegh's inspiration. These adventurers made their landfall where they could find no good inlet, and so sailed north, searching, until at last they reached the sounds on the North Carolina coast, and tarried awhile. Satisfied with the quality of the country, they returned to England; and their recitals so pleased Ralegh and the Queen that the country was named Virginia, and preparations were made to dispatch a colony. It went the next year, but its history is of no farther importance to our present purpose than that it marks the commencement of English colonization, disastrous though it was, on the North American continent, and the beginning of detailed English cartography of its coast, in the map, already referred to, which seems to open a passage, somewhere near Port Royal, to an interior sea.

In 1585–86 John Davis had been buffeting among the icebergs of 1585-86. Greenland and the north in hopes to find a passage by the John Davis. northwest; on June 30, 1587, he reached 72° 12′ on the Greenland coast, and discovered the strait known by his name, and in 1595 when he published his *World's Hydrographical Description,* he maintained that he had touched the threshold of the northwest passage. He tells us that the globe of Molineaux shows how far he went.

Seamanship owes more to Davis than to any other Englishman. In English seamanship. 1590, or thereabout, he improved the cross-staff, and giving somewhat more of complexity to it, he produced the backstaff. This instrument gave the observer the opportunity of avoiding the glare of the sun, since it was used with his back to that luminary; and when Flamsteed, the first astronomer royal at Greenwich, used a glass lens to throw reflected light, the first approach to the great principle of taking angles by reflection was made, which was later, in 1731, to be carried to a practical result in Hadley's quadrant.

BACK-STAFF.

The art of finding longitude was still in an uncertain state. Gemma Frisius, as we have noted, had as early as 1530 divined the method of carrying time by a watch; but it was not till 1726 that anything really practicable came of it, in a timekeeper constructed by Harrison. This watch was continually improved by him up to 1761, when the method of ascertaining longitude by chronometer became well established; and a few years later (1767) the first nautical almanac was published, affording a reasonably good guide in lunar distances, as a means in the computations of longitude.

In 1676 the Greenwich observatory had been founded to attempt the rectification of lunar tables, then so erroneous that the 1676. calculations for longitude were still uncertain. In 1701 Edmund Halley had published his great variation charts. These dates will fix in the reader's mind the advance of scientific skill as applied to navigation and discovery. It will be well also to remember that in 1594 Davis published his *Seaman's Secrets*, the first manual in the English tongue, written by a practical sailor, in which the principles of great circle sailing were explained.

The first marine atlas had been printed at Leyden in 1583-84; but the Dutch had not at that time taken any active part in 1583-84. the development of discovery in the New World. Their Earliest marine atlas. longing for a share in it, mated with a certain hostile inten- tion towards the Spaniards, instigated the formation of the 1592. Dutch West India Company. West India Company, which had first been conceived in the mind of William Usselinx in 1592, though it was not put into execu- tion till twenty-five years later. It was claimed by the Dutch that in 1598 the ships of their Greenland Company had discovered 1598. the Hudson River, though there can be little doubt that the French, Spanish, and perhaps English had been there much ear- lier. It is also claimed that the straits shown in Lok's map in 1582 had instigated Heinrich Hudson to his later search. But the truth in all these questions which involve national rights is very much per- plexed with claim and counter-claim, invention and perversion, in which historical data are at the beck of political objects.

By the end of the sixteenth century the Dutch began to appear on the coasts of the Middle and New England States, and the 1598. The Dutch on the North cartography of those regions developed rapidly under their American coasts. observation; but it was through the boating explorations of Captain John Smith in 1614 that it took a shape nearer the truth. It is to him that the northerly parts owe the name The English. of New England, which Prince Charles confirmed for it. The reports from Hudson, May, and others instigated a plan marked out in 1618, but not directly ordered by the States General till 1621, which led to the Dutch occupation of Manhattan and the neighboring regions, intro- ducing more strongly than before a Dutch element into the maps.

When the seventeenth century opened, the English had come well to
the front in maritime explorations. A large-minded and
patriotic man, Sir Thomas Smith, did much in his capacity
as governor of the "merchants trading into the East Indies " to direct contemporary knowledge into better channels. Dr.
Thomas Hood gave public lectures in London on the improvements in methods of navigation. Richard Hakluyt,
the historiographer of the new company, had already shown that he
had inherited the spirit of helpful patronage which had characterized
the labors of Eden.

We find the peninsula made by the St. Lawrence and the Atlantic
insularized from the beginning of the seventeenth century,
the transverse channel being now on the line of the Hudson,
then of the Penobscot, then of the St. Croix, and when the
seventeenth century came in, it was not wholly determined
that the longed-for western passage might not yet be found
somewhere in this region. On July 24, 1601, George Waymouth, a
navigator, as he was called, applied to the London East India Company to be assisted in making an attempt to discover a
northwest passage to India, and the company agreed to his
proposition. The Muscovy Company protested in vain against such
an infringement of its own rights; but it found a way to smother its
grief and join with its rival in the enterprise. Through such joint
action Waymouth was sent by the northwest "towards Cataya or
China, or the back side of America," bearing with him a letter from
Queen Elizabeth to the Emperor of " China or Kathia." The attempt
failed, and Waymouth returned almost ignominiously.

In 1602, under instructions from the East India Company, he again
sailed, and now pushed a little farther into Hudson's Strait than
any one had been before. In 1609 Hudson had made some
explorations, defining a little more clearly the northern
coasts of the present United States; and in 1610 he sailed again from
England to attempt the discovery of the northwest passage, in a small
craft of fifty-five tons, with twenty-three souls on board. Following
the tracks of Davis and Waymouth, he went farther than they, and
revealed to the world the great inland sea which is known by his
name, and in which he probably perished.

In 1612–13 Sir Thomas Button developed more exactly the outline
in part of this great bay, and in 1614 the *Discovery*, under
Robert Bylot and William Baffin, passed along the coasts of
Hudson's Strait, making most careful observation, and Baffin took
for the first time at sea a lunar observation for longitude, according to
a method which had been suggested as early as 1514. It was on a

voyage undertaken in the next year, 1615, that Baffin, exceeding the northing of Davis, found lying before him the great expanse of Baffin's Bay, through which he proceeded till he found a northern exit in Sir Thomas Smith's Sound, under 78°. Baffin did all this with an accuracy which surprised Sir John Ross, who was the next to enter the bay, two centuries later. It was in these years of Hudson and Baffin that Napier invented logarithms and simplified the processes of nautical calculations.

1615. Baffin's Bay.

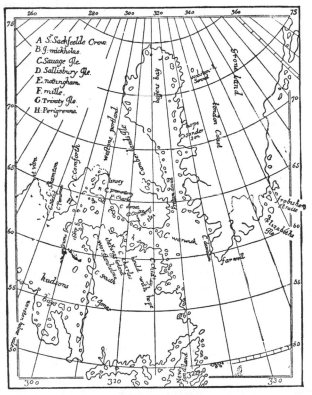

LUKE FOX, 1635.

The voyage of Luke Fox in 1631 developed some portions of the western shores of Hudson's Bay, and he returned confident, from his observation of the tides farther north, that they indicated a western passage; and in the same year Thomas James searched the more southern limits of the great bay with no more success. These voyages put a stay for more than a hundred years to efforts in this direction to find the passage so long sought.

1631. Luke Fox.

Thomas James.

Up to 1602 the explorations of our northern coasts seem to have been ordinarily made either by a sweep northerly from Europe, striking Newfoundland and then proceeding south, or by a southerly sweep following the Spanish tracks and coasting north from Florida. In this year, 1602, the Englishman Gosnold, without any earlier example that we know of since the time of Verrazano, stood directly to the New England coast, and in the accounts of his voyage we begin to find some particular knowledge of the contour of this coast, which opens the way to identifications of landmarks. The explorations of Pring (1603), Champlain (1604), Waymouth (1605), Popham (1607), Hudson (1609), Smith (1614), Dermer (1619), and others which followed are of no more importance in our present survey than as marking further stages of detailed geography. Even Dermer was dreaming of a western passage yet to be found in this region.

*1602. Gosnold.*

We must now turn to follow the development during the seventeenth century of the discoveries on the Pacific coast. Sebastian Viscaino, in his voyage up the coast from Acapulco in 1602, sought the hidden straits as high as 42°, and one of his captains reporting the coast to trend easterly at 43°, his story confused the geography of this region for many years. This supposed trend was held to indicate another passage to the Gulf of California, making the peninsula of that name an island, and so it long remained on the maps, after once getting possession, some years later (1622), of the cartographical fancy.

*Discoveries on the Pacific coast.*

*1602. Viscaino.*

Some explorations of the Dutch under De Vries, in 1643, were the source of a notion later prevailing, that there was an interjacent land in the north Pacific, which they called "Jesso," and which was supposed to be separated by passages both from America and from Asia; and for half a century or more the supposition, connected more or less with a land seen by João da Gama, was accepted in some quarters. Indeed, this notion may be said to have not wholly disappeared till the maps of Cook's voyage came out in 1777–78, when the Aleutian Islands got something like their proper delineation.

*1643. De Vries.*

In fact, so vague was the conception of what might be the easterly extension of the northern sea in the latitudinal forties that the notion of a sea something like the old one of Verrazano was even thought in 1625 by Briggs in Purchas, and again in 1651 in Farrer's map of Virginia, to bathe the western slope of the Alleghanies.

*Confused geographical notions of a western sea.*

Early in the eighteenth century, even the best cartographers ran wild in their delineations of the Pacific coast. A series of

*1700.*

multifarious notions, arising from more or less faith in the alleged explorations of Maldonado, Da Fuca, and De Fonte, some of them assumed to have been made more than a century earlier, filled the maps with seas and straits, identified some- Maldonado, Da Fuca, De Fonte. times with the old strait of Anian, and converting the northwestern parts of North America into a network of surmises, that look strangely to our present eyes. Some of these wild configurations prevailed even after the middle of the century, but they were finally eliminated from the maps by the expedition of that James Cook who first saw the light in a Yorkshire cabin in 1728.

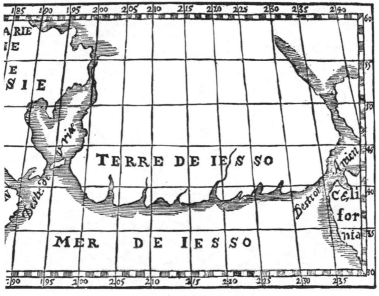

JESSO. [After Hennepin.]

In 1724 Peter the Great equipped Vitus Bering's first expedition, and in December, 1724, five weeks before his death, the Czar gave the commanding officer his instruction to coast 1724. Bering. northward and find if the Asiatic and American coasts were continuous, as they were supposed to be. There were, however, among the Siberians, some reports of the dividing waters and of a great land beyond, and these rumors had been prevailing since 1711. Peter the Great died January 28, 1725 (old style), just as Bering was beginning his journey, and not till March, 1728, did that 1728. navigator reach the neighborhood of the sea. In July he spread his sails on a vessel which he had built. By the middle of August he had

The Sea of China and the Indies.

S.ᵣ Francis Drake was on this sea and landed Aᵒ: 1577 in 37 deg: where hee tooke Possession in the name of Q: Eliza: Calling it new Albion.

Whose happy shoers, (in ten dayes march with 50 foote and 30 horsmen and through the rich adiacent Valleyes beautyfied with as profitable an Indian sea, may be discovered ,to the exceeding benefit of Great Brittan.

Ould RAWLIAN

Meridies

VIRGI

Apalatcy Cy

Montes C.

Carolana

Ca Feare

Sassafras trees

Roanok Ile

MARE SAT LIN

Capa Chara

Smiths Ile

Iohñ Goddard Sculp     Domina Virginia Farrer Collegit     Are sold by I. Stephenson at

DOMINA FARRER'S

MAP, 1651.

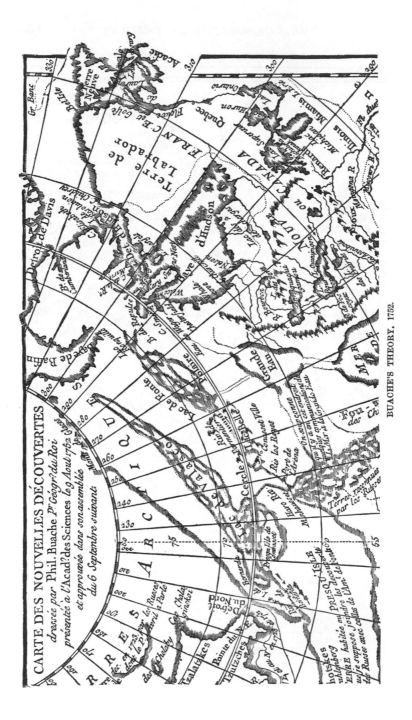

BUACHE'S THEORY, 1752.

passed beyond the easternmost point of Asia, and was standing out into the Arctic Ocean, when he turned on his track and sailed south. Neither in going nor in returning did he see land to the east, the mists being too thick. He had thus established the limits of the Russian Empire, but he had not as yet learned of the close proximity of the American shores. His discoveries did not get any cartographi-

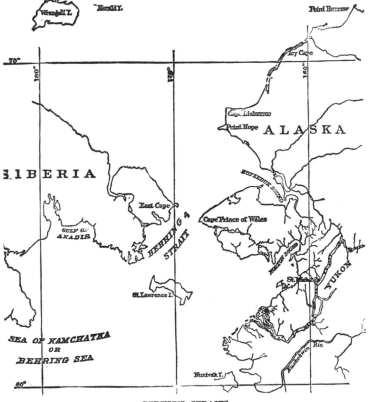

BERING'S STRAITS.

cal record till Kiriloff made his map of Russia in 1734, using the map which Bering had made in Moscow in 1731. The follow- 1732. ing year (1732), Gvosdjeff espied the opposite coast; but it 1741. Ber- was not till 1741 that Bering sailed once more from the ing. Asiatic side to seek the American coast. He steered southeast, and soon found that the land seen by Da Gama, and which the Delisles' had so long kept on their maps, did not exist there. Thence sailing northward, Bering sighted the coast in July and had Mount St. Elias before him, then named by him from that saint's day in the calendar.

Aleutian Islands.   On his return route some vague conception of the Aleutian Islands was gained, the beginning of a better cartography, in which was also embodied the stretch of coast which Bering's associate, Chirikoff, discovered farther east and south.

In 1757 Venegas, uninformed as to these Russian discoveries, con-

Northern Pacific.   fessed in his *California* that nothing was really known of the coast line in the higher latitudes, — an ignorance that was the source of a great variety of conjectures, including a large inland sea of the west connecting with the Pacific, which was not wholly discarded till near the end of the century, as has already been mentioned.

The search for the northwest passage to Asia, as it had been begun

The search for the northwest passage.   by the English under Cabot in 1497, was also the last of all the endeavors to isolate the continent. The creation of the Hudson Bay Company in 1670 was ostensibly to promote "the discovery of a new passage into the South Sea," but the world knows how for two centuries that organization obstinately neglected, or as far as they dared, the leading purpose for which they pretended to ask a charter. They gave their well-directed energies to the amassing of fortunes with as much persistency as the Spaniards did at the south, but with this difference: that the wisdom in their employment of the aborigines was as eminent as with the Southrons it was lacking. It was left for other agencies of the British government successfully to accomplish, with the aid of the votaries of geographical science, what the pecuniary speculators of Fen Church Street hardly dared to contemplate.

The spirit of the old navigators was revived in James Cook, when

1779. James Cook.   in 1779 he endeavored to pass eastward by Bering's Straits; but it was not till forty years later that a series of arctic explorations was begun, in which the English races of both continents have shown so conspicuous a skill and fortitude.

While the English, French, and Spaniards were dodging one another

Kendrick in the "Columbia."   in their exploring efforts along this upper coast, a Boston ship, the "Columbia," under Captain Kendrick, entered the Columbia River, then named; and to these American explorations, as well as to the contemporary ones of Vancouver, the geographical confusion finally yielded place to something like an intelligible idea.

It had also been the aim of Vancouver in 1790–95 "to ascertain

1790–95. Vancouver.   the existence of any navigable communication between the North Pacific and the North Atlantic Oceans," and the correspondence of the British government leading to this expedition has

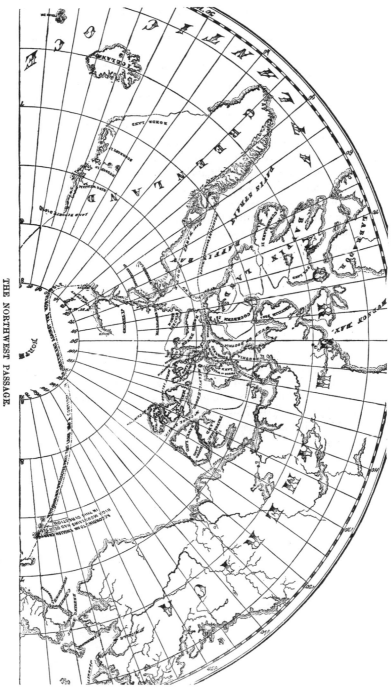

THE NORTHWEST PASSAGE.

only been lately printed in the *Report* of the Dominion archivist, Douglas Brymner, for 1889.

The names of Barrow, Ross, Parry, and Franklin, not to mention

Arctic explorers. others of a later period, make the story of the final severance of the continent in the arctic seas one of conspicuous interest in the history of maritime exploration. Captain Robert L. McClure, in the "Investigator," late in 1850 passed into Bering's

1850. Mc-Clure finds the northwest passage. Straits, and before September closed his ship was bound in the ice. In October McClure made a sledge journey easterly over a frozen channel and reached the open sea, which thirty years before Parry had passed into from the Atlantic side. The northwest passage was at last discovered.

We have seen that within thirty years from the death of Columbus the outline of South America was defined, while it had taken nearly two centuries and a quarter to free the coast lines of the New World from an entanglement in men's minds with the outlines of eastern Asia, and another century and a quarter were required to complete the arctic contour of America, so that the New World at last should stand a wholly revealed and separate continent.

Nor had all this labor been done by governments alone. The private merchant and the individual adventurer, equipping ships and sailing without national help, had done no small part of it. Dr. Kohl strikingly says, " The extreme northern limit of America, the desolate peninsula Boothia, is named after the English merchant who fitted out the arctic expedition of Sir John Ross ; and the southernmost strait, beyond Patagonia, preserves the name of Le Maire, the merchant at whose charge it was disclosed to the world ! "

# INDEX.